Attention

Attention
Theory and Practice

Addie Johnson
University of Groningen, The Netherlands

Robert W. Proctor
Purdue University

SAGE Publications
International Educational and Professional Publisher
Thousand Oaks ▪ London ▪ New Delhi

For information:

Sage Publications, Inc.
2455 Teller Road
Thousand Oaks, California 91320
E-mail: order@sagepub.com

Sage Publications Ltd.
6 Bonhill Street
London EC2A 4PU
United Kingdom

Sage Publications India Pvt. Ltd.
B-42, Panchsheel Enclave
Post Box 4109
New Delhi 110 017
India

Printed in the United States of America

Library of Congress Cataloging-in-Publication Data

Johnson, Addie.
Attention: Theory and practice / Addie Johnson, Robert W. Proctor.
    p. cm.
Includes bibliographical references and index.
ISBN 0–7619–2760-3 — ISBN 0–7619–2761–1 (pbk.)
    1. Attention. 2. Information processing. 3. Memory.
I. Proctor, Robert W. II. Title.
BF321.J56 2004
153.7′33—dc22

                                                        2003016015

07   08   09   10   9   8   7   6   5   4   3   2

Acquiring Editor:	Jim Brace-Thompson
Editorial Assistant:	Karen Ehrmann
Production Editor:	Diana E. Axelsen
Copy Editor:	Toni Zuccarini Ackley
Typesetter:	C&M Digitals (P) Ltd., Chennai, India
Cover Designer:	Michelle Lee Kenny

CONTENTS

PREFACE

Attention is one of the fastest growing research areas in cognitive psychology. In light of the growing importance of this topic, there are surprisingly few courses in attention at the undergraduate level, and courses at the graduate level often concentrate on just a few topics. One reason for the dearth of courses on attention is the lack of suitable textbooks. Several current books on attention are too specialized for an introductory course, focusing too heavily on just one research group's work, or emphasizing only one aspect of attention research, such as the neuropsychology of attention. Several edited books contain excellent chapters on different aspects of attention, but none of these books contains a selection of chapters suitable for an introduction to or overview of the field.

This situation led us to write the present book. This book is intended as a textbook for cognitive psychology courses or seminars on attention and as a resource for researchers and practitioners (e.g., ergonomists and neuropsychologists) who wish to gain an overview of the field of attention. Our goal in writing this book was to present a coherent view of the field of attention that highlights the important issues and major findings while giving sufficient details of experimental studies, models, and theories so that the results and conclusions are easy to follow and evaluate. We have tried to provide a readable overview of attention and how theories and paradigms for the study of attention have developed. However, rather than brushing over tricky technical details, we try to explain them clearly. In other words, we give readers the benefit of understanding the motivation and techniques of the experimenters in order to allow them to think through results, models, and theories for themselves. We always attempt to present a technically correct picture, but without getting bogged down in controversies that have turned out not to be too important in the long run.

In contrast to other books on attention, this book gives approximately equal weight to theory, experimental paradigms and results, neuropsychology, and applications. The book as a whole provides an overview of the major studies, findings, and applications in the field of attention and is intended to be accessible to readers with a limited background in psychology while remaining interesting to researchers and practitioners with expertise in some aspects of the field. In addition to basic attentional theories and paradigms, we discuss the current state of understanding of the neuropsychology of attention, including clinical deficits, diagnosis, and rehabilitation. We also discuss theory and applications within the field of human factors and ergonomics, including applications of attentional research and theory for display of information, design of human–machine systems, and developing training programs. Wherever appropriate we have broadened our approach to include other topics within cognitive and social psychology, such as in our treatment of attention and memory, and attention and emotion.

Given our goal of presenting a coherent view of the field written in an accessible and consistent style, we did not want an edited book. However, we also wanted to draw on the expertise of authors in specific areas. This led us to our rather unusual construction of having guest authors on some of the chapters, but with the two main authors each reading and revising the entire text to ensure coherence.

A word of thanks is in order for the more than 700 Utrecht University students and many teaching assistants who read and commented on the first version of the book and to the students at Purdue University who used a revised version in Fall 2002. We especially thank Rob van der Lubbe for helping to shape early versions of Chapters 2 and 3, Julie Smith for helping with the indexing, and Edward de Haan, Roy Kessels, Bob Melara, Mark Nieuwenstein, and Kim Vu for coauthoring specific chapters.

Thanks also to the following reviewers: Tom Busey, Indiana University; Richard Carlson, Pennsylvania State University; Steven Yantis, The Johns Hopkins University; Art Kramer, University of Illinois; and Mark Faust, University of South Alabama.

Addie Johnson
Robert W. Proctor

CHAPTER 1

HISTORICAL OVERVIEW OF RESEARCH ON ATTENTION

with Kim-Phuong L. Vu

At any moment in time, we are bombarded with various stimuli, only some of which are relevant to current goals and only a few of which will ever reach our consciousness. The many stimuli present may each require a different action—actions that often are incompatible with each other. Consider, for example, what is going on in the cockpit during a commercial flight. The pilot must process information from visual displays and the outside world, while at the same time listening to and talking with air traffic controllers and other members of the flight crew. He or she must select and operate appropriate controls, and be prepared to detect and identify emergency warning signals. Flying requires selection among competing stimuli, concurrent performance of several subtasks, and the monitoring of instruments for changes. The study of attention is concerned with how people are able to coordinate perception and action to achieve goals such as successfully flying an aircraft.

The study of attention is a major part of contemporary cognitive psychology and cognitive neuroscience. Attention plays a critical role in essentially all aspects

attn coordinates perception; action to achieve goals.

1

attn.
perception
cognition
action

of perception, cognition, and action, influencing the choices you make. For example, when performing a memory task such as remembering the name of someone you have met only once before, attention must be given to the retrieval cue (the person's face or who they are with) and then shifted to evaluating the possible candidates (names) for retrieval. In a more complex task, such as deciding which car to buy, attention must be directed to the different properties that the new car should have, and the most important goals (e.g., staying within budget) must be kept in mind. As these examples illustrate, the study of attention should be of interest to anyone who wants to learn more about human behavior and cognition, and to gain insight into how attention guides their own behavior.

Attention has been of interest to the field of psychology since its earliest days. This research was first summarized in the book *The Psychology of Attention,* by Ribot (1890). Eighteen years later, two landmark texts devoted to the topic of attention were published: Titchener's (1908/1973) *Psychology of Feeling and Attention* and Pillsbury's (1908/1973) *Attention.* These texts put the study of attention in experimental psychology on a firm footing. In fact, Titchener described the discovery of attention as one of three major achievements of experimental psychology to that point. He acknowledged that many ideas about attention could be traced to philosophers in the 18th and 19th centuries, stating:

> But what I mean by the "discovery" of attention is the explicit formulation of the problem; the recognition of its separate status and fundamental importance; the realization that the doctrine of attention is the nerve of the whole psychological system, and that as men judge of it, so they shall be judged before the general tribunal of psychology. (p. 173)

Pillsbury (1908/1973) provided a similarly strong assessment of the importance of attention, asserting, "The manifestations of the state that we commonly call attention are protean. No part of the individual is untouched by them. They extend to every part of the physical organism, and are among the most profound facts of mind" (p. 1). The statements of Titchener and Pillsbury make clear the central importance placed on attention in the early days of psychology and also, in part, why the topic of attention has continued to be the focus of considerable research to the present.

The history of research on attention can be broken into five periods:

1. Philosophic work preceding the founding of the field of psychology

2. The period from the founding of psychology until 1909

3. The period from 1910 until 1949, during which behaviorism flourished and interest in attention waned to some extent

Time Period	Attention as a Topic According to Lovie (1983)	Attention in the Title	Attention as a Keyword
1911-1915	60	20	101
1916-1920	28	21	102
1921-1925	29	22	384
1926-1930	94	66	1,356
1931-1935	127	78	1,805
1936-1940	90	38	3,090
1941-1945	59	30	1,706
1946-1950	69	23	979
1951-1955	97	39	782
1956-1960	147	53	739
1961-1965		105	1,017
1966-1970		353	2,432
1971-1975		586	3,458
1976-1980		712	4,009
1981-1985		932	5,733
1986-1990		1,573	8,050
1991-1995		2,258	11,392
1996-2000		3,391	17,835
2001-2002		1,189	6,845

Table 1.1 Number of publications on attention as indicated by Lovie's (1983) survey of Psychological Index and Psychological Abstracts and a PsycINFO search conducted on November 29, 2002

4. The resurgence of widespread interest in attention during the period of the cognitive revolution from 1950 to 1974

5. Contemporary research dating from 1975 to the present

Table 1.1 shows estimates of the number of articles concerning attention published during the latter three periods up until 2002. In the sections that follow, we summarize the major research and theories of attention during each of the five periods. This historical overview is intended to provide the reader with a foundation on which the more detailed treatments of specific topics in subsequent chapters will build.

▲ THE PHILOSOPHICAL PERIOD

Interest in attention began in the field of philosophy, prior to the founding of psychology as a scientific discipline. Because the topic of attention was originally discussed by philosophers, many ideas about the nature of attention held today can be traced back to the views of various philosophers. Among the issues considered were the role of attention in conscious awareness and thought, and whether attention was directed voluntarily or involuntarily toward objects and events. The characterization of attention provided by each philosopher reflected that individual's larger metaphysical view of the nature of things and how we come to know the world. In this section, we briefly describe the treatments of attention provided by a few eminent philosophers.

Watson (1915) refers to Vives (1492–1540) as the father of modern psychology. Vives was among the first to recognize the importance of empirical investigation, publishing his book, *De Anima et Vita,* in 1538. He is most well known for his views on memory (Murray & Ross, 1982), in which attention played a significant role. According to Vives, the more closely one attends to stimuli, the better they will be retained. Learning consists of the formation of associations, and retrieval from memory occurs through automatic activation of associated ideas or through intentional, effortful search.

Berlyne (1974) attributes the first extended treatment of attention to Malebranche (1638–1715), in his book, *The Search After Truth* (1674/1980). Malebranche held that we have access to ideas, or mental representations of the external world, but not direct access to the world itself. He considered attention to be necessary to prevent ideas from becoming confused and to make them clear. According to Malebranche, understanding is no different than simple perception, but

> because it often happens that the understanding has only confused and imperfect perceptions of things, it is truly a cause of our errors. . . . It is therefore necessary to look for means to keep our perceptions from being confused and imperfect. And, because, as everyone knows, there is nothing that makes them clearer and more distinct than attentiveness, we must try to find the means to become more attentive than we are. (pp. 411–412)

Malebranche also noted,

> The mind does not pay equal attention to everything it perceives. For it applies itself infinitely more to those things that affect it, that modify it, and that penetrate it, than to those that are present to it but that do not affect it and do not belong to it. (p. 412)

Leibniz (1646–1716) was responsible for introducing the concept of *apperception,* which refers to an act that is necessary for an individual to become conscious of a perceptual event (Leibniz, 1765). Events can be perceived unconsciously, but will not enter conscious awareness without apperception. Leibniz emphasized a reflexive view of attention, in which attention is directed automatically to events and ideas that demand it (McRae, 1976). However, attention also has a voluntary and directed aspect, according to Leibniz, who said, "Attention is a determination of the soul to know something in preference to other things" (1948/1985, p. 525).

Herbart (1776–1841) agreed with Leibniz that an event had to be apperceived to enter conscious awareness. However, he stressed that apperception involved relating newly perceived ideas to ones already contained in the mind (Herbart, 1824–1825). In other words, all new perceptual experience occurs in relation to prior perceptions. This apperceptive process occurs through associations among mental contents. Herbart also was the first person to stress the importance of applying mathematical modeling to the study of psychology.

A popular view in the first part of the 19th century was that people are incapable of attending to more than one thing at once. Hamilton (1788–1856), however, argued that the span of attention is more than one object. He proposed measuring its size by throwing marbles on the floor and determining how many of them could be apprehended at once (Hamilton, 1859). Hamilton's idea for testing the span of apprehension was followed up by Jevons (1871), who estimated it to be four items.

In summary, many philosophers gave attention a central role in perception and thinking. They introduced several important issues, such as the extent to which attention is directed automatically or intentionally, that continue to be examined and evaluated in contemporary research. Although they conducted little experimental research themselves, their conceptual analyses of attention laid the foundation for the scientific study of attention in ensuing years.

THE PERIOD FROM 1860 TO 1909 ▲

The philosophical analyses of attention led to some predictions, as in Hamilton's work, that could be tested experimentally. In addition, in the mid-1800s psychophysical methods were being developed that allowed measurement of the relation between physical stimulus properties and the psychological perceptions of them (Fechner, 1860/1966; Weber, 1846/1978). Consequently, it was a relatively small step to infer that attention could be systematically investigated using an experimental approach.

Speed of Mental Processes

Wilhelm Wundt, who is credited with establishing the first laboratory devoted to psychological research in 1879, was also responsible for introducing the study

Wundt

of attention to the field. As a laboratory assistant in physiology at Heidelberg, he became interested in the issue of the astronomers' "personal equation" (see Woodworth, 1938). This refers to systematic individual differences between astronomers in their measures of the time for the transit of stars. Astronomers in the late 18th and early 19th centuries measured time by determining when the stars and planets crossed the meridian. This was measured with a special telescope that had an eyepiece equipped with a number of equidistant vertical wires. The astronomer recorded the times at which a particular star crossed each of the wires and averaged these times to find the time at which the star crossed the meridian. This was a generally accepted method that had the advantage of allowing comparison across different observatories. However, individual differences in the judgment of when the star crossed each of the wires resulted in different readings from one astronomer to another. In an attempt to compensate for differences in timing among the astronomers, a personal equation was developed in which a constant "correction" was made in order to equate their readings. Around 1860, Wundt set up an apparatus to simulate this situation. As described by Blumenthal (1980):

> Wundt suddenly realized that he was measuring the speed of a mental process, that for the first time, he thought, a self-conscious experimental psychology was taking place. The time it takes to switch attention voluntarily from one stimulus to another had been measured—it varied around a tenth of a second. (p. 121)

This insight led Wundt to emphasize the voluntary control of attention (see Box 1.1).

F. C. Donders (1868/1969) and his students conducted the first detailed investigations of the speed of mental processes. De Jagger's (1865/1970) dissertation provided the first account of the experiments conducted in Donders's lab. The experiments described in the dissertation focused on measuring the time required to identify a stimulus and to select a motor response. In one set of experiments, subjects were required to respond to a red light with the right hand and a white light with the left hand. The mean reaction time (RT) was 356 ms, which was 172 ms longer than a simple reaction (executing a single response when a stimulus is presented) to the same stimuli. De Jagger interpreted this time as the duration of the central processes involving stimulus discrimination and response initiation.

Donders (1868/1969) formalized the method used by De Jagger, known as the *subtractive method,* emphasizing specifically that the time for a particular process could be estimated by adding that process to a task and taking the difference in RT between the two tasks. He distinguished three types of reactions: *a* (simple reaction), *b* (choice reaction), and *c* (go or no-go reaction; respond to one stimulus but not another). These types of reactions allowed separate measures of the stimulus identification and decision processes that were assessed together by De Jagger.

| Box 1.1 | A Reappraisal of Wundt's Contribution to Psychology |

Wilhelm Wundt is typically given credit in introductory psychology and cognitive psychology textbooks for having developed the first experimental psychology laboratory in 1879. He is also portrayed as having a view called "structuralism," which had the goal of determining the elements of conscious experience and how these elements are combined into more complex experiences. The method of choice for Wundt is described as introspection, or reports of the structures of conscious experience by trained observers. These views are often attributed to both Wundt and his student, E. B. Titchener. For example, Lahey (1995) says,

> Because they were interested in the elements of the mind and how those elements are organized, Wundt and Titchener are known as the first proponents of a school of thought called *structuralism;* that is, they sought to determine the *structure* of the mind through controlled introspection. (p. 11)

Because structuralism as a school of thought in psychology and introspection as a method were rejected and replaced by behaviorism and objective behavioral measures, Wundt's specific contributions are depicted as being of little relevance to contemporary psychology.

However, beginning in the 1970s, several authors have emphasized that this prototypical characterization of Wundt is inaccurate (see the edited books on Wundt by Rieber & Robinson, 2001, and Rieber, 1980), being much closer to that of Titchener. Blumenthal (1975), in an article titled, "A Reappraisal of Wilhelm Wundt," states, "To put it simply, the few current Wundt-scholars (and some do exist) are in fair agreement that Wundt as portrayed today in many texts and courses is largely fictional and often bears little resemblance to the actual historical figure" (p. 1081). Blumenthal goes on to note, "Contrary to frequent descriptions, Wundt was not an introspectionist as the term is popularly applied today" (p. 1081).

This point can be illustrated by descriptions of the research being conducted in Wundt's lab in 1886, written by two visiting French academics, Alfred Grafé and Emile Durkheim (Nicolas, Gyselinck, Murray, & Bandomir, 2002). Grafé and Durkheim independently described the same five projects, with Grafé's list being:

1. The effect of expectation on the time taken to perceive something;

2. The measurement of how well time intervals can be discriminated;

3. The verification of Weber's Law in the perception of lightness [grayness] using the method of bisection;

4. Experiments in auditory sensations using the method of just noticeable differences;

5. Experiments on auditory sensations using the method of bisection (Nicolas et al., 2002, p. 210, parenthetical acknowledgments of collaborators excluded).

(Continued)

Box 1.1 | (Continued)

The first project refers to one by Ludwig Lange, mentioned in the chapter, that used reaction-time methods to evaluate the effects of expectancy, or preparation, on perception of sensory input. The other four used psychophysical methods, similar to those used today, to examine fundamental issues in sensation and perception. Note that introspection was not the primary method for any of these projects. Moreover, Wundt was highly critical of Titchener's reliance on introspection, stating:

> Introspective method relies either on arbitrary observations that go astray or on a withdrawal to a lonely sitting room where it becomes lost in self-absorption. The unreliability of this method is universally recognized. . . . Clearly, Titchener has himself come under the influence of the deceptions of this method. (Wundt, 1900, p. 180, cited in Blumenthal, 2001)

As noted in the text, Wundt called his approach to psychology "voluntarism", and Blumenthal (1975) and others have noted that Wundt never used the terms "structuralist" or "structuralism," which were introduced by Titchener. In contrast to a search for mental elements, Wundt emphasized mental processes. In fact, he was highly critical of the British associationist philosophers' approach of describing mental experience in terms of associations of mental elements. In his emphasis on apperception, Wundt stressed that "mental synthesis" had a creative aspect that could not be predicted on the basis of a simple combination of mental elements (Danziger, 2001). Also, as implied by the term "voluntarism," volition was at the heart of Wundt's views. His studies of volition "amounted to an elaborate analysis of selective and constructive attentional processes" (Blumenthal, 1975, p. 1083). In sum, Wundt's views were much closer to those of contemporary cognitive psychology than is typically realized.

The difference between the c- and a-reactions was presumed to reflect the time for stimulus identification, and the difference between the b- and c-reactions was considered to be the time for "expression of the will" (p. 424). Donders's assertion that the time for distinct mental processes can be measured and his method for modeling human information processing are precursors to contemporary methods that are described in Chapter 2.

Reaction-time research in general, and the study of action selection in particular, continued to flourish throughout the remainder of the 19th century (see Jastrow, 1890; Robinson, 2001). Wundt (1883) criticized Donders for using the c-reaction as a measure of stimulus identification, reasoning that subjects must distinguish between whether to respond or not, and suggested what he called the "d-reaction" instead as a pure measure of identification time. The d-reaction is assessed by presenting subjects with the same stimulus and having them make the same response every time, as in the a-reaction, with the difference being that they are instructed not to respond until they have identified the stimulus. Wundt's d-reaction attracted criticism because it is subjective and highly variable, and after practice, the d-reaction time does not differ from the a-reaction time.

Other classic reaction-time experiments include those of Exner (1882), who noted that performance of simple reaction-time tasks was characterized by voluntary preparation that occurs prior to presentation of the stimulus, with the reaction itself being a reflexive response to the stimulus. L. Lange (1888) extended this work further by distinguishing between preparatory sets that focused on the sensory and motor stages of the task. A motor set, which involved focusing attention on the response, produced fast, reflexive responses of the type described by Exner. In contrast, a perceptual set, which involved focusing attention on the stimulus, required apperception and an intentional act of will to initiate the response, resulting in slower responses. Merkel (1885), described in Woodworth (1938), provided the initial demonstration that choice RT increases as a function of the number of possible stimulus–response alternatives—that is, as a function of uncertainty regarding which response will be required. In Merkel's experiment, the Arabic numerals 1–5 were assigned to the left hand and the Roman numerals I–V to the right hand, in left to right order. Results showed that when the number of alternatives increased from 2 to 10 choices, mean RT increased from approximately 300 ms to a little over 600 ms. This relation, which indicates that the probabilities of occurrence of stimuli influence the time to respond to whichever one occurs, was rediscovered in the early 1950s by Hick (1952) and Hyman (1953). Their work resulted in the formulation of what is now known as Hick's law, or the Hick-Hyman law, which is described in detail in Chapter 2.

Effects of Attention

The relation between attention and perception was one of the first topics to be studied in experimental psychology. At the end of the 19th century, von Helmholtz (1894a) argued that attention is essential for visual perception. Using himself as subject and pages of briefly visible printed letters as stimuli, he found that attention could be directed in advance of the stimulus presentation to a particular region of the page, even though the eyes were kept fixed at a central point. In his own words, "With a subsequent discharge [of the tachistoscope used to briefly illuminate the letters] I could direct my perception to another section of the field, while always fixating on the pinhole, and then read a group of letters there" (von Helmholtz, 1894a, p. 259). He also found that attention was limited: The letters in by far the largest part of the visual field, even in the vicinity of the fixation point, were not automatically perceived. Based on these observations, von Helmholtz (1894a, p. 259) concluded:

These observations demonstrated, so it seems to me, that by a voluntary kind of intention, even without eye movements, and without changes of accommodation, one can concentrate attention on the sensation from a particular part of our peripheral nervous system and at the same time exclude attention from all other parts.

Wundt held that attention was an inner activity that caused ideas to be present to differing degrees in consciousness. He distinguished between perception, which was the entry into the field of attention, and apperception, which was responsible for entry into the inner focus. He assumed that the focus of attention could narrow or widen, a view that has also enjoyed popularity in recent years. Wundt (1907a) said, "Attention contains three essential constituents: an increased clearness of ideas; muscle sensations, which generally belong to the same modality as the ideas; and feelings, which accompany and precede the ideational change" (p. 249). Wundt used the word *voluntarism* to describe his school of psychology, which emphasized volition, or the study of conscious decision and choice. He held that psychological processes could be understood only in terms of their goals or consequences, and that apperception and attention are processes of active synthesis. (See http://psychclassics.yorku.ca/Wundt/Outlines/sec2.htm.) According to Wundt (1907b),

Psychological voluntarism . . . looks upon empirical volitional processes with their constituent feelings, sensations, and ideas, as the types of all conscious processes. For such a voluntarism even volition is a complex phenomenon which owes its typical significance to this very fact that it includes in itself the different kinds of psychical elements.

Lotze (1885) did not accept the view that "attention is simply a more intense illumination of the content" (p. 35). He proposed, instead, that conscious attention occurs to varying degrees, with lower processes such as a simple sensory experience not always accompanied by higher processes involving comparison of relations between the simple sensations or between them and previous experiences. In his words, "Various stages [of attention] may thus, indeed, be distinguished in the consciousness according as simply the thing itself and its own nature is conceived; or its connection with others; or, finally, its significance and importance to our personal life" (p. 35).

Pillsbury (1908/1973) emphasized that the conditions of an act of attention are to be found both in the environment and in the past experience of the individual. He based this conclusion in part on demonstrations of the importance of *task set* on performance. Task set refers to the readiness to carry out an instructed action in response to a given stimulus. One of the earliest investigations of task set was carried out by Külpe (1904), who used briefly displayed nonsense syllables of different colors as stimuli. The instructions were to determine the number of letters displayed, the colors and their positions, or the letters and their positions. Performance was best when the judgments that had to be made coincided with the task for which the observer had been set. Other early experimental research investigated the role of attention in periodic fluctuations of faint stimuli between perceptibility and imperceptibility. N. Lange (1888) attributed these fluctuations to the waxing and waning of attention or apperception, although others attributed them to sensory fatigue.

William James's (1890/1950) views on attention are probably the most well known of the early psychologists. His definition of attention is widely quoted. According to James,

> It is the taking possession by the mind, in clear and vivid form, of one of what seem several simultaneously possible objects or trains of thought. Focalization, concentration, of consciousness are of its essence. It implies withdrawal from some things in order to deal effectively with others. (pp. 403–404)

James's definition mentions *clearness*, which Titchener (1908/1973) viewed as the central aspect of attention. Titchener placed even more emphasis on clearness, stating, "It seems to me beyond question that the problem of attention centers in the fact of sensible clearness" (p. 182). He attributed this view of attention to Wundt, saying,

> And as we connect the name of Helmholtz with the doctrine of sensible quality, and the name of Fechner with that of sensible intensity, so must we connect the name of Wundt with the doctrine of attention, which, as I see it, is that of sensible clearness. (p. 173)

Pillsbury (1908/1973) agreed with Titchener, indicating, "The essence of attention as a conscious process is an increase in the clearness on one idea or a group of ideas at the expense of others" (p. 11).

Researchers at the beginning of the 20th century debated how this increased clearness is obtained. Mach, Stumpf, and others favored the view that this increase in clearness was direct, whereas Wundt, Külpe, and others held the view that the increase was accomplished indirectly by inhibiting the sensations that were not attended to (Pillsbury, 1908/1973). One problem with resolving the issue of how attention influences clearness is illustrated by an experiment conducted by Mach and Stumpf. They agreed that attention to a stimulus increases its perceived intensity, but whereas Mach thought that this effect of attention occurs for all stimuli, Stumpf thought that attention benefits only weak sensations. As described by Titchener (1908/1973), to resolve this issue, Mach and Stumpf listened to a harmonium together to determine whether attention to one of the clearly audible component tones in a chord increases its strength. Regrettably, Mach concluded that it did, but Stumpf concluded that it did not. Thus, their introspections did not allow them to agree on an answer to this question. The debate about whether attention increases the clearness of attended events or decreases the clearness of unattended events presaged the current argument in psychology regarding whether attending is accomplished primarily through excitatory or inhibitory mechanisms (see, e.g., Tipper, 2001; see also Chapters 5 and 11).

As evident in the above quote from James, he considered clarity to be a central feature of attention, going so far as to say, "My experience is what I agree to attend to" (1890/1950, p. 402). However, James is known for taking a functionalist view that emphasized the selective aspect of attention, as illustrated in the last sentence of the earlier quote. Judd (1917) also emphasized the selective aspect of attention, stating, "The word 'attention' refers more especially to the selective character of the organizing process, whereby one particular group of sensory factors is emphasized more than any other group" (p. 191). It is this functional, selective aspect of attention that has been emphasized in most research of the past 50 years (see, e.g., Pashler, 1998). However, the issue of conscious awareness remains important and is attracting increased interest (see, e.g., Rosetti & Revonsuo, 2000).

James (1890/1950, p. 416) suggested several ways in which attention could be classified:

It is directed either to

    a. Objects of sense (sensorial attention); or to
    b. Ideal or represented objects (intellectual attention).

It is either

    c. Immediate; or
    d. Derived. . . .

Attention may be either

    e. Passive, reflex, non-voluntary, effortless; or
    f. Active and voluntary.

The first distinction stresses that attention can be directed to stimuli that are not physically present, as well as ones that are present. The second means that attention can be removed from the present event. The third foreshadows a distinction that is currently popular between *exogenous control*, in which attention is drawn automatically toward a stimulus, and *endogenous control*, in which attention is directed toward the stimulus voluntarily (see, e.g., Yantis, 2000).

According to James (1890/1950, pp. 424–425),

The immediate effects of attention are to make us

    a. perceive—
    b. conceive—
    c. distinguish—
    d. remember—

better than otherwise we could—both more successive things and each thing more clearly. It also

    e. shortens "reaction time."

Perceiving, conceiving, and distinguishing all contribute to our immediate perceptions. Studies of the role of attention in perceiving and identifying stimuli constitute the largest part of contemporary research on attention. Remembering comes into play when actions are delayed until some time after the relevant stimulus information has been displayed. According to James, "an object once attended to will remain in the memory, whilst one inattentively allowed to pass will leave no traces behind" (1890/1950, p. 427). Pillsbury (1908/1973) was more explicit about the role of attention in memory, stating, "Retention is dependent on the degree of attention that was given at the moment of learning." He also emphasized the role of attention in retrieving information, asserting, "Recall is always directed by attention," and "recognition is influenced by attention both in its quickness and correctness" (p. 148).

The majority of contemporary research on attention has focused on perception. However, as Pillsbury (1908/1973) noted, "There is no act of attention that is unaccompanied by some motor process" (p. 12). Motor responses include both voluntary and involuntary orienting toward a source of stimulation, as well as other more overt actions. In agreement with Pillsbury, James said, "Organic adjustment, then, and ideational preparation or preperception are concerned in all attentive acts" (p. 444). The former refers to "the accommodation or adjustment of the sensory organs" and the latter to "the anticipatory preparation from within of the ideational centers concerned with the object to which the attention is paid" (p. 434).

Lotze (1852) introduced the idea that the links between movements and their mental representations are bi-directional, thus allowing the representations to directly produce the movements. This idea came to be called "ideomotor action," a term first coined by Carpenter (1852) to explain the effect of suggestion on muscular movement independent from conscious intent. Carpenter was interested primarily in explaining phenomena such as dowsing, in which a divining rod might be "pulled" to the earth by the presence of water under the ground, that were attributed to unknown or supernatural forces. His basic idea was that the individual's expectancies and thoughts affected the motor system and thus unintentionally caused the movements.

James elaborated on Carpenter's views and was a strong advocate of the *ideo-motor theory of action*. According to James:

> The question is this: Is the bare idea of a movement's sensory effects its sufficient mental cue, or must there be an additional mental antecedent, in the shape of a fiat, decision, consent, volitional mandate, or other synonymous phenomenon of consciousness, before the movement can follow? (1890/1950, p. 522)

His answer is that sometimes the idea is sufficient, and sometimes it is not. For James, "Wherever movement follows unhesitatingly and immediately the notion of it in the mind, we have ideo-motor action" (p. 522). In more recent years, Greenwald (1970) and Hommel, Müsseler, Aschersleben, and Prinz (2001) have advocated ideomotor theories of action.

A common idea is that if a task requires attention, it will interfere with simultaneous performance of another task that also does (Keele, 1967). Binet (1890) was one of the first individuals to suggest that attention could be understood in terms of interference. He found that mental addition interfered with a task of rhythmically squeezing a rubber ball a specified number of times. However, this interference did not occur when the timing and number of squeezes did not have to be monitored. In another demonstration of the link between action and attention, Welch (1898) found that a strong grip could not be maintained while performing demanding mental tasks.

Around 1860, the philosophical approach dominated the study of psychology in general and attention in specific. During the period from 1860 to 1909, the study of attention was transformed, as was the field of psychology as a whole, to one of scientific inquiry with emphasis on experimental investigations. By 1909, many phenomena of concern to contemporary attention researchers had been discovered and investigated, and the study of attention was central to the field of psychology. However, the situation was one captured by Ribot (1890) in the first sentence of his book: "Psychologists have given much study to the effects of attention, but very little to its mechanism" (p. 7). Unfortunately, because behaviorism came to dominate psychology in the next period, at least in the United States, the study of attentional mechanisms was largely delayed until the middle of the 20th century.

▲ THE PERIOD FROM 1910 TO 1949

One often reads that research on attention essentially ceased during the period of 1910–1949. For example, Neisser (1976) states that from World War I to the 1960s,

"There was no research on attention" (p. 5). Similarly, Moray (1969) states, "Research on attention disappeared virtually completely from about 1930 onwards" (p. 2), and Keele (1967) says, "For many years, little work was done on attention, but since the mid 1950s there has been a resurgence of interest in the problem" (p. 5). However, Lovie (1983) made a strong case that attention research never disappeared, although there was an increase in interest in the topic with the advent of contemporary cognitive psychology. He compiled tables showing the numbers of papers on attention listed in *Psychological Abstracts* and its predecessor, *Psychological Index*, in 5-year intervals from 1910 to 1960 (see Table 1.1 earlier in the chapter). As illustrated in the table, work on attention and related topics was published continuously during the entire 50-year period. Work on attention reached a low point in the period of 1945–1955, but numerous studies were still conducted during this period.

Not only was research on attention conducted continuously during the 20th century, but this research also provided a close link both to the work prior to 1910 and to contemporary work. Lovie (1983) notes that research by Titchener, Dallenbach, and others pursued the ideas expressed in Titchener's (1908/1973) book, and he indicates links between the work done during this period to the work of Broadbent and others following the increased interest in attention in the 1950s.

Among the important works on attention was that of Jersild (1927), who published a classic monograph, "Mental Set and Shift," in which he began by saying, "The fact of mental set is primary in all conscious activity. The same stimulus may evoke any one of a large number of responses depending upon the contextual setting in which it is placed" (p. 5). The monograph reported a series of experiments in which subjects had to make a series of judgments regarding each stimulus in a list as a function of whether a single task was to be performed for all stimuli or whether two tasks were performed in alternating order. The major finding was that in many situations the time to complete the list was longer for mixed lists than for pure lists of a single task. Although Jersild's study did not generate much interest for many years, since the mid-1990s there has been a resurgence of interest in *task-switching costs*, making it one of the hottest areas of research on attention (see, e.g., the special issue of the journal *Psychological Research,* 2000, Volume 63, Issue 3/4, devoted to executive processing; see also Chapter 6).

Another significant contribution during this era was the discovery of the *psychological refractory period effect* by Telford (1931). He noted that numerous studies showed that stimulation of neurons was followed by a refractory phase during which the neurons were less sensitive to stimulation. Telford conducted an experiment to answer the question, "Do voluntary responses, judgments and simple associative processes produce effects in the organism which serve as a barrier against immediate repetition, that can be identified with a refractory phase" (p. 7)?

Figure 1.1   A monochrome version of the Stroop task.

One of Telford's tasks required subjects to make a simple reaction by pressing a key whenever a tone occurred. The interval between successive tones varied between 0.5, 1, 2, and 4 seconds. Responses were considerably slower when the stimulus followed the preceding one by a short interval than when the interval was longer. This general finding, that RT to the second of two stimuli or tasks is increased when the interval between their onsets is short, was shown subsequently to be a pervasive phenomenon that occurred for choice reaction tasks as well. This psychological refractory period effect has been a constant source of research and theoretical speculation for the past 50 years (see, e.g., Pashler, 1998; see also Chapter 6).

Stroop (1935/1992) published what is certainly one of the most widely cited studies in the field of psychology, in which he demonstrated that stimulus information that is irrelevant to the task can have a major impact on performance. He had subjects name the ink colors for a list of 100 stimuli. In the crucial list, the stimuli spelled incongruent color words, and the subjects were instructed to name the ink color while ignoring the color word (see Figure 1.1). Subjects took an average of 110 seconds to name a list of this type, compared to 63 seconds to name the colors when presented in the form of solid squares. Thus, the naming time nearly doubled in the presence of conflicting color words, an effect that is known as the Stroop effect. Another finding reported by Stroop was that the time to name the color words was essentially unaffected by the presence of incongruent ink colors. The time to read 100 words for that list was 43 seconds, compared to 41 seconds to read those words presented in black ink. Thus the interference with color naming was asymmetric: Irrelevant words interfered with naming ink colors, but irrelevant ink colors did not interfere with naming color words. The Stroop task has provided one of the best methods for examining a variety of issues pertaining to attention in young adults and in numerous more specialized populations of people. When the article was reprinted in 1992, MacLeod (1992) referred to the Stroop task as the "gold standard" of attentional measures and noted that citations of the article actually increased over the period of 1974 to 1990, from a low of 25 in 1974 to 80 in 1990. In MacLeod's words, "The Stroop effect . . . continues to play a key role in the understanding of attention" (p. 12).

Paschal (1941) conducted a review of the research on attention in the preceding years. According to Paschal,

> Two theories have come into the foreground, then, out of the thinking of the past quarter of a century. The one, the mental set theory, looks upon attention as a vague, diffused term for phenomena which are adequately covered by mental set, as defined in terms of the tonic-postural augmentation of the stimulus impulse, with or without the end-organ adjustments, and with or without a reflexive sensitizing of the receptor cells. The other theory, a selective theory, sees in attention a preparatory act of adjustment which serves to pave the way for a particular stimulus. (p. 396)

Among the research conducted in the 1930s and 1940s, that on preparatory set or mental set was among the most important. Gibson (1941) noted, "At about the turn of the century it began to be realized that the events in a psychological experiment—reactions, associations, judgments or thoughts—were determined by something other than the reportable events themselves and that this was itself a psychological problem" (p. 783). Mowrer, Rayman, and Bliss (1940) established that preparatory set does not necessarily involve motor adjustments such as body posture and muscle tension. They reached this conclusion based on the finding that expectancy for one of two possible stimulus events was a critical factor influencing reaction time. They noted the consistency of their findings with those of Wundt (1880), who found that reaction time was slower when the subject did not know whether the stimulus would be visual, auditory, or tactual than when the subject knew the sense that would be stimulated because of the need to attend to a particular sense. Gibson (1941) provided a thorough, highly critical, review of the literature on set, noting, "The concept of set or attitude is a nearly universal one in psychological thinking despite the fact that the underlying meaning is indefinite, the terminology chaotic, and the usage by psychologists highly individualistic" (p. 781).

In sum, although the proportion of psychological research devoted to the topic of attention was less during this time period than during preceding decades, many important discoveries were made. In fact, much of the recent literature on attention has been concerned with developing theoretical explanations of the phenomenon of task-switching costs, the effects of irrelevant information in the Stroop and related tasks, and the psychological refractory period effect in dual-task performance, which were discovered during this time.

▲ THE PERIOD FROM 1950 TO 1974

The period from 1950 to 1974 saw a revival of interest in the characterization of human information processing. This revival, which is sometimes called the "cognitive revolution," was stimulated by developments in communication theory and by renewed interest in measuring and characterizing stages of information processing. Research on attention in this period is characterized by an interplay between technical applications and theory. N. Mackworth (1950) reported experiments on the maintenance of vigilance that exemplified this interaction and set the stage for extensive research on the topic over the remainder of the 20th century. This research originated in concerns about the performance of radar operators in World War II detecting infrequently occurring signals. It has continued to generate considerable interest because of its relevance to industrial monitoring tasks and to theoretical issues in attention. Mackworth introduced a "clock" test in which a pointer moved in steps of 12 minutes of arc per second, but 12 times in 20 seconds it made a double jump of 24 minutes. The subject was to report the double jumps by pressing a key whenever one occurred. The proportion of double jumps detected decreased sharply across the first half hour or so of the vigil. Research on the nature of this *vigilance decrement,* and on the factors that affect its magnitude, has been conducted continuously since Mackworth's influential study.

Cherry (1953) conducted one of the seminal works on attention during this period. He studied the problem of selective attention or, as he called it, "the cocktail party phenomenon." He was concerned with the issues of how we can select one voice to which to attend among several, and what information is remembered from the unattended messages. Cherry used a procedure called *dichotic listening* in which he presented different messages to each ear through headphones. Subjects were to repeat aloud, or *shadow*, one of the two messages while ignoring the other. This was a relatively easy task for them to do. Moreover, when subsequently asked questions about the unattended message, subjects were unable to describe anything about it except physical characteristics, such as gender of the speaker. They were even unaware of a change in language of the words in the unattended ear from English (their native language) to German.

Broadbent (1958) conducted an experiment that produced converging results with those of Cherry (1953). He presented subjects with a set of three digits one after the other to one ear and another set at the same time to the other ear, with instructions to recall as many digits as possible. Subjects tended to recall all of the digits presented to one ear before trying to recall the digits presented to the other ear. To account for findings such as his and Cherry's, Broadbent developed the first complete model of attention, called *filter theory* (see Chapter 3). He proposed that the nervous system acts as a single communication channel of limited capacity. According to filter theory, information is held in a preattentive temporary store, and only sensory events that have some physical feature in common (e.g., spatial location) are selected to pass into the limited capacity processing system. Broadbent's filter theory implies that the meaning of unattended messages is not identified. He also proposed that an amount of time that is not negligible is required to shift the filter from one channel of events to another.

Later studies showed that the unattended message could be processed beyond the physical level, in at least some cases (Treisman, 1960). To accommodate the finding that the meaning of an unattended message can influence performance, Treisman (1960) reformulated filter theory into what is called the *filter-attenuation theory.* According to filter-attenuation theory, early selection by filtering still precedes stimulus identification, but the filter attenuates the information only on unattended channels. This attenuated signal may be sufficient to allow identification if the stimulus is one with a low identification threshold, such as a person's name or an expected event. Deutsch and Deutsch (1963) took an alternative approach, proposing that unattended stimuli are always identified and that the bottleneck occurs in later processing. This view is called *late-selection* theory, in contrast to the filter and filter-attenuation theories, which are called *early-selection* theories. The issue posed by the distinction between the early- and late-selection theories is whether meaning is fully analyzed. This issue continues to be debated, with, for example, Pashler (1998) concluding in a recent thorough review that the evidence favors the early selection/attenuation view.

In the early 1970s, there was a shift from studying attention mainly with auditory tasks to studying it mainly with visual tasks. A view that regards attention as a limited-capacity resource that can be directed toward various processes became popular. Kahneman's (1973) model is the most well known of these *unitary capacity,* or *resource,* theories. According to this model, attention is a single resource that can be divided among different tasks in different amounts. The available supply of this resource varies as a function of arousal and task demands, and voluntary allocation strategies determine the tasks and processes to which the resource should be devoted when the demand exceeds the supply. Unitary-resource models provided the impetus for dual-task methodologies, such as *performance operating characteristics* and *secondary-task* measures of mental workload (see Chapter 9). The basic idea behind these models is that multiple tasks should produce interference when they compete for the limited capacity resources.

In the early 1970s, the first controlled experiments that used psychophysiological techniques to study attention were conducted on humans (see, e.g., Hillyard, Hink, Schwent, & Picton, 1973). These experiments used methods that allow brain activity relating to the processing of a stimulus, called *event-related potentials,* to be measured using electrodes placed on the scalp. The difference between event-related potential patterns obtained under different conditions, such as when a person is attending to a stimulus versus when the person is not, can provide evidence about the nature of the mechanisms underlying the processing of specific stimuli.

The research during this period yielded considerable information about the mechanisms of attention, specifically those involved in auditory attention. The most important development was the introduction of detailed information processing models of attention, beginning with Broadbent's (1958) filter theory. The realization that models of attention can be developed and tested paved the way for many advances in our understanding of attention.

▲ THE PERIOD FROM 1975 TO PRESENT

Research on attention burgeoned during the last quarter of the 20th century. This is clearly evident in Table 1.1, in which it can be seen that the number of articles with "attention" in the title increased to more than 3,000 for the period from 1996 to 2000. Researchers continued to conduct behavioral (and psychophysiological) research directed toward many of the tasks, issues, and phenomena of the previous period, but the range of research expanded.

Although unitary resource models held sway in the mid-1970s, they began to give way to *multiple resource* models in the latter part of the decade (see Chapter 9). Many studies showed that it is easier to perform two tasks together when the tasks use different stimulus or response modalities than when they use the same modalities. Performance is also better when one task is verbal and the other is visuospatial than when they are the same type. Based on these types of findings, Navon and Gopher (1979) proposed that attention was better viewed as multiple resources. Wickens (1980) extended the multiple resource view to the area of human factors by proposing that different attentional resources exist for different sensory modalities, coding modes, and response modalities. Multiple resource theory captures the fact that multiple task performance typically is better when the tasks use different input-output modes than when they use the same modes. However, it is often criticized as being too flexible because new resources can be proposed arbitrarily to fit any finding of specificity of interference (Navon, 1984).

Another distinction that has become prominent is between *space-based* and *object-based* approaches to attention. In the space-based approach, a widely used metaphor for visual attention is that of a spotlight that is presumed to direct attention to everything in its field (see, e.g., Posner, 1980). The attentional spotlight can presumably be dissociated from the direction of gaze (a view proposed by von Helmholtz many years earlier). Studies show that when a location is cued as likely to contain a target stimulus, but then a probe stimulus is presented at another location, a spatial gradient surrounds the attended location such that items nearer to the focus of attention are processed more efficiently than those farther away from it (Yantis, 2000). Evidence suggests that two types of cues, exogenous and endogenous (Klein & Shore, 2000) can trigger movement of the attentional spotlight to a location. As mentioned earlier, an exogenous cue is an external event such as the abrupt onset of a stimulus at a peripheral location that involuntarily draws the attentional spotlight to its location. Exogenous cues produce rapid performance benefits, which dissipate quickly, for stimuli presented at the cued location. An endogenous cue is typically a symbol such as a central arrowhead that must be identified before a voluntary shift in attention to the designated location can be made. The performance benefits for endogenous cues take longer to develop and are sustained for a longer period of time when the cues are relevant, indicating that their benefits are due to conscious control of the attentional spotlight (Klein & Shore, 2000).

Treisman and Gelade (1980) developed a highly influential variant of spotlight theory called the *feature integration theory* to explain the results from visual search studies, in which subjects are to detect whether a target is present among distractors. Feature integration theory assumes that basic features of stimuli are encoded into feature maps in parallel across the visual field at a preattentive stage. Search for a target distinguished from distractors by a single feature can be based on processing occurring during this preattentive stage. The second stage involves focusing attention on a specific location and combining features that occupy the location into objects. A search for a target distinguished from distractors by a conjunction of features requires attention for integration of the features. Thus, performance in conjunctive search tasks decreases as the number of distractors increases because attention must be moved sequentially across the search field until a target is detected.

Object-based models of attention view objects as being the primary unit on which attention operates. The primary reason for proposing such models is that numerous findings suggest a processing cost when attention must be directed toward two different objects, even when spatial factors are controlled. Duncan and Humphreys (1989) developed an object-based model of attention. According to this model, in the first stage of selection a visual representation is formed that is segmented into object-like units and that contains meaning codes. This stage of perceptual grouping and description operates in parallel across the visual field and is followed by competitive interaction between inputs, which guides selective access to awareness and action. Input is weighted relative to the degree to which it matches a representation of the information needed for current behavior.

Priming studies have also been popular during the most recent period of attention research. In such studies, a prime stimulus precedes the imperative stimulus to which the subject is to respond; the prime can be the same as or different from some aspect of the imperative stimulus. Posner and Snyder (1975) and Neely (1977) provided evidence for two types of priming effects. One is an automatic facilitation effect when the stimulus is the same as the prime, even though the prime has no predictive value. This benefit occurs without any cost for those trials on which the prime is different from the stimulus. When the prime indicates which target is likely to follow, it also produces a benefit at longer priming intervals, but with a cost for trials on which the prime is misleading. More recently, interest has developed in a phenomenon called *negative priming*. In a negative priming task, participants must respond on prime and probe trials, each of which contains one stimulus that should be ignored and one stimulus that should be responded to. Negative priming refers to slower responding on the probe trial when the stimulus that had to be ignored on the prime trial is now the relevant stimulus. This phenomenon was originally attributed to inhibitory processes active at the prime trial affecting performance on the probe trial, but there continues to be considerable controversy about the cause of negative priming (Tipper, 2001).

Another view that has become increasingly popular in recent years is called the *selection-for-action view*. According to this view, first advocated by Neumann (1987) and Allport (1987), attentional limitations should not be attributed to a limited capacity resource or mechanism. Instead, the limitations are byproducts of the need to coordinate action and ensure that the correct stimulus information is controlling the intended responses. A recent application of this approach is the Executive-Process/Interactive Control (EPIC) model presented by D. E. Meyer and Kieras (1997a, 1997b), which attempts to account for limitations in multiple-task performance in terms of strategic factors, rather than in terms of structural capacity limitations.

During the most recent period of research, a major focus has been on gathering neuropsychological evidence pertaining to the brain mechanisms that underlie attention. Cognitive neuroscience, of which studies of attention are a major part, has made great strides due to the continued development of neuroimaging technologies. These include the measurement of event-related brain potentials with scalp electrodes (mentioned earlier), positron emission tomography, and functional magnetic resonance imaging. These neuroimaging techniques, described in Chapter 2, allow the activity of different brain regions during performance of a variety of tasks to be examined (see, e.g., Leonards, Sunaert, Van Hecke, & Orban, 2000). The converging evidence provided by neuropsychological and behavioral data promises to advance the study of attention significantly in the first half of the 21st century.

Significant advances have also been made toward expanding the theories and methods of attention to address a range of applied problems. Applications of research on attention are many, but two major areas can be identified. The first concerns ergonomics in its broadest sense, ranging from human–machine interactions to improvement of work environments. Examples include mental workload (the measurement of the mental demands placed on a person; Gopher, 1994) and situation awareness (a person's understanding of the situation in which he or she is involved; Endsley, 1995b), for both of which measurement has become increasingly sophisticated during the period (see Chapter 9). The second major area of application is clinical neuropsychology, which has benefited substantially from adopting cognitive models and experimental methods to describe and investigate damaged systems in neurological patients. These clinical ramifications of fundamental research into the cognitive and physiological basis of attention will be described in Chapter 12.

SUMMARY ▲

There has been considerable interest in the topic of attention over the centuries. Attention was treated initially as a component of general philosophical systems concerning the mind and body. For the most part, concern was with the role of attention in determining what entered conscious awareness, and how. Empirical investigations of attention began in the last half of the 19th century. One of the major methodological advances at that time was the use of reaction time procedures to study attention. Most of the early studies dealt with issues arising from the philosophical analyses of attention, and these studies produced findings that are still of concern in contemporary research. In part because of a lack of theoretical tools for characterizing the mechanisms of attention, much research shifted to a behavioral emphasis in the first half of the 20th century, with the study of attention relegated to a secondary role. Despite this reduction in importance, many significant findings occurred during this period. Attention research has flourished since the middle of the 20th century, in large part due to the development of theories and models that characterize human information processing in detail. This period has seen progressive refinement of theory and methods as our understanding of attention has progressed.

We have tried to make clear in this chapter that contemporary research on attention owes a considerable debt to the work on attention conducted since the earliest days of the field of psychology. Posner (1982) made this point eloquently, stating:

One can see emerging from psychological research in the area of attention a cumulative development of theoretical concepts that rely on principles, some over 100 years old, that are now elaborated in ways that were essentially unavailable to earlier researchers. (p. 168)

He also notes,

The cumulative nature of work on attention is not widely appreciated, in part because of a failure to recognize that the methods used in current studies arose in empirical findings of the past and also because attention is a concept that can be studied at many levels. (p. 168)

Among the findings to which Posner refers are that each mental operation requires a period of time that can be measured (Donders, 1868/1969), that two events occurring close together in time are processed sequentially (Wundt, 1912), that internal events can have facilitatory or inhibitory properties (Pavlov, 1960), and that reflexive orienting to stimuli may occur (Sokolov, 1963). It is our hope that this chapter will help you to appreciate the history of research on attention in its own right, as well as provide a foundation for understanding ongoing investigations.

▲ PREVIEW OF THE BOOK

Our goal in this book is to provide the reader with a comprehensive treatment of the study of attention. The intent of Chapter 1 was to provide a historical background for the study of attention and to introduce many issues that are covered in detail in later chapters. Chapters 2–7 describe the methods used to study attention, the theories that have been proposed for various aspects of attention, and the evidence relevant to them. Chapters 8–10 develop the implications of the basic research on attention for specific applied problems. Finally, Chapters 11–12 address the neurological bases for attentional processes and disorders of attention. In the following paragraphs we provide an overview of the chapter contents.

Chapter 2 introduces the human information processing approach that provides a framework for studying the effects of attention. The information processing approach focuses on the processes by which information in a stimulus is translated to a response and on methods to improve our understanding of these processes. We also introduce the concept of arousal and its relation to information processing. This chapter also describes the behavioral tools and paradigms that have been developed to determine the nature of the processes involved in task performance. Finally, we consider psychophysiological and brain imaging methods that have been used in recent years to examine the neurophysiological basis of attention.

Chapter 3 is concerned with the topic of selective visual attention. Selectivity is needed if we are to be able to produce coherent behavior in the face of competing and distracting sources of stimulation in the environment. We can be aware of only a small portion of our surroundings at a given moment, and only a limited range of objects can be attended to and acted on at any time. In this chapter, we focus on the level of processing, early or late, at which attention comes into play and on the nature of selection, be it space- or object-based. We also examine the influence of task demands on the processes of selection.

In Chapter 4, we review much of the research on auditory attention. Research on attention in the late 20th century focused on the visual modality; however, research in the 1950s and 1960s used primarily auditory stimuli to address critical issues such as the nature of selective and divided attention and whether selection occurs early or late in processing. Although the conclusions of both the early researchers of auditory attention and their current counterparts in the study of visual attention often assume that general properties of attention are the object of investigation, an increasingly interesting question is whether there are separate sorts of attention corresponding to different sensory modalities. The corresponding question is, of course, how information from different modalities can be integrated and whether there is such a thing as a central, supra-modal attentional controller.

In Chapter 5, we discuss the range of processes involved in suppressing irrelevant information and inhibiting inappropriate actions. That is, when we "pay attention" to what we are doing, we actively attempt to attend to task-relevant information and to monitor our actions to be sure that appropriate responses are made. Equally important for successful task performance, though, are the suppression of irrelevant information and the exclusion of inappropriate actions.

Chapter 6 addresses our ability to attend to more than one thing at a time— in particular, our ability to divide attention across multiple tasks. For most of us, demands on our attention first become evident when we are required to attend to several things at once. In some cases, however, attention can be divided almost effortlessly among many sources of stimulation. In this chapter, we also explore the concept of cognitive control in terms of task set and scheduling different tasks.

In Chapter 7, we attempt to bridge the research on memory and attention, examining in detail the moments at which attention is required for memory, and vice versa. Many of the experiments concerned with attention have been, directly or indirectly, dependent on memory. If an observer is able to report what he or she has seen, we can also assume that the information is remembered, however briefly. Sometimes it is difficult to sort out whether memory or attention is responsible for a certain effect. For example, some priming effects can be attributed to memory (e.g., semantic priming effects assume the engagement of either an implicit or explicit memory system), whereas others might be attributed to a change in stimulus processing (e.g., a rejected location may be subject to temporary inhibition).

Chapter 8 concentrates on how display organization affects sampling and search behaviors, while surveying the types of displays in use today. Issues of display design have been explored extensively in the area of human factors and ergonomics. Display types are often chosen on the basis of their alerting properties, and the success of a display can be measured by whether it attracts and holds attention. Rather than being just an application of research on attention, display design has driven and continues to guide research on attention.

In Chapter 9, we review the theoretical construct of mental workload and the assumptions about attention that underlie the concept. Mental workload is another major topic in the field of human factors and ergonomics. System and product designers, developers of training programs, and accident investigators all concern themselves with the measurement of the cognitive demands placed on the human operator of a system. Situation awareness, also examined in the chapter, goes beyond mental workload in addressing the operator's understanding of the dynamic aspects of a situation. Our discussion focuses on the cognitive correlates of situation awareness and, in particular, on the attentional strategies that lead to an up-to-date (and updateable) mental model of an operational environment.

Chapter 10 addresses individual differences in attention. In addition to describing differences in basic attentional abilities between individuals and across the lifespan, it addresses the relationship between attention and intelligence. Also discussed are implications of individual differences in attentional ability for selection and training.

Chapter 11 describes cognitive neuroscience investigations of attention that focus on how attentional functions are implemented in the human brain and how the brain's physiology might inform or constrain the theories of attention. Electrophysiological and neuroimaging measurement techniques introduced in Chapter 2 are described in more detail, and examples are provided of how studies using these techniques, as well as lesion techniques, have increased our knowledge of the brain structures and pathways that are involved in attention. Issues of attention that are discussed include detection of change, filtering of irrelevant information, and the sources of excitatory and inhibitory control. This chapter also outlines various proposals regarding the attentional systems and networks of the brain.

Finally, Chapter 12 summarizes the typical impairments in attention seen in various patient groups, describes the neuropsychological tests that can be used to assess attention deficits, and outlines procedures for the treatment and rehabilitation of patients. Attention deficits are frequently reported in patients with brain disease, dementia, or trauma, and can have enormous impact on everyday-life functioning. Even mild head injury (e.g., whiplash) can result in decreased information processing speed and impairments in divided attention and concentration.

It is our hope that after completing this book the reader will have a firm grasp of (1) what research on attention involves, (2) why and how it is conducted, (3) what has been learned from attentional research, (4) issues that remain to be resolved, and (5) how our knowledge of attention informs, and is informed by, applied problems and issues. The topics in the book sometimes require effort on the reader's part for comprehension of complicated experimental designs or thorny theoretical issues, but this effort should be rewarded with an understanding and appreciation of the varied and diverse aspects of attention and their relation to theoretical and practical concerns.

CHAPTER 2

INFORMATION PROCESSING AND THE STUDY OF ATTENTION

I t is apparent that attention takes many forms and has many roles. Specifying in detail the function of a particular aspect of attention requires an understanding of exactly what is involved in performing an act. That is, to specify the role of attention in performance, it is necessary to describe the course of information processing. For example, attention might act as a sort of amplifier, making processing of stimulus information in an attended region more efficient. That is, attention may affect perception by enhancing stimulus processing or by filtering out distracting information. Attention might also affect later stages of information processing. For example, paying attention to certain aspects of a scene might cause you to remember other information associated with the perceived information. It also is the case that a certain level of physiological arousal, or alertness, is necessary in order to perform any task.

The *information processing approach* focuses on the processes by which information in a stimulus is translated to a response. Because these processes are unobservable, a variety of techniques have been developed to gain insight into their nature. This chapter describes the techniques and paradigms that have been developed to determine the processes involved in perceiving, classifying, and acting upon stimuli. Traditionally, the most important measures of performance have been speed and accuracy. Currently, however, psychophysiological measures are taking an increasingly important role in making the unobservable observable. For example, by measuring the electrical activity produced in the brain during the performance of a task, it is often possible to determine more directly the stage of processing influenced by an experimental manipulation. Finally, recently developed neuroimaging techniques are allowing us to determine not just the processes of cognition, but also how these processes are implemented in the brain.

▲ THE INFORMATION PROCESSING APPROACH

A basic model of information processing distinguishes just three processing stages: perception (or stimulus identification), decision making and response selection (or stimulus–response translation), and response programming and execution. As shown in Figure 2.1, it is often assumed that the stages occur one after the other, and that the results of one stage of processing form the input to the next one. In order to fully describe human performance, this framework would, of course, have to be supplemented with an attentional system that selects some sources of information for processing over others, and a memory system that maintains the information of immediate relevance to the task at hand and stores knowledge that may be brought to bear on task performance. However, the basic three-stage framework serves as a useful means of describing the effects of a number of factors on performance.

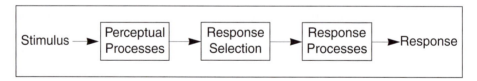

Figure 2.1 The information processing framework. Stimuli are processed in three distinct stages: perceptual, response selection (also called stimulus–response translation), and response processing.

Although specific models differ in the proposed properties of the stages of information processing—such as whether attention is required for processing, whether particular processes can be carried out concurrently or must be performed sequentially, and the extent to which one process affects another—they all rest on the basic idea that processing can be usefully described in terms of more-or-less separate activities. In this section, we will describe methods for determining what the stages of processing are and which processes are affected by various experimental manipulations. We will then discuss the place of energetical concepts such as arousal, alertness, and effort in models of information processing.

Information Theory

A central idea in the human information processing approach is that the human is not just a receiver of information, but also a transmitter of information. In this sense, the human can be described as an information channel (Shannon & Weaver, 1949). As with any other information channel (e.g., a modem or a telephone line), it is possible to talk about the rate of information transfer and the efficiency of transmitting information. For example, an operator at a central switchboard might have the task of relaying information from different sources to workers in the field. The performance of the operator will depend on the quality of the information from different sources and on the speed and reliability of his or her equipment. However, it will also depend on how quickly and accurately the information is relayed. In order to describe the rate of transmission of information, we first need to quantify the information, after which we can examine the time it takes to receive and transmit a given amount of information.

Technically, information is available whenever there is some uncertainty about what will occur. If the switchboard operator makes a mistake and gives a message received from one source back to that same source, the original source does not hear anything he or she did not already know, and we can say that no information has been transmitted. In other words, if no reduction of uncertainty has taken place, no information has been transmitted. The amount of information in a stimulus depends in part on the number of possible stimuli that could occur in a given context. For example, if the same stimulus occurs repeatedly, there is no room for reduction in uncertainty about what stimulus will occur. On the other hand, if different stimuli are possible, there will be some uncertainty about what will happen next, and the stimulus will, by definition, convey information. The amount of information in a stimulus is usually expressed in *bits* (*bi*nary uni*ts*). When stimuli are equally likely, the number of bits in a stimulus is computed as the base 2 logarithm of the number of stimulus alternatives, that is, $\log_2(N)$,[1] where N is the number of alternatives. For example, a flip of a fair coin has two equally possible outcomes: heads or tails. When the coin lands, the uncertainty about the outcome is reduced by half, and one bit [$\log_2(2)$] of information is conveyed. If two coins are flipped together, there are four possible outcomes (where H represents heads and T represents tails, these are HH, HT, TH, and TT), and two bits of information [$\log_2(4)$] are conveyed when the outcome is made known.

Just as information contained in the stimulus can be expressed in bits, so can information in the operator's responses. If the responses are perfectly correlated with the stimuli, such that an observer can know what the stimulus was if told the response, then all of the stimulus information is said to be transmitted by the operator. For example, in the coin-flipping example, imagine that you cannot see the coins being flipped, but that an observer reports the outcome of each flip. If the observer is able to see each and every outcome and is careful in reporting the results, the information transmitted by the observer will be the same as the information in the stimulus (that is, you will know the outcome of each flip simply by listening to the observer's reports). However, if the observer makes a mistake, for example, calling "heads" when the outcome was "tails," the information that was contained in the stimulus will be lost and the information transmitted will be reduced.

In the 1950s and 1960s, many experiments were conducted concerning the information processing efficiency of the human operator. Human processing efficiency was often described as the rate of information transmission expressed in bits per second. This measure was used to compare the effectiveness of different coding schemes or the efficiency of one operator compared with another. In Chapter 1, we mentioned one general law of human performance, the Hick-Hyman law, that relates task performance to information transmitted (Hick, 1952; Hyman, 1953). According to the Hick-Hyman law, reaction time (RT) in a task is linearly related to the amount of information transmitted. That is, given equally likely stimuli and perfect performance, RT will increase by a constant amount each time the number of possible stimuli is doubled, with the slope of the line reflecting the efficiency of information processing. For example, as shown in Figure 2.2, the slope will be steeper (as with the open circles) when the relation between stimuli and responses is arbitrary (e.g., when "John" is the correct response to the number "6") than when the response is compatible with the stimulus (closed circles; e.g., say "six" when the stimulus is "6").

Information and Stages

A common idea in models of information processing is that information builds up over time following stimulus presentation. In its simplest form, the buildup or accumulation of evidence over time can be conceived of as occurring continuously from the moment of stimulus presentation to the execution of a response. For extremely simple, reflexive actions, something like this might be the case. However, most behavior is more complicated, and evidence must be evaluated, weighted, or combined before an appropriate action can be selected.

As mentioned earlier, a common approach to human information processing is to suppose that information is processed in a series of discrete stages or modules (see Figure 2.1). In this approach, a stage can be viewed as a processing module in which the output of one module serves as the input for the next. A stage

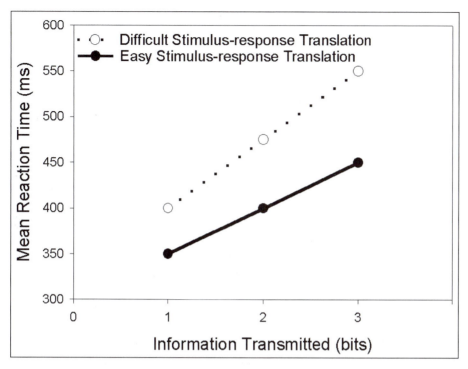

Figure 2.2   The relationship between reaction time and information transmitted according to the Hick-Hyman Law.

does not necessarily correspond to a particular circuit or structure in the brain, but indicates a function (or process) carried out during a period of time. One topic of interest is the measurement of the time needed to complete various processes (i.e., mental chronometry). A more fundamental question concerns the number and nature of the stages themselves.

One of the most important events in experimental psychology was the realization that the time to complete mental processes could be measured. The development of this idea since the establishment of psychology as a science was discussed in Chapter 1, beginning with Wundt's observations of the time to switch attention from one stimulus to another. The measurement of information processing time was set on a firm footing with Donders's (1868/1969) *subtractive method* for measuring the duration of processes. Recall that this method consists of comparing tasks that differ only in the processing stage of interest, and taking the difference in completion times for the two tasks as a measure of the time needed to complete the process of interest. For example, in a relatively recent application of this technique, Posner and Mitchell (1967) measured the time to name letters. They did this by comparing the time needed to make a same/different classification of two letters that were identical in form (e.g., RR) with the time needed to make the classification when the letters were identical only in name (e.g., Rr). Posner and Mitchell found that judgments were 75 ms faster in the former case than in the latter. Reasoning that the letters with the same form could be judged as being the same or different on the basis of visual information alone, whereas the letters presented in different cases required in addition that the name of each form be determined, Posner and Mitchell concluded that the naming process takes approximately 75 ms.

It should be noted that application of the subtractive logic, as in the example in the previous paragraph, depends on the assumptions that the processing stages (e.g., perceive letters, name letters, select response "same" or "different," make response) are distinct and independent, and that the insertion of the additional process does not alter the basic task structure. The latter assumption has been called the *assumption of pure insertion*. Posner and Mitchell's application of the subtractive method in determining the time to name letters could be questioned because the time to process the letters might be affected by the forms of the letters, with processing proceeding more efficiently when the same stimulus occurs twice, rather than when there are two different stimuli (Proctor, 1981).

Conditions that might lead to the violation of the assumption of pure insertion were observed relatively soon after Donders published his landmark paper. For example, L. Lange (1888) noted that emphasizing the response to be made—rather than the stimulus to be processed—led to faster RTs. Thus, the addition of stages that change the focus of the subject from the stimuli to the responses might lead to changes in one or more other stages of processing. Other studies have shown that although, as Donders claimed, responses to simple and choice reaction tasks have similar characteristics, more physical force is exerted in responding in the go or no-go task than in simple or choice reaction tasks (Ulrich, Mattes, & Miller, 1999).

The subtractive method is used to compute the time needed to complete a known process. That is, the researcher makes assumptions about what the processes are, and then compares tasks to measure the duration of the process of interest. The *additive factors method*, developed by Sternberg (1969), is a method for determining which stages are involved in a particular information processing task. That is, it can be used to infer the presence of particular stages. In this method, several factors (i.e., independent variables) are manipulated, and the effects of these manipulations on time to perform the task are examined. If two factors have additive effects (i.e., if the effect of one factor does not depend on the level of another factor), they are assumed to affect different stages (see Figure 2.3, left panel). If the factors interact, such that the effect of one factor depends on the level of the other, the two factors are assumed to affect the same stage of

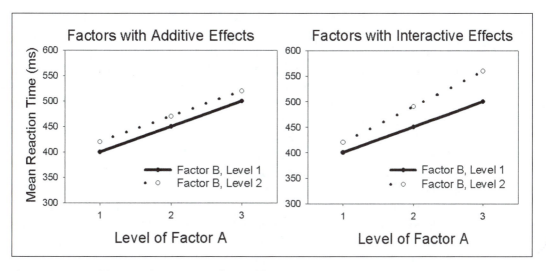

Figure 2.3   Additive and interactive effects of factor manipulations.

processing (see Figure 2.3, right panel, in which the effect of changing Factor B is relatively small at Level 1 of Factor A, larger at Level 2, and largest at Level 3). When it is known which processing stage is affected by one of the factors (e.g., stimulus clarity most likely affects perceptual processing time), it is possible, by examining the patterns of interactions, to infer the underlying processing stages (e.g., if the frequency with which a stimulus occurs interacts with stimulus clarity, the effect of frequency can be localized at the perceptual stage).

An example of an everyday activity like going from your home in, say, Amsterdam, to the university in, say, Utrecht, may be helpful in understanding the principles of the additive factors method. In this example, after leaving home you might cycle to the train station, where you take the train from Amsterdam to Utrecht. Once in Utrecht, you then take the bus from the train station to the university. Excluding any time spent waiting for the train or the bus, the actual travel time to get from home to the university (T_{total}) is equal to the sum of the time to bicycle ($T_{bicycle}$), the time spent on the train (T_{train}), and the time spent on the bus (T_{bus}). Assuming that these stages are independent, the total travel time, T_{total}, is simply the sum of the times to complete each leg of the journey ($T_{bicycle}$ + T_{train} + T_{bus}). The additive factors method assumes that if the duration of one stage is increased by some amount (e.g., T_{train} might increase because of work being conducted on the overhead wires), the total time increases by the same amount as the prolonged stage (i.e., $\Delta T_{total} = \Delta T_{train}$), and all other stage durations remain unchanged (i.e., $\Delta T_{bicycle} = 0$, $\Delta T_{bus} = 0$).

As mentioned earlier, factors have additive effects when they affect different stages. In our example, the effect of a flat tire and the effect of work being done on the overhead wires will have additive effects on travel time (e.g., if it takes 10 minutes to fix the tire and 5 extra minutes on the train, the total delay will be 15 minutes). When two or more factors affect a common stage, the effect of a factor can depend on the levels of the other factors. For example, strong winds might normally slow your cycling time by about 10 minutes, and being tired in the morning might slow you by 2 minutes. However, if you are tired and it is windy, you might need to get off your bike and walk, which will slow you by 20 minutes, more than the 12 (10 + 2) minutes of the effects of each factor when they occur in isolation.

Our example is quite simple because it excludes any waiting time from the calculation of total travel time. If waiting time is included, we can no longer speak of three separate stages in the trip from Amsterdam to Utrecht. For example, trouble with the bicycle can lead to missing an express train, with the result that a local train has to be taken instead. Local trains take more time to reach their destinations than express trains, so the effect of manipulating some factor thought to affect only one stage (e.g., the effect of a flat tire on cycling time) also affects the duration of another stage, the train ride. If we want to persist in thinking of cycling, riding the train, and taking the bus as separate stages, the additive factors method cannot be validly applied to estimations of total trip time. This example points out the importance of *stage robustness*. Stages are said to be robust if a number of experiments produce data consistent with the proposed stages, and if when two factors show additive effects, the addition of a third factor does not result in a higher-order (i.e., three-way) interaction. If the three factors interact, then the initial conclusion based on the additive effects of the two factors is proven incorrect, and it must be concluded that all three factors affect a stage in common (Van Duren & Sanders, 1988).

According to the additive factors method, additive effects of two factors indicate that the two factors affect different processing stages, and it is assumed that these stages are sequential and that the processing associated with one stage is completed before that associated with the next stage begins. Despite the likelihood that these assumptions do not always hold (e.g., processes may operate concurrently or a given process may output partial rather than complete information; McClelland, 1979; Roberts & Sternberg, 1993), a fairly consistent picture of the stages of information processing has emerged from applications of the additive factors method (Sanders, 1990). Figure 2.4 shows a diagram of the stages suggested by a wide range of experiments and some of the factors that have been shown to affect one or more of these stages. For example, the effect of the number of stimulus alternatives interacts with that of stimulus quality and with that of stimulus–response compatibility. However, the effects of stimulus quality and

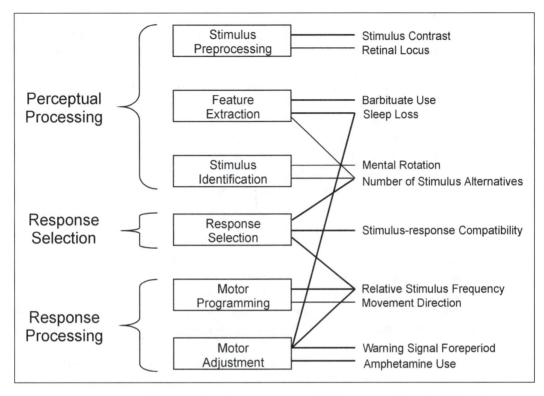

Figure 2.4   Summary of conclusions drawn from additive factors studies of human information processing.

SOURCE: Adapted from Sanders, 1990.

stimulus-response compatibility are additive, suggesting that they affect different stages. It can therefore be concluded that the effect of the number of stimulus alternatives affects more than one stage of processing.

MENTAL RESOURCES ▲

Up to this point, our treatment of information processing has been structural in the sense that information is assumed to be passed as a matter of course from one stage to the next. However, it seems likely that all processes will, to some extent, depend on the amount of energy, capacity, or mental resources devoted to processing. At a biological level, all processes depend on the availability of oxygen and glucose in the blood. At a more cognitive level, we are often aware of having to "try harder" to achieve some goals.

The relation between *arousal level* (i.e., one's general level of stimulation or readiness to act) and performance was first described nearly a century ago by Yerkes and Dodson (1908). Yerkes and Dodson trained mice to discriminate between two passageways, a light one and a dark one. The mouse's task was simply to enter the lighter of the boxes. The researchers varied the difficulty of the task by increasing or decreasing the contrast between the two boxes, and they encouraged the mice to select the correct box by giving them a shock whenever they entered the wrong one. As one might expect, the easier the discrimination between the light and dark box, the faster the mice learned to enter the lighter box and avoid the darker one. Also, when the discrimination was easy, the speed with which the mice learned was roughly proportional to the intensity of the shock delivered to the mouse when it entered the wrong box (see Figure 2.5, Condition II). However, when the discrimination was more difficult, increasing the intensity of the shock did not always lead to faster learning. In this case, the time to learn the discrimination was a U-shaped function of the intensity of the shock (see Figure 2.5, Conditions I and III), with an intermediate shock leading to the optimal learning time. In other words, whereas the easy task could be learned under strong stimulation as well as under weak stimulation, the difficult one was more readily learned under relatively weak stimulation.

Yerkes and Dodson's findings regarding the relation between performance and arousal levels have come to be called the *Yerkes-Dodson Law*. Although Yerkes and Dodson plotted their results in terms of trials needed to learn a task, which results in a U-shaped relation with arousal, the Yerkes-Dodson Law generally states that performance is an *inverted* U-shaped function of arousal, with the optimal arousal level (i.e., the level at which the inverted U peaks) being lower the more difficult the task. In Yerkes and Dodson's original experiments, motivating the mice by raising the shock level brought them closer to the arousal level that was optimal for the simple task, but clearly pushed them "over the top" in the more difficult task.

Easterbrook (1959) argued that arousal level affects performance by determining the number of sources of information ("cues") that the organism can effectively monitor. According to this *cue-utilization theory*, high arousal leads to greater selectivity and is thus beneficial only when relatively few cues have to be monitored (and especially when other, potentially distracting cues have to be ignored). In contrast, low arousal will lead to better performance when many cues have to be monitored. The notion of cue utilization can be equated with attentional selectivity. High arousal favors high selectivity, for example, focusing attention on one source of input while ignoring others. In contrast, low arousal favors low selectivity, or dividing attention across many sources of input.

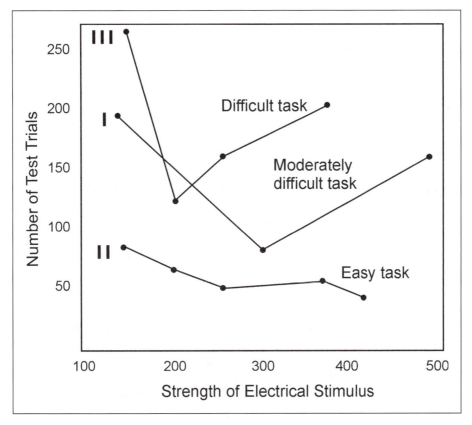

Figure 2.5   The relation between the strength of electrical stimulation and task difficulty on the number of trials necessary to learn a task.

SOURCE: Adapted from Yerkes & Dodson, 1908.

Arousal and Performance

The concept of cortical arousal is closely related to that of *vigilance* (i.e., a
state of readiness to detect and respond to infrequent, randomly occurring
events). Both terms are often used to refer to a general state of wakefulness, and
factors that increase or decrease arousal level are associated with corresponding
increases or decreases in vigilance task performance. However, the association
between cortical arousal and vigilance performance is not perfect, suggesting that
vigilance is a multidimensional construct (Parasuraman, Warm, & See, 1998). In
particular, although arousal level seems to determine the overall level of vigilance
performance, it cannot explain why vigilance performance typically decreases after
a short (20–30 minute) period of vigilance task performance (see discussion of this

vigilance decrement in Chapter 8). The regulation of arousal has long been linked to the reticular formation of the brain (Moruzzi & Magoun, 1949), although other subcortical areas have since been shown to play a role in regulating arousal level (see Parasuraman et al., 1998). A state of alert attentiveness is reflected in brain activity, in particular with relatively fast electroencephalogram (EEG) beta (14–30 Hz) activity. Slower EEG activity (e.g., alpha activity in the range of 8–13 Hz) is associated with poorer performance on vigilance tasks and lower levels of arousal.

One popular task for studying the relation between arousal and performance in both humans and nonhuman animals is the *serial reaction time task* (Wilkinson, 1963; see also Chapter 6), in which subjects respond to whichever of five lights comes on by pressing a corresponding response key. Variables that negatively affect the state of arousal of the subject, such as time on task, noise, sleep loss, and alcohol, reduce accuracy and, somewhat less consistently, speed on the serial reaction time task. Variables that are associated with a higher level of arousal, such as performance incentives and testing at a later time of day, improve performance (see, e.g., Parasuraman, 1984).

Performance in a serial reaction time task under conditions of noise and sleep loss was studied by Wilkinson (1963). Noise led to a decrease in performance in subjects who had had a normal night's sleep, whereas it benefited the performance of sleep-deprived subjects. This is consistent with the inverted U-shaped relation between arousal and performance—if it is assumed that noise compensates for the arousal-reducing effects of sleep loss, but results in excessive arousal after normal sleep. Another effect that may seem counterintuitive, but that is consistent with the hypothesized effects of arousal, is that performance incentives exacerbated the detrimental effect of noise, presumably by further increasing the already excessive amount of arousal.

If the negative effect of noise is due to its increasing the arousal level of the performer, time on task should also interact with noise, such that the detrimental effects of noise should be counteracted by the arousal-reducing effect of progressive time on task. However, this is not the case, as was noted by Broadbent (1971), who proposed an extension of the notion of unitary arousal to account for this seeming contradiction. He called the two proposed types of arousal *lower arousal* and *upper arousal*. Lower arousal was equated with the notion of cortical arousal and was hypothesized to be affected by state variables such as noise and sleep loss. Upper arousal was assumed to facilitate controlled, strategic operations that correct sub- or superoptimal levels of lower arousal, and corresponds to the concept of "effort" (Kahneman, 1973; Sanders, 1983). Broadbent hypothesized that upper arousal becomes depleted as time on task increases, thus reducing the ability of the subject to compensate for deficient lower arousal. Thus, whereas effects of sleep loss and noise are effectively compensated for during the early trials of task performance, they are not during later trials.

Box 2.1 | **Impulsivity and Arousal**

It may seem counterintuitive that impulsive people are thought of as having low basic arousal. This seeming paradox is especially evident in the case of *attention deficit hyperactivity disorder* (ADHD; see Chapter 12 for a clinical description). People with ADHD suffer from excessive impulsivity, impairments in focusing attention, and hyperactivity. About 70% of these individuals can be treated successfully with methylphenidate (Ritalin), an amphetamine. That is, children who are excessively active, impulsive, and distractible are less so when taking a stimulating substance that, by definition, increases spontaneous motor activity. One key to this apparent paradox lies in the nature of distractibility. When organisms are given stimulants their arousal is heightened. In turn, they become more selective, and therefore less distractible. They may also become less impulsive, because impulsivity is strongly related to the capacity to inhibit undesired (but possibly potent)

tendencies to act or respond. Hyperactivity and distractibility are also related; excessive distraction may result in excessive activity (orienting, approaching, etc.).

Further evidence that low levels of arousal are associated with ADHD and impulsivity comes from a recent study on the prevalence of sleep disorders and symptoms of ADHD in children. Sleep deprivation is strongly associated with arousal and may also lead to (or be caused by) symptoms of ADHD. Chervin et al. (2002) found that sleepiness during the day is linked to hyperactive behavior in both boys and girls throughout childhood and early adolescence. Children who snore face nearly double the risk of being inattentive and hyperactive. This suggests a rather unorthodox intervention for some sufferers of ADHD: Snoring is often caused by apnea, which in turn may be caused by large tonsils, so removing the tonsils might in some cases improve behavior.

Anderson and Revelle (1982) also demonstrated that different factors that affect arousal can exacerbate or ameliorate the effects of other factors while confirming that the optimal level of arousal depends on task demands. They manipulated task difficulty by comparing performance in a task requiring that attention be focused on a small area (search of a text for spelling errors) with that in a task requiring a broader focus of attention (search for syntax errors). Arousal was manipulated by choosing subjects high or low in impulsivity (see Box 2.1), as measured by a questionnaire, and by the administration of caffeine (versus placebo). Impulsivity is thought to reflect low arousal whereas caffeine generally increases arousal (Lorist & Tops, in press). Caffeine improved the performance of high impulsivity subjects, presumably by increasing their arousal to a more optimal level, whereas the performance of the low impulsivity subjects was worse with caffeine, presumably because their arousal levels were already optimal. The combination of low impulsivity and caffeine was more detrimental in the syntax

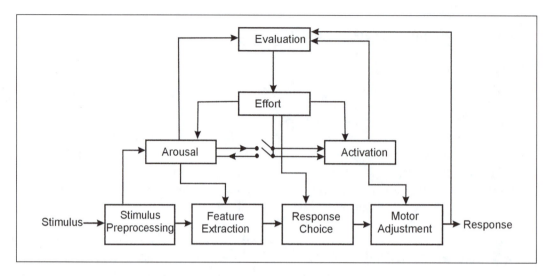

Figure 2.6   Sanders's model of energetic mechanisms and their relation to human information processing.

SOURCE: Sanders, 1983. Copyright 1983; reprinted with permission of Elsevier.

task (requiring a broader focus of attention) than in the spelling task (in which attention could be more focused), consistent with the idea that high arousal can increase selectivity to the point that performance in tasks requiring divided attention or a broader focus actually suffers. The results of Anderson and Revelle's study are also consistent with the idea that "sustained information transfer" (requiring focused attention on a single input stream) improves under conditions of higher arousal whereas "short-term memory" function does not (M. S. Humphreys & Revelle, 1984; see also Chapter 10 for a discussion of these processes).

An Energetic Systems Model of Information Processing

Sanders (1983, 1997) suggested how a stage model of information processing might be augmented by energetical systems. As shown in Figure 2.6, Sanders suggested that different stages of information processing have different relations to effortful processing. In the model, perceptual processing is divided into two stages, stimulus preprocessing and feature extraction, the response-selection stage is relabeled "response choice," and what is usually called the response stage is called motor adjustment. Sanders proposed that there are three different energetical mechanisms: arousal, activation, and effort. An evaluation mechanism monitors arousal and activation and can increase effort (which then increases the potential arousal and activation). Stimuli themselves can increase arousal at the early stages of stimulus processing, and this arousal will facilitate later stages of stimulus processing. On the other hand, effort, which can be roughly equated with conscious processing, directly influences the efficiency of response selection, and activation affects response processing. This conception of activation at the response stage (e.g., preparation to respond) can be interpreted as general alertness.

BEHAVIORAL MEASURES ▲

Most of the tasks used to study attention and information processing are speeded; that is, subjects are asked to respond as quickly as possible to a given event without sacrificing accuracy. Although other measures, such as the force with which a response is made, may be used to quantify performance, by far the most commonly used measures of performance are RT (reaction time) and accuracy.

Reaction Time

Reaction time, usually measured from the onset of stimulus presentation until the participant's response, is one of the most commonly used behavioral measures in experimental psychology. Although usually measured using an all or none response (e.g., the time required to press a button or to start to say a word), it can also be based on the time to initiate a movement or to exert a minimal amount of force.

The making of a response can be considered the outcome of a cognitive process initiated by a specific stimulus. One factor that can affect RT is the readiness (or preparedness) of the responder. For example, the RT of a runner in a race can be defined as the time interval between the starting shot and the moment at which the starting block is left. The athlete's recognition of the need for a high degree of preparedness in getting off to a good start is evident in the occurrence of "false starts." In order to trim milliseconds from their racing times, athletes enter a high state of preparedness to run, which sometimes results in the execution of a response before the actual stimulus is presented. Preparation to respond is usually studied by presenting a warning signal at various intervals prior to the onset of the relevant stimulus. The warning signal does not indicate what the stimulus will be, but only that it is about to occur. Presenting a warning signal very shortly (less than 150 ms) before a stimulus has been shown to decrease RT (see, e.g., Bertelson, 1967) and increase error rates. Thus, in experiments—as on the starting block— readiness to respond can result in faster RTs, but at the expense of accuracy.

Reaction time to a stimulus is not constant, but varies from trial to trial. Figure 2.7 shows an RT distribution for one subject in a simple reaction time task. As is

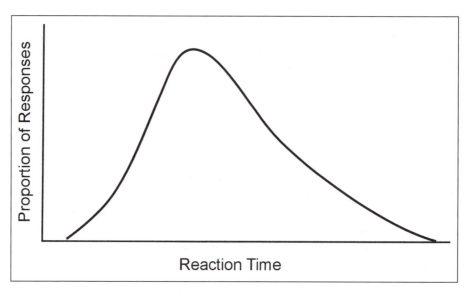

Figure 2.7   A typical reaction time distribution.

typical, the distribution is skewed to the right rather than following a normal, bell-shaped curve. In other words, the median of the distribution is to the left of the mean of the distribution. Part of the reason for the skew apparent in RT distributions has to do with the nature of the measurement: Time is bounded by 0 on the left and unbounded on the right. Even when this consideration is taken into account, the best description of an RT distribution is that the random variations in RT do not follow a normal distribution. Even though RT distributions are expected to tail off to the right to some degree, many researchers use an RT cut-off to remove "outliers" arising from factors such as momentary loss of attention (or even falling asleep during an experiment) from the data before analyses are done. Reactions that are too fast to be logically possible (e.g., faster than 100 ms) are considered to be anticipations, rather than deliberate responses, and are removed as well.

Accuracy

In addition to (or in place of) RT, accuracy of performance is often used as a dependent variable. Either the proportion or percentage of correct responses or the proportion or percentage of errors may be reported. An important consideration when interpreting accuracy is that the probability of making an error depends on the number and probability of the response alternatives: The more alternatives, the lower the percentage correct expected by chance alone.

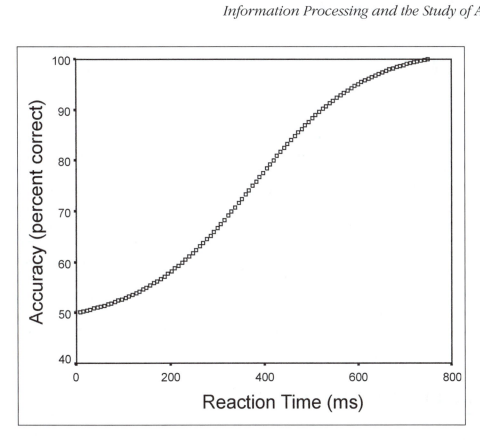

Figure 2.8   A speed–accuracy trade-off function.

It has been known since at least the end of the 19th century that the speed and accuracy of responding are closely linked (Woodworth, 1899), such that either speed or accuracy can be emphasized to the detriment of the other. Thus, even when RT is the primary dependent measure in an experiment, accuracy (based on the trials remaining after any outliers have been removed) is also measured. Having measures of both RT and accuracy is important in order to determine whether *speed–accuracy trade-off* has occurred. In general, RT and accuracy are inversely related such that, in a given task, increases in response speed are generally accompanied by reduced accuracy of performance. Figure 2.8 shows a typical speed–accuracy trade-off function. The S-shaped form of the function reflects that when RTs are relatively fast, any decreases in RT are accompanied by large costs in accuracy. Similarly, when accuracy is already high, it can be increased only at large costs in time to respond. Asking subjects in an experiment to "respond as quickly as possible without making too many errors" is essentially asking them to find an optimal point on the speed–accuracy trade-off function. Speed–accuracy trade-off is said to occur when relatively fast RTs are accompanied by relatively high error rates, and vice versa. When this occurs, it is impossible to know whether differences between conditions are due to differences inherent in the task, or simply due to the adoption of a different setting on the speed–accuracy trade-off function.

A distinction has been made between two types of speed–accuracy trade-off: macro-trade-off and micro-trade-off (Pachella, 1974). Macro-trade-off is the most commonly studied type of trade-off, and refers to the setting on the speed–accuracy trade-off function within a particular condition or experiment. For example, some participants might adopt a risky strategy, resulting in fast reactions and many errors, whereas others may be more conservative, making few errors but taking a relatively long time to respond. Thus, macro-trade-off reflects the strategy (risky or conservative) adopted by the subject and corresponds to adopting a setting on the speed–accuracy trade-off function. The influence of macro-trade-off has been examined by using instructions that emphasize speed or accuracy, or by using deadlines to induce different levels of time pressure (see, e.g., Wickelgren, 1977). Micro-trade-off refers to the relation between speed and accuracy from one trial to the next. For example, trials following error trials are often slower than the mean RT for a condition, and may reflect a temporary shift to a more conservative setting on the speed–accuracy trade-off function (see Box 2.2).

▲ SIGNAL DETECTION METHODS

In the previous section, we discussed the need to consider both speed and accuracy to check for any effects of speed–accuracy trade-off due to adopting a more liberal or conservative criterion on the speed–accuracy trade-off function. In this section, we describe a method for more generally separating effects due to the sensitivity of the observer (i.e., the ability to perceptually process information) from effects due to the setting of a response criterion. This method, based on *signal detection theory* (see, e.g., Green & Swets, 1966; Swets, 1998), has been used with a wide variety of tasks, ranging from perceptual discrimination to recognition memory, in order to determine whether differences in performance between subjects or tasks can be attributed to differences in the ability to discriminate among stimuli, to a change in response bias, or to both.

Signal detection methods are applied in situations in which a subject has to indicate whether a stimulus (the signal) was present or not. For example, in a perceptual discrimination experiment, the signal might be a flash of light or a tone of a specific frequency; in a memory experiment the "signal" might be a word that was presented earlier in the experiment. A basic assumption is that signals are not equally clear on all trials, but contain a random amount of noise that can detract from their discriminability. Noise might be due to external sources, such as the visual or auditory background, or to internal sources, such as physiological

| Box 2.2 | Modeling Speed-Accuracy Trade-Off |

Several classes of models have been proposed to account for speed-accuracy trade-off (Sanders, 1998). In so-called random walk models, decisions to respond are made when the evidence for a particular event, starting at an initial baseline, has accumulated sufficiently over time to reach a criterion. The criterion and baseline may vary not only between conditions, thereby accounting for macro-trade-off, but also from trial to trial, resulting in a specific micro-trade-off function.

The "fast-guess" models (see, e.g., Ollman, 1966; Yellott, 1967, 1971) are based on the assumption that mean RT reflects a mixture of trials in which a stimulus was correctly recognized and "guess" trials that are fast and at chance accuracy. Accuracy decreases as RT decreases because the proportion of guess trials increases. Thus, according to these models, the micro-trade-off function has the same form as the macro-trade-off function.

"Deadline" models (see, e.g., Yellott, 1971) assume that responses are made on the basis of the information that has accumulated up to the point in time that a response is made. If insufficient evidence is available for an accurate response at the moment at which a deadline (e.g., 500 ms) is reached, then a guess is made on the basis of the information available at that moment. Thus, according to deadline models, guesses are generally slow, because they are made only after the deadline is reached. The setting of a late deadline will result in relatively accurate responses because a late deadline reduces the percentage of guesses, whereas the setting of an early deadline results in more guesses and, hence, more errors.

An important difference between the fast-guess model and the deadline model is the predicted speed of error trials, which is fast according to the fast-guess model and slow according to the deadline model. Furthermore, according to the fast-guess model, macro-trade-off will be most evident on trials with fast responses, whereas according to the deadline model, it will be most evident for trials with slow responses.

An important difference between the random walk models and the other models is that, in random walk models, an error is made when a specific amount of evidence has accumulated, and not when a specific amount of time has elapsed. Thus, the model presupposes no direct relation between errors and the speed of error trials. However, the use of a liberal criterion (i.e., a criterion close to the initial baseline) will generally lead to relatively fast reactions and high error rates; in contrast, a conservative criterion (which demands more evidence) will lead to relatively slow reactions and low error rates.

variations due to changes in blood pressure. It is assumed that the quality of the signal varies along a single continuum of sensory evidence, ranging from relatively little evidence that a stimulus is present on a given trial to relatively convincing evidence. So-called "noise" trials, on which no stimulus is present, are also assumed

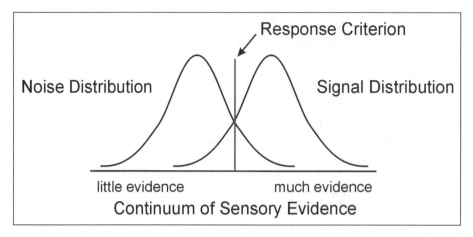

Figure 2.9   The distributions of noise and signal along the continuum of sensory evidence. Whenever the evidence exceeds the response criterion, the response "signal present" is given.

to contain some evidence that a signal is present. Thus, both signal and noise trials can be represented by distributions along the continuum of sensory evidence (see Figure 2.9). Signal detection methods can be applied only when the distributions overlap, such that there are some trials on which it cannot be said with certainty whether the signal was present. If the signal and noise distributions overlap completely, it is impossible to ever know for certain whether a signal was present, and performance will be at chance.

In a typical signal detection experiment, the stimulus is presented on some proportion of the trials, and observers indicate on each trial whether they think that the target stimulus was present. The experiment can be described as shown in Figure 2.10. On each trial, the signal was either present or absent, and the observer responded either "yes" (the signal was present) or "no" (the signal was not present). Thus, there are four possible outcomes on given trial: a "hit," a false alarm, a correct rejection, or a miss (see Figure 2.10). Because the miss rate and the correct rejection rate can be derived from the hit rate and false alarm rates, respectively, performance can be completely described by focusing on just the hit rate and the false alarm rate.

Although it might seem that a high hit rate indicates good performance, this is not always the case. For example, if the task is to detect tumors in a mammogram, the observer will not want to miss any tumors, but will also not want to order surgery unless it is necessary. In order to assess the sensitivity of the observer, it is thus necessary to take the false alarm rate into account. We say that the sensitivity of the observer is high when the hit rate is high relative to the false alarm rate;

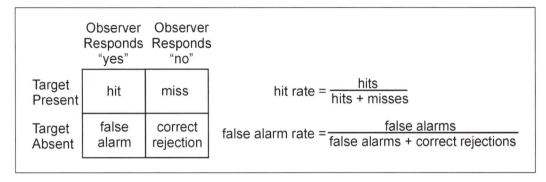

	Observer Responds "yes"	Observer Responds "no"
Target Present	hit	miss
Target Absent	false alarm	correct rejection

$$\text{hit rate} = \frac{\text{hits}}{\text{hits + misses}}$$

$$\text{false alarm rate} = \frac{\text{false alarms}}{\text{false alarms + correct rejections}}$$

Figure 2.10 Possible outcomes in a signal detection experiment and the computation of the hit and false alarm rates.

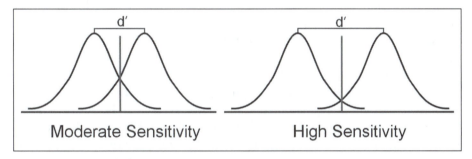

Moderate Sensitivity   High Sensitivity

Figure 2.11 Observer sensitivity conceptualized as overlap between the noise and signal distributions.

that is, when the observer is good at discriminating signal and noise trials. High sensitivity can be conceptualized as indicating that there is little overlap between the signal and noise distributions (see Figure 2.11). The most common measure used to describe sensitivity is d' (pronounced "dee-prime"), which is the distance between the means of the two distributions.

A key assumption of signal detection methods is that the results of a given experiment do not depend on the sensitivity of the observer alone, but also on the decision criterion used by the subject. The decision criterion is defined as the point along the continuum of sensory evidence at which the subject perceives enough information to make a "yes" response (see Figure 2.11). A liberal observer requires less information than a conservative observer. For example, a radiologist examining a mammogram from a woman at high risk for breast cancer may interpret any slight anomaly as a tumor, whereas the same radiologist may require more information before making such a diagnosis of a mammogram from a low-risk woman. The more liberal the criterion setting, the more often the observer will say

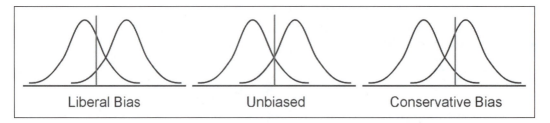

Figure 2.12   Response bias conceptualized as the location of the response criterion.

"yes," and the higher the hit and false alarm rates will be (see Figure 2.12). A common measure of response bias is β (beta), which is the ratio of the height of the signal distribution to the height of the noise distribution at the location of the decision criterion. Response bias has traditionally been assumed to be influenced by a number of factors, including payoffs that encourage observers to be more liberal (e.g., pay 20 cents for a hit and penalize 1 cent for a false alarm) or more conservative (e.g., pay 10 cents for a hit and penalize 10 cents for a false alarm), and the use of different probabilities for signal and noise (i.e., changes in signal base rate). Both the degree of overlap of the distributions and the location of the response criterion can be computed from the observed hit and false alarm rates.

Signal detection methods have been used extensively to study the effects of variables such as drugs, alcohol, and sleep loss on performance. The major question is whether such variables affect the sensitivity of the observer or the response criterion. For example, Maylor and Rabbitt (1987) studied the influence of alcohol on recognition memory. Participants in the study had to judge whether items had or had not been presented earlier in the study (a hit was correct recognition of a word as having been previously presented). Participants who had ingested alcohol (1 ml per kg body weight) were both less sensitive (as indicated by a decrease in d') and more conservative (as indicated by an increase in β). Thus, alcohol not only impaired memory, but also introduced a more conservative bias.

Despite the successes of signal detection methods in isolating effects of sensitivity and bias on performance, some of the basic assumptions have recently been criticized. For example, the assumption that the setting of the response criterion is at least partly under subject control has been put into question by recent studies that show little correlation between observers' perceptions of their decision strategies and their actual performance in signal detection tasks. For example, Balakrishnan (1998) showed that both hit and false alarm rates decreased when the chance that a signal was present decreased, as well as when the time observers had performed a task (i.e., time on task) increased. However, neither of these factors affected observers' judgments of the accuracy of their decision making. Balakrishnan (1999) has also argued, on the basis of distribution-free estimates of the proportion of biased responses, that the response criterion set by observers is almost always unbiased, and is not necessarily affected by changes in base rates or payoffs. He argues that the strong influence of changes in base rate and payoffs on hit and false-alarm rates may be due to their effects on the distributions of signal and noise rather than, as commonly assumed, on the setting of the response criteria. For example, observers may maintain a more accurate internal representation of the target when the base rate is higher.

PSYCHOPHYSIOLOGICAL MEASURES ▲

Behavioral measures of human information processing, such as response time and accuracy, are increasingly being supplemented by more direct measures of the physiological processes that underlie such processing. The most widely used of these psychophysiological measures is based on the voltage fluctuations within the brain that can be measured by electrodes placed on the scalp (i.e., the EEG). The EEG reflects all neural processing occurring within a given time interval and, as such, is not very informative as to what specific processes are occurring. In order to narrow down the range of activity examined at a given moment, *event-related potentials (ERPs)* are generally computed. The ERP is computed by averaging together many single-trial EEGs starting from (i.e., time-locked to) a particular external event, usually the onset of a stimulus. Averaging of many trials is necessary in order to eliminate random noise and any electrical activity that is not temporally related to the processing of the stimulus. The resulting average waveform is the ERP, and reflects only the neural activity associated with the information processing performed in response to the stimulus.[2] As shown in Figure 2.13, electrical activity is generally recorded at several scalp sites. The different sites are denoted by their positions above brain areas. For example, in Figure 2.13, positions above frontal areas include F3, Fz, and F4; those above central areas C3, Cz, and C4; those above parietal areas P3 and P4; and those above occipital areas O1 and O2. ERPs may be computed for each of the sites.

An important advantage of the ERP relative to behavioral measures is that it is measured throughout the time intervening between the presentation of the stimulus and the making of a response, allowing precise measurement of the time course of attentional processes. Typical ERPs in reaction to a visual stimulus are shown in Figure 2.13. Both the magnitudes and latencies of several components of the ERP can be associated with specific cognitive events. The components of the ERP are designated by the letters N or P, to indicate whether the component is negative-going or positive-going, and a number indicating the serial order in the event sequence (e.g., N1 is the first negative-going component). Because different research groups follow different conventions, it is always important to look at the

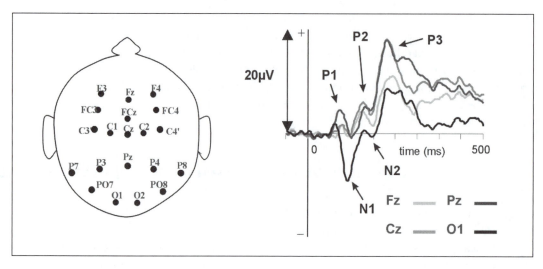

Figure 2.13   (Left) The positioning of electrodes for EEG measurements at the scalp according to the system of Pivik et al. (1993). (Right) ERPs to a visual signal as a function of the site of the electrodes.

y-axis of an ERP plot to determine whether the ERP has been plotted with positive going downwards and negative going upwards, or vice versa.

Stimulus-locked ERPs in visual tasks show several positive (P) and negative (N) deflections (components), which are denoted as NP80 (a small negative-positive complex peaking at 80 ms after stimulus onset; also denoted as C1), P1, N1, P2, N2, and P3, in their temporal order of appearance. The earliest components (NP80, P1, and N1) are assumed to reflect mainly bottom-up (i.e., stimulus-driven) processing. For example, the polarity of the NP80, which appears to be generated in the cortical areas involved in early visual processing (the striate visual cortex), depends on the position of a stimulus (Clark & Hillyard, 1996). The P1 component is sensitive to the side of stimulus presentation, such that it is larger when measured at the brain hemisphere contralateral to the side of presentation (Heinze et al., 1994). The N1 component seems to arise from several sources (V. P. Clark & Hillyard, 1996; Wijers et al., 1997), and could reflect the operation of a process that discriminates relevant from irrelevant stimuli (Vogel & Luck, 2000). The N1 is also greater for attended than for ignored stimuli, which suggests that attention enhances early perceptual processing (Luck & Girelli, 1998).

One of the most widely studied ERP components is the third positive component, or P3 (also denoted as P300, or P3b) component, which reaches its largest amplitude at the Cz electrode and usually peaks between 330 and 600 ms after stimulus onset. The peak latency of the P3 component is assumed to reflect the endpoint of stimulus evaluation (Donchin et al., 1978), although some studies have shown this component to be sensitive to variables that are thought to affect response-related processing (Verleger, 1997). Stimuli falling within the focus of attention elicit a P3 component only when the stimulus is relevant for performance, that is, when it is a target rather than a distractor (Hillyard & Kutas, 1983).

The dependency of the P3 component on target relevance can be observed very clearly in the *oddball paradigm*, widely used in ERP research (see Chapters 4, 9, and 11 for applications using the oddball paradigm). In this paradigm, one *standard* stimulus is repeated in a series. Occasionally, a different stimulus (the oddball) is presented, and the participant should either make an overt response or covertly count the occurrences of the oddball stimulus. In trials in which an oddball occurs, a clear P3 component is evoked. The amplitude of this P3 component has been interpreted as reflecting processes involved in *memory updating* (Donchin & Coles, 1988), because only when the oddball stimulus appears does memory for the target need to be updated. It should be noted that P3 amplitude may be affected by many variables, including task complexity and stimulus intensity (see, e.g., R. Johnson, 1993).

The oddball paradigm has also been used to examine the influence of changes in unattended auditory stimuli. In this case, a series of tones of short duration (e.g., 60 ms) is presented while participants perform a relatively passive task such as reading a book, or even while they sleep (see, e.g., Atienza, Cantero, & Gomez, 2000). Most of the time a standard tone of a given frequency (e.g., 1000 Hz) and duration is presented, but occasionally a deviant (oddball) tone of a slightly different frequency (e.g., 1032 Hz), intensity, or length is presented. The difference between the ERPs elicited by the standard and deviant tones is largest over the fronto-central brain areas and has been denoted as the *mismatch negativity* (see, e.g., Näätänen, 1992; see also Chapter 4). The mismatch negativity has been interpreted as the outcome of a preattentive process that registers the "mismatch" between new sensory input and the representation of the standard stimulus, which is stored in auditory sensory memory (Näätänen, 1992). The mismatch negativity arises from the auditory cortex, and it has been argued that the mismatch negativity can be modulated by attention (Woldorff et al., 1998).

Another frequently used measure derived from the EEG is the lateralized readiness potential (LRP). The LRP seems to be a pure measure of motor preparation (see, e.g., J. Miller & Hackley, 1992). The LRP is measured above the primary motor areas, and is obtained by means of a double subtraction procedure to remove activity that is not related to the side of the required response. Relatively high activity contralateral to the hand used to make the required response indicates that motor activation is larger for the required response, whereas higher ipsilateral activity indicates that motor activation is larger for the incorrect response. The LRP can be computed time-locked to either the onset of the stimulus or to the response (i.e., it can be either stimulus- or response-locked). The interval between the stimulus and the stimulus-locked LRP is related to the duration of the processes that occur before the start of the LRP (and thus before readiness to respond), and the interval between the response-locked LRP and the actual response is related to the duration of processes that occur after the start of the LRP (Osman & Moore, 1993). Exclusive effects of factors on either the stimulus- or response-locked LRP suggest that the time interval before or after the LRP can be selectively influenced. Thus, when an experimental manipulation (e.g., varying signal quality) has an effect on the start of the stimulus-locked LRP but not on the start of the response-locked LRP, it can be concluded that a process prior to the moment of correct motor activation is affected. In contrast, an influence of a manipulation on the start time of the response-locked LRP but not on the start time of the stimulus-locked LRP (e.g., varying speed-accuracy instructions, see Osman et al., 2000; Van der Lubbe et al., 2001), indicates that processes after correct motor activation are affected.

▲ BRAIN IMAGING TECHNIQUES

Although ERPs provide precise temporal data about the time course of information processing, they generally do not provide much information about which brain areas are involved in particular activities. New methodologies for human brain imaging allow us to see brain activity as tasks are being performed. The techniques most often used to provide information about the localization of particular processes are *positron emission tomography (PET)* and *functional magnetic resonance imaging (fMRI)*. In both techniques, people perform a cognitive task (e.g., a task requiring selective attention) while in a scanner. Brain activity during this task is subtracted from the activity present during baseline testing (i.e., without the specific cognitive aspect of interest) in order to isolate the activity that is unique to the process of interest. In this way, cerebral activity associated with specific task components can be visualized

In PET research, a radioactive marker is inhaled by or injected into the participant. These marker molecules (in most cases $H_2^{15}O$) can be used to measure brain metabolism as the markers move with the regional cerebral blood flow (rCBF). Images of the locations of the markers thus reveal where blood flow was necessary to provide oxygen. Areas that show an increase in rCBF during a cognitive task are presumed to be actively involved in the underlying process. Although it is a widely used, important technique, PET can be extremely sensitive to methodological differences between tasks and, because of the nature of the vascular response, is limited in spatial resolution (Corbetta, 1998).

Functional magnetic resonance imaging is based on the magnetic characteristics of the so-called blood oxygen level–dependent (BOLD) response. Brain regions that are active during a given task or process require more oxygen, supplied through the blood. This increase in blood oxygen is measured by fMRI using the specific magnetic properties of blood and the surrounding tissue (see Haxby, Courtney, & Clark, 1998, for a detailed overview of the use of fMRI as a research method to study attention). Unlike PET, fMRI does not require invasive measures, although being in the scanner can be unpleasant. Functional magnetic resonance imaging has a fairly high spatial resolution of about 1 cm, and is becoming more and more accurate in the temporal domain. Recently, it has also become possible to study the BOLD response to a single event (e.g., with different stimulus types within a task), using a technique known as event-related fMRI (D'Esposito, Zarahn, & Aguirre, 1999).

A more recently introduced technique to map neural activity is *magnetoencephalography (MEG)*, which is based on the electromagnetic characteristics of the electric field produced by firing nerve cells (Downing, Liu, & Kanwisher, 2001). Although the temporal characteristics of the activity of the brain revealed by these methods are relatively detailed and accurate, their spatial resolution generally is not. In other words, it is difficult to link the electrical signal to a specific structure in the human brain, other than in general terms such as "left posterior" or "right posterior" activity.

Another technique for localizing brain function is *transcranial magnetic stimulation (TMS)*. This technique uses brief electromagnetic pulses that are applied over a given area of the skull either before or during a cognitive task by means of a current-producing coil that interferes with the underlying neural tissue (Stewart, Ellison, Walsh, & Cowey, 2001). Low-frequency TMS (<1 Hz) is thought to produce a so-called virtual lesion, that is, a transient dysfunction in the affected brain area. High-frequency TMS (>5 Hz) might enhance neural activity, thus improving performance on a specific function (Wassermann & Lisanby, 2001).

In short, imaging techniques can be applied to study in detail the functional characteristics of the healthy human brain with relatively high resolution. Although the temporal resolution is not as high, it is becoming progressively more precise as the imaging techniques increase in sophistication. With the help of such techniques, our knowledge of the neural basis of attention has greatly improved over the last few decades. However, because this work is in its infancy and many issues remain to be resolved, it is still an open question as to how much detail about localization of function the imaging techniques ultimately can provide (Uttal, 2001).

SUMMARY

This chapter provides a primer of the techniques used to conduct research on attention and performance. The concept of the human as an information processor plays an important role in empirical research and in theory development. A simple three-stage model of information processing provides an adequate framework for organizing discussion and debate of issues such as the purpose and effects of attention. The three-stage framework will recur throughout the book as we address topics such as the locus of attentional selection, the location of processing bottlenecks, and the performance of multiple tasks. As new topics are addressed, details about the sort of processing that occurs—and the role of attention in that processing—will be discussed.

A range of techniques is available for delineating the processes involved in the selection and processing of information and the factors that influence them. Behavioral techniques focus on the outcome of information processing by measuring overt performance such as the speed and accuracy with which a task is performed. Electrophysiological and neuroimaging techniques can be used to examine intermediate steps of processing, providing a picture of brain activity during task performance. These techniques can also be used to explore and confirm hypotheses about attentional systems and their brain basis. The techniques introduced in this chapter recur throughout the book as we describe the nature of attention and its role in human performance.

▲ NOTES

1. The probability of different events influences the amount of information conveyed. For example, if one event is twice as likely as another, the occurrence of that event conveys less information than the occurrence of the other. The information conveyed by stimuli with unequal probabilities of occurrence is $\log_2 (1/P_i)$, where P_i is the probability of occurrence of stimulus i).

2. Because the ERP is time-locked to the stimulus, only processing that is also consistently time-locked to the stimulus is revealed. Aspects of processing that are variable in onset or duration may be blurred or lost in the ERP.

CHAPTER 3

(pg 59-66)

SELECTIVE VISUAL ATTENTION

T o produce coherent behavior in the face of competing and distracting sources of stimulation in the environment, some things must be selected and others ignored. If we *were* able to attend to everything going on around us, we would be constantly distracted and unable to carry out any action at all. In this sense, it is a useful adaptation that we are aware of only a small portion of our surroundings at a given moment, and that only a limited range of objects can be attended to and acted upon at any one time. As James (1890/1950) pointed out, concentration and focus are the essence of attention. However, although it seems clear that selective attention is necessary, the locus of selective attention—and even the objects of selection—remains a controversial topic. For example, some-times selection seems to occur at an early, perceptual stage of processing, such that some stimuli are processed and others are not. At other times, selection does not seem to occur until perceived information has achieved some degree of semantic processing, such that information conveyed by stimuli that should have been ignored nonetheless influences performance. This chapter will focus on selective visual attention as we address such questions as the following: At what stage of information processing is attention required to select information? What is selected, regions of space or the objects in it? What makes selection easy or difficult?

▲ THE FUNCTION OF SELECTIVE ATTENTION

Questions commonly asked about attention concern what effects attention has and how these effects are manifested. A more basic question is why attention is necessary. In Chapter 1, we discussed changing views of attention throughout the history of psychology. In this section, we review three of the major conceptions of attention.

Attention for Perception

It has been proposed that attention is necessary for perception; that is, because the perceptual system has limited processing capacity (see, e.g., Broadbent, 1958), attention is necessary to select a subset of items to receive perceptual processing. In this view, attention is needed to restrict the input to the perceptual system in order to prevent overload. Another hypothesis is that the task of combining all the separate features of objects, such as their contours, colors, and locations, if undertaken for all objects at the same moment, would result in a combinatorial explosion of the number of different possible reconstructions (see, e.g., Treisman & Gelade, 1980). This problem, called the *binding problem,* can be solved with attention by selecting only a limited spatial area for processing, so that only the features within that area will be combined to reconstruct the objects present there.

Attention for Awareness

As discussed in Chapter 1, an initial view regarding the function of attention was that it is needed to bring perceptual information to conscious awareness. James (1890/1950) described this role of attention as "anticipatory preparation" for the stimuli to come. As James put it, "The image in the mind is the attention; [this] preperception . . . is half of the perception of the looked-for thing" (p. 442). In James's view, preperception (as a variety of attention) refers to the preparation for, or anticipation or expectation of, a to-be-perceived object. Thus, attention plays an important role in becoming aware of an object (see also Wundt, 1907b). In this view, unattended objects are present on the retina, and may even be processed to the level of identification (e.g., to a semantic level), but attention is needed to register the results of this processing. In other words, "attention" serves the function of enabling us to become conscious or aware of the presence of objects or events (see Chapter 7 for more discussion of the role of attention in fixing items in consciousness).

Attention for Action

Some researchers argue that rather than being linked to the limited capacity of the visual system, attentional selection is needed to constrain possible actions. The basis for this view is that although the senses are capable of registering many different objects together, effector systems are typically limited to carrying out just one action at a time (see, e.g., Allport, 1987). For example, Neumann (1987) has argued that the limits of attention are not due to perceptual processing limitations but, rather, result from the way in which the brain solves selection problems for the control of action (see also Gibson, 1941). In most tasks, just one category or mode of action is given priority. This instruction, according to Neumann, prevents "the behavioral chaos that would result from an attempt to simultaneously perform all possible actions for which sufficient causes exist" (p. 374). Attention is thus needed to constrain the selection of the appropriate action on the basis of the incoming information.

THE LOCUS OF SELECTION ▲

As suggested by the differing viewpoints about why selection is necessary, a long-standing controversy in the literature on attention concerns the level of processing at which attention comes into play, or, in other words, the extent to which stimuli can be processed without the application of attention. It is commonly assumed that information processing starts with basic feature information, such as the orientation, form, and color of items in a display. At this level, information is precategorical in the sense that the meaning of the stimuli has not yet been processed (i.e., the items have not been assigned to categories). At a later moment in time, and higher level of processing, stimuli are interpreted. This interpretation may involve assigning a name (e.g., apple), a category (e.g., fruit), or an action (e.g., ripe for the picking) to the stimulus. This later level of processing is often denoted as postcategorical or semantic processing.

The Early-Selection View

The first proponent of the *early-selection view* was Broadbent (1958), who characterized the human information processing system as an information channel with limited capacity. Broadbent's views about the human as a limited capacity information channel were inspired by new developments in communications engineering. Information theory (see Chapter 2) provided an elegant way to model the transfer of information, and Broadbent was quick to see the possibilities of using this theory to

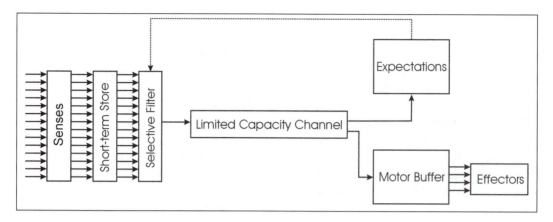

Figure 3.1   Broadbent's early-selection model (filter theory) of attention.

precisely quantify human information processing. Broadbent's first concern was specifying the point at which information processing is limited. Relying primarily on experiments in which it was found that subjects could select information presented to one "information channel" (in this case, an ear) and ignore information presented to the other (see Chapter 4 for details), Broadbent hypothesized that attention operates to select information at an early, precategorical level based on attributes such as the location of the stimuli, or basic perceptual features such as pitch or loudness. According to his *filter theory* (see Figure 3.1), a selective filter protects the information-processing channel from being overloaded by too much information. This filter, which is "set" for basic stimulus characteristics such as location, color, pitch, or loudness, allows only some information to enter the system, and excludes the rest. For instance, when driving a car along a crowded road one is usually able to concentrate on the traffic sign boards (which can be distinguished by location, color, or shape) and ignore billboards and other advertisements along the wayside.

As shown in Figure 3.1, filter theory assumes that information from the senses first enters a buffer in which it can be held for a short time. Information that fits the filter is then passed along to the limited capacity channel, where it can be identified. The results of this analysis are then sent on to a response system and may also be used to update expectations about what is likely to occur in the given situation. Filter theory is an early-selection theory in that information is assumed to be selected by attention at a relatively early stage of processing.

Although the powers of selection are impressive, selection is not perfect. For example, when driving your car along the highway, a particularly flashy or interesting billboard might distract you. Such distraction is most likely to occur when something relevant to you or highly practiced, such as your own name, is present.

In other words, potentially relevant information sometimes gets past the selective filter. This finding (discussed at more length in the following chapter) led Treisman (1960) to propose the *filter attenuation theory.* According to this theory, the early, selective filter does not completely block out unwanted information, but only attenuates or reduces the strength of unattended stimuli. Under normal conditions, this attenuated information does not reach consciousness, but when the information is familiar or fits the context of attended information, it manages to pass the threshold for identification.

The Late-Selection View

Not long after the development of the early-selection viewpoint, Deutsch and Deutsch (1963) and Norman (1968) argued that there is no serious processing limitation up to a categorical level of processing. In other words, they suggested that selection does not occur on the basis of an early-selection filter (which sometimes fails), but after stimuli have already been identified. According to this *late-selection view,* attention is not needed to perceptually process and identify items, but it is needed to create a more durable representation of the information. That is, information that is not explicitly attended will be seen or heard, but this information will decay rapidly in the absence of attention, and will not usually reach the level of conscious perception. The point at which information reaches consciousness and the manner in which this occurs will be discussed in more detail in later chapters. The basic contribution of late-selection theories is that the assumption that all information is processed to a semantic level can explain why relevant, though initially unattended, information sometimes is identified.

Is Selection Early or Late?

Many studies show evidence for early selection—and perhaps as many show evidence for late selection. An example of a study showing that processing does not proceed effortlessly to the point of stimulus identification (and thus depends on attention at an earlier stage) is that of Pashler (1984a). In these experiments, subjects were required to identify as quickly as possible a letter at one location of a visual display. The letters in the display were either high contrast (white on a black background) or low contrast (dark gray on a black background). Pashler found a typical effect of stimulus contrast in that low contrast letters took about 40 ms longer to identify than high contrast letters. He also found that this contrast effect did not depend on whether the location cue indicating which letter should be identified was presented 200 ms before the letter array, simultaneous with the

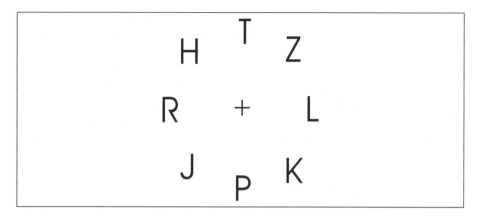

Figure 3.2   Example of the type of circular display often used to study the deployment of attention.

letters, or 300 ms after the array. The lack of dependence of the contrast effect on the presentation time of the cue suggests that even when observers have time to process many items, they still do not identify the cued item until after the cue arrives (see also Pashler, 1998). As we will discuss at more length in Chapter 7, we do seem to be able to briefly hold on to sensory information even after it is no longer physically visible. Apparently, we do not tend to hold on to the *results* of perceptual processing of that information.

Many studies have supported von Helmholtz's (1894a) view that attention is needed to fully process information from visual locations (see Chapter 1). Rather than acting as subjects themselves and simply deciding where to look on a given trial, as did von Helmholtz, most researchers conduct experiments in which instructions or cues indicate to participants where they should focus their attention. Often, a circular display is used so that all possible stimuli are an equal distance from the point of fixation (see Figure 3.2). For example, Yantis and Johnson (1990) used a display like that shown in Figure 3.2 to determine whether unattended information has any effect on the perception of attended information. The task was simply to look at one of the eight positions of the display, as indicated by a location cue (a line under one of the positions), and to indicate whether that position contained a particular target, for example, the letter *T*. On some trials, an extra target was present somewhere in the display. If this redundant target was in a position adjacent to the cued location, responses to the target at the cued position were faster than when no redundant target was present. However, if a redundant target was anywhere else in the display, it had no effect on performance. Yantis and Johnson thus concluded that attention was effectively allocated to a small region of space and that only stimuli present in that region were processed.

Although the results of Yantis and Johnson's (1990) study are consistent with the hypothesis that attention is needed in order to perceive stimuli, Shiffrin, Diller, and Cohen (1996) argue that basic visual information is processed in parallel across the visual field, and that attention is applied to a location only when a response must be selected. Shiffrin et al. used a procedure similar to that of Yantis and Johnson, but instead of sometimes presenting a second target in the same display as the relevant target, they presented it first in a separate *prime* display (see Figure 3.3). As in previous studies, they found that the benefit of a redundant target and the cost associated with having a conflicting target (i.e., a target assigned to a different response) in the display were limited to locations adjacent to (or the same as) the target. However, these costs and benefits were essentially the same when the location cue appeared *after* the prime display as when it appeared before the prime display. This suggests that all items in the prime display were processed to some extent, even though the observer had not yet been cued as to where to direct attention. Based on this finding, Shiffrin et al. suggested a model of attention in which perceptual processing proceeds without attention to specific locations, but in which attention to locations is needed to select the appropriate response. In other words, they argued that the results using the cuing paradigm of Yantis and Johnson could be explained in terms of response competition (i.e., stimuli that are associated with the same response benefit performance and those associated with a different response hinder it) rather than perceptual interference.

The study by Shiffrin et al. (1996) and many other studies have found that unattended stimuli are processed up to a semantic level. Such results favor the view that selection occurs after information has been categorized. A partial explanation for the conflicting results regarding whether selection is early or late may be that the level of selection depends on perceptual load (see, e.g., N. Lavie & Tsal, 1994; Treisman, 1969). According to Treisman, early selection is necessary whenever perceptual load is high in order to prevent interference within the various perceptual analyzers. Lavie and colleagues have argued that selection is inefficient under conditions of low perceptual load. Thus, when perceptual load is high, selection can occur early and only selected items are fully identified. When perceptual load is low, processing proceeds unhindered to the point of identification of all elements in a display. That is, when perceptual load is low, early selection often fails and even irrelevant information is processed to the point of semantic identification. As we will discuss in Chapter 5, perceptual load can mediate the extent to which subjects suffer interference from other elements in a display, which suggests that whether selection is early or late is to some extent determined by the perceptual processing required.

Electrophysiological support for the role of perceptual load in determining the level of selection comes from the finding that the event-related potential (ERP) components associated with early, perceptual processing, P1 and N1, are larger in amplitude when perceptual load is high than when it is low. Handy and Mangun

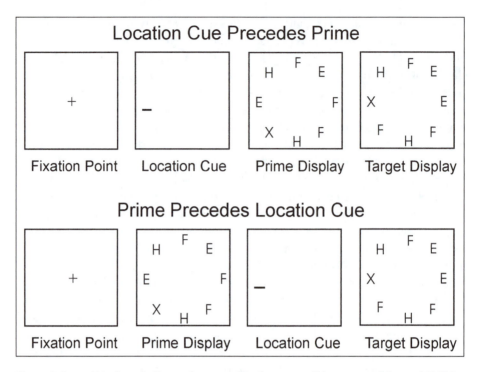

Figure 3.3   Displays similar to those used in the compatible cue conditions of Shiffrin, Diller, and Cohen (1996). The target is the letter X in the target display. The time between location cues, prime displays, and target displays varied across experiments.

(2000) had subjects identify whether a letter to the left or right of fixation was an A or an H. A left- or right-pointing arrow presented in the center of the screen 600–800 ms prior to the onset of the letter cued its location. The cue was valid on 73% of the trials and invalid on 27% of the trials. On low-load trials the letter A or H was intact, making the two highly discriminable; on high-load trials, the arms of the A were pulled apart slightly and the arms of the H were tilted inward slightly, making the two more difficult to discriminate. The important finding was that in the high-load condition P1 and, to a lesser extent, N1 were larger when the letter occurred in the cued location than when it did not, but in the low-load condition the two components were unaffected by expectancy. These findings suggest that increasing perceptual load indeed induces more efficient early selection in visual processing. Another technique for assessing the point in processing at which attention comes into play is described in Box 3.1.

| Box 3.1 | Using External Noise to Assess Internal Noise Suppression |

The great benefit of models is that they allow us to pose questions that we might otherwise not be able to answer. A good example of this is the question posed by Z.-L. Lu and Dosher (1998), "Is the effect of attention on performance in visual tasks due to signal enhancement, distractor exclusion, or internal noise suppression?" This question is based on Lu and Dosher's perceptual template model (PTM) of a human observer, and its answer is made possible by the model's predictions regarding the effects of adding external noise to the stimulus signal. According to the model (see Box Figure 3.1), performance can be affected by external noise and two sources of internal noise. The external noise can be presented in a variety of ways, depending on the stimulus. In Lu and Dosher's experiment, the targets were Gabor patches (spatial frequency stimuli) oriented to the left or right, and the noise was randomly distributed light and dark pixels. The two sources of internal noise are additive and multiplicative. Additive noise does not vary with signal strength, but multiplicative noise does. Multiplicative noise is consistent with the fact that the ability to perceive a difference between two stimuli depends on the magnitude of the stimuli, such that the greater the magnitude, the greater the just noticeable difference (Stevens, 1975). Other features of the PTM are a perceptual template that can be tuned to specific aspects of stimuli, such as their spatial frequency, and a decision module, which allows detection or discrimination responses to be determined on the basis of signal-noise ratios.

In the PTM, attention may affect performance in one of three ways: by enhancing the stimulus, by excluding distractors, or by reducing multiplicative noise. These three possible effects of attention can be distinguished by examining the effects on performance of adding external noise to the signal. Specifically, attention as signal enhancement, which intensifies the perceptual strength of the stimulus (signal plus external noise), is predicted to affect performance only when external noise levels are low because the enhancement affects both the signal and the external noise. Attention as distractor exclusion, which works as a filter tuning the template to exclude distractors, is predicted to affect performance only at relatively high external noise levels because internal noise dominates performance at low external noise levels. Because multiplicative internal noise can affect performance at all levels of external noise, effects of attention as internal noise reduction should be observable regardless of the quality of the stimulus.

Lu and Dosher (1998) had observers perform a discrimination task under varying levels of external noise to determine how attention affected performance in such a task. On each trial, two Gabor patches, each oriented slightly to the left or right, were shown, and the task was to report the orientation of the two patches. In different trials, observers were instructed to attend to the right, left, or both sides of the display. Performance was

(Continued)

Box 3.1   (Continued)

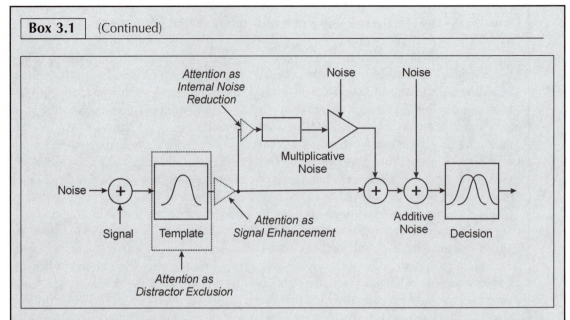

Figure 1   The perceptual template model of Lu and Dosher (1998) and three possible loci of the effects of attention (indicated by the dotted lines).

compared for stimuli on the attended side, the unattended side, and for the case when both sides were attended. Discrimination performance was the best for attended stimuli, intermediate for the case where equal attention was given to both stimuli, and poorest for unattended stimuli. However, this relation held only when the noise levels were relatively low. As the noise level increased, the effects of attention disappeared. This pattern of results is consistent with the hypothesis that attending to a spatial location reduces the signal quality (in this case, contrast level) required to perform the discrimination task. Thus, according to the PTM, attention improved performance by enhancing the signal (or, equivalently, according to the model, reducing additive internal noise).

▲ THE SPOTLIGHT OF ATTENTION

A popular metaphor of attention is that it is like a spotlight, highlighting selected information and leaving information outside the focus in the dark (Eriksen & Hoffman, 1973). Like a spotlight, attention can be moved to different regions of space in order to "illuminate" anything that might be present there. Less obvious is whether the movements of attention are continuous and are of either constant or variable

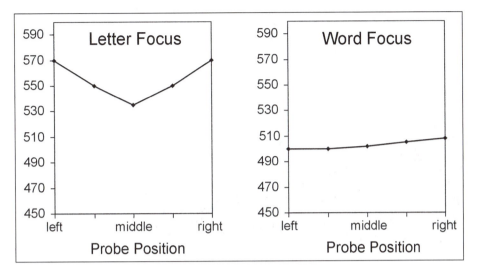

Figure 3.4   The results of LaBerge's (1983) experiment on the focus of the attentional spotlight.

SOURCE: Data from LaBerge (1983).

speed, or whether attention is "turned off" at one location before being applied at another. The spotlight metaphor has inspired a wealth of research on focusing and moving attention.

Focusing the Attentional Spotlight

Many studies have shown that the spotlight of attention can be adjusted to focus on a relatively small region or on a larger region of space (see, e.g., Eriksen & Yeh, 1985). For example, LaBerge (1983) found that attention could be focused on just one letter of a five-letter word, or on the whole word. He showed this by having people perform a task that required them to focus on just one letter (i.e., indicate whether the middle letter in a word was from a certain range of the alphabet) or on a whole word (i.e., indicate whether a word was a proper noun). On some trials, in place of a word, a row of four #s with a probe letter or digit was presented (e.g., ###7#), and the subject had to respond to the probe as quickly as possible. LaBerge found that response time depended on the focus of attention: If attention was focused on the middle letter, response times were fastest to the middle letter, intermediate to the letters adjacent to the middle letter, and slowest to the letters farthest away from the center (see Figure 3.4, left panel). On the other hand, if attention was devoted to the whole word, response time to the probe did not depend on its position (see Figure 3.4, right panel).

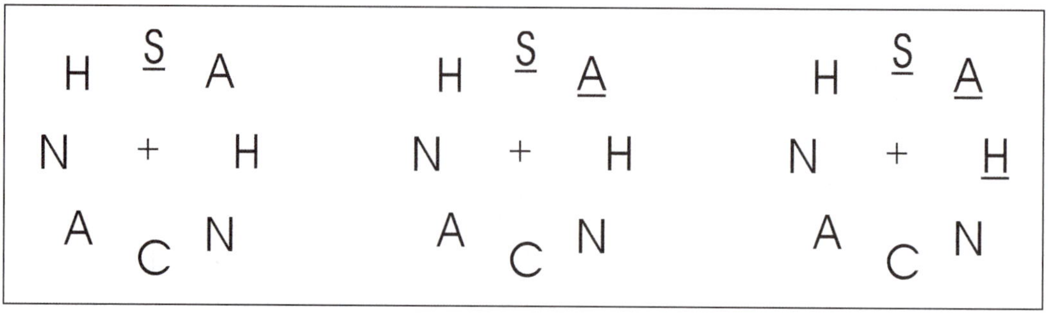

Figure 3.5   Displays like those used by Eriksen and St. James (1986). One, two, or three adjacent positions were cued in order to change the size of the subject's attentional focus.

SOURCE: Data from Eriksen & St. James (1986).

The size of the attentional focus can also be manipulated by cuing different numbers of locations in a circular display. Using this method, Eriksen and St. James (1986; see Figure 3.5) found that response times to a target letter increased when the number of cued positions was larger. Moreover, the costs associated with incompatible items (noncued items that, if cued, would require a different response) depended on the size of the attentional focus, such that when the focus was larger, items in positions farther away from the target showed more interference than when the focus was smaller. As shown in Figure 3.6, the benefit in reaction time for cuing a smaller number of positions increased as the cue-display onset interval (cue-onset asynchrony) increased, indicating that it takes time to focus attention. Eriksen and St. James proposed that focused attention is like a zoom lens for which there is an inverse relation between the illuminated area and the concentration of attentional resources. According to this metaphor, when the attended area is small, the concentration of attention is greater (see also Castiello & Umiltà, 1990).

Moving the Attentional Spotlight

If attention is like a spotlight (or a zoom lens), it should be possible to move it across regions of space. Moreover, the spotlight should illuminate the area over which it passes. These assumptions of the spotlight metaphor have been tested by examining movements of attention. For example, using location cues (i.e., cues at the to-be-attended location) and targets at three distances from fixation, Tsal (1983) found that the time needed to focus attention at a location increased as the eccentricity of the target increased. This finding led Tsal to propose that attention

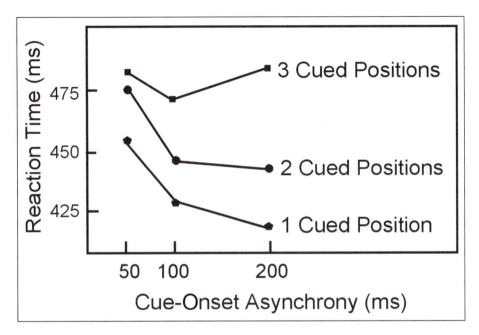

Figure 3.6   Time to focus attention in Eriksen and St. James's (1986) Experiment 1.

SOURCE: Data from Eriksen & St. James (1986).

travels through space at a constant velocity. However, this assumption has been criticized because the results can also be interpreted in terms of the time needed to identify peripheral targets: More time is needed to identify more distant targets (and their cues) because of poorer visual processing in the periphery of the visual field (Eriksen & Murphy, 1987). Using a central cue to tell subjects where to look, Remington and Pierce (1984) showed that attention could be moved just as quickly to a position 2 degrees of visual angle away as to a position 10 degrees away. In general, attention shifts can be well described by models that assume that the time taken to move attention is independent of the distance to be moved (e.g., Yantis, 1988). Rather than moving around the display in an analog fashion, it appears that attention jumps from one position to another such that resources are allocated to a new location as they are released at the old location (see also Eriksen & Webb, 1989).

The Resolution of the Attentional Spotlight

The implication of the spotlight metaphor—that everything within the focus of the attentional spotlight is attended—may not be correct. For instance, regions of space that contain objects may be processed differently than empty regions of space. Cepeda, Cave, Bichot, and Kim (1998) used a *probe dot procedure* in which a small dot, which appeared only on some trials, had to be responded to as quickly as possible, to test whether attention is allocated differently to objects than to empty space. In general, detection of a probe is faster when attention is directed at the probe's location than when it is not. That is, the probe response time gives an indication of where attention is currently allocated. The primary experimental task of Cepeda et al. was to select and identify one digit of a four-digit circular display based on its color, while keeping the eyes fixated at the center of the display. Rather than responding to the digit right away, participants made their responses after an interval of 1,400 ms. On 50% of the trials, the dot probe was presented in the interval between the primary-task stimulus and response. It could occur with equal probability at any of the digit positions or in one of the blank positions between the digits (for a total of eight possible locations). Response times to the probes were fastest when the probe occurred at the position of the to-be-reported digit, and slowest at the position of any other digit. An additional finding, namely, that responses were faster when the probe occurred on blank positions far from the target than when the probe occurred on the position of a distractor digit, was interpreted as showing that the nonselected digits were inhibited. Responses to probes at blank positions near the target were faster than to probes at blank positions farther away, consistent with the spotlight metaphor. However, this experiment clearly shows that rather than illuminating all areas within its focus, attention operates differently on objects than on empty space.

We saw in the previous section that a display may be searched by moving attention from cue to cue in a serial search of target positions, and that movement time does not depend on the distance to be moved. The fact that some studies do, however, support the conclusion that the focus of attention can be changed to concentrate on a larger or smaller area suggests that the ability to jump from cue to cue or target to target depends on the nature of the display. The ability to change the size of the attentional focus to include different numbers of items seems to depend on the presence of perceptual groups in the display (e.g., Kramer & Jacobson, 1991). It might thus be concluded that attention moves from item to item, but that the "items" (such as the words vs. the letters in LaBerge, 1983) might sometimes be perceptual groups.

▲ AN ATTENTIONAL GRADIENT?

It has been suggested that a better metaphor of selective visual attention is that of a gradient of resources that is allocated to a region in space rather than a spotlight that can be moved from place to place (e.g., LaBerge & Brown, 1989). Such a gradient may vary in size, and resources are assumed to fall off from the center of the gradient to the edges.[1] A more substantial difference between a spotlight and a gradient metaphor is that the gradient may reflect not only the current focus of attention, but also the results of previous attentional allocation. That is, activation in the gradient can build up (and decay) over time and across more than one attentional fixation. This view was tested by LaBerge, Carlson, Williams, and Bunney (1997), who used a series of three displays to test the buildup of attentional resources. At the beginning of a trial, subjects focused on one position of the display (i.e., one position in a horizontal row of letters and distractor characters). On subsequent trials, attention had to be refocused to find targets at other positions. LaBerge et al. found that the time to detect a target depended not only on where attention had just been allocated, but also on where attention was at the beginning of the trial. Their results were generally consistent with a gradient model in which a concentration of resources remained allocated to the initially attended position. Thus, the allocation of attentional resources at any particular time and place may reflect the history of attentional allocation across a short period of time (see also Breitmeyer et al., 1999).

ATTENTIONAL CONTROL ▲

Directing attention to a particular object or region increases the efficiency of processing at that point. This fact makes it clear that attention can select some items for preferential processing, but how does this selection occur? As we saw earlier, selecting some objects or regions of space can have a "dark side" in that nonselected objects or regions may be actively inhibited. Recent positron emission tomography (PET) studies suggest that the frontal cortex may exercise attentional control by inhibiting areas or objects that should not be attended. This inhibition, which can be supposed to decrease the attentional "weighting"[2] of unwanted inputs, or, alternatively, to reduce the noise from unwanted inputs, aids selection by accentuating the difference in activation between the wanted and unwanted inputs. Vandenberghe et al. (1997, 2000) directly measured cortical attentional weighting by asking observers to attend to one dimension of an object located on the left or right of a visual display while a PET scan was made. The PET scans revealed that activation in the frontal areas was higher on the side ipsilateral to the attended stimulus. Because visually presented information is processed in the hemisphere contralateral to the hemisphere of presentation, this finding suggests that the frontal areas were involved in actively inhibiting processing of the contralateral (ignored) visual field. In other words, paying attention to one thing can imply decreasing the weights of unwanted inputs rather than simply increasing the weights of desired inputs (Duncan, 2001; but see Kimberg & Farah, 2000, for a different view).

▲ OVERT AND COVERT ORIENTING

When you want to draw someone's attention to an object, you might say, "Hey, look here!" In doing so, you will have made the not unreasonable assumption that the direction of one's attention is linked to the direction of gaze. However, this assumption is not always valid. Even when the eyes are fixed, it is possible to select only a subset of the available information for perceptual processing. For example, in reading a text one is normally aware only of the information on the current line. However, if you focus on a word (e.g., "here") you will find that it is possible, without changing your focus, to read the words on the lines above and below. Although it is possible to focus attention on items not within the eye's focus, it is seldom necessary to do so (unless you are trying to read over someone's shoulder without being noticed). Nonetheless, dissociations between *overt orienting* (changes in the positioning of the senses to improve perception, for example, by making head or eye movements) and *covert orienting*, in which attention is directed to a location other than the focus of the eyes, are interesting from a theoretical viewpoint.

Overt movements of the eyes occur quite frequently. A rough distinction can be made between two types of eye movements: reflexive and controlled. Reflexive eye movements, which are controlled by the superior colliculus of the midbrain, are fast and are triggered automatically by the sudden appearance of stimulation. Controlled eye movements are slow, controlled by areas in the frontal lobe, and are made voluntarily.

Covert (hidden) orienting refers to the changes in the focus of attention that are not due to overt orienting. Thus, covert orienting does not affect which information is registered by the senses, but may affect the output of perceptual processes by directing attention to specific locations or items (see von Helmholtz, 1894a). The role of covert orienting in selecting information is often studied with "filtering" tasks, in which participants are shown a number of stimuli and asked to attend to just one of them. Filtering tasks abound in real life. For example, when you search for your own name on a list of test scores, or when you read a train schedule to find out when your train is expected, you do your best to select relevant information and ignore irrelevant information.

Some of the most compelling evidence for covert orienting and attentional selection comes from studies in which people watched superimposed video clips, attending to one video and ignoring the other. Neisser and Becklen (1975) used this procedure to study the extent to which people could selectively attend to one set of events in the face of distracting information. In their experiments, one video image (a hand game) was superimposed on another (a ball game) by means of a half-silvered mirror (the effect produced was like watching an image in window glass at night). Neisser and Becklen asked people to attend to certain events (e.g., throwing a ball) in just one of the videos and found that they could attend to either the "actual" or the reflected image with excellent results. Not only were participants good at monitoring the attended video, they were unlikely to notice events (such as a person walking across the room) in the other video. Apparently, the differences in the quality of the images served as an effective cue for selecting information.

A study by Heinze, Luck, Mangun, and Hillyard (1990) provides electrophysiological support for the assumption that covert orienting affects early perceptual processing. These authors examined the effect of attention on the different components of the ERP. Subjects were instructed to direct their attention to one side of a display for the duration of a block of trials, but to keep their eyes fixed at a central fixation cross. Four-letter arrays that covered an equal part of the left and right visual fields were used as stimuli, and a response was required only when a specific combination of letters occurred on the attended side (this was the case on 25% of the trials). On these trials, the occipital P1 ERP component, which is associated with early stimulus processing, was enhanced on the contralateral side (indicating processing of the attended side) relative to the ipsilateral side (which would indicate processing of the unattended side). Thus, it appears that covert orienting of attention affects early visual processing.

EXOGENOUS AND ENDOGENOUS ORIENTING ▲

Just as overt eye movements may be reflexive or controlled, so are there two ways that covert orienting can occur. Reflexive orienting is commonly denoted as *exogenous orienting*, to indicate that it is driven by stimuli (i.e., it is data driven); controlled orienting is commonly denoted as *endogenous orienting*, to indicate that it is controlled by endogenous (within the observer) factors. Because exogenous cues are usually presented in the periphery of the display, they are often called peripheral cues. Exogenous cuing effects are found even when observers are aware that the cues do not provide reliable information about where a target will occur. That is, just the appearance of an exogenous cue will affect responses to other stimuli subsequently presented in the cue's former location. In fact, by definition, the presence of an exogenous cuing effect can be determined only when the cue is not informative. If the cue is informative, endogenous cuing may also play a role in performance. Endogenous cues have to be processed by the observer and intentionally acted upon in order to have an effect. They are often called central cues because they are usually presented at the center of the display, where the eyes are fixated. For example, an arrow presented in the center of a display might "tell" you where to look, but you have to move your attention to the indicated location yourself.

As mentioned earlier, reflexive eye movements will tend to be made to stimuli that appear suddenly. Exogenous cuing effects reveal that, even when reflexive eye movements are suppressed, attention will move reflexively to the place of onset (or offset) of a stimulus in the visual field. Because sudden changes may not only attract attention, but also increase alertness (e.g., Posner, 1978; Van der Lubbe, Keuss, & Stoffels, 1996), cuing benefits are usually measured using a cost-benefit analysis (Jonides & Mack, 1984). In this procedure, a cue is presented on every trial so that any alerting effect of the cue is held constant. Trials on which the cue appears on the same side of the display as the target (i.e., the stimulus to which the subject has to respond) are considered "valid" trials because they correctly predict where the target will appear; trials that appear on the side opposite to the target are called "invalid" (i.e., they give misleading "information" about the location of the target). Cuing benefits (or costs) are computed by comparing the reaction time and accuracy on valid trials with that of invalid trials. When performance is better for valid trials, we can speak of a cuing effect on attention.

Many studies have shown that valid peripheral cues benefit performance, with the benefit being greatest when the time interval between the onset of the cue and the onset of the target (cue-target asynchrony) is only about 100 ms (Cheal & Lyon, 1991; Jonides, 1981; Müller & Rabbitt, 1989; Posner, 1980; Tsal, 1983; Yantis & Jonides, 1984). Importantly, a reversal of this benefit occurs when the cue-target asynchrony is longer than about 300 ms (Posner & Cohen, 1984). This reversal of the cuing benefit, such that valid cues produce longer reaction times than invalid ones, has been called *inhibition of return*, and will be discussed in Chapter 5.

Theeuwes (1991) found that not only stimulus onsets, but also stimulus offsets can attract attention. The attention-attracting effect of abrupt onsets or offsets may be due to the changes in luminance that they create. This is suggested by Theeuwes's (1995) finding that abrupt changes in equiluminant color do not attract attention. However, simple luminance changes do not always directly attract attention. Yantis and Hilstrom (1994) showed that whether or not luminance changes result in a cuing effect depends on whether an object is present at the moment of the luminance change. If no object is present, attention will not be directed to the location of the luminance change.

ERP studies using peripheral cues with short cue-target intervals have shown an enhancement of the components associated with early stimulus processing when the target is presented at the location of a valid exogenous cue. Effects on the P1 component are seen for both nonpredictive (Hopfinger & Mangun, 1998) and predictive (Van der Lubbe & Woestenburg, 1997) exogenous cues. Namely, valid exogenous cues enhance the P1 component when the cue-target interval is short (less than about 300 ms; see Figure 3.7). ERP studies with endogenous, symbolic cues of 75% validity (e.g., Mangun & Hillyard, 1991) have also revealed an

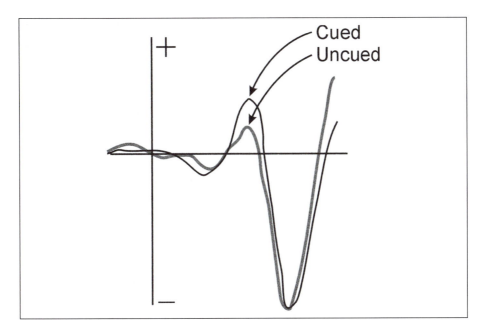

Figure 3.7   The difference in the P1 component of the ERP to a stimulus at a cued or uncued location.

enhancement of the P1 component on valid trials at the site contralateral to the target, but this effect is found only with a relatively long cue-target interval (e.g., 800 ms). On the basis of these ERP data, it may be concluded that both endogenous and exogenous cues affect early stages of stimulus processing, but that the effects of the respective cues interact with the length of the cue-target interval.

When the locus of attention varies from trial to trial, which is the case in most studies using peripheral and symbolic cues, transient aspects, or phasic changes of attention, can be studied. Sustained attention to a location can be examined by instructing participants to attend to one side of the visual field for the duration of a block of trials. The mechanisms controlling transient and sustained aspects of attention need not be the same. For example, Posner, Snyder, and Davidson (1980) compared the costs and benefits of cuing attention in a simple detection task. The attentional cues either remained the same for a block of trials or varied from trial to trial. The target could occur in any of four locations. In one condition, each target position was equally likely to be used, and in the other condition the target was more likely to occur in one position (79% of the trials), and less likely in each of the three remaining locations (7% of the trials per position). When the cued position was blocked, significant costs relative to a neutral cue were found, but there was no significant benefit relative to the neutral cue. In contrast, when the cued side changed on a trial-to-trial basis, significant costs and benefits were found. Posner et al. attributed the absence of benefits in the blocked conditions to an inability or unwillingness of participants to focus their attention at the expected position. However, the study by Heinze et al. (1990), discussed earlier, in which effects of attending to one side of a display for a block of trials were found, suggests that sustained attention can sometimes be allocated to visual locations.

Exogenous orienting is often described as being under control of the stimulus in the sense that orienting occurs reflexively in response to the onset of the cue. Several studies, however, have examined whether exogenous attention can be affected by instructions. Theeuwes (1991) and Koshino, Warner, and Juola (1992) both showed that cuing effects of abrupt onsets disappeared when participants were instructed to attend to a specific region and when the cue appeared outside the attended area. This suggests that exogenous orienting—like reflexive eye movements—can be prevented by top-down attentional control. Furthermore, although ERP studies suggest that both exogenous and endogenous orienting affect the same, early level of processing (i.e., in both cases a validity effect has been observed for the P1 component, although a longer cuing interval is needed with endogenous cues), some behavioral studies suggest that nonpredictive peripheral cues and symbolic cues may affect different levels of processing. For example, Riggio and Kirsner (1997; see also Juola, Koshino, & Warner, 1995) found that the effects of the two types of cues were additive, which suggests (according to additive factors logic; see Chapter 2) that endogenous and exogenous cues have their primary effects at different levels of visual processing.

▲ SPACE-BASED VERSUS OBJECT-BASED ATTENTION

The early work on cuing attention assumed that attention is allocated to regions of space. As we saw earlier, however (see also Cepeda et al., 1998), objects in space might be attended to differently than the regions of space that they occupy. An important issue in the field of visual attention is whether selection (i.e., directing of attention) can occur on the basis of features other than spatial location. Many theories assume that selection takes place via a representation of visual space (see, e.g., Cave & Pashler, 1995; Eriksen & St. James, 1986; LaBerge & Brown, 1989; Posner et al., 1980; Treisman & Gelade, 1980; Van der Heijden, 1992). However, some theories of visual attention argue that stimulus features (e.g., location, color, or form) can also be used as the basis for selection (Baylis & Driver, 1992; Bundesen, 1990; Kahneman, 1973).

Is Space Special?

An early examination of the effects of cuing an aspect other than spatial location was performed by Posner et al. (1980). In this study, participants monitored a display for the appearance of 1 of 10 uppercase letters presented to the left or right of fixation. On each trial, a cue with 80% validity was presented, with the cue-target interval varying from 800 to 1,200 ms. The cue indicated the identity of the target letter, its location, both the identity and the location, or neither. Posner et al. found that knowing the probable location of the letter speeded responses when the cue was valid (reactions were fastest when the letter gave valid location information [249 ms], intermediate when the cue was uninformative [266 ms], and slowest when the cue was invalid [297 ms]). However, no effects of cuing the letter itself were found.

Similar cuing effects with spatial but not with nonspatial cues were found by Theeuwes (1989), who tested the effects of location and form cues in a discrimination task. The target form was either a circle or a diamond in which a horizontal or vertical line segment was positioned, and responses were based on the orientation of the line. In different conditions, either the most likely target location (left or right) or the most likely target form (circle or diamond) was cued with 75% validity. The location cue resulted in costs and benefits on performance, but no cuing effects were found with the form cue.

These findings support the view that space is more important for selection than is form. However, failures to find effects of form, identity, or color cues in detection and discrimination tasks do not necessarily rule out the possibility that selection can be based on nonspatial features. It could be argued, for example, that the forms or letters were too similar to be effective selection cues. Indeed, a number of studies have shown that efficient selection can take place on the basis of features (e.g., color and form) other than spatial location (see, e.g., Bundesen, 1990; Bundesen, Pedersen, & Larsen, 1984; Von Wright, 1968). Although these latter results support the view that other features may also provide effective selection cues, it may also be the case that selection by color or form takes place via spatial selection. For instance, given a cue to attend to red letters, it is possible that attention is automatically directed to the locations containing red letters, rather than being directed to the color red without selecting location.

A recent study conducted by Tsal and Lamy (2000) provides support that attending to a nonspatial feature of an object (e.g., its color) implies that its location is also selected (see also Cave & Pashler, 1995). Tsal and Lamy presented subjects with circular arrays of six letters of different colors. Three of the letters were enclosed by or superimposed on a colored shape (e.g., a red, green, blue, or yellow square, circle, or triangle). Participants were instructed to report a shape of a given color (e.g., the shape of any yellow objects) and any letters from the array. The results showed that people tended to report letters that shared the location of the target shape, rather than preferentially reporting letters that shared the same color as the shape. Thus, attending to an object of a relevant color did not facilitate the identification of objects with the same color, but objects that were near the location of the attended object.

Attending to an object with a specific color can also have an effect on processing a subsequently presented object (a probe stimulus) at the same location. For example, Luck, Fan, and Hillyard (1993) presented a target, defined by color, in an array of irrelevant stimuli (distractors), with the task of identifying the target. Either the target or one of the distractors was replaced by a probe (which did not have to be responded to) 250 ms after the presentation of the array. ERPs elicited by the probe showed an enhanced P1 component when the probe occurred on the position of the target relative to when the probe was presented on the position of a distractor. This suggests that the location, and not only the color, of the target was attended.

In conclusion, spatial position does seem to have a special role in visual selection (see also Van der Heijden, 1993). In other words, attention seems to operate on a spatial representation of visual space. This is not surprising given that attention is generally oriented to a location. Although it may be handy (and possible) to maintain an attentional set for color or form, identifying objects seems to entail their localization.

Allocating Attention to Objects

According to purely space-based models of selection, attention directly operates on a spatial representation of visual space. For instance, in feature integration theory (see Chapter 1 and "Feature Integration Theory" later in this chapter) attention is allocated to regions of space and acts to bind features in those regions to form objects. Thus, objects are identified only after attention has been directed to regions of space. However, other models of attention assume that attention selects objects rather than regions of space (see, e.g., Desimone & Duncan, 1995; G. W. Humphreys & Müller, 1993; for a review see Goldsmith, 1998). Such object-based theories of visual selection assume that attention selects only regions of space that are occupied by objects. Space-based theories assume that attention can select regions of space whether they are occupied by objects or not.

Several findings suggest that objects may be the target, and not just the outcome, of attention. Duncan (1984) reported a series of studies in which participants were presented with two superimposed objects and were required to identify either two dimensions of a single object or one dimension on each of the objects. Performance was better when both of the dimensions were on the same object. Duncan proposed that we attend to objects and not to space, and that when judgments are made about two objects, attention must be switched from one object to the other, which takes time. According to this object-based conception of attentional selection, space or spatial proximity is not the dominant factor in the control of attention, but attention operates on objects formed on the basis of earlier perceptual processes. For example, the visual field may be preattentively segmented into separate objects on the basis of Gestalt properties such as continuity, proximity, similarity, and movement. After this preattentive stage, focal attention is employed to analyze objects in more detail (see, e.g., Neisser, 1967).

C. M. Moore, Yantis, and Vaughan (1998) argued that if attention is truly object-based, then it should operate not only on object representations that are explicit in the image, but also on representations that are the result of earlier perceptual completion processes (i.e., processes that infer the presence of an object on the basis of Gestalt principles). In one experiment, two vertical rectangles were presented that were either occluded by a third horizontal rectangle (see Figure 3.8, p. 80) or not. The task was to indicate whether a T or an L was presented in a display of four characters. The four characters were presented on the lower and upper ends of the vertical rectangles, and consisted of three T-L hybrid characters, and one T or L. Shortly before the display was presented, an end of one of the rectangles was briefly illuminated. On 80% of the trials, the T or L was presented at the cued location. In both the occluded and nonoccluded conditions, RTs were fastest when the cue was valid, intermediate when the target occurred on the other end of the cued rectangle, and slowest when the target occurred on the other rectangle. The fact that the results were the same in both the occluded and nonoccluded conditions supports the view that selection can occur on object-based representations that are formed by perceptual completion processes.

Another way of creating virtual objects in a display is to use Gestalt grouping principles to create perceptual groups. Prinzmetal (1981) used the proximity principle (objects that are close together in space will be perceived as belonging to a common group) to create displays that would be processed as two groups. An "object" in these displays was a group composed of a row or column of four of five circles; two groups were shown in each display. On a given trial, the display was shown briefly, followed by a mask, and subjects had to report whether a target was present. Figure 3.9 (p. 81) shows sample displays for the task of determining whether a target, a cross formed by the conjunction of a horizontal and a vertical line segment, was present in any of the eight circles in the display. Prinzmetal reasoned that if attention is devoted to objects, then illusory conjunctions (falsely combining two features to create a nonpresent object) of features on nontarget trials would be more likely to occur when the two features were in the same row of the display (and hence in the same perceptual group) than when each feature was in a different row (with the Euclidean

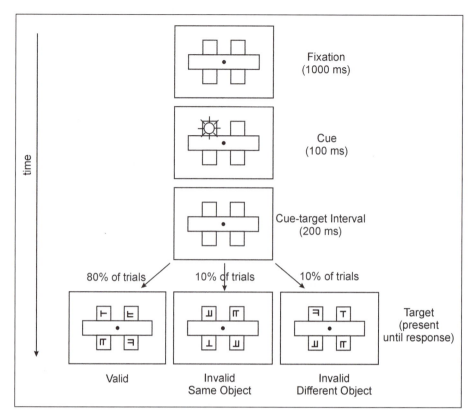

Figure 3.8   The occluded-object display used by Moore et al. (1998). In the nonoccluded condition, the horizontal bar was removed, revealing the two vertical bars.

SOURCE: Moore, Yantis, & Vaughan, 1998. Reprinted with permission from Blackwell Publishers.

distance between the two features held constant). This is just what was found. Subjects rarely reported seeing a target when the two features in the display were the same (the "target-absent feature display"; see Figure 3.9). When one horizontal and one vertical line segment were present (the "target-absent conjunction display"), participants were more likely to mistakenly report having seen a target. When the two features were in the same group, illusory conjunctions were reported on nearly 25% of target-absent conjunction trials. However, when the two features were in different groups, illusory conjunctions occurred on about 18% of the trials. These results suggest that people process all of the features of a perceptual group at once, as suggested by object-based theories of attention.

    Evidence abounds that attention operates on objects, even when these objects are only virtually present. However, at the same time, spatial location and distance

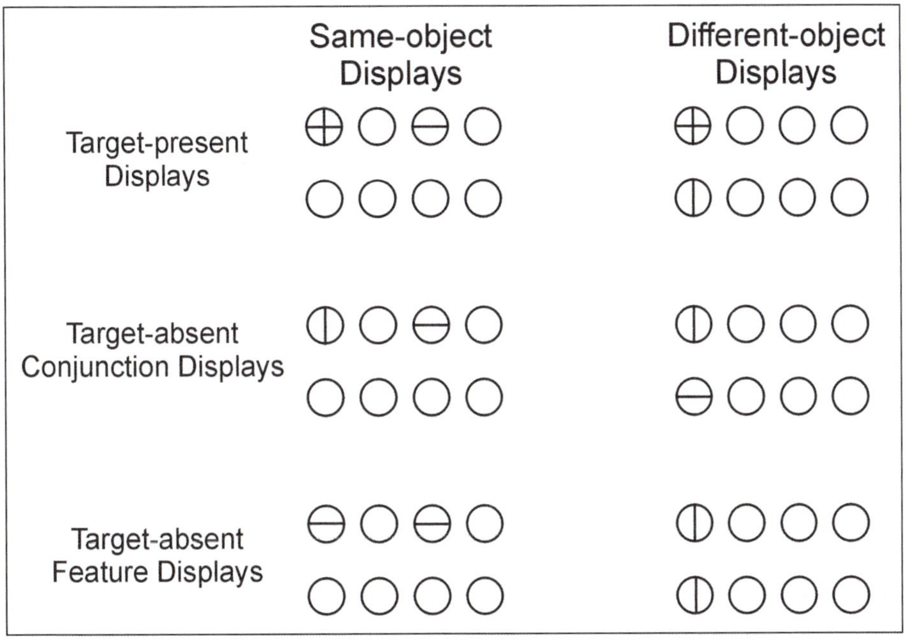

Figure 3.9 Displays like those used by Prinzmetal (1981). Two rows of four circles were shown on each trial, and the task was to indicate whether a cross was present.

SOURCE: Adapted from Prinzmetal, 1981.

play important roles in selection. A possible conclusion is that attention may be either space-based or object-based depending on task demands. For example, Tipper and Weaver (1998) argued that the use of object-based or space-based selection is flexible. Alternatively, selection, although spatial, may be driven to a large extent by top-down expectations from object-based representations (e.g., see Treisman, 1998). Support for this view comes from the finding that object-based selection seems to activate features at a spatial representational level (Weber, Kramer, & Miller, 1997).

VISUAL SEARCH ▲

Just about all visual attention tasks in the real world involve search. Even in simple detection tasks, like waiting for a green light at an intersection, the correct signal must be found and attended to. Most search tasks are more complicated, like searching for a tumor in an X-ray film or for a friend in a crowd. In laboratory

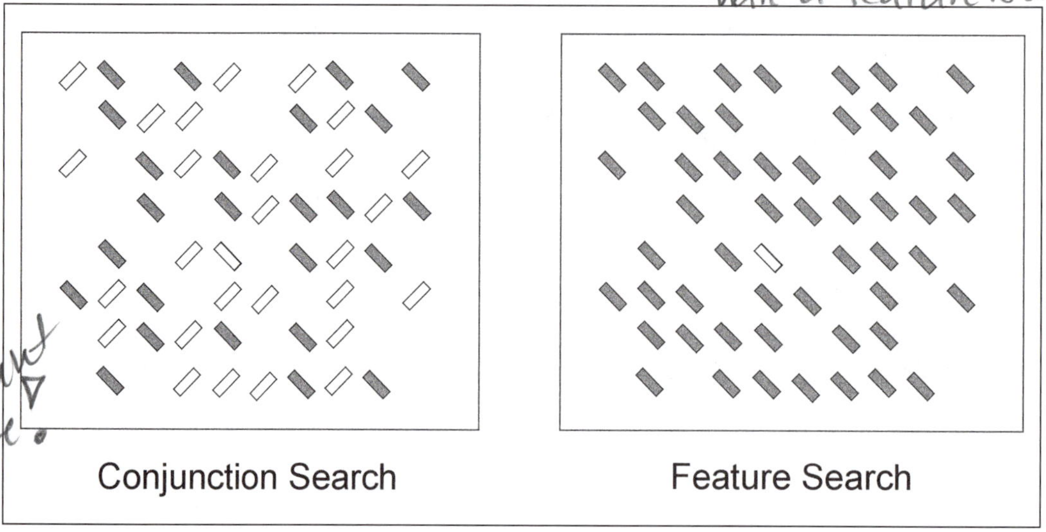

*pop out muns loc we
make a feature: solid or
not

Conjunction Search   Feature Search

*important
figure

Figure 3.10 Visual search displays. In both displays, the target is a white bar oriented 45 degrees to the left. The target "pops out" in the feature display, but is difficult to find in the conjunction display.

search tasks, the task is usually to search for a particular target (e.g., a white bar) in a display with distractors (e.g., gray bars). On some trials a target is present; in other trials there is no target. As a rule, search is easier when the target can be defined by one *feature*, such as the color of the target (see Figure 3.10, right panel), than when it is defined by a *conjunction* of two or more features, such as color and orientation (see Figure 3.10, left panel), in part because with conjunctions the targets and distractors tend to be more similar to each other. One way to characterize search performance is to measure the time needed to determine whether a target is present in the display. Another method is to present displays for a limited amount of time and to measure the accuracy with which observers report whether there was a target present.

In general, the time taken to determine whether a target is present depends on the number of items in a display in conjunction search, but not in feature search. Moreover, in conjunction search, search times are generally longer when there is no target present than when there is. The fact that conjunction search time depends on the number of items in the display has led some researchers to suppose that such search proceeds serially. That is, every item in the display must be checked to see if it is a target. The faster search times for target-present than for target-absent trials can be explained by assuming that observers stop searching when the target is found. According to this serial self-terminating search model, on average, half of the items will need to be checked before the target is found on

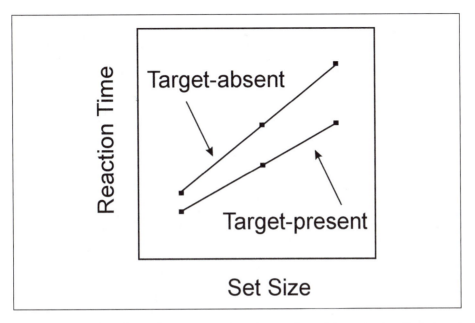

Figure 3.11   The relation between set size (the number of items in the display) and reaction time in a serial self-terminating visual search.

target-present trials, but all items will need to be checked on target-absent trials. That is, because for some target-present trials the target will be the first item checked, on others the last, and on others somewhere in between, on average attention will need to visit only half the items. Thus, the function relating search time to the number of items in the display should be twice as steep for target-absent trials (see Figure 3.11). The notion of serial self-terminating visual search is consistent with many visual search studies. By examining the slope of the reaction time × set-size function (i.e., the function relating search time to the number of items in the display), it is possible to estimate how much time is needed to process each item in the display.

Conjunction search is well described by the serial self-terminating search model (although this is not the only model possible; see Wolfe, 1998; also see Box 3.2), but what about feature search? In the early days of visual search research, it was assumed that feature search could be performed by processing everything in the display in parallel. In fact, feature search is sometimes termed parallel search, whereas conjunction search is termed serial search. The distinction between parallel and serial search has formed the basis for theories of visual search (see, e.g., Triesman & Gelade, 1980). However, this dichotomy has lost importance in some theories (see, e.g., Treisman, 1998), and is explicitly rejected by others (see, e.g.,

Box 3.2 Model Identifiability and Mimicking

One of the major goals of research on human information processing is to identify which of several alternative models best characterizes a particular process. Because these models often are based on different assumptions about the process in question, identifying which model is best provides fundamental knowledge about the nature of the process. To accomplish the goal of identifying the best model, researchers frequently try to conduct experiments for which one model (or class of models) predicts an outcome that is different from that predicted by another model. Although such a research strategy seems simple on the surface, it is complicated by the problem of mimicking. Mimicking is said to occur when at least some members of one class of models can generate results, often mean reaction times, that on the surface seem to support another class of models (Van Zandt & Ratcliff, 1995). Analyses of mimicking problems and model identifiability focus on the general properties of models that can generate particular patterns of results and on finding approaches and measures that can be used to distinguish between alternative models.

The issue of mimicking first arose in the context of search tasks (Townsend, 1972). In a memory-search task, the subject is given a set of some number of items (e.g., letters) to be held in memory, and is to make a "yes" or "no" reaction regarding whether a subsequent target item is in the memory set. A visual search task is similar, except that a single target item held in memory is compared against a set of items in a subsequent visual display.

Two of the major issues concerning search are whether the comparison process is (a) serial (the target is compared to one item at a time) or parallel (the target is compared to all items simultaneously), and (b) self-terminating (comparison is stopped when a match occurs) or exhaustive (comparison continues until the target has been compared to all items). In both memory and visual search tasks, reaction time typically increases linearly as the size of the set to be searched increases. Sternberg (1966) and others originally interpreted this linear increase in reaction time as a function of set size as indicating that the comparison process was serial and not parallel, with the supposition that reaction time should not be a linear function of set size if search were parallel. However, Townsend (1972) showed that parallel models with certain assumptions can generate linearly increasing RT functions. Consequently, the serial versus parallel issue cannot be resolved by examining the effects of set size on mean RT alone.

Sternberg (1966) also concluded that the search process was exhaustive because he obtained equal slopes for "yes" and "no" responses in memory search tasks. A self-terminating search model would seem to predict slope ratios of 2:1 for "no" and "yes" responses because all items must be searched to determine that the target item is not present, but only $(n + 1)/2$ items must be searched on average when the target item is present. Many other studies of visual and memory search have reported slope ratios approximating this 2:1 value. Based on a mimicking analysis,

(Continued)

| **Box 3.2** | (Continued) |

Van Zandt and Townsend (1993) concluded that the results could be interpreted as favoring the view that the search process is self-terminating because exhaustive search models cannot produce the 2:1 slope pattern, but self-terminating search models can generate the parallel functions predicted by exhaustive models.

Van Zandt and Ratcliff (1995) showed that mimicking arises even when models do not make the exact same predictions. Many models make predictions that are different but so similar that it is difficult statistically to tell them apart. They suggest that one of the best ways to deal with the mimicking problem is to test predefined models, for which certain constraints are specified, rather than working backwards from the data to try to fit the models in an unconstrained manner. They also suggest that the tests should involve large data sets, with several independent and dependent variables, because a single one of the predefined models is more likely to be identified as providing the most adequate account of the entire data set. More generally, sophisticated models can often generate data that on the surface seem inconsistent with their basic assumptions, and care must be taken when interpreting results as favoring one model over another.

Duncan & Humphreys, 1989; Wolfe, 1994). Rather than thinking in terms of a dichotomy of search types in which search is either serial or parallel, Wolfe (1998) argues that is better to think of search as being more or less efficient and to examine the factors that influence efficiency. Very efficient search (such as search for a vertical line among horizontal lines) results in search slopes of zero; that is, the time to determine whether a target is present does not depend on the number of items in the display. Very inefficient search (such as search for a conjunction of two orientations) can take more than 30 ms per item, resulting in a much steeper search slope.

Feature Integration Theory ⭐

In visual search, the observer is faced with the task of sifting through multiple features of stimuli in order to find a target. The most robust finding from decades of visual search research is that search efficiency depends on the nature and combinations of features in the display. Based on these findings, models of visual search, and models of selective attention in general, ascribe a special role to the processing of features. The *feature integration theory*, put forward by Treisman and Gelade (1980), assumes that features receive a sort of preferential processing. In

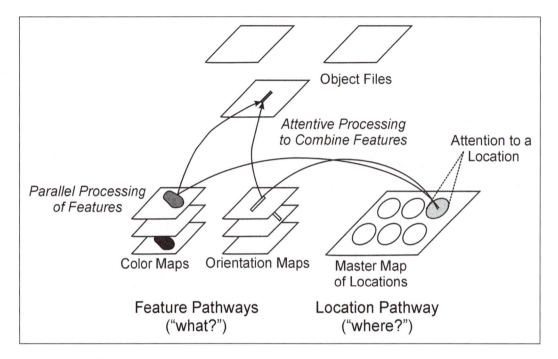

Figure 3.12   Feature integration theory.

this model (see Figure 3.12), features, such as color, orientation, spatial frequency, brightness, and direction of movement, are assumed to be registered early, automatically, and in parallel across the visual field. In this sense, all the elemental bits of information present in a display (patches of color, line segments, etc.) are also present in the early stages of information processing. Feature information must then be combined in order to re-create the objects of the display. This process of "gluing" features back together is assumed to require attention, and attention is allocated on the basis of spatial location. More specifically, selection takes place on the basis of a master map of locations, which contains all locations in which features have been detected. Each location within the master map has access to the feature maps (which indicate whether a specific feature is present at that position) created during the early, parallel processing of the feature information. Focusing attention at a position automatically activates the features that are present at the attended position. These features are then assembled into a temporary object file. Finally, features in the object file are compared with representations of objects in memory (the object frames). Identification takes place when the object file matches an object frame.

Treisman and Gelade (1980) give focused attention a central role in visual perception. In the absence of attention, feature conjunction is likely to go awry, with the result that objects are incorrectly identified. For example, Treisman and Schmidt (1982) conducted an experiment in which subjects had to search for a yellow "O" in a display containing letters of different colors. When only the search task was performed, detection accuracy was quite high; however, when attention demands were increased by adding a secondary task (comparing digits presented to the left and right of the search display), detection performance decreased in an interesting way. With attentional distraction, subjects were more likely to report that a yellow O had been present when it was not, but when a letter O of a different color and another letter with the color yellow had been present in the display. In other words, an illusory conjunction of letter and color seemed to take place.[3]

The usefulness of models that contain separate modules or maps for different feature dimensions depends on a means for determining what the basic features are. Treisman and Gelade (1980) suggested an empirical method for defining features: They should pop out during search, mediate texture segregation (i.e., the perception of object boundaries on the basis of texture differences), and hold the possibility of recombining to form illusory conjunctions. Features defined according to these criteria include obvious candidates such as orientation and color, but also a few surprises, such as perceived direction of lighting (Enns & Rensink, 1990). Feature integration theory includes a number of feature maps for each basic dimension, and attention is required to combine features into objects. However, attention might be needed to combine different values of the same feature, as well. For example, "purple" is, subjectively, a combination of blue and red. Treisman (1998) suggests that feature maps within a dimension such as color might be limited in number, and that purple has to be constructed as a conjunction of blue and red. The finding that search for a purple target is much less efficient when the distractors are red and blue, as compared to when they are other colors matched for similarity, suggests that the number of feature maps within a stimulus dimension may, indeed, be limited.

The original version of feature integration theory (Treisman & Gelade, 1980) assumed that features were represented independently of their locations, and that locations were used only to bind different features together. Subsequent experiments have shown that features are often localized—as well as identified—even in very efficient feature searches. This led Treisman (1998) to conclude that the dissociation between "what" and "where" in feature processing is less extreme than she and Gelade originally supposed. Cohen and Ivry (1989) take a stronger stance, and maintain that features are preattentively bound to coarsely defined locations.

To account for the fact that conjunction search can sometimes be very efficient (see, e.g., Nakayama & Silverman, 1986; Wolfe, Cave, & Franzel, 1989), Treisman

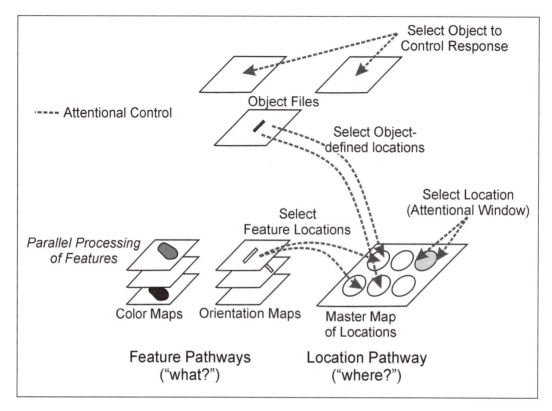

Figure 3.13   Feature integration theory revised to allow stimulus-based attentional control.

and Sato (1990) proposed that attention may modulate activity in the master map of locations via the feature maps (see Figure 3.13). For example, attention may operate to inhibit irrelevant features, and thereby the locations in the master map containing these features, so that search can be restricted to locations containing relevant features. Treisman (1991) suggests that such a mechanism can explain why Duncan and Humphreys (1989) found that the difficulty of finding a target depends on both the similarity of the target to the distractors (such that greater target–distractor similarity makes finding the target more difficult) and on similarity between the distractors themselves (such that search is more efficient when distractors are similar to each other). According to Treisman, inhibition or activation of feature maps can influence search only when either the target or the distractors activate a unique set of features. Treisman (1998) suggests that attention might also operate by allowing object files to influence the master map of locations. This sort of top-down influence may explain constancy of objects in case of movement or changes of the object.

Guided Search 2.0

According to Wolfe (1998), attention can be directed to the locations of interesting objects in the visual field by means of preattentive processes. That is, before attention is directed to locations or objects, preattentive processes are at work. Preattentive processes might direct attention in a bottom-up (stimulus-driven) way, such as when a unique feature pops out of a display even when one does not know in advance what or where the target will be. Preattentive processes might also direct attention in a top-down (observer-driven) way. For example, a red stripe will not pop out of a display in which every stripe is of a different color, but if one knows in advance that a red stripe should be found, search is nonetheless quite efficient. The idea that preattentive processing can occur is suggested by the finding that basic features presented in the periphery of a display can still be identified even when attention is tied up in a demanding task that requires fixation (see, e.g., Braun, 1994). That is, even when attention is busy elsewhere, preattentive processes may be at work.

In Wolfe's guided search model (Wolfe, 1994) information from top-down and bottom-up analyses of the stimuli is used to rank items according to their attentional priority. These attentional priorities guide search (and make it more efficient) by directing the application of attention. As in feature integration theory, attention is needed to bind features together in order to identify objects.

COMBINING OBJECT- AND SPACE-BASED SELECTION IN THEORIES OF VISUAL ATTENTION ▲

Comprehensive models of attention face many challenges. They must describe how attention is allocated to both locations and objects. They must also describe how objects and groups are formed from features present in the display. In this section we will describe efforts to model selection in all its complexity.

A Theory of Visual Attention

One model of how selection might proceed on the basis of different stimulus features is Bundesen's (1990) *theory of visual attention* (TVA). In this model, two things are selected simultaneously, a perceptual item and a categorization for the item, and selection is seen as a choice among categorizations of perceptual inputs. Bundesen's theory can be considered both an early-selection theory (selection based on perceptual features) and a late-selection theory (selection based on the category of the items). Perceptual information is represented at one level, and consists of the features of the display items. A separate, conceptual level of representation consists of categorizations of display items and features. These two sorts of representation are linked by a parameter that indicates the amount of sensory evidence contained in a given item for membership in a given category. This parameter, η, is the bottom-up component of the theory; it is determined for each item on the basis of the quality of the data and the set of possible categories.

In Bundesen's model, location is a feature of an item, as are color, form, and so on. The categories used in the theory can be basic qualities such as "red," "round," or "top-left corner," and can be applied to each feature of the stimulus. Selection is a race between the different possible categorizations of stimulus features. The outcome of this race is determined by the evidence parameter η, modified by two attentional parameters, one called β that reflects the subject's bias to categorize the display in a certain way, and one called w that focuses attention on a particular item in the display. The parameter β is under the subject's control and can affect the outcome of categorization by determining the initial (but not necessarily the final) categorization of an item. For example, if you are waiting for a friend in a crowded station you might think you see him several times before he actually appears, whereas when you are just walking through the same station you will rarely be deceived into thinking you have seen him. The parameter w, on the other hand, does not affect what the categorization is, but affects the probability that a given item will be categorized. For example, your search for your friend might lead you to focus on tall people, and lead to their categorization as "my friend" or "not my friend." A final parameter in TVA is π. Like β, π is under subject control. Combined with η, π helps determine the attentional weights, w. A high value of η suggests that an item contains much information, and a high value of π suggests that it is pertinent (i.e., relevant to current goals). Thus, attention is most likely to be allocated to meaningful, pertinent information.

Bundesen (1990) showed that the theory can account for a wide variety of findings including the effects of object integrality in selective report and the number and spatial positions of targets in divided-attention paradigms. More recently, the theory has been incorporated into even more ambitious theories of visual attention.

The CODE Theory of Visual Attention

Space-based and object-based approaches to visual attention are more explicitly integrated in the CODE theory of visual attention (CTVA) presented by Logan (1996). Logan describes CTVA as a fusion of Bundesen's theory of visual attention and his own contour detection (CODE) theory of perceptual grouping by proximity (Compton & Logan, 1993; Van Oeffelen & Vos, 1982; see Figure 3.14). The theory begins attempting to explain selection in the early stages of visual processing,

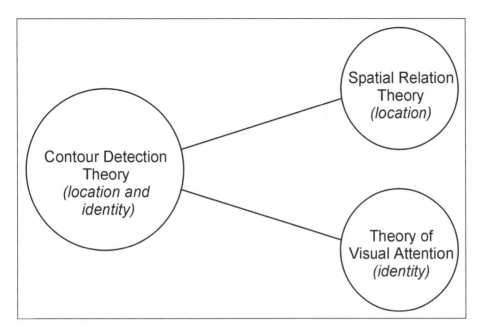

Figure 3.14 The CODE theory of visual attention.

SOURCE: Logan, 1996.

in which location and object information are processed together (anatomically, this takes place in area V1 in the visual cortex). Processing at this level occurs according to the processes described in the CODE theory, which operate to form perceptual groups. This information is passed on to the late identity processes, which are assumed to work as in Bundesen's theory of visual attention (taking place in the inferotemporal cortex), and to a processing module that is less well-defined, but based on Logan's (1995) spatial relation theory, which accomplishes late processing of location (which takes place in the posterior parietal cortex) by determining the spatial relations between items in the display.

CODE theory represents space in terms of an analog representation of locations of items and a quasi-analog, quasi-discrete representation of objects and groups of objects. The analog representation of location is the result of bottom-up processes that depend only on the proximity of various items in the display. The representations of objects and groups result from an interaction of the bottom-up processes that generate the analog representation and top-down processes that apply a threshold to the analog representation. Logan (1996) gives a detailed mathematical description of how these representations might be created. The results of the application of CODE theory to a display such as that shown in Figure 3.9 are shown in Figure 3.15. As can be seen in the figure, before a threshold

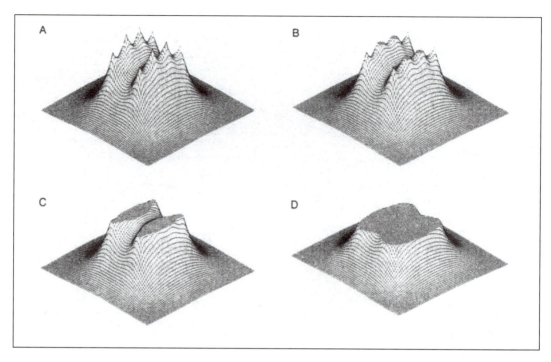

Figure 3.15   CODE surfaces. The figure illustrates how lowering the threshold (from A to D) reveals perceptual groups.

SOURCE: Logan, 1996. Copyright 1996 by the American Psychological Association; reprinted with permission.

*KNOW

has been set, the representation is simply the analog representation of space and the features that occupy it. Changing the threshold changes the representation, such that the lower the threshold, the larger the groups that are formed. The hierarchical structure of groups is revealed when different thresholds are applied to the analog representations.

The distributions that make up the CODE surface represent item features distributed over space. The height of the surface at any point represents the probability of sampling the features of the items at that point. Attention chooses among the above-threshold regions and samples from the features present there. In this sense, the CTVA is object-based (because objects drive the CODE surface above the threshold). However, because the CODE surface is affected by all objects present, CTVA is also location-based in the sense that features from objects other than the one selected will also be processed if there is some overlap in the distributions corresponding to the features of the different objects (i.e., the representation of items in space is fuzzy).

The identity system of the theory, following the theory of visual attention, interprets the representation created by CODE theory in terms of features and categories. When the threshold is changed, the search will be either more parallel (in the case of a low threshold) or more serial (in the case of a high threshold). For the location system, the second representation defines the perceptual organization of the display. Selection on the basis of identity is assumed to take place in a similar way as in the model of Bundesen, but rather than selecting items (i.e., rather than treating items as discrete units), CTVA treats items as spatial distributions, and sensory evidence and attentional weights are attached to parts of the distributions. Moreover, rather than treating location as just another feature (as in the theory of visual attention), CTVA represents objects embedded in their locations and space is represented across the whole display, not just as features of objects. Selection of locations occurs outside of the part of the system described in the theory of visual attention, and depends on both the perceptual relations in the display and a conceptual representation of propositions that express the spatial relations between objects (e.g., A is above B or above B is A).

The CODE theory of visual attention is just one "incarnation" of a series of theories of grouping and selection in visual search. Such theories are quite exciting because they offer the promise of modeling search, which allows the testing of predictions about the effects of changing various stimulus or subject parameters. Eventually, these theories may provide the basis for testing new display techniques (see Chapter 8) or for describing deficits of visual processing behavior (see Chapter 12).

SUMMARY ▲

Selection is arguably the essence of attention. Knowing what is selected, and how and why, is a prerequisite for understanding any subsequent aspect of information processing. Research on selection, perhaps more than any other aspect of attentional processing, has dictated how attention is characterized. In this chapter, we discussed the major metaphors of attention and the research stimulated by them. This research has explored how attention can be moved or focused, and how the direction and degree of focusing of attention influences stimulus (or response) processing. One of the major findings of this research is that although attention can be focused on specific regions of space, its purpose can be better described as one of highlighting objects for selection.

Although visual attention usually coincides with the direction of gaze, the two can be dissociated. The orienting of attention (often followed by the orienting of the eyes) may be controlled by the environment (exogenous orienting) or by instructions or intention (endogenous orienting). These processes often interact in tasks such as visual search for a target among distractors. Numerous models have been proposed to characterize both bottom-up and top-down aspects of selection. In fact, such models have been proposed since the beginning of the modern era of research on attention in the 1950s.

In 1890, William James said that everyone knows what attention is. When it comes to contemporary views of visual selective attention, one might say that everyone has a model of it. Although these models differ in details and in the range of findings they accommodate, they share many commonalities.

▲ NOTES

1. Some spotlight models also assume that the edges of the spotlight are weaker than the center.

2. A popular metaphor for selective attention is that of selection based on competition between inputs. The task of attentional control is then to bias the selection of some inputs while preventing other inputs from being selected. Selection is assumed to occur on the basis of the weight or strength associated with each input; the input with the strongest weight wins the competition. Attentional control operates by using task context or goals to bias competition among inputs by setting the weights appropriately.

3. Illusory conjunctions play a central role in feature integration theory; however, the notion of illusory conjunctions as the result of imperfect binding of features has been questioned. For example, Donk (1999) argues that evidence for illusory conjunctions can be interpreted as target–nontarget confusion. Although such confusion and guessing may account for some illusory conjunctions, the evidence supports the view that imperfect feature binding does occur (Prinzmetal, Ivry, Beck, & Shimuzu, 2002).

CHAPTER 4

Pg 95-104

AUDITORY AND CROSSMODAL ATTENTION

A glance at the literature on attention (and at the previous chapter) makes it obvious that much of the research on attention in the late 20th century focused on the visual modality. However, this has not always been the case, nor, we suspect, will this remain so. Much of the early research on attention used auditory stimuli to address critical issues such as the nature of selective and divided attention and whether selection occurred early or late in processing. A question that is increasingly receiving interest is whether there are separate types of attention corresponding to different sensory modalities. The corresponding question is, of course, how information from different modalities can be integrated and whether there is such a thing as a central, supra-modal attentional controller.

Hearing differs from vision in several ways; for example, the spatial aspect of auditory processing is much different than that of visual processing. Whereas in vision, different stimuli distributed in space stimulate different, specific positions on the retina, the influence of auditory stimuli is combined, as it were, before sensory processing begins. This fact constrains the type of research that can be conducted using auditory stimuli. For example, whereas it is possible to conduct visual search experiments with hundreds of different stimuli, a number of which can be presented at one time, it is impossible for subjects to process more than a few simultaneously presented auditory stimuli. On the other hand, different streams of stimuli can be presented much more easily to two ears than to two eyes, making it easier to examine abilities to combine or keep separate different sources of information.

We begin this chapter by reviewing research using the *dichotic listening paradigm,* in which separate messages are presented at the same time, each to a different ear. We review the major findings for both selective attention, in which listeners attend to only one message, ignoring the other, and divided attention, in which the messages presented to both ears must be reported. We also discuss the theories of attention based on this work. Next, we examine the relation between the alerting effects of auditory stimuli and the information contained in the signal, and the implications of this distinction for discrimination between concurrent stimuli versus simple detection of sounds. We then examine the role of attentional set, focusing (although not exclusively) on the processing of auditory stimuli. We conclude with a discussion of recent research on crossmodal attentional links between hearing, vision, and touch.

▲ AUDITORY SELECTIVE ATTENTION

Understanding auditory messages or detecting auditory targets depends on the analysis and partitioning of complex sounds into perceptual components. This process of separating sound elements into different auditory objects is known as *auditory stream segregation.* Stream segregation enables us to distinguish between different streams, or sources of information. For example, in baroque music one instrument is often used to play two melodic lines by alternating low and high tones in a rapid sequence. Given a sufficient pitch difference between the low and high tones, the sequence will be perceived as two melodic lines—one consisting of the low tones and the other consisting of the high tones (Bregman, 1990). Stream segregation is an ongoing topic of research in hearing. In this section, we examine attentional effects on the ability to distinguish among and select different sources of information, as in the example of streams of high and low pitch tones.

The Dichotic Listening Paradigm

We have all had the experience of trying to follow two conversations at the same time, such as when we hear our own name at a party and try to hear what is being said while trying to carry on the current conversation. A related task, but with a different goal, is trying to ignore one conversation in order to focus on another, such as when trying to follow the dialogue of a film in a noisy theater. In both of these examples, two sources of auditory information are presented to both ears more or less simultaneously. We try to follow one of the conversations while filtering out the other, relying only on our attentional capacities.

In order to more carefully control the presentation of the stimuli used to study the ability to select information, researchers in the 1950s developed the *dichotic listening* paradigm, in which two separate sources of auditory information are presented to the two ears of the listener. For example, one might hear a list of spoken digits in one ear and a list of spoken letters in the other ear. Selecting one message is easier in dichotic listening than in monaural listening, in which two messages are presented with equal intensity to both ears (Egan, Carterette, & Thwing, 1954). In dichotic listening, each message is presented with an unnaturally great intensity difference (in each case, zero for one ear and easily audible for the other), but even more moderate intensity differences improve selective listening considerably (Treisman, 1964a). Dichotic presentation gives the impression of two separate streams of sound, each localized roughly at the input ear. The localization is stronger than in monaural listening, and also of a different nature. Normally, localization rests on a number of cues, one of the most important being the difference in time (and phase of the sound waves) at which the information reaches each of the two ears, respectively. These cues are absent in the dichotic listening task because each ear receives only one message. Nonetheless, the task has often been used to study the limits of attention in selecting information.

Cherry (1953) was the first to use the dichotic listening technique to study attention. In his experiments, participants were required to *shadow* (repeat back without delay) one of the messages. People could do this surprisingly well. When asked about the information presented to the other, unattended ear, however, they were able to report nothing more than that sounds had been present. Cherry manipulated the message on the unattended ear in order to determine how much of the information was processed despite the instruction to attend to the opposite ear. He found that almost no one noticed when the unattended message changed from English to German, or when English speech was played backward. On the other hand, when the gender of the speaker (and, hence, the pitch of the voice) changed, or when a 400-Hz auditory tone was presented, listeners almost always noticed it. Cherry concluded that "certain statistical properties [of the rejected message are] identified, but that detailed aspects, such as the language, individual words, or semantic content are unnoticed" (1953, p. 978).

To test whether people really were as insensitive to the unattended channel as it seemed in Cherry's (1953) study, Moray (1959a) played the same word list to the unattended ear 35 times. He found that listeners were no more likely to report having heard the repeated words than words that were never presented. However, when the message played to the unattended ear is the same as that played to the attended ear, listeners notice the repetition so long as the lag between the repeated words does not exceed a few seconds (Cherry, 1953; Treisman 1964b).[1] This result poses a problem for theories of attention that propose early selection of information on the basis of a filter that monitors sounds fitting a certain criterion, be it location, pitch, or intensity (e.g., filter theory; Broadbent, 1958). It also shows that more information may be processed than we are normally aware of. One account of this finding states that all unattended information is processed automatically to some point just below conscious awareness (e.g., Deutsch & Deutsch, 1963), that is, before the point that it can be reported. When the information receives just a bit more activation—either because it has recently been heard or because it is highly pertinent—it attracts attention and we become aware of it (Treisman, 1964a; see Chapter 3).

Factors Affecting the Ease of Selection

Early work with the dichotic listening paradigm led researchers to conclude that ears were like information channels and that information could be more or less independently presented to each of these channels. As we mentioned earlier, the localization of the message in dichotic listening is much more extreme than in normal listening conditions. In the real world, location can be an effective cue for auditory selection, but the resolution of auditory localization has severe limits. For example, when several stimuli are presented simultaneously to both ears, it is difficult to tell more than a few apart (Scharf & Buus, 1986). Even under dichotic listening conditions, the number of messages that can be effectively isolated (and ignored) is limited. Treisman (1964a) showed this by creating a third "channel" as a result of presenting a message with equal intensity to both ears. This procedure creates the impression of a voice in the middle of one's head. Treisman found that shadowing of one of the three channels was possible when a message was presented in only one of the other channels, but performance was severely impaired when speech messages were presented in all three channels.[2] Ears may be like channels, but there is a high potential for interference among them.

Even when just two messages are played separately to the two ears, selection is not always efficient. In fact, sometimes shadowing by ear is nearly impossible. For example, Treisman and Riley (1969) showed that it is also necessary to be able to separate the two streams of information on the basis of temporal cues. In the relevant experiment, they synchronized the words presented to each ear by first digitally processing each word so that it lasted precisely 250 ms. Words were presented simultaneously, one list of words to each ear. Listeners in these experiments made many shadowing errors and words that should have been unattended often intruded into the listener's report. Apparently, it is not just the physical localization of the voices that makes selection easy in dichotic listening—the differences in onset times of the words in the messages also play an important role in enabling selection.

We mentioned in the previous section that participants in Cherry's (1953) study noticed when the gender of the speaker on the unattended channel was changed. This suggests that people can be aware of the pitch of a message without actively attending to a channel. According to Broadbent (1958), this suggests that pitch can be used to filter information. Because pitch is used as a filter, people notice when pitch is changed and the filter is no longer effective. In general, it is much easier to tell simultaneously presented auditory messages apart if the different messages are presented in different pitches (Treisman, 1964c). For example, it is much easier to attend to one voice in the presence of another if the two voices are of different gender (and hence of different pitch) than if the second message is spoken by a member of the same sex as the speaker of the first.

Processing of Unselected Information

Although early work with the dichotic listening paradigm focused on the efficiency of selection, later work focused more on what could "get through" on the unattended channel. One famous result is that people are much more likely to hear their own name on the unattended channel than other names or information. For example, Moray (1959a) found that when the words "you may stop now" were presented on the unattended channel, only 8% of the participants actually stopped. However, when this message was preceded by the participant's name (e.g., "Neville, you may stop now"), 33% of the participants stopped.

In another examination of the breakthrough of unattended information, Treisman (1960) presented two messages to listeners using dichotic listening, but the messages, both logical sentences and both recorded in the same voice, were split such that the first half of the message was presented to one ear and the second half to the other ear. Although participants were instructed to shadow everything presented to one ear, they often "jumped" to the other channel at the point at which the messages changed channels. When this occurred (about 30% of the time; see Pashler, 1998, for more discussion), listeners would usually switch back to the appropriate channel after just one or two words—and without even noticing what had happened. For example, when the stimuli presented to the left ear were the words "I saw the girl song was wishing . . ." and the words presented to the right ear were "me that bird jumping in the street . . . ," one listener shadowed, "I saw the girl jumping wishing. . . . ." This result shows that information on the unattended channel is analyzed to the level of meaning (at least under conditions when the attended message stops making sense). Just as your own name may capture attention, so can words that fit into a sentence context.

Corteen and Wood (1972) conducted an ingenious experiment that suggests that unattended words are processed to a semantic level. These researchers first conditioned people to expect a mild but unpleasant shock after hearing the names of certain cities. Next, they tested the participants in a dichotic listening task in which the unattended message contained the conditioned city names, other city names, and unrelated nouns. The participants did not report having heard any city names, but they did exhibit a physiological response (a change in the *galvanic skin response*, a measure of the conductivity of the skin that has been shown to be associated with stress) to the conditioned names on about 38% of the trials on which they were presented, compared to 23% of the presentations of other city names and only 10% of the presentations of unrelated nouns. Thus, even though the conditioned names did not reach conscious awareness, they did seem to reach semantic analysis.

Although the results of Corteen and Wood (1972) are consistent with the idea of semantic analysis of words on the unattended channel, they do not imply that all information on the unattended channel is fully processed. As is also suggested by the fact that one's own name is recognized only about 33% of the time in a dichotic listening task, Corteen and Wood's results could be at least partly due to occasional lapses in selective attention wherein the to-be-ignored channel is monitored. That this may have been the case is suggested by a replication of the Corteen and Wood study conducted by Dawson and Schell (1982). Dawson and Schell replicated the main finding of Corteen and Wood, but also found that the galvanic skin responses to conditioned words on the unattended channel were often accompanied by evidence of attention lapses (shadowing errors or reports of having heard items on the unattended channel). It should also be noted that evidence of semantic processing does not mean that the stimuli were fully processed. The finding that participants in Corteen and Wood's experiment were not aware of having heard the conditioned city names that elicited the galvanic skin response suggests that even when semantic information breaks through, attention is required to further process this information to a reportable form. This issue will be discussed in more detail in Chapter 7.

As you know yourself if you have ever tried to block out one conversation while keeping up your end of another conversation, attending to only one source of information seems to require an active effort to inhibit the information in the other channel. We have already seen that selection is not perfect; however, people do tend to be fairly successful in blocking out irrelevant auditory information. One measure of the success of inhibiting information in the unattended channel is a phenomenon called negative priming. *Negative priming*, which will be discussed in detail in Chapter 5, is the finding that information that has to be ignored at one point in time, but attended at a later point in time, is responded to more slowly at the later point (usually ranging from 0.5 to 3 seconds later) than if it had never been presented. Banks, Roberts, and Ciranni (1995) used a dichotic listening task in which one channel was shadowed to show that information in the unattended ear is actively suppressed. When information from the unattended channel was subsequently presented in the to-be-shadowed ear, shadowing performance was worse than for words that had never been presented before.

DIVIDED AUDITORY ATTENTION ▲

In many tasks, the problem is not to attend to just one source of information, but to divide attention across different sources. For example, if the telephone rings as you are trying to listen for the daily weather forecast on the local televised newscast, you may try to answer the phone and respond appropriately to the caller, while at the same time monitoring the newscast for the weather report and listening to the forecast. For most people, this is a difficult feat to accomplish. In this section, we describe paradigms that have been used to study the ability to divide attention across different auditory sources and discuss the major findings in the field.

The Split-Span Technique

The selectivity observed with the dichotic listening paradigm shows that people can direct attention to just one source of stimulation when the source is well defined by a basic characteristic such as location. Variations on this paradigm have been used to ask how efficiently people are able to divide their attention across different sources or channels. An example of this other type of dichotic listening task is the *split-span technique*. This technique gets its name from the memory span (the number of items that can, on average, be remembered without rehearsal), with the list of items to be remembered split into two shorter lists for presentation to the two ears. In this type of experiment, the listener is instructed to report all items heard in both ears.

Broadbent (1954) used this procedure to present two lists of three spoken digits, one list to each ear, at a rate of two digits per second. He found that listeners tended to report all the items presented to one ear first, followed by the items presented to the other ear (see Figure 4.1), rather than reporting them as pairs grouped by presentation time. This seemed to suggest that selection of information occurs quite early in the course of information processing, at the level of the physical properties of the stimuli (e.g., location or pitch; Broadbent, 1956). Broadbent (1954) proposed that while the message presented to one ear was attended to, the other was held in a sort of "preperceptual" storage (see Chapter 7 for more discussion of early

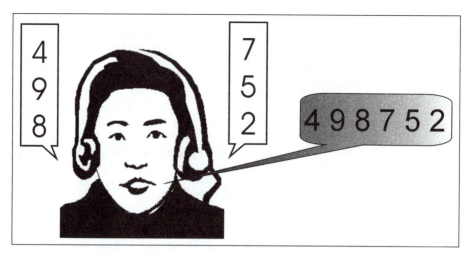

Figure 4.1   A split-span experiment. Listeners tend to report the items presented to one ear, followed by the items presented to the other ear, rather than reporting together pairs of items presented at the same time (i.e., 4-7, 9-5, 8-2).

auditory stores). After the items in one ear were reported, the attentional "filter" would switch to the other ear, allowing report of those items. However, later experiments showed that selection of items for report can be based on higher-level, semantic properties of the stimuli, and not just on physical properties such as location or frequency. For example, Bartz, Satz, and Fennell (1967) found that listeners tended to report lists of digits and nondigit monosyllabic words according to the ear in which the lists were presented, but when instructed to report the digits first, followed by the nondigits, they could do this easily. Furthermore, when a message such as "who-3-there" is played to the right ear and the message "2-goes-9" is played to the left ear, some people spontaneously report the familiar phrase, "who goes there," followed by the digits "2 3 9" (J. A. Gray & Wedderburn, 1960).

Auditory Monitoring

The split-span technique can be viewed as a special case of an *auditory monitoring* task. In auditory monitoring, participants listen to streams of auditory stimuli and indicate when they have heard a target. In the split-span technique, all words are targets and the task is to report everything; in contrast, auditory monitoring tasks are usually performed under more noisy conditions. For example, Pohlmann and Sorkin (1976) studied the ability of people to divide their attention using a paradigm in which up to three targets had to be detected in a stream of auditory noise presented to one ear. In a single-channel condition, participants had to monitor short intervals of noise for the presence of a target of a given frequency. In the multiple-channel condition, one, two, or three targets (of widely spaced different frequencies) could be presented, which meant that participants had to simultaneously monitor for different frequencies. In each of the conditions, a target was present on half of the trials. Pohlmann and Sorkin's participants were quite good at detecting any one of the three targets in the multiple-target condition when only one target was presented at a given moment (in this case, their performance was comparable to the single-target condition); however, their performance was much worse when two or three targets were presented simultaneously. Other studies also have shown that the ability of people to monitor both ears depends on whether multiple targets are presented at the same time (Sorkin, Pohlmann, & Gilliom, 1973). Performance in monitoring information in both ears is quite good as long as only one target is present at a time and as long as the different targets are easy to tell apart. Thus, it seems that auditory attention can be "set" to monitor a number of channels, but that limitations on the ability to simultaneously identify multiple targets prevent perfect time-sharing on the multiple channels. Moray (1975) reached the same conclusion based on studies using continuous presentation of stimuli (tones or speech) rather than discrete intervals during which a target may or may not occur: Attention can be directed to multiple possible stimuli, but a bottleneck occurs at the point where multiple identifications are required.

Gilliom and Sorkin (1974) conducted a number of studies to determine why people are so poor at detecting two simultaneous auditory targets. They found that even when one observation interval (a 100-ms interval during which a predefined target could be presented to one ear) followed the other (at the other ear), detection of a second target was much worse when a target was present in the first interval. This two-target deficit was still present when listeners knew which ear would be used for the first target interval. Interestingly, when both targets are different features of the same stimulus, people are just as good at detecting two targets as they are at detecting only one. For example, J. J. Moore and Massaro (1973) showed that listeners were just about as accurate in making simultaneous judgments about the amplitude (loudness) and quality ("sharp" or "dull") of a tone as they were in judging only one dimension. Furthermore, Puleo and Pastore (1978) found that increasing the difference in intensity between two targets could cancel out the two-target deficit. Thus, it is not really clear whether the two-target deficit results from an inability to hear the two targets, to monitor the two targets, or to select the appropriate responses.

Monitoring for single targets cannot always be accomplished without costs. This can be illustrated by a study by Ninio and Kahneman (1974) in which two lists of words were presented dichotically (i.e., one list to each ear), and targets (animal names) could appear in either list. When participants were instructed to monitor only one list, they were quite good at detecting any animal names (96% hit rate). Performance dropped slightly (to about 90%) if an animal name was presented in the unattended channel shortly before a target was presented in the attended channel, suggesting that, as we saw earlier, exclusion of information from the unattended channel is not perfect. However, when the instructions were to monitor the messages presented to both ears, the hit rate dropped to 77% and responses were slower (the false alarm rate also rose slightly), even though only one target was presented at a time. As in visual search (see, e.g., Schneider & Shiffrin, 1977), dividing attention across different channels is more difficult than attending to just one source of information.

stop ✱

▲ ALERTING AND ORIENTING FUNCTIONS OF AUDITORY ATTENTION

Although turning the head or cupping a hand around the ear can result in a slight increase in the loudness, and, thus, the salience, of auditory stimulation, auditory attention is in large part independent of the position of the head and ears. This makes the auditory system quite different from the visual system. Although visual attention can be de-coupled from the direction of gaze, the normal state of affairs is that we attend only where we look (or look where we wish to attend). According to Scharf (1998, p. 75), "This neutrality with respect to the spatial aspects of sound makes the auditory system an excellent early-warning system, one that is ready to receive and process stimuli from all directions regardless of the organism's current orientation."

Despite the inability to move the ear to catch wanted sounds in the way that the eyes can be moved to catch wanted sights, the ear does seem to have some built-in attentional control. The cochlea of the ear, where the sensory receptors are located, receives input from the brain that may control the direction of attention. In fact, some 1,400 nerve fibers (the olivocochlear bundle) travel from the brainstem to the cochlea, delivering input from the auditory centers in the temporal lobe of the brain. This input might help to tune the sensory receptors to favor one sound over another (G. Rasmussen, 1946; Scharf, 1998). Such efferent control might be necessary to protect us from distraction. That this is so is suggested by the finding that cats that have undergone surgery to sever the olivocochlear bundle are more easily distracted by irrelevant noise than are other cats. When efferent input is intact, cats, and perhaps people, too, are less susceptible to distraction and interference from noise. However, such efferent control seems to be limited to near-threshold stimuli and may not play a great role in orienting auditory attention. In particular, changes in auditory stimulation typically break through any sort of cognitive control of the receptors.

Given that sounds are often associated with important, potentially life-threatening events (e.g., the sound of a crashing tree, oncoming predator, or, in modern life, an approaching automobile), it makes sense that we have a strong tendency to localize sounds and orient our attention to the supposed source of the sound. Sounds can have strong effects on the orienting of visual attention. For example, responses to a visual target on the left or right of a display are faster when an auditory cue is presented from a speaker on the corresponding side (Buchtel & Butter, 1988). Spence and Driver (1996; see also Schmidt, Postma, & De Haan, 2000) showed that even an uninformative auditory cue (i.e., a cue with only 50% validity in a two-choice discrimination task) results in faster responses to a visual stimulus presented on the same side as the auditory cue as compared to the opposite side, although this result may be due to interference from the auditory stimulus when it is presented opposite to the target rather than to facilitation from an auditory signal on the same side as the target.

J. J. McDonald, Teder-Sälejärvi, and Hillyard (2000) presented more convincing evidence that the involuntary orienting of attention to sound enhances the perceptual processing of visual stimuli. In their experiments, an auditory cue was followed by a briefly presented, masked visual stimulus. The auditory cue was played on the left or the right, but was completely unpredictive of the location of the visual target (a single green LED, see Figure 4.2), which was presented on only half of the trials. Lights (four red LEDs) surrounding the target were used to mask the targets. Because the target was masked, it was difficult to detect, but because the mask surrounded the target, the participant knew the position of the target, had it been presented. The response was simply to press a key if a target was detected, regardless of the side of the target. Thus, response uncertainty was minimized. McDonald et al. found that whether speed and accuracy (Experiment 1) or accuracy alone (Experiment 2) was emphasized, people were faster and more likely to detect the target when the target was on the same side as the cue (see Figure 4.3 for the results from Experiment 1). Furthermore, signal detection analyses (see Chapter 2) showed that observers were more sensitive to signals on the cued side, as well as being biased to respond to stimuli on that side. The authors suggest that crossmodal attentional links play a role in enhancing the perceptual salience of multisensory stimuli. Increasing the salience of events that co-occur in space (and occur close together in time) may help us to integrate information from different senses in order to construct a stable representation of environmental events.

Studies in which both reaction times and event-related potentials (ERPs) were measured also attest to the attention-capturing nature of sounds. For example, Schröger (1996) had people perform a dichotic listening task in which pairs of tones were presented to the left and right ears. The tone in the left ear, which was presented first, was to be ignored, and listeners were to make a go or no-go

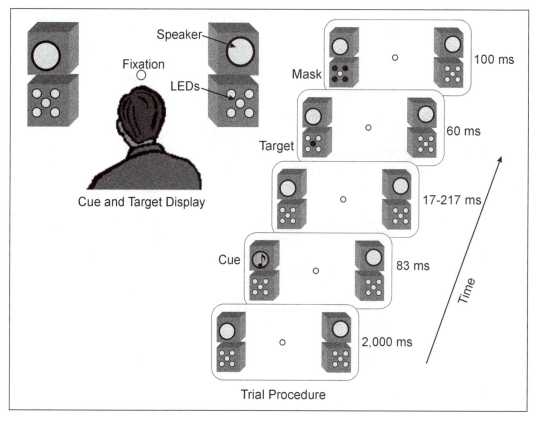

Figure 4.2   The displays and trial procedure used by McDonald, Teder-Sälejärvi, and Hillyard (2000) to show the influence of auditory cuing on visual perception. The LEDs filled a 1-degree square; the distance from the center of the loudspeaker and the lights was 2 degrees.

response to the tone in the right ear, which was presented after a short (200-ms) or long (560-ms) delay. On most trials, the to-be-ignored tone presented to the left ear was of a single, standard frequency. On some trials, however, the tone deviated from the standard. Schröger found both electrophysiological and behavioral evidence for the capture of attention by these deviant tones. Targets presented shortly after a deviant tone were responded to more slowly—and less often—than targets after the standard tones, and the N1 component of the ERP (associated with perceptual processing) to the target was smaller. Schröger also found that the deviant tone elicited the *mismatch negativity* that is associated with the detection of a change in stimulus information (see Chapter 11 for a discussion of this difference in waveform to unexpected stimuli). He concluded that the auditory system contains a change-detection system that monitors acoustic input and interrupts

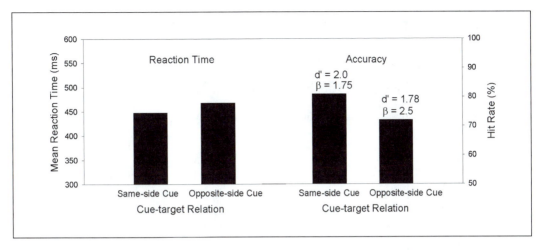

Figure 4.3   Reaction time and accuracy data from McDonald et al. (2000) for valid (same-side) and invalid (opposite-side) cues. (Data averaged by eye across left- and right-side stimuli.)

other processing when a change occurs. This interruption, or attentional capture by the deviant stimulus, in turn results in impoverished processing of closely succeeding stimuli.

ATTENTIONAL SET ▲

If listeners know in advance the frequency of a tone that must be detected, their detection performance is better than under conditions of uncertainty (Green, 1961) or when the particular frequency is unlikely rather than likely to occur (Greenberg & Larkin, 1968; see also Sorkin et al., 1973, discussed earlier). For example, people with some musical ability asked to listen to five-note melodies are better at judging the pitch of one target note when the target is at an expected frequency—in terms of the musical scale—than at an unexpected frequency (Dowling, Lung, & Herrbold, 1987). Tanner and Norman (1954) also concluded that listeners are better at detecting what they expect. These researchers showed that after performing a number of trials in which a 1,000-Hz tone had to be detected in a background of noise, listeners were then very poor at detecting a 1,300-Hz signal. As soon as they had heard a few examples of the 1,300-Hz signal, however, performance rose considerably. These findings suggest that it is possible to set an attentional filter at a relevant frequency just as it is possible to focus visual attention on a particular region of space (see Chapter 3).

Many researchers have used what is called the *probe-signal paradigm* to study auditory detection. In this paradigm, the target signal is first played loudly enough

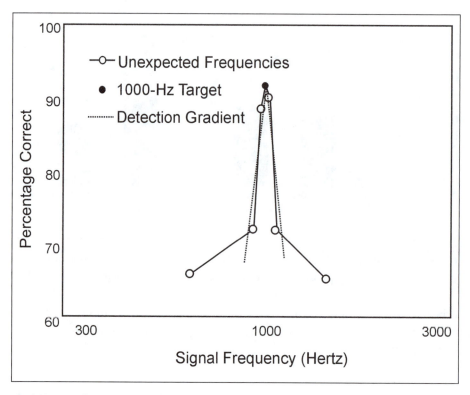

Figure 4.4   Percentage correct detection for an expected (1,000 Hz) frequency and unexpected frequencies using the probe-signal paradigm. The dotted line shows the detection gradient (see text).

SOURCE: Data from Scharf, 1998.

to be clearly audible several times to familiarize the participant with the target. Then, a two-interval forced choice task is used in which the participant listens to two short intervals of noise, one of which also contains the target (now presented at an intensity that makes it difficult to detect), and then reports whether the first or the second interval contained the target. Greenberg and Larkin (1968) found that the range of frequencies that could be detected using this paradigm was rather narrow. For example, when the target tone was 1,100 Hz, only tones between 1,000 Hz and 1,200 Hz were detected. In other words, the listener seems to set an attentional "filter" to detect the target tones. It should be noted that all of the stimuli used in these experiments were difficult to discriminate (even the target tone was detected only 65–80% of the time); if tones out of the range of the filter are presented loudly enough, they will be heard. Figure 4.4 shows typical probe-signal results for a target tone of 1,000 Hz. The dotted line in the figure shows results from other experiments, such as masking experiments, that mapped the extent to which listeners are able to detect a 1,000-Hz tone in the presence of noise (i.e., the detection gradient; see, e.g., Patterson, 1974). The high degree to which the probe-signal results conform to the detection gradient suggests that auditory attentional set has its effect at a relatively low, perceptual level.

Some researchers have argued that the tones outside the immediate range of the target are heard, but are misidentified as belonging to the noise. According to this "heard but not heeded" hypothesis, attentional set does not necessarily make us more sensitive to particular stimuli, but has its effect by reducing response uncertainty. Scharf et al. (1987) provided evidence disputing this hypothesis. They showed that people who had been explicitly told that some of the targets would be quite distant in frequency from the prototypical target did not improve in their detection of distant target probes. Moreover, skilled observers were not much better at detecting out-of-range targets than were beginners (Dai, Scharf, & Buus, 1991). It has also been shown that after people have practiced detecting one target (e.g., a 600-Hz tone) and then are switched to a different target (e.g., a 400-Hz tone), they are no better at detecting the old target than tones that differ from the new target in the other direction (e.g., a 200-Hz tone). Interestingly, and consistent with the results from auditory monitoring experiments, reported earlier, if listeners are told to expect several targets, for example, a 700-Hz tone and a 1,600-Hz tone, they are quite good at detecting both of these tones, but not tones in between the target frequencies (Dai, 1989; see Figure 4.5). This shows that people can set an attentional filter (or filters) for multiple target frequencies. This result corresponds to the finding that decrements in multiple-target detection are usually not found unless multiple targets are presented at the same time or very shortly after one another.

It seems that auditory attention can also be set for stimulus location, or, as Ward, McDonald, and Golestani (1998) put it, "that the appropriate alignment of auditory attention with the spatial location of auditory events aids processing of those events" (p. 239). Despite the strength of this statement, it seems to hold only when the stimulus environment or the task is fairly complex. It has often been found that simple detection accuracy of a target does not benefit from knowledge of where an auditory target will occur (e.g., Lowe, 1968; Scharf, 1988), although reaction time (RT) to detect a tone is sometimes faster when the observer knows in advance the direction from which to expect the tone. One reason to suspect that specifying location may not show much benefit to detection of an auditory signal is that auditory signals elicit a strong orienting response. Thus, auditory signals may be so quick to capture attention that any effects of knowing location in advance may be too small to be reliably measured. Alternatively, it may simply be the case that spatial position is not very important to auditory perception. Given

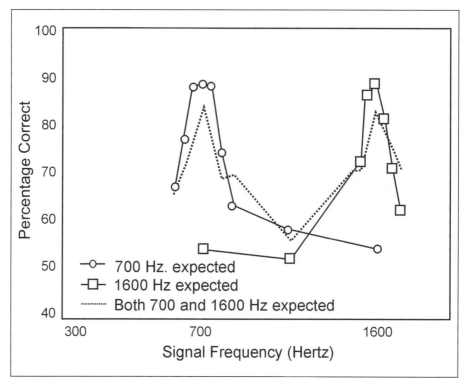

Figure 4.5   Percentage correct detection for expected (700 Hz and/or 1,600 Hz) and unexpected frequencies using the probe-signal paradigm.

SOURCE: Data from Scharf, 1998.

the fact that the auditory cortex is arranged tonotopically (such that stimuli of adjacent frequencies are processed in adjacent areas and other attributes of sounds are integrated within these frequency bands; Moss & Carr, 2003) rather than spatiotopically as is the visual cortex, the human brain may be wired to orient visual and auditory attention in distinct ways.

Some evidence that advance knowledge of location might speed detection—at least when the targets are relatively far from the ears of the observers[3]—is reported by Scharf (1998). When a warning cue presented on each trial predicted the location of a target, which was about 2 meters away from the listener, responses were faster than when it did not. When the task was to discriminate which of two targets was presented, rather than simply to detect a target, advance knowledge of location seemed to reliably speed performance. For example, people instructed to respond to a tone at one frequency (1,000 Hz) and to ignore a different frequency (800 Hz) were faster when they knew the side on which the tone would be presented (see Figure 4.6). They were also faster with location cuing

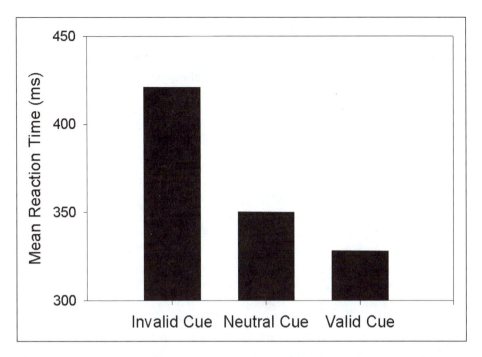

Figure 4.6   Mean reaction time to an auditory tone after a neutral (central), valid (target side), or invalid (side opposite to target) cue.

SOURCE: Data from Scharf, 1998.

when the task was to discriminate between target locations (i.e., respond to a tone located 60 degrees to the right or left and ignore a tone presented 45 degrees to the right or left). In these experiments, the location cue consisted of a short (40-ms) tone burst and a 300-ms flash of light located either to the right, in front, or to the left of the participant. A question that will be addressed in the section "Effects of Visual Information on Auditory Localization" is whether a crossmodal cue (in this case, the light) can affect performance in the target modality. However, because the experiments reported by Scharf used both an auditory and a visual cue, that question cannot be answered here.

Consistent with the hypothesis that frequency may be more important than spatial position in orienting auditory attention, D. L. Woods et al. (2001) showed that frequency is often a better cue for selection than is location. Woods et al. also found that directing attention to a relevant location does not necessarily speed detection of other stimulus properties, such as frequency or duration, or of conjunctions of these features. In short, spatial attention does not seem to play a central role in auditory processing.

Attending to Multiple Locations or Modalities

Multisensory processing is so ordinary we are often not aware that we are doing it. As you type, for example, you are normally aware only that letters appear on the screen, and you may use this visual feedback to monitor your progress. If you shift your attention to your fingers, you become aware of the pressure of the keys on your fingers and you can monitor that feedback, along with texture information (such as the shape of the keys and the ridges on the "f" and "j" keys). A third ready source of information is the sound that is created when you press on the keys. It is possible to make a silent keyboard, but research has shown that people prefer to have auditory (as well as tactile) feedback.

Some tasks require that information from different senses be integrated. In cooking, for example, the appearance of a dish might be used along with its smell and taste to determine if it is ready to serve, and in riding a bicycle, visual information (e.g., the presence of pedestrians) is combined with auditory information (e.g., sounds of approaching traffic) to decide if it is safe to cross an intersection. A number of issues concerning the use of information from different modalities can be considered. Most of the questions revolve around the degree to which information from one modality can be processed independently of information from another modality. One aspect of this question is whether one source can be selected and another ignored; another aspect is whether information can be processed more efficiently when multiple modalities, rather than just one, are used to present information.

Several studies have shown that it is sometimes possible to attend to information in two separate modalities relative to just one without any apparent costs. For example, Shiffrin and Grantham (1974) found that people were just as good (or even slightly better) at detecting three different brief signals—one visual, one auditory, and one tactile—when all three stimuli were presented at the same time as when the three signals were presented successively. There can even be an advantage for crossmodal over unimodal presentation. For example, Treisman and Davies (1973) showed that observers could more easily monitor one auditory and one visual stream for the presence of a target (e.g., an animal name) than either two visual streams or two auditory streams. This finding can be attributed to greater perceptual load within rather than across modalities, and has led some researchers to assume that there are separate pools of processing resources for the different modalities (e.g., Wickens, 1980; see Chapter 9). That is, if auditory and visual processing resources, for example, are to some extent separate pools of resources, high information loads will be dealt with more effectively when they are spread across the processing resources. On the other hand, it has been argued that when processing loads are low, more interference from to-be-ignored information might be expected from a different modality than from the same one, simply because the potential pool of processing resources is greater (see, e.g., Lavie,

1995). When excess capacity is available, irrelevant stimuli may have a greater chance of capturing attention.

Many studies have shown only limited effects of attention on early, perceptual stages of auditory processing (see Scharf, 1998, for a review), but some researchers have suggested that attention can play an important role in auditory perception. Lukas (1981) conducted one study relevant to the role of attentional set. Participants in this experiment were presented with a stream of visual stimuli (Os and Qs) as well as a stream of auditory stimuli (short and long pips). In the "look" condition, participants were required to count the Qs and could ignore all other stimuli, both visual and auditory; in the "listen" condition they were to count the long pips and ignore everything else. The stimuli were always the same; only the instruction to attend to either the visual or the auditory stimuli differed. Lukas's important finding was that the auditory targets (the long pips) were processed differently within just three milliseconds after target presentation when the task was to attend to the auditory stimuli. That is, recordings of auditory nerve activity showed enhanced activity when auditory targets were presented. When the task was to count the Qs, no difference was found in the response to target and nontarget pips. This result suggests that attentional set can influence the early processing of auditory stimuli.

Research conducted by Spence and Driver (1997b) shows that knowing which modality to expect produces measurable effects on the performance of detection and discrimination tasks. In their experiments, targets could be either auditory or visual signals. A cue (which was valid 64% of the time) was presented on each trial to inform the participant which modality, visual or auditory, to expect. The cue itself was presented in the visual modality, and consisted of the illumination of red (for visual targets), green (for auditory targets), or both red and green (either an auditory or a visual target should be expected) LEDs. Whether the task was detection, intensity or color discrimination, or spatial discrimination, responses were faster when the target was in the expected modality rather than in the unexpected modality. Figure 4.7 shows the results of Spence and Driver's experiments with detection and color (visual) or intensity (auditory) discrimination tasks. As can be seen in the figure, the cuing effect for auditory targets is largely a cost when the cue is invalid rather than a benefit when the cue is valid, whereas for the visual stimuli, a benefit for valid cues relative to a neutral cue is present. Thus, although both visual and auditory targets show modality-cuing effects, the nature of the effect is different. One possible explanation for this difference, not tested by Spence and Driver, is that the use of a visual cue may have had a direct priming effect for visual targets but not for auditory ones.

Even when one task demands auditory resources and another demands visual resources, additional restrictions on information processing may eliminate any benefits of bimodal presentation. For example, Eijkman and Vendrik (1965) found that listeners were able to divide attention between visual and auditory stimuli

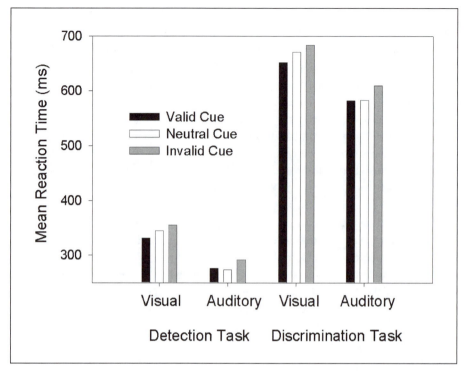

Figure 4.7   Mean reaction time as a function of the validity of a modality cue and task type for auditory and visual detection and discrimination

SOURCE: Data from Spence & Driver, 1997b.

such that they were just as good at detecting a change in the intensity of either a light or a tone when the two stimuli were monitored simultaneously as when only one of the stimuli had to be monitored.[4] When the task was to detect a change in the duration of the stimuli, marked interference was found when both modalities had to be attended to rather than just one. This suggests that temporal judgments may draw on the same processing system.

Visual Dominance

The relationship between processing in the visual and auditory modalities is asymmetric: Auditory and visual stimuli do not, in general, have an equal influence on each other. In many cases, the visual information gets the upper hand and a phenomenon called visual dominance is observed. *Visual dominance* refers to situations in which, given competing visual and other (e.g., auditory or proprioceptive) stimulation, the visual information captures, as it were, perception. A common example of visual dominance can easily be observed in a train or a car. If you are parked next to another vehicle (preferably a large one that fills the field of view outside your window), and that vehicle starts to move forward, you will feel as if your own vehicle is moving backwards. Despite information from other senses (e.g., proprioception) that you are not moving, you believe what your eyes are telling you. Another example is that visual information from a speaker's lip movements can profoundly modify the auditory perception of natural speech. For example, if a listener hears the utterance /ipi/ while watching a video of a person uttering /iki/, he or she is likely to report having heard /iti/ (McGurk & MacDonald, 1976). This effect may contribute to the difficulty some people experience in understanding dubbed speech in films.

Visual dominance has been demonstrated in the laboratory using tasks such as making a response with one hand to a tone and with the other hand to a light. On most trials, only the light or only the tone is presented. On the critical trials, both stimuli are presented. When both stimuli are presented, people will generally respond to the visual stimulus, and may not even hear the tone (Colavita, 1974). Visual information can also disrupt the processing of proprioceptive information. Jordan (1972) reported that people were slower to respond to a proprioceptive stimulus when it was accompanied by a visual stimulus. Apparently, the visual stimulus captured attention that was necessary for efficient processing of the proprioceptive information.

The location of simultaneously presented visual lights can also distort the localization of tactile stimulation. In their "rubber hands" experiments, Pavani, Spence, and Driver (2000) showed that people were slower to report whether the finger or the thumb of their own right or left hand was stimulated (by small vibrators located within a cube that was grasped by the thumb and forefinger) when a visual distractor was presented at a conflicting location (e.g., a light on the upper edge of a cube placed on a shelf presented simultaneously with vibrotactual stimulation at a lower location). In these experiments, the participants' own hands were concealed beneath a shelf, and the lights were in full view on top of the shelf. The effect was even stronger when rubber hands holding cubes such as those held by the participants were placed on the shelf (see Figure 4.8). Despite knowing that the rubber hands were not their own, they often reported feeling as if the rubber hands were their own and that the vibration seemed to occur at the location where the rubber hands were seen. These sensations—and the cuing effect—diminished when the rubber hands were placed in an orientation different than that of (orthogonal to) the participants' hands.

Visual dominance is not universal (see, e.g., Heller, 1992), and it should be noted that auditory stimuli have a stronger natural tendency to "draw attention to themselves" (Wickens & Hollands, 2000) than do visual stimuli. However,

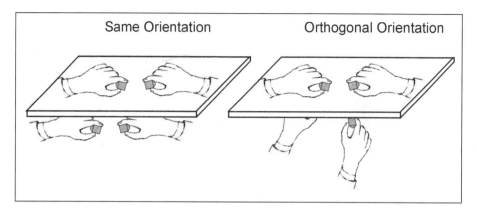

Figure 4.8   The experimental set-up used in the "rubber hands" experiments of Pavani, Spence, and Driver (2000). The subject's hands were out of sight below the shelf and the rubber hands were placed on the shelf.

when visual stimuli have equal importance and provide at least as much information as other stimuli present at the time, a bias toward the visual information is likely.

Effects of Visual Information on Auditory Localization

Anyone who has seen a ventriloquist at work has also seen (whether they knew it or not) an influence of visual information on the localization of sound. The ventriloquist cannot throw his or her voice any more than the loudspeakers used in a movie theater can project the voices of actors onto the movie screen. In both cases, however, we attribute the location of the sound to a source other than the actual one—the dummy's mouth in the case of the ventriloquist and the actors' mouths in the case of a movie. This ventriloquism effect provides support for crossmodal attentional cuing. In particular, it shows that our perception of sound can be influenced by visual information. The ventriloquism effect is strongest when the actual source of the sound is difficult to localize, and localization of sound is more difficult in the vertical than in the horizontal plane. This has implications for the placement of both the ventriloquist's dummy and speakers in the movie theater.

A technique for masking the location of an auditory stimulus was used by Spence and Driver (2000) to show that spatial attention can be cued to the illusory source of a sound. In the experiments of Spence and Driver, a visual cue (a set of lights arranged in a grid; see Figure 4.9) was combined with either an

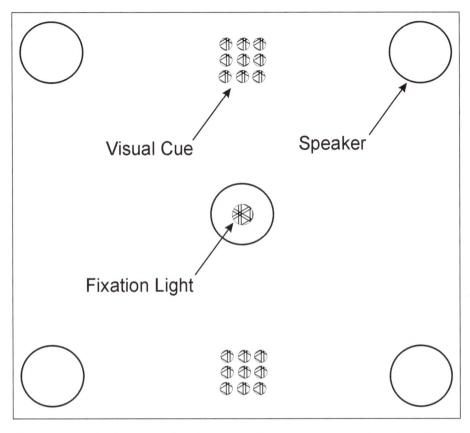

Figure 4.9   The display used by Spence and Driver (2000) to test for cuing effects of ventriloquized sounds.

easily localized sound (a burst of white noise from one loudspeaker) or a hard to localize sound (a 2,000-Hz pure tone presented simultaneously from multiple locations). After the presentation of the cue, which was located in the upper or lower visual field, a second auditory stimulus, the target (four short bursts of white noise) was presented. The target could come from any one of four loudspeakers located at the corners of the display, and the participant's task was to indicate whether it came from one of the speakers to the right or one of the speakers to the left by pressing a key located to the right or left, respectively. The most important finding was that, at short cuing intervals, responses to the target were slightly but significantly faster when the vertical position of the target (e.g., upper right or upper left) coincided with the vertical position of the visual cue (e.g., upper middle) than when it did not (e.g., upper-right or upper-left target combined with a cue at the lower-middle position)—but only when the auditory cue was hard to localize. This implies that it was not the visual cue that cued spatial attention to the source of the target, but the illusory location of the auditory cue. Spence and Driver concluded that although a visual cue normally does not attract auditory attention to its location, it does do so when the sound is hard to localize. Furthermore, because the attentional cuing effect depended on the nature of both the visual cue and auditory cues, their study implies that integration of visual and auditory information occurs prior to the directing of attention.

More evidence that the direction of visual attention can influence the perceived location of sound comes from a study of selective listening conducted by Driver (1996). Here, participants listened to difficult to distinguish target and distractor messages and attempted to follow the target message. Both the target (random words) and the distractor (also random words, and spoken in the same voice) messages were presented from the same loudspeaker. Together with the two messages, a videotape of a person speaking the words of the target message was played. When this video was presented off to the side of the auditory presentation (above a dummy loudspeaker rather than above the speaker broadcasting the stimuli), selective listening to the target message improved considerably (see Figure 4.10). Presumably, the target sounds were "relocated" by the participant due to ventriloquism. The resulting illusory spatial separation between the target and distractor messages improved selective listening just as actual spatial separation does.

Effects of Attention on Pain Perception

Most of the research on attention has focused on the visual and auditory modalities; however, some research has looked at the effects of attention within the tactile modality, and, in particular, at the role of attention in the perception of pain. Just as focusing visual attention on a particular region of space leads to enhanced perception of targets presented in that region, knowing where to expect tactile stimulation lowers the threshold of perception for that stimulation (see, e.g., V. Meyer, Gross, & Teuber, 1963). Similarly, when the stimulation is painful, knowing where to expect the painful stimulus makes one more sensitive to an increase in the aversiveness of the stimulus (Bushnell et al., 1985). In one experiment in which participants either saw a visual stimulus or were given a painful dose of heat on each trial, the thermal stimulus was rated as more intense and unpleasant when the thermal stimulation was expected than when it was not (Miron, Duncan, & Bushnell, 1989). Such findings suggest that distracting a patient about to receive a painful treatment may make the experience more bearable.

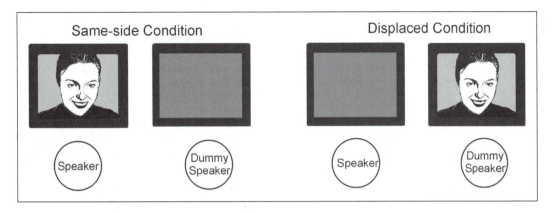

Figure 4.10   The experimental set-up used by Driver (1996).

CROSSMODAL ATTENTION ▲

If attention is to make sense as a construct, it must be possible to think of it as directing behavior in the broader environment; this obviously requires the integration of different sensory information. There are enough differences between visual and auditory processing to support the view that "auditory attention" is distinct from "visual attention." However, it has also been argued that substantial interactions exist between the mechanisms that control visual and spatial attention and that a crossmodal approach to the study of attention is likely to reveal more about attention than within-modality studies (Ward, McDonald, & Golestani, 1998). Perhaps the best way to think about crossmodal connections is with regard to the perception of space and the construction of spatial frames of reference. Because each of the senses collects information from only one set of receptors, and because these receptors move about with respect to each other and things in the world, connections between different modalities may be necessary in order to support a stable representation of the external environment (Driver & Spence, 1998).

Effects of the direction of visual attention on the ability to select auditory information have been known for some time. For example, Reisberg, Scheiber, and Potemken (1981) found that it was easier to attend to a target message broadcast from one loudspeaker and ignore a distractor message from another loudspeaker when looking at the loudspeaker that delivered the target message rather than the loudspeaker on which the distractor message was played. Although Wolters and Schiano (1989) were unable to replicate this particular result, direction of gaze does seem to have reliable effects on the ability to process auditory information, especially (and perhaps only) when the auditory information is difficult to localize (Driver, 1996).

Although most studies of crossmodal attention have focused on the direction of attention and representation of space, some studies have looked at cross-modality effects from the point of view of the processing resources required by auditory and visual information processing. For example, Puel, Bonfils, and Pujol (1988), using a task similar to that of Lukas (1981), found that otoacoustic emissions (weak sounds produced by the cochlea in response to external sounds) were smaller when participants performed a visual task (counting the Qs in a stream of Os and infrequent Qs) than when they were just relaxing. Apparently, performing visual tasks can have a direct (although small) effect on auditory processing. Another way in which visual and auditory information processing can interact is as *crossmodal facilitation*. Crossmodal facilitation can be studied by comparing the neural responses to each of two unimodal stimuli (e.g., one visual and one auditory) presented alone with the response to the bimodal presentation of both stimuli together. If the bimodal response is greater than the combined response to the two unimodal stimuli, facilitatory intermodal integration can be said to have taken place. Teder-Sälejärvi, McDonald, Di Russo, and Hillyard (2002; see also Stein & Meredith, 1993) subtracted the ERPs for unimodal visual (a flash of light) and auditory (a burst of noise) targets from the ERP to an audiovisual combination of the two targets and found an interaction effect beginning around 40 ms after stimulus presentation, at the earliest stages of perceptual processing.

Crossmodal Attention Cuing

The major question addressed in crossmodal cuing studies (i.e., presenting a cue in one modality to draw attention to some aspect of a stimulus in another modality) is whether the direction of attention to stimuli in one modality is affected by stimulation in another modality. This question is a bit tricky, because there are also nonattentional factors that may be responsible for crossmodal effects. For example, if it is found that responses to the location of a tone are faster when it occurs on the same side as a recent visual event, one could conclude that auditory attention was directed to the location of the visual stimulus, but it could also be the case that the visual stimulus primed the response associated with the tone. For example, a sound on the left might automatically be coded as "left," and if a left key-press response is then to be made to a visual stimulus presented on the left, the response will benefit from this activation of the spatial code (see Chapter 5).

To avoid such problems, Spence and Driver (1994, 1996, 1997a; see Driver & Spence, 1998, for a review) developed what they called an orthogonal cuing paradigm (see Figure 4.11). In the exogenous cuing version of this paradigm, an uninformative, abrupt onset cue is presented either to the right or to the left. The target stimulus may also occur on the right or left, but at more than one elevation. The

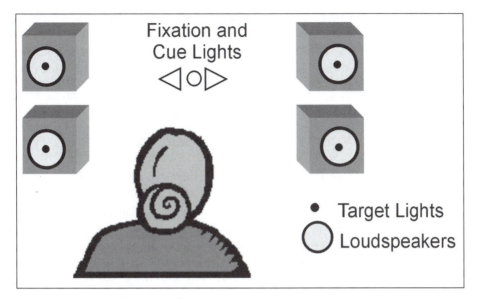

Figure 4.11 Orthogonal cuing with endogenous cues. Attention is cued to the left or to the right by one of the central arrows. Stimuli can then be presented at any of the four locations in either modality.

participant's task is to judge whether the target was presented in a high or low position, ignoring whether the target was on the right or left. Crossmodal cuing is said to have occurred when responses to the target (i.e., judgments of the elevation of the target) are faster on the cued than on the uncued side. This procedure minimizes the chance that response priming or expectancy effects are the basis for any evidence of crossmodal cuing. The same paradigm can be used to study the effects of endogenous cues—cues that are symbolic in nature (such as a centrally presented arrow) and can be used to direct attention to the probable location of an upcoming event.

As previously mentioned, even uninformative auditory cues can facilitate responses to a visual stimulus presented on the same side as the auditory stimulus (Spence & Driver, 1996; but see Ward, McDonald, & Lin, 2000). Somewhat more debatable is whether visual processing has an effect on the orienting of auditory attention. Spence and Driver, for example, found that visual cues had no effect on auditory discrimination. In direct contrast to Spence and Driver, Ward (1994) found that spatially uninformative visual cues orient auditory attention in a discrimination task, but that spatially uninformative auditory cues do not orient visual attention. The reason for the divergent results of Ward (1994) and Spence and Driver (1996) may lie in the types of targets and cues used (see Ward, McDonald, & Lin, 2000). In the experiments of Ward and colleagues, the cuing environment was rather complex (consisting of cues in different modalities, in different locations, and in different combinations) and the target was simple (light or tone to the right or the left), whereas in Spence and Driver's experiments, the cuing environment was simpler and the targets were more complex. Despite occasional conflicting results, it is clear that crossmodal cuing effects occur.

A Single Supra-Modal Spatial Attention Controller?

Spatial location has a large effect on performance in many situations. Spatial separation in sounds can make it easier to attend to one source and ignore another. It has also been suggested that the proximity of visual and auditory displays can affect performance. Driver and Spence (1994) found that participants were better at monitoring both a visual and an auditory display when both displays (a speaker and a computer monitor) were located on the same side of the participant, as compared to when one display was located to the left of the participant and the other to the right. Although the effects of display location were quite small, such effects suggest that some aspect of spatial attention may be supra-modal.

A similar conclusion can be reached on the basis of ERP experiments. Eimer and Schröger (1998) found that the direction of spatial attention had an effect on auditory ERPs when hearing was relevant, but there were no effects of cued attention on auditory ERPs when vision was relevant (see Box 4.1). Tactile attention, on the other hand, can influence auditory (as well as visual) processing. Eimer, Cockburn, Smedley, and Driver (2001) conducted two experiments in which participants had to focus their attention on either their right or left hand to detect infrequent tactile targets. In their first experiment, visual stimuli were also presented on some trials. ERPs were measured, and it was found that a visual target on the tactually attended side elicited enhanced N1 and P2 components at the occipital sites. Similarly, auditory stimuli presented in the second experiment were responded to differently (the N1 component was enhanced) when the sounds were on the side where the participant expected a tactile target. This suggests that crossmodal links exist both between touch and vision and between touch and hearing. Eimer et al. also looked at auditory and visual ERPs when the hands were crossed. In this case, it was the stimuli in the same physical side of space (and not the same side of the body) that showed enhanced responses. This result shows that it is the common external location of the stimuli that determines crossmodal attentional links, and not hemispheric projections within the brain.

Based on results like these, Driver and Spence (1998) concluded, "Attention operates on spatial representations that are subject to crossmodal influence, [and] not merely within the receptor space of the relevant modality" (p. 260). Ward (1994) has interpreted crossmodal cuing effects as evidence for a supra-modal representation of space. In this view, the mechanisms underlying visual and auditory shifts of attention are not completely independent, but share information at some level of processing. This conclusion is consistent with evidence of visual dominance, such as the ventriloquism effect discussed earlier, the finding that the presentation of a visual stimulus (or the direction of gaze) can affect the localization of auditory signals (e.g., Bertelson & Aschersleben, 1998), and an absence of auditory dominance effects.

Can the fact that crossmodal effects on attention have been found between the visual, auditory, and haptic modalities, and for both exogenous and endogenous cues, be interpreted as evidence for supra-modal attentional control? The fact that the deployment of attention in one modality can modulate attentional effects in another modality does not necessarily imply that attention is directed in a supra-modal manner. Crosstalk between information processes seems to be possible at just about any level of information processing. Although this may argue against a strict modularity of processing systems, it does not prove the existence of a master controller.

SUMMARY ▲

Together, the two ears function as an early warning system and facilitate omnidirectional orienting. Separately, the two ears offer the advantage of two distinct channels for studying information processing. Much early research on attention took advantage of the availability of two separate processing channels for hearing to study a range of issues, including the locus of attentional selection and the fate of unattended information. This research showed that despite the fact that people can select information on the basis of simple features, such as stimulus location or auditory pitch, the semantic content of nonselected information is also processed.

Whereas visual stimuli can be detected and identified only in the region to which the person is attending, auditory stimuli originating from any direction relative to the person can be perceived with approximately equal ease. Once alerted to the presence of something by its sound, a person generally will want to look in the direction of the sound for further investigation. Thus, auditory attention may play a role in visual selection. Because the functions of auditory and visual attention are clearly linked, much research has focused on interactions in processing between the two modalities. One important finding is that capacity limits in recognition are more pronounced when multiple stimuli must be processed within one modality rather than across different modalities. This suggests that there may be separate attentional resources for visual and auditory information. On the other hand, crossmodal cuing effects suggest that modality specificity may be graded or that there may be a supra-modal attentional controller. As will be discussed in later chapters, even if stimuli from different modalities may be attended to independently up to a point, attentional limits involved in the selection of responses are indifferent to whether multiple stimuli originate in the same or different modalities.

Box 4.1   Using ERPs to Measure Crossmodal Attention

In a typical crossmodal ERP study, sounds and lights are presented to the left and right of the participant, who maintains fixation centrally (at the "+" in Panel A of Box Figure 4.1). Two streams of successive sounds, one coming from the left and one from the right, are accompanied by two visual streams, also to the left and right. Stimuli in the four streams are desynchronized by pseudorandom amounts so that a target occurs in only one stream at a time, enabling ERPs to be time-locked to single events in each of the streams. Participants are instructed to attend to either visual or auditory targets on just one

side. The task is to detect occasional *deviant* events (e.g., longer than normal stimuli) in the relevant modality on the relevant side, ignoring any events in the other three stimulus streams. The ERP waveforms are averaged for each electrode on the scalp, starting from the moment of deviant stimulus presentation (i.e., time-locked to the stimulus). Because ERPs are computed for all target stimuli in all four streams, the effects of attention can be assessed by comparing the ERPs for stimuli on the attended and unattended sides, and in the currently relevant and irrelevant modalities.

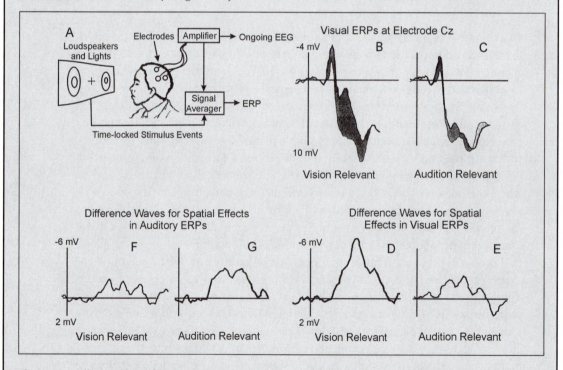

Figure 1   Effects of attending to targets of a specific modality at a specific location on the ERP for auditory and visual stimuli.

Source: Data from Eimer & Schröger, 1998.

| Box 4.1 | (Continued) |

The data shown in Box Figure 4.1 are for one electrode (Cz, a central midline site at the vertex of the head) in a study by Eimer and Schröger (1998, Experiment 2). Effects of the direction of endogenous spatial attention (as shown by the gray shading of the difference between responses to stimuli on the attended and unattended sides) were found for the currently relevant modality (see Panel B). Small effects of covert spatial attention were also present for visual events when the task was to monitor sounds (see Panel C). Panels D and E show the *difference waves* derived from subtracting the waveform for the attended side from the waveform for the unattended side. (Panel D plots the difference between the two waves in Panel B; Panel E plots the difference between the two waves in Panel C.) The resulting difference waves can be interpreted as the amplitude modulation due to spatial attention. For ERPs to auditory events, the results corresponded to those found for visual stimuli. In this case, analogously derived difference waves (for ERPs to auditory stimuli) showed larger amplitude modulation of auditory ERPs by spatial attention when hearing was relevant (Panel G) than when vision was relevant (Panel F).

NOTES ▲

1. Treisman (1964b) showed that when the attended message led (i.e., was started first), repetition was noticed for lags of up to 4.5 seconds. However, when the unattended message led, the greatest lag at which repetition was noticed was only 1.5 seconds. The difference in lag times suggests that the unattended message enters only auditory sensory memory, whereas a more durable short-term memory holds the attended message.

2. Performance improved considerably when speech-like sounds, rather than speech, were presented. This indicates both that the limitations with three channels are not solely due to auditory masking and that the statistical or semantic properties of the messages are critical.

3. When sounds are presented from earphones or at locations close to the listener, cuing effects are typically much smaller.

4. In this study, the increment in intensity lasted 1 second, which was enough time to switch attention from one sensory channel to another. Nonetheless, representations of both stimuli would have to have been kept current in memory in order for the comparison to be made.

CHAPTER 5

ATTENTION AND INHIBITION

In most cases, attention is used to select information. When we "pay attention" to what we are doing, we actively attempt to attend to task-relevant information and to monitor our actions to be sure that appropriate responses are made. Equally important for successful task performance, however, is the shutting out of irrelevant information and the exclusion of inappropriate actions. In this chapter, we discuss the range of processes involved in suppressing irrelevant information and inhibiting inappropriate actions.

Like attention, inhibition is not a unitary construct. In some cases, inhibition operates at a subconscious level as an automatic countereffect of acts of selection. An example of this is *inhibition of return* to exogenously cued locations, which is seen when a target appearing in the location where a cue stimulus has been shown is actually detected less readily than one at an uncued location when the interval between cue and target is more than a few hundred milliseconds. The requirement to select one item while ignoring others may trigger active processes of inhibition that can last for some time, as in the *negative-priming* paradigm, in which targets that have served as distractors on previous trials are more slowly responded to than are items that were not previously ignored. Other types of inhibition are presumably under conscious control, such as when a prepared response must be inhibited in response to a "stop" signal or when conflicting stimulus information must be ignored in order to respond appropriately.

According to Rafal and Henik (1994):

> The brain goes about the business of coordinating reflexive responses with goal-directed behavior through inhibitory mechanisms. . . . these inhibitory processes serve to provide a coherent experience of the world, as well as flexibility and efficiency in skilled performance. (p. 43)

Because inhibitory processes form a vital part of skilled performance, understanding inhibitory processes is central to issues of control and automaticity, as well as to basic questions of information processing.

▲ TYPES OF INHIBITION

In behavioral research, the term *inhibition* may be used whenever decreases in some activity (such as pressing response keys) are seen as a result of manipulating some aspect of the task environment. Although it may suffice to say that inhibition occurs, a deeper understanding of the nature of task performance can sometimes be gained by describing the processes by which inhibitory effects arise.

Inhibition That Counters Activation

At a neurological level, inhibition can be viewed as negative activation. In this sense, it works by lowering the activation level of neurons (or, in neural network models, "units"). This so-called *neurological inhibition* occurs as a result of the interconnectivity of the network and does not require (although it may be influenced by) conscious effort. Neurological inhibition has been called a sculpturing process, in which "the inhibition, as it were, chisels away at the diffuse and rather amorphous mass of excitatory action and gives a more specific form to the neuronal performance at every stage of synaptic relay" (Eccles, 1977, p. 92). An example of inhibition by cortical control is the development of reflex suppression. Damage to cortical areas is often accompanied by a return of reflexes that have not been seen since infancy. For example, the sucking and rooting responses of the nursing infant can reappear in elderly Alzheimer's patients. The development of inhibition of reflexes—and the disinhibition of reflexes following damage to cortical control systems—provides support for the idea that attentional control may be exercised by neuronal systems separate from the systems that are responsible for the involved actions (Rafal & Henik, 1994).

HHHHHAHHHHH

A

Figure 5.1   Lateral masking by flanking stimuli. (See text for instructions.)

Another example of the workings of inhibition can be easily demonstrated. In Chapter 3, we discussed visual search and the factors that affect how easily a target can be found among distractors. Sometimes, however, the presence of distractors affects performance even when the location of the target is known. One way that distractors can affect target detection is through lateral masking, which refers to the fact that items located to either side of a target can affect whether the target can be seen. The effect of lateral masking becomes more evident as the target is moved into the periphery of the visual field (N. H. Mackworth, 1965). For example, look at the string of letters in the top part of Figure 5.1. You should have no trouble seeing the letter "A." Now move the book to the left, but keep your eyes fixated straight ahead. At a certain point, you will no longer be able to see the "A," even though you may be able to see the letters to both sides of it. To illustrate that your inability to see the "A" is not just a lack of acuity, try to see the "A" that stands by itself at the bottom of the figure. You will probably be able to see the lone letter at a greater eccentricity than the letter flanked by distractors. The exact causes of lateral masking are not known, but it seems to occur in part as a result of lateral inhibition between sensory neurons. There is considerable evidence that both feature and position information are disrupted under lateral masking (see, e.g., Butler & Currie, 1986). The effects are robust and have even led to the development of a "conspicuity meter" for the measurement of the conspicuousness of colors, shapes, and objects (Toet, Kooi, Bijl, & Valeton, 1998; Wertheim, 2002). This meter has been used by the military to determine both easy and hard to mask colors and patterns; for example, camouflage clothing is good to the extent that it blends in with the surroundings, whereas a life raft should "pop out" against the range of colors seen on the open ocean.

Reactive Inhibition

Inhibition that arises as a result of performing some process can be described as *reactive inhibition*. Some examples of reactive inhibition that are discussed in this chapter include inhibition of return and negative priming. Reactive inhibition has been described as a side effect of executing a process that must subsequently be overcome. The process that produces the inhibition may itself be engaged deliberately, such as when observers intend to select one target for further processing, but the inhibitory effect of this active selection on other concurrent or subsequent processes is not usually intended (Logan, 1994).

Both neurological and reactive inhibition depend to some extent on excitatory processes. In the case of neurological inhibition, activation and inhibition both build up in the interconnected network of neuronal units and spread automatically. The activation of any one unit can be determined by summing up the positive and negative (i.e., inhibitory) activation of neighboring units. Reactive inhibition builds up across one processing episode and can be observed as a slowing effect on activation processes in a subsequent processing episode.

Behavioral Inhibition

It is not always possible (or necessary) to describe the way in which inhibition arises or exercises its effects. Throughout much of this chapter, the term "inhibition" is used in a descriptive way. In this sense, increases in reaction time or decreases in performance may be referred to as inhibition without specifying how that inhibition occurs.

▲ INHIBITION OF IRRELEVANT INFORMATION

Research on selective attention often uses paradigms in which irrelevant information must be ignored and relevant information selected. In this section, we discuss the major paradigms that explore specifically the ability to inhibit the processing of irrelevant information.

The Stroop Effect

As anyone who has read an introductory psychology book knows, the *Stroop effect* is one of the most robust demonstrations of our inability to completely filter out irrelevant information. If you can read well enough to be reading this, your word recognition skills are developed to the point where you cannot suppress reading at will. The classic Stroop effect (Stroop, 1935/1992) refers to the interference of words on naming colors: When the task is to name the color of ink that a word is printed in, and to ignore the meaning of the word, performance will be much more labored and cumbersome when the ink happens to form the name of a color other than that of the ink (i.e., when the color word and ink color are incongruent) relative to a color-neutral word or patch of color (neutral trial), or the name of the ink color (i.e., when the word and color are congruent). For example, naming the color "pink" is much more difficult when pink is the color of the word "purple" than when it is the color of a row of X's or a non–color-related word. The Stroop effect can be measured by computing the difference in response time and accuracy on congruent versus incongruent trials or as the difference between incongruent and neutral trials. Some researchers have found a benefit for performance when word and word color are congruent rather than neutral; however, this effect is not always found. A Stroop effect can also be found for spatial stimuli; for example, if people are asked to report where the word "right" or "left" was presented, they will be much slower to respond "right" when the word "left" is presented on the right side of a display than when the word happened to spell "right" (see C.-H. Lu & Proctor, 1995, for a review).

An important property of Stroop interference is that it is asymmetric (Virzi & Egeth, 1985). For example, incongruent color words slow color naming, but incongruent ink colors do not tend to slow color-word reading. Similarly, naming the locations of stimuli is slowed when the stimuli are incongruent location words, but the reading of location words is not slowed significantly by incongruent physical locations. However, this asymmetry in processing spatial word stimuli or their locations is reversed when the responses are manual keypresses: Manual responses to location words are interfered with by incongruent physical locations, whereas responses to the locations are not interfered with by incongruent location words (see Figure 5.2). Findings such as these are generally consistent with the conclusion that when the irrelevant stimulus dimension is processed within the same system as responses, or relies on a similar manner of coding, interference can occur.

Although Stroop effects are generally interpreted as reflecting the result of automatic processes of word reading on another task, such as color naming, some authors have argued that the effect does not imply a pure form of automatic processing in which words can never be ignored. For example, if only one letter of a word is colored, color-naming responses are less influenced by the presence of incongruent color words than if the whole word is colored (Besner, Stolz, & Boutilier, 1997). It seems that the requirement to focus attention on just one letter of a word unshackles the "automatic" reading of the entire word. As will be discussed in the section "A Response-Selection Basis for Spatial Compatibility Effects," Stroop effects can also be affected by changing the proportion of congruent and incongruent stimuli, and by other factors that affect the strategic processing of word information.

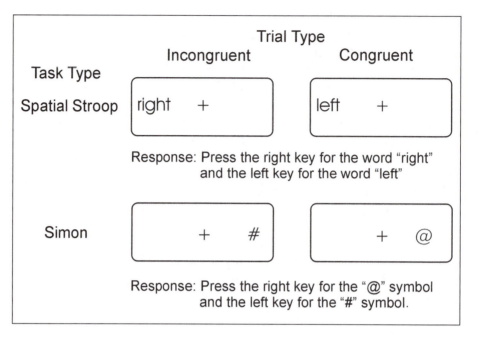

Figure 5.2   The spatial Stroop and Simon tasks.

The Simon Effect

In the spatial Stroop task, performance is impaired when the stimulus location is incongruent with the location information inherent in the stimuli. However, it is not necessary that stimuli convey spatial information in order for effects of stimulus position to occur. In a typical Simon task (see C.-H. Lu & Proctor, 1995; Simon, 1990), nonspatial stimuli, such as tones of high and low pitch or visual stimuli of different colors or shapes, are presented on either the right or left side of a display and are responded to by pressing either a left or a right key (see Figure 5.2).[1] The subject is instructed to respond to the identity of the stimuli and to ignore their locations. The *Simon effect* refers to the finding that responses are faster when the stimulus appears on the same side as the assigned response than when it does not. Like the Stroop effect, the Simon effect seems to be due to the inability to exclude irrelevant information. The Simon effect thus illustrates that it is not necessary that the relevant and irrelevant dimensions of the stimuli be related (as are colors and their names) in order for interference effects to occur.

The Simon effect is primarily due to interference effects that occur when stimulus and response locations do not correspond, rather than to facilitation when they do. This implies that the effect is the result of conflict between the action indicated by the relevant stimulus information and the irrelevant stimulus location information. Simon and Small (1969) first explained the effect as the result of a natural tendency to respond to the direction of stimulation. Subsequent experiments show that a Simon effect occurs even when both stimulus locations are on the same side of fixation (e.g., one location is simply more to the right than the other one), indicating that such a response tendency cannot adequately explain the effect (see, e.g., Umiltà & Nicoletti, 1985; see also Eimer, Cockburn, Smedley, & Driver, 2001). Another idea is that the location of the stimulus automatically results in the formation of a spatial code. Because this spatial code is related to the response, which is coded in terms of its spatial position, response competition can occur on trials in which the spatial code for stimulus position is different than the spatial code for the response to the relevant stimulus dimension. Although theories differ regarding how this code is formed (e.g., as a result of attention shifting, Nicoletti & Umiltà, 1989; or as a result of coding of relative position, Hommel, 1993b), most researchers agree that the Simon effect is the result of conflicting spatial codes.

According to Hommel (1993a), the spatial code associated with stimulus position forms rapidly when the stimulus is presented and then decays automatically, without the application of voluntary inhibitory strategies. Thus, if something is done to delay the response (such as increasing the difficulty of stimulus discrimination), the Simon effect should be—and generally is—reduced in size (see, for further discussion of automatic activation in the Simon effect, Roswarski & Proctor, 2003; Wascher, Schatz, Kuder, & Verleger, 2001). However, it seems likely that a voluntary inhibitory strategy is also needed to fully explain the Simon effect. To see why this is necessary, consider the Simon effect that occurs when responses are identified in the same way as the stimuli; for example, when a red key located on the right is pressed in response to a red stimulus and a green key located on the left is pressed in response to a green stimulus. If the mapping of stimulus color to response color is reversed, such that red stimuli are responded to with the green key and vice versa, so is the Simon effect. That is, with a reversed mapping, responses are actually faster when the stimulus appears on the side opposite to the response key. This can be explained by a logical recoding account in which performers keep in mind that the logical relation between stimuli and responses must be reversed. Thus, "red" comes to mean "green" and, as the logical recoding is also applied to the irrelevant dimension, "right" comes to mean "left" (see Hedge & Marsh, 1975). The fact that the Simon effect is greatest when responses are relatively fast suggests that it may depend primarily on a briefly active spatial code. However, the reverse Simon effect is also evident when responses are relatively slow, suggesting that an additional process—such as logical recoding—is responsible for the effect (De Jong, Liang, & Lauber, 1994).

A Response-Selection Basis for Spatial Compatibility Effects

Color and spatial Stroop effects, as well as the Simon effect, have been attributed to the stage of processing commonly called response selection (see Chapter 2). In general, both the relevant and irrelevant stimulus dimensions are assumed to be processed in parallel, and both result in the activation of a response code. When the response code for the irrelevant dimension is different than that for the relevant dimension, the irrelevant response code must be suppressed (or must decay in strength) before the correct response can be selected. In order for irrelevant information to interfere with selecting a response, it must be processed before the processing of the relevant stimulus information is complete. Based on this fundamental idea, many different "race" models of the Stroop and similar effects have been proposed (see C.-H. Lu & Proctor, 1995, for a review). Race models have in common that they presume that the relevant and irrelevant stimulus dimensions are processed in parallel and then queue up for entry into a sort of single-channel central processor (see Chapter 6 for a detailed discussion of central-bottleneck models). Whichever stimulus dimension is finished processing first gains entry into the channel, where it then conveys information to a response buffer. Interference arises when the irrelevant information enters the response buffer before the relevant information.

Although the idea of information racing to activate responses is attractively simple, several important findings suggest that race models of spatial compatibility effects are fundamentally wrong. One problem is that, contrary to the predictions of a race model, the effects of irrelevant information depend on the relation between the stimulus dimensions and the type of response. For example, Virzi and Egeth (1985) had people respond to the words "LEFT" and "RIGHT," presented on either the left or right, by either saying "left" or "right" or by pressing a left or right response key. Spatial Stroop effects were found for vocal responses to word position and for manual responses to word meaning, but not for manual responses to position and verbal responses to meaning. Both manually responding to positions and verbally responding to words (i.e., reading aloud) are high in what Greenwald (1972) called *ideomotor compatibility*. That is, in both cases the stimuli closely resemble their assigned responses.[2] According to ideomotor compatibility theory, response selection occurs directly, without cognitive mediation, when ideomotor compatibility is high, bypassing the usual bottlenecks. Effects of ideomotor compatibility are problematic for race models because if a given dimension "wins the race" in one case, it would also be expected to win the race in other cases. Clearly, other aspects of correspondence between stimuli and responses play a role in performance.

Another line of evidence against race models is provided by the effects of pre-exposure of the irrelevant information. Several experimenters have given the irrelevant information a "head start" by displaying the irrelevant dimension before the relevant one (e.g., Virzi & Egeth, 1985). Contrary to predictions of the race model, pre-exposure often reduces Stroop effects (see Lu & Proctor, 1995). In the case of spatial Stroop effects, this may be because irrelevant spatial codes (see, e.g., Hommel, 1993b) decay rapidly, or, more generally, it may be that the early presentation makes the irrelevant information more distinctive and easier to isolate from the relevant information.

The usual account of the classic Stroop effect rests on the assumption that it is an involuntary consequence of the inability to effectively inhibit the processing of the meaning of the word, or, in other terms, of the inability to decouple the meaning of the word from control of action (Allport, 1987; Neumann, 1987). However, several demonstrations have shown that failure to inhibit word reading is not the only factor in the Stroop effect. For example, changing the proportion of congruent and incongruent trials can affect the magnitude of the Stroop effect (compatible stimuli are processed faster when conflicting trials are rare, but conflicting stimuli are processed faster when they are frequent; Logan & Zbrodoff, 1979), as can varying the proportion of neutral words (Stroop interference decreases as the percentage of color words increases; Tzelgov, Henik, & Berger, 1992). The advantage for conflicting stimuli when they are relatively frequent can be taken as evidence for a strategy involving dividing attention between reported and unreported dimensions (Logan & Zbrodoff, 1979). Furthermore, simply speeding up the pace of the trials can essentially eliminate the Stroop effect. De Jong, Berendsen, and Cools (1999) found that a spatial Stroop effect (in which the words "high" and "low" were presented either above or below a fixation mark) was eliminated by reducing the inter-trial interval (the time between the response on one trial and the presentation of the stimulus on the next trial) from 2,000 to 200 ms. They argued that the fast pace enabled performers to remain focused on the task of naming the location of the words, thus inhibiting any tendency to read the words. When the pace is slow, attention falters and the meaning of the words is able to get past, as it were, the intended attentional set.

Lu and Proctor (1995) summarize the literature on the Stroop and Simon effects as follows. First, the dependence of the effects on the manner in which the responses are made suggests that there are pre-existing associations of stimulus attributes to various response characteristics, and that these associations differ in strength. Although some stimuli seem to activate responses automatically, automaticity seems to be a matter of degree, rather than an all-or-none characteristic. Second, the effects depend on spatial coding, even though there is still some debate about how these spatial codes are formed. Third, the relative timing of the buildup of relevant and irrelevant information can influence the effects, though not always in the way a race model would predict. It seems likely that automatically created spatial codes dissipate with time, whereas intentional processing (such as logical recoding) has longer lasting effects. Finally, effects of the relative frequency of

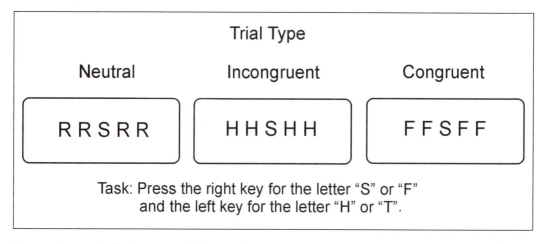

Figure 5.3   The flanker-compatibility paradigm. The task is to respond to the central letter, ignoring the flanking letters.

congruent and incongruent trials (as well as the effects of timing discussed earlier) suggest that the application of an attentional strategy can modulate the effects.

Flanker-Compatibility Effects

Another example of an interference effect caused by the inability to fully inhibit irrelevant information is the *flanker-compatibility effect*. In the flanker-compatibility paradigm, first popularized by B. A. Eriksen and C. W. Eriksen (1974), a target letter is presented in the center of a display, flanked by two or more distractor letters. Usually, there are two or more different targets, and the targets are assigned to different responses. For example, the letter "S" might require that a lever be moved to the left, and the letter "H" might require the lever to be moved to the right. The flanker compatibility (or "response compatibility") effect is that responses are relatively slow and inaccurate when the target is flanked by incongruent letters (i.e., letters assigned to a different response), intermediate when the flankers are neutral letters (i.e., letters that are never used as the target), and fastest when the flanker letters require the same response as the target (i.e., when they are congruent; see Figure 5.3).

Numerous studies have shown that the response associated with incongruent flankers is activated along with the correct, target response. That is, not only are the flanker letters perceptually processed (even though instructions are to focus on only the central, target letter), but also information is often processed to the point of producing a lateralized readiness potential, which is indicative of motor preparation (see, e.g., Gratton, Coles, Sirevaag, & Eriksen, 1988; Heil et al., 2000).

The presence of such preactivation of responses seems to be the critical factor in accounting for the costs and benefits associated with flankers; however, this does not imply that only response production processes are subject to flanker effects. The flankers may also produce interference at the response-selection stage of information processing (Botella, 1996).

The fact that flankers assigned to an incompatible response produce more interference than flankers not assigned to any response suggests that the interference arises because of conflicting response information. Incongruent letters activate response-selection or response processes, and this irrelevant activation must be suppressed or overcome in order to fully activate the correct response. The flanker-compatibility effect is a classic example of the failure of early selection in that, despite the negative effects of processing flankers on performance, people are not able to filter out flanker information. In fact, Miller (1987) showed that the semantic information contained in the flankers could be used to learn predictive relationships between the identity of the flankers and the correct response on a given trial. In Miller's experiments, people made faster target identification responses when targets were consistent with a probabilistic relation to the flankers (i.e., when the flankers could be used to predict target identity based on an imperfect, but positive, correlation), even though they had been instructed to ignore the flankers and were unable to report having noticed any correlation between flankers and targets. This so-called *flanker validity effect* is found even when stimuli are consistently mapped to target and flanker sets such that the flankers never belong to a response category (i.e., when certain letters are used only as targets and other letters are used only as distractors).

The finding that, under many circumstances, flankers are not or cannot be ignored has led to a search for conditions that might facilitate early selection and thus reduce the flanker-compatibility effect. The only factor that has a strong, consistent effect on selection of the target and suppression of the flankers is spatial separation: Increasing the distance between flankers and targets beyond 1 degree of visual angle (about the width of your thumbnail at arm's length) decreases the compatibility effect (see, e.g., B. A. Eriksen &. C. W. Eriksen, 1974). However, reductions in the flanker effect are sometimes found when the physical similarity between flankers and targets is reduced by, for example, changing the color of the distractors (Kramer & Jacobson, 1991). It can be concluded that spatial separation is especially effective in facilitating visual selective attention, although other factors that increase the distinctiveness of the target may also reduce the flanker-compatibility effect.

At least one researcher has suggested that making the task easier actually makes selection more difficult. According to the perceptual load hypothesis (N. Lavie, 1995; see Chapter 3), the degree to which flankers will interfere with performance depends on the perceptual processing load imposed by the task. When the processing load is low (e.g., when there are only a few items in the display), such that the relevant stimuli do not demand all of the available processing capacity, irrelevant

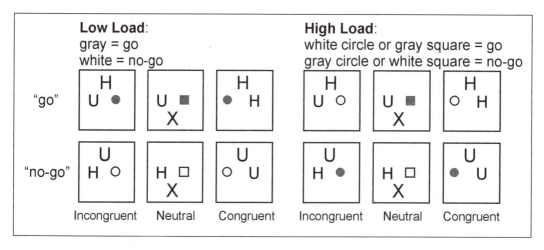

Figure 5.4   A schematic depiction of the displays used by N. Lavie (1995). The task was to respond to the letter in the middle row (ignoring the letter above or below the middle row) when a "go" signal was present.

stimuli will, according to Lavie, "unintentionally capture spare capacity, consequently enabling their processing" (p. 452). In one of her experiments, Lavie used a go or no-go task to show that, consistent with this hypothesis, increasing attentional demands can reduce interference from an irrelevant distractor. She did this by cuing the "go" response (i.e., respond to target identity, ignoring any distractors) in either a nondemanding (i.e., make a response if there is a blue shape next to the target but not if the shape next to the target is red; see Figure 5.4) or a demanding way (e.g., "go" if the shape is a blue square or a red circle, but withhold the response if the shape is a blue circle or a red square). When the more demanding cuing condition was used, smaller flanker interference effects were found. Although some results provide support for the perceptual load hypothesis, evidence against the hypothesis has been found, as well. For example, Paquet and Craig (1997) showed that attentional capture by irrelevant distractors does not always occur automatically in the flanker task even when the perceptual load is low.

In summary, flanker effects reflect difficulty in suppressing irrelevant information. The robustness of flanker effects has led to their use as a diagnostic tool in assessing difficulties in suppressing irrelevant information (C. W. Eriksen, 1995). The flanker task has also been used to study the nature of visual neglect, a syndrome in which information from one side of the visual field is ignored (see Chapter 12). People who suffer from visual neglect sometimes appear to be completely blind to items in the neglected hemisphere; for example, they may neglect to eat all the food on the right side of their plate. However, A. Cohen, Ivry, Rafal, and Kohn (1995) have shown that flankers presented in the neglected side of space cause just as much interference as flankers in the intact visual field. Because flanker effects stem from response competition, this shows that "neglected" information not only is perceived, but also is processed to the level of response activation even when observers are not aware of having seen the flankers.

INHIBITION OF RETURN ▲

In order to comprehend visual scenes, we have to move our attention from object to object, or from one region of space to another. Focusing attention at a particular point leads to quicker detection of changes in the information presented at that point and, more generally, to quicker processing of information at the attended location. Posner, Snyder, and Davidson (1980) demonstrated this by showing that when attention is cued to move to a location, identification of a target at that location is accomplished more quickly than otherwise—even when the eyes are still focused elsewhere.

As discussed in Chapter 3, attention can be cued to move to a location in two different ways. Exogenous cues (also called "peripheral" or "location" cues) are cues that attract attention to themselves. For example, a flicker or a flash at a particular location will draw attention to that location in what has been described as "reflexive orienting." Endogenous cues are cues that have to be processed by the observer in order to have an effect. Both endogenous and exogenous cues are effective in directing attention, but they seem to operate in quite different ways. One of the major differences between the two types of cues is the time course of the facilitation produced by the cue. When the task is simply to detect a target, both types of cues show a gradual buildup of effectiveness over time, with the maximum benefit usually being reached by about 300 ms. When the task is to discriminate between different targets, exogenous cues often have a larger and faster acting effect on performance (see Figure 5.5). More strikingly, the facilitation produced by an exogenous cue can turn to inhibition.

Posner and Cohen (1984) were the first to show that observers were slower to detect a target at an exogenously cued location when 300 or more milliseconds elapsed between the presentation of the cue and the presentation of the target (see Figure 5.6). That is, after an interval of about 300 ms (and lasting as long as 3 seconds), responses to targets at a cued location are often slower than responses to objects at uncued locations. It seems that exogenously triggered attention has a rather short lifetime and is biased not to return to a location where it has recently been. According to Klein and Taylor (1994, p. 136), "As endogenous control over visual orienting brings attention back to fixation, an inhibitory process develops that operates to repel attention from returning to the cued/stimulated location (where nothing of interest had been 'found')." This so-called *inhibition of return*

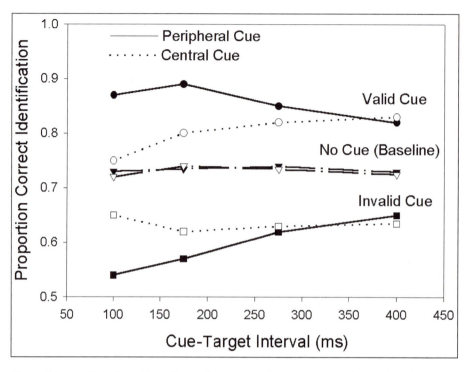

Figure 5.5   Cuing benefits and costs for peripheral (exogenous) and central (endogenous) cues as a function of cue-target interval.

SOURCE: Data from Müller & Rabbitt (1989).

has been observed in a wide variety of contexts, with both visual targets (see, e.g., Posner & Cohen, 1984) and auditory targets (see, e.g., Mondor, Breau, & Milliken, 1998), for detection and identification tasks (see, e.g., Kingstone & Pratt, 1999), and for both manual responses (see, e.g., Posner & Cohen, 1984) and eye movement responses (see, e.g., Abrams & Dobkin, 1994). Inhibition of return is greatest at the location of the cue, but can apply to the entire cued hemifield. Bennett and Pratt (2001) have shown that inhibition of return follows a sort of spatial gradient, with inhibition around the cued location gradually giving way to facilitation in the hemifield opposite to the cue.

Inhibition of Return and Visual Search

It has been suggested that the function of inhibition of return may be to ensure efficient search of complex environments by creating a bias against returning to locations that have already been investigated. One way that inhibition of return might serve to integrate attention and eye movements, and thus serve to

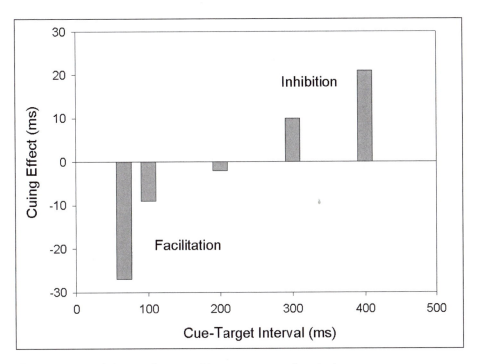

Figure 5.6   Inhibition of return with an exogenous (location) cue.

SOURCE: Data from Wright & Richard (1998).

favor novelty in visual scanning, is by producing either a motor or an attentional bias (or both) that influences where the eyes travel next. In addition to encouraging us to attend to new objects or new regions of space, inhibition of return might also serve the function of suppressing distraction. That is, the flashes and flickers that originally draw our attention may lose their ability to do this because of inhibition of return, thus allowing us to direct our attention elsewhere.

The hypothesis that inhibition of return supports efficient search has been tested directly using a search task in which multiple locations have to be checked in order to see if a target is present. Inhibition of return is measured by presenting a faint probe at one of the checked locations or at a different location. Snyder and Kingstone (2000) have shown that inhibition of return effects, measured by longer reaction times (RTs) or higher error rates to probes at checked locations, can persist across at least five different locations. The magnitude of the inhibition of return effect is largest at the most recently searched location and declines in an approximately linear fashion as one works back in time. It should be noted that inhibition of return at multiple locations using a search paradigm is found only when the searched items remain in view. Blanking out the screen before presentation of the probe eliminates inhibition of return (Wolfe & Pokorny, 1990).

Inhibition of return to locations in a search display has been called *inhibitory tagging*. Not surprisingly, given its suggested role in visual search, inhibitory tagging seems to be bound to the objects of search. In real life, unlike the typical search paradigm, the objects of our search are seldom stationary. In an attempt to mirror real-life, dynamic search, Tipper, Driver, and Weaver (1991) used moving peripheral cues. Inhibition of return was bound to the current location of a cued square, even though it had moved since cuing (by brief illumination). According to Tipper et al., inhibitory tagging of the locations of objects—rather than of fixed spatial coordinates—is an important adaptation that provides the foundation for efficient search through dynamic scenes. The importance of objects—and not just their spatial locations—in triggering inhibition of return is supported by the finding discussed earlier that inhibitory tagging occurs only when the items of the search task remain present until the responses to the probes are made (see also Takeda & Yagi, 2000). Inhibition of return is, however, larger in static displays than in dynamic ones (Tipper, Weaver, Jerreat, & Burak, 1994). Tipper et al. interpret this as evidence that environment- and object-based inhibition of return effects combine when an inhibited object remains at the inhibited location. In general, object-based inhibition of return is less pronounced than location-based inhibition of return.

Attentional and Motor Effects in Inhibition of Return

The different effects of exogenous and endogenous cues have led some researchers to propose that the cues engage two different attentional systems. In this view, the exogenous attentional system orients attention reflexively to external signals. Such reflexive attention seems to share the brain system that controls saccadic eye movements (the rapid movements that occur between fixations; as opposed to pursuit movements, in which the eye smoothly follows a moving target). Some researchers have suggested that inhibition of return is generated by activation of the oculomotor system (Rafal & Henik, 1994). For example, although inhibition of return is generally associated with exogenous cues, it can occur for endogenous cues if eye movements are required to the cued location, and even if observers prepare themselves to make an eye movement to the periphery (Rafal, Calabresi, Brennan, & Sciolto, 1989). However, the finding that inhibition can be associated with many locations at the same time (see, e.g., Wright & Richard, 1996) shows that a purely oculomotor account of inhibition of return is oversimplified. After all, we can only program and execute eye movements to one location at a time.

Inhibition of return seems to result from a delay in activating attentional, as well as motor, processes to a previously cued stimulus. If inhibition of return were a pure motor phenomenon specific to localizing targets, it should occur only when the task is to localize a target, and not when the task requires merely target identification and no spatially directed response. Kingstone and Pratt (1999) found that inhibition of return does occur when the task is to identify a target, rather than to indicate its location, supporting an attentional account. However, inhibition of return is larger when eye movements are executed rather than withheld, which indicates that a motor component also contributes to inhibition of return. In summary, inhibition of return seems to consist of both an oculomotor component and an attentional component.

VISUAL MARKING ▲

In the preceding section, we saw how inhibition of return might facilitate search processes by discouraging eye movements or attention shifts back to already checked locations. Relatively new work suggests that top-down inhibition can also influence search performance. As discussed in Chapter 3, visual search is much more laborious when targets are defined by a conjunction of features (e.g., a blue circle among green circles and blue triangles) than when they are defined by just one feature (e.g., a blue circle among green circles and triangles). In conjunction search, search time increases as the number of items in the display increases (i.e., there is a set-size effect; see Chapter 3). It has recently been shown that when some of the distractors are presented (i.e., "pre-exposed") before the entire search display, new objects can be prioritized for visual attentional processing by the top-down attentional inhibition of old objects already in the field, thus reducing the set-size effect.

difficult

think

should circle an area not stare at one specific area.

Watson and Humphreys (1997, 1998) attribute the effects of pre-exposure of distractors to a mechanism they call *visual marking* (not to be confused with inhibitory tagging). This marking process results in the active inhibition of the distractor locations, as demonstrated by the fact that detection of a dim probe dot is impaired when it falls at the location of an old object in conditions in which it is advantageous to mark (inhibit) old objects (Watson & Humphreys, 2000). As is the case for inhibition of return, inhibition due to visual marking is also found for dynamic displays in which the old items move (Watson & Humphreys, 1998). However, static items can be marked even when old and new stimuli contain the same features, but moving items can be inhibited only when the old items have a unique feature. This suggests that the marking of static items can be location-based, whereas the marking of moving items depends on a feature map (see Chapter 3 for a description of how feature and location maps might be used in visual processing). Unlike inhibition of return, visual marking seems to be able to be flexibly applied (or withheld), depending on the goals of current behavior.

vis. marking not in exam

▲ NEGATIVE PRIMING

*[handwritten margin notes: *KNOW* / look for smiley face ...then next time, find fish / takes you longer to press the button, bc you were told to ignore fish last time]*

Even simple acts like reaching for a saltshaker at a crowded table require selection. Attention must be directed to the saltshaker in order to guide the action of your hand, but attention is also required to prevent any number of misdirections of action along the way. You have to be careful not to knock over the wine or bump into the flowers, and you want to be sure to grasp the salt, and not the pepper. Some ideas about how such an action is initiated and carried out are discussed in Chapter 9. What we will discuss here is the consequences of inhibiting attention (and action) to objects and locations.

Selecting a target often requires rejecting distractors. For example, in the classic Stroop task words have to be ignored—in so far as possible—in order to be able to name colors. Similarly, in the flanker-compatibility paradigm, responses to distractors have to be suppressed in order to respond to a target. The negative-priming paradigm was developed to examine the nature and time course of the inhibition of distractors. In a common version of this paradigm, participants are told simply to respond to the identity of a target. One or more distractors typically accompany the target. For example, a participant might be told to name the object presented in red on each trial (e.g., a cat), and to ignore the object presented in green (e.g., a kite). Across trials, the effects of the relation between the distractors on one trial (the "prime" trial) to the target on the next trial (the "probe" trial) are examined. On so-called ignored repetition trials, an object that served as a distractor on the previous trial is now presented as the target. *Negative priming* is said to occur when responses to a target are slower when the target was present as a distractor on the previous trial (e.g., the kite) than if the target was unrelated to the previous trial (e.g., a fish; see Figure 5.7; note that, in the figure, black is used as the target color instead of red, and the gray items should be ignored). This effect provides evidence that the selection of a target is accompanied by suppression of the distractors. This suppression, or inhibition, can have long-lasting effects that make subsequent selection of the item more cumbersome.

Negative priming also occurs when the task is to respond to the location of an object rather than its identity (see, e.g., Tipper, Brehaut, & Driver, 1990). If only one, target, stimulus is presented, responses to the stimulus location (e.g., pressing a response key corresponding to the location where the stimulus occurred) are faster than if there is a distractor present in the display (see also Kahneman, Treisman, & Burkell, 1983). The presence of a distractor on the prime trial also affects response times on the probe trial. In this case, people are slower to respond to the location of a target (e.g., a triangle) if the current target location was previously occupied by a distractor (e.g., a circle). As illustrated in Figure 5.8, on the ignored-repetition trials, when the target on the probe trial is presented at the location of a distractor from the prime trial, responses are slower than on the control

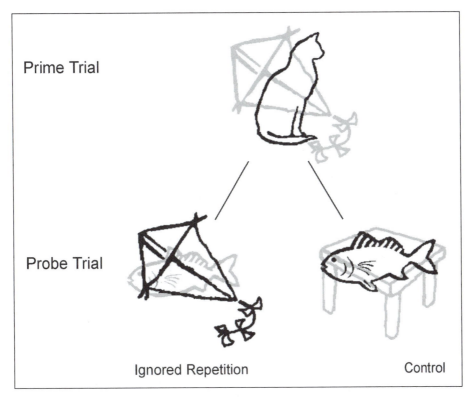

Figure 5.7   Negative priming for identity. The task is to name the item presented in black. When the gray item from the prime trial is presented as the black (target) item on the probe trial, reaction times are longer than in the control condition, in which both items are new.

trials in which the probe target is presented in a previously unoccupied location. The RT difference between the ignored-repetition and control trials is taken as the measure of negative priming.

✳ Negative priming can have far-reaching effects. This is illustrated in a study by Shiu and Kornblum (1996) in which participants saw either a word or a picture and had to respond with a different word or picture name. For example, if the stimulus was "bike," the subject had to say "car." If the stimulus on the probe trial was the same as the response on the prime trial, facilitation (positive priming) was found. However, if the response on the probe trial was the same as the stimulus on the prime trial, negative priming was found. For example, when participants saw "car" and said "plane" on the prime trial, and then saw "bike" and had to say "car" on the probe trial, responses were slower than when all stimuli and responses were different. This finding suggests that the congruent response (i.e., the name of the

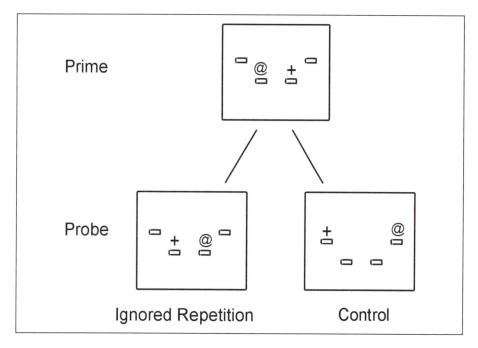

Figure 5.8   Negative priming for location. The task is to respond to the location of the target "@". A target presented at the location of the prime-trial distractor is responded to more slowly than when presented in a different location.

word or picture) was activated, even though it would have been an incorrect response, and then had to be inhibited. A similar negative priming effect is obtained when the stimuli are different spatial locations and the responses are keypresses, but only if the mapping is not one for which the assigned response can be selected by a simple rule (e.g., respond at the mirror-opposite location; Read & Proctor, in press).

All of the experiments we have discussed so far used two-dimensional stimuli and simple responses. We suggested, however, that the function of negative priming might be to facilitate goal-directed action. In an attempt to address the role of negative priming in action control, Tipper, Lortie, and Baylis (1992) developed a selective reaching paradigm in which participants had to reach to one of nine targets (see Figure 5.9). Each target was marked with two lights: a red light that indicated the target and a yellow light that had to be ignored. In one condition, participants started each trial with their hand on a start button close to their body, at the bottom of the display, and reached toward the target. In this case, yellow lights produced distraction (and produced negative priming) only when they appeared next to targets along the reach path (e.g., for responses to buttons in the middle row, only front-row

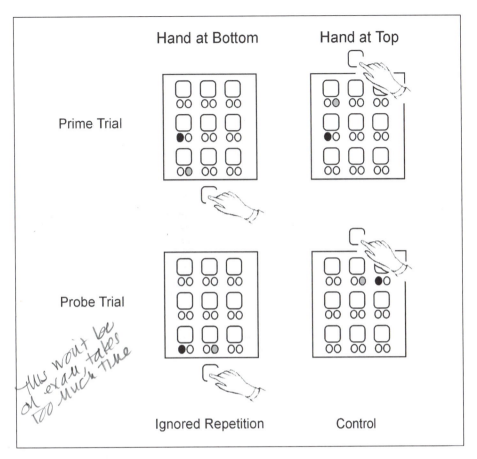

Figure 5.9   The selective reaching paradigm of Tipper, Lortie, and Baylis (1992). The task is to move the hand to the key corresponding to the target light (here shown as the darker circle). Note that control and ignored-repetition trials occurred with both hand placement conditions.

lights produced interference). In the other condition, participants started with their hands at the top of the display such that they had to move the hand toward the body in order to make a response. In this case, only distractors in the back row interfered with responses to the middle row (see Figure 5.10). The finding that only distractors on the path for making a response (i.e., distractors over which the hand had to move) caused interference led Tipper et al. to conclude that negative priming is action-centered; that is, when actions are directed at objects in the environment, attention is directed to action-centered representations in which the relationship between the target and the effector takes center stage.

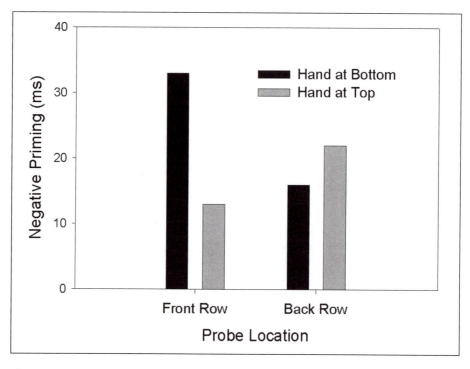

Figure 5.10   Negative priming in the selective reaching task of Tipper, Lortie, and Baylis (1992).

Object-Based Negative Priming

Because objects tend to move around from place to place, and because most action is undertaken with the goal of reaching an object (e.g., catching a ball, shaking an acquaintance's hand, or picking up a coffee cup), it makes sense to think that inhibition might be tied to objects instead of (or in addition to) locations. Tipper, Brehaut, and Driver (1990) tested this hypothesis by examining location-negative priming with either stationary or moving stimuli. In the two relevant experiments, there were eight possible display locations (see Figure 5.11). In one case, the eight positions were marked by small pieces of tape, and the target and distractor were shown above the marked positions. In the other case, the positions were marked by four long pieces of tape, and the targets could occur either at the top or bottom end of each piece. The target and distractor appeared in the top row of the display on the prime trial and in the bottom row on the probe trial. The critical manipulation was that the targets and distractors appeared to move from the top to the bottom position in the second display, but not in the first display. Negative priming was found only with the moving targets. In this case, negative

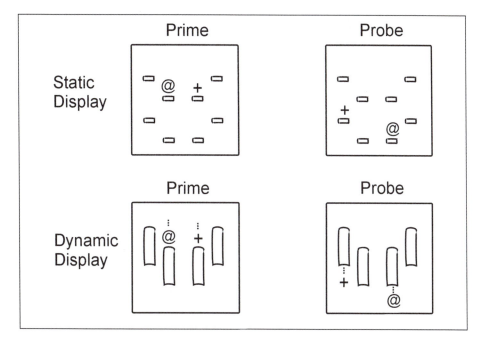

Figure 5.11   A negative priming paradigm with static and "dynamic" (apparent motion) displays. The task was to respond to the position of the target "@" by pressing a key corresponding to the lateral (left-to-right) position of the target.

SOURCE: Adapted from Tipper, Brehaut, & Driver, 1990.

priming occurred when the target on the probe trial appeared in the same relative lateral position (e.g., far right) as the distractor on the prime trial, even though its absolute position was different. Thus, when objects move, inhibition moves with them. This shows that inhibition can be based on objects even when location is responded to.

[handwritten margin note: This is what obj.-based neg priming is]

Connelly, Hasher, and Kimble (1992) showed that both identity and location priming can play a role in performance. Participants in their experiments either reported the name of a letter printed in a target color or pressed a response key to indicate its location. When required to identify the letter, responses on ignored-repetition trials were affected by both the location and the identity of the prime. In fact, the effects of the two factors were additive, suggesting that identity- and location-based inhibition may affect different aspects of target processing. Further evidence that the two types of inhibition are different is the fact that location responses (i.e., responding to the location of the target letters) were affected only by the location of the prime and not its identity. Although this latter result seems

> **Table 5.1   Some Conclusions About Negative Priming**
>
> 1. Negative priming can be associated with any perceptual feature of an ignored object (e.g., color, location, identity). It occurs for words, Stroop color words, local-global letters, letters, pictures, random shapes, and across languages.
>
> 2. Negative priming is flexible, depending on the behavioral goals of the task. Only those properties of the distractor that directly compete with the target in terms of the goals to be achieved will be inhibited.
>
> 3. The magnitude of negative priming tends to decrease as the number of objects to be ignored increases, probably because inhibition has to be spread over a number of distractors.
>
> 4. Negative priming sometimes depends on the presence (or anticipation) of distractor stimuli on the probe trial.
>
> 5. Negative priming takes time to develop and dissipates over time, sometimes surviving despite other intervening events.
>
> 6. Negative priming increases as the difficulty of selecting the target (whether on the prime or probe trial) increases.

to conflict with that of Tipper et al. (1990), in which location inhibition was shown to move with the stimulus object, it should be noted that participants in Tipper et al.'s experiments had to identify the target in order to respond to it. In Connelly et al.'s task, selection of an object or location was based on color, making it unnecessary to process the letter name. It has been suggested that the level of analysis of ignored stimuli corresponds to the level of representation required by the task (Fox, 1995; see Table 5.1).

Ease of Selection and Degree of Negative Priming

We saw earlier that when responses were based on location, there were no effects of ignored repetition of target identity. This was interpreted as a lack of negative priming due to the fact that the identity of the distractors could be completely ignored, rather than activated by selection, however fleeting, and then repressed. MacDonald, Joordens, and Seergobin (1999) suggest, in fact, that the degree of negative priming increases directly as a function of selection difficulty. In their experiments, participants saw two animal names (e.g., DONKEY and

CAMEL) on a computer screen, one printed in red and the other in white. In the "easy-selection" condition, the task was to read the red word. In the "difficult-selection" condition, the larger of the two animals had to be named. When selection was more difficult, much larger negative priming effects were observed. A similar suggestion that negative priming depends on the ease of selection is present in a series of studies by N. Lavie and Fox (2000), although those authors came to rather different conclusions. Lavie and Fox investigated the effect of perceptual load on negative priming by presenting various numbers of distractors during the prime trials. They found that increasing the number of distractors during the prime trial decreased negative priming. They argued that the high perceptual load at the prime trial exhausted resources that would otherwise be used to inhibit distractors, and, because the distractors could not be inhibited, they also did not give rise to negative priming. However, it could also be the case that negative priming was weak because attention (and inhibition) was distributed across all the distractors. More work is needed to determine whether perceptual load, per se, influences negative priming and has effects distinct from the need to inhibit multiple distractors.

Inhibition Accounts of Negative Priming

According to inhibition accounts, negative priming results from having to suppress distractor information in order to select a target. As such, it should not arise when selection is between two or more targets. Neill, Valdes, Terry, and Gorfein (1992) tested this implication of the inhibition account of negative priming using a location-negative priming paradigm in which two targets were sometimes shown on the prime trial. On these trials, the subject could respond to either target. Neill et al. found that no negative priming occurred at the nonselected target location. It seems the participants did not "reject" the extra target; they simply did not respond to it. In other words, because a response to the nonselected target would have been valid, there was no need to actively suppress it.

The selective inhibition account of negative priming assumes that distractors are, in fact, attended and receive some initial activation, and that this activation must then be suppressed or inhibited. An important question is, "What is inhibited?" One finding that must be taken into consideration in order to answer this question is that ignored distractors sometimes produce positive priming (i.e., faster or more accurate identification) when they are presented on the probe trial with no accompanying distractors (C. M. Moore, 1994). That is, when the need to suppress distractors on the probe trial is eliminated, the activation of the previously ignored target is still evident. This finding suggests that the overall activation level of the distractors is not decreased by their suppression on the prime trial. It may be that the inhibition is directed at the point where the representation of the distractor and the response are linked, that is, at the point of response selection (Tipper & Cranston, 1985). According to this hypothesis, response selection proceeds differently when no distractors are present, perhaps because no choice between "distractor" and "target" has to be made. Inhibition does not appear to be at the point of response suppression; changing the response to be made (e.g., a keypress response on the prime trial and a vocal response on the probe trial) does not eliminate negative priming (Tipper, MacQueen, & Brehaut, 1988).

Driver and Tipper (1989) showed that negative priming cannot be attributed to response competition between distractors and targets during the prime trials. They found that ignored distractors that were presented as flankers to the target did not produce a flanker-compatibility effect at the prime trial, but did produce negative priming at the probe trial. However, there does seem to be an important relation between selective filtering (as in the response-compatibility paradigm) and negative priming: People who are relatively good at filtering out irrelevant information show relatively large negative priming effects. Moreover, particular groups of people who have more difficulty inhibiting distractor information show less negative priming. Reduced negative priming has been found (but not always reliably) for children, children with attention-deficit hyperactivity disorder (ADHD), elderly people, obsessionals, people who report high incidence of cognitive failure, schizophrenics, depressed individuals, and Alzheimer's patients (see Houghton & Tipper, 1994). This suggests that inhibition of distractors is the mechanism of both selection and negative priming effects: Distractors are inhibited on the prime trial, and this inhibition has to be overcome on the probe trial.

Episodic Retrieval Accounts of Negative Priming

Some researchers (e.g., Neill & Valdes, 1992) have argued that it is inappropriate to think of negative priming as the result of an inhibition process and suggest instead an episodic retrieval account of negative priming. According to this account, negative priming results when the target was previously a distractor because of the way that it was encoded into memory. That is, a distractor on a prime trial is encoded along with the information that it is a distractor and should not be responded to. When the ignored distractor then is presented as a target, this "do not respond" information is also recalled. In other words, the target on an ignored-repetition trial includes both the information that the target should be ignored (due to retrieval of the previous processing episode) and that it should be attended (due to its designation as the target on the present trial). The mismatch between the encoded "do-not-respond" feature and the requirement to respond to the target produces conflict that takes some time to resolve.

Although this explanation can easily account for findings such as the fact that an extra target (which could have been responded to) does not produce negative priming, it cannot easily account for differences in negative priming across different groups or for relations between skill in selecting information and negative priming. An account that integrates inhibition and retrieval processes in a way that helps to explain how targets can be efficiently selected from competing distractors and how previous distractors can be efficiently dealt with would seem to provide the best account of negative priming (see, e.g., Milliken, Tipper, & Weaver, 1994).

INHIBITION OF THOUGHT AND MEMORY ▲

The research discussed thus far in this chapter focused on people's ability to suppress processing of unwanted stimulus information. In this section, we describe the suppression of information that is not physically present, but that is called to mind by associative processes in memory.

Intentional Forgetting

Memory depends on attention in several ways (see Chapter 7). To-be-remembered information must be attended to in the first place, and the appropriate retrieval cues must be attended if recollection is to occur (even though recollection itself may be unintended or even unconscious). In some memory-based tasks, the goal is not to remember information, but to forget it, such as when a jury is asked to disregard remarks made by the prosecutor, or one tries to forget information after learning that the source was unreliable. Forgetting is a critical activity. For example, imagine how hard it would be to find your car in a parking lot if you still remembered where you had left it the day—or even the week—before.

In typical laboratory research on such *intentional forgetting,* people are asked to learn items, and then are cued to forget some of the items. In order to study forgetting, it is, of course, necessary to first remember the items of interest. Thus, the cue to forget an item is usually not presented simultaneously with the item itself. Intentional forgetting is demonstrated whenever the recall protocol contains a higher proportion of to-be-recalled items than of to-be-forgotten items. The success of intentional forgetting depends on how well the information is learned, the nature of the instruction to forget, and the type of retrieval task used (H. M. Johnson, 1994).

From the standpoint of this chapter, the most important question is whether intentional forgetting involves the inhibition of items in memory. One account of intentional forgetting (similar to the episodic retrieval account of negative priming described earlier) is that the instruction to ignore is encoded along with the memory item. In a retrieval context, if the "ignore tag" is detected, retrieval processes for that item are stopped (Johnson, 1994). This account does not include an inhibitory process, per se, but assumes that the instruction to forget the item is part of the memory trace for that item. Some authors have argued that to-be-forgotten items are actively inhibited, probably at the time of retrieval. For example, Geiselman and Bagheri (1985) presented a list of words, with each word displayed for 5 seconds and followed by an instruction to either forget or remember that word. After a test in which selective remembering (i.e., intentional forgetting) was demonstrated, the same list was presented a second time, but this time all items were cued as items to be remembered. The subsequent recall test found that items that were to be forgotten in the first presentation of the list were relatively better recalled than to-be-remembered items after the second presentation of the list. The authors suggest that this was due to release of inhibition, although it could also be the case that the presentation of the "forget" instruction actually led to more rehearsal during the first presentation.

Suppression Processes in Reading

Research on skill in reading suggests that the act of reading is dependent on processes of suppression (Gernsbacher, 1993). When we read or perform other cognitive tasks, comprehension builds up over time. As information is processed, information in memory is activated automatically or retrieved either consciously or unconsciously. Along with the appropriate representations that lead to the eventual understanding of a situation, related, but task-inappropriate, representations may be activated and lead to distortions in our perception of the situation. For example, reading the sentence: "While placing her bet, she glanced at the spade held in her hand" is likely to bring to mind the image of a playing card, perhaps the ace of spades. However, another sort of spade, one used for digging the garden, may also have been brought to mind. Successful comprehension depends on determining the appropriate meaning of ambiguous words and suppressing inappropriate meanings.

The degree to which irrelevant meanings of words are suppressed can be measured by having people read sentences containing ambiguous stimuli, such as homophones, and then requiring readers to judge whether a word related to the inappropriate meaning of the word fits into the sentence context (see, e.g., Gernsbacher, 1993). For example, the sentence "He dug with the spade" might be followed with the question of whether the word "ace" fits into the context of the sentence. When this question is posed immediately following the reading of the sentence, both skilled and unskilled readers have more trouble determining whether the word "ace" fits the sentence context relative to when the same judgment is made after reading the sentence with an unambiguous word such as "shovel." However, after a delay of 1 second, the unskilled readers have much more trouble rejecting the inappropriate word than do skilled readers. The ability of skilled readers to more quickly suppress irrelevant meanings is also found for latencies to reject homophones (e.g., reject "patients" after reading the sentence "She treated the dog with great patience") and words related to pictures that were to be ignored.

It seems that the ability of more skilled readers to suppress information extends to suppressing "appropriate" meanings as well. Gernsbacher and Robertson (1995) showed that skilled readers could more easily suppress the influence of context in order to judge the similarity of a word to a word meaning inappropriate to that context. For example, skilled readers instructed to ignore the context of a sentence and only judge whether or not the last word was related to a test word were better able to accept the inappropriate meaning of a homonym and more quickly judge "ace" as related to "spade" after hearing the sentence, "He dug with the spade." This suggests that more skilled readers will also be quicker to "get the joke" after hearing a story such as, "Two men walked into a bar. The third man ducked."

RESPONDING TO A SIGNAL TO STOP ▲

It is a fact of life that goals change and actions must sometimes be modified to follow them. If you are reaching for something tasty just out of the oven and your friend calls out, "That's hot!" you will probably withdraw your hand rather than put the hot item into your mouth. A driver thinking about getting to work on time will have to both change his priority (from speed to safety) and stop the car when a railroad barrier descends in front of him. When the current course of thought or action is no longer appropriate, it must be replaced by a new one, and the first step in changing a course is to stop the present one. According to Logan (1994), stopping processes are especially interesting because they are a general requirement in cognitive control. In other words, "stopping is a clear case of executive intervention. It gives us a chance to see executive processes in action, a chance to discern their nature" (Logan, 1994, p. 190).

Actions such as stopping a car or rephrasing a remark are fairly complex. In order to look at just the stopping component of changes of plan, it is necessary to use a simpler, more direct task. The *stop-signal paradigm* (Logan, 1981, 1994) was developed to isolate stopping processes from other aspects of performance. In this paradigm, people are asked to perform a simple task, such as pressing one of two keys when they see an "X" and the other key when they see an "O." On trials in which a "stop signal" is presented (e.g., a tone), the response to either letter is to be withheld. The primary dependent variable of interest is whether people can withhold responses after receiving a stop signal.

It has been hypothesized that a stop signal initiates an inhibitory "stop" process that then races against an excitatory "go" process that is set off by the primary task stimulus. In the so-called "race model" of stop-signal performance, these two processes operate independently of each other (Logan & Cowan, 1984). If the stop process finishes before processing on the first task has reached a point of no return (i.e., a point beyond which the response can no longer be withheld), it "wins" and the response is inhibited.

Much research has focused on finding the point of no return by manipulating factors that have been shown to affect different stages in the primary task and then examining the effect of these manipulations on stopping time. The reasoning is as follows: If a stage before the point of no return is made to last longer, there will be more time for the stopping process to finish its course, and thus the percentage of successful stops will be higher. If the process affected is after the point of no return, no change in the percentage of successful stops is to be expected (see Figure 5.12). For example, stimulus-response compatibility (i.e., the "naturalness" of the assignment of responses to stimuli) affects the time required to select a response. If response selection and the processes after it are ballistic (i.e., if, once started, they always run to completion), changing the compatibility of the task will not affect the probability of correctly stopping (see Figure 5.12, Panel C). If response selection is not ballistic, making the response less compatible and, thus, lengthening the time needed for response selection allows the stopping process more time and should lead to a higher percentage of correct stops (see Figure 5.12, Panel B). Logan (1981) found that the latter was the case, and, thus, concluded that response-selection processes can be interrupted. Given that response selection is under inhibitory control by stop processes, it is not surprising that increasing stimulus discriminability, which affects perception, an earlier stage of processing, also allows more time for stopping. More surprising is that response planning (i.e., motor programming) also seems to be before the point of no return. This is indicated by the finding that one factor that affects the time required to initiate a movement (and is generally assumed to reflect the time required to set up a motor program), response complexity, also affects a stage under controlled processing (Osman, Kornblum, & Meyer, 1990).

Some researchers have argued that there is no point of no return. De Jong, Coles, Logan, and Gratton (1990) used sophisticated measurement techniques to measure both brain and muscle electrical activity on trials that were successfully stopped and on trials that should have been stopped, but were not. Primary task responses were made by squeezing a dynamometer (a device that registers the force applied to it). Electrodes placed on the arms were used to record the electromyogram (EMG) from the muscles that would be used in making a response.

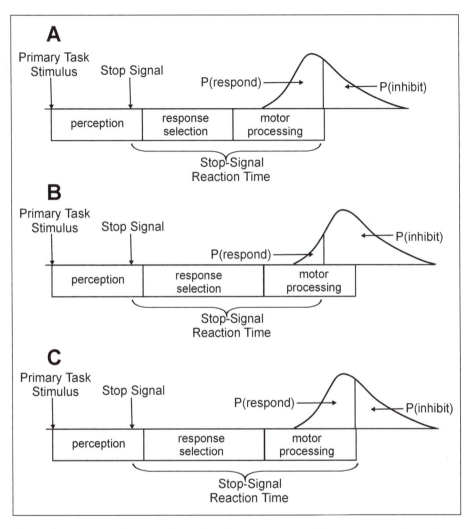

Figure 5.12   Hypothetical effects of prolonging a stoppable (Panel B) and a ballistic (Panel C) process on stop-signal responses compared to a control condition (Panel A). Logan (1981) found that response selection can be aborted when a stop signal is presented, such that the probability of making a response is lower when response selection is more difficult (Panel B).

Finally, electrodes placed on the scalp measured the lateralized readiness potential, assumed to reflect brain activity associated with the differential involvement of the right and left motor cortex in preparing to make unimanual movements, on each trial. Using these measurement techniques, De Jong et al. were able to determine whether there was any point of activation beyond which the response could no longer be inhibited. Information processes, as measured by lateralized readiness potentials, forearm muscle activation, and even the squeezing of the response meter itself, could all be stopped once begun. If there is a point of no return, De Jong et al. argued that they were not able to find it. If the point of no return is defined as the beginning of a response, then it might be the case that once muscle activation has started, a response cannot be completely withheld. In fact, De Jong et al. found that in all cases where there was activation in the forearm muscles, there was also at least a partial squeeze on the dynamometer. Some would interpret this finding as evidence that muscle activation is the point of no return (see, e.g., Osman, Kornblum, & Meyer, 1990).

Stopping Times

A wide variety of primary tasks and stop signals have been used. Whether the action to be withheld is a button press, a hand movement, speech, or a squeeze, a normal, healthy young adult will be able to stop the response in about 200 ms (Logan & Cowan, 1984; see Box 5.1 for a description of how to compute stop-signal reaction time). The consistency of stopping times for different tasks and effector systems suggests that stopping relies on a single, central, amodal process, although one recent study (Logan & Irwin, 2000) suggests that the inhibition of eye movements and the inhibition of hand movements are governed by separate processes (and even these processes are assumed to operate according to the same principles).[3]

Like many other inhibitory processes, the response to a stop signal depends on age. Both young children (see, e.g., Ridderinkhof, Band, & Logan, 1999) and elderly adults (see, e.g., Kramer et al., 1994) take more time to react to a stop signal than do young adults. Interestingly, the stopping times for elderly people and young (6- to 8-year-old) children are about the same, with estimates for both groups being about 300 ms. Ridderinkhof et al. found a decrease in stopping time from 305 ms for 6–8 year olds, to 234 ms for 10–12 year olds, to 188 ms for young adults (university students with a mean age of 21.7 years). The longer stopping times for children and the elderly may be due to developmental changes in frontal lobe functioning. The frontal lobes, which play an important role in cognitive control processes (see Chapter 12), are the last parts of the brain to fully develop and the first parts of the brain to show age-related decay.

The Nature of the Stopping Process

According to the race model, stopping an action depends on a separate sort of processing than selecting and executing an action. Both behavioral and electrophysiological evidence for this assumption has been found. Naito and Matsumura (1996),

Box 5.1 | Measuring the Stop Process

Measurement of the stop process is complicated by the fact that it is not directly observable. All that we can observe is whether subjects are successful in withholding a response after receiving a stop signal. However, with the help of the race model, it is possible to determine stopping times. Two rules determine the outcome of the race between the stop process and the go process. First, if the stop process is faster than the go process, the response is inhibited. Second, if the go process is faster than the stop process, the response is executed. Both the stop process and the go process are *stochastic*; that is, their finishing times vary probabilistically from trial to trial. Thus, there will be a distribution of stopping times and a distribution of finishing times. However, for the purposes of determining stopping times, it is often assumed that the stopping time is constant.

On every trial, there is some probability that the subject will respond, P(respond), and some probability that the response will be stopped, P(inhibit). Note that even when we assume that the stop process has a constant duration, variability in primary-task reaction times will mean that sometimes the response is made before the stop process is finished, and that sometimes the stop process will finish before the response is made.

The time at which the stop process finishes can be calculated by considering the stop-signal delay (i.e., the time elapsed between the presentation of the primary-task stimulus and the stop signal), the probability of responding on stop-signal trials, and the distribution of primary-task reaction times on no stop-signal trials. When an experiment is being run, the stop-signal delay is often manipulated until the probability that a primary-task response is made, even though a stop signal is presented, is equal to 50%; that is, until P(respond|stop signal) = .50. In this case, the finishing time of the stop process would fall at the 50th percentile of the distribution of primary-task reaction times (see Box Figure 5.1). Thus, we can determine the finishing time of the stop process by finding the primary-task reaction time at the 50th percentile, which is simply the median of the distribution. The duration of the stop process is found by subtracting the stop-signal delay from the finishing time of the stop process.

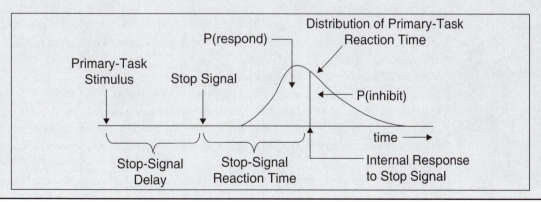

for example, found that some aspects of motor activation in preparation for a response were unaffected by a stop signal, and that the stopping process itself was associated with an independent "no-go" specific EEG component. Normally, when two stimuli require different responses, the response time to the second of the two stimuli is longer if it is presented before the response to the first stimulus is made, than if the two tasks do not overlap (see Chapter 6). However, withholding responses after a stop signal does not show the usual effects of overlap with the processing of another task. As Logan and Cowan (1984) assert, stop signals do not seem to be subject to the same bottlenecks in performance that affect responses to other stimuli.

Some factors that affect response selection do seem to affect stopping time. In particular, it has been shown that stopping time depends on whether the primary task requires the inhibition of irrelevant information. For example, Ridderinkhof, Band, and Logan (1999) combined a stop signal with a flanker task (see also Kramer et al., 1994). The primary task was to press a key corresponding to the direction of a centrally presented arrow (i.e., press the right key if the arrow points right and the left key if the arrow points left). On each trial, four flanker arrows were presented to the left and right of the central, target arrow. On congruent trials, the flankers pointed in the same direction as the target arrow, and on incongruent trials the flanker arrows pointed in the opposite direction. In such a task, RTs to the arrow are longer on incongruent trials than on congruent trials. Ridderinkhof et al. found that stopping times were also longer on incongruent trials (208 vs. 182 ms for congruent trials). Thus, it may be that the act of suppressing conflicting information uses some of the same processes or resources needed for suppressing a response. The reverse seems to be true as well. When a stop signal was presented, but the response was not inhibited in time, the difference in response time to the incongruent versus the congruent trials was greater (39 ms) than on trials with no stop signal. This suggests that suppression of the flankers was less efficient when stop processes were initiated (even though they were not successful in inhibiting the response) than when they were not. The operation of response inhibition due to the presence of conflicting flankers in the primary task and response inhibition triggered by the stop signal affect each other negatively (i.e., the inhibition is less effective), which suggests that the two types of inhibition either occur sequentially, such that only one type of inhibition can be exercised at a time, or both compete for activation.

If the control exercised by the stop process operates outside the system that controls go processes (Logan, 1994), it could be the case that stop processes intervene when it is necessary to stop an action, but are not otherwise involved in control. Although the stopping process seems to operate independently of primary-task "go" processes, it may nonetheless influence the way these processes operate. For example, when a stop-signal paradigm in which only some trials are followed by stop signals is used, RTs on the trials following stop-signal trials are longer than otherwise. It seems that invoking the stopping process has a sort of inhibitory aftereffect that carries over into the processing of the next trial (Rieger & Gauggel, 1999).

In many everyday situations, either a stopping of action or a change in action may accompany a change of plan. This raises the interesting question of whether it is necessary to stop an action before a change can be made, or whether the changing process has a separate, independent function. The evidence thus far is that stopping is qualitatively different than changing. For example, in making reaching movements, it takes less time to switch to a new target than it does to simply stop a movement. This suggests again that, indeed, stop processes provide a different sort of control than that needed for go processes.

SUMMARY ▲

In this chapter we reviewed a number of tasks that require the inhibition of unwanted information, associations, or actions. As is clear from the range of tasks discussed, inhibition may have many different purposes and can take different forms. It should be kept in mind that the term "inhibition" reflects a phenomenon—the suppression of information or action—and that a range of processes might be responsible for producing the inhibition of information or responses. Tasks such as the Stroop and Simon tasks examine the ability of people to focus on a relevant dimension while ignoring an irrelevant dimension. Inhibition may play a central role in visual search as well, making search more efficient by preventing return to previously checked locations. The aftereffects of selecting a relevant stimulus, as seen in negative priming tasks, reveal that selection in general implies rejecting irrelevant stimuli or locations.

Failure to inhibit irrelevant information can make a person distractible and forgetful, and thus less able to pursue goals, learn new information or skills, and comprehend and remember information. The ability to terminate actions once it becomes apparent that they are no longer appropriate is central to adaptive behavior. Research using the stop-signal paradigm has shown that there is no point-of-no-return in information processing. Up until a response is actually made, intentions can be modified and the course of action can be changed. An understanding of inhibition is important because of its implications for understanding cognitive control and the choice of one course of action among many, a topic that will be further explored in the following chapters.

NOTES ▲

1. In the first demonstration of the Simon effect, Simon and Small (1969) had participants make right or left keypress responses to high- or low-pitched tones. Tones were presented in the right or left ear. When the location of the tone corresponded with the location of the required response, responses were faster than when it did not.

2. Strictly speaking, stimulus and response are ideomotor compatible when the sensory feedback resulting from making the response closely resembles the stimulus. See Chapter 1 for a discussion of early views of ideomotor compatibility.

3. Logan and Irwin (2000) found that stopping eye movements was 45 ms faster than stopping hand movements, and that the compatibility of the primary-task response (respond by pressing a key or moving the eyes on or to the same or different side of space) had an effect only on eye movements; eye movements, but not hand movements, were suppressed more quickly in the same-side condition. Of course, because Logan and Irwin used a discrete button pressing response for the "hand" response, the differences in results might also reflect a difference between discrete and continuous responses.

CHAPTER 6

MULTIPLE-TASK PERFORMANCE

The critical feature of divided attention is that it ALWAYS leads to a performance decrement.

For most of us, demands on our attention first become evident when we are required to do several things at once. A classic example of this is driving while carrying on a conversation. This is quite easy most of the time, but when driving conditions become difficult, conversation screeches to a halt. Just about every skilled activity involves performing multiple tasks. For example, a skilled musician must divide his attention between reading a score, playing the instrument, and following the directions of a conductor, and a tennis player must move to intercept the ball while planning her following shot.

Although information from multiple sources must often be attended to and acted upon, only a fraction of the many sources of stimulation present in the immediate environment is, as a rule, relevant to current task demands. Focused attention is therefore required to attend to the relevant subset of the possible information sources and to ignore all else, whereas divided attention is required to attend simultaneously to the two or more important sources of information. Most real-world tasks, ranging from reading a book in a crowded waiting room while monitoring the time so that one's appointment is not missed, to taking notes while listening to a lecture and ignoring the activities of fellow students, have both divided and focused attention components.

This chapter addresses our ability to perform multiple tasks. Several topics from previous chapters come up again in this one. One of these topics is the nature of attention itself. The concept of attention as a single capacity or resource will be discussed and contrasted with multiple-resource models of attention. The relation between controlled and automatic processing will be discussed as an important factor in skilled multiple-task performance. Another important topic in this chapter is the role of goals and intentions in guiding performance of tasks. The interacting roles of memory, intention, and attention are taking an increasingly prominent role in models and theories of human performance, and will be discussed in both this and the following chapter.

▲ MANAGING ATTENTIONAL RESOURCES

Even if a task is well understood from the researcher's point of view when it is performed singly, taking that task out of isolation and placing it in the context of other tasks means that additional factors will come into play. The need to do two or more things at once brings with it problems of coordinating task strategies and, often, dividing attention between different aspects of the tasks. In other words, specialized skills are required in order to become good at performing multiple tasks. One such skill has been called *time-sharing*, which refers to efficiently allocating processing resources to component tasks at the appropriate times. It seems to reflect a basic ability that generalizes across a variety of task combinations (Salthouse & Miles, 2002). Sometimes, however, multiple-task performance improves because performers learn to restructure two or more tasks that are performed together, such that the multiple tasks are effectively treated as a single task. The ability to restructure tasks will depend on the components of the tasks that are to be performed together. For example, task interactions, such as interference in making a manual response for one task from the execution of a similar response for another task, may prevent two tasks from being combined into a smoothly executable, coherent unit. Although such structural interference may be a major determinant of the ability to perform different tasks together, interference can also arise when senses and effectors used in the two tasks differ.

Given the limited nature of attentional resources, performing a task adequately often depends on the ability to allocate attention appropriately (see also Chapters 9 and 10). That is, optimal performance may require devoting less attention to some aspect of the task in order to devote more attention to a different aspect of the task. It is clear that only some combinations of strategies will lead to optimal performance. For example, moving the head or eyes about to collect peripheral information needed for planning ahead can be useful, but can also result in accidents, such as falling off a curb when walking or rear-ending the car in

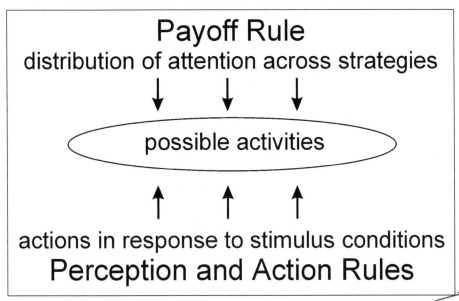

Figure 6.1   Schematic depiction of Erev and Gopher's (1999) game-theoretic model of attention and control. The payoff rule determines how much emphasis will be given to each strategy for attending to stimulus information. Perception-action rules determine how this information will be used.

front when driving. Optimizing performance requires finding the right combination of attentional strategies (attending to different sources) and perceptual strategies (acting on the minimal effective amount of information). For example, when jogging along a path, it is sufficient to notice that there is a tree in the way; it is not necessary to continue focusing on the tree until one has enough information to know whether it is a maple or an ash.

One theoretical account of optimizing performance by changing attentional strategies is that of Erev and Gopher (1999). These authors proposed that attention control is subject to two constraints: the cognitive strategies available to the performer and the incentives (payoff rule) for applying these strategies. Their approach is based on the assumption that, at each point in time, behavior is controlled by a cognitive strategy made up of at least two components: an executive control (top-down) component that determines which information will be attended to (according to a payoff rule; see Figure 6.1) and a data-driven perception and action (bottom-up) rule component that controls the execution of a response to the attended information.

The roles of both bottom-up processing and executive control are nicely illustrated in a study that was concerned with the development of training programs for helicopter pilots. In this study, Seagull and Gopher (1997) based the development of training exercises on the assumption that a certain level of divided attention is optimal. The helicopter pilots in Seagull and Gopher's study had to learn to move their heads (which were fitted with helmet-mounted displays; see Chapter 8) to collect data in order to be able to fly safely. Strategic executive control determined the amount and type of information collected by the pilots, who could choose to limit their head movements in order to focus on a narrow field of view (e.g., in order to focus on a potential crash situation), or move their heads in order to get a broader perspective (e.g., to facilitate planning for the future). An example of using a data-driven perception and action rule would be to move to the left in order to avoid crashing into a rock on the right. As will be discussed in more detail in Chapter 10, Seagull and Gopher were able to train pilots to adopt efficient strategies by having them perform a secondary task requiring head movements concurrently with the piloting task.

▲ SETTING GOALS AND INTENTIONS

All experimenters assume that their participants are willing to pursue the goals that they, themselves, are interested in. It is assumed that participants are able to grasp the task instructions and do their best to carry out the assigned tasks. However, participants in even very simple experiments are not always able to keep the goals of performance current. For example, in an anti-saccade experiment, in which a saccadic eye movement is moved to a location opposite to a cued location, participants may lose their concentration or their ability to maintain the cue–action relationship and nonetheless allow their eyes to move to the cue. The ability to maintain and modify task goals has received increasing attention in recent years. These executive control functions have been most extensively studied in situations in which participants must switch from one simple task to another, or perform a series of steps in a multi-step task.

Task-Set Switching

Efficient, coordinated performance of complex tasks often depends on the ability to switch from one task or task component to another. For example, the baseball player waiting at bat must be prepared to quickly switch from the task of hitting the ball to the task of running to first base. In the case of the baseball player, years of practice will have had an influence on the ability to make the transition from hitting the ball to running to first base. It seems likely that successful players will have developed what researchers call *advance reconfiguration* (Rogers & Monsell, 1995) processes to facilitate this transition. According to this idea, performers can intentionally prepare for a task switch, thus eliminating the costs of having to change tasks. *Switching costs*, increases in reaction time (RT) and error rates on the task after the switch, have been taken as an index of the control processes involved in reconfiguring and reconnecting various "modules" in the brain so as to perform the appropriate action with a given stimulus (Monsell & Driver, 2000). In other words, they seem to reflect the time needed to adopt the appropriate task set.

Switching costs have most often been studied in paradigms in which participants have to switch between two simple tasks, for example, between classifying either the digit member of a pair of characters as even or odd or the letter member as a consonant or vowel (Rogers & Monsell, 1995). In such experiments, participants switch between the two tasks in a predictable way (e.g., on every second or fourth trial). Switching costs reflect poorer performance for task-switch trials (i.e., the first trial after a switch) than for consecutive same-task trials (i.e., trials in which the same task is performed as in the preceding trial). Rogers and Monsell found that when people knew that there was going to be a task switch and had sufficient time to prepare for it (i.e., when the interval between the response to a previous trial and the presentation of the stimulus for the current trial was long enough), task-switching costs were substantially reduced. However, they also found evidence that the reconfiguration of task set for the new task was only partial: Even with 1.2 seconds available for preparation, a large cost in RT remained for the first trial of the new task. They attributed this residual cost to an exogenously triggered reconfiguration component. In other words, they suggested that the presence of the task-relevant stimulus was necessary in order to fully evoke the appropriate task set.

In Rogers and Monsell's (1995) view, task-set switching depends on two components: a top-down, control component and a bottom-up component in which the imperative stimulus triggers the appropriate set. Other researchers have argued that residual switch costs reflect a failure to fully discard or inhibit the previous task set. Common assumptions in models of task-set switching are that (1) task set depends on a configuration of processing pathways or modules in the brain through which some operations are facilitated and others inhibited, and thus reflects the degree of "readiness" to perform a task; and (2) that the processing system stays in this state of readiness until it is switched again. However, as we have already begun to see, these assumptions are often violated. The most problematic finding for the view that task set can be preconfigured is that even predictable, well-prepared switches show residual switching costs (see, e.g., Arbuthnott & Frank, 2000). Thus, it does not seem to be the case that task-set switching is always an all-or-none action,[1] and it may be the case that task-set inhibition is an important executive control process. A similar view has been proposed by Sohn and Carlson (2000), who argue that switch costs primarily reflect persisting activation from previous task sets rather than inadequate preparation for the new task (see also Allport, Styles, & Hsieh, 1994). Although foreknowledge allows preparation for both repeated and switched tasks, repeating the same task has benefits over task switching regardless of foreknowledge.

Task-Set Switching and Executive Control

The suggestion that both executive control and automatic activation play roles in task switching is consistent with the finding that people cannot "plan away" all switch costs. It may be that executive control is responsible for determining which task will be performed, but that readiness (and, thus, RT) to perform the task depends on more automatic processes of inhibition and activation from preceding trials. One such idea about residual costs in task-set switching is that they primarily reflect competition from earlier stimulus–response mappings. This could be the case whenever the two tasks use the same stimuli but require different responses—although competition may be a problem only when there is meaning-related similarity between the relevant stimulus dimensions for the two tasks (see Meiran, 2000, for a model that addresses these issues). For example, Allport and Wylie (2000) reported a series of experiments using Stroop-type stimuli (see Chapter 5) in which participants had to switch between naming the color of the ink in which the color words were printed and reading the color word itself. One of the most impressive findings from these experiments was that reading times were greatly increased when the word-reading task had been preceded by the color-naming task. This effect was even more pronounced when the particular word to be read had previously appeared as a color to be named. The magnitude of this negative transfer from the color-naming task to the word-reading task was greatest on the first trial of the word-reading blocks of trials. Importantly, reading times on the first trial of a block were still relatively slow even after several blocks of word-reading trials. This "restart" effect may reflect a general need to reinstate the stimulus–response mapping (e.g., to retrieve it from memory) for the task after any sort of interruption. Thus, traditional estimates of switching costs may be too high: Switching seems certain to contain restart costs and may also reflect negative transfer.

De Jong (2000) proposed a model of residual switching costs based on limitations in the ability to fully prepare for a new task before the presentation of the first stimulus and on the failure to take advantage of opportunities for advance preparation. Unlike accounts of residual switching costs that suggest that preparation cannot be completed until the stimulus appears and exogenously triggers the completion of the reconfiguration process (see, e.g., Rogers & Monsell, 1995),[2] De Jong proposes that residual switch costs rest largely on a "failure to engage" in advance preparation for an upcoming task. According to an exogenous triggering account, residual switch costs should be present on all switch trials. According to the failure-to-engage account, however, residual switch costs should be observed only on trials for which performers fail to prepare for the new task (e.g., because the stimulus–response mapping is not activated strongly enough in working memory to be able to be retrieved). Because the results of any experiment will contain a mixture of prepared and unprepared responses, the results should be able to be modeled by what is called a *mixture distribution*. In a mixture distribution, a distribution of responses (in this case, RTs) is assumed to reflect the combined result of two different underlying processes (in this case, a process producing prepared responses and a process producing unprepared responses).

The details of how such a distribution can be fitted are described by De Jong (2000), but the general idea is to estimate the response times for prepared and unprepared trials, and then to estimate the number of trials in which participants were or were not prepared. An estimate of prepared response time is available simply by looking at the mean RT on nonswitch trials. An estimate of unprepared response time can be found by looking at switch RTs for trials with a very short preparation interval (i.e., with a short response–stimulus interval [RSI]). The next step in evaluating the failure-to-engage model is to look at the entire distribution of RTs. This is done by rank ordering all RTs from fastest to slowest and then averaging the RTs in each decile (i.e., each 10% of trials) of the distribution. According to the model, very fast RTs (e.g., the fast RTs in the first decile of the RT distribution) for switch trials with long preparation intervals should be just as fast as the fast RTs on nonswitch trials. This is because fast RTs can be assumed to reflect that part of the distribution of RTs that is primarily made up of prepared trials. Because unprepared RTs are longer than prepared RTs, slow RTs (e.g., the slowest RTs in the tenth decile) should consist mainly (or only) of unprepared RTs and thus should be just as slow as RTs in the unprepared (short-RSI) condition. As shown in Figure 6.2, the fast part of the RT distribution for switch trials with a long preparation interval does indeed resemble the distribution of prepared (nonswitch) RTs, whereas the slow part of the distribution approaches the distribution of unprepared RTs. Although the good fit of the failure-to-engage model does not prove that there is no exogenous triggering process involved in residual switch costs, it does suggest that the effect of such a process is small in at least some sorts of task switches.

CONTROL OF MULTI-STEP TASKS ▲

Even in simple laboratory experiments like pressing a key in response to a light, a goal (e.g., respond as quickly and accurately as possible) must be maintained. In everyday life, the goals (e.g., build a career) are generally more complex, as are the

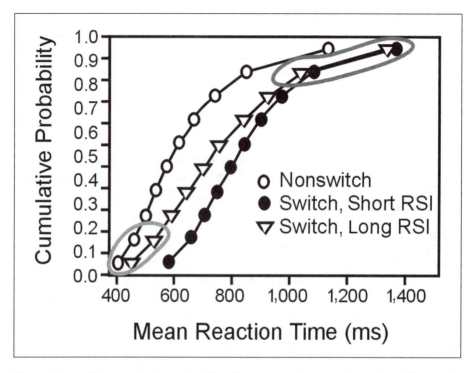

Figure 6.2   The cumulative probability distributions for nonswitch, short-RSI switch, and long-RSI switch trials and the model predictions from De Jong (2000). As predicted by the model, RTs of the fastest long-RSI switch trials resemble those of nonswitch trials (lower left), whereas the longer RTs resemble those of the short-RSI trials (upper right).

steps needed to perform the tasks that lead to the achievement of the goals. Often, subgoals must be created and prioritized in order to break more complex tasks into manageable pieces, and planning is needed to assure completion of the goals. For example, in order to go to work in the morning (in order to build your career) you have to set a number of subgoals. Some subgoals are rather personal, and will not be discussed here. Others have to do with not forgetting to take work-related papers with you, finding your keys, and so on. In order to accomplish even this mundane task, you have to keep your goals in mind, remember to perform certain acts at the appropriate moments, and avoid falling into habitual acts that may not be appropriate at the time.

Performing sequences of actions is heavily dependent on attentional control. We will discuss the failures and errors that can be attributed to lapses in control in Chapter 9. Multi-step tasks also place considerable demands on working memory.

One aspect of memory in this context is prospective memory; that is, remembering to do something at a distant point in time based on planning in the present. For example, while showering you might remember that you need to feed the cat before leaving, but you will need to retrieve that thought in the kitchen. Setting goals, attending to actions and monitoring progress, and remembering to perform acts are all examples of cognitive control.

One approach to studying the control of multi-step tasks is to embed series of component tasks in a cascaded sequence and to study the nature of information processing in these tasks. This approach was used by Elio (1986) to study the relative contributions in learning to solve complex mental arithmetic problems of (1) performing intermediate calculations, and (2) integrating and combining these intermediate results. Participants in these experiments practiced solving particular intermediate calculations (e.g., $x = a * (c - d)$, and $y = \text{maximum}[(b/2), (a/3)]$) and integrative structures for combining the intermediate results (e.g., $x + y$). They then completed a transfer session with new problems using the same intermediate calculations, the same integrative structure, or neither. Performance was better in the transfer session when either the component steps or the integrative structure was the same, relative to completely new problems, although the benefit was longer lasting for the problems with the same integrative structure. A second experiment showed that the amount of transfer to new problems with the same intermediate components was greater when a familiar integrative structure was used, suggesting that the integrative structure provides a context for applying the component steps that aids learning.

More recently, Carlson and Sohn (2000) have studied in more detail the manner in which the information processing tasks involved in solving multi-step problems are carried out. In particular, they tested the theory that the intention to apply operators (i.e., the actions to be carried out) can be considered as the instantiation of task goals. According to the *procedural frame hypothesis* (Carlson, 1997; see also Anderson & Lebiere, 1998), forming task goals "provides a frame to which operands are assimilated to perform mental activities" (Carlson & Sohn, 2000, p. 444). That is, knowing what one needs to do (and how to do it) provides a framework for more quickly processing particular information. Performing a multi-step task fluently is assumed to require the coordination of goals with information given at the beginning of the task and new information computed during the task. Keeping track of previous and current states and goals can put heavy mental demands on the person performing the task. According to the procedural frame hypothesis, which equates the intention to apply operators with goals that organize and drive task performance, participants will benefit when they know in advance what operators will be required.

We have already seen that having learned an integrative structure leads to greater transfer of learning of component steps (Elio, 1986). Carlson and Sohn

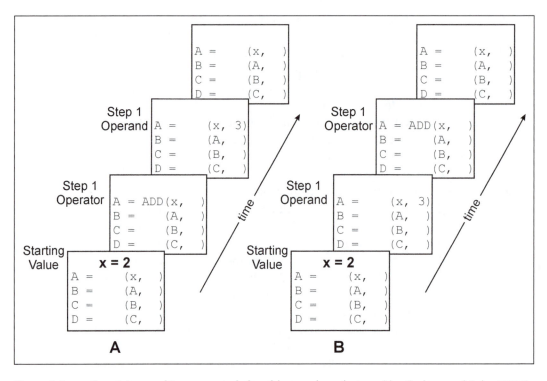

Figure 6.3   Step 1 in a multi-step, cascaded problem such as that used by Carlson and Sohn (2000).

(2000) more directly tested the benefit of having formed intentions to perform certain actions in a series of experiments using so-called cascaded tasks, in which the results of one step were used as input to later tasks, and in which some steps could begin (e.g., goal formation) before other steps (e.g., computing a calculation) were completed. Carlson and Sohn compared the effects of giving participants advance knowledge of operands (i.e., digits to be operated upon) versus operators (e.g., add, subtract, etc.) in multi-step arithmetic problems in which the value computed at one step was used as the starting value for the next step. They hypothesized that performance would be better with advance knowledge of operators than of operands because these allow the formation of intentions to act, and thereby provide a basis for interpreting operands.

For each task, a starting value was displayed that was to be updated through four steps in which each of four different operations was performed in a randomly determined order. The operations were:

▲ *ADD*—Add the current value and the displayed operand.
▲ *DIFF*—Obtain the absolute difference between the current value and the displayed operand.

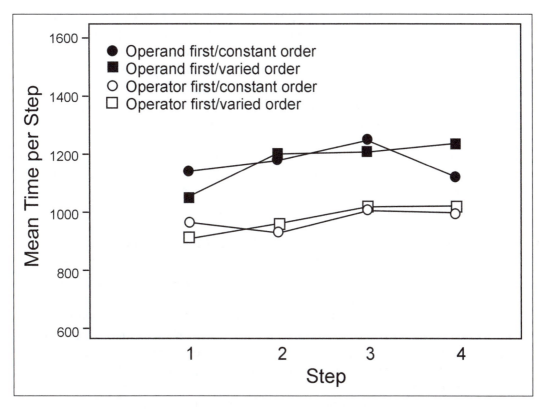

Figure 6.4   Mean time to perform a step (measured from the point at which all information was available for the step) in multi-step arithmetic as a function of condition (operator first or operand first) and fixed or varied order.

SOURCE: Data from Carlson & Sohn, 2000.

▲ *MIN*—Take the smaller of the current value or the displayed operand as the new value.

▲ *MAX*—Take the larger of the current value or the displayed operand as the new value.

Figure 6.3 shows one step in which either the operator is available before the operand (Panel A) or the operand is available first (Panel B). Participants view the first display (starting value) as long as necessary and then press a key to see the next display. The following two displays are shown for 500 ms each. Answers to the problem are given after four steps have been completed. As predicted, solution time was faster in the operator-first condition than in the operand-first condition (see Figure 6.4). Furthermore, the benefit of knowing the operator beforehand did not depend on whether the steps followed in a constant or varied order, suggesting that the effect is not dependent on a strategy for solving a problem (which would be the same for each problem when order is constant, thus eliminating any extra effect of operator foreknowledge), but on the instantiation of goals at each step. Additional experiments showed that the benefit of knowing what to do before knowing what to do it with is a general phenomenon, also being present when the operators for all steps were held in memory, and when the task was spatial (computing the position of a dot in a grid) rather than arithmetic. For example, having the intention to eat a piece of cake is more important in directing your actions than knowing that a spoon or fork is available but not knowing the use to which it will be put.

▲ INTENTIONAL CONTROL AND MULTITASKING

Two of the most important elements in multitasking are keeping current goals activated and remembering what to do both in the current situation and in the future. Shallice and Burgess (1991) developed a test called the "six element test" to study the ability of people to maintain and realize intentions to perform a task. In the six element test, participants are given three different tasks (describing memorable events, writing the answers to simple arithmetic problems, and writing the names of objects depicted in simple line drawings), each of which is split into two sections, A and B. Participants are then told that the first few items in each section are worth the most points and that they have 15 minutes to score as many points as possible, given the constraint that Section B of a task cannot be completed immediately following Section A of the same task. Shallice and Burgess were primarily interested in pinpointing the reason why former patients who had suffered frontal lobe damage, but seemed, on the basis of various tests of information processing, to have fully recovered, nevertheless had difficulties in leading a normal life. They found that these former patients were able to perform each of the component tasks of the six element test at a level comparable to age- and IQ-matched control participants, but that they showed great difficulty in switching between tasks (as required to maximize the number of points earned) and following the rule that Section B of a given task not be done immediately following completion of Section A of the same task.

Additional research (Burgess et al., 1998) has shown that performance on the six element test is statistically related to the tendency to make errors associated with forming and realizing intentions (e.g., deficits in planning, distractibility, poor decision making). Such work is promising in terms of delineating the component processes of multitasking, and may well pave the way for a better understanding of the attentional and memory systems involved in multiple-task performance.

In a study concerned with the role of memory in forming intentions, Allport and Styles (1990) showed that loading working memory with items to be remembered did not interact with the number of tasks to be switched between in a task-switching paradigm. This suggests that memory for intentions may be represented differently than memory for items. Similar conclusions were reached by Burgess and colleagues (see Burgess, 2000), who found that the brain areas shown to be active using positron emission tomography (PET) scanning techniques depended on whether expected items appeared or not. When participants were told to react if a particular event should occur, more activation was found in frontal and parietal regions relative to a baseline condition. This elevated activation was found even on trials in which the particular event did not occur. When the event did occur, however, activation in the thalamus was found, and activation in an area of the pre-frontal cortex (the right dorsolateral prefrontal cortex) was reduced relative to the condition in which the event was expected but did not occur. It seems that the brain areas responsible for holding the intention to react are different than those involved in the actual recognition of the event.

ATTENTION AND SKILL ▲

According to James (1890/1950), "habit diminishes the conscious attention with which our acts are performed" (p. 114). In other words, performance becomes automatic in the sense of becoming independent of attentional control. There are two sides to the withdrawal of attention as actions become skilled: reductions in capacity demands, such that skilled operations can operate without experiencing interference from or causing interference to other ongoing operations, and independence of voluntary control, in that, once started, automatic operations run to completion. In some cases, automatic operations also seem to operate outside of conscious awareness.

According to resource views of attention, in which attention is viewed as a limited-capacity resource (or, in multiple-resource views, as a collection of limited-capacity attentional resources), two tasks can be performed together only to the extent that sufficient attentional resources are available. Both single- and multiple-resource views imply that if one of two tasks is automatized, such that it does not require any attentional resources, it should be possible to perform the two tasks simultaneously with little or no cost, even if they initially placed overwhelming demands on a common resource. One impressive demonstration of the bypassing of attentional limitations was reported by Allport, Antonis, and Reynolds (1972), who found that skilled pianists showed almost no decrement in playing sight-read music (which should be highly automatized for them) when the requirement to shadow auditorily presented words was added.

As another example of the effects of automatization on dual-task performance, consider the tasks of reading while copying down auditorily presented words or sentences. Although reading is highly automatized, it proceeds more slowly in this dual-task context than when it is done in isolation (Hirst et al., 1980). However, after several weeks of extensive practice, people who practice reading while copying down text have been shown to be able to read equally fast in the dual- and single-task contexts. To test the hypothesis that reading while taking dictation is a skill, and is not dependent on the specific sort of material read, Hirst et al. tested the ability of people to read while taking dictation with two types of reading material: short stories and encyclopedia articles. One of the materials was introduced after the other, once the performance criterion with one type of material had been met. Excellent transfer to the new type of text was found, suggesting that a general skill at reading while taking dictation had been acquired.

Another impressive illustration of overcoming apparent processing limitations is Underwood's (1974) comparison of the performance of a skilled shadower (the attention researcher, Neville Moray) to that of average performers on a dichotic listening task (see Chapter 4). In this task, which had originally led to the view of the human as a single-channel processor of limited capacity, Moray was able to detect 66.7% of digit targets embedded among letters in the nonshadowed message—nearly seven times as many as that normally found.

On the basis of such results, Spelke, Hirst, and Neisser (1976) concluded:

> Although individual strategies may have their own limitations, there are no obvious, general limits to attentional skills. Studies of attention which use unpracticed subjects, and infer mechanisms and limitations from their performance, will inevitably underestimate human capacities. Indeed, people's ability to develop skills in specialized situations is so great that it may never be possible to define general limits on cognitive capacity. (p. 229)

Some researchers have argued that this statement may be overly general (see, e.g., Cowan, 1995), and others have argued that the improvements in skill seen in studies such as the one just mentioned, although quite impressive, should not be overstated (see, e.g., Broadbent, 1982). For example, more errors were made in Hirst et al.'s (1980) study when taking dictation while reading than in taking dictation alone.

In most studies of the ability to divide attention across ongoing tasks (or information channels), there is no hard evidence that either task was completely automatized (see, e.g., Allport, Antonis, & Reynolds, 1972; Spelke, Hirst, & Neisser, 1976; Underwood, 1974). In particular, it cannot be ruled out that the primary skill developed by participants in these studies was that of switching attention between the two tasks (as suggested by Broadbent, 1982; Welford, 1980). Although switching takes time, it is plausible to suppose that responses to one task can be buffered, and this buffering provides the participant with the chance to select information or responses on the other task. The presence of response buffers (which are assumed to queue both responses and the instructions for emitting the responses) provides the participant with the opportunity to switch central processing resources between the tasks while still giving the impression of continuous performance on both tasks (see Pashler, 1998, for a detailed description of how this might work).

The effects of automaticity on multiple-task performance were tested in a more strictly controlled study by Schneider and Fisk (1982). Schneider and Fisk used a combination of visual search tasks (see Chapter 3) to examine whether two tasks could be carried out without time-sharing costs when one of the tasks was automatized. They combined a task in which automaticity would be expected to develop (i.e., a visual search task with a consistent mapping of items [numbers and letters] to either the target or distractor sets) with a task in which automaticity would not be expected to develop due to a varied mapping of items to the target and distractor sets so that, for example, digits may have been the target for one trial but distractors for the next. Both tasks were practiced in isolation, with periodic dual-task test sessions in which participants had to monitor two search displays (although only either a consistently mapped or a variably mapped target occurred on any particular trial), and instructions emphasized attending to the varied-mapping task.

It was found that performance of the consistent-mapping task, in which automaticity had developed as a result of practice, was initially worse in the dual-task condition than in the single-task condition. This important finding demonstrates that automatized processes are not entirely "encapsulated" and immune to interference (see, e.g., Neumann, 1987). However, with practice in the dual-task setting, performance of the consistent-mapping task improved to the level of the single-task condition, as did that of the varied-mapping task. Because varied-mapping performance should still be sensitive to available resources, it can be argued that the relative improvement with the varied mapping in the dual-task context was due to a freeing up of resources as the consistently mapped task became automatized. This hypothesis is further supported by the results of subsequent experiments in which subjects were instructed to emphasize the consistent-mapping task, if we assume that this instruction causes people to devote attention to a task that otherwise would be performed without it. In this case, performance of the varied-mapping task seriously deteriorated in the dual-task context. Hoffman, Nelson, and Houck (1983) argued that visual attention is not freed up after large amounts of consistent practice. They found that when a supposedly automatized search task was combined with a visual discrimination task, interference between the two tasks was the result. Apparently, visual attention was still required in the skilled search task.

A CLOSER LOOK AT DUAL-TASK PERFORMANCE ▲

Broadbent (1956) noted that interference between two tasks does not occur just because two stimuli are presented and two responses have to be made. Rather, interference occurs at moments when response selection must occur in both tasks, that is, when events have to be noted and decisions taken to launch actions. In this section, we will examine this notion in detail.

The Psychological Refractory Period Effect

The task-set switching effects discussed in the previous section suggest that it is not possible to fully prepare two separate tasks at the same time. In fact, when people are asked to prepare and execute two tasks at more or less the same time, responses to one or both of the tasks are typically slower than when the respective tasks are performed in isolation. In a typical dual-task paradigm, performers are instructed to identify two separate stimuli and to make a separate response to each of the stimuli. If the tasks involve responding to two widely separated visual stimuli, dual-task performance may suffer because both stimuli cannot be fixated at the same time. Similarly, if the tasks involve responding to two different stimuli using the same motor effector, dual-task performance may suffer because the motor effector can initiate only one response at a time. To avoid peripheral limitations such as these, the stimuli for the two tasks are often presented in different sensory modalities and the responses are made with different effectors. For example, a tone that may be either high or low in pitch might be followed by a white square shown on either the left or right side of the display. The participant's task would be to say "high" or "low" to indicate whether the tone was high or low in pitch and then to press one of two response keys to indicate whether the square was on the right or the left. A very robust finding in such a dual-task paradigm is that RT to the second stimulus (the square, in this example) is slowed relative to when that stimulus is presented alone. Furthermore, the increase in RT is a decreasing function of the interval between the two stimuli; that is, when the time interval between the presentations of the two stimuli (i.e., the stimulus onset asynchrony, or SOA) is short, the relative delay in making the second response is greater than when the SOA is long. This slowing of the response to the second stimulus has been called the *psychological refractory period* (PRP) effect (Smith, 1967; Telford, 1931). As the name suggests, early theorists thought that the first stimulus had a physiological inhibitory effect on the processing of the second, stemming from the refractory properties of neurons. Although this explanation has long been discredited, the name has been retained.

The PRP effect reflects a basic limitation in the ability to perform two tasks at once, implying instead that at least some processes may be carried out for only one task at a time. Major questions of interest from the information processing perspective are how and where (and why!) this limitation occurs. With regard to these questions, De Jong (2000) has suggested:

Serial organization of activities should perhaps be viewed not as the result of resource scarcity prohibiting a presumably more efficient parallel organization, but as an efficient solution to the problem of getting a powerful parallel processing device, the human brain, to support coherent behavior in environments that provide multiple affordances for action. (p. 357)

Consistent with Broadbent's (1956) observation that interference between tasks seems to occur only when a response must be selected, it has been suggested that the PRP effect can be attributed to a bottleneck in processing such that only one response can be selected at a time.

The Response-Selection Bottleneck Model

Most accounts of the PRP effect assume that the slowing of the response to the second stimulus occurs because there is some point in the information-processing sequence at which only one stimulus at a time can be processed. About half a century ago, Welford (1952) and Davis (1957) proposed that there was indeed a bottleneck in dual-task performance, and that this bottleneck had its locus at the stage of response selection. They suggested that the stimuli for two tasks could be processed in parallel, but that the selection of the appropriate response for Task 2 could not occur until the response to Task 1 had been selected. The bottleneck model was inspired by the finding that the slope of the function relating Task 2 RT to the interval between the onsets of the two stimuli tended to be linear with a slope of -1.0. Thus, it seemed that Task 2 RT (RT2) could be captured by a simple model (when the SOA is less than or equal to the time to complete perceptual processes and response selection to the first stimulus) in which: $RT2 = RT_n + RT1 - SOA$, where RT_n refers to the time to perform Task 2 in isolation and RT1 is the mean RT to Task 1. The fact that RT2 is sometimes prolonged even when the SOA is longer than RT1 was explained by Welford as being due to the need to process proprioceptive information about the Task 1 response.

Since the introduction of the response-selection bottleneck model, techniques have been developed to test hypotheses about the existence and location of any bottlenecks in dual-task performance. Basically, the locus of any processing bottlenecks can be determined by selectively influencing the time it takes to complete the processing stages involved in performing each of the tasks. A pioneering technique for interpreting the effects of selectively influencing stages of processing, Sternberg's additive factors method, was introduced in Chapter 2. However, it is not always the case that processes are to be carried out in series, as assumed by the additive factors method. In fact, the finding that RT2 in a dual-task situation is often less than RT1 + RT2 when the two tasks are performed in isolation shows that the dual-task condition can result in a savings in total time to do the two tasks, and therefore suggests that some parallel processing occurs. A technique for determining how processes are arranged is presented in Box 6.1.

Box 6.1 | **Latent Network Theory**

An important technique for determining how processes are arranged is that of examining the patterns of interaction or additivity resulting from the manipulation of stimulus and response factors according to *latent network theory* (Schweickert, 1983; Schweickert & Wang, 1993; Townsend & Ashby, 1983). This technique can be applied to determine whether the processes affected by a set of manipulated factors are executed sequentially or concurrently. Sequential processes imply bottlenecks (because they allow only one operation at a time), whereas concurrent processes indicate that processes can be carried out in parallel. A latent network analysis is carried out by manipulating several factors, such as SOA and the difficulty of the perceptual processing of the stimuli, and then examining the interaction contrasts for these factors. An interaction contrast has the form: $T_{ij} - T_{1j} - T_{i1} + T_{11}$, where T_{ij} is the time taken to respond at level i of one factor (e.g., perceptual discriminability) and

level j of the other factor (e.g., SOA), and the factor levels are numbered in order with respect to the length of the prolongation produced (e.g., easy, medium, and hard discriminations would produce short, medium, and long RTs, and would be numbered 1, 2, and 3, respectively).

The usual finding is that the interaction contrasts are monotonic with increases in the factor levels, and all of the contrasts have the same sign. If the values of the interaction contrasts are positive or zero, the processes are sequential. If the interaction contrasts are negative, they are not. Another way to describe the interaction contrasts is to speak of additivity and underadditivity. Additivity means that the interaction contrasts are zero. This implies serial processing and is the same as saying that there is no statistical interaction between two factors. Underadditivity implies that the interaction contrasts are negative and, thus, that the processes are carried out in parallel.

According to the response-selection bottleneck model, the arrangement of processes in a dual-task situation looks like that shown in Figure 6.5. Starting and stopping points for each process are shown by the small circles (which overlap when the end of one process coincides with the beginning of the next). Stimulus and response processing can occur in parallel in this model; however, as shown by the arrow from Task 1 to Task 2, response selection for Task 2 cannot be carried out until the response to the first stimulus has been selected.

An important construct for our examination of the response-selection bottleneck model is that of slack (Schweickert, 1983), which can be defined roughly as the time during which task information is not being processed. Slack implies a "down time" in information processing caused by the need to wait for a bottleneck to be available. According to the response-selection bottleneck model, slack occurs for Task 2 whenever the time it takes to identify the Task 1 stimulus and select the Task 1 response is greater than the SOA plus the time to identify the second stimulus (see Figure 6.6). Increasing the difficulty of perceptual identification

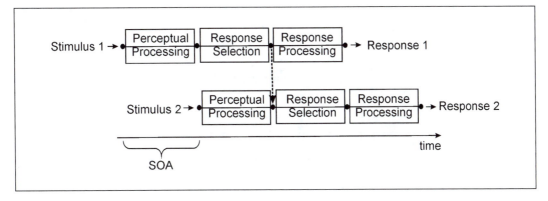

Figure 6.5 The response-selection bottleneck model. Task 1 is shown at the top of the figure and Task 2 at the bottom. The arrow from Task 1 to Task 2 indicates that Task 2 response selection cannot begin until Task 1 response selection is finished.

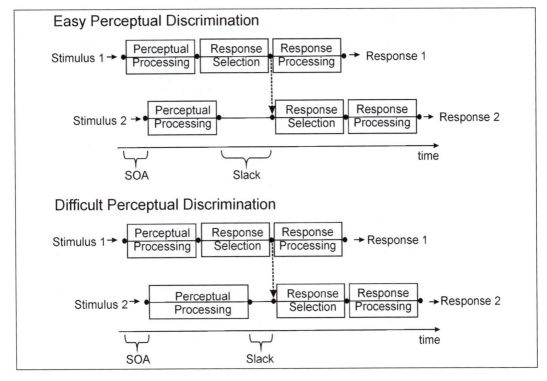

Figure 6.6 Possible prediction of the response-selection bottleneck model for the effects of increasing perceptual difficulty. At short SOAs, slack between processes can hide any effect of changing perceptual difficulty.

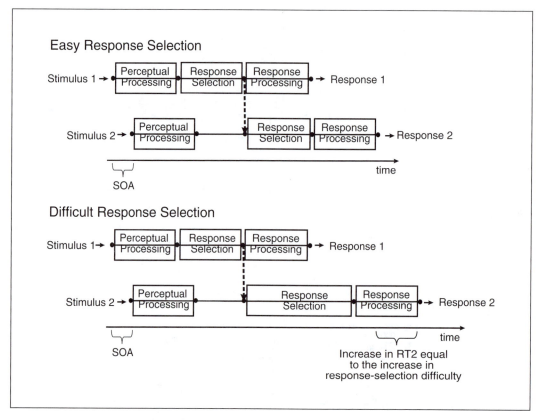

Figure 6.7   According to the response-selection bottleneck model, increasing the difficulty of Task 2 response selection will always have additive effects on Task 2 reaction time (RT2).

of the Task 2 stimulus would thus reduce the amount of slack in the network because increasing difficulty increases identification time. Importantly, there will be no observable effect on Task 2 RT until the slack is used up. However, because there is no slack in the system after Task 2 response selection begins, factors influencing Task 2 response-selection difficulty should be additive with SOA (see Figure 6.7).

One prediction of the response-selection bottleneck model is that increasing the difficulty of Task 2 stimulus identification should be underadditive with the effect of changing SOA between the stimuli for the two tasks (see Figure 6.8). That is, because stimulus identification for the second task can be carried out in parallel with perceptual identification and response-selection in the first task, the effect of increasing Task 2 discrimination time by making the stimuli more difficult to process should be partially absorbed by the slack in the system. Because the

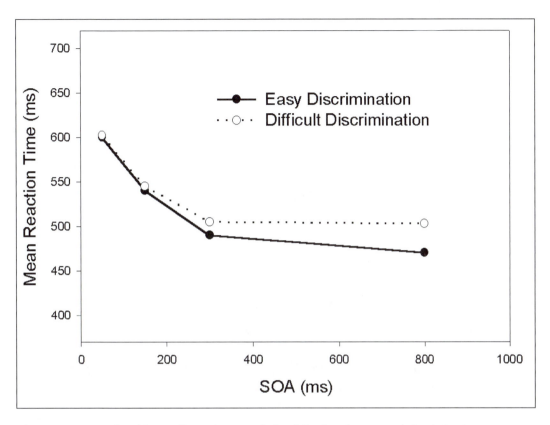

Figure 6.8 Underadditive effects of SOA with the difficulty of perceptual discrimination.

SOURCE: Based on Pashler & Johnston, 1989.

amount of slack increases as SOA decreases, the delay in Task 2 RT will be less at the shorter SOAs than at the longer ones. Pashler (1984b) used a visual search task in which the characters were of high (easy discrimination condition) or low (difficult discrimination) contrast to test this prediction. He compared the performance of a group of people who performed the task by itself with that of a group who performed the search task in conjunction with another task. Consistent with the model, the effect of reducing the contrast of the search array was smaller when the search task was performed in the dual-task context than when performed alone. The negative interaction contrasts (i.e., the underadditivity of stimulus contrast with SOA) imply that stimulus processing for the two tasks can be carried out concurrently. Thus, it does not seem to be the case that perceptual capacity is limited in these simple tasks.

Another important prediction of the bottleneck model is that processes that require the bottleneck—or occur after it—will exert the same effect on RT regardless

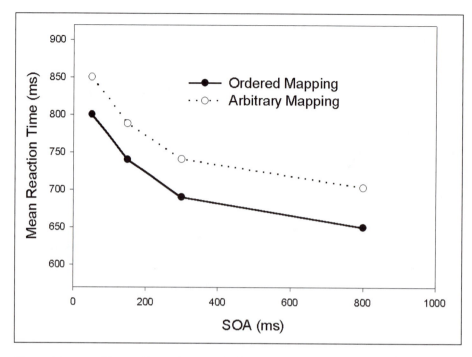

Figure 6.9   Additive effects of SOA with the difficulty of response selection.

SOURCE: Based on McCann & Johnston, 1992.

of the SOA. That is, because the slack prior to the bottleneck is of no consequence for factors that affect response selection or motor processes that occur after the bottleneck, the effects of such factors should be additive with SOA (see Figure 6.7). One factor that strongly influences the ease of response selection is stimulus–response compatibility. Stimulus–response compatibility effects are differences in RT and accuracy that result from the manner in which responses are assigned to stimuli. For example, if the two stimuli in a two-choice task are red and blue circles, performance will be better when the response to the red circle is to say "red" and the response to the blue circle is the word "blue" than vice versa. McCann and Johnston (1992) used the PRP paradigm with two tasks of different stimulus–response compatibility to test the response-selection bottleneck model. Making response selection more difficult by reducing the compatibility of the stimuli and responses should have the effect of prolonging the duration of the response-selection stage. Increasing the difficulty of Task 2 response selection by decreasing stimulus–response compatibility resulted in additive effects (i.e., zero interaction contrasts) of compatibility and SOA (see Figure 6.9), consistent with a bottleneck located at response selection and serial selection of responses in the two tasks.

Modifications of the Response-Selection Bottleneck Model

Although the response-selection bottleneck model has received much support, several of its basic assumptions have been questioned. Some researchers have argued that response selection is not the only locus of a bottleneck; others have argued that there are no bottlenecks at all.

Distinguishing Response Activation From Response Selection

Strictly speaking, the response-selection bottleneck model implies that the two tasks in the PRP paradigm are processed in two separate information-processing streams, with the only effect of one task on the other being that response selection for the second task cannot begin until response selection for the first task is completed. However, several studies have shown that crosstalk between the two tasks can occur as a function of their respective stimulus–response mappings (Hommel, 1998; Lien & Proctor, 2000; Logan & Schulkind, 2000). For example, in Hommel's Experiment 3, the stimulus for Task 1 was a red or green rectangle, and the stimulus for Task 2, which was presented 50, 150, or 650 ms after the first stimulus, was the letter *H* or *S* presented in the same color as the rectangle. For Task 1, subjects were to respond to the color of the rectangle by pressing a left or right key (e.g., "left" for red and "right" for green), and for Task 2 they were to respond to the letter identity by saying "red" or "green" (e.g., "green" for H and "red" for S). Thus, the *response* for Task 2 was conceptually similar to the distinguishing feature of the stimulus for Task 1. At the shortest SOA of 50 ms, both Task 1 and Task 2 RTs showed effects of crosstalk such that RTs were shorter when the stimulus color for Task 1 corresponded with the response "color" for Task 2 than when it did not. It may not seem surprising that subjects were slower to respond when a color they were processing for one task conflicted with a color name they had to produce for another, but this finding does suggest that processing in the two tasks is not strictly parallel and independent. One way that such crosstalk effects might be accounted for is if the stimulus for one task generates activation in the processing stream for the other task prior to the processing bottleneck, which is at the point where the ultimate choice based on the activation is made. Tasks can then affect each other whenever the stimulus and response sets share some similarity, much as for the Stroop and Simon effects in single tasks (Hommel, 1998; Lien & Proctor, 2002).

Graded Capacity Allocation

A characteristic of the response-selection bottleneck model is that response-selection processing is all-or-none. As long as response selection is being performed for one task, it cannot be performed for the other. An alternative view is that although the capacity to perform response selection is limited, it is not all-or-none. According to this resource- or capacity-sharing view, the limited capacity resources required for response selection can be allocated to Task 1 and Task 2 in graded amounts. Recently, detailed analyses of capacity sharing and all-or-none bottleneck models have shown that capacity-sharing models can account for most of the data from the PRP paradigm just as well as the bottleneck models (Navon & Miller, 2002; Tombu & Jolicoeur, 2002, 2003), and thus provide a viable alternative to the response-selection bottleneck model. Moreover, the capacity-sharing models predict that RT for Task 1 should increase as SOA decreases and should be affected by the difficulty of response selection for Task 2, findings that have been observed in several studies.

Bypassing the Response-Selection Bottleneck

Greenwald and Shulman (1973) reported a widely cited study from which they concluded, "The psychological refractory period (PRP) effect of interference between 2 choice reaction time tasks at short intertask intervals was eliminated when both of the tasks were ideomotor compatible" (p. 70). Ideomotor compatibility, mentioned in Chapter 5, refers to situations in which the stimulus is similar to the sensory feedback from the response. For example, the auditory word *dog* is similar to the sensory feedback from speaking "dog," but not from pressing a key. Thus, the spoken response is ideomotor compatible with the stimulus in this example, whereas the keypress response is not. In Greenwald and Shulman's study, the two ideomotor tasks were moving a switch left or right in response to a left- or right-pointing arrow and speaking the letter "A" or "B" in response to the auditory letter *A* or *B*. Their Experiment 2 in fact showed no PRP effect, as they concluded, but their Experiment 1, which differed in several respects, did show an effect. Moreover, although the concept of ideomotor compatibility seems to imply that the PRP effect should also be eliminated when only one task is ideomotor compatible (because that task bypasses the response-selection bottleneck, leaving it free for the other task), substantial PRP effects were still evident.

Elimination of the PRP effect under conditions of ideomotor compatibility seems to be the exception rather than the rule. The PRP effect has been found to occur in most studies for which one or both tasks could be classified as ideomotor compatible (see Lien & Proctor, 2002, for a review). Recently, Lien, Proctor, and Allen (2002) conducted four experiments that were close approximations of Greenwald and Shulman's (1973) Experiment 2 and obtained a significant PRP effect in all experiments, regardless of whether one or both tasks were ideomotor compatible. Greenwald (in press) has argued that in addition to both tasks being ideomotor compatible, it is necessary to use instructions that emphasize responding as fast as possible and, when the stimuli are separated by a short SOA, responding to the two tasks simultaneously. However, with this speed emphasis, a PRP effect was evident in the error rate (which was higher at the short SOAs than at the longer ones), suggesting that the primary influence was on the speed-accuracy criterion (Lien, Proctor, & Ruthruff, in press). Regardless, although ideomotor compatibility is a factor influencing the magnitude of the PRP effect, it is clear that its presence for one or both tasks is not sufficient to eliminate the effect.

A Dual-Bottleneck Model

Although evidence for a response-selection bottleneck of some type is compelling, some studies suggest that there may be additional bottlenecks in performance. For example, not all studies have found additive effects of stimulus–response translation difficulty and SOA. One early study (Karlin & Kestenbaum, 1968) manipulated response-selection difficulty for the second task by requiring either a simple or a two-choice reaction. In this study, the number of stimulus–response alternatives had a larger effect at long SOAs than at short SOAs. A model with only one bottleneck—at response selection—cannot explain these results, but, as De Jong (1993) showed, the results can be accounted for if there is an additional bottleneck at the stage of response initiation that prevents two responses from being initiated in close succession. Normally, Task 2 response selection lasts longer than Task 1 response initiation, with the result that the response-initiation bottleneck is almost always free by the time it is needed for Task 2 processing. However, when Task 2 response selection can be completed very quickly (as when there is only one possible response), the information produced at the response-selection stage may have to wait until the Task 1 response has been initiated before it can be passed along to the motor stage. De Jong obtained additional evidence for such a response-initiation bottleneck by combining a go or no-go Task 1 with different second tasks, including simple and choice reaction tasks. He reasoned that the response-initiation bottleneck would not be a factor in performance on no-go trials because no response was required, even though response selection was required in order to determine whether a response should be made. Thus, any effects of a response-initiation bottleneck should be apparent only on go trials, for which responses for both Task 1 and Task 2 had to be made. Indeed, De Jong found that the difficulty of response selection in Task 2 interacted with SOA on go trials, but had additive effects with SOA on no-go trials.[3]

Other findings consistent with the existence of a response-initiation bottleneck have been obtained with callosotomy patients (i.e., individuals who have had an operation severing the corpus callosum that connects the two cerebral hemispheres). These individuals show substantial PRP effects when one of two keys is pressed with the left hand to a stimulus in the left visual field and the right hand to a stimulus in the right visual field (Ivry, Franz, Kingstone, & Johnston, 1998; Ivry & Hazeltine, 2000; Pashler et al., 1994). However, several variables affect their performance differently from that of control participants for whom the corpus callosum is intact. For example, one callosotomy patient showed a smaller additional cost than control participants of maintaining inconsistent stimulus–response mappings for the two tasks compared to maintaining consistent mappings (Ivry et al., 1998). Moreover, this effect of inconsistency on Task 2 RT was underadditive with SOA for the patient, whereas it was not for the control participants. In addition, when Task 2 was different from Task 1, the callosotomy patient showed no task-switching cost compared to when the two tasks were the same, again in contrast to control participants (Ivry & Hazeltine, 2000). These and related findings led Ivry and Hazeltine to conclude that "processes involved in the establishment and maintenance of stimulus–response codes can be independently supported in the two cerebral hemispheres" (p. 420), with the PRP effect in callosotomy patients possibly reflecting a late bottleneck associated with response initiation and execution.

Effects of Practice on the PRP Effect

If the PRP effect is the result of a fundamental constraint on processing capacity, it would be expected to remain despite long periods of practice. In one early study of the effects of practice on the PRP effect, Gottsdanker and Stelmach (1971) found that the PRP effect was reduced considerably when extensive practice (lasting 87 days) with one SOA was given, but that there was little transfer of this benefit to shorter or longer SOAs. Gottsdanker and Stelmach concluded that the decrease in the PRP effect over the course of practice was due to a strategy specific to coordinating responses at short intervals, rather than to a more general improved ability to perform two tasks in rapid succession. The persistence of the PRP effect over extended practice has since been demonstrated in a number of experiments using a variety of stimuli, responses, and SOAs (Dutta & Walker, 1995; Van Selst, Ruthruff, & Johnston, 1999). Although reductions in the PRP effect are sometimes quite dramatic, especially when the stimuli (e.g., tones in Task 1 and visually presented numbers and letters in Task 2) and responses (vocal for Task 1 and manual for Task 2; see Van Selst et al., 1999) do not seem to share common resources, the effect itself typically does not disappear entirely. Ruthruff, Johnston, and Van Selst (2001) and Ruthruff et al. (2003) presented evidence that the reduction of the PRP effect with practice is primarily due to a decrease in the duration of the bottleneck stage for Task 1. According to Ruthruff et al., the bottleneck may essentially be latent—that is, have little effect on Task 2 performance—when the operations of the bottleneck stage for Task 1 are fast enough to be completed before the stage is ready to begin for Task 2. Thus, it appears that bottlenecks in response selection, initiation, or both cannot be bypassed even when the joint tasks are practiced extensively.

Alternatives to Bottleneck Models

Although the evidence for a true, structural bottleneck in performance is compelling, at least one research group maintains that the essential aspects of multiple-task performance can be captured by a theoretical framework in which multiple tasks are executed concurrently and information processing (including response selection) occurs in parallel (Kieras, Meyer, Ballas, & Lauber, 2000; Meyer & Kieras 1997a, 1997b). Their explanation of the PRP effect is based on an information-processing architecture, the executive-process interactive control (EPIC) framework, which assumes no attentional capacity limitations. Instead, emphasis is placed on executive control functions, that is, "how people schedule tasks, allocate percep-tual-motor resources, and coordinate task processes" (Kieras et al., 2000, p. 681). Hence, within the EPIC framework, the psychological refractory period effect is attributed to a task strategy, specifically one of response deferment for Task 2, without recourse to the idea of a structural processing bottleneck. According to the strategic response deferment account, prior to the start of a trial only Task 1 is given priority, or, in the terminology of the EPIC framework, put into an "immediate" mode. Task 2, on the other hand, is put into "deferred" mode, meaning that no information pertaining to response selection will be sent to motor processors. According to this view, Task 1 execution can act as an "unlocking" event that then shifts Task 2 to immediate mode so that motor activation and execution can occur.

The EPIC framework has been used to account for a large number of experimental results (see, e.g., Kieras et al., 2000) and has the attractive feature of considering higher-level, executive processes. However, numerous alternative models can be generated within the framework, and any specific model developed within it, such as the response deferment model, has many parameters, making the formulation and testing of specific predictions difficult. Moreover, it could be argued that the need to shift from "deferred" to "immediate" mode in EPIC is essentially equivalent to renaming either the response-selection or the response-initiation bottleneck. The essential difference between those researchers who favor a bottleneck account of the PRP effect and those who argue against a bottleneck, therefore, is not whether there is a point in processing at which some operation for the two tasks typically is carried out sequentially, but whether this sequential processing is a "built-in" limitation of the basic information-processing architecture or a strategy that subjects adopt in order to comply with the task instructions.

SUMMARY ▲

In this chapter, we discussed fundamental limits on performing some aspects of information processing, as well as the manner in which skill in allocating attentional resources can develop. Whether or not particular tasks can be performed together has been shown to depend on the nature of the tasks, the level of skill attained in each component task, and the relative amount of attention allocated to the respective tasks. People can learn to make tradeoffs between certain pairs of tasks that require attentional resources. The ability to time-share is a skill that develops with practice in multiple-task contexts, and, if performance for one of two tasks has been automatized, dual-task performance may show little loss in efficiency.

Although it seems that in skilled performance of complex tasks, competing goals can be held active such that different task components can be integrated into smooth performance, some experiments reveal limits on the ability to do two things at once. Even in ostensibly simple tasks like naming a digit when it is presented on the left in a display and saying whether it is odd or even when it is presented on the right, people have trouble keeping the instructions straight (i.e., keeping the task goals current). Moreover, when several stimuli, each requiring a speeded response, are presented in close succession, a bottleneck in selecting responses is revealed. Basic limits in doing two or more things at once seem to be a fundamental aspect of human performance. Other findings indicative of such limits are encountered in the remaining chapters.

▲ NOTES

1. Preparation, when it occurs, may indeed be all-or-none (De Jong, 2000), but for some types of tasks, additional, inhibitory effects are likely to exert an influence on performance.

2. In this view, the stimulus can be seen as a cue that triggers the appropriate stimulus–response mapping. It could be argued that this cue can also be internally generated.

3. Recent electrophysiological measures of the lateralized readiness potential suggest that findings that led to the formulation of the dual-bottleneck model, namely the under-additivity obtained with simple versus choice reaction tasks, may be due to the tendency of people to make response anticipations (i.e., to begin response initiation processes before the stimulus has been processed) at long SOAs. Because anticipations are more likely to be correct in the simple reaction task (where only one response is possible) than in the choice reaction task, the difference between simple and choice RT increases as SOA increases (Sommer, Leuthold, & Schubert, 2001).

CHAPTER 7

MEMORY AND ATTENTION

with Mark Nieuwenstein

M any of the research findings concerned with attention are, directly or indirectly, dependent on memory. If an observer is able to report what he or she has seen, we can assume that the information is remembered, however briefly. Sometimes it is difficult to determine whether memory or attention is responsible for a certain effect. For example, some priming effects can be attributed to memory (e.g., semantic priming effects assume the involvement of either an implicit or explicit memory system), whereas others might be attributed to a change in stimulus processing (e.g., a rejected location may be subject to temporary inhibition) that may or may not involve memory processes. In this chapter, we attempt to bridge the research on memory and attention, examining in detail the moments at which attention is required for memory, and vice versa.

Without memory, we would be unable to recognize objects, sounds, and smells, to experience continuity in an ever-changing world, to understand complex sentences, or to perform sequences of behavior such as those involved in tying shoelaces or driving a car. Attention plays a prominent role in determining what, and how well, information is learned. For example, if, while reading this text, your attention is distracted by a conversation being held next door, you may still be able to read, but your chances of being able to recall what it was you were reading decrease, with the result that you may have to return to the top of the page to discover what the text was about. However, as you go through a particular segment of the text for a second time, you may recognize parts of the text as having been read before. These feelings of familiarity indicate that inattention does not always prevent the acquisition of information, and that the failure to recall information at will does not necessarily imply that the information has not been stored in memory.

The fact that memory can be evidenced by performance on one test but not on another, as illustrated by the difference between recall and recognition of text, indicates that different sorts of memory tests may be needed to determine whether something was actually stored in memory. Memory tests have in common a learning phase, during which the to-be-learned information is presented, and a subsequent retrieval phase, during which the learned information is recalled or used in performing a particular task. One important distinction concerns the difference between so-called *explicit* and *implicit memory tests*. Explicit tests require that one consciously refer back to the learning phase. For example, one may be asked whether one has seen a particular face before, or to recall all words presented earlier in the experiment. On the other hand, implicit tests indirectly assess memory by presenting tasks that do not seem to be related to the information presented during the learning episode. However, performance on these tasks may nevertheless be influenced by whether that information is retained in some form of memory. For example, an experiment may begin with the task of classifying words as being either nouns or verbs. An explicit test of memory for these words would be to ask participants to write down all the words they can remember. An implicit test of memory for these words would be to ask participants to solve anagrams (e.g., "ERTE"). Memory for the words from the learning episode would then be evidenced by faster solving times when the solutions (e.g., "TREE") were presented in the classification task than when they were not. The difference between explicit and implicit memory tests is a methodological one in that it refers to the nature of the test demands. The primary distinction between explicit and implicit tests is that people are instructed to retrieve specific information in the former case, but not in the latter. Retrieval of specific information might occur consciously or unconsciously in either case.

In this chapter, we explore the extent to which different tests tap into different aspects of memory while focusing on the role of attention in forming, storing, and retrieving memories. We begin the chapter with a brief overview of sensory and short-term, or working, memory. We explore the extent to which attentional selectivity determines the contents of memory, and try to answer the question of whether attentional selection is a prerequisite for remembering information over various periods of time. We then explore how memories of perceived information are formed and stored in such a way that we can report them. Subsequently, we discuss the attentional demand of the different processes that are involved in the consolidation and retrieval of previously presented information. Here, we revisit the dual-task bottleneck model introduced in Chapter 6 as we explore whether these processes depend on the same central bottleneck revealed in dual-task performance. We then examine the intertwining roles of attention and memory in the control of ongoing behavior, focusing on how these cognitive processes contribute to the adaptability and flexibility of human performance.

SENSORY MEMORY ▲

One way to study the relation among perception, memory, and attention is to design experiments in which information is presented only very briefly and to study the processes involved in reporting the information. Such research has focused on determining both the amount of information that can be perceived and retained and the rate at which this information decays from memory. As you will see in the following sections, perceived information may initially be stored in modality-specific sensory memory stores from which attention can select the information that is relevant to current intentions and goals.

Iconic Memory

In 1960, Sperling showed that when observers were asked to report all the letters they could see from a briefly flashed display consisting of 9 to 12 letters, they could usually report only 4 or 5 letters—the same number of items that could be reported in the early experiments on the span of apprehension (i.e., the number of items that can be apprehended during a single glance), described in Chapter 1. In spite of their failure to report more than approximately four letters, observers in Sperling's experiments often reported the feeling of having seen all of the letters in the display. This led Sperling to hypothesize that there must be a sort of visual memory that holds all the items in the display for a period of time, but that this representation faded before all items could be reported. In other words, the simple question, "What did you see?" implies that observers should report both what they remember and what they may already have forgotten. Sperling therefore devised a so-called *partial-report procedure* (in contrast to the whole-report procedure used initially) to determine whether more items could be apprehended from the display than initially seemed to be the case.

The partial-report procedure consists of briefly presenting an array of letters that is then followed by a cue (e.g., a high-, middle-, or low-pitched tone) that

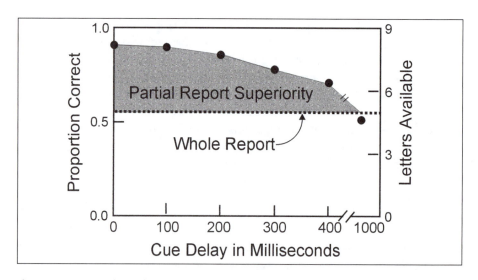

Figure 7.1   Decline of the partial-report superiority effect.

indicates which row of the array must be reported. Sperling found that when the cue was presented shortly after the display, observers were able to report all of the letters in the cued row. Because they did not know in advance which row would be cued, it could be concluded that all of the letters present in the display were stored in some manner, and that representations of the letters were still available at the time of the cue. The higher percentage of reported letters obtained with the partial-report procedure is called the *partial-report superiority effect.* By varying the interval between the display and the cue, Sperling showed that the availability of the letters decreases as the cue is delayed. Specifically, after a delay of 500–800 ms, the partial-report superiority effect disappears, and performance is no better than with whole report (see Figure 7.1). This indicates that the lifespan of the iconic image is less than a second. A similar conclusion has been reached on the basis of the so-called *temporal integration paradigm,* in which two visual displays are briefly presented at different temporal intervals and observers are required to judge an aspect of an image that can only be inferred from the information integrated from both displays. For example, each display may consist of a random configuration of dots that, together, make up a 5 × 5 matrix of dots with one dot missing (see, e.g., Di Lollo, 1977). By asking the observer to report the location of the missing dot, one can determine whether the displays were integrated into a single percept. When more than one second intervenes between the presentation of the two displays, performance falls to the level of chance.

The partial-report superiority effect shows that all items from a briefly flashed array are initially stored in some kind of memory buffer in which they may reside for up to 800 ms. This memory buffer has been called *iconic memory* (Neisser, 1967). Neisser suggested that all items are initially held in iconic memory, and then transferred to a more durable store at the time of the cue. The relatively small number of items that can be reported in the whole-report condition can be taken to indicate that either the transfer process or the durable store is of limited capacity. Sperling (1960) found that increasing the presentation duration of the display from 15 to 500 ms (thus increasing the time available for the transfer of items from the iconic to the durable store) did not affect the number of reported items in a whole-report procedure. Thus, it seems that the locus of the limitation lies in the capacity of the durable store.

The iconic image itself has two stages of representation, a retinal afterimage and a later stage of representation that combines the images from the two eyes (Turvey, 1973). The retinal afterimage is specific to the eye on which the presented information is projected, as is evidenced by the fact that presenting a bright blank field (e.g., a brightness mask) to one eye has no disruptive effect on the retinal afterimage retained on the other eye. Apparently, this earliest form of representing visual information that is no longer physically present in the environment is computed before the information from both eyes is combined. This early iconic image can be distinguished from a second stage of representation in which the information from both eyes is combined into a single representation that can be used as input for subsequent stages of information processing. Together, these two stages of iconic memory contribute to a memory system that has a relatively large capacity (at least 12 items, based on experiments with 3×4 arrays), but a short duration (based on the disappearance of the partial-report superiority effect within 800 ms).

In addition to providing insight into both the amount of information that can be retained in iconic memory and the rate at which this information decays, the partial-report procedure has been used as a technique for assessing the level of processing achieved by the information retained in iconic memory. If a particular cue can be used to select target information from the iconic image, and thus results in a partial-report superiority effect, it can be concluded that the information that distinguishes the cued from the noncued items is represented in the image. For example, the success of location cues (Sperling, 1960) in increasing the proportion of letters reported indicates that the location of the items is represented in the iconic image.[1] Following this line of reasoning, the effectiveness of a number of cues has been investigated. For example, some studies investigated whether a difference in color or brightness between the to-be-reported items and the distractor items would result in a partial-report advantage, even though the target items were randomly positioned in the display. In this case, items are originally presented in different colors or luminances, and the cue indicates which items should be reported (e.g., a high tone might be the cue to report the items that were presented in red). The results from studies using perceptual characteristics such as color and luminance to differentiate between target and distractor items

Figure 7.2   A demonstration of iconic memory at work.

consistently reveal a partial-report superiority effect (see, e.g., Van der Heijden, 1992). Results using the category of the stimuli as a cue (e.g., report letters and ignore digits) are mixed. In general, selection by category is effective only when subjects know beforehand which category of items should be reported (see, e.g., Bundesen, Pedersen, & Larsen, 1984).

It has been argued that iconic memory might serve the function of contributing to a stable perception of the world (Cowan, 1995). To demonstrate how this might work, cut a long, narrow slit (about 3 mm × 4 cm) in an index card. Now, hold the card still in your hand and move the book back and forth so that you see the image in Figure 7.2 behind the slit. You should be able to see the whole image, and it should even look a bit better than it does in the figure. As McCloskey and Watkins (1978) reported, images viewed this way (with the help of iconic memory) tend to look narrower than in real life. Iconic memory has been likened to an integrative visual buffer in which the visible contents of successive fixations are superimposed according to their environmental coordinates to produce a stable, overall, image of the environment (McConkie & Rayner, 1976). However, when iconic memory is "erased" by presenting a mask (e.g., rows of X's) after the letter display, so is the partial-report superiority effect, and it has been argued that the overwriting of the iconic buffer with every new fixation makes the integrative visual buffer interpretation of the function of iconic imagery implausible (see, e.g., Tatler, 2001). Whether iconic memory has a function remains an elusive issue; it may simply be a byproduct of physical limitations of the visual system.

Echoic Memory

The discovery of visual sensory memory naturally led to the question of whether such a sensory memory buffer also exists for auditory information. Many studies have indicated that there are broad similarities between visual and auditory sensory memory. First of all, analogous to the visual modality, two separate forms of early auditory memory can be distinguished. The first form of auditory sensory memory appears to reflect an ear-specific representation of the physical characteristics of the stimulus (Deatherage & Evans, 1969). This representation can be thought of as an "echo" of the heard information that may last 150–350 ms after the auditory stimulation has been terminated. This early memory store has been called echoic memory (Neisser, 1967). The second form of auditory sensory storage is a representation of information that was previously heard that may last up to several seconds. In contrast to the initial ear-specific echo, this representation combines the input from both ears, and may store multiple previously presented items at the same time (Glucksberg & Cowan, 1970).

In an attempt to apply the partial-report procedure of Sperling (1960) to auditory sensory memory, Moray, Bates, and Barnett (1965) devised a paradigm referred to as the "four-eared man." In one experiment, participants were presented with four sequences of consonants at a rate of two items per second, with each sequence being presented from a different location (one sequence was presented in front of the participant, one behind, and the other two to the left and right of the participant). In the whole-report condition, participants were simply asked to report as many consonants as possible. In the partial-report condition, participants were first presented with the sequences and afterwards cued to report the consonants presented from just one direction. Although a partial-report superiority effect was observed, it was markedly smaller than that observed with visual stimuli. As Pashler (1998) points out, one reason for the relatively small partial-report advantage may be that the cue used to differentiate between the different sequences (e.g., relative location of presentation) may not be as effective in segregating auditory information as it is for visual information. Instead, auditory attention may be more easily directed on the basis of acoustic properties such as pitch and frequency than on the basis of location because of the low spatial resolution of the auditory system (see, e.g., Scharf & Buus, 1986; see also Chapter 4). However, this hypothesis has not yet been tested empirically.

In addition to confirming a significant, albeit weak, partial-report superiority effect for auditory information, subsequent studies in which the temporal interval between the termination of the auditory stimulation and the presentation of the cue was varied showed that the advantage for partial report could last as long as 5 seconds, nearly an order of magnitude longer than for visual stimuli (Darwin, Turvey, & Crowder, 1972). Norman (1969) used a dichotic listening task (see Chapter 4) to show that auditory information can be retrieved for several seconds after its presentation. In one of his experiments, participants were presented with two messages, one to each ear, and were instructed to shadow (i.e., repeat out loud) one of the messages. When asked to report what had been presented to the unattended ear, participants showed virtually no memory for the unattended message. However, when the presentation of the messages was interrupted and participants were immediately asked to report two digits that had been presented to the unattended ear, they were able to do this perfectly. Using a similar procedure, Glucksberg and Cowan (1970) found that the digits presented to the unattended ear could be reported for up to 5 seconds after presentation.

In summary, there is abundant evidence in favor of the existence of memory systems that represent and briefly maintain information generated in the early stages of information processing. These systems exist in both the auditory and the visual modality, and for both domains they can be fractionated into ear- or eye-specific sensory aftereffects and a later representation of the combined input from both sensory organs. Sensory memory is characterized by a large capacity, susceptibility to masking, and a short lifespan. By prolonging the persistence of perceived information, sensory memory may play a role in making our perceptions more stable.

▲ WORKING MEMORY

Perhaps no concept so well reflects the interplay between attention and memory as that of working memory. The term *working memory* is often used synonymously with the term *short-term memory* to refer to a memory system that holds information relevant to current goals and activities. The adjective *working* implies that this kind of memory, in contrast to the iconic and echoic sensory memory stores, encompasses more than just passive storage of information. According to Baddeley (1998a; see also Baddeley & Hitch, 1974), working memory can be defined as "the alliance of temporary memory systems that play a crucial role in many cognitive tasks such as reasoning, learning, and understanding" (p. 6). It can be distinguished from *long-term memory,* which is the more or less permanent collection of facts, knowledge, and records of experiences. The working memory model proposed by Baddeley consists of three components: a *visuo-spatial sketchpad,* a *phonological* (or articulatory) *loop,* and a *central executive* (see Figure 7.3). The visuo-spatial sketchpad and phonological loop are often described as "slave" systems. The visuo-spatial sketchpad is responsible for storing and manipulating visual images, and the phonological loop is called upon to store and manipulate speech-based information. The central executive is an all-purpose attentional controller that is presumed to supervise and coordinate the work of the slave systems.

The Phonological Loop

As its name implies, the phonological loop is thought to contain phonological information; that is, it represents information according to how it sounds. This has implications for measuring memory span (i.e., the length of a list of items that can be correctly repeated back 50% of the time) and for information processing. People can accurately report back more phonologically dissimilar items than similar items. For example, if memory span for dissimilar words (e.g., mat, fir, nut,

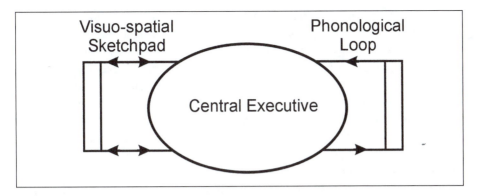

Figure 7.3   Baddeley's (1996) model of working memory.

SOURCE: Based on Badderley (1996).

log, cup) is seven items, memory span for phonologically similar words (e.g., top, pop, shop, ship, tip) may be only five items (see, e.g., Conrad & Hull, 1964). Memory will also be impaired if recall is accompanied by the presence of spoken syllables, even when the syllables are irrelevant and should be ignored. It seems that the presentation of speech or speech-like sounds directly interferes with the information held in the phonological loop, and the more similar it is in sound, the greater the interference (see, e.g., Salamé & Baddeley, 1987). The fact that the phonological loop is unable to deal with multiple sources of conflicting information indicates that it has only limited capacity for processing information. This limited capacity of the phonological loop is also reflected in the dependence of memory span on the time it takes to pronounce the items to be remembered. The more time it takes to pronounce an item (because of either the speaker's rate of speech, the language used, or the type of item), the fewer items that can be remembered (see, e.g., Schweickert & Boruff, 1986). In general, people can remember the amount of information that they can pronounce within about 2 seconds (Baddeley, 1998a).

The role of the phonological loop in performing various tasks has been explored by loading the phonological loop with words to be remembered and then testing people's ability to perform other tasks. This secondary-task methodology has proved to be an important tool for studying the nature in which complex tasks are performed (see Chapter 9 for more examples of the application of secondary-task techniques). Using loading tasks that are thought to selectively interfere with either verbal or spatial memory, for example, it is possible to investigate whether different task processes draw on the same mechanisms or resources.

With regard to the phonological loop, it has been found that even when the phonological loop is heavily loaded, people are able to comprehend and learn new information—although performance on these tasks is impaired (see Baddeley, 1998a, for a review). Thus, although the phonological loop seems to be critical for holding and manipulating verbal information, it appears to be only one part of the working memory system. Complex behavior (such as solving arithmetic problems while remembering a list of digits) likely depends heavily on attentional allocation strategies (see discussion of working memory capacity in Chapter 10). Keeping information current in the phonological loop requires rehearsal, and rehearsal would seem to require attention. With practice, however, one can learn how long it is possible to leave off rehearsing without losing the information in the phonological loop. Such a strategy of "refreshing" information periodically, rather than rehearsing it constantly, can free up resources so that other tasks can be performed concurrently (Naveh-Benjamin & Jonides, 1984).

Even though we are able to learn new information or perform complex tasks while using our working memory for other activities, just holding information in working memory can influence the nature of information processing. For example, presenting a cue before presentation of a stimulus display can enhance processing. Holding information in working memory can also tie up processing resources that are needed for task performance. For example, the imposition of a memory load can tie up resources that would otherwise be used to keep task goals current. The importance of the availability of memory resources for keeping us on track is demonstrated by the fact that conflicting information is more difficult to ignore when memory is loaded. De Fockert, Rees, Frith, and Lavie (2001) showed this by requiring subjects to remember either an easy (e.g., 01234) or difficult (e.g., 03241) series of numbers while performing a Stroop-like task. The Stroop-like task was to read the names of famous people imposed on distractor faces. On congruent trials, the face matched the name. On incongruent trials, the face was familiar, but different than the name. Neutral trials in which the face was unfamiliar to the subject were also included. When the more difficult series of numbers had to be remembered, subjects showed more interference (as measured by the difference in reaction time on incongruent and congruent trials) than when the easy sequence had to be remembered. This finding is interesting because increasing perceptual load in such a task has been shown to actually decrease the amount of interference found (see, e.g., N. Lavie & Tsal, 1994; see also Chapter 5)—a result that is exactly opposite to the effect of increasing memory load. This suggests that memory processes may be required to actively inhibit irrelevant information. Perceptual load may have the effect of sharpening the ability (or highlighting the need) to selectively attend to relevant information, but memory resources must be available to suppress distraction.

The Visuo-Spatial Sketchpad

Not all information can be easily represented in a phonological code. For example, imagine a block letter F. Without looking at the F on the page, and starting at the bottom left corner, count how many "outside" (right turn) and how many "inside" (left turn) corners there are (there are seven outside and three inside corners). Tasks such as this have been used to study the existence and nature of spatial memory, or, in terms of Baddeley's (1998a) model, the visuo-spatial sketchpad. One important finding is that such tasks can be efficiently combined with tasks that require verbal memory (e.g., shadowing words), but suffer when a spatial task (e.g., judging whether rotated letters are normal or mirror-reversed images) must be performed concurrently.

Logie et al. (1988) used the secondary-task methodology described in the previous section to analyze aspects of performance in a complex video game (the Space Fortress game, a video game developed specifically to study complex task performance; Mané & Donchin, 1989) and to evaluate the role of working memory in the game. They used a battery of secondary tasks that included tasks that required paced generation of responses, verbal working memory tasks, and visuo-spatial working memory tasks (e.g., remember a sequence of movements through a 4 × 4 matrix). The task battery was administered both early and late in practice with the Space Fortress game. Early in practice, performance was more affected by a visuo-spatial than by a verbal memory load, whereas verbal and visuo-spatial tasks produced equal effects later in practice. Additionally, experienced players actually showed more interference from a concurrent, paced response task than did less experienced players, suggesting that strategies to control the timing of game responses developed with practice.

Awh and Jonides (1998; Awh, Jonides, & Reuter-Lorenz, 1998) have argued that an intimate link exists between spatial working memory and spatial selective attention. In particular, they argue that the processes involved in keeping a representation active in working memory are the same as those used in selectively attending to locations. In Chapter 3, you saw that there is an interaction between spatial attention and visual processing such that focusing attention on a region of space enhances visual processing at that location (see, e.g., Mangun, Hansen, & Hillyard, 1987). That attention to location may be involved in rehearsing information in spatial working memory is suggested by the fact that maintaining locations in memory (e.g., trying to remember where a dot had been presented) results in faster RTs to another, unrelated visual stimulus when that stimulus is presented at a remembered location than when presented at a location nearby (Awh, Smith, & Jonides, 1995). Another line of evidence that there may be a process of rehearsal for spatial memory that resembles spatial selective attention comes from brain imaging studies and scalp recordings of electrical activity in the brain. Brain imaging studies show a high degree of overlap between the areas involved in spatial working memory and the areas involved in selective attention to spatial regions (Awh & Jonides, 1998). Similarly, both remembering and actively attending to specific locations lead to enhancement of the N1 and P1 components (both associated with early stimulus

---

Box 7.1 | **Memory and Attentional Networks**

New evidence regarding the relation between attention and memory comes from recent work using fMRI (see Chapter 2 for a description of this technique). For example, Cabeza et al. (2003) directly compared brain activation during episodic memory retrieval and sustained attention. The episodic memory task was to report whether a displayed word had been present on an earlier presented list, and the sustained attention task required that participants monitor a single character for a period of 12 seconds to determine whether it flickered once, twice, or not at all. Both of these tasks were performed in a scanner, and fMRI images were made and compared for the two tasks.

Cabeza et al. found some differences between the two tasks, including relatively more activation of the left prefrontal cortex in the memory task (presumably reflecting semantic processing) and relatively more right prefrontal cortex activation in the attention task (presumably reflecting monitoring processing). However, there were striking similarities. Both tasks made demands on a fronto-parietal-cingulate-thalamic network. Because the attentional task made essentially no demands on working memory, Cabeza et al. argued, on the basis of parsimony, that the right prefrontal cortex and parietal activation commonly seen during the performance of memory tasks reflects attentional processes. In particular, they argued that the right prefrontal cortex may reflect the sustained attention demands of evaluating the output of retrieval processes, and the lateral parietal, thalamic, and anterior cingulate activations may reflect shifts of attention from the processing of the retrieval cue to the processing of the recovered information. More studies directly comparing memory and attention tasks are needed to shed light on the interactions between these two fundamental processes.

---

processing) of the event-related potentials (ERPs) to a probe stimulus (e.g., a checkerboard pattern flashed on a screen) presented at the attended or remembered location (Awh, Annlo-Vento, & Hillyard, 2000). See Box 7.1 for more physiological evidence of links between attention and memory.

The Central Executive

Perhaps no concept so well reflects the interplay between attention and memory as the question of how memory is controlled. This question could be phrased in a much broader manner: What is control and how is it achieved? This question was addressed in part in Chapter 5, where we considered the role of inhibition in assuring smooth control of information processing. It was also addressed in Chapter 6, in the discussions of goal setting and task-set switching. In this section, we consider the nature of the processes that mediate between memory systems, or, that are responsible for selecting and maintaining strategies.

The working memory model of Baddeley and Hitch (1974) gave a central place to executive processes. As described earlier, the model consists of a central executive, a visuo-spatial sketchpad, and a phonological loop, with the central executive being viewed as the "controller" of the two slave systems. Much research has been done on the slave systems—the visuo-spatial sketchpad and the phonological loop—but the nature of the central executive has remained rather vague. In his 1998 book, *Human Memory: Theory and Practice,* Baddeley describes the central executive as more of an attentional system than a memory store. Unfortunately, giving the system a different label does not make its function any more explicit. One thing should be clear to the reader by now: Attention is a multi-faceted collection of different processes that may facilitate (or inhibit) detection, identification, and even memory and response selection.

Much of the research on cognitive control (i.e., executive functioning) has been performed with so-called frontal patients—patients who have suffered injury to the frontal lobes of the brain (see Chapters 11 and 12). However, even healthy persons often exhibit symptoms of poor cognitive control (see also Chapters 9 and 10), particularly when executive aspects of memory are taxed by the requirement to perform a secondary task. For example, Humphreys, Ford, and Francis (2000) loaded the working memory of subjects by having them perform a version of the trails test (a sort of connect-the-dots test used to assess neurological functions; Heaton, Grant, & Mathews, 1991) while performing everyday acts such as wrapping a gift or making tea. In their version of the trails test, subjects had to both work their way through the alphabet and count, starting with an arbitrary letter-digit pair. For example, if the experimenter said "B8," the participant would continue with "C9," "D10," "E11," and so forth. This test was considered to place demands on both verbal working memory and on central executive aspects of memory because of the demand to both say the letters and digits aloud and keep track of the last letter and digit produced. Participants in another condition (the articulatory suppression condition) were simply required to repeat the word "the" as quickly as possible in order to tax only verbal memory. Humphreys et al. reasoned that the differences in performance between subjects in the two conditions should reveal the role of executive control in performing familiar multi-step tasks.

Participants in the trails test condition made many more errors than those in the articulatory suppression condition—though not nearly as many errors as frontal patients. Most of the errors involved omitting steps. Unlike patients, these participants rarely added unnecessary steps, repeated actions, or committed spatial (e.g., using too little paper) or semantic (e.g., wrapping the bow instead of the gift) errors. Furthermore, unlike the patients, they were also observed to correct

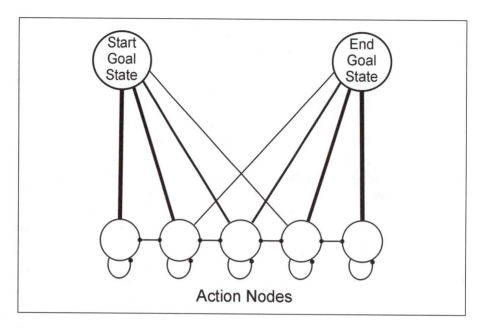

Figure 7.4   A competitive queuing network model of sequential errors in a multi-step task.

SOURCE: Humphreys, Forde, & Francis, 2000. Reprinted with permission from MIT Press.

erroneous actions (e.g., stop in mid-reach when reaching for the wrong item). Almost all of the observed errors occurred on the step following the commission of an error on the trails test. The correlation between errors on the two tasks suggests, not surprisingly, that executive memory is involved in multi-step tasks.

G. W. Humphreys, Ford, and Francis (2000) proposed a "competitive queuing" network (see Figure 7.4) to account for the pattern of sequential errors that was observed in patients performing the trails test. In this model, actions are represented by "nodes." Goal states send activation to each of the nodes, with the most activation being to the first step for the "start" goal unit and to the last step for the "end" goal unit. In addition to receiving top-down activation from goal units, nodes also receive "bottom-up" activation due to the presence of previously learned associations between the objects present in the environment and the actions represented by the nodes. The action represented by the node that currently has the most activation is executed, and after an action has been executed, the node is inhibited, allowing the next action to take place. According to the model, temporary loss of the goal state caused by the need to devote working memory to correcting errors on the trails task may have led to the loss of activation for component actions and to increased competition from other objects present for actions in a different part of the sequence. Such an account is consistent with errors such as omitted actions, out-of-sequence actions, and the "capture" of action due to the bottom-up activation getting the upper hand (e.g., if an action in the sequence is more commonly associated with another, more familiar action, that action may be performed instead of the one associated with the current goal). In normal subjects, the goal state can be reinstated quickly enough to correct most actions before they result in an overt error.

THE ROLE OF ATTENTION IN ENCODING AND RETRIEVAL ▲

As you will see in the section on conceptual short-term memory, the process of extracting semantic information from perceived inputs seems to proceed automatically, that is, without being restricted by attentional limitations. On the other hand, later processes associated with consolidating information into reportable representations in working memory are subject to severe capacity limitations. These observations are consistent with late-selection models of attention (see, e.g., Deutsch & Deutsch, 1963; Duncan, 1980) that make assumptions tantamount to saying that the level of processing at which attentional selection occurs can be equated with the limits of short-term memory. According to these models, recognition of familiar objects proceeds unselectively and is not subject to capacity limitations. Limitations occur at the point where the results of this (unconscious) analysis must be further processed. Attention is thus needed to ensure that processed information is remembered. More recently, *working memory capacity* has been defined as the ability to control the allocation of attention (Engle, 2002; see Chapter 10).

One model of short-term memory that incorporates the idea of attention as a selection mechanism is that of Cowan (1988, 1995). Cowan attributes the capacity limits of short-term memory (following James, 1890) to the limit on the number of items to which attention can be allocated at the same time. In addition (following Hebb, 1949), he attributes the time limits in holding information current in memory to limits in the activation of items in memory. This dichotomy of processes (attention to items and activation of items; see Figure 7.5) allows for separate effects of attention and simple exposure to items. For example, in the dichotic listening paradigm (see Chapter 4), a change in the physical properties of the stimulation on the unattended channel can capture one's attention from the attended channel (Cherry, 1953). In Cowan's view, this would indicate that physical features of the stimulus activate a part of the memory system outside of the current focus of attention.

MEMORY CONSOLIDATION AND ATTENTION ▲

In order to be able to interact with the environment, we need to identify and interpret the information that surrounds us. We do this by linking our current percepts

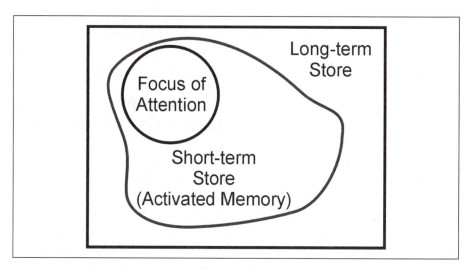

Figure 7.5   Cowan's (1988, 1995) theory of short-term memory capacity as the number of items that can be attended.

of the different items around us, such as objects and faces, to their representations in long-term memory. Matching percepts to their corresponding object representations enables recognition of objects and people, and we can use the associated knowledge to guide our actions towards or away from them. Given that the input of information from our senses changes almost continuously, either because we ourselves move around or because of changes in the source of the information itself (i.e., when the person we are looking at turns his or her head), interpretations must be integrated over time in order to experience continuity. Clearly, both the activation of representations stored in long-term memory and the integration of currently perceived information with previously perceived information must occur rapidly on a moment-to-moment basis.

Conceptual Short-Term Memory

The processes of identification and categorization are thought to occur "on the fly" and rapidly; that is, they commence as perceptual information from the stimulus accumulates during its presentation, and they are completed during the first second after a particular stimulus has been presented. It has been proposed that the initial identification and categorization of stimuli are mediated by a so-called *conceptual short-term memory* system (Potter, 1993, 1999). This memory system differs from iconic memory in that it enables the rapid computation of postcategorical, meaningful representations of perceived stimuli. In this regard, the conceptual short-term memory system is similar to the idea of a durable store (Coltheart, 1983) mentioned earlier. According to Potter (1999), the conceptual short-term memory system enables the identification of perceived stimuli by means of activating the semantic knowledge that corresponds to the stimulus being processed.

Substantial evidence supports the view that identification and interpretation are rapidly completed; for example, subjects are able to read, understand, and recall sentences that are presented word for word with *rapid serial visual presentation* (RSVP; for a review see Potter, 1999). During RSVP, simple visual items such as letters, words, or pictures are presented one after the other, at the same location, at a rate of about 10 items per second. In this way, RSVP mimics the way in which we perceive the world, that is, as a sequence of brief snapshots (i.e., fixations separated by saccades), but without requiring that the observer make eye movements. The fact that people are able to read sentences presented with RSVP indicates that a presentation duration of 100 ms is sufficient for each word to be identified. Furthermore, observers can easily detect a particular, verbally specified, picture (e.g., a boat) presented in RSVP (Potter, 1976).

The Attentional Blink

In many tasks, potentially relevant information must be selected by rapidly distinguishing between target information (e.g., a number) and nontarget information (e.g., words). For example, we are not interested in the meaning of the words of a text when we are searching that text for the presence of a particular telephone number. As discussed in the previous section, in order for selection to be based on the identity or category of a particular stimulus, that stimulus must have entered conceptual short-term memory. As you shall see, such identification and categorization is not always sufficient for the stimulus to be recalled.

A common technique for investigating the attentional requirements of identifying and storing visual information is to require participants to search RSVP sequences for the occurrence of particular, prespecified targets items that are to be either detected or identified and reported. In a detection task, observers may simply be asked to report whether a particular item (e.g., a black "X") was presented. More often, targets are specified on the basis of a feature such as color or category, and the task is to identify the targets (e.g., name the red words or report any letters in a stream of digits). Implicit tests, such as determining the threshold for identification of words related to the target (see, e.g., Martens, Wolters, & Van Raamsdonk, 2002) might also be used to determine whether targets that could not be reported were nevertheless identified.

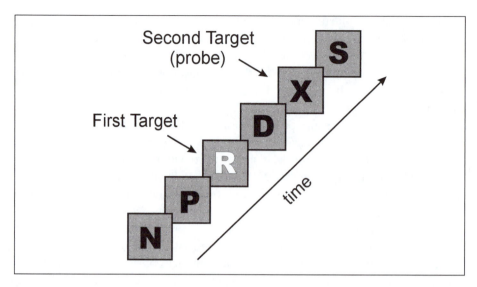

Figure 7.6   An RSVP task used to study the attention blink. The task is to name the white letter and to report whether an X was present. The figure shows a Lag 2 trial.

We mentioned earlier that subjects could read whole sentences presented in RSVP. However, this exceptional performance is largely dependent on the context provided by the sentence. When the task is to read unrelated words, performance often shows a pronounced dip after only one word has been identified. For example, Broadbent and Broadbent (1987) found that people often could not detect a second word, defined either by a physical feature or category, when it appeared within half a second of the first one.

The limits of identification in RSVP sequences have since been studied in a large variety of experiments in which two targets (often denoted T1 and T2) are presented in a stream of distractors. The number of distractors (and, hence, the time interval between the two targets) is varied in order to study the time necessary to process the targets (see Figure 7.6). The temporal interval between the first and second target is generally called the "lag"; that is, the number of items that the second target "lags" behind the first one. For example, at Lag 1 there is no intervening distractor, and, in this case, the second target follows the first in the RSVP stream. At Lag 2 there is one intervening distractor, and so forth.

The typical finding obtained with this procedure is that, although participants are able to identify and report a single target in RSVP, report of the second target often fails. For example, Raymond, Shapiro, and Arnell (1992) showed that when an "X" (i.e., the probe shown in Figure 7.6) had to be detected after identification of another target (e.g., the white letter shown in Figure 7.6), probe detection was

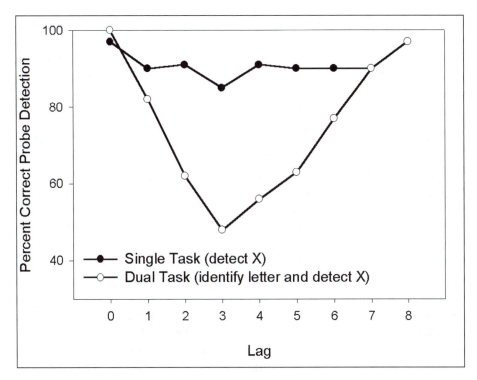

Figure 7.7   Detection of the second target (the probe) as a function of lag and whether the first target had to be reported.

SOURCE: Based on data from Raymond et al. (1992).

far worse than when the first target could be ignored (see Figure 7.7). Furthermore, when the target was identified, detection of the X depended on the lag, with performance following a U-shaped function across lags. As shown in Figure 7.7, probe detection was quite good when it was the white letter (i.e., when the white letter was the letter "X"; shown by performance at Lag 0) and relatively good when the probe was presented directly after the target (i.e., at Lag 1). Performance dropped dramatically up to Lag 3, and then increased as a function of lag until the level of performance seen in the condition in which only the X had to be detected was again achieved at Lags 7 and 8. Because this transient impairment in probe detection could not be caused by perceptual limitations, but, instead, seemed to stem from interference of the processing requirements of the target, Raymond et al. termed this deficit the *attentional blink*.

The attentional blink is a robust phenomenon (see Visser, Bischof, & Di Lollo, 1999, for a review). In addition to letters, both spoken and written words or word-like stimuli (see, e.g., Duncan, Martens, & Ward, 1996), and even pop-out features

(Joseph, Chun, & Nakayama, 1996), can trigger or suffer from an attentional blink. Several models have been proposed to account for the attentional blink. Consistent with late-selection models of attention (see, e.g., Deutsch & Deutsch, 1963; see also Chapter 3), each of these models assumes that selection occurs late in processing, that is, after the stimuli have been identified and categorized. In this section, we will discuss one model of the attentional blink, the two-stage model proposed by Chun and Potter (1995).

Chun and Potter's (1995) two-stage model of the attentional blink provides a parsimonious account for most of the experimental findings. Following Potter (1993), Chun and Potter proposed that the first stage of processing the items presented with RSVP consists of the identification of the items within the conceptual short-term memory system. This is assumed to occur rapidly and without being restricted by attentional limitations; therefore, all items in the RSVP sequence should initially be identified. Indeed, several studies have shown that both the distractors presented in the interval between the two targets and second targets that could not be identified because of the blink produce priming effects on subsequent implicit memory tests. The presence of priming effects indicates that these items must have been processed up to a semantic level, even though they were not reported. For example, Maki, Frigen, and Paulson (1997) showed that when a distractor word that was semantically associated with the second target was presented during the attentional blink, performance on the second target improved relative to a condition in which none of the distractors was related to the second target.

The fact that a second target is often not reported when it is presented within half a second of a first indicates that, even though the second target may be processed to a certain extent, the resulting representation requires further processing in order to be stored in memory. Such further processing occurs in Stage 2 of the two-stage model, and is assumed to draw upon limited attentional capacity. Because of this limited capacity, efficient processing requires that only relevant items be transferred into this stage. The selection of relevant items is described as occurring by means of matching the conceptual representation of a perceived item to a target template. If a match is found, the conceptual representation is selected for Stage 2 processing and is stabilized and consolidated into a memory trace that can be reported. However, if a previous item is still receiving Stage 2 processing, selection of a new item has to wait because Stage 2 processing is limited. As a consequence, the short-lived conceptual representation of a to-be-selected second target is vulnerable to decay and may be overwritten by new information while the first target is being processed in Stage 2.

As shown in Figure 7.7, performance on the second target is relatively unaffected by the blink when the two targets are presented in direct succession, thereby giving the curve of second target performance across lags its characteristic U-shaped form. The relatively good second target performance at Lag 1 has been termed *Lag-1 sparing*. The two-stage model accounts for Lag-1 sparing by assuming that the selection process that is initiated upon detection of the first target is sluggish. That is, although selection may begin as soon as the first target is detected, it does not shut off rapidly enough for the item that follows T1 to be excluded from access to Stage 2 processing. In this regard, the selection process can be likened to an attentional "gate" that opens rapidly upon detection of a target, but takes approximately 150–200 ms to close. Because the gate is open longer than the actual duration of the first target, the immediately following item may automatically gain access to Stage 2. If this item happens to be the second target, both targets gain access to Stage 2 processing, with the consequence that the limited capacity for consolidating information is shared between the two targets. This results in the second target being spared from the attentional blink.[2] However, if a distractor immediately follows the first target, the second target arrives after the gate has been closed. Because this gate remains closed until Stage 2 processing of the first target is completed, the second target is often lost before it can be selected for Stage 2 processing. The gradual increase in T2 performance across longer lags indicates that the chance to gain access to Stage 2 gradually increases as more time elapses.

In summary, it appears that reporting a particular item briefly presented in an RSVP sequence (when that RSVP sequence lacks intrinsic structure) requires that the item be identified, selected, and consolidated. The attentional blink phenomenon reflects a limitation in the process of consolidating information from an unstable conceptual representation into a stable representation in memory. This limitation is evidenced by the fact that no new inputs can be consolidated while a previous item is being consolidated. On the other hand, this limitation does not affect the first stage of identification that is mediated by conceptual short-term memory, as indicated by the finding that items that cannot be reported nonetheless influence performance on implicit memory tests.

The two-stage model of the attentional blink (Chun & Potter, 1995) is supported by measurements of the ERPs taken during performance of an RSVP task. Vogel, Luck, and Shapiro (1998) examined several ERP components that correspond to different aspects of information processing: The N1 and P1, both of which reflect sensory processing; the N400, which reflects semantic analysis; and the P3, which reflects the updating of working memory. Vogel, Luck, and Shapiro designed a number of experiments in which an enhanced ERP component would or would not be expected if a stimulus was processed up to the point at which the particular component occurred. By comparing waveforms time-locked to second targets presented either at Lag 1 (before the attentional blink), Lag 3 (during the attentional blink), or Lag 7 (after the attentional blink; see Figure 7.8, left panel), Vogel et al. showed that only the P3 component was affected by the blink (see Figure 7.8, right panel). That is, whereas the sensory and semantic analysis of the second target proceeded unimpeded by the attentional blink, the ERP component that is assumed to

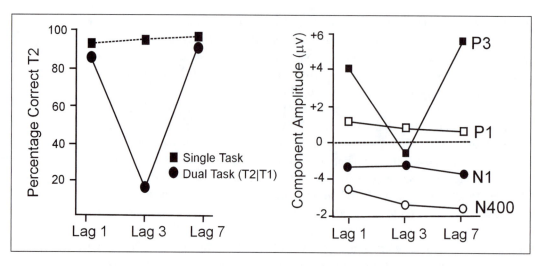

Figure 7.8   Performance in an attentional blink task (left panel) in single-task (detect only second target) and dual-task (detect two targets) conditions and the voltage differences for ERP components elicited by the second target when presented before (Lag 1), within (Lag 3), and after (Lag 7) an attentional blink (right panel).

SOURCE: Adapted from Vogel, Luck, & Shapiro, 1998.

reflect the updating of working memory was significantly attenuated during the attentional blink. These findings are in agreement with both the fact that distractors that are presented during the attentional blink facilitate the processing of semantically related targets (Maki, Frigen, & Paulson, 1997) and the assumption of the two-stage model that the attentional blink reflects a deficit in the consolidation phase of storing information in working memory (Chun & Potter, 1995).

Change Blindness

One of the impressive features of the mind is that, in spite of the fact that the input from our senses changes almost continuously, it enables us to experience continuity and stability in our perception of the world. Although it has been assumed that the ability to experience such continuity is the result of storing and updating detailed representations of the environment, recent findings showing failure to detect changes in visually presented scenes indicate that these representations may actually contain far less information than was previously assumed.

The failure to detect changes in the visual environment is a robust phenomenon that can be observed in a variety of tasks. In each case, the task of the observer is to detect a single difference between two images. An important prerequisite for so-called *change blindness* to occur is that the presentation of the two images be separated by a disruptive visual event, or mask. If disruption of visual processing does not occur (e.g., when the two images are presented in direct succession), the change can easily be detected because it results in a local transient (change in color, luminance, or form) at the location of the retinal image that corresponds to the location of the changed item. Such a local transient is somewhat like a motion signal that captures attention, and, hence, facilitates change detection. Presenting a visual event that results in either a global transient (e.g., a bright blank screen after an image display) or in multiple transients across the whole image obscures the effect of a local transient. When the difference between two images does not pop out because of a local transient, observers have to compare their representation of the previous image with the currently perceived image in order to detect a change. The critical assumption in studies of change blindness is that change detection depends on whether the relevant element was in the attentional focus at the time of the switch between images. If the representation of the first image does not contain a focused view of the changed element, no change will be detected.

A common technique for studying change detection is the "flicker" paradigm, which involves presenting two versions of a visual scene that have one difference. Some examples of differences between pictures are that a particular object is present in one picture but not in the other, that a particular object is colored differently, or that a particular object has changed position. The pictures are presented briefly, for approximately 200 ms each, and each is followed by a blank screen. Participants are instructed to search for the change and to press a key as soon as they detect it. The sequence is repeated until a response has been made. (Figure 10.2 in Chapter 10 shows an example of such a change detection task.)

A robust finding in such experiments is that observers rarely detect the change during the first cycle. In fact, sometimes the sequence must be repeated for more than a minute before the change is detected. How fast the change is detected depends on which object has been changed, with changes being detected more easily in objects that form the center of interest in a picture (Rensink, O'Regan, & Clark, 1997). Although this finding suggests that change detection is more likely to occur when the changed object is attended, it has also been demonstrated that change blindness can occur even when observers apparently attend to the object being changed. Simons and Levin (1998) provided a striking example of change blindness for presumably attended information under naturalistic conditions. They showed that people in conversation with an unfamiliar person who asked them for directions failed to notice that this person was replaced by a different person when their view of this person was interrupted by two people carrying a door. This finding is rather counterintuitive because one can assume that people pay attention to the people they are talking to. Nevertheless, the participants in Simons and Levin's study often failed to notice the substitution of the old person by the new person, even though they wore different clothes, had different faces, talked differently, and so forth.

As indicated by a recent review of the change blindness literature (Simons, 2000) that details no fewer than five possible accounts of the change-blindness phenomenon, the effect has generated much interest but is still not well-understood. It appears that attentional limitations restrict the amount of detail we perceive in such a way that these details are not retained in memory from one moment to the next. There are, however, different views on the exact nature of the processing limitations that underlie the inability to detect changes.

▲ THE BOTTLENECK MODEL REVISITED

In Chapter 6, we discussed a model of dual-task performance that assumes that a response can be selected for only one task at a time. In this section, we discuss whether retrieval of items from memory is also subject to this bottleneck.

The Attentional Blink and the PRP Effect

The RSVP paradigm used to study the attentional blink can be viewed as a double-task paradigm because at least two targets must be detected and responded to. However, because the response to both targets is unspeeded, psychological refractory period (PRP) effects like those discussed in Chapter 6 are not generally a factor in performance. When the paradigm is modified, so that a speeded response is required to the first target, PRP effects are found. In this case, the requirement to make a speeded response to the first target causes a profound deficit in the detection of the second target, even when the first target is a relatively easy auditory discrimination (e.g., classifying a tone as high or low) and the second target is visual (e.g., detecting an "X" or "Y" in a stream of letters; Jolicœur, 1999). This is an interesting result given that other researchers have found that perceptual processing can occur in parallel with other processes. Thus, since the response to the second target is unspeeded, one could predict that no particular decrement in second task processing would occur. An explanation for the deficit in detection of a visual target presented shortly after a tone requiring a speeded response is that the memory consolidation processes needed to fix the visual target in a reportable form require access to the same limited, central bottleneck that is required to select the appropriate response to the tone target. This interpretation is consistent with the idea that the attentional blink has a relatively late processing locus. Thus, even if perceptual processing of the second target does occur, the early perceptual information is lost before it can be consolidated in memory.

The process that ensures that perceived information is remembered and reported has been called *short-term consolidation* (Jolicœur & Dell'Acqua, 1999). Short-term consolidation seems to be dependent on the same limited capacity

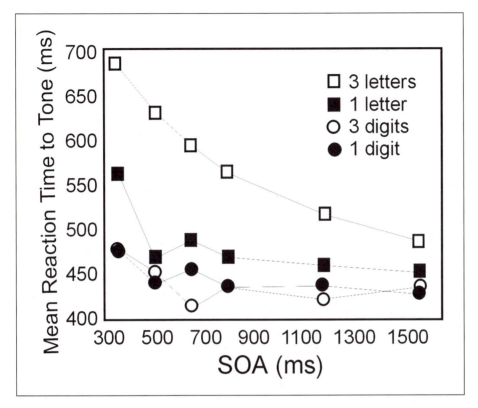

Figure 7.9   Mean reaction time to a tone (Task 2) as a function of SOA between the visual stimulus and the tone and Task 1 stimulus type (1 vs. 3 letters to be remembered or digits that could be ignored).

SOURCE: Adapted from Jolicœur & Dell'Acqua, 1999.

central bottleneck that is revealed in studies of dual-task performance. For example, Jolicœur and Dell'Acqua combined a memory task (remember one or three letters) with a speeded response to a tone. Subjects were first shown one or three letters to remember, or one or three digits, which did not have to be remembered. After a delay of 350–1,600 ms, a high- or low-pitched tone was presented, and a speeded classification response had to be made. Finally, subjects reported which letters, if any, had been presented at the beginning of the trial. The time to make a speeded response to the tone depended on the number of letters to be encoded and on the stimulus onset asynchrony (SOA) between the letters and the tone. At the shortest SOA (350 ms between the presentation of the letters and the presentation of the tone), response times to the tone were elevated for both the one- and three-letter conditions (see Figure 7.9). When three letters had to be remembered, tone RT was affected for much longer intervals. This result suggests that the time to complete short-term consolidation depends on the amount of information to be remembered. Short-term consolidation causes interference in the sense that it delays speeded responses to other stimuli. It is also subject to interference. Stimuli that are briefly presented during the interval required to make a response to another stimulus are sometimes remembered more poorly than if they are presented alone (Jolicœur & Dell'Acqua, 1999; but see Pashler, 1998).

Do Memory Operations Occupy the Central Bottleneck?

It has been shown that just holding items in memory sometimes has little effect on the performance of other tasks. However, when the information in memory has to be searched through in order to find the right data to perform a task, response times are slower than if the information is simply present (Carlson, Sullivan, & Schneider, 1989). In other words, accessing working memory may require the same limited resource processes that are required by other information processing tasks, such as making judgments, performing mental arithmetic, or simply selecting a response. It has been shown that memory scanning (i.e., searching through a set of remembered items to determine whether a presented item is in the memory set) cannot be carried out concurrently with even the simplest arithmetic tasks (Ehrenstein, Schweickert, Choi, & Proctor, 1997), and that memory scanning is subject to the same central bottleneck revealed in the psychological refractory period paradigm (Heil, Wahl, & Herbst, 1999).

Retrieval of items from long-term memory also seems to be subject to the central bottleneck. Carrier and Pashler (1995) combined a tone classification task (manual response to a tone) with a memory retrieval task (recall of the second member of a pair in a paired associates task in which pairs of words were learned). The difficulty of the retrieval was manipulated by giving subjects more practice with some word pairs than with others before the dual-task trials were begun. The effect of retrieval difficulty of the second word of a pair in response to the first word was additive with SOA, suggesting that retrieval had to wait until the response to the tone task had been made. Pashler (2000) argues that the central bottleneck comes into play whenever a retrieval operation has to be performed. In other words, two retrievals cannot be carried out concurrently. Whether one is retrieving the action plan for making a response or a word that has been learned earlier in the experiment, one of the retrieval operations will, according to Pashler, have to wait until the other one can be carried out. This limitation on retrieving two responses also applies when both responses are made to the same stimulus.

As discussed in Chapter 6, perceptual operations do not seem to be subject to the central bottleneck. However, when subjects have to perform other operations on the identified stimuli, such as mental rotation (e.g., determining whether a rotated image is a letter or its mirror image), limitations that could be due to the central bottleneck sometimes emerge (Ruthruff, Miller, & Lachman, 1995). Not all studies find the additive effects of SOA and mental rotation that would suggest that mental rotation occupies the central bottleneck. For example, Heil, Wahl, and Herbst (1999) found that the effects of SOA and degree of rotation were under-additive. This underadditivity could be interpreted as indicating that the rotation task also makes use of perceptual processes, and that the increase in perceptual difficulty is absorbed into the slack created by Task 1 response selection. In fact, studies using the additive factors method attribute mental rotation to stimulus identification, a stage hypothesized to occur before response selection (Sanders, 1990).

Whether or not memory retrieval occupies the central bottleneck remains a tricky question. One of the problems is defining the nature of retrieval. Earlier, we discussed the process of transferring early representations of stimuli into short-term memory. In terms of memory retrieval, one can ask whether retrieval processes begin before the final transfer of the accumulated information to short-term memory takes place. Evidence that some retrieval of information occurs in parallel, before retrieval reaches a central bottleneck, is found in recent studies (see, e.g., Logan & Delheimer, 2001). These studies show that some aspects of retrieved information about the second stimulus presented in a dual-task paradigm can influence judgments about the stimulus presented for the first task. In Logan and Delheimer's experiments, for example, both tasks required subjects to judge a word as having been presented in a study list or not. They found that recognition judgments about the first word were faster if both words were either targets (i.e., if both words had been presented earlier) or lures (i.e., both words had not been previously presented), than if one word had been previously presented and one had not. This congruence effect was found when both words were presented simultaneously and when the second word was presented after an SOA of about 250 ms. The presence of this crosstalk between the stimuli is inconsistent with the assumption that retrieval of the second item cannot begin until retrieval of the first item has finished (see Chapter 6). Crosstalk between the stimuli indicates that sub-jects began processing the second stimulus before finishing processing of the first. This suggests that at least some aspects of retrieval can occur in parallel.

PROCEDURAL MEMORY ▲

It is an old adage that once you learn how to ride a bike you never forget it. It seems that the old knowledge resides in the very bones and muscles that carry out the action. A skill such as bicycle riding illustrates that there are different ways of learning and knowing how to do something. The two forms of "knowing" are sometimes described as "knowing that" versus "knowing how" (Squire & Cohen, 1984). Memory may be explicit, that is, based on the conscious directing of attention to the act of recall for remembering facts (e.g., knowing that one should sit astride a bicycle or that the front brake should not be used alone at high speeds), or it might, although reflecting past experience, proceed without active attention or conscious recall, as in the performance of a skilled action (e.g., knowledge of how one should balance the bicycle even in turns). *Procedural learning,* or learning evidenced by improvements in the execution of task elements, may involve a different, *procedural memory* system than the declarative learning of facts and instructions. Tulving (1985) defines procedural memory as a memory system that "enables organisms to retain learned connections between stimuli and responses, including those involving complex stimulus patterns and response chains, and to respond adaptively to the environment" (p. 387). Procedural memory is based on different methods of acquiring, representing, and expressing knowledge than is declarative memory, and is characterized by a different kind of conscious awareness. According to Tulving, procedural knowledge can only be overtly expressed, and is not available for conscious introspection. Procedural memory is also assumed to provide knowledge that can be used to guide action even though it contains no specific information about the past. This assumption is largely based on the finding that amnesics often show an ability to acquire information at a normal rate, and can maintain normal performance across delays, even in the absence of the ability to recognize having seen the particular stimuli or task before.

▲ IMPLICIT LEARNING

When you want to learn how to perform a complex task, such as using a copy machine to create a booklet, you read the instructions or, better yet, find someone who can show you how to perform the task. You clearly intend to learn the task, and you pay attention to the relevant pieces of information. In recent decades, researchers have started to examine whether and how learning occurs without intention—and without conscious awareness of what is being learned. Learning without intention is often called implicit learning. A hallmark of implicit learning is that learners often are not aware of any performance improvements and cannot state what they have learned. Implicit learning has also been observed in amnesic patients. These individuals may not even remember having performed the task before, yet they show close to normal performance improvements as a function of practice.

One of the tasks most often used to study implicit learning is the *serial reaction time task*. In this task, the observer is to press an assigned key whenever a stimulus appears. The response may be made to the position of the stimulus, its color, or some other stimulus attribute. Two conditions are usually compared—a random condition, in which stimulus position is chosen randomly from trial to trial, and a repeating sequence condition, in which the position of the stimulus is

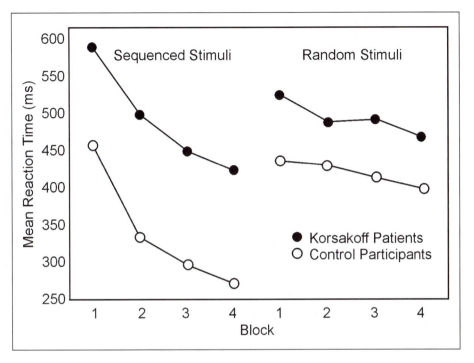

Figure 7.10   Sequence learning in normal and amnesic subjects.

SOURCE: Adapted from Nissen & Bullemer, 1987.

predictable. For example, Nissen and Bullemer (1987) assigned keypresses to the spatial location of targets. They compared the performance of subjects who practiced the task with a repeating sequence (designating the positions from left to right as A, B, C, and D, the repeating sequence was D-B-C-A-C-B-D-C-B-A) with that of subjects who received the stimuli in random order. People who practiced the task with the 10-element repeating sequence showed much more improvement than those who practiced the task with a random presentation of stimuli, even though they were neither informed that there was a repeating sequence nor instructed to look for repetitions while performing the task.

Although they had not been instructed to look for regularities in the stimulus presentation, the participants in the repeated-sequence condition of Nissen and Bullemer's (1987) study did report being aware of the sequence. In order to determine whether awareness was necessary for learning, Nissen and Bullemer repeated the experiment with Korsakoff patients, a group of individuals characterized by a profound amnesia that prevents them from recognizing and recalling material to which they have been exposed. As expected, the Korsakoff patients reported no awareness of the repeating sequence; however, their performance showed a degree of learning of the sequence comparable to that of the normal subjects (see Figure 7.10).

Apparently, learning can and does occur without awareness, although persons with intact memory function do seem to pick up verbalizable knowledge, as well.

Given that learning can occur without awareness, it is interesting to ask whether it also can occur when attention is diverted from the task. One way to assess the role of attention in learning is to compare learning in a single-task condition, where only the task to be learned is performed, with a dual-task condition, in which a secondary task is performed. The requirement to perform a secondary task should take attention away from the primary task. Cohen, Ivry, and Keele (1990) used a serial reaction time task in combination with distractor tasks of different difficulties to examine the role of attention in implicit learning. The sequences they used contained either unique associations, in which each stimulus uniquely specified the following (e.g., A always followed by C), ambiguous associations (e.g., A might be followed by C when preceded by B and by D when preceded by C), or both. Ambiguous sequences were not learned under the dual-task conditions, but unique associations were. This suggests that sequence learning depends on two processes, an automatic association process that links adjacent items and an attention-demanding higher-order process that builds hierarchical codes based on grouping elements of the sequence at a higher level.

The attentional demands of implicit learning have also been explored using sequences that are unlikely to be explicitly learned and secondary tasks designed to produce little disruption. Jiménez and Méndez (1999) showed that general attentional demands do modulate sequence learning using a serial reaction time task like the one described earlier, in which subjects responded to stimulus location, but in which the identity of a stimulus on a given trial gave probabilistic information about where the next stimulus would appear. In some conditions, participants also had to count target shapes and report the total at the end of each block. Participants in both the single- and dual-task conditions appeared to learn the sequence of stimulus locations. However, only subjects in the dual-task conditions, in which the identity of the target had to be attended to in order to perform the counting task, learned the predictive relationships between stimulus identity and stimulus location. Thus, selective attention to the relevant dimensions does seem to be necessary for learning to occur. In other words, it is necessary to pay attention to a predictive dimension if this dimension is to enter into a predictive relationship.

In summary, sequence learning can occur implicitly, and this learning occurs at least partly as the result of automatic associative processes. Associative processes operate independently of mental load, but only on events that are active in working memory. Although some simple associative learning occurs automatically, learning involving specific episodic contexts for events depends on attention (see also Cowan, 1988, 1995).

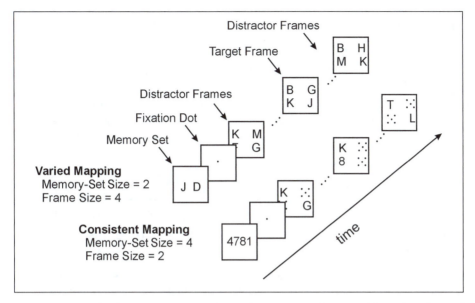

Figure 7.11   The hybrid memory and visual search paradigm used by Schneider and Shiffrin (1977).

SOURCE: Data from Schneider & Shiffrin, 1977.

ATTENTION, MEMORY, AND SKILL ▲

Although attention is central to acquiring the information on which learning is based, much research has focused on showing that attention may not be necessary at all once a skill has been learned. As mentioned in previous chapters, there is an ongoing debate in cognitive psychology as to whether skilled actions can be performed automatically, without the need for attention. Supporters of the distinction between automatic and "controlled" behavior describe automatic processes as those processes that (1) are under control of the stimulus, (2) once started, cannot be stopped, and (3) neither suffer from nor cause interference with other processes. Posner and Snyder (1975) defined automatic processes as those that may occur "without intention, without any conscious awareness and without interference with other mental activity" (p. 81). Controlled processing (Atkinson & Shiffrin, 1968) is relatively slow, requires effort, and involves consciousness of one's actions. According to the controlled/automatic processing dichotomy, the development of skill is characterized by a freeing up of processing resources and a shift to a capacity-free, stimulus-driven mode of performance that is not dependent on conscious control.

Much of the research directed towards understanding the proposed shift from controlled to automatic processing has used search tasks in which one searches a display for one or more targets held in memory (see Figure 7.11). Using such

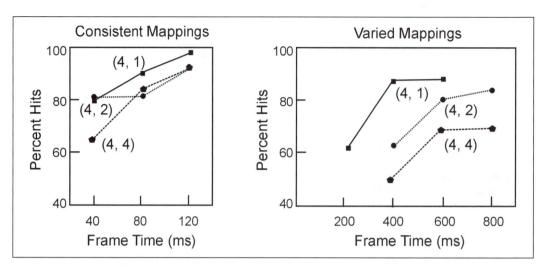

Figure 7.12   Automatic and controlled processing. When mappings are consistent, automatic processing can develop such that performance does not depend on perceptual or memory load.

SOURCE: Data from Schneider & Shiffrin, 1977.

hybrid memory and visual search tasks, Schneider and Shiffrin (1977; Shiffrin & Schneider, 1977) performed an extensive series of experiments that seemed to support the idea that there are two different modes of processing: controlled and automatic. In Schneider and Shiffrin's experiments, processing seemed to occur automatically when stimuli were mapped to responses in a consistent way; that is, when some items (e.g., digits) were always distractors, and other items (e.g., letters), if present, were always targets (see Figure 7.12). Automaticity is evidenced by the finding that performance depends on the size of the memory set or the number of items in the display for varied mappings, but not for consistent mappings.

One influential theory of skill acquisition describes the development of skill as the acquisition of instances. In this *instance theory of automaticity* (Logan, 1988), instances are episodes in which attention was directed to relevant information, with the result that the information was encoded into memory. Performance speeds up as a function of practice because more and more instances are collected as time goes on, which has the effect of making retrieval of the appropriate information faster and easier as a function of practice. In this theory, the only hallmark of automatic processing is that it is based on the retrieval of instances, rather than on the results of algorithm-based computations. For example, a child learning to add might first count on her fingers in order to compute a sum such as 4 + 5. After

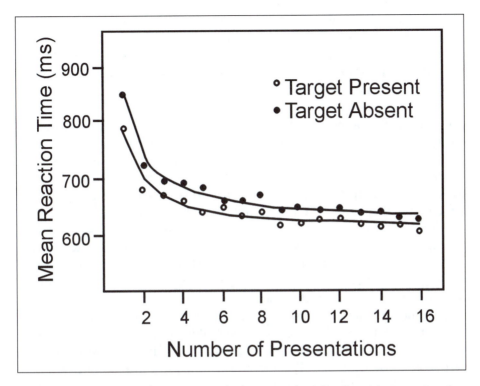

Figure 7.13   Power law of practice applied to target-detection data. Mean reaction time decreases as a power function of the number of trials of practice.

several presentations of the sum and computations of the correct answer, she will no longer need to count, but will remember the correct answer.

The instance theory of automaticity predicts one of the most robust findings in skill acquisition, the power law of practice. The power law states that performance will improve as a power function of the number of trials of practice (see Figure 7.13). Power-law improvement follows from the instance theory because of mathematical properties of response-time distributions: As the number of instances increases, the mean time to retrieve an instance decreases, and this decrease follows a power function.

According to Logan's (1988) instance theory, "attention drives both the acquisition of automaticity and the expression of automaticity in skilled performance" (Logan & Compton, 1998, p. 114). Selected information becomes part of instances, but ignored information does not. Moreover, attention must be paid to the right cues, if associations dependent on those cues are to be retrieved (Logan & Etherton,

1994). Thus, attention is needed at both the time of encoding and the time of retrieval. In this sense, and within the framework of the instance theory, attention can be viewed as the interface between memory and events in the world. The dependence of memory on attention means that knowing (or learning) what to attend to is a critical component in the development of skill (A. Johnson, 2003).

The view of automaticity embodied in Logan's (1988) instance theory is very different than that proposed by Shiffrin and Schneider (1977). According to Logan, processing is automatic when it depends on the retrieval of instances rather than the application of a general algorithm for performing the task. Attention remains important for attending to relevant cues. In fact, the view that controlled and automatic processing are qualitatively distinct has come under more general attack. Even within the realm of visual search, most researchers now refer to the "efficiency" of search, rather than supposing that some targets can be found without the involvement of attention (see Ehrenstein, Walker, Czerwinski, & Feldman, 1997). Others (e.g., Neumann, 1987) reject the view of automaticity as a form of processing, and describe automaticity instead as a phenomenon arising from a conjunction of input stimuli, skill, and the desired action. In this view, performance is automatic when all information needed to perform a task is present in the input information (stimulus information available in the environment) or in long-term memory. This view is somewhat similar to Logan's (1988, 1990), in which automatic processing is based on memory retrieval, and attention forms the cues necessary for retrieval. It seems that attention retains an important role even in highly practiced tasks.

Recently, Logan, Taylor, and Etherton (1999) presented a unified account of attention, memory, and learning. This account is an integration of Logan's instance theory of automaticity and Bundesen's (1990) theory of visual attention. According to Bundesen's theory (see Chapter 3), attentional selection is based on the outcome of a race between various categorizations of the stimuli in a display. Stimuli are assumed to activate representations in memory, and the stimulus that most quickly reaches an activation threshold is selected. Attention to stimuli is assumed to speed up the activation process, enabling the attended stimuli to win the race for selection. Three factors combine to determine which stimuli will be selected: the quality of the sensory evidence that a given stimulus belongs to a given category (e.g., that the lines ∧ belong to the letter *A* and not to the letter *H*); the bias for categorizing stimuli as members of a category (based on the goals of the observer or the context, such as C ∧ T vs. T ∧ E); and the attentional weight applied to features of the stimulus (e.g., the color "red" would receive a higher attentional weight when the task is to identify red items). According to Logan et al.'s interpretation and use of Bundesen's theory, the first type of information—which relates sensory evidence to particular stimuli—is the result of learning. The instance theory describes how the retrieval of instances can predict the speed of retrieval of the correct interpretation of the object. The bias to classify objects as belonging to a particular category determines what, exactly, will be learned. For example, in an experiment in which words must be classified as belonging to different categories, practice will result in faster categorization judgments. The attentional weight, which can be viewed as a criterion for selection, does not directly result in learning. For example, if subjects are told to classify the top word in a display and to ignore the bottom word, they use position to select the word to be categorized, but position is not encoded or learned. However, as demonstrated in the experiments of Logan et al., if subjects are required to also classify the position of a word belonging to a certain category, they will show learning of both the categorization and the position response.

SUMMARY ▲

This chapter makes clear that both attention and memory are simple terms for describing complex sets of more or less interrelated functions of information processing. "Memory" refers to various kinds of representations of information that are retained in different formats and processed in different stores. Perceptual information is retained briefly in modality-specific sensory stores but must be further processed, or consolidated, if it is to reach conscious awareness. Information is held active and can be operated on in working memory, which is commonly supposed to be capable of processing both spatial and phonological information. Attention and memory come closely together in the executive control of working memory. The role of attention in memory can be described as being that of a selective agent that regulates the flow of information and restricts the operation of memory processes.

Just performing a task is sufficient to learn much about the task. However, some information that we learn escapes our awareness. Subtle regularities in the task itself may lead to better performance of the task, even when we are not able to verbalize what these regularities are. Thus, although successful episodic memory depends on attention to what is being encoded and what is being retrieved, implicit learning can occur without conscious selection of information. Short-term memory is sometimes defined as that part of memory that is currently available for conscious introspection. Paradoxically, much processing that would seem to require retrieval from memory seems to go on outside of consciousness.

▲ NOTES

1. Although location is an effective cue in increasing the total number of letters reported, the specific locations of the items are not always remembered. In fact, when only items recalled in the correct order are counted as correct, partial report is not any better than whole report. Assuming that the processes of transferring information to a durable store are the same for cued and uncued letters, this indicates that the iconic image is not a "snapshot" of the display.

2. This account can also explain why the two targets are often reported in the wrong order when one target succeeds the other in the RSVP stream.

CHAPTER 8

ATTENTION AND DISPLAYS

with Kim-Phuong L. Vu

The previous chapters have focused primarily on basic research concerning mechanisms of attention. Although knowledge about attention for its own sake is an admirable goal, ultimately this knowledge needs to be applicable to situations outside of the laboratory. In the present chapter, we shift to an emphasis on how the methods, phenomena, and models of attention described in the previous chapters can be applied in practical situations.

Display design, the focus of this chapter, illustrates that contemporary basic research on attention has been intertwined with applied research on the topic. The role of attention in processing the information provided by the natural and constructed environments, and how this information can best be represented in displays, has been of central concern for more than half a century. Display types are often chosen on the basis of their alerting properties, and the success of a display can be measured by whether it attracts and holds attention. Rather than being just an application of research on attention, display design has guided research on attention as well. For example, the development of displays that need to be monitored for long periods of time (e.g., radar displays) led to the discovery of the *vigilance decrement* (the decrease in detection of infrequent target stimuli over the first half-hour of performance) and spawned much research on vigilance behavior. More recently, developments in three-dimensional sound, head-up displays, and virtual reality have inspired research on spatial representation and spatial cognition.

Issues in display design include alerting and holding attention, supporting both selective and divided attention—depending on task requirements—and supporting the maintenance of appropriate situation models and integration of information. Other issues include the ability to orient attention in three dimensions and moving attention between "real" and display spaces. This chapter will concentrate on sampling and search behavior, while surveying the types of displays in use today.

One area of particular concern to the study of attention is that of automation. Technological advances have allowed many tasks to be automated, which enables certain functions previously performed by the operator to be performed by the mechanical system. For example, automation in the flight deck of a modern aircraft includes flight management and instrument systems, autopilots, and warning systems. A benefit of automation is that it reduces the attentional and cognitive demands placed on the operator by allowing actions to occur, and potential problems to be detected, without requiring operator intervention. Another benefit is that systems can be programmed to adapt to the behaviors of specific users. One consequence of automation is that many jobs have been transformed from ones of direct involvement in performing tasks to ones of monitoring whether the automated tasks are performed correctly. Intervention and direct involvement of the operator with such systems is required primarily when automation fails or the system alerts the operator to a potential problem.

In addition to the benefits provided by automation, there are several drawbacks. Because the operator must input information into the automated system in many cases, errors may result during information entry. A common error of this type is a *mode error,* in which the interface has several modes for information entry and the operator mistakenly enters the information thinking that one mode is in effect when really another is. These mode errors often are due in part to the interface not signaling the mode change effectively to the operator. An over-reliance on automation may lead operators to fail to detect and correct problems. Another drawback of automation is that operators may be "out of the loop," and therefore not understand the situation fully when an emergency occurs that requires their involvement. In this chapter, we will consider ways in which attentional guidance can be provided to the operator to assist in the detection and awareness of unintended events that occur as a consequence of the automation.

VISUAL DISPLAYS ▲

Modern displays rely heavily on visual information. They vary from simple to complex, often cover a large portion of the visual field, and may require operators to monitor more than one display or a single display consisting of several components. Because the displays and their components are usually more than the operator can attend to at any given moment, he or she must selectively attend to important or relevant features of the displays, while filtering out or ignoring the remaining features. Thus, most research on the attentional demands required to perform tasks with displayed information uses visual displays.

Because high visual acuity is restricted to only a small area around the fixation point, the control of eye movements is essential for good performance. Pursuit eye movements (those in which the eyes move together to track a visual target, as in following an object as it moves through the visual field) are important in tasks, such as driving, that require following a variable "track." Saccadic eye movements (those for which the eye shifts fixation rapidly from one fixed position to another) occur when an operator checks individual instruments on a display panel. They can be triggered automatically by a salient event such as the onset of a stimulus or intentionally as a consequence of the operator's goals. Although the beam of attention can be directed toward a location other than the fixated location (see Chapter 3), in many cases gaze patterns can be used as a measure of which displayed information the observer is attending to. For example, the percentage of time that a driver spends looking outside of the vehicle versus looking at the instrument panel can be used to evaluate the amount of attention devoted to monitoring in-vehicle and out-of-vehicle activity.

Visual Search

Because many tasks involve operators searching for information in a display, factors that influence search time have been studied extensively with respect to display design. Basic characteristics of visual search were discussed in Chapter 3, and only points that are relevant to issues of display design will be discussed here. Search time can be very long when complex, multi-element displays must be scanned for target information because search is, in general, an attention-demanding, slow process. Because search can be terminated whenever the target information is found, factors that direct attention to the targeted information will reduce search time and improve performance. For example, search time will typically be shorter if the target information is in central (foveal) vision, where it is most likely to be identified early in the search. Use of a distinctive feature for the target information, such as a unique color, can have a similar beneficial effect because the feature will "pop out," enabling attention to be directed to the information at that location.

Search Patterns

When an operator monitors multiple sources of information, or displays on which critical events occur periodically, the relative frequency with which the operator will sample particular displays is a function of the frequency with which the critical events occur (the *event rates*). If the event rate for one display is higher than that for another, the operator will sample the former display more often than the latter. According to normative models of sampling behavior (i.e., models that dictate the sampling strategies that should lead to the most efficient performance; Senders, 1983), the frequency of inspections of individual displays, and therefore, the transitions between looking at different displays, should depend only on the event rates of the display instruments. However, Donk (1994) showed that subjects engage in predictable search patterns, and that they use these patterns regardless of whether they are beneficial to performance. In Donk's Experiments 1 and 3, subjects monitored displays in which four instruments were arranged in two rows and two columns. The instruments differed in terms of their informativeness, and the spatial arrangement of the different instruments within the array was varied. Consistent with normative models, instruments with higher event rates were sampled more than those with lower rates. However, regardless of the event rates, subjects were more likely to scan the displays horizontally, and to a lesser extent vertically, than diagonally. This outcome suggests that human monitoring is biased towards sampling by way of horizontal transitions, regardless of the relative informativeness of the particular instruments.

Mudd and McCormick (1960) also showed that people engage in predictable search patterns, but that these patterns can be broken if an auditory cue is used to direct attention to a region of the display that contains the target. The task was to locate one dial, from among 32 dials arranged in 4 quadrants, for which the pointer deviated from its normal position. The mean search time for subjects to locate the deviant dial was more than 18 seconds. The primary reason for this long search time was that, as in Donk's (1994) more recent study, participants tended to search the display in a manner consistent with reading habits (i.e., from left to right and top to bottom). Because the target was in the upper left quadrant on only one-fourth of the trials, at least one quadrant would be searched prior to the one containing the target on the remaining three-quarters of the trials, causing mean search time to be long.

On some trials, an auditory cue occurred simultaneously with the display. The cue was a tone in the left or right ear that signaled whether the target was in the left or right half of the display. In some cases, the tone also varied in pitch, with a high pitch signaling top half and a low pitch signaling bottom half, specifying the exact quadrant to be searched. Search time was reduced to about 10 seconds with the left-right location cue and about 6 seconds with the combined cue. This decrease in search time occurred because the auditory cue reduced uncertainty about the location of the deviant dial, allowing search to be directed initially to the appropriate side or quadrant of the display.

Computer Menus

Structuring search can be beneficial for computer menu design. A menu is a set of options that is displayed to users in which the selection of an option or sequence of options would result in a change in the interface (Paap & Cooke, 1997). This change in the interface may be the desired output or may allow the user to obtain the desired output. A good menu should be composed from unambiguous descriptors that accurately convey each option to the user, with the options organized in a manner that will lead to short search times.

When a user intends to execute a goal, the user directs his or her fixation at an option on the display and evaluates whether selecting that option would help him or her achieve the goal. If the user decides to select the option, it is executed; if not, the user must redirect his or her attention to searching other options. When the user knows exactly what option to search for, *identity matching* can be used and search time is fastest. When the user knows exactly what option to search for, *identity matching* can be used and search time is fastest. When the user knows what option should be executed but does not know how the option is labeled, the user can use *equivalence search*. Finally, *inclusion matching* can be used to find an option that is classified within a menu when the user does not know under which class a specific option would be categorized. To structure the options of menus in an optimal manner, designers must take into account the type of search in which the user would most likely be engaged.

When identity search is used, the interface should organize menu options in alphabetical order rather than in random order (Perlman, 1984). Furthermore, options that are organized by functions also reduce search times compared to randomized options (Card, 1982). With equivalence matching, alphabetical and categorical organization yield shorter search times than randomized organization, but if users are uncertain about the exact label of the option, categorical organization leads to shorter search times than alphabetical organization (J. E. McDonald, Stone, & Liebelt, 1983). With inclusion matching, problems arise when an option can fit into two or more classifications or is not a well-known exemplar of the category. Somberg and Picardi (1983) showed that it took longer to identify the category to which an option belonged if the option was a less-familiar example of the category than if it was more familiar.

Recently, menus have been designed to be adaptive in order to reduce search times for finding the desired item and to reduce movement time to select the item (Jameson, 2002). *Smart menus* display only those commands from a menu that have been used most often and most recently. The remaining commands from the menu are hidden, and the user must indicate that he or she wants to view them if they are to appear. The advantage of smart menus is that only the few options that the user is likely to consider are displayed, eliminating the need to search the full menu and move the cursor a long distance. If the desired command is not displayed, then the user can position the cursor on an "expand" symbol, and the full menu will appear, allowing the user to search for the command in the normal manner. One drawback of smart menus, however, is that the mapping of commands to specific locations is variable because the location depends on how many and which commands were used recently. As discussed in Chapter 7, practice and experience with a variable mapping does not yield the benefits in performance that would be obtained with a consistent mapping. Another drawback is that a desired command may be embedded in the menu hierarchy, and locating it may require additional expansion steps along the way.

When designing menus, a decision must be made regarding whether to have few menus with many commands under them (broad design) or a hierarchical organization of many menus, each with fewer commands underneath them (deep design). This issue is known as the *breadth versus depth tradeoff.* A broad design has the benefit of requiring fewer steps to complete a task but longer search times and movements within a menu level. In contrast, a deep design reduces the search and movement times but at the expense of having users work through more intermediate steps. Lee and MacGregor (1985) analyzed the expected search time for a menu interface, and their results indicated that deep hierarchies are preferred over broad ones. This preference for deep hierarchies is because the time associated with searching for the desired option within a large list is longer than the time associated with moving through the steps of a deep menu hierarchy.

Multifunctional and Gaze-Contingent Multiresolutional Displays

Multifunctional displays consist of multiple display options mapped to a limited number of keys. Such systems are used for, among other things, interactions with automatic teller machines and helicopter control. Because the information in multifunctional displays is typically organized in a hierarchical manner, Francis (2000) introduced a computational method of mapping labels to buttons (used to execute functions) in an optimal manner. According to Francis, two steps are involved in creating an optimal mapping of hierarchy labels to buttons: (1) development of a quantitative model of the time needed to search through the hierarchy, and (2) application of an optimization algorithm to determine the best mapping according to the model. The model assumes that the time needed to reach a target is a function of the button-path time (sequence of buttons that need to be executed, including the time for the user to reach the button) and the label time (time that is needed in addition to button-path time). Francis used a hill-climbing method for optimizing the design in which the costs of different mappings are calculated by the computer, and if the new cost is smaller than the old cost, the mapping is adopted. Using this method to model user search time and obtaining necessary parameters for the model, Francis tested the optimized mappings against a random assignment of labels to button paths and found that the optimized mapping resulted in a 32% reduction of search time.

Another recent display technology is that of *gaze-contingent multiresolutional displays* (GCMRDs; see Reingold, Loschky, McConkie, & Stampe, in press). Many purposes require operators to search for information on large computerized screens and monitors. Because items are more easily identified when the display has high resolution, the use of high-resolution displays is desired in many instances. However, the amount of processing capacity required for such displays often exceeds the capacity of the system, making the use of high-resolution displays unfeasible. One solution to this problem has been the development of GCMRDs. Such displays have a limited region of high resolution, with the remainder of the display presented at lower resolution. The display dynamically changes as the observer moves his or her eyes so that the area of high resolution always corresponds to the part of the image falling on or around the fovea. The basic idea is that the operator needs high resolution only in central vision and can utilize the peripheral cues as effectively from a low-resolution display as from a high-resolution display.

Loschky and McConkie (2002) investigated this issue by manipulating the size of the high-resolution area to see how it affected performance in a visual search task. A smaller area led to saccades of shorter distance, which in turn led to longer search times because more saccades had to be made to cover the same distance. The apparent reason why more saccades had to be made with the smaller high-resolution area is that the salience of the target object was less in the low-resolution region. Thus, although GCMRDs may be useful, Loschky and McConkie's findings indicate that performance of tasks that require visual search may not be as good with such displays as it would be with a high-resolution display. Moreover, given that display technology is constantly improving, a feasible high-resolution display may be available shortly after a GCMRD is developed. Thus, in the long term, GCMRDs may be more valuable as tools to study visual attention than as general display media.

ORGANIZATION OF DISPLAYS ▲

The way in which a display is organized can have a great influence on the amount of attention required to perform a task, as well as on the speed and accuracy with which it can be performed. In this section, we review several perceptual grouping principles that can be used to make critical information easier to apprehend. We also emphasize that, for performance to be maximized, the display organization must be matched to the type of processing that is to be performed on the displayed information, and to the organization of the response environment.

Grouping Principles

When organizing a display, the way individual elements are grouped is of extreme importance; when these elements are grouped in an optimal manner, performance will be better and the attentional demands will be less. Grouping of displays can be accomplished by following the Gestalt perceptual-organization principles (Palmer, 2003). These include, among others:

1. *proximity*: components in close spatial proximity tend to be grouped together;

2. *similarity*: components that are similar in appearance tend to be grouped together;

3. *continuity*: components that follow a continuous contour tend to be grouped together;

4. *closure*: gaps between contours tend to be filled in; and

5. *common fate*: components that move in the same direction or at the same speed will tend to be grouped together.

With a good display organization, the operator should be able to get all information regarding a certain aspect of a task while focusing his or her attention on one area of the display rather than switching between multiple areas. Elements of a display should be grouped together when they (1) are related, (2) are usually monitored in sequence, or (3) can be clustered together in a way that allows the operator to attend to particular groups of elements at once.

The benefit of a good organization is illustrated by studies conducted by Banks and Prinzmetal (1976; Prinzmetal & Banks, 1977). In their experiments, participants judged whether a T or an F was presented among hybrid T-F distractors. They found that performance was worse when the target letter was clustered into the same group as the distractors than when it was not. For example, one experiment demonstrated an effect of continuity. In all cases, the target was presented among five distractors. In one condition, the target was placed in line with four of the distractors, so that continuity grouped it as part of the line (as in Figure 8.1a). In a second condition, the target was placed separately from the line of five distractors, so that they were grouped separately from it (as in Figure 8.1b). Reaction times to identify the target were longer in the former case than in the latter.

Displays should also be organized in a consistent manner in order to minimize the amount of attention that needs to be allocated to searching for the information. When operators interact with a display, they can intentionally or unintentionally remember where certain elements of the display are located and can easily divert their attention to the particular location when desired. However, if the

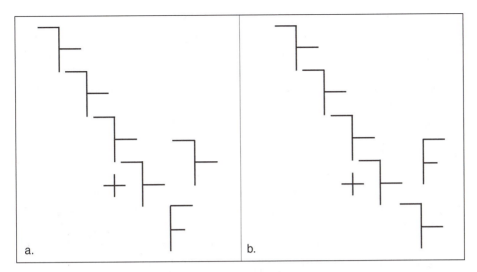

Figure 8.1   Two sample displays used by Banks and Prinzmetal (1976; Prinzmetal & Banks, 1977). The task was to judge whether a T or an F was presented among hybrid T-F distractors.

SOURCE: Prinzmetal & Banks, 1977, p. 390. Copyright 1977 by the Psychonomic Society; reprinted with permission.

display is not consistent, then the operator may divert his or her attention to the wrong location and must search for the desired information.

Finally, displays should also be organized to minimize clutter. If there is too much information on the display, the operator will be overloaded with information. Too much information also reduces the benefit of grouping displays because the groups may not be easily identified. Thus, there should be an adequate amount of space between all groups of elements in a display. Minimizing clutter is especially important when the task requires letter identification in the periphery of a display because crowding causes neighboring letters to be perceived as an integrated signal of overlapping letters (Palomares, Pelli, & Majaj, in press). The letter that is perceived most easily changes as a function of size, distance, and eccentricity, making correct identification difficult. To avoid effects of crowding, letters that need to be identified should be spaced adequately far apart, with the minimum separation distance increasing as eccentricity increases.

Object Displays and Emergent Features

Object displays are multidimensional displays that can be perceived and monitored as a single object. The advantage of object displays is that attention does not have to be divided among the individual components and that the information provided by the components can be processed in parallel. The *proximity compatibility principle* and *emergent feature view* provide frameworks for evaluating the effects of object displays.

Wickens and colleagues (e.g., Wickens & Andre, 1990; Wickens & Carswell, 1995) developed the proximity compatibility principle to emphasize that there is a relationship between different types of displays and the way in which information from the displays has to be used. According to Wickens and Andre, the proximity compatibility principle asserts that tasks in which "close mental proximity" is required (i.e., information integration) will be best served by more proximate displays, whereas tasks that require "low mental proximity" (i.e., the independent processing of two or more variables, or the focusing of attention on one while ignoring others) will benefit from more separate displays.

Wickens and colleagues specify two types of proximity: perceptual and processing. *Perceptual proximity* refers to the perceptual similarity that exists between different components of the display. This type of proximity includes *spatial* (distance), *chromatic* (color), *form* (shapes), *measurement* (physical dimensions), and *code* (analog or digital). Spatial proximity refers to the distances between the items of the displays. For example, the flanker compatibility effect (B. A. Eriksen & C. W. Eriksen, 1974; see Chapter 5), that reaction time (RT) is longer when a target letter is flanked by letters assigned to an alternative response than letters that are not, decreases as the spatial separation between the target and flankers increases. An example of chromatic proximity is that there is a tendency for items with the same color to be grouped together. Carter and Cahill (1979) showed that search for a set of targets is easier if they are the same color. Treisman and Gelade (1980) showed that search for a single target is easier if the target is a different color than the display because it "pops out."

Processing proximity refers to how much attention must be focused on the different components of a display in order to obtain the information necessary to complete a task (Wickens & Carswell, 1995). Processing proximity can be characterized by three different categories: *integrative processing, nonintegrative processing,* and *independent processing.* Integrative processing involves active integration of the components through computational integration (using mathematical operations) or Boolean integration (satisfying more than one parameter; e.g., X "and" Y). Nonintegrative processing involves similarity among the components of the display such as metric similarity (displays that are measured in the same units), covariance similarity (changes in one display can predict changes in another), functional similarity (multiple displays that yield information about a class of information), and so forth. Finally, independent processing does not require processing of components together. That is, separate decisions are made for each display component (e.g., determining the speed with which one is driving from a speedometer and evaluating whether there is enough gas in the vehicle from the gas gauge).

In summary, the proximity compatibility principle states that the display proximity should match the task proximity. That is, object displays should facilitate performance on integrated tasks and produce a cost with selective tasks. Similarly, separate displays should facilitate performance on selective tasks and produce a cost with integrated tasks.

In some cases, multiple elements of a display or multiple displays can be aligned or grouped in such a way that certain properties of the monitoring task will "emerge." A unique property of an *emergent display* is that it reduces the attentional demands that a user must devote to a multi-element display because the operator can monitor the global property rather than the individual components. Treisman (1986) indicates that emergent features can lead to quicker processing of information about the system because recognition of the overall pattern can be done quickly, but it can impair performance if information regarding individual elements needs to be analyzed.

D. D. Woods (1991) distinguished between displays that are designed for *information availability* and those designed for *information extraction*, such as those with emergent features. Displays that are designed to make information available alone are not optimal because the operator must collect, remember, and integrate the information to interact with the system. Displays that are designed to maximize the ability of operators to extract information are better because "performance can be improved by providing displays that allow the observer to utilize the more efficient processes of perception and pattern recognition" (Bennett & Flach, 1992, p. 514).

Both selective and divided attention tasks can be affected by the dimensional relationships between the display types. Emergent displays can be classified into *integral* and *configural displays* (Bennett & Flach, 1992), and these displays are often compared to *separable displays.* Separable displays allow each component to maintain its unique perceptual properties in such a way that processing of these components can be done independently. In integral displays, emergent properties of the components are so strong that the perceptual properties of the individual components are not distinguishable. Although this display provides an excellent depiction of a system's overall status, it affects the operator's ability to selectively attend to an individual component or divide attention to monitor different components of the system. Configural displays have emergent features, but maintain the individual perceptual properties of the components. For example, the emergent features can be of vertical symmetry (e.g., [ ]), but the individual components, left and right brackets, can be maintained. With configural displays, there is a smaller cost of divided attention but a larger cost of selective attention.

Bennett and Flach (1992) maintain that the emergent features view provides a better account for performance data than does the proximity compatibility principle.

First of all, they point out that performance for integrated tasks improves more as a function of the presence of emergent features or configurality of the display than of the use of object displays, although they do acknowledge that subsequent modifications of the proximity compatibility principle incorporated the importance of emergent features. Second, the tradeoff in performance between tasks and displays that is predicted by the proximity compatibility principle is not always found: Object and configural displays usually lead to a benefit for integrated tasks but usually do not show a cost for selective tasks.

Display-Control Relations

For a display to be arranged for optimal selection, its arrangement should correspond to the configuration of the controls (see, e.g., Fitts & Seeger, 1953). In a classic study of stove configurations, Chapanis and Lindenbaum (1959) evaluated four control-burner arrangements (see Figure 8.2). An experimenter demonstrated the individual pairings of burners to controls for one of the four stoves to subjects, and then instructed subjects to push the control assigned to the burner that was lit. Subjects responded more quickly with design 1, for which correspondence between the horizontal locations of the burners and controls was maintained, than with designs 2–4, for which it was not. Furthermore, no errors were made with design 1, whereas the overall error rates were 6%, 10%, and 11% for designs 2, 3, and 4, respectively. Practice significantly reduced response time and errors for design 2 compared to designs 3 and 4, but performance was still worse than with design 1. This study illustrates that not only is display arrangement important, but also the way in which the display maps onto any responses that must be made is vital.

Salience of Display and Control Features

A factor contributing to the effectiveness of a display at conveying information is the salience of the display components. An operator's central visual area is the region where the operator focuses most attention, and it is usually the area directly in front of the operator. Because the operator is more likely to detect small changes in displays in this area than in the peripheral areas, the most important and frequently used information should be displayed in this area.

The salient features of a display can also predict what response will be made to the stimuli. As noted in Chapter 5, stimulus–response compatibility refers to the fact that people respond faster and more accurately to some mappings of displays to controls than others (Proctor & Reeve, 1990). For example, if a left or right response must be made to a stimulus appearing in a left or right location, the

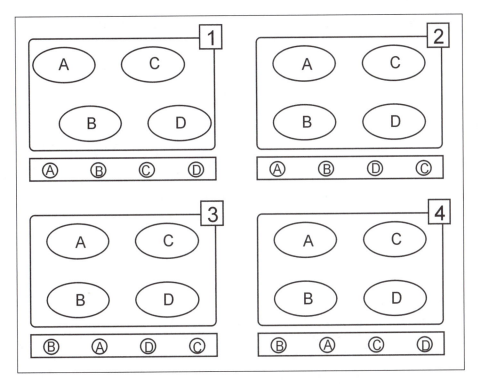

Figure 8.2   Stove configurations with different mappings of burners to control knobs.

compatible mapping of right stimulus to right response and left stimulus to left response yields better performance than the alternative incompatible mapping. This spatial compatibility effect is primarily a function of relative location of stimuli and responses, or, in other words, of an environmental frame of reference. However, for situations in which an egocentric frame of reference, such as the distinction between the left and right hands, is made more salient, compatibility effects as a function of this frame of reference can be obtained as well (Heister, Schroeder-Heister, & Ehrenstein, 1990).

The importance of salience can be illustrated for situations in which stimuli and responses vary along both horizontal and vertical dimensions, thus allowing compatibility to be maintained for both, one, or neither of the dimensions. Figure 8.3 illustrates situations of this type examined in a study by Nicoletti and Umiltà (1985). The stimuli could occur in the upper-left or lower-right corners of the display panel, and responses were made by pressing one of two buttons with the left or right thumb. The two response alternatives were arrayed along the same diagonal as the stimuli (upper-left, lower-right) or the opposite diagonal (upper-right, lower-left). When aligned on the same diagonal, the mapping of stimuli to

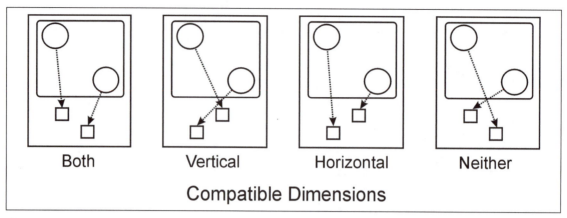

Figure 8.3   Stimulus-response configurations used by Nicoletti and Umiltà (1985).

responses was compatible on both the horizontal and vertical dimensions or on neither dimension. When located on opposite diagonals, the mapping of stimuli to responses was compatible on only the horizontal dimension or only the vertical dimension. Not surprisingly, performance was best when both dimensions were mapped compatibly and worst when both were mapped incompatibly. More important, performance was better when compatibility was maintained along the horizontal dimension than along the vertical dimension, a phenomenon called the right-left prevalence effect.

Based on these results, Andre and Wickens (1990) concluded, in their guide-lines for cockpit layouts, "The left-right dimension preferentially attracts atten-tion . . . , and because of this, determines compatibility effects at the expense of the above-below dimension" (p. 31). However, recent studies demonstrate that right-left prevalence occurs only for situations in which the environment provides a salient frame of reference for the horizontal dimension. That is, right-left preva-lence is obtained when the stimuli are neutral and responding is made with left-right effectors, most likely because the effectors provide a salient frame of reference for horizontal coding. Vu and Proctor (2001) had subjects respond to stimuli displayed along a diagonal using an ipsilateral (e.g., right hand and right foot) or contralateral (e.g., right hand and left foot) hand and foot. The right-left prevalence effect was obtained when responses were made with the contralateral hand and foot, but a top-bottom prevalence effect was evident when responses were made with the ipsilateral hand and foot. This latter finding is most likely due to the fact that the ipsilateral effectors could be coded easily in terms of the verti-cal dimension but not in terms of the horizontal dimension, because they were from the same side of the body. Furthermore, Vu and Proctor (2002) illustrated that the advantage for horizontal—or vertical—compatibility is largest when the salient features of the display and response configurations both favor the same dimension than when only one does. Thus, although in many situations it is more important to maintain compatibility on the right-left dimension than on the top-bottom dimension, this will not be the case for situations in which the task environment provides a more salient frame of reference for coding on the vertical dimension.

AUDITORY AND MULTISENSORY DISPLAYS ▲

Based on the treatment of visual displays discussed to this point in the chapter, it should be clear that visual displays are the design of choice for many applications. Visual displays can convey large amounts of information and provide detailed pictorial and spatial information, and the displayed information can be mapped compatibly onto spatial control operations. However, there are situations in which other types of displays are more beneficial to performance. Box 8.1 discusses research and applications using tactile displays. In this section, we discuss displays designed to capitalize on a more commonly used modality, hearing.

Auditory Displays

Auditory displays are more effective than visual displays when the lighting is of low intensity or visibility is poor. Also, whereas an operator must be looking at a visual display in order to process any information presented there, auditory displays can be detected regardless of the operator's orientation, and they attract attention more automatically.

Auditory displays can utilize speech to present information (see Brewster, 2003). Speech sounds share many benefits of nonspeech sounds, such as being able to be perceived regardless of orientation and reducing the cognitive demands placed on visual attention. However, there are drawbacks to speech output, including the serial nature of speech, its length, and intelligibility. To comprehend a message, the operator must attend to the entire message, from start to finish. Furthermore, information presented with speech tends to be lengthy in that many words may be required to describe information that could be depicted in a simple image. The use of artificial speech in many computerized displays may suffer from lack of intelligibility, requiring the operator to pay more attention to decode the message.

Modern technological advances have allowed use of computerized auditory representations to augment visual displays. Most computer programs utilize stereo sounds produced through speakers or headphones. By manipulating auditory cues such as interaural-time differences and interaural-intensity differences, the generated sounds can provide the users with spatial cues to direct their

Box 8.1	Tactile Displays

Historically, tactile displays have been developed and used extensively as sensory substitution systems for the blind and deaf. For example, Braille characters are often placed on directional signs, room numbers, and automatic teller machines to enable blind individuals to navigate through buildings and perform daily transactions. More recently, vibrotactile aids have been developed to allow blind individuals to scan and read written text (see, e.g., Tan & Pentland, 2001). In the past, tactile displays have been used relatively infrequently for individuals with normal vision and hearing. However, this situation is changing because of technological developments in the design of vibrotactile displays and the fact that such displays have some advantages over visual and auditory displays. These advantages include the ability of a vibrotactile signal (1) to summon and direct attention, (2) to convey spatial information, (3) to be perceived from any posture or orientation, if attached to the operator, and (4) to be processed simultaneously with visual and auditory stimulation (see, e.g., Sklar & Sarter, 1999).

Because the tactile sense is underused, few competing demands are typically placed on it. Consequently, one potential use of tactile displays is for environments like the inside of an automobile in which there is already considerable visual and auditory stimulation. In such environments, the tactual modality should be considered for displaying additional signals or directing attention to specific locations at which relevant visual or auditory information will be displayed. A use with which many readers may be familiar is the vibrator mode on a pager or cellular phone. This alerts the person that a message or call is waiting even in a noisy environment, without distracting other people with unwanted sound.

One potential use of tactile displays is to cue locations at which visual or auditory information may be displayed. Spence, Nichols, Gillespie, and Driver (1998) provided evidence that even an uninformative tactile cue can produce exogenous orienting that affects both vision and hearing. In their experiment, subjects judged the elevation (high vs. low) of auditory or visual stimuli by raising the toes or heel of the right foot. The stimuli could be presented to either the left or right side of the subject, and were preceded at a variable interval by a tactile precue to the left or right index finger. Although the precue was uninformative regarding the side at which the visual or auditory stimulus would occur, performance was better when the stimulus was presented to the same side as the tactile cue. This suggests that attention was oriented toward the cued side. Spence et al. also showed that uninformative visual and auditory cues have a similar benefit on identification of tactile stimuli at the cued side, indicating that processing of information from a tactile display may also benefit from cuing in another modality.

Box 8.1 | (Continued)

Gray and Tan (2002) showed a similar crossmodal attentional link between dynamic tactile stimuli and identification of a visual stimulus. In their study, a column of five vibro-tactile simulators (tactors) was strapped to the subject's left forearm and wrist. The tactors were stimulated in sequence, beginning at one end or the other of the array, causing a perception of movement toward the wrist or toward the shoulder. The number of tactors used in the sequence varied from trial to trial. Two light emitting diodes (LEDs) were attached to the left or right side of each tactor. At a variable interval after the offset of the last tactor, one of the 10 LEDs was lit and subjects responded to its left-right location by pressing a left or right key using the right hand. When the interval between tactor offset and LED onset coincided with the time that the next tactor in the sequence was to be stimulated, RT was shorter when the LED onset occurred at that location and slowest when it occurred at the location prior to the last activated tactor (i.e., in the location opposite the direction of expected movement). Gray and Tan obtained similar results when the visual stimuli were used for dynamic cues and the tactile event was used as the target stimulus.

Among the applications for tactile displays that are currently being explored are wearable computers and virtual reality systems. Wearable computers provide a discreet form of display that can be used to provide information to complement that provided by visual and auditory displays (Tan & Pentland, 2001). For virtual reality systems, tactile displays can be used to provide force feedback consistent with the visual environment to provide a more complete user experience (Iwata, 2003).

attention (see Chapter 4). More recently, there has been an emphasis on the development of *auditory icons* and *earcons* for display designs (Brewster, 2002). Auditory icons are sound effects for computers that map everyday sounds to computer events (Gaver, 1997). For example, different sounds are used to characterize common objects (e.g., a metal sound for applications and a wood sound for files) and their properties (e.g., the deepness of the sound represents the size of the object). Different sound combinations are also used to describe events taking place in the system. When an object is selected, the auditory icon will let users identify its type and properties, allowing users to determine whether the selected object matches the characteristics of the object that they were intending to select.

Earcons are short, nonverbal, audio messages that convey information to the user regarding characteristics of objects or events in the system (Blattner, Sumikawa, & Greenberg, 1989). The major difference between earcons and auditory icons is that the latter attempt to map the computer objects and events to everyday sounds, whereas the former do not. As a result, earcons must be learned. Earcons utilize different combinations of sounds, called *motives,* that can vary in terms of rhythm, pitch, timbre, position, or volume (see Brewster, 2002). Objects or events in the system can be represented by different earcons (e.g., the "create" command can be represented with a high-pitch sound that increases in volume). Earcons can also convey structural information to the user because they can be organized hierarchically. Brewster notes that auditory icons have an advantage over earcons in that they are easier to remember because they represent natural sounds. However, earcons have an advantage of conveying structure that auditory icons cannot. Auditory icons may be more effective for displays intended for novice users, but earcons may have an advantage for more experienced users (Hempel & Altinsoy, in press).

Warning and Alerting Signals

The auditory channel is ideal for the use of alarms that warn operators of malfunctions and emergencies. The intensity of the sound can be used to differentiate between levels of urgency. Signals need to be between 6 and 10 dB above the hearing threshold for the given background noise environment in order to be easily detectable. However, to attract immediate attention for emergency situations, the warning signal should be about 15 dB above the threshold (Sorkin, 1987). Auditory warning signals can also use pitch to signal different levels of priority and to avoid being masked by the noise in the environment. In addition, the speed of presentation and repetition of sound units in a warning can convey urgency (Hellier, Edworthy, & Dennis, 1993).

Most uses of auditory signals are to direct the operator's attention to a specific part of a visual display that needs to be attended to. A benefit of using auditory cues to direct visual attention is that they do not impose additional demands on the visual system. Many researchers have shown that auditory spatial cuing can reduce visual search time because the cue directs attention to the target (see, e.g., Rudmann & Strybel, 1999; see also Chapter 4). Such benefits of auditory spatial cues in reducing visual search times depend on the factors surrounding the environment such as target distance from fixation, distractor density, and size of the visual search field (Strybel, Boucher, Fujawa, & Volp, 1995). Auditory spatial cuing effects have also been examined with simulated two-dimensional cues that signaled the location on the horizontal plane and three-dimensional cues that also signaled elevation (Perrott, Cisneros, McKinley, & D'Angelo, 1996) Perrott et al. showed that the two types of cues were of equal benefit in reducing the time to locate and identify a visual target located on the inner surface of a geodesic sphere. They attributed this reduction in search time to the auditory spatial cues signaling the general area in which the target is located, limiting the visual information that needs to be searched to identify the target (see also Mudd & McCormick's [1960] study described earlier in the chapter).

Alerting Signals for Mode Changes

As mentioned in the introduction to the chapter, automated mode changes often go undetected. As a result, *mode errors* have been the cause of numerous aviation accidents. Thus, there is concern about how best to alert pilots to mode changes. Sarter and Woods (1995) asked pilots what strategies they use for monitoring automated flight deck systems. The pilots reported that instead of scanning all standard navigation instruments, they allocated their attention to the instruments they expected to be relevant for the automated flight mode that was in effect. This strategy of allocating attention based on mode places importance on signaling changes in mode to the pilots. Sarter (2000) noted that the reason why pilots may miss automated mode changes is because the transition is signaled by a rectangular outline box that appears around the new flight mode for a short period of time and then disappears. Thus, if pilots are not looking directly at the display, they will miss the signaling of a mode change. Fortunately, under most circumstances, pilots are able to realize at a later time, on the basis of feedback from subsequent interactions with the system, that the mode has changed. However, Sarter described one case where this correction was not made:

> The crew did not realize that due to the coupling of lateral and vertical modes, their selection of a new lateral mode had the indirect unintended effect of a transition from the flight path angle to the vertical speed mode. When a target descent rate was subsequently entered, the systems interpreted the pilot-entered digits, 33, to mean 3,300 fpm [feet per minute] instead of the desired 3.3° angle of descent . . . the [team] members approached and ultimately crashed into a mountainside. (p. 234)

Nikolic and Sarter (2001) provided evidence that a better way to alert pilots to mode changes is to signal the mode change with a distinct stimulus presented in the periphery of the display panel. They had pilots detect and identify mode changes with three mode transition displays: the standard flight mode display just described, an enhanced version of that display in which the box was made more salient by using solid and distinct colors, and an ambient colored strip that appeared across the bottom of the screen. Both the enhanced version of the display and the ambient strip resulted in better detection of mode changes and did not interfere with performance of the other visual flight tasks. Sarter (2000) suggests that auditory and tactual cues may also be effective in signaling mode changes.

Multisensory Interfaces

Although the effective use of auditory cues as warning signals is well documented, having operators monitor both auditory and visual information at the same time also has drawbacks. Spence and Driver (1996) showed that, although it is possible to direct auditory and visual attention to different locations, there is a cost associated with shifting attention between visual and auditory modalities (see Chapter 4). Spence and Driver proposed a "separable-but-linked" hypothesis to explain these crossmodal interactions. In their study, an orthogonal cuing method was used, in which participants were asked to make elevation judgments (up or down discriminations) of targets that were presented to either the left or right side of fixation. In two experiments, participants were instructed to direct either their auditory or visual attention to one side of fixation. Results showed that RTs for the elevation judgments were shorter when the targets appeared on the cued side compared to when they appeared on the uncued side, even if the target was in a different sensory modality. This finding indicates that when attention for one modality is directed to one side of fixation, there is a corresponding shift of attention for the other modality to that location.

In another experiment, Spence and Driver (1996) instructed participants to direct their auditory attention to one side of fixation and their visual attention to the other side for a whole block of trials. Results showed effects of spatial expectancies for both modalities, although these effects were reduced relative to unimodal conditions. This finding indicates that participants were able to split auditory and visual attention when the targets for the two modalities were expected on opposite sides of fixation, but this splitting reduces the cuing effects within each modality. An implication of this research is that, although people can direct auditory and visual attention to separate locations, it is best to design displays that use attentional cues that are consistent across modalities.

When stimuli have two dimensions, crosstalk between dimensions may occur. *Crosstalk* can be defined in this context as the influence of one stimulus dimension on another. For example, if observers have to judge whether a dynamically changing auditory stimulus is increasing or decreasing in pitch, their judgments will be influenced by the absolute pitch of the stimulus (Walker & Ehrenstein, 2000). Similarly, when observers have to judge the saturation (purity) of a color, their judgments will be affected by the color's brightness. Garner (1974) developed a paradigm and a terminology for describing interactions between stimulus dimensions. He made a distinction between *integral* and *separable* dimensions. Two dimensions are integral if classifications of one dimension are hindered by variations in the other dimension. In other words, stimuli made up of integral dimensions (such as color saturation and brightness) are perceived as unitary wholes, and it is difficult to selectively attend to either dimension. In contrast, if dimensions are separable, variation on one dimension (e.g., color) will not be affected by the value on the other dimension (e.g., shape).

Although Garner focused on perceptual interactions between stimuli, interactions between stimuli can occur at a later, decisional, level of processing. Dimensions sometimes interact because of meaningful, learned relationship between them. For example, Melara and Marks (1990b) showed that the time to respond to the visually presented word "high" or "low" (the actual stimuli were the letter groups "HI" and "LO") depended on whether a simultaneously presented tone was high or low in pitch. When a high-pitched tone accompanied the word "high" and a low-pitched tone accompanied the word "low," classification responses were faster than if these pairings were reversed, even though subjects were instructed to ignore the tones. Thus, crosstalk can occur at both sensory and meaning-based levels of processing, indicating that selective attention to only one dimension of a stimulus is often not possible. These findings have important consequences for the display of information.

When selective attention is not required, that is, when the task does not require attending exclusively to one feature while ignoring others, a redundant signal in a different modality can improve performance. For example, if subjects are required to respond to an auditory tone, they will perform more quickly when the tone is accompanied by a light (and to a light when it is accompanied by a tone; see, e.g., Stein, London, Wilkinson, & Price, 1996). Just as with the speeded classification task discussed earlier, this redundancy gain depends on the relation between the stimuli. If stimuli are coded along some similar dimension, the effect of signal redundancy will depend on the particular pairings of the two signals. For example, both positions of visual stimuli and auditory pitch are coded along a vertical spatial dimension (see Walker & Ehrenstein, 2000). J. Miller (1991) found a redundancy gain for presenting a tone along with a visual signal when the task was to indicate the position of the visual stimulus, and the benefit of the auditory cue was greater when a high-pitched cue accompanied a high spatial location and a low-pitched cue accompanied a low spatial location than when these relations were reversed.

SUPERVISORY CONTROL ▲

Selective attention has been studied for supervisory control tasks in which the operator must selectively attend to some instruments among others on a complex display panel. A skilled operator will select relevant display information at appropriate times. Highly overlearned skills, as well as task requirements and goals, contribute to sampling and search from complex displays. Several factors have been found to influence an operator's sampling strategies (Moray, 1986; Wickens & Hollands, 2000).

Mental Models

The concept of a *mental model* refers to a representation of some aspect of the world (e.g., a system) that reflects the individual's understanding of it (van der Veer & Puerta Melguizo, 2002). The concept is somewhat ambiguous, but mental models are presumed to allow operators to use past experiences to simulate the behavior of the system of interest and make predictions about future events. When interacting with a system, operators interpret the information provided by the display in terms of their expectancies and use their knowledge to direct sampling from the display. That is, the operators have mental models of how the system with which they are interacting operates, what displayed information will be pertinent to the current situation, and where and how that information is displayed.

An example using a Web browser is as follows. If a user must perform tasks using a browser, the user would expect the layout of the Web page to match "typical" Web pages: The home page hyperlink is located at the top-left corner, the major navigation controls or links for the major sections of the site are located across the top of the page, the local navigation within each major section is along the left side of the page, and so forth (see Najjar, 2001). The user also has a functional understanding of how the browser operates and takes actions dependent on this understanding. For example, most users expect to be able to navigate backwards to previous Web pages by clicking on the back button. However, the links for some Web pages are designed to open the page in a new window, and clicking on the back button does not yield the expected outcome. Because the user is likely to have considerable experience with Web pages and have developed a strong mental model for them, Web pages that are not formatted in a manner consistent with the operator's mental model may lead to poorer performance. For instance, a user expects text that is colored and underlined to be hypertext, for which a click on the text will open another page relating to the topic. Displays that underline and color text solely to emphasize a word or concept that is not hyperlinked may cause confusion to the user.

A user's mental model may not contain complete information about the system, and it may include concepts that are not part of the system (G. Fischer, 1991). To format the display in a manner consistent with the operator's mental model, Wickens, Gordon, and Liu (1998) suggest that the design principles of pictorial realism and moving components be incorporated. The *principle of pictorial realism* is that the display should visually depict the item it is supposed to represent. Windows Explorer uses pictorial realism where folders containing files can be organized into sections like a physical file cabinet. The *principle of moving components* refers to the notion that moving elements of a display should move in the direction that is consistent with the user's mental model. For example, when displaying how much fuel is remaining in a vehicle, the fuel gauge bar should move from top (full) to bottom (empty) as the fuel is used up.

Ecological Interface Design

The notion of designing displays consistent with the mental models of the users provides a foundation for *ecological interface design*, which focuses on the idea that displays should not be arbitrary symbolic representations of the "real" environment but should impose lawful constraints that are representative of the actual environment (Flach, 2001; Vicente & Rasmussen, 1992). Ecological interface design begins by considering the constraints in the task environment that are relevant to the user (Vicente, 1999). It is based on two conceptual tools developed by Rasmussen, the *abstraction hierarchy* (Rasmussen, 1985) and the *skill-rules-knowledge behavioral taxonomy* (Rasmussen, 1983). The abstraction hierarchy distinguishes five levels of representation of a work domain (e.g., a power plant) that can be characterized in terms of lower-level physical information concerning the equipment, its physical appearance, and layout, and higher-level functional information concerning the purposes and functions of the equipment.

In the behavioral taxonomy, the *skill-based* mode is relatively automatic behavior that occurs when the situation is a familiar one in which overlearned procedures are applicable. For example, an aircraft pilot is highly trained at the basic operation of an aircraft and can automatically execute the required actions under normal flying conditions. Behavior is *rule-based* when a rare event occurs, but the event is one for which a previously learned rule can be retrieved and applied. Rule-based behavior may occur for the pilot when an emergency signal comes on indicating that one of two engines is on fire. Because this situation is not routine, the pilot cannot behave in an automatic mode. However, the pilot may remember that during training he or she was instructed to shut down the engine if this situation occurred. Finally, behavior is *knowledge-based* when an event is unfamiliar, no simple rule applies, and the user must engage in problem solving. Knowledge-based behavior may occur for the pilot if the aircraft control becomes erratic but there is no obvious indicator as to the nature of the problem. In that situation, the pilot must develop and evaluate alternative hypotheses about the cause of the problem and what action should be taken. Clearly, in this type of emergency situation, it is important that the pilot be able to arrive at an appropriate understanding of the problem as quickly as possible.

The basic idea behind ecological interface design is that the information that needs to be represented in a display varies as a function of the appropriate behavior mode. The display should highlight the goal-relevant information in a way that changes dynamically to reflect the real world. Because skill-based and, to a lesser extent, rule-based behavior require less cognitive effort than knowledge-based behavior, the interface should encourage their use whenever possible. For skill-based behavior, the user should be able to respond directly to the display, with the structure of the displayed information being isomorphic to the required actions. Hansen (1995) describes the example of using landing lights to mark the runway for night flights. Landing lights provide reduced information relative to the visible runway in daylight, but the information that they do provide is the functional information needed to control the landing. For rule-based behavior, the interface should signal the appropriate rules to be applied with a consistent mapping between the constraints of the work environment and the information provided by the display.

When the operator must engage in knowledge-based behavior, the interface should guide the problem-solving and decision-making process so that the operator reaches an appropriate solution. For this purpose, the work environment should be represented in the form of an abstraction hierarchy. This hierarchy serves as a model of the system that emphasizes the functional and physical components, and their relations. For example, STEAMER, a processor display to simulate steam plant operation and maintenance, uses a graphical interface that conveys the conceptual components of the steam plant and how they interact (Holland, Hutchins, & Weitzman, 1984). STEAMER can present simplified versions of subsystems that enable the operator to develop an understanding of what is occurring within each specific subsystem.

Because ecological interface design is a relatively recent development, its value has yet to be fully evaluated. Vicente (2002) summarizes the progress to date and the challenges facing the enterprise. Ecological interface designs have been shown to yield better performance than alternative designs, but this superiority is primarily for more complex tasks that require knowledge-based behavior. The improved performance is due largely to providing the higher-level functional information, in addition to the physical information, in a visuo-spatial format rather than a verbal format. Many important issues concerning implementation of this technology remain to be addressed, including the form in which to display the functional information, the potentially negative impact of sensor noise and failure, and how to integrate the interface into the full system design.

Memory-Related Factors

As described in Chapter 7, working memory refers to representations that are currently being used or have recently been used, and that last for a short duration. The main characteristic of working memory is that it is of limited capacity, a point emphasized by G. A. Miller (1956). Displays that exceed the operator's limited capacity can lead to errors. Long-term memory refers to representations that can be

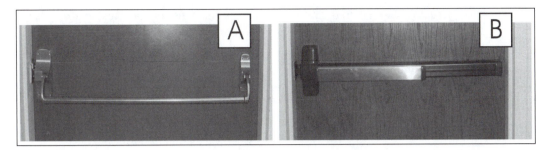

Figure 8.4   Example of door pushbars: (A) bad design and (B) good design.

remembered for durations longer than can be attributed to working memory. The information provided by a display often is interpreted in terms of knowledge from long-term memory. For example, an operator's mental model of the system is dependent in part on the expectancies derived from long-term memory. However, an operator's sole reliance on long-term memory may lead to error because information can be forgotten or misremembered.

Wickens, Gordon, and Liu (1998) suggested three memory principles that should be incorporated into the design of displays. First, the display should have an anticipatory property. When operators are overloaded, they do not have the mental resources to devote to predicting what will occur in the future and anticipating what action to take next. Performance can be aided by the use of displays that make these predictions for the operator. Second, the display should provide knowledge in the world, that is, explicit reminders or prompts that will minimize memory retrieval problems for the operator. Finally, the display should be designed to be consistent with automatic human action tendencies. All three of these points are illustrated in Figure 8.4, which shows two types of push bars for opening doors. Both are designed in a manner to signal that they should be pushed, rather than pulled, to open the door. However, only door B signals unambiguously which side should be pushed. Thus, a person who uses the door does not need to remember which side the door will open to, will tend to automatically respond appropriately, and will be able to predict the future state of the door after pushing on it.

COMPLEX TASKS AND DISPLAY ARRANGEMENTS ▲

In complex tasks, a person must direct his or her attention to multiple sources of information and multiple task components in an appropriate, coordinated manner.

These tasks can vary in their goals, from integrating instructional text with associated displays and diagrams to monitoring instruments and controlling a vehicle.

Cognitive Load and Instructional Learning

When a display or diagram alone does not provide a learner with sufficient information to understand its meaning, the learner must integrate instructional or textual information with the displayed information to achieve this understanding. Performance suffers in this case because the learner must split his or her attention between both sources of information and mentally integrate them. Sweller (1994) interpreted this split-attention effect in terms of *cognitive load theory*. According to cognitive load theory, performance decreases when the task requires attention to be split between the textual and displayed information because cognitive workload increases. A prediction of cognitive load theory is that designing the display in a manner that promotes information integration can reduce costs associated with splitting attention. Consistent with this prediction, Chandler and Sweller (1996) showed that physically integrating instructional material with its associated diagrams reduces working memory load and, as a result, improves learning.

Another way to reduce the costs of splitting attention is to use auditory presentation for the textual material that needs to be integrated with the information in a diagram (Kalyuga, Chandler, & Sweller, 1999). This benefit in performance can be attributed to the fact that working memory is enhanced by the use of both visual and auditory modalities, and that less interference occurs when, in Baddeley's (1998a) terminology (see Chapter 7), one source of information can be maintained in the phonological loop and the other in the visuo-spatial sketchpad. However, Kalyuga et al. found that providing the textual material that needs to be integrated with the diagram to both the auditory and visual modalities concurrently increases cognitive load and decreases performance. Kalyuga et al. also demonstrated that when the textual information is presented visually and separate from the diagrammed information, the cost of splitting attention can be reduced by using a computerized display to color-coordinate the textual material with its related components in the diagram.

Thus, the results of split-attention studies show that attentional demands for tasks requiring mental integration of information can be reduced if the pieces of information to be integrated are located in close physical proximity, presented in distinct modalities, or color-coded. It should be noted, however, that presenting redundant textual information in different modalities decreases, rather than increases, performance, and that color-coding is beneficial only if the number of colors does not impose extra mental demands.

Vehicle Control and Operation

Driving a vehicle is a task for which attention must be time-shared between the road and in-car tasks such as monitoring the speedometer and other instruments, operating a cassette/compact disc/radio player, and dialing and talking on a cell phone. Because the driver needs to attend to visual information from outside of the vehicle to keep the vehicle from going off the road or colliding with obstacles, increases in the time for which gaze is directed toward the interior of the vehicle will increase the likelihood of an accident. To drive effectively while performing secondary tasks, the driver must employ appropriate strategies regarding when, and for how long, she needs to divert attention from the roadway to one of the other tasks to accomplish that task while not placing the vehicle at risk. Glances of less than 0.5 seconds are probably too short to gather information about most in-car tasks, whereas glances longer than 2 seconds keep attention away from the road for too long (see, e.g., Zwahlen, Adams, & DeBald, 1988).

Wikman, Nieminen, and Summala (1998) examined whether novice drivers show less adequate supervisory control strategies than more experienced drivers, as would be expected if the strategies were learned. They tested groups of inexperienced (mean age 19 years) and experienced (mean age 36 years) drivers, with driving as the primary task. Driving was performed alone or while inserting and removing a cassette from a cassette player, dialing a cell phone, or searching for a station playing "soft" music on the radio. Lateral displacements of the car were measured, as were the number and duration of glances to the inside instrument. As in previous studies (Nieminen & Summala, 1994), the mean glance lengths did not differ between the experienced and novice drivers. However, the novice drivers showed more variability in their glance durations than did the experts, showing larger numbers of glances that were too short to be effective and too long to be safe. The novices also showed larger lateral displacements of the car as a consequence of their glances.

Aircraft pilots similarly must attend both to the outside environment and to the internal cockpit displays. As new instruments are added to which the pilot must attend, these instruments could reduce that time devoted to attending to the outside environment or the time attending to other instruments. A proposed change in the air traffic control system is to increase pilot authority over flight path selection and reduce the role of the air traffic controller, an approach that is called user-preferred routing (or "free flight"). Allowing the pilot to select the flight path requires awareness of the status of air traffic near the pilot's aircraft; this information will be provided by a *cockpit display of traffic information (CDTI)*. Wickens, Helleberg, and Xu (2002) had pilots fly a simulator using a CDTI or following air traffic control instructions. The flight route involved maneuvers necessary to avoid air traffic. The pilots looked at the CDTI 25% of the time, with all of this time coming from the time that otherwise would be devoted to looking outside of the aircraft. Thus, use of the CDTI requires considerable attention, and problems may arise if events occur in nearby airspace that are not easily detectable by the CDTI.

Head-Up Displays

One solution to the problem of having to divide time looking outside vehicles (the far domain) and monitoring inside instrumentation (the near domain) is to use *head-up displays (HUDs)*. HUDs superimpose a virtual image of the information display on the central area in which the outside world is viewed in order to place important display information in close proximity (Weintraub & Ensing, 1992). The basic idea is that superimposing the displays for the near and far domains will allow more parallel processing of the two images, reducing the need for scanning both domains. Head-up displays were initially developed for use in aircraft, where the pilot must maintain visual contact with the external environment and monitor displays at the same time. More recently, their use has been extended to automobiles for similar reasons. The advantages of HUDs are that (1) they allow both the environment and the display to be monitored simultaneously, minimizing "head-down" time during which the pilot or driver is looking away from the outside environment; (2) a display can be aligned with its actual counterpart in the environment; and (3) the display can be collimated to appear at "optical infinity" to match the environment so that the lens of the eye does not have to refocus when switching focus between the environment and display. The disadvantages of HUDs are that they (1) create clutter, (2) may not be seen against the environmental background, and (3) reduce visibility of environmental objects that are located behind them. Thus, the cost-benefit ratio must be evaluated before determining whether to implement HUDs (see Newman, 1995).

According to Weintraub and Ensing (1992), the costs and benefits of HUDs must be based on the three dimensions by which they differ from conventional head-down displays: their optical distance, their location, and their symbology. Tasks can require focusing on the near domain or the far domain, or integrating information across the two (see Figure 8.5; Wickens & Long, 1995). Attention may thus be focused on one domain, divided between the two domains, or switched between the domains.

A supposed benefit of HUDs is to minimize cognitive switching because the eyes do not need to be moved or refocused. However, Weintraub and Ensing (1992) noted that all of the cues that a switch is occurring that are present with a head-down display are absent with a HUD: looking up, changing focus, and changing convergence.

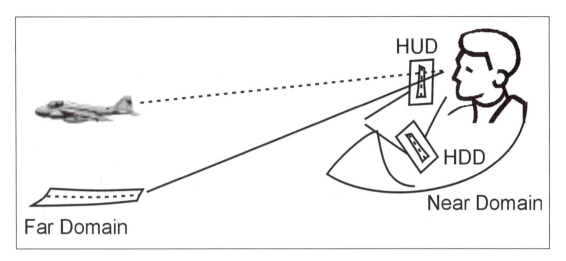

Figure 8.5   Symbolic representation of pilots' attention processing between near and far domains using head-up versus head-down displays.

SOURCE: Wickens & Long, 1995. Copyright 1995 by the American Psychological Association; reprinted with permission.

Consequently, it is possible that a HUD will produce *cognitive capture* (or *cognitive tunneling*), and actually make it difficult to shift attention to the environment. Several studies have found faster switching times between the near and far domains with HUDs than with head-down displays (see, e.g., McCann, Foyle, & Johnston, 1993; Weintraub, Haines, & Randle, 1984, 1985). Moreover, HUDs have been shown to yield better flight-path control (Larish & Wickens, 1991; Wickens, Martin-Emerson, & Larish, 1993) and taxiing (Lasswell & Wickens, 1995). However, in these studies, all of the benefits were associated with normal, expected tasks.

Evidence for cognitive tunneling has been found for unexpected events. Fischer, Haines, and Price (1980) had pilots land with the HUD for many trials, before an aircraft unexpectedly moved onto the runway in front of them. The pilots did not notice the aircraft blocking the runway and continued their landing. Wickens and Long (1995) extended these findings, confirming that the unexpected nature of the missed event was crucial.

Brickner (1989) and Foyle, Sanford, and McCann (1991) found a performance tradeoff between maintenance of altitude (a HUD task) and path-tracking performance. Path-tracking performance was better with no HUD digital altitude information than with a centered HUD display, whereas altitude maintenance was better with the HUD display than without. Foyle, McCann, Sanford, and Schwirzke (1993) found that this performance tradeoff was evident only when the HUD symbology was presented near the out-of-the-window path information. When the HUD symbology was more than 8° of visual angle from the path information, processing was efficient both for the path-tracking task and the HUD task. They proposed that the eye movements required at large separations reintroduced a cue that a shift was in progress. Foyle, Dowell, and Hooey (2001) eliminated several confounds in Foyle et al.'s (1993) study by controlling HUD background contrast and independently assessing HUD background complexity and motion. Their results confirmed that cognitive tunneling is eliminated by placing the HUD display at least 8° away from the out-of-window information.

Tufano (1997) reviewed the literature for HUDs in automobiles and concluded that the issues of focal distance and cognitive capacity have a greater impact on safety in the automotive context than in aviation. He noted that the recommended guidelines to focus automotive HUDs at 2.0–2.5 m were based on findings showing that older adults had difficulty extracting information from the HUD at closer focal distances (Inuzuka, Osumi, and Shinkai, 1991; Kato et al., 1992). However, possible influences on perception of outside objects were not considered. Tufano notes that the problems of positive misaccommodation, where outside objects appear smaller than they are, should be exacerbated with the closer focal distance used for automotive displays. Tufano notes, "One of the paradoxes of HUDs is that they may do their job too well. Their salience, legibility, and head-up location may command too much of the operator's visual attention" (1997, p. 306), consistent with the earlier description of cognitive tunneling.

Intelligent Transport Systems and In-Vehicle Navigation Aids

One area in which rapid technological change is occurring is that of traffic systems. The advanced technologies coming into use include in-vehicle navigation and control systems, digital maps, and highway-to-vehicle communication systems, among others. These technologies, collectively known as *intelligent transport systems* (ITS), have the potential to reduce many of the problems associated with overcrowded roadways and to improve driving safety. However, these systems increase the complexity of the driver's task and, consequently, the mental workload imposed on the driver. In order for the potential benefits of ITS to be attained, the interfaces that are developed must take into account the way that humans perform complex tasks (Noy, 1997).

Virtual Reality Environments

Virtual reality environments manipulate sensory stimuli, such as visual, auditory, and haptic stimuli, to provide the observer with a sensation of interacting with the actual world. Such environments can be constructed using several different technologies, including simulators, head-mounted displays, and desktop display screens (Wilson, 1997). If the virtual environment is designed optimally, the observer will report that there is a strong "presence of reality." When interacting with the system, the observers must focus their attention on the coherent set of stimuli simulated by the environment. As a result, several authors (see Nash, Edwards, Thompson, & Barfield, 2000, for a review) have suggested that the amount of attention allocated to the virtual environment is an important factor in determining the degree of presence that a user will feel. Stanney and Salvendy (1998) indicated that users typically report the perceived degree of presence by dividing attention between their interaction with the environment and their memories or expectations of the real world.

Users must also be able to navigate through the virtual environment in order to reach a desired location or object. Navigation is a cognitive task that requires much attention for unfamiliar routes and less attention for familiar ones. Nash et al. (2000) indicated that current virtual environment technology has not been able to provide the user with a high fidelity simulation of the real world, causing many users to become lost in the environment, report feelings of disorientation, and be dissatisfied with their interaction. The ability of a user to navigate the virtual environment successfully is also dependent, in part, on the user's spatial ability.

SUSTAINED ATTENTION AND VIGILANCE ▲

Vigilance tasks have become increasingly common in the work environment with the increasing automation of many jobs. With automation, the operator's job changes from one of actively controlling the system to one of monitoring a display for occasional malfunctions or unexpected events. In a typical vigilance task in the laboratory, a subject is asked to monitor a display for certain changes in it (e.g., the occurrence of a rare stimulus event). Performance of the task thus requires sustained attention for long periods of time. The most common finding for vigilance tasks is the *vigilance decrement*: The hit rate decreases as the time on the task increases.

The vigilance decrement was first noticed during World War II. After 30 minutes in a shift, radar operators in the Royal Air Force began to miss the signals on their screens that indicated possible enemy submarines (N. H. Mackworth, 1948). Mackworth (1950, 1961) developed a task called the *clock test* in which a pointer moved around a blank clock face jumping 0.3 inches every second. Occasionally, the pointer would make a double jump of 0.6 inches, and the participant was to respond to this target event by pressing a key. About 85% of the targets were detected early in the session, but this decreased to about 75% over the first 30 minutes and continued to decrease slightly more after that time. This decrement in performance has been confirmed numerous times with a variety of tasks in subsequent research.

The vigilance decrement is affected by several factors that can be classified into three broad categories: task parameters, environmental or situational factors, and subject characteristics (Ballard, 1996). Performance usually declines less when the target event is salient than when it is not. Detection performance also varies inversely with the background event rate and directly with signal event frequency. When spatial uncertainty exists about where a signal event may occur, performance is worse than when the event can occur in only a single location. Similar results are obtained when the number of displays that must be monitored increases. Performance also improves if participants are cued verbally that a signal will occur soon, just prior to the occurrence of one. Environmental factors include auditory noise, heat, and vibration. Their effects seem to be complex, varying as a function of situational factors such as intensity, duration, and quality of the environmental factor. Subject characteristics associated with the vigilance decrement include age, with performance being an inverted U-shaped function of age across the life span.

Many of these findings are consistent with the possibility that the vigilance decrement is due to underarousal (that is, a low level of alertness or preparation; see Chapter 2), a view that was held for many years (see, e.g., Frankmann & Adams, 1962). That is, because the task is monotonous, it was thought that the operator could not maintain a sufficient level of alertness. However, recent evidence has suggested the opposite, that the information processing required for vigilance tasks is highly demanding and that the vigilance decrement reflects depletion of information resources over the period of the vigil (Warm, Dember, & Hancock, 1996).

Warm et al. (1996) used the NASA-TLX as a measure of mental demands (see Chapter 9). Perceptual sensitivity (i.e., responding to the target event and not to nontarget events) was greater when the target was of high salience than when it was of low salience, and the former condition was judged to be less demanding than the latter. Moreover, ratings of mental demand increased linearly over the period of the vigil. In a series of other experiments, Warm et al. showed that other variables (e.g., low background event rate and spatial uncertainty) that reduce vigilance performance also lead to higher ratings of mental effort.

One issue of concern in the research on vigilance has been whether the decrease in signal detection across time is due to a change in perceptual sensitivity or to a shift in response bias. This issue can be addressed by examining the frequency of false detection responses on noise trials and performing a signal detection analysis, as described in Chapter 2. If the proportion of correct detections decreases across the vigil but the proportion of incorrect detections does not, then the decrement would reflect a decrease in perceptual sensitivity. If, however, the proportion of incorrect detections also decreases, then a shift to a more conservative response criterion is implicated. Based on such analyses, Parasuraman and Davies (1977) concluded that, for many situations, signal detection analyses show little change in sensitivity as indexed by d′ across time but a shift in the decision criterion, β, to a more conservative response criterion. That is, the false alarms as well as the correct detections decrease as a function of time on task. However, perceptual sensitivity seems to be affected as well when the task requires the subject to compare rapidly presented events to information in memory in order to identify the events as signals or nonsignals. Judgments that require comparing a signal to a standard in memory are much more attention demanding in general than are tasks for which the judgments can be based entirely on information available in the stimuli themselves. Apparently, the effort required to satisfy the high attention demands of rapid memory-comparison tasks is responsible for the decline in perceptual sensitivity when the task is performed for long periods of time. Signal discriminability and task type (cognitive vs. sensory) can also influence whether the decrement will be primarily one of a more conservative bias or a decrease in sensitivity (See, Howe, Warm, & Dember, 1995).

SUMMARY ▲

This chapter shows that many tasks in everyday life require directing attention to critical aspects of information at appropriate points in time. Displays that are designed in accordance with human attention capabilities will be easier to use than ones that are not. In this chapter, we showed that strategies and control processes play an important role in the sampling of displayed information. For a display to be effective, it must take advantage of task constraints and automatic response tendencies, as well as the user's expectancies and mental model of the situation. Search of a complex display can be facilitated by structuring the display so that the most important information will tend to be examined first and by using cues to signal locations of relevant visual information. The full capabilities of new display technologies will be realized only if they are designed in a way consistent with the characteristics of human attention.

CHAPTER 9

MENTAL WORKLOAD AND SITUATION AWARENESS

Attention, more than any other topic in cognitive psychology, exemplifies the interplay of basic and applied concerns. The need to solve practical problems was at least partly responsible for the resurgence of interest in attention in the 1950s and, by extension, for the central place that attention research has taken in modern cognitive psychology. Topics such as the ability of air traffic controllers to divide attention among multiple aircraft and of radar operators to maintain vigilance while on the lookout for enemy submarines led to a renewed interest in attention as a topic of research. Interest in topics such as the limits of divided attention, selective attention, and vigilance has spawned extensive research in both theoretical and applied contexts. In fact, it could be argued that theoretical work has left applied work behind in the development of detailed processing models of attention. However, theoretical work in attention is still often driven by the need to solve practical problems. Some of these problems, regarding the display of information, were discussed in Chapter 8. Equally important, and not entirely unrelated, problems are how to measure and describe the attentional demands of task performance and how to predict when errors are likely to occur.

One of the biggest changes in society in the last 100 years has been the nature of work. Comprehensive and impressive technological developments have transformed both the variety of jobs needing to be done and the way in which work is accomplished. A major trend has been a reduction in the physical requirements of work. This can be seen even in a relatively straightforward job such as that of a secretary, where paper files are being replaced with computer files, thus reducing considerably the amount of walking, carrying, and handling of material involved in the job. Instead of typing on a typewriter, most secretaries (like the rest of us) now use powerful word processing programs on a computer for even the simplest tasks. Thus, whereas the physical demands of work have steadily decreased, the cognitive demands of work have shown a remarkable increase. Just using a modern telephone can bring with it the requirement to remember numerous codes and special functions—and these functions must be carried out while monitoring e-mail messages, fax transmissions, and, of course, the demands of people needing information or assistance. The focus of this chapter is on measuring and evaluating the mental demands imposed by tasks and describing how people cope with multiple demands on their attention. A related issue is, of course, why performance sometimes breaks down such that errors occur.

Mental workload refers to the information processing demands imposed by the performance of cognitive tasks. According to Gopher and Donchin (1986), mental workload reflects "the difference between the capacities of the information-processing system that are required for task performance to satisfy expectations and the capacity available at any given time" (p. 41-3). This definition implies that the mental workload experienced by one person may be different than that experienced by another; workload depends on the match between task requirements and capacities, and different people have different capacities. Gopher and Donchin also imply that the workload imposed by a task or task combination will depend on the capacities called upon. An important question is, what are these capacities? An equally important question is, how can mental workload best be measured?

▲ PROCESSING RESOURCES

Defining mental workload as the difference between available and required capacities requires a definition of what those capacities are. Some of the key terms that are used in describing mental workload are *effort, arousal,* and *resources.* Effort is a general term and simply refers to conscious exertion. Arousal is generally used in the physiological sense of readiness for activity, and resources may be viewed as hypothetical processing reserves or sensory, motor, or information processing capacities. All three terms are sometimes interrelated. We can think of resources as reflecting arousal level and being directed, as effort, to various activities, such as in the definition of a resource according to Wickens (1991) as "one of a small set of scarce commodities within the human information processing system, which is associated with a distinct physiological structure, and with physiological arousal changes as increased demands are placed on it" (p. 22).

In a general sense, workload is caused by the need to exert effort or make use of available processing resources. Not all tasks, however, will impose measurable mental workload. As long as the processing requirements are well within the capacities of the performer, no feelings or manifestations of load will be present. The experience of mental workload arises when sufficient stress is placed on various capacities. Sources of mental workload might include energetical limitations on processing such as having to perform difficult work when sleep deprived, structural limitations such as not being able to attend to information both in front of and behind you, scarcity of resources, the need for controlled versus automatic processing, and top-down regulation of perceptual processes.

Arousal and Workload

The relation between the concept of arousal and mental workload has been the subject of intense study, and, as you will see, many measures of workload are essentially measures of arousal. As is the case for arousal, performance seems to benefit from a minimal amount of imposed mental workload. Low levels of workload can lead to boredom and a lack of alertness that influence performance negatively. Also, as is the case with arousal, too much workload hurts performance. The goal, then, is to design systems that demand optimal levels of workload.

The concept of mental workload has its foundations in a unitary-resource model of attention, and arousal has a central role in this model. Perhaps the best-known unitary-resource model is that of Kahneman (1973). According to Kahneman, the arousal of an individual determines the capacity available to engage in different activities (see Figure 9.1). Attention is viewed as a limited-capacity resource that can be allocated to a variety of processes and tasks. Whenever the demands on attentional resources exceed the available capacity, performance suffers.

Kahneman (1973) introduced the idea of an allocation policy for distributing attentional resources. The existence of an allocation policy implies that there is a sort of "comparator" that assesses current resources and the active intentions and activities of the performer. The need for attentional allocation ability is most evident when situations are complex or dangerous. When performance demands are high, stability of performance depends on the effectiveness of attentional control in maintaining the current priorities. One mundane example of this is driving a car while talking on a mobile phone. When driving demands are routine, the driver is able to carry on a conversation without too much trouble. However, when conditions

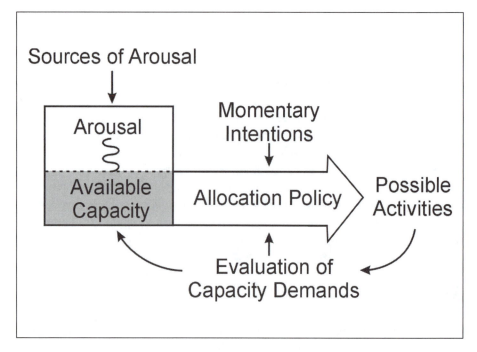

Figure 9.1   Kahneman's (1973) unitary-resource model of attention.

are demanding, such as when the weather is bad or when unfamiliar streets have to be navigated, the driver will not be able to keep up his or her end of the conversation, and may even terminate the conversation. In many situations, performance must be "protected" from environmental disturbance, and this can be accomplished only through maintaining the priority of task-oriented goals. It has been suggested that this need to monitor and protect task performance may be a significant factor in feelings of load or fatigue: Protecting primary-task performance may produce costs in terms of decreased stability in other energetic systems, such as affective states, emotional stability, and autonomic activation (Hockey, 1993).

The operation of a "performance-protection strategy" can make it difficult to demonstrate overt decrements in primary-task performance (Hockey, 1993). Only when primary tasks are quite sensitive (such as some vigilance tasks; see Chapter 8) is it possible to measure direct effects of a variety of stressors. But even when primary-task performance is not affected, it may be possible to measure the load placed on the operator. One way of doing this is to measure *compensatory costs,* such as increased sympathetic activation or feelings of effort or strain. Several studies have shown that people who make more mistakes under stressful conditions show less evidence of compensatory costs (e.g., relatively low production of catecholamines, a group of hormones commonly used as measures of workload and stress, or reports of subjective effort), whereas people who perform well show more evidence of such costs (see, e.g., Lundberg & Frankenhaeuser, 1978; Wilkinson, 1962). Sloppy performance may be a protective strategy!

Another possible indicator of stress or high workload is *strategy adjustment*. When demands are high, people will, if possible, switch to using less effortful strategies for performing a task. A phenomenon called *attentional narrowing* is an example of such a shift. This refers to the tendency of people in high-stress situations to restrict their attention to an inappropriately small set of displays or information sources. Even people who only think that they are going to experience a stressful situation (e.g., after having been told by an experimenter that they were going to experience the conditions of a deep dive in a pressure chamber) have been shown to restrict their attention to central cues, ignoring peripheral stimuli in a detection task (Weltman, Smith, & Egstrom, 1971).

More serious consequences of attentional narrowing can be seen in environments such as aircraft cockpits, where pilots experiencing a problem with an indicator will focus their attention on that display, ignoring other indicators that are necessary for flight (Wickens & Hollands, 2000). Such attentional narrowing has probably been responsible for more than one "controlled flight into terrain." A final possible side effect of protecting performance is *fatigue aftereffects*. After having performed a fatiguing or stressful task, people show a preference for using low-cost strategies for performing other, unrelated tasks (see Hockey, 1993).

One experiment that suggests that there is a close relation between capacity and performance was carried out by P. Lavie, Gopher, and Wollman (1987). In this experiment, participants were first deprived of sleep for 28 hours. Following this, they were required to alternate between performing a choice-reaction-time task with different levels of movement difficulty for 13 minutes and lying on a bed for 7 minutes for a total of 36 hours. The experiment was conducted twice with each person. In one version of the experiment, participants were instructed to sleep when they were lying down, and in the other version they were told to try to stay awake. The instruction to sleep or stay awake did not affect the amount of time actually spent sleeping during the 7-minute periods, but it did affect reaction time (RT) and the coordination with which responses were made. It appears that trying to stay awake, even unsuccessfully, exhausts resources that can otherwise be used for task performance.

Multiple-Resources Framework

The idea that there is just one general resource or capacity for performing all sorts of tasks cannot account for some important aspects of task performance, such as the fact that two tasks of apparently equal difficulty may have completely different effects when combined with a third task, with one of the tasks causing interference and the other causing none. Such a finding suggests that the tasks draw on multiple, different resources, and that only when the same resources are required by another task will performance show a decrement. Three different sorts of effects stimulated the development of the *multiple-resources* concept (Wickens, 1980, 1984): difficulty insensitivity, structural alteration effects, and perfect time-sharing. *Difficulty insensitivity* refers to the fact that allocating more resources to one of two tasks does not always hurt performance on the other one. This is in violation of the idea that only one pool of resources or capacity is drawn upon. *Structural alteration* refers to changing the structure of a task without changing its difficulty, for example, by changing the stimulus modality and then seeing corresponding changes on the ability to perform the task concurrently with another one. If there were only one general resource, all tasks of the same difficulty should use up the same amount of capacity. Finally, *perfect time-sharing* is anomalous when two tasks shown to interfere with other tasks can nonetheless be performed together without decrement.

Many current workload measurement techniques are more closely linked to multiple-resources models than to unitary-resource models of attention. The multiple-resources view is that different sorts of tasks, or different task components, draw on separate resources with their own distinct capacity reserves. This implies that if two tasks draw on different resources, they may be performed together more efficiently and their combined mental workload may be lower than if they rely on the same resources. Wickens (1980, 1984) proposed that there are separate processing resources corresponding to the basic information processing stages of perception, central processing, and responding, as well as separate resources for spatial and verbal processing codes, visual and auditory modalities, and manual and vocal responses. These resources for processing stages, codes, and input and output modalities can be represented as a three-dimensional model (see Figure 9.2). Evidence for separate visual and auditory attentional modalities, reviewed in Chapter 4, is generally supportive of the proposal that visual and auditory information may be processed independently, at least up to a point. The model is also consistent with the idea that working memory is based on both a phonological loop and a visual-spatial sketchpad (Baddeley, 1986; see Chapter 7), and with the finding that dual-task performance cannot always be predicted on the basis of single-task difficulty. However, the multiple-resources model is mute on the subject of executive control and possible interactions between codes and modalities, beyond suggesting that switching attention brings with it a "mental cost" that may influence how often different sources in the environment are sampled.

Although inadequate as a model of attention, the multiple-resources view can serve as a useful framework for predicting operator performance in complex tasks. The major strength of the multiple-resources framework is that it allows tasks to be

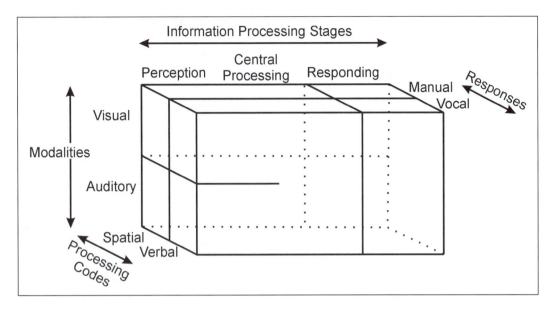

Figure 9.2 Wickens's multiple-resources framework. The different modalities, processing codes and stages, and response modalities are assumed to each have a separate pool of attentional resources.

SOURCE: Wickens, 1984. Reprinted with permission from Academic Press.

defined in terms that are relatively easy to represent. Researchers can use the framework to develop task descriptions that allow the prediction of time-sharing performance: Better time-sharing between two tasks is expected to the extent that they use separate rather than common resources because demand increases in one will be less likely to affect the other. A weakness of the framework with regard to modeling performance is its inability to offer clearly defined scales of the amount of demand for resources that generalize across different tasks.

PROCESSING STRATEGIES ▲

When a task is complex and consists of multiple, concurrent processing demands, different task components can be scheduled and carried out in many ways. The possible variations in the scheduling and carrying out of tasks means that operator strategies may vary from one person or situation to another. The existence of multiple processing strategies can complicate the task of measuring mental workload because task demands might be met in different ways, thereby modifying the workload or resource expenditure involved in performance. *Strategy shifts,* themselves, can be used as an indicator of changes in operator mental workload. For example, higher time demands might lead to speed–accuracy trade-off. A more specific example of a strategy shift comes from a study of air traffic controllers conducted by Sperandio (1971). Controllers in that study were found to use one of two different strategies for landing aircraft, depending on the workload imposed by the situation. When the workload was relatively low, the controllers used an efficient (in terms of time and elegance of the routing) strategy of having each aircraft land directly—that is, take the shortest route to landing. When the imposed workload was higher, they used the strategy of sending the aircraft to a standard route consisting of entering a holding pattern and then following a standard set of procedures. The second strategy required more time per aircraft and was less efficient by objective measures, but it was successful in helping the controllers to better cope with high workload levels.

One factor that has a large influence on the methods or strategies employed is the skill level of the performer. Training and experience not only can influence the strategies adopted by the operator, but also can lead to fundamental changes in the way that stimuli are processed and, thereby, influence the processing resource demands of a task. In some tasks, skilled operators show evidence of automaticity of processing, such that processing is "rapid, parallel, and effortless" (Eggemeier, Wilson, Kramer, & Damos, 1991, p. 212) and not subject to capacity or resource limits normally associated with performance. Tasks that have been automatized through extensive, consistent training can show very high levels of time-sharing with other tasks (see, e.g., Strayer & Kramer, 1990; see also Chapter 6). Therefore, it is important to test operators who possess a level of skill representative of that of the target population.

▲ MEASURING MENTAL WORKLOAD

Meeting the goal of maintaining mental workload at an optimal level depends on designing environments and tasks that make appropriate demands on the operator. In order to determine whether one design or another is more acceptable, it is necessary to measure the mental workload of the operator. Three classes of techniques have been developed and extensively tested for these purposes: physiological, performance-based, and subjective measures.

Physiological Measures

Physiological measures of mental workload are direct measurements of various body or brain responses to task performance. There are two classes of physiological measures: ones that presume to measure general arousal and ones that reflect brain activity associated with specific processing activity (Gopher,

1994). The basic assumption underlying the use of general arousal measures is that various bodily systems are activated or aroused whenever the demand for mental effort increases. Increases in arousal lead to cardiovascular and respiratory changes, and influence brain electrical activity. Although many different measurements of these changes have been used in the study of the effects of work, the physiological responses to arousal that seem to be the most suited for examining changes in mental workload are changes in pupil diameter and heart-rate variability.

Parasympathetic activation in the autonomic nervous system is reflected in changes in pupil diameter: The greater the workload demands, the larger the size of the pupil. The relation between pupil size and arousal has a long history. In the 19th century, for example, some women would put an extract of belladonna ("pretty lady"), a poisonous plant containing atropine, into their eyes to dilate their pupils—thus indicating their arousal to those they were trying to arouse. The changes in pupil size as a result of exertion are small compared to the changes associated with variations in light level and changes in the depth of focus, such that the measurement of changes in pupil diameter, or *pupillometry*, requires special measurement techniques and strict environmental and stimulus control. Pupil diameter has been shown to be sensitive to a variety of sources of mental workload, including memory load, classification requirements, and motor-response difficulty (Beatty, 1982).

Cardiovascular changes are also associated with arousal levels and both mental and physical work. Although increased heart rates generally show a correlation with increased workload, heart rate itself depends primarily on physical workload and arousal level. A better indicator of mental workload is heart-rate variability—the changes in heart rate within brief time intervals. As mental effort increases, one of the components (around 0.10 Hz) of heart-rate variability decreases (Vicente, Thornton, & Moray, 1987).

Event-related potentials (ERPs) have been shown to be effective indicators of mental load. As described in Chapter 2, ERPs are measured by placing electrodes on the scalp and then measuring the electrical response to an externally presented stimulus. Variations in the properties, demands, and difficulty of tasks can be revealed by the elicitation or disappearance of certain components, or by changes in component amplitude. ERPs have also been shown to be sensitive to the priority given to a task. For example, when a task is designated as the primary (most important) task in a dual-task paradigm, the intensity of ERP components associated with primary-task events is greater than when the task is designated as the secondary (lower priority) task (see, e.g., Strayer & Kramer, 1990). It has been suggested that "such reciprocal changes in the intensity of activation demonstrate the expected competition and trade-off between concurrent tasks sharing a common limited pool of processing facilities" (Gopher, 1994, p. 273).

Compared to measures of general workload, such as pupil diameter and heart-rate variability, ERPs give an indication of more specific processing activity. One ERP component that appears to be clearly related to workload is the P3 (also

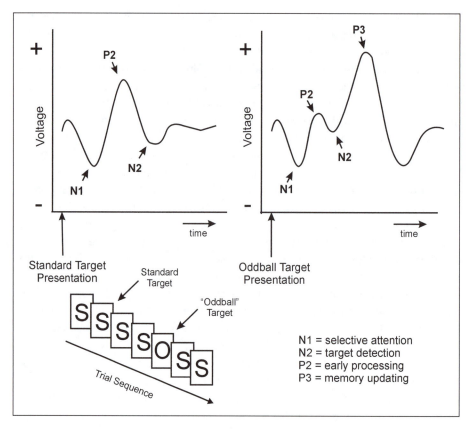

Figure 9.3   The oddball paradigm and effects on the processing associated with ERP components. The magnitude of the P3 component, associated with memory updating, is sensitive to mental workload.

called the P300; a positive component that occurs about 300 ms after stimulus onset). The P3 has an especially great amplitude when an unexpected stimulus occurs. For example, in the so-called oddball paradigm the same target is repeated many times, during which time the P3 becomes smaller. When an odd-ball (infrequent) target is then presented, it elicits a large P3 (see Figure 9.3). The P3 seems to reflect the amount of cognitive processing performed on a stimulus, and may best be described as reflecting memory updating (see Chapter 7). The P3 is diagnostic of the type of demand that contributes to workload because it is sensitive to stimulus-evaluation processes (and, thus, to perceptual and central processing resources; Isreal, Wickens, Chesney, & Donchin, 1980), but not to motor-output processes. For example, the amplitude of the P3 to an infrequent stimulus tone decreases as the difficulty of a concurrent visual-search task increases. Thus, it seems that not only do visual search and auditory discrimination require some of the same resources, but also the particular point of interference may be in memory updating.

Measuring the amplitude of ERP components may be a good indicator of workload even when the event used to elicit the ERP is totally irrelevant to the task. In a study in which radar operators performed a simulated radar monitoring task, irrelevant auditory probes—which the operators were instructed to ignore—were presented, and the effects of various task characteristics on the amplitude of several ERP components were measured relative to the onset of the tones (Kramer, Trejo, & Humphrey, 1995). It was found that the amplitude of several early ERP components (the N1, N2, and early and late mismatch negativity) decreased relative to baseline in the low load radar-monitoring task and decreased as a function of increasing radar-monitoring task difficulty. Moreover, P3 amplitude was sensitive to the introduction of the radar-monitoring task. Under very high loading levels, where the operator may be simply too busy or not have sufficient resources available to make responses, such a measurement technique may be effective.

Performance-Based Measures

One way to assess the mental workload imposed by a task is to simply measure some aspect or aspects of task performance. In this so-called *primary-task technique*, performance will suffer when performance demands exceed available resources. As described in the section "Arousal and Workload," when difficulty is below a certain level, primary-task performance will not show any decrements even though the operator may experience feelings of workload. For this reason, it is often preferable to use a *secondary-task methodology*, in which a second task is performed at the same time as the primary task, and the extent to which performance on one of the tasks suffers is measured. For example, operators might be asked to press a key as quickly as possible whenever they hear a tone. This is a simple-reaction-time task, because the participant need only decide whether the tone has been heard and then make a keypress response. Despite the simplicity of the task, RT to the tone (usually called a "probe" because it is a probe of the momentary attentional demands of the primary task) has been shown to depend on the processing resources required in the primary task.

Posner and Boies (1971) used this so-called *probe-reaction-time task* to examine capacity limits in a letter-comparison task. In this task, a warning signal was followed by the presentation of a letter. After a short interval, a second letter was presented and participants had to indicate, by pressing one of two keys, whether the two letters were the same or different. There were large differences in RT depending on when the probe was presented, with RTs being longest when the probe was presented around the time that the second letter was presented (see

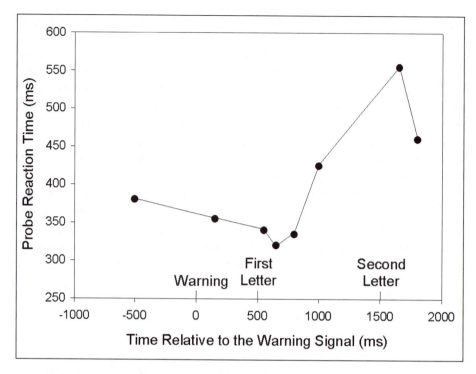

Figure 9.4   Probe-reaction time during a letter-matching task. Reaction time to the probe is assumed to reflect the capacity demands of the primary task.

SOURCE: Data from Posner & Boies, 1971.

Figure 9.4). This led Posner and Boies to conclude that response-selection processes required more general attentional resources than did encoding or preparatory processing. Whether probe-reaction time is a pure measure of central processing capacity is debatable, as shown by McLeod's (1978) finding that RT to the probe depends on whether the response to the probe is made verbally or manually. The finding that probe-reaction time depends on the nature of the probe-reaction-time task indicates that there may be multiple resources for different sorts of responses. Alternatively, structural interference due to the requirement to make similar sorts of responses may sometimes be confused with general processing requirements.

The probe-reaction-time task can be considered to be an example of a dual- or secondary-task measure. In general, a secondary-task measure of workload consists of adding a second task to the performance of a first one—thus increasing or manipulating the load on a certain component—and measuring the effects of this on performance. The purpose of the secondary task is to use up any additional capacity that might be available so that changes in the difficulty of the primary task will be reflected in performance changes (in either the primary or secondary task) and cannot be compensated for simply by trying harder. It is also possible to selectively influence the load or resource demands on specific components, and thereby to assess the contributions of different resources to task performance.

Some of the more frequently used secondary tasks are choice-reaction-time tasks (similar to the probe-reaction-time technique, but with two or more probes each requiring a different response), time estimation (estimation of the duration of a specified interval of time) or time-interval production (e.g., tap a key every 15 seconds), memory search (i.e., indicate whether a probe is a member of a set of items seen at the beginning of a trial), and mental arithmetic (e.g., perform sums; see Wickens et al., 1986, for a review). Although each of these tasks has been shown to be sensitive to the workload imposed by different task conditions, they are not completely interchangeable. For example, time estimation is more sensitive to demand manipulations than is time-interval production, but time-interval production is a better indicator of workload in tasks with a high degree of motor output (Eggemeier & Wilson, 1991).

In a secondary-task paradigm, performance on either the primary task (i.e., the task of interest) or the secondary task may be measured. In a *loading-task paradigm,* the emphasis is placed on the secondary task, and different aspects of primary-task performance are measured. Brown, Tickner, and Simmonds (1969) used this method in a study of driver performance. While driving, participants in the study listened to and evaluated sentences presented over a telephone. Automatized tasks, such as gear shifting, were not affected by the need to carry on a conversation, but more cognitive tasks, such as distance estimation, were. In a *subsidiary-task paradigm,* the emphasis is placed on the primary task, and performance on the secondary task is measured. For example, drivers can drive effectively while performing mental addition or subtraction, but the time required to perform sums or differences depends on whether one is driving or not, and on how demanding the driving conditions are (Eggemeier & Wilson, 1991).

In complex environments, loading or subsidiary tasks may be perceived as bothersome or too irrelevant to be given serious notice. This problem of poor operator acceptance can sometimes be circumvented by using an embedded task. *Embedded secondary tasks* are tasks that can occur naturally in the task environment under consideration, but are not part of the primary-task performance. For example, radio communication has been used as an embedded task to measure pilot workload. Eggemeier and Wilson (1991) suggest that embedded tasks may be used as either loading or subsidiary tasks, depending on instructions to the operators.

Because many factors may contribute to mental workload, it is important to use a variety of secondary tasks to form a complete picture of the mental load involved in performance. By pairing the task of interest with a variety of secondary tasks, it is possible to construct a load profile of the primary task that gives more complete information about the load imposed by a task than any one measure can. In general, it is important to choose secondary tasks on the basis of their overlap with the information resources required for the primary task (e.g., in accordance with the multiple-resources framework; Wickens, 1980, 1984).

Performance Operating Characteristics

The extent to which two tasks can be performed together can be graphically represented as a *performance operating characteristic* (POC; Navon & Gopher, 1979), in which performance on one task is plotted against performance on a second task. As shown in Figure 9.5, the POC depicts the combined influences on performance of task difficulty and allocation policy. Given that two tasks compete with each other for a limited pool of resources, the more difficult a task, the harder it will be to combine with a second task and the more performance will suffer to the extent that resources are withdrawn from it and allocated to the other task. If two tasks can be perfectly timeshared, performance on both tasks will remain at single-task levels despite instructions to emphasize one task or the other, and performance will fall at the so-called independence point, P. A diagonal line from the upper left-hand corner to the lower right-hand corner would indicate that any allocation of resources to Task B will detract from performance on Task A, and vice versa. Most task combinations will result in a more or less gradual drop in the performance of one of the tasks as more and more resources are allocated to the other task. In this case, performance at different *allocation policies* (e.g., "devote 50% of resources to Task A and 50% to Task B") will fall along a curve, the POC. The distance of the POC from the independence point reflects the efficiency with which two tasks can be combined.

To plot a POC, it is first necessary to measure single-task performance for both tasks. Performance on the single task is considered to have a score of "100%," and dual-task performance is measured relative to single-task performance (e.g., if a single-task score on a task is "52," this score would be considered 100%, even though actual scores could be higher; if performance on the same task receives a score of "44" in a dual-task condition, this would be scored as [44/52] * 100 = 85%). The two tasks are then performed under different "priority" conditions, in which the emphasis placed on the two tasks is varied (e.g., 80% emphasis on Task A, equal emphasis on both tasks, and 80% emphasis on Task B).

With the appropriate feedback and training, performers can learn to prioritize their performance of two tasks such that one is performed better at the cost of the other (see, e.g., Gopher, Brickner, & Navon, 1982). However, augmented feedback, in which details of the nature of the performance are given, may be required in

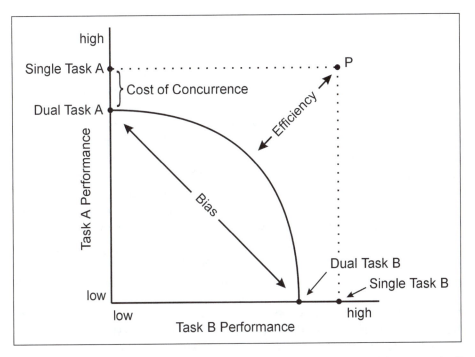

Figure 9.5 A hypothetical performance operating characteristic showing tradeoff between two tasks.

order to learn to trade off performance and to allocate attention according to instructions (Spitz, 1988).

The training of attentional allocation and prioritization strategies can have a strong and long-lasting influence on performance. It seems that dual-task performance can be improved by training with variable priority settings (e.g., Task 1 priority of 25, 50, or 75%), relative to training without priority instructions or with only one priority (e.g., 50%). Performers who train under variable priorities become better at detecting changes in task difficulty and are able to better adjust their efforts to cope with changing task demands (Gopher, 1993). Gopher, Weil, and Siegel (1989) showed that variable-priority setting can be an effective training method. Participants in their study learned to change their emphasis on different aspects of a complex task (the "Space Fortress" video game; Mané & Donchin, 1989), which forced them to explore different strategies of performance, thus overcoming limitations that arise when learners lock onto a non-optimal strategy early in performance of a task. Performing under variable instructions also improved the performers' ability to evaluate their own peripheral attention abilities and thus to discover minimal control levels (see Chapter 10 for other applications of variable-priority training).

Subjective Measures

The most popular form of workload measurement is based on the assumption that people can accurately report how much workload they experience during the performance of a task. Performers may be asked to compare tasks and to report the relative effort experienced in each, or they may rate different aspects of tasks on an absolute scale. In any case, these *subjective measures* are relatively easy to implement, nonintrusive and inexpensive, and have high face validity. One of the most widely used measures is the National Aeronautic and Space Administration Task Load Index (NASA-TLX; Hart & Staveland, 1988). The NASA-TLX is an example of a multidimensional workload measure. It consists of six different scales, each of which has been shown in preliminary research to make an independent contribution to the subjective impression of workload (see Table 9.1). In most applications, ratings are made on each of the scales after a task has been performed. Raters are also asked to judge the relative importance of each of the scales to task performance. These ratings are then used to weight the individual scale ratings, and the weighted ratings are added together to give an indication of overall workload. Comparisons of different weighting methods have, however, shown that weighting the ratings does not add to the sensitivity of the NASA-TLX (Hendy, Hamilton, & Landry, 1993). This finding suggests that simply adding together the ratings on the different scales may be just as effective as calculating a weighted sum, and that the step of calculating weightings could just as well be skipped.

The Subjective Workload Assessment Technique (SWAT; Reid, Shingledecker, & Eggemeier, 1981) requires that raters first rank-order the workload that would be assumed to result from all combinations of levels of the three SWAT load dimensions: time, mental effort, and stress load. Each of these load dimensions has three levels. For example, one combination of the three dimensions to be rated is the load that would be imposed by a task that "occasionally allows spare time" (interruptions or overlap among activities occur frequently; Time Scale, Level 2), "requires very little conscious mental effort or concentration" (activity is almost automatic, requiring little or no attention; Mental Effort Load, Level 1), and induces "very high stress due to confusion, frustration, or anxiety" (high to extreme determination and self-control required; Stress Load, Level 3). After all 27 combinations of the three levels of the three scales have been rated, a scaling technique is used to create an individualized mental workload scale for the rater. Once this scale has been derived, simple ratings for individual tasks can be made (e.g., Level 1 Time Load, Level 2 Mental Effort Load, and Level 1 Stress Load) and these ratings can be combined, on the basis of the individualized scale, to give a single estimate of mental load. One possible benefit of the SWAT over other subjective measures is that the ratings have been shown to have interval-scale properties, which makes comparisons between different ratings more meaningful.

Table 9.1   The NASA-TLX Rating Scales and Definitions

Scale	Description
Mental demand	How much mental and perceptual activity was required? (e.g., thinking, deciding, calculating, remembering, looking, searching, etc.)? Was the task easy or demanding, simple or complex, exacting or forgiving?
Physical demand	How much physical activity was required (e.g., pushing, pulling, turning, controlling, activating, etc.)? Was the task easy or demanding, slow or brisk, slack or strenuous, restful or laborious?
Temporal demand	How much time pressure did you feel due to the rate or pace at which the tasks or task elements occurred? Was the pace slow and leisurely, or rapid and frantic?
Performance	How successful do you think you were in accomplishing the goals of the task set by the experimenter (or yourself)? How satisfied were you with your performance in accomplishing these goals?
Effort	How hard did you have to work (mentally and physically) to accomplish your level of performance?
Frustration level	How insecure, discouraged, irritated, stressed, and annoyed versus secure, gratified, content, relaxed, and complacent did you feel during the task?

One factor that must be taken into consideration when subjective measures are used to compare different tasks is the range of conditions experienced during a session. Subjective measures are based on judgments, and are therefore subject to the judgmental tendencies of the raters. A general finding is that raters are influenced by both the range and frequency of different possible stimuli. People seem to divide the stimulus range into categorical intervals and use all categories equally often (Parducci, 1965). Thus, even when stimulus variability is relatively low, raters still tend to use the whole rating scale. This means that ratings of a task with a relatively restricted range of difficulty conditions will tend to overestimate workload whereas a high range of task difficulties will result in an underestimation of task workload.

Colle and Reid (1998) verified this prediction using both the SWAT and NASA-TLX to measure workload in a categorization task (deciding whether two words belonged to the same category). They manipulated the task load by varying the presentation rate of the stimuli. Using a small range of presentation rates led to higher mental workload ratings for a given rate than when the same rate was embedded in a context of greater variability of presentation rates (e.g., the SWAT rating of a presentation rate of 22 word pairs per minute was "6" in the high-variability condition and "33" in the low-variability condition). Fortunately, Colle and Reid also presented a possible solution to this problem. When all possible conditions were first presented in a practice session, along with the instruction to use the whole scale, the effect of task variability disappeared. Just as it is necessary to describe the rating scales before using subjective measures, it may also be necessary to give raters examples or practice with the task to be rated.

Gopher (1994) points out that the "emotional" components of the NASA-TLX and SWAT ("frustration" and "stress load," respectively) cannot easily be related to any theory of processing capacity. Perhaps partly for this reason, some researchers have argued that simpler, unidimensional measures are just as appropriate as, or better than, multidimensional methods. One unidimensional method is magnitude estimation (Gopher & Braune, 1984), in which raters are asked to compare the workload experienced in one version of a task with other versions, assigning numbers to the various task versions according to their relative load. This method assumes that workload reflects the magnitude of the investment of processing resources made during a task and that these magnitudes can be experienced and judged just like other perceptual qualities such as color and loudness. Hendy, Hamilton, and Landry (1993) reviewed a series of studies and concluded that unidimensional methods can be more sensitive to task demands than multidimensional scales. One way to improve the effectiveness of multidimensional methods might be to delay ratings until all conditions have been experienced, thus allowing performers to make comparisons between the conditions (Tsang & Vidulich, 1994).

Another simple, unidimensional method is to simply ask people to rate the degree of effort they experienced. This method is essentially equivalent to just looking at one of the scales of the NASA-TLX, the "effort" scale. However, at least one study (Veltman & Guillard, 1993) found low correlations between the NASA-TLX effort scale and ratings on a unidimensional scale. More research is needed to determine exactly what simple, unidimensional rating scales measure and how well they do it.

Dual-task performance is determined by a number of factors, including the resources invested in the task and competition for common resources. It has been argued that subjective measures, however, are primarily influenced by the amount of invested resources and by demands (such as those imposed by time-sharing) on working memory. This suggests that a dissociation may be found for performance and subjective measures when multiple-task configurations involving time-sharing are compared with single-task conditions and when comparisons are made between task combinations that differ in terms of competition for common resources. In fact, there are many examples of dissociations in the literature (see Yeh & Wickens, 1988). For example, comparisons of easy, dual-task conditions with harder, single-task conditions show that performance is indeed better in the dual-task condition, but workload ratings are higher. Although it is important and interesting to note that the requirement to time-share sometimes affects subjective workload more than it does performance, comparisons between single- and dual-task conditions should be made with caution.

Criteria for Selecting and Evaluating Workload Measures

In order to be useful, a workload measure must be *reliable*. That is, it must give similar ratings in similar situations. Another major factor in choosing a measure is *ease of use*. This factor may be a major reason why subjective measures are so popular. *Sensitivity* is also vital. A workload measure is sensitive when ratings made with it reflect significant variations in the workload imposed by a task. For example, the SWAT has been shown to be sensitive to workload increases caused by sleep deprivation and time-on-task, as well as task difficulty (Hankey & Dingus, 1990). If an instrument is not sensitive, it may not be possible to detect differences that exist between tasks or system functions. "Temporal" sensitivity is also important: When the task changes in difficulty during performance, ratings should reflect when these changes occurred.

A measure is *diagnostic* when it not only reflects changes in load, but also discriminates between the amounts of load imposed on various operator capacities or resources (such as perceptual versus memory load). In terms of a multiple-resources framework, diagnosticity refers to a measure's ability to identify which resources are at risk. For example, pupillometry might be used to provide a global measure of resource allocations, whereas secondary tasks can be chosen to tax either spatial or verbal, perceptual or central processing resources. The optimal degree of diagnosticity depends on the question of interest. If one is interested in adding an information display to an already complex task, it might be worthwhile to find out which resources are the most loaded already so that an appropriate method of displaying the new information can be chosen.

Intrusiveness refers to any disruption in performance of the task of interest as a result of the application of the mental workload measurement technique.

Depending on the situation, a given measure of workload can be more or less intrusive. For example, a secondary task may be viewed as intrusive if it affects the resource-allocation policy of the operator, but might be deemed unobtrusive if it is embedded in primary-task performance. In general, secondary tasks will be too intrusive if they cause a fundamental change in the way that a task is carried out. Finally, workload measures must be accepted by the operator. If operators are not convinced of the utility and acceptability of a given measure, they may not do their best to provide precise and adequate data.

▲ SITUATION AWARENESS

Imagine yourself in a situation where everything around you is changing every minute. Objects come in and out of view. People jostle for position around you. You try to keep your goal in mind as you avoid obstacles, look for breaks, and maneuver for position. The situation just described is not a high-tech video game. It could describe something as simple as making your way through a crowded train station or a casual game of football. The point is, many activities require that we keep track of large amounts of changing information, predict changes in the environment around us, and choose an appropriate course of action. In other words, we must maintain a dynamic situation model. Such a model includes all the information that is necessary for task performance, as well as the processes of perceiving and comprehending this information, and using it to make predictions about what is going to happen next. The result of maintaining an accurate dynamic picture of the situation has been called *situation awareness,* or "the perception of the elements in the environment within a volume of time and space, the comprehension of their meaning, and the projection of their status in the near future" (Endsley, 1995b, p. 36).

A commonsense description of situation awareness is being aware of and understanding both the current situation and the way in which it is evolving, such that appropriate decisions can be made or actions taken. For example, a driver must be aware of road conditions, the presence of other cars or obstacles, and the rate of change of the traffic in the area in order to predict whether it is safe to change lanes or to pass another car. Two of the leading causes of driving accidents, "improper lookout" and "inattention" (Treat et al., 1979), can best be described as failures to maintain situation awareness. Unfortunately, people often fail to "look ahead" (and behind) and to keep track of traffic and environmental changes. In fact, the ability to shift attention is a good predictor of driving ability (Elander, West, & French, 1993).

Situation awareness is supported by attention, working memory, and long-term memory, but it cannot be equated with any of these processes. In a sense, situation awareness is as difficult to describe as consciousness—it is the awareness that arises when attention is paid to relevant information and when both working and long-term memory support the interpretation and maintenance of the attended information. Situation awareness can also be de-coupled from response processes. Sometimes situation awareness seems to be very low, yet responses continue to occur appropriately, such as when a driver suddenly realizes that he or she cannot remember traveling a stretch of road.

Cognitive Factors in Situation Awareness

How and where attention is directed will determine which elements in the environment are incorporated into the situation awareness, and both the salience of information (see Chapter 8) and the individual's goals and priorities in directing attention (see Chapters 3 and 6) will influence perception and performance. In fact, the failure to attend to readily available information (e.g., because of attentional narrowing) is the single most frequent causal factor in losing situation awareness (Jones & Endsley, 1996).

Given that situation awareness involves keeping track of events and objects in the environment, it makes sense that memory may play an important role in maintaining it. One investigation of the role of working memory in maintaining situation awareness was carried out by Gugerty (1997), who examined the relation between memory and driving performance in a driving simulator. To obtain an indication of situation awareness, Gugerty introduced hazardous situations into the driving task and measured people's responses to these hazards. One task was to respond to "hazard" cars. These were cars that entered the path of the driver such that a collision would occur if the driver did not take appropriate action. The other situation involved the driver's blind spot (the area to the side of the car where another car cannot be detected by looking in the rear-view and side mirrors). Drivers had to be aware of traffic to know whether a car was in the blind spot before they could move to the right or the left in order to avoid a hazard car. Because the experiment was done in a driving simulator, the number of crashes could be used as an indicator of situation awareness. Explicit memory for the situation was measured by asking participants to re-create the driving situation just experienced by placing the correct number of cars in their correct positions on the road after a trial had ended. Gugerty found high correlations between explicit memory and driving performance, a result that emphasizes the role of memory in maintaining situation awareness. The high correlations between explicit memory and performance suggest that only information that people pay attention to and are aware of influences their situation awareness. This research shows that people do not, as a rule, drive on "automatic pilot": Attention is needed to attend to and remember necessary information.

Wickens and Hollands (2000) maintain that the link between situation awareness and working memory is a direct one, and that situation awareness is bound to become worse when working memory resources are overtaxed. Consistent with this idea, Gugerty (1997) found that when the memory load was high, people paid attention only to the car directly in front of them. This finding, coupled with the fact that lapses of attention and failures to shift attention appropriately are leading causes of accidents (Treat et al., 1979), suggests that drivers could benefit from special training in scanning strategies for high-load situations.

Working memory plays an important role in maintaining situation awareness, but it is obvious that long-term memory also is important. One of the basic assumptions about expert performance is that it depends heavily on long-term memory (see, e.g., Proctor & Dutta, 1995). Experts have abstract knowledge of what to expect, as well as a repository of previous situations that can be matched to the situation at hand. Perhaps more importantly, experts in many domains have been shown to possess strategies to quickly encode information into long-term memory and to have highly efficient retrieval strategies. This makes it possible for an expert to depend more on long-term memory, thus freeing up working memory resources for other tasks. In this respect, the mental model of a situation serves as a schema that guides the allocation of attention to important aspects of the situation and helps in the interpretation and storage of relevant information. Mental models have a dark side, too. Jones and Endsley (1996) found that 18% of pilot errors involving a loss of situation awareness were due to overreliance on a poor, incorrect, or inappropriate mental model, or because information inconsistent with the mental model was ignored in favor of an interpretation that would be consistent with the mental model. Another aspect of expertise, domain specificity, is also reflected in situation awareness. People who evidence a high level of situation awareness in one environment do not necessarily evidence good situation awareness in other environments.

Situation Awareness and Mental Workload

Although situation awareness may suffer when workload is so high that necessary information cannot be processed, or when workload is so low that operators lose vigilance (see, e.g., Endsley & Kiris, 1995), mental workload and situation awareness are essentially independent constructs. Design changes intended to increase situation awareness do not necessarily reduce mental workload, and vice versa. In a review of 15 studies in which both situation awareness and mental workload were measured before and after the implementation of a new interface, Vidulich (2000) found that situation awareness was improved in 80% of the studies, but mental workload was reduced in only 47% of the studies.

Measurement of Situation Awareness

The same criteria applied to mental workload measurement (sensitivity, diagnosticity, reliability, intrusiveness, acceptance, and ease of use) also apply to the measurement of situation awareness. Up to now, situation awareness has most commonly been assessed by using subjective self-report questionnaires (the best of which appears to be the Situation Awareness Rating Technique [SART]; Selcon & Taylor, 1990) or memory-probe techniques. Memory-probe measures, such as the tasks used by Gugerty (1997), described earlier in the chapter, are most sensitive when they include a wide variety of questions. The Situation Awareness Global Assessment Technique (SAGAT; Endsley, 1995a) is an example of a broad memory-probe technique. The SAGAT consists of stopping task performance (usually in a simulator) and asking performers various questions about their current perception of the situation. The SAGAT is based on an in-depth, goal-based task analysis in which the goals of the particular activity are identified, as are the subgoals that support achievement of each goal. Questions asked during the pauses in simulator action are related to the goals and subgoals. For example, the air traffic controller has the goals of avoiding near misses and collisions and landing aircraft safely. Subgoals involve collecting information about each of the aircraft in the controlled space. SAGAT questions might include reporting details, such as airspeed and heading, of aircraft in the controlled space.

Improving Situation Awareness

Some of the same factors that improve routine performance have a negative effect on situation awareness. For example, displays designed to support routine tasks may not present enough information to allow the operator to maintain situation awareness (Wickens, 1999). Similarly, automation in process control may improve performance and reduce workload, but at the same time reduce situation awareness (Sarter & Woods, 1995).

Much research has focused on how to enhance the situation awareness of teams. This question is an important one because many of the tasks for which situation awareness is a limiting factor in performance (such as flying aircraft, steering ships, and managing chemical processes) depend on the combined efforts of team members. Situation awareness in a team depends on a shared mental model (see, e.g., Salas & Cannon-Bowers, 1997) that allows team members to anticipate each other's actions and to maintain an accurate, up-to-date picture of the current situation. One way to promote the development of a shared mental model is *crosstraining,* in which team members receive information and training in the tasks of other team members. In addition to providing the team with backup knowledge should a team member be absent, this strategy has been shown to contribute to the development of more efficient communication strategies and enhanced task performance (Volpe et al., 1996). In addition to crosstraining, teams who must function in high-workload environments may benefit from special training to recognize high-stress conditions and to adapt their behavior accordingly. One of the most important adaptive strategies seems to be learning to anticipate the information needs of other team members (Entin & Serfaty, 1999).

Analyses of near-misses and other reported incidents in aviation show that about half of the reported errors involve loss of situation awareness (defined as loss of either spatial, temporal, or system awareness; Pew, 1995). In aircraft with two pilots (e.g., a captain and a first officer who take turns piloting the airplane), incidents involving loss of situation awareness are more likely to occur when the captain is flying the aircraft than when the first officer is in control (Jentsch et al., 1999). The finding that the captain is more likely to become disoriented when he or she is at the controls seems to run counter to the finding that involvement in controlling a system tends to lead to higher situation awareness (see, e.g., Sarter & Woods, 1995). However, there may be a simple explanation for this. The captain has the primary responsibility for the flight and all decision making, and is most directly faced with the task of integrating information and assessing the situation. When required to fly the aircraft, resources that could be spent collecting and communicating information must instead be devoted to the task of flying. The best way to improve the situation awareness of the crew may, therefore, be to have the first officer take over the controls during problem situations and to put the captain in the co-pilot's seat.

▲ HUMAN ERROR

Error is an inescapable part of action. In fact, it has been argued that error arises according to exactly the same principles that are responsible for skilled performance. Take the example of meaning to do one thing but doing something else. An example of this is opening a new package of tea with the intention of filling the empty tea canister, but instead of pouring the tea into the canister, pouring the whole package into the waiting teapot. In this case the correct action was performed (that of pouring), but the object of the action (the teapot) was the inappropriate one. Reason (1979) was one of the first researchers to systematically describe this kind of error, which he called a "slip of action." He argued that such errors arise because much of our behavior is performed more or less automatically, without conscious mediation or monitoring. In other words, slips of action occur because of the way action is organized and automated.

Although much of our behavior is under conscious control or shaped by feedback from the environment, we are also able to perform some actions on the basis of

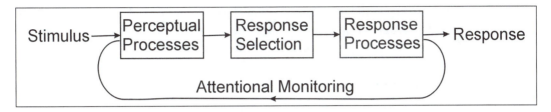

Figure 9.6   The basic three-stage model of information processing augmented with closed-loop control.

motor programs. The original idea of a motor program was that of a set of muscle commands put in place before an action is begun that allows the action to be carried out uninfluenced by peripheral feedback. In other words, actions controlled by motor programs can be performed in an open-loop manner—that is, without feedback. Actions under conscious control, on the other hand, are said to be performed in a closed-loop manner (i.e., feedback or conscious monitoring "closes" the perception-action loop; see Figure 9.6). A more general description of a motor program is a "functional state that allows particular movements, or classes of movements, to occur" (Rosenbaum, 1991, p. 109). A motor program thus implies a readiness to perform an action. In the example at the beginning of this section, it seems that the motor program took over and was responsible for the tea ending up in the wrong container.

Reason (1979) inventoried a large number of *action slips* (in just 2 weeks his 35 subjects committed over 400 unintended acts) and categorized them according to the type of information processing error made.[1] For example, putting shaving cream on a toothbrush was classified as a failure of discrimination, and unwrapping a sweet and throwing the sweet in the wastebasket and the wrapper in one's mouth is an example of a program assembly error, in which two actions in a sequence appear to have been transposed. Some errors seem to be due to a failure to test or monitor the progress of an action, such as in the case of going into the bedroom to change into comfortable clothes and, instead, putting on pajamas and going to bed. This latter type of error, the test error, illustrates Reason's ideas about the interaction between control and motor programs nicely. The person's action was "captured" by the context, and the presumably stronger program of getting ready for bed was activated. Going back to the tea problem, it seems that the recently de-activated, but generally more common, plan for filling the teapot superceded the newer, less common plan of filling the tea canister.

Slips of action seem most likely to occur during the automatic execution of highly practiced, routine actions. Therefore, skilled or "routinized" behavior, which can operate under open-loop control, is most likely to be subject to action slips (Reason, 1979). Action slips can be described as failures of attention, with slips occurring either because the wrong action plan is maintained or because attention is switched to the wrong elements of a plan or aspects of the environment. It has long been suggested that paying too much attention to a highly practiced task can actually disrupt action (Freud, 1922)[2]; paying too little attention (i.e., failing to switch to closed-loop control) also can lead to errors.

Initiating and Maintaining Action Plans

Norman (1981) extended the work of Reason (1979) and used his analysis of action slips as the basis for a theory about how intentions are represented and acted upon. Whereas Reason explained slips in terms of failures to control motor programs, Norman based his theory on the idea that actions are based on schemas that embody the procedural knowledge needed for carrying out an act. Basically, *schemas* are generalized procedures for carrying out actions; they embody both motor programs and rules for selecting between specific versions of motor programs. According to Norman, any complicated act requires a number of schemas, arranged in a particular control structure. In order for actions to be performed correctly, the right schemas must be activated at the right time—and with the right information. Norman's *activation-trigger-schema (ATS) system* assumes that actions are governed by high-level parent schemas. For skilled actions, Norman assumes that once the parent schema is activated, the child schemas that control component parts of the action are initiated automatically. Thus, intention can be equated with the activation of the parent schema, and attention is needed only when critical choice points are reached.

Because a number of schemas may be active at any one time, some means of triggering the appropriate schema for a particular act is needed. For example, most drivers have a schema for "drive home from work." Deviations from the schema, such as "pick up the dry cleaning on the way home," require a separate subschema that must be triggered at the appropriate time. Once on the way, the task of driving occurs more or less automatically. The driver must, however, pay sufficient attention to the errand schema if it is to be activated at the appropriate moment. If the activation for the schema is not sufficiently high, the better-known "drive home" schema will prevail and the dry cleaning will be forgotten. Table 9.2 summarizes the types of action slips that occur due to errors in the formation of intentions, or activation and triggering of schemas.

Control of action can be described as the transition from intention to schema triggering. In the view that actions are controlled by schemas, well-learned schemas can be considered to be lying in wait, pending the appropriate set of conditions that will enable their selection. Once a schema is in place, attention is not necessarily required to perform an action. In fact, it can be argued that attention is incapable of controlling action because of the timescale involved. Deliberate conscious control takes more time than is available for skilled action. The idea that attention is not involved in much skilled performance is also supported by the fact that deliberate

---

Table 9.2   A Classification of Action Slips

Slips due to errors in the formation of intentions:

Mistakes in goal determination or cognition

- *Mode errors:* Erroneous classification or interpretation of the situation
- *Description errors:* Ambiguous or incomplete specification of the intention

Slips that result from faulty activation of schemas:

Unintentional activation (activation of schemas not part of a current action plan)

- *Capture errors:* Capture of control by a better learned, but currently inappropriate schema
- *Data-driven activation:* Schemas inappropriately triggered by outside events
- *Associative activation:* Activation by another, currently active schema

Loss of activation

- Forgetting an intention (but continuing to perform the action)
- Misordering the components of an action sequence
- Skipping steps in an action sequence
- Repeating steps in an action sequence

Slips due to faulty triggering of schemas:

False triggering: Correct schema triggered at inappropriate time

- *Spoonerisms:* Reversal of event components
- *Blends:* Combinations of components from two competing schemas
- *Thoughts leading to actions:* Triggering of schemas only meant to be thought, not executed
- Premature triggering

Failure to trigger: When an active schema never gets invoked because:

- Action is preempted by competing schemas
- There is insufficient activation as a result of forgetting or initial activation is too low
- Trigger condition does not match due to insufficient or faulty specification

---

control of skilled performance can lead to deterioration of that performance. The view that skilled performance is relatively independent of attentional control is consistent with Neumann's (1984) view of automaticity, according to which processing

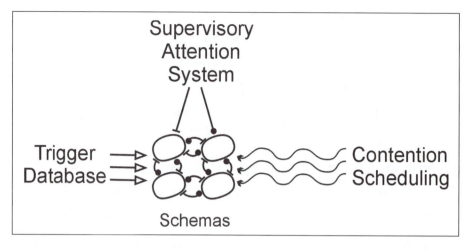

Figure 9.7   Norman and Shallice's (1986) model of action control. The small black circles represent excitatory connections and the short lines represent inhibitory connections.

is automatic when all aspects or parameters of an action are specified in long-term memory or are directly available in the environment. If there is insufficient information to perform an action, attentional mechanisms are needed for parameter specification. It is these attentional mechanisms that give rise to conscious awareness of action and can cause interference with other actions.

Norman and Shallice (1986) propose that two systems influence schema activation, a *contention-scheduling system* and a *supervisory attentional system*. The basic mechanism of action control, according to Norman and Shallice, is contention scheduling. Contention scheduling is a more or less passive process that emerges naturally as a result of the way schemas are learned and performed. The contention-scheduling system can directly activate and order action schemas that are linked to each other with both inhibitory and excitatory connections (see Figure 9.7). For example, a schema for tying shoelaces might have inhibitory connections to other schemas involving fine motor control of the hands, but excitatory connections to a schema for pulling down pant cuffs. The precise timing of schema activation occurs through "triggers." A schema is triggered for execution when environmental conditions match the triggering conditions incorporated in the schema. The notion of triggering provides an explanation for the capture errors described earlier: When intentions are not actively maintained, schemas can become activated simply because their triggering conditions are present in the environment.

Schemas operate whenever their activation exceeds a threshold, whether this activation comes from contention scheduling, the activation of other schemas, or environmental conditions. Top-down mechanisms also play an important role in schema activation and action control. In Norman and Shallice's (1986) model, top-down control of action is performed by the supervisory attentional system (SAS). The SAS works by modulating the contention-scheduling system, as is necessary whenever a less familiar version of an action sequence must be performed in place of a more familiar one.

The Supervisory Attentional System

Whenever no schema exists for performing an action—as in novel or complex tasks—contention scheduling alone will be insufficient to guide action. In these cases, a higher level of control is needed, and this control is provided by the SAS. The SAS can directly activate or inhibit schemas, but cannot select them directly. Control always proceeds through the process of contention scheduling, with the SAS biasing selection by inhibiting some schemas and activating others. Although Norman and Shallice (1986) view the SAS as a control system, its output is called simply "attention." Thus, activation by the SAS consists of allocating attention to schemas. When attentional activation by the SAS is withdrawn, the activation value of the schema will decay back to the value determined by the other sorts of activational input. Absent-mindedness, as in forgetting why you entered a room or what you are looking for, can be viewed as a failure to keep the SAS engaged. Without the SAS, attention is withdrawn from goals or actions, and the relevant schemas may suffer from lack of activation.

Resisting a habitual or tempting action, or performing aversive actions, also requires the intervention of the SAS. The involvement of the SAS in overcoming habits or resisting temptation led Norman and Shallice to think of the SAS as embodying the "will." For example, you may intend to nurse a beer while waiting for a friend, but lapses of attention often result in the beer being drunk "before you know it." The SAS is needed to overcome reluctance to perform an action or to overcome a bad habit. However, being creatures of habit, continued application of will can eventually result in the learning of new schemas for actions that initially were difficult to perform.

The control of action as described by Norman and Shallice (1986) is analogous to the distinction between automatic and controlled processing in perception (see, e.g., Schneider & Shiffrin, 1977; see also Chapter 7). In a sense, the automatic execution of action can be considered the default mode of performance. Most actions occur too quickly to be the product of conscious deliberation; attention is needed only to initiate processes or to override automatic processing. Such deliberate attentional resources are needed whenever a less familiar action must be substituted for a more familiar one. Tasks that require planning, decision making, or troubleshooting; those that are ill-learned, contain novel sequences, or are difficult or dangerous; and those that require resisting temptation or overcoming a strong, habitual response all exceed the reach of normal, automatic control of behavior.

Attentional resources are needed for stopping actions as well as initiating them. Control may be necessary whenever schema selection is required, and schemas are apparently necessary for both starting and stopping movements. Probe-reaction-time studies show that if (and only if) an external stop is provided for a hand movement, attentional resources are required only at the initiation of the movement (Posner & Keele, 1969).

If the SAS is not intact or not functioning properly, as is the case of patients with frontal-lobe lesions, two very different-looking sorts of disorders may result. The same patient might show both increased perseveration (an inability to switch from a current action or goal to a newer, more appropriate action) and heightened distractibility. Without the input of attention from the SAS, strong schemas may remain active too long, thus resulting in the prolongation or repeated application of a schema characteristic of perseveration, or many schemas of similar activation values may compete for control, thus producing disorganized behavior.

▲ SUMMARY

One way to view attention is as one or more resources that are in limited supply. Whenever the demand for resources exceeds the supply, performance will suffer and decisions must be made about where to allocate the available resources. It is important to measure resource demands in order to determine whether the mental workload imposed by a particular task is within tolerable limits. Using techniques ranging from self-report questionnaires to continuous measurement of physiological variables, system and product designers, developers of training programs, and accident investigators measure the cognitive demands placed on the human operator within a system. Situation awareness goes beyond mental workload in addressing the operator's understanding of the dynamic aspects of a situation. Maintaining a dynamic model requires attending to the relevant cues in the environment and continually updating one's situation assessment.

Whether because of excessive mental workload, understimulation, or just plain distractibility, human error is an inescapable aspect of human performance in both everyday situations and high-performance environments. Errors occur when lapses of attention result in the activation of inappropriate action plans. As is apparent in the following chapters, supervisory attentional control is vital to coordinating goals and actions whenever our behavior deviates from the routine.

NOTES ▲

1. If you are interested in determining how often you make such errors, fill out the questionnaire in Box 9.1.

2. A recent experimental demonstration of the negative effects of attention to performance on skilled action (Beilock, Carr, MacMahon, & Starkes, 2002) showed that the requirement to focus on a specific aspect of an action (such as which side of the foot was in contact with the ball in soccer dribbling) narrowed the difference between experts and novices.

Box 9.1	The Short Inventory of Minor Lapses (SIML)

Inventory Item	Norm
1. How often do you forget to say something you were going to mention?	2.3 (0.79)
2. How often do you have the feeling that you should be doing something, either now or later, but you can't remember what it is?	2.0 (0.78)
3. How often do you find your mind continuing to dwell upon something that you would prefer not to think about?	2.5 (0.97)
4. How often do you find you can't remember what you have just done or where you have just been (e.g., when walking or driving)?	1.5 (0.71)
5. How often do you leave some necessary step out of a task (e.g., forgetting to put tea in the teapot)?	1.5 (0.64)
6. How often do you find that you cannot immediately recall the name of a familiar person, place, or object?	2.4 (0.92)
7. How often do you think you're paying attention to something when you're actually not (e.g., when reading a book or watching TV)?	2.2 (0.82)
8. How often do you have the "what am I here for" feeling when you find you have forgotten what it was you came to do?	2.1 (0.82)
9. How often do you find yourself repeating something you've already done or carrying out some unnecessary action (e.g., flicking on the light when you're done leaving the room in daylight)?	1.6 (0.73)
10. How often do you find you've forgotten to do something you intended to do?	2.0 (0.77)
11. How often do you decide to do something and then find yourself sidetracked into doing something different?	2.4 (0.89)
12. How often do you find yourself searching for something that you've just put down or are still carrying with you?	2.1 (0.92)
13. How often do you forget to do something that you were going to do after dealing with an unexpected interruption?	2.2 (0.83)
14. How often do you find your mind wandering when you're doing something that needs your concentration?	1.9 (0.86)
15. How often do you make mistakes in which you do the right actions but with the wrong objects (or people; e.g., unwrapping a sweet, throwing the sweet away, and putting the paper in your mouth)?	1.3 (0.56)

SOURCE: Reason, 1993, Table 20.1, p. 408. Reprinted by permission of Oxford University Press.

NOTE: Questions are rated on a scale from 1 (hardly ever) to 5 (nearly all the time). Norms (means and, in parentheses, standard deviations) are from a survey of 1,656 car drivers (847 males and 809 females, aged from 17 to 69 years); reported in Reason (1993).

CHAPTER 10

INDIVIDUAL DIFFERENCES
IN ATTENTION

Human performance is intrinsically variable. Despite this obvious fact, modern cognitive psychologists have tended to emphasize mean performance. Commonalities of human performance are taken to the extreme in engineering models of human performance, where estimates of mean time (sometimes including a parameter for variability) are used to model performance in real-world tasks. Failures to take human variability into account can have disastrous effects in some technical applications. For example, Casey (1993) describes a design flaw in a machine designed to administer radiation treatments that resulted in several deaths. In one case, a radiotherapy technician mistakenly typed the letter X, which stood for high-power X-ray mode, instead of E, which stood for electron beam mode, the desired mode for the particular patient. The technician quickly saw her mistake, corrected it by entering the edit mode of the program and changing the X to an E, and then restarted the procedure. However, although the display showed that the system was now set to deliver the electron beam treatment, the power setting of the high-power X-ray mode was left unchanged due to the speed with which the correction was made. The designers of the machine had not adequately taken variability in response time to correct mistakes into account. The technician's correction was completed before the machine had time to readjust, and a lethal dose of radiation was delivered.

Examples abound of the effects of failure to understand human variability. Fortunately, not all individual differences in information processing lead to lethal results. For example, the boxing competition of the 1992 Summer Olympic Games was marred by controversy over the scoring system. The system required that each of five judges record the blows of each boxer by pressing one of two keys (corresponding to each of the boxers) on an electronic box. The scoring system was such that a blow had to be registered by at least three judges during a 1-second interval in order to be counted. This time restriction resulted in problematic decisions such as awarding the fight to one boxer even though each of the five judges had, independently, recorded more blows for the opponent boxer (see Proctor & Dutta, 1995). Many factors can be presumed to influence performance in this task, including intrinsic variability in the performance of a given judge and the effects of repetitions of stimuli (a given boxer's blows) and responses (the actual keypresses). Other factors rest on the differences between the judges, such as speed of information processing and the ability to switch attention from one event to another. Chapter 9 introduced some techniques and theoretical frameworks for measuring and describing attentional demands and people's responses to them. In this chapter we examine the evidence for and the nature of individual differences in basic attentional processes such as filtering out irrelevant information, maintaining vigilance, and dividing attention between two tasks.

▲ ATTENTIONAL ABILITY

As any primary school teacher (or university professor) can tell you, there are large individual differences in the ability to pay attention to the task at hand. Some students seem to always be focused on the teacher, to understand and follow instructions, and to monitor their own understanding, asking questions when necessary. The ability to focus on relevant information (such as what the teacher is saying) and to filter out irrelevant stimulation (such as what the classroom rabbit—or a student seated nearby—is eating) may depend on a multitude of social, motivational, and cognitive factors.

Selective attention, or the ability to attend to one subset of items while ignoring others, is necessary for the performance of both simple and complex tasks. A range of tasks has been developed to test the limits of our ability to select some stimuli (see Chapters 3 and 4) and to ignore others (see Chapter 5). The overwhelming majority of these studies have been devoted to describing commonalities in the ability to select information, such as the average size of the attentional spotlight or the number of auditory channels that can be monitored. When differences are examined, comparisons are usually made between groups of people, such as the differences between young and old or between children with or without attention deficit hyperactivity disorder (ADHD). However, even "normal," healthy adults vary in their ability to attend to information.

Various attentional paradigms have revealed differences in attentional abilities and limitations. A widely used task is that of dichotic listening, discussed in detail in Chapter 4. It has been suggested that the ability to shift attention between two or more tasks can reliably be measured and used to predict performance in complex tasks. Gopher, Kahneman, and colleagues (Gopher, 1982; Gopher & Kahneman, 1971; Kahneman, Ben-Ishai, & Lotan, 1973) put this suggestion to the test. They developed a test of selective attention and validated it on several populations, including flight cadets in the Israeli Air Force and bus drivers. In one version of the test, spoken lists of unconnected words and digits were presented dichotically, with pairs of items being presented simultaneously to the two ears. The task was to write down the digits that were presented to just one, relevant ear, ignoring any words or digits presented to the ear designated as irrelevant. A brief tone of high or low frequency was presented at the beginning of each list to indicate whether the right or left ear was relevant for the first portion of the list. Sixteen word-digit pairs of items were then presented, one item to each ear, with at most one digit in each pair. After the presentation of the 16 word-digit pairs, another tone signaled the right or left ear as relevant for the remainder of the list. After this signal tone, zero, one, or two pairs of words, followed by three pairs of digits, were presented dichotically.

If people are good at selecting which ear to attend to, they should have no trouble reporting the relevant digits from the second part of the list. However, Gopher found that some people made mistakes by reporting the incorrect digit when an attention shift was required (e.g., when the right ear was relevant for the first part of the list and the left ear for the second part). The number of selective attention errors in the second phase of the experiment was found to be a good predictor of future complex task performance, correlating negatively with successful completion of flight school and positively with the accident rates of bus drivers. It should be noted that few errors of selective attention occurred when digit pairs were presented in isolation, without the requirement to switch attention from a previous task. Thus, it seems that the ability to switch attention from one ear to the other was the important factor in performance. This could explain why automobile drivers who have had more accidents also have been found to have more difficulty rapidly reorienting their attention than drivers who have had fewer accidents (Avolio, Kroeck, & Panek, 1985).

Differences in visual attention have also been investigated. One measure of the ability to select visual information is the functional field of view (FFOV). The

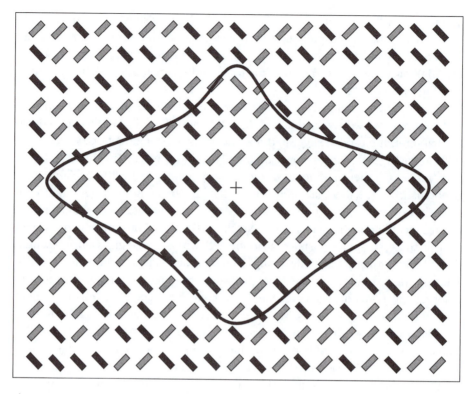

Figure 10.1   The functional field of view (FFOV) in a target detection task. The task was to determine whether a bar with a unique combination of color and orientation was present while keeping the eyes fixated on the central cross.

FFOV is the spatial area in which an individual can perform a given task without making head or eye movements. It is typically measured by means of a target-detection task in which participants search a briefly presented display for the presence of a target among distractors. The FFOV is defined as the eccentricity at which targets can be detected with a given level of accuracy. Figure 10.1 shows the average FFOV for a group of college students in a visual identification task. Functional field of view can be considered a measure of the breadth of attention because it measures the ability to "notice" targets in the absence of eye or head movements—that is, on the basis of attention.

Pringle, Irwin, Kramer, and Atchley (2001) examined the relation between the FFOV and performance in a change-detection task using the flicker paradigm (see Chapter 7) in order to assess the contribution of attentional ability to change-detection task performance. In the change-detection task, two versions of a traffic scene were presented to observers in rapid alternation, with each scene

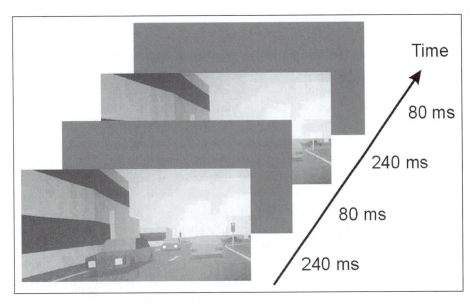

Figure 10.2   Schematic version of the change detection task used by Pringle et al. (2001). The two scenes were alternated for a total of 1 minute, or until a response was made.

followed by a blank gray screen (see Figure 10.2). Recall that a typical finding in a change-detection task is change blindness, that is, the inability to detect even simple changes in the scene unless attention happens to be focused on the particular point of the change.

In order to maximize FFOV differences, Pringle et al. (2001) tested both young and older adults in the change-detection task. Reliable differences in the size of the FFOV were found, with older adults tending to have a smaller FFOV than younger adults. Younger adults also performed better in the change-detection task. Much of the variance in change-detection performance could be explained by the size of the FFOV: A larger FFOV was related to faster detection (r = −.68). Based on this result, Pringle et al. concluded that the breadth of attention plays an important role in change detection, presumably because it reduces the number of areas of the scene that need to be attentionally fixated before the change is detected.

Differences in selective attention may be related to everyday absent-mindedness and failures of attention. Many everyday mishaps (such as meaning to return a library book on the way home but heading home instead; see Chapter 9) can be attributed to the capture of action plans by environmental stimuli. That is, planned, intended actions (such as walking to the library) may be captured by stimuli in the environment (such as the familiar route home) such that an action is carried out with inappropriate objects. Models of attentional modulation of action planning (see, e.g., Norman & Shallice, 1986) suggest that there may be a positive relationship between the ability to ignore irrelevant stimuli and the ability to avoid making everyday errors. The tendency to make everyday errors can be assessed by means of questionnaires in which individuals are asked how often they make certain types of errors, such as misplacing keys or forgetting why they entered a particular room. The two most often used questionnaires are the Short Inventory of Mental Lapses (SIML; Reason, 1993; see Chapter 9) and the Cognitive Failures Questionnaire (CFQ; Broadbent, Cooper, FitzGerald, & Parkes, 1982). The relationship between selective attention and cognitive lapses can be studied by comparing the performance of low or high scorers on the SIML or the CFQ on a range of selective attention tasks.

Tipper and Baylis (1987) investigated individual differences in ignoring irrelevant information with a task that required selectively responding to a target word of one color, while ignoring a distractor of another color. The distractor could be either a word or a random-letter string. People who scored high on the CFQ (i.e., who made relatively many everyday errors) responded just as quickly as low scorers when the distractor was a random-letter string, but took significantly longer to respond when a distractor word was present in the display. Assuming that only the distractor word has to be actively inhibited, this suggests that more absent-minded people have more difficulty inhibiting irrelevant semantic information. Tipper and Baylis also found that only the low scorers on the CFQ showed negative priming effects. As discussed in Chapter 5, negative priming (a slowing of a response to a target on one trial as a result of it having appeared as a distractor on a previous trial) is an indicator of efficient selection in the sense that it reflects the inhibition of competing information. Thus, Tipper and Baylis concluded that individual differences in the efficiency of selective attention may result from differences in the ability to actively inhibit distractors. A similar conclusion was reached by Conway, Tuholski, Shisler, and Engle (1999), who found that people high in working memory capacity (which the authors equate with attentional control; see the section "Attention and Working Memory Capacity" later in the chapter) showed negative priming effects, whereas low working memory capacity individuals did not.

It has been hypothesized that people who have difficulty resisting visual capture (attentional capture by a sudden-onset stimulus) may also be more prone to the capture of actions by stimuli in the environment. That is, people who find it difficult to resist capture of action by sudden-onset stimuli may be more prone to making capture errors (see Chapter 9). Larson and Perry (1999) found that individuals who scored high versus low on the CFQ performed similarly in a visual discrimination task with valid spatial cues, but differently in the anti-saccade task, in which the task is to withhold eye movements to a peripheral cue and to identify a target presented in the location opposite to that cue. Error-prone people were more likely to fall victim to visual capture (i.e., made more involuntary eye movements to the cue position in the anti-saccade task) than less error-prone people, and were also faster to initiate a saccade following the cue. Thus, it appears that individuals with high CFQ scores have difficulty inhibiting fast, reflexive saccades in the direction of a distracting cue. People who score lower on the CFQ were able to hold their eyes (and, presumably, their attention) at fixation for the brief period of time necessary to inhibit reflexive eye movements and then to move their eyes to the position of the target. Although the CFQ scores accounted for only a relatively small amount of the variance in capture errors (the correlation between capture errors and CFQ score was .3), Larson and Perry suggest that the anti-saccade task could be useful in screening individuals for tasks in which capture errors are likely and have serious consequences. Given that individuals involved in accidents have also been shown to have difficulty ignoring irrelevant messages in a dichotic listening task (Kahneman, Ben-Ishai, & Lotan, 1973; Mihal & Barrett, 1976), it may be possible to develop a battery of tests to this end.

ATTENTION AND INTELLIGENCE ▲

An intriguing idea regarding attention and individual differences is that the ability to control or apply attention may be intimately related to what we call intelligence. The idea that attention is a basic factor in intelligence dates back at least to Spearman (1927), who suggested that attentional capacity may be a source of the general intelligence component, g.[1] This view has been revived and extended in the past few decades, although the exact nature of the relationship between intelligence and attention (like the nature of intelligence and attention, themselves!) remains a matter of debate.

Galton (1883) put forward the more general idea that differences in basic cognitive operations—such as the time needed to make a simple discrimination—underlie differences in intelligence. Galton's original ideas were rejected when the simple tests he employed were shown to be incapable of predicting differences in IQ. But despite generally having fallen out of favor, the search for elementary processing accounts of IQ differences continues to have proponents. Perhaps the most well known of these is Jensen (e.g., 1998), who has suggested that mental speed—that is, aspects of brain physiology that affect the sensitivity, efficiency, or effectiveness of basic information processing—is directly related to general intelligence. Attempts to measure mental speed directly have been mixed. For example, some studies have shown positive correlations between measures such as the form of the auditory-evoked potential or the speed of nerve transmission and general intelligence, whereas other studies have shown no or negative correlations (see Mulhern, 1997, for a

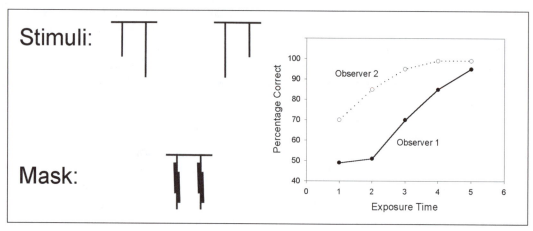

Figure 10.3   (Left) Representative stimuli in an inspection task. The task is to indicate whether the left or the right vertical line is longer. (Right) Performance of two hypothetical observers. Observer 2 has the shorter inspection time.

review). PET studies (see, e.g., Haier et al., 1988) measuring the brain's glucose use (and, hence, it is supposed, its activity) during performance of relatively brief tasks have shown that relatively intelligent people (as measured by general intelligence tests) metabolize less glucose while solving problems. Of course, this finding of a correlation between efficient processing at a physiological level with intelligence does not necessarily imply that more efficient processing is the cause of intelligence differences; more intelligent individuals may develop more efficient processing.

Some behavioral measures of mental speed have shown more stability than physiological measures. One of these paradigms is *inspection time*. In this procedure, the minimum exposure time for making a simple discrimination at a given level of accuracy is measured. A typical stimulus consists of two lines, one obviously longer than the other, followed by a mask (see Figure 10.3, left). The observer's task is to indicate which of the lines was longer. The observer repeats the task many times with different exposure times in order to determine the exposure time at which a given level of accuracy (e.g., 95%) is reached. The exposure time is then taken as a measure of the observer's inspection time (see Figure 10.3, right). Inspection time is considered by some to be a direct reflection of mental processing, reflecting the speed or efficiency of the activity of the brain (see Bors, Stokes, Forrin, & Hodder, 1999, for a discussion of this view). However, some studies suggest that the determining factor of inspection time is not, strictly speaking, mental speed. For example, Bors et al. (1999) presented evidence that suggests that performance in the inspection time task is largely dependent on the ability to maintain attention to the task. They showed that when inspection time scores were corrected for attentiveness (by partialing out accuracy in an above-threshold condition), the correlations between inspection time and IQ were substantially reduced. Regardless of what it is measuring, inspection time has repeatedly been shown to be negatively related to IQ (i.e., the quicker the inspection time, the higher the IQ), with correlations ranging from −.2 to −.9.

Sustained attention (or mental concentration) has been related to general intelligence in several other tasks in addition to the inspection time task. One task used in this context is a so-called temporal tracking task. In such a task, two sets of items are presented, and the task is to report a difference between the two sets. For example, the letters *RTX* might be presented in the first set and the letters *TYR* in the second set. The task is to report the letters that were unique to one set (*X* and *Y*, in this example). Although such a task, when repeated many times, would seem to make demands on sustained attention, it obviously also makes demands on working memory. The finding that such tasks seem to form a factor of intelligence (see Stankov & Horn, 1980) cannot, thus, be unambiguously related to attention. In fact, performance in another variety of sustained attention task, the vigilance task (see Chapter 8), has been shown to be unrelated to IQ (J. F. Mackworth, 1969). The difference in results for tasks such as the temporal tracking tasks and vigilance tasks can be attributed to task complexity or, perhaps, to decreasing arousal in the vigilance conditions but not in the complex task conditions.

Performance on tasks that involve keeping instructions, or task set, active also seems to be related to intelligence. In fact, tests that require making a specific response (e.g., crossing out or circling an item) according to directions and the type of test material presented are included in some intelligence test batteries. In such tasks, participants must keep alternate sets of instructions in memory and must apply the right instruction when task conditions demand it. Several studies have shown that people of relatively low intelligence have more difficulty initiating shifts of attention from one stimulus dimension to another when the shifting rules have to be maintained in memory (see, e.g., Duncan, Emslie, et al., 1996).

The ability to divide attention has often been described as basic to cognitive functioning and intelligence (see, e.g., Stankov, 1983). Many studies have shown that the ability to divide attention between two tasks (as measured by the variability in dual-task performance that cannot be attributed to either single-task performance or random error) is related to general intelligence. In fact, it has even been argued that some dual tasks could be used as replacements for IQ tests (Stankov, 1983). Although some dual-task studies are confounded by other factors that could also explain the relation between dual-task performance ability and intelligence (such as increased memory requirements in the dual-task conditions), a number of studies provide results consistent with a specific, divided attention element of intelligence. For example, Ben-Shakhar and Sheffer (2001) showed that the reaction time (RT) variability attributable to dual-task performance was consistent across practice, suggesting that the ability to allocate processing resources is a distinct ability. Furthermore, they found that dual-task performance was more predictive of a general measure of cognitive performance (the Israeli college entrance exam) than was single-task performance. However, this relation held only for dual-task performance early in practice, suggesting that, at least in the tasks used in this study, the ability to allocate attention between the two tasks was quickly automated. That is, the ability to flexibly allocate attention in novel situations seems to be indicative of intelligence. The tasks used by Ben-Shakhar and Sheffer were quite simple (a lexical or category membership decision combined with a location verification task in which participants had to respond according to whether a word correctly indicated the position of a briefly presented visual stimulus), thus virtually eliminating the possibility that the results were due to other cognitive factors, such as processing complexity or memory load. In short, there is promising evidence that the ability to divide attention is related to intelligence.

Duncan et al. (1996) suggest that the particular aspect of attention that best describes general intelligence is attentional control exercised by the frontal lobes. Duncan et al. measured *g* using standard tests of fluid intelligence, and then examined the relation between *g* and a phenomenon called *goal neglect*. Goal neglect is commonly seen in patients who have suffered injury to the frontal lobes. It can perhaps best be described as the failure to carry out a task requirement even though the instruction to do so has been understood. For example, Luria (1980) described a frontal-lobe patient who, instead of following the instruction to squeeze her hand when a light went on, failed to act but said, "I must squeeze!"

Duncan et al. (1996) adapted the dichotic listening task used by Gopher and Kahneman (Gopher, 1982; Gopher & Kahneman, 1971) to study goal neglect in healthy individuals. Their decision to do so was based on the finding that some individuals completely fail to carry out the instruction to switch attention from one channel to another (see, e.g., Kahneman, Ben-Ishai, & Lotan, 1973). They developed a visual analog of the task (see Figure 10.4) in which letter or digit pairs were presented one at a time in a display. The task was to read the letters from only one side of the display. A trial began with the instruction to read either the left or right letters; after 10 pairs of stimuli, a second instruction (a "+" for the right letters or a "−" for the left letters) indicated which side was relevant for the last three pairs. Goal neglect was said to have occurred when participants failed to switch sides when that was required (e.g., when the instruction "watch right" was followed by the cue −, which indicated that left was now the relevant side). Duncan et al. found that *g* was inversely related to goal neglect in this task (see Figure 10.5) in both older and younger adults.

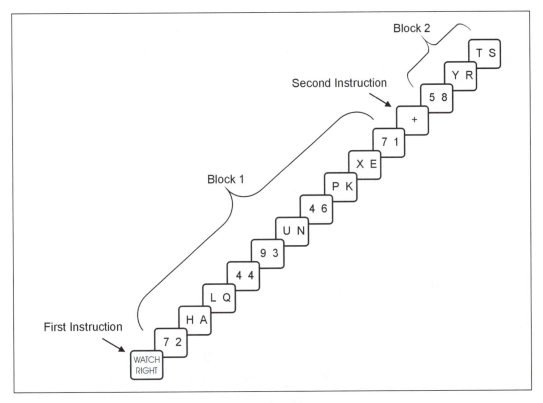

Figure 10.4   The visual attention-switching task used by Duncan, Emslie, et al. (1996). The task was to read the letters from only the indicated side of the display. Goal neglect is said to occur when the subject fails to switch sides when the second instruction (a "+" for "right" or a "−" for "left") indicates that it is necessary to do so.

    In an additional experiment, Duncan et al. added a dot-detection task to the letter-detection task. In this case, a dot appeared above or below a letter or digit pair once or twice during each trial, and one of two keys had to be pressed as quickly as possible to indicate the dot's position. The addition of the dot task resulted in higher correlations between *g* and goal neglect as compared to performance in the letter-detection task alone. Interestingly, the dot itself was almost never neglected when participants were first instructed about the dot task and then about the letter-detection task. In contrast, neglect of the dot was common, and related to *g*, when the dot task was described last. This result suggests that a major factor in goal neglect is the number of instructions that have to be borne in mind, and that a new task requirement is likely to be ignored when other requirements are already activated. This finding has practical implications that should be further

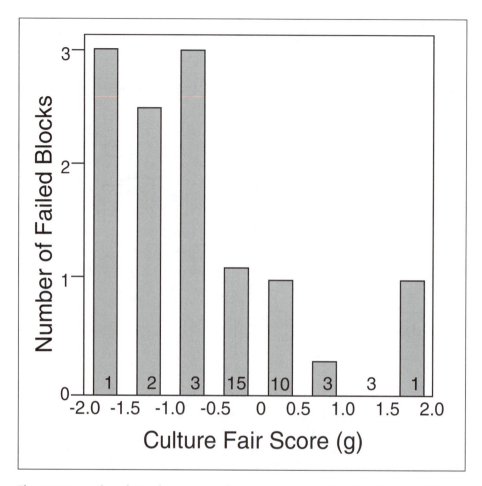

Figure 10.5   The relation between intelligence (*g*; measured with a "culture fair" test) and goal neglect in Experiment 3 of Duncan et al. (1996), p. 324, Table 10.1. The numbers on the bars indicate the number of participants tested of a given *g* (expressed in *z* scores). With only minor exceptions, the results are consistent with a strong relation between *g* and goal neglect.

SOURCE: Data from Duncan et al., 1996.

researched. For example, it could be concluded that when several instructions are given, such as when a doctor is counseling a patient, the most important instruction should be given first.

Intelligence has also been related to controlled processing, in general. Recall that controlled processing (Atkinson & Shiffrin, 1968) is defined as being relatively slow, requiring effort, and involving consciousness of one's actions, whereas automatic processing is often described as a capacity-free, stimulus-driven mode of performance that is not dependent on conscious control. Comparisons of performance on tasks that require controlled processing, such as search for a target defined by a conjunction of features (e.g., a red T among blue Ts and red Os) with performance on tasks that do not require such processing, such as search for a target with a unique feature (e.g., a T among Os), suggest that the ability to exercise controlled attention is related to intelligence (Ackerman, 1988). A similar conclusion was reached by Tuholski, Engle, and Baylis (2001), who examined the relation between controlled processing and intelligence in a study in which people of relatively low or high intelligence performed a task in which different numbers of targets had to be counted. The targets were presented either alone or in the presence of distractors. The study was based on the assumption that counting consists of an automatic and a nonautomatic component. The automatic component, called *subitizing*, supports recognition of small numbers of objects. Most people can accurately subitize three to four items (a number that is consistent with the span of apprehension).

In a first experiment, with no distractors in the display, Tuholski et al. (2001) found no difference between low and high intelligence individuals in their ability to subitize. In contrast, counting more than four items (which presumably depends on controlled processing to keep track of which items have already been counted) was performed more efficiently by high than by low intelligence individuals. Similar results were found when distractors that could be distinguished from the target on the basis of a unique feature were added to the display. However, the results were different when the added distractors differed from the targets on the basis of a conjunction of features. In this case, the results (increasing RT as a function of the number of items to be counted) indicated that even small numbers of items had to be counted, rather than automatically subitized. With conjunction targets requiring controlled search, high intelligence individuals outperformed those of lower intelligence even in the subitizing range of one to three items. The simplicity of the counting task lends strength to the argument that fundamental processes are at the core of differences in intelligence. The relation of controlled, but not automatic, processing to intelligence is also consistent with the finding that performance early in practice in attention-demanding tasks is more highly correlated with intelligence than is performance later in practice.

It seems clear that more intelligent individuals are also better at performing tasks requiring attention. Intelligence is associated with a broad range of attention tasks. Tasks that require controlled attention or active maintenance of goals seem to be the most strongly associated with general intelligence. The question remains, however, whether attention is a basic ability that determines how intelligent a person is.

▲ INTRA-INDIVIDUAL DIFFERENCES IN ATTENTION

Although the focus of this chapter is on inter-individual differences (differences between individuals or groups), there are also important intra-individual differences in attention. Most obvious are changes across the lifespan. Some differences between younger adults and older adults, and some differences between adults and children, have already been mentioned elsewhere in the book. In the following section, we will summarize and complement what has already been said about the effects of aging on attention. But first, we will look at changes in attention on a much shorter time scale, that is, within the course of one day.

Arousal and Circadian Rhythms

Most of us are familiar with the sensation of feeling drowsy upon awakening, despite just having had a night's rest. At the time of awakening, most people are still experiencing the rising portion of the daily cycle of body temperature and readiness for action. Body temperature changes over the course of the day, and arousal level changes with it (see Figure 10.6). Temperature increases throughout the day until about 10:00 P.M., at which point it starts to drop, usually reaching a minimum around 5:00 A.M. Performance of simple, perceptual-motor tasks improves as body temperature rises (see, e.g., Kleitman & Jackson, 1950), although a deviant "post-lunch dip" often occurs in the performance function. That is, whereas body temperature rises monotonically throughout the day, performance usually shows a temporary drop around 1:00 P.M. On the other hand, tasks with significant short-term memory components, such as verbal reasoning and mental arithmetic, typically show better performance in the morning than later in the day, with the best performance around midmorning (see, e.g., Folkard, 1975; Folkard & Monk, 1980). In short, tasks with minimal short-term memory demands show peak performance late in the day and tasks with heavy short-term memory demands are performed best early in the day.

The relation between arousal changes as a function of time of day and performance as a function of task type is consistent with M. S. Humphreys and Revelle's (1984) multiple-resources model. According to this model, sustained information transfer resources (which encompass all of the processes involved in identifying a stimulus and selecting and executing a response to it) increase as a function of arousal throughout the day, whereas short-term memory resources (which encompass the processes required to retain and retrieve information in the short-term store) decrease as a function of increases in arousal. Performance on tasks with little or no short-term memory demands, such as many vigilance and sustained attention

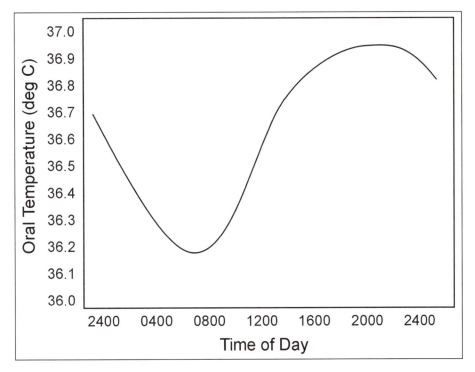

Figure 10.6   Schematic view of body temperature as a function of time of day.

tasks, should be solely a function of the sustained information transfer component and, hence, should increase with arousal level. Performance on tasks with significant short-term memory demands, such as digit span and running memory tasks, should reflect both increases in sustained information transfer and decreases in short-term memory resources, and, thus, should follow an inverted U-shaped function of arousal, with optimal performance occurring at intermediate levels of arousal. Moreover, as the demands for short-term memory resources increase relative to those for information-transfer resources, the arousal level at which optimal performance is obtained should decrease.

The morning advantage for tasks with a substantial short-term memory component is not solely a function of arousal. Different cognitive strategies may also be adopted at different times of day. For example, Folkard and Monk (1979) found that articulatory suppression (i.e., counting aloud or repeating a given syllable in order to tie up phonological processing resources; see Chapter 7), which typically is thought to prevent maintenance rehearsal, eliminates the advantage for immediate recall early versus late in the day. Moreover, Folkard and Monk (1980) found an evening advantage for delayed recall, which depends more on elaborative than on maintenance rehearsal. Such findings led Folkard and Monk to propose that people tend to engage in relatively more maintenance rehearsal (e.g., simply repeating items) in the morning and relatively more elaborative rehearsal (e.g., attempting to form meaningful chunks of items) in the afternoon. This suggests that it may be best to perform tasks that rely on maintenance rehearsal (such as some simple arithmetic tasks) early in the day, and to learn material that requires elaborative rehearsal (such as studying this chapter in preparation for an exam) later in the day.

Energetic Arousal and Performance

One aspect of arousal that has been specifically related to attention is subjective feelings of energy versus fatigue, also described as *energetic arousal*. Energetic arousal is moderately correlated with indices of autonomic arousal, as is tense arousal (feelings of tension versus calmness; Matthews & Westerman, 1994). Higher levels of energetic arousal are associated with improvements in performance in a range of tasks, including relatively simple information processing tasks (Matthews, Davies, & Lees, 1990) and more complicated tasks, such as simulated flight (Singh, Molloy, & Parasuraman, 1993). However, the relation between performance and energetic arousal does not follow the prediction of the Yerkes-Dodson Law that the simpler the task, the higher the level of optimal arousal. Contrary to this, higher levels of energy are more facilitative as task complexity increases (Matthews, Davies, & Lees, 1990). It has been suggested that this effect is directly related to the attentional demands of the task. Specifically, it may be that subjective feelings of energy reflect the availability of attentional resources that can then be allocated to different aspects of task processing.

Matthews and Davies (2001) tested the hypothesis that energetic arousal reflects the availability of general attentional resources by combining a digit-detection task with a probe-reaction time task. The digit-detection task required that observers monitor a stream of digits presented visually at a rate of one per second for the presence of a target digit (the digit 0). Each digit was presented for 40 ms, in either a less degraded (23% of the pixels making up the digit reversed in polarity to match the background) or more degraded (30% of the pixels reversed) form. The probe for the probe-reaction time task was easy to discriminate and was either auditory (a 70-dB tone presented for 200 ms over headphones) or visual (a small square presented in the same location as the digits). Both probes and targets were to be responded to as quickly as possible. To preclude psychological refractory period effects (see Chapter 6), probes appearing directly after targets were not included in the analysis. Energetic arousal was measured by means of a mood description checklist (the UWIST mood adjective checklist [UMACL]; Matthews,

Jones, & Chamberlain, 1990) in which participants rated their current mood in terms of feelings of energy, tenseness, and pleasantness.

Measures of response time and sensitivity to the targets showed that performance was better for individuals reporting high energy rather than low energy. However, this relation held only for the condition in which the digit-detection stimuli were more degraded and the probe was visual—that is, under the highest level of perceptual load within one modality. No effects of energy were found on probe-response times. These results were interpreted as evidence that high levels of energy lead to a greater availability of processing resources. The finding that only performance with the visual probe was influenced by the level of energy of the participants is consistent with other findings of restricted attentional capacity within, but not between, modalities (Duncan, Martens, & Ward, 1996; Wickens, 1984). Of course, it could be argued that perceptual processing, in particular, rather than resource availability, in general, benefits from high levels of energy.

ATTENTION ACROSS THE LIFESPAN ▲

Like other basic cognitive functions, attention changes across the lifespan. Many have argued that effortful cognitive abilities that consolidate relatively late in childhood are also the first to weaken in old age. Thus, understanding the development of attentional processes in children paves the way for an understanding of deficits of attention in old age.

Attentional Control in Children

Many things that we take for granted (such as moving our eyes to an object of interest) cannot be performed at all by very young infants. Somewhat less obvious are differences in attentional resources or abilities between children and adults. One factor complicating the study of the development of attentional processes is that other cognitive processes, such as short-term memory, are also subject to developmental changes. The ability to keep task instructions in mind and to sustain attention in a task also changes radically throughout childhood. For example, in one study (Levy, 1980), it was found that the percentage of children who could perform a relatively simple go or no-go vigilance task (press a key on the relatively few occasions when the letter "x" is shown and ignore all other letters) increased monotonically from just 27% of children between 3 years and 3 years 5 months of age to 100% of children 4 years 6 months of age and older. The speed and accuracy of responding continued to improve up to the age of 7 years, the oldest group tested. Although a number of abilities change throughout childhood, studies that control for other cognitive abilities do show clear differences in many aspects of attention, ranging from the development of covert orienting in infants to the final stages of the development of cognitive control in adolescence.

The development of the ability to orient both the eyes and attention in infancy is dependent on the stage of development of the brain (see M. H. Johnson, 1998, for a review). For example, visual orienting is contingent on the emergence of functioning of cortical oculomotor pathways between the ages of 2 and 3 months. Up to about 6 months of age, volitional control of eye movements develops, as infants become increasingly able to inhibit automatic saccades, produce anticipatory saccades, and delay making a planned saccade (see Box 10.1, p. 312). Covert shifts of visual attention first emerge around 4 months of age. However, the ability to direct and sustain attention continues to develop into childhood.

Many studies have shown that children are more sensitive to interfering information than are adults (Lane, 1982). For example, younger children (6–8 years old) are more sensitive to the spatial separation of two stimuli when they are required to ignore one, spatially distinct, stimulus in order to make a judgment about another than are older children (9–11 years). That is, they show more interference than older children when the stimuli are closer together. When the judgment requires attending both stimuli, younger children are hurt more by a greater spatial separation. Taken together, these results suggest that the ability to narrow or broaden the attentional focus is still developing in this period of childhood (Enns & Girgus, 1985). More recently, children's performance in a selective attention task was tested under conditions of high and low perceptual load (Huang-Pollock, Carr, & Nigg, 2002). When perceptual load is low (e.g., when a display of just one or two items has to be searched for the presence of a target), it has been argued, processing is actually less efficient than when perceptual load is high (e.g., when the display contains five or six items), as measured by interference from an irrelevant, peripheral distractor. N. Lavie (1995) has argued that high load mobilizes early-selection processes that enable selection of the relevant information for further processing and preclude the processing of the distractor, whereas low load conditions are such that all present information (relevant or irrelevant) is processed to a semantic level (see Chapter 3). Huang-Pollock et al. (2002) found that when perceptual load was high, children performed the task of determining whether a particular letter ("X" or "N") was present in a circular display, while ignoring a letter to the right or left of the display and not making eye movements (see Figure 10.7), in a way that was qualitatively similar to adults. However, when perceptual load was low, they did not. In particular, children showed evidence of early selection (i.e., a decrease in the interference effect, defined as the difference in accuracy or reaction time between trials with an incompatible peripheral letter

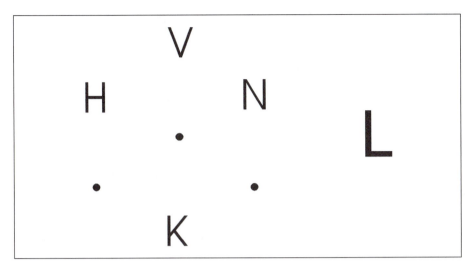

Figure 10.7   A display of the type used by Huang-Pollock et al. (2002). The letter to the side of the display could be neutral (a letter that never occurred as a target), compatible (the same letter as the target present in the display), or incompatible (the same letter as the target *not* present in the display). In the figure, the perceptual load is four items, and the peripheral letter is neutral.

and a compatible peripheral letter) at lower perceptual loads than did adults. The authors argue that children implement early selection at lower perceptual loads than do adults in order to compensate for immature interference control processes.[2] Age differences in the development of the ability to abort actions in response to a stop signal, described in Chapter 5, also suggest that inhibitory processes continue developing well into childhood.

Studies using the dichotic listening paradigm (see Chapter 4) have shown that selective attention (attending target words on one channel while ignoring input to another channel) improves during childhood. For example, Geffen and Sexton (1978) found that 10 year olds were much better able to select relevant auditory information than were 7 year olds (i.e., they were able to selectively listen to a speaker presented in one voice or just one ear while ignoring information presented in another voice or the other ear). The older children in this study also showed better divided attention, as evidenced by higher target detection rates when both channels had to be monitored. Not all researchers have found that older children are better able to divide attention than younger children. When single-task performance is equated for the groups studied, a common finding is that younger and older children perform equally well when two tasks are performed with equal priority. However, even when performance on the component tasks is equated, older children are better able to differentially allocate

Box 10.1 Measuring Attention in Infants

Studying attention in infants and very young children is complicated by the fact that one cannot rely on verbal instructions nor collect manual responses. This led Luria (1954; cited in Levy, 1980) to conclude that "firm regulation of the motor system by verbal instruction" (as indicated by children's ability to perform a go or no-go task) first appears at the age of 5 years. Fortunately, it is possible to capitalize on the tendency of infants to orient to (look at) stimuli that are especially attractive, being novel, dynamic, or colorful. For example, H. M. Johnson (1994) found that 4-month-old infants learned to perform an anti-saccade task when a boring peripheral stimulus (which should be ignored) was followed by a colorful, dynamic second stimulus. Similarly, Butcher, Kalverboer, and Geuze (1999) were able to test for inhibition of return (IOR) in infants as young as 6 weeks old. The first step in testing infants is to make sure that they are awake. Measurements can be made when infants are in state 3 or 4 of Prechtl's scale of alertness (Prechtl & Beintema, 1964); that is, they are awake, their eyes are open, and they show some spontaneous movements. The equipment necessary to run the tasks and record eye movements, as well as the experimenter, must be concealed so that the infant can see only the stimuli themselves.

The task used by Butcher et al. (1999) is shown in Box Figure 10.1. Each trial began with the appearance of a fixation stimulus (a brightly colored, high-contrast cross whose arms changed in length or intensity of color six times per second), accompanied by a brief melody.

One to two seconds after the infant shifted gaze to the fixation stimulus it disappeared, and a cue was displayed 10° to the left or the right for 100 ms. The fixation stimulus reappeared as the cue disappeared. It was replaced after 900 ms by targets identical to the cue, located 10° to the left and the right. The targets remained in view until the infant looked away from the fixation stimulus, or for 10 seconds. After a short intertrial interval, the fixation stimulus reappeared and the next trial began. Cues and targets were bicolored bars whose colors reversed six times per second. The task included 24 trials, with 12 left and 12 right cues in pseudorandom order. The onset and direction of the first eye movement after the target appeared was scored on each trial. Eye movements to targets at cued locations were considered to indicate facilitation. Eye movements to targets at uncued locations were considered to indicate IOR. As can be seen in the graph in Box Figure 10.2, IOR responses increased in frequency between the 6- and the 12-week sessions. Infants looked significantly more frequently to uncued targets than to cued targets from the 16-week session on, and significantly faster to uncued targets from the 18-week session on. The gradual emergence of IOR between 12 and 16 weeks has been interpreted as evidence of increasing attentional control over looking behavior (probably mediated by the parietal lobe, which undergoes a period of rapid development during the second and third months), as the infant develops the ability to inhibit the oculomotor priming initiated by the cue.

(Continued)

Box 10.1 (Continued)

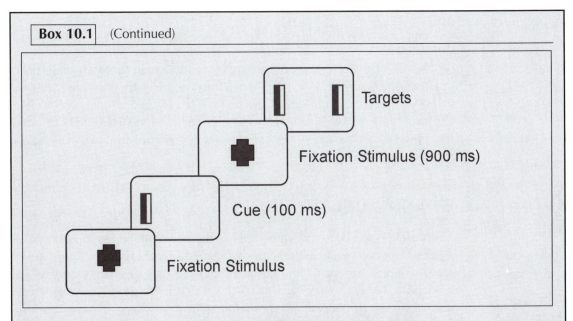

Figure 1 The trial procedure used by Butcher, Kalverboer, and Geuze (1999).

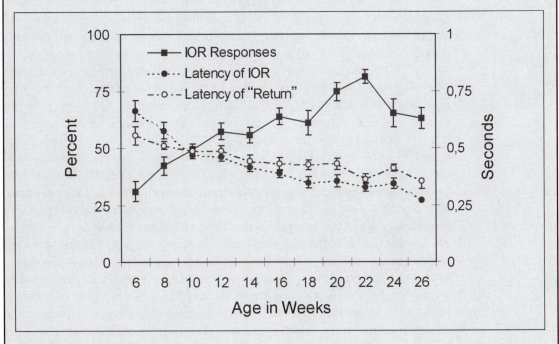

Figure 2 Inhibition of return in infants aged 6 to 26 weeks.

attention to the two tasks. That is, older children are better able to vary the amount of attention they place on one task at the cost of another (Irwin-Chase & Burns, 2000).

The role of attention in cognitive development is critical (M. H. Johnson, 1998). An interesting point in this regard is that aspects of infant attention are correlated with later measures of intelligence. Even at a very early age, attention determines what aspects of the environment an infant or child will learn about. As attention develops, children become better able to monitor both their own performance and events in the world.

Attentional Control and Aging

In some respects, aging can be seen as the downside of development. Many abilities that develop and improve in childhood decline in old age. On the bright side, a lifetime of experience and learning compensates in large part for age-related deficiencies, but understanding why these deficiencies occur is still a major topic of research. Elderly people have shown impairments in a range of attention tasks. The most robust effects of attention on aging are seen in tasks requiring executive control of attention, which has been defined as the processes of selection, scheduling, and coordination of the processes of perception, memory, and action. Control of attention is needed to control resource allocation whenever more than one task must be carried out at a time, and when different task goals must be kept active.

In 1977, Craik concluded, "One of the clearest results in the experimental psychology of aging is the finding that older people are more penalized when they must divide their attention" (p. 391). Although the underlying mechanisms for this finding have been debated, the basic result has been replicated many times (see, e.g., Crossley & Hiscock, 1992; Korteling, 1991, 1993). Older people experience more difficulty than younger people in rapidly redeploying attention among two or more tasks or processes (see, e.g., Korteling, 1991) and exhibit less flexibility than younger adults in varying their speed-accuracy criteria (see, e.g., Strayer, Wickens, & Braune, 1987; see also Chapter 2). Elderly people have particular difficulty with timesharing, or allocating resources to different tasks at the same time. For example, Ponds, Brouwer, and van Wolffelaar (1988) examined the ability of young, middle-aged, and elderly people to drive in a driving simulator while performing a second task, counting dots presented unobtrusively on the windshield display. As shown by the performance operating characteristics plotted in Figure 10.8, elderly people tend to show a greater divided-attention deficit than younger people. The divided-attention deficit for older people in comparison to younger adults also has been shown to be resistant to dual-task practice (McDowd, 1986).

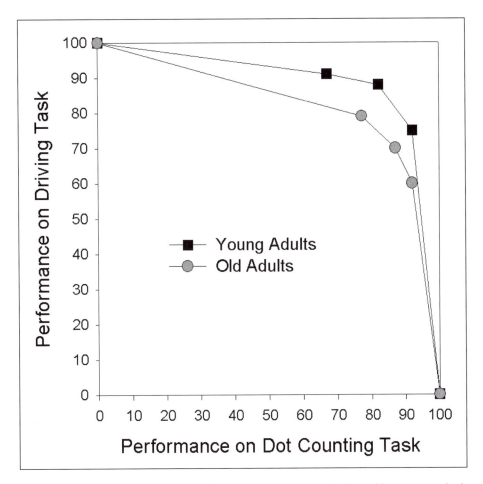

Figure 10.8 A divided-attention deficit in elderly drivers as indicated by a greater dual-task decrement.

SOURCE: Data from Ponds, Brouwer, & van Wolffelaar, 1988.

In an attempt to determine whether the dual-task performance decrement among the elderly could be overcome through appropriate training (an important question given the relation between the ability to allocate attention and to perform complex tasks, such as driving), Kramer, Larish, and Strayer (1995; see also Kramer, Larish, Weber, & Bardell, 1999) made use of the variable-emphasis training technique developed by Brickner and Gopher (1981). They compared the ability of young and old participants to deploy their attention to two tasks, and examined whether training could reduce the age-related dual-task deficit. Participants in their study practiced performing two tasks together, and then were tested with two different tasks to determine whether any timesharing skill would transfer to a new situation. Two training regimens were contrasted. Half of the participants received a fixed-priority instruction in which they were always instructed to divide their attention equally between the two tasks. The other half of the participants practiced with a variable-priority strategy in which 20–80% of the emphasis should be placed on one of the tasks, with the remaining emphasis placed on the other task.

The display used in the training conditions in Kramer, Larish, and Strayer's (1995) experiment is shown in Figure 10.9. One task was to monitor the six gauges and to press one of six keys whenever one of the gauges reached "9" or higher. In order to check the state of a gauge, one of six keys had to be pressed in order to cause the current reading of the gauge to be shown (the indicator then remained visible for 1.5 seconds). The other task was to perform "alphabet arithmetic." In this task, participants had to work their way forward or backward in the alphabet in order to solve problems such as "H − 3 = E." In order to help participants to allocate their attention appropriately, feedback bars were integrated into the display. The bars indicated the proportion of single-task performance that should be striven toward in each condition. A marker placed between the two bars indicated the criterion for each condition. For example, in the 20–80 condition for the variable-priority group, a marker was placed in between the bars for the two tasks so that criterion performance was reached when performance was 20% of single-task performance on the monitoring task and 80% of single-task performance on the alphabet arithmetic task.

Kramer, Larish, and Strayer (1995) found that older participants were slower than younger ones on single-task performance of each of the tasks. They also found that older participants showed a larger dual-task decrement than younger ones. Performance in the dual-task conditions improved when variable-priority training was given, but not when the training was with only one priority setting. Although older participants benefited from the training as much as did younger ones, there was still a substantial age-related difference in the dual-task decrement after training. Both older and younger participants in the variable-priority condition showed transfer to the two new tasks, suggesting that a generalizable skill in dual-task processing was learned. Most importantly, the size of the dual-task decrement in the transfer session (unlike in the training sessions) did not depend on age. Thus, there is some evidence that older people can benefit from divided-attention training.

Inhibition and Aging

One notable effect of aging is a general slowing in information-processing speed. It has been hypothesized that this slowing is in part due to declines in the

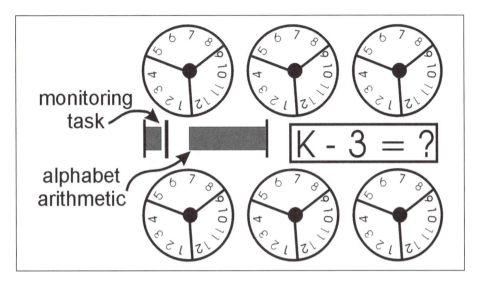

Figure 10.9   The monitoring and alphabet arithmetic tasks used by Kramer, Larish, and Strayer (1995). The arrows point to the feedback display. In this example, performance is optimal when the monitoring task is performed at 20% of the single-task level and the arithmetic task at 80% of the single-task level.

SOURCE: Kramer et al., 1995.

control of inhibitory processes. For example, stop-signal RTs (see Chapter 5) are longer in elderly people than in young adults (Kramer et al., 1994), suggesting that older people have more difficulty controlling the stopping process than do younger people.

Older people are also disproportionately susceptible to Stroop interference. Compared to younger adults, older adults show more interference from color words in a color-naming task. Some researchers have argued that the increase in the Stroop effect in older people can be attributed to general decreases in information-processing speed. For example, Salthouse and Meinz (1995) argued that increases in the Stroop effect could be accounted for by variability in the speed to perform simple perceptual-motor tasks. Other researchers have argued that the increase in the Stroop effect is due to a decline in the efficiency of inhibitory processes in older adults. For example, Spieler, Balota, and Faust (1996) showed that variations in the magnitude of the Stroop effect could be explained in terms of an increased influence of the words used in the task. More evidence for an inhibition account of increases in the Stroop effect as a function of aging is that the magnitude of the difference in the Stroop effect for older and younger people depends on the demand placed on inhibitory processes. For example, West and

Baylis (1998) showed that an abnormally large Stroop effect was seen only when the proportion of incongruent trials was high. Recall that Logan and Zbrodoff (1979) found that increasing the proportion of incongruent trials usually decreases the Stroop effect, which they attributed to an attentional strategy to attend to the relevant dimension and inhibit the irrelevant dimension.

In general, decreases in inhibitory control could result in inefficient selective attention, which could, in turn, lead to the intrusion of irrelevant information in working memory. In this way, poor inhibition can lead to what would be manifested as memory problems. The most prominent account of the relation between inhibition and performance declines associated with aging is that of Hasher and colleagues (Hasher, Zacks, & May, 1999). According to this account, inhibition plays a critical role in determining what gains access to working memory. Because working memory is limited in capacity (see Chapter 7), it is important to restrict its contents to only relevant information. Inhibition is often required to keep unwanted information out of working memory. When inhibition fails, working memory can become "cluttered" and difficulties arise in the selection of appropriate goals, thoughts, or actions. According to Hasher, Zacks, & May, 1999), inhibition is central to cognitive control. They define control as "the degree to which an activated goal determines the contents of consciousness" (p. 653). Inhibition serves the function of suppressing the activation of extraneous, goal-irrelevant information by controlling the activation of items in working memory. Hasher et al. describe the different functions of inhibition as (1) facilitating access of relevant information to working memory resources, (2) enabling the deletion of irrelevant or no-longer-relevant information, and (3) restraining the activation of responses until all courses of action have been considered.

Research using the negative-priming paradigm inspired much work on the role of inhibition in cognitive processes and possible declines in inhibition as a function of aging. Connelly and Hasher (1993) reported that older people show normal levels of negative priming for location-based tasks, but reduced negative priming for responses based on object identity (although this finding is not always replicated; see Kramer et al., 1994). The finding that older people show reduced negative priming for responses based on object identity, but not for location, suggests that only some aspects of inhibition are impaired. Studies examining inhibition of return in older people also suggest that impairments to inhibition are selective. In general, inhibition of distractors, as in the response-compatibility paradigm, or of location, as in inhibition of return or location-based negative priming, seems to remain intact. On the other hand, inhibition of identity information, as in object-based negative priming, shows an age-related deficit.

Age-related differences have also been found in directed forgetting tasks. In a task in which "true" and "false" statements about a simulated criminal report were read, older people were less successful than younger ones in ignoring the false information when making a judgment about the severity of the crime (Chen & Blanchard-Fields, 2000). Language comprehension shows the same pattern: Older adults are less efficient in suppressing no-longer-relevant word meanings (May, Zacks, Hasher, & Multhaup, 1999). Both of these examples can be attributed to differences in managing the contents of working memory.

Difficulty in inhibition at a more basic level has been demonstrated in a task in which observers have to suppress eye movements to peripheral cues and instead move their eyes to the corresponding location in the opposite visual field (i.e., in the anti-saccade task). Older people are slower than younger observers in this task, and are more likely to move their eyes to the cue itself (see, e.g., Nieuwenhuis et al., 2000). Nieuwenhuis et al. suggest that inhibition to the location of the cue fails because of inadequate activation of the cue-response representation. That is, inhibition fails because older people have more difficulty keeping the task goals in mind.

Although many researchers have found age-related differences in the ability to inhibit information or responses, Kramer et al. (1994) caution that the support for a general decrease in inhibitory efficiency is limited. They compared the performance of young and old on tasks ranging from the stop-signal task to learning new rules in a categorization task (which requires inhibiting previously learned rules) to negative priming. The only strong differences between older and younger participants were on the stop-signal and categorization tasks. It should be noted that both of these tasks depend on frontal lobe function, whereas other neural pathways (in particular, the dorsal and ventral pathways involved in location processing and object processing, respectively) are relied upon in the other tasks. Kramer et al. also found relatively low correlations between the different tasks in their test battery, which reflects the nonunitary nature of inhibition. Interestingly, though, they did find that most tasks correlated with participants' self-reports of making errors in daily life (as measured by the Cognitive Failures Questionnaire; Broadbent et al., 1982). This suggests that everyday performance (and the cognitive failures associated with it) depends on a range of inhibitory processes.

Frontal Lobe Function and Monitoring Performance

Deficits in inhibition among elderly people provide support for the hypothesis that reduced frontal lobe function may be responsible for differences in performance between younger and older adults (see, e.g., West, 1996). According to the *frontal lobe hypothesis*, older adults are disproportionately disadvantaged on tasks that require cognitive processes supported by the frontal and prefrontal lobes of the brain. More support for the frontal lobe function hypothesis for aging deficits is found in the literature on dual-task performance and divided attention, discussed earlier, and in work using the task-switching paradigm (see Chapter 6). In their study of age differences in task switching, Kramer, Hahn, and Gopher (1999) compared the performance of young (18–25 years old) and old (60–75 years old) adults at different levels of practice in a task consisting of judging either the number of digits present on a trial or the value of the digits. The task was performed in blocks of 15 trials. At the beginning of each block, subjects were told which of the two tasks (counting digits or determining their value) should be performed, and whether they might have to switch tasks during the block. Partway through each block, subjects saw a message indicating which task should be performed for the remainder of the trials. In the first session of performing the task, the older adults showed a much larger switch cost (i.e., elevation in reaction time on the first trial after a switch in task) than did the younger adults (switch costs in the first session were about 850 and 220 ms for older and younger adults, respectively). However, after just one session of practice, the switch costs for older and younger adults were essentially the same (switch costs of about 300 and 220 ms for older and younger adults, respectively). When working memory load was increased (by requiring subjects to keep track of the number of trials performed in order to make a switch), age-related differences in switch costs were more robust. Moreover, regression analyses showed that age was responsible for at least part of the switching costs. Thus, although older adults can sometimes switch between tasks almost as well as younger adults, the ability to switch tasks (or the ability to learn to switch between tasks) does seem to decline with age.

Another important executive function is monitoring one's actions. Error recognition and recovery are thought to be dependent on frontal lobe function, and, as in other executive control tasks, elderly people show deficits in monitoring performance. The ability to recognize and correct errors is an important factor in the performance of many tasks. Incorrectly judging one's competence can be risky, such as when drivers overestimate their level of alertness in driving at night. The ability of people to catch their errors is often studied using an error-signaling paradigm. Typically, participants are asked to press a button or make another response when they recognize that an error has been made. According to Rabbitt (1990), "Error recognition, error correction, and error signaling appear to represent a hierarchy of progressively less 'automatic'—and increasingly slow and decreasingly reliable—processes" (p. 1296). Thus, one could expect that error signaling would be particularly sensitive to deficits in frontal lobe function. Rabbitt (1990) found reliable age and IQ differences in the number of errors signaled (by pressing a special key when an error had been made) in a choice-reaction task. However, all participants in the study were apparently equally aware of their errors in that they all showed the characteristic slowing of a response on a trial after an error had been made and were equally likely to correct their errors. Rabbitt argued that the difference between the number of errors corrected, on the one hand, and signaled, on the other, was a result of the relative automaticity of corrective (i.e., press the key that should have been pressed when an error was detected) versus signaling (i.e., press a key unrelated to the primary task when an error is committed) responses. However, another interpretation of the finding is that the error-signaling response was treated as a second task and that the difference in corrective and signaling responses could be viewed as a dual-task decrement. Whether due to controlled processing failures or a dual-task decrement, older people are less able to overtly report their errors. Even though correcting one's mistakes is arguably the more important process, it is necessary to recognize one's mistakes as such in order to revise one's estimates of the accuracy of one's performance. Like many executive control functions, the ability to report one's mistakes declines with age.

TRAINING AND ATTENTION ▲

To the extent that attentional strategies can be learned, attentional control, such as is used to switch between sources of information or to focus on relevant information, can be viewed as a skill. This conception of attentional control suggests that attentional strategies can be trained. Moreover, because most complex, real-world tasks require selective attending to different information sources, the ability to allocate attention might be a good predictor of success in many tasks.

Controlling Attention

A number of studies have shown beneficial effects of training attentional control. For example, people who are instructed to emphasize some aspects of task performance over others are able to learn to do this, and their ability to do so improves with practice (Brickner & Gopher, 1981). It also has been shown that training people to use particular attentional strategies can have long-lasting effects on performance. One example of this is that people trained to perform a task by giving variable priority to different task components often outperform learners who have had more practice on the criterion task (see, e.g., Gopher, 1993; Gopher, Weil, & Siegel, 1989; see Chapter 9 for details) and show better transfer to new task variations (Gopher, 1993; Kramer, Larish, & Strayer, 1995). Even more convincing is that training in variable priority setting (i.e., in allocating attention differentially to different aspects of a task) in the context of a video game has been shown to increase the flight school completion rates of future pilots (Gopher, Weil, & Bareket, 1994).[3] The importance of learning efficient attentional control strategies is also illustrated by the fact that too much information can lead to worse performance. For example, the introduction of new information or displays designed to improve performance can initially reduce performance because operators must learn how attention should be allocated over old and new information sources (Gopher & Barzilai, 1993; see also Chapter 9).

One way to force people to abandon inefficient attentional strategies is to train them with an appropriate secondary task that is to be performed concurrently with the primary task of interest. For example, in the helicopter flight-training program mentioned in Chapter 6 (Seagull & Gopher, 1997), many pilots were found to make inefficient use of their helmet-mounted displays. Pilots tend to avoid head movements because they can lead to orientation problems, yet efficient use of the displays required that the head be moved. In order to push pilots beyond their self-imposed limits in making head movements, Seagull and Gopher included a training condition (in a flight simulator) in which a secondary task requiring the making of head movements in order to collect information was performed concurrently with the task of piloting the helicopter. Pilots who performed the secondary task requiring head movements subsequently outperformed those who either performed no secondary task or whose secondary task did not require head movements. Apparently, forcing the pilots to make additional head movements allowed them to adopt a more efficient information-collecting strategy and made it possible for them to choose between limiting their head movements in order to focus on a narrow field of view and moving their heads in order to get a broader perspective.

Automaticity and Training

The usual view of automaticity is that it develops gradually and inexorably as a function of practice in consistently mapped tasks. It is characterized by a gradual freeing up of resources and increased independence from competing tasks. A great challenge for training programs is to identify those components of complex tasks that should be able to become automatized and to present training in such a way that consistent relations are highlighted and can benefit from growing automaticity of processing.

Not all training strategies have a beneficial effect. For example, in an exploration of training methods using the video game Space Fortress (see Chapter 7), some methods actually had a negative effect on game performance. One method of training was to slow down the presentation of the hostile elements in order to allow players more time to react to them. When the hostile elements (the mines) were slowed to half their normal speed, some positive transfer to whole-game performance occurred. However, when they were slowed even more, to one-fourth the normal speed, no benefit of the training was found (Mané, Adams, & Donchin, 1989), presumably because the disruption of the normal timing of the elements changed the task to such an extent that necessary strategies did not develop. Similarly, Newell, Carlton, Fisher, and Rutter (1989) found that training just the motor components of the task independent of a strategy for integrating these components in overall task performance led to only fleeting transfer to whole-game performance. These examples illustrate that it is necessary to under-stand the interplay between task components in order to create training programs to develop specific skills.

It has been argued that it is inappropriate to think of automaticity as the end-point on a continuum of gradually developing skill. Instead, there seems to be a constant interplay between automatic and controlled processing throughout levels of skill. The interplay between automatic and controlled processing may occur partly because different components develop automaticity at different rates (Shebilske, Goettl, & Regian, 1999). This could result from differing complexities of the subprocesses, or because regularities in some components become evident only after skill has developed in other components. As discussed at length in Chapter 9, automaticity in processing can lead to a range of errors in the perfor-mance of even simple tasks. Thus, controlled processing is necessary to monitor behavior and modify automatized routines when necessary. The finding of high correlations between both tests of general reasoning and performance on visual attention tests with skilled performance on the Space Fortress game (Rabbitt, Banerji, & Szymanski, 1989) lends further support to the idea that attentional monitoring remains important despite increased automaticity of some task components.

Schneider and Detweiler (1987, 1988) developed a simulation model that attempts to capture the distinction between controlled and automatic processing. Their primary goals were to characterize the development of multitasking skill and to provide support for the design of training programs for complex, high-performance skills. At a technical level, the model combines both connectionist (parallel distributed processing) and rule-based (production system) modeling. Skill acquisition is modeled as occurring in five phases. In the first phase, perfor-mance is determined by strictly controlled processes of comparing information held in working memory. As a function of learning, context information is gradually used (Phase 2), followed by goal-driven processing (Phase 3), and automatic activa-tion with controlled transfer of information (Phase 4). In Phase 5, processing is fully automatic, and able to bypass the usual control systems for processing information. In addition to the learning phases just described, the development of multitasking skill is dependent on specialized compensatory strategies (see Table 10.1).

Table 10-1   Compensatory Strategies in Dual-Task Performance Implemented in Schneider and Detweiler's Connectionist / Control Architecture

1. Abandoning, delaying, and preloading tasks

2. Abandoning suboptimal, high-workload strategies

3. Utilizing noncompeting structures and processes

4. Multiplexing control actions

5. Optimizing the transfer of information

6. Learning new associations between processing modules

7. Chunking and recoding information

Attention and Working Memory Capacity

As discussed in Chapter 7, the relationship between memory and attention is an intimate one. In fact, it has been argued that some aspects of memory are essentially aspects of attention, or vice versa. A strong proponent of the view that memory and attention are intimately linked is Engle (see, e.g., Engle, 2002). Engle has argued that executive attention and working memory capacity are the same thing. Importantly, his definition of working memory capacity as the ability to control and sustain attention in the presence of interference or distraction (Engle, Kane, & Tuholski, 1999) is different from that of memory span, discussed in Chapter 7. Memory span is basically a passive measure, which simply requires that items be remembered and reported back in either the same or reverse order in which they were presented. Working memory capacity is also measured by testing recall for a list of items (e.g., words), but the presentation of these items is interleaved with another, attention-demanding task. For example, in the operation-span task, words to be remembered are interleaved with a task requiring the evaluation of arithmetical expressions. The expressions are presented visually, read aloud, and evaluated (e.g., "Is $4 / 2 + 3 = 6$ [yes or no]"), after which a visually presented word (e.g., DOG) is read aloud. After a number of such trials, the words are recalled and the number of words recalled is taken as the capacity of working memory. In another measure of working memory capacity, the reading-span task, subjects read aloud a series of two to seven sentences, each followed by a letter that is also read aloud. After all sentences and letters have been read aloud, subjects are asked to recall as many of the letters as possible, the number of letters recalled being the measure of working memory capacity.

Engle, Tuholski, Laughlin, and Conway (1999) used structural equation modeling[4] techniques to show that working memory capacity is not the same as short-term memory capacity (e.g., digit span), although the two constructs are highly correlated. Importantly, when the variance common to short-term memory and working memory is statistically removed, working memory—but not short-term memory—capacity is correlated with general fluid intelligence. Engle et al. go on to argue that the variance that is shared by working memory and short-term memory is due to memory processes such as grouping, chunking, and rehearsal, and that the variance left in working memory capacity is attributable to executive attention. Following this reasoning, executive attention is predictive of general intelligence. Engle (2002) reviews the evidence that has shown that working memory capacity is predictive of the abilities to ignore irrelevant information, solve new problems, and suppress inappropriate responses.

Engle's definition of working memory capacity as executive attention suggests that working memory capacity should be related to performance in tasks requiring attentional control. One such task is the anti-saccade task, described earlier in the chapter. Kane, Bleckley, Conway, and Engle (2001) found that observers with a high working memory capacity were better able to resist attentional capture (i.e., made fewer saccades to the cue in the anti-saccade condition) than those with a low working memory capacity. The two groups performed similarly when the cue was valid, suggesting that the ability to suppress eye movements to the invalid cues was the only process affected by working memory capacity.

The ability to selectively listen to one channel in a dichotic listening task has also been related to working memory capacity, with the percentage of subjects hearing their own name on the to-be-ignored channel depending on working memory capacity (65% versus 20% for subjects with low and high working memory capacity, respectively; Conway, Cowan, & Bunting, 2001). Finally, Kane and Engle (described in Engle, 2002) showed that high working memory capacity individuals are also better able to suppress word reading in a Stroop color-naming task. They compared the performance of subjects with low versus high working memory capacity in a color-naming task with varying percentages of congruent (word color same as color word name) and incongruent (word color different than color word name). Kane and Engle reasoned that the goal of naming the colors and ignoring the color words would be easier to maintain when the number of congruent trials (on which the word name is the same as the response) was smaller, because the presence of many incongruent trials requires that the goal of ignoring the words be kept current. Indeed, when all trials were incongruent, high and low working memory capacity individuals performed similarly. Both groups made more errors when the percentage of congruent trials was increased to

50%, and both groups showed similar degrees of interference. However, when the percentage of congruent trials was increased to 75%, the low working memory capacity group made nearly twice as many errors as the high capacity group. Apparently, when the context makes it difficult to maintain the appropriate task goal, people with a high working memory capacity outperform those with a low working memory capacity.

The results and conclusions of Engle and colleagues regarding the relation between memory, attention, and intelligence are compelling, but a broader look at the literature suggests that much work remains to be done. For example, Larson and Perry (1999), who found a relation between visual capture in the anti-saccade task and the tendency to fall victim to capture errors in everyday life, found no evidence for a relation between working memory capacity and the ability to resist capture errors in an anti-saccade task. They used the mental counters test (Alderton, Wolfe, & Larson, 1997) to measure working memory capacity. This test requires that the test-taker keep a running tally of three different counters, each of which is displayed as a line on a computer screen. A box presented above the line means that the counter should be increased by one; a box presented below the line indicates that the counter should be decreased by one. All counters start at zero, and a series of five or seven boxes (each indicating an adjustment to be made) is presented on each trial, after which the participant is to report the current counter values. Working memory capacity is measured as the total number of correct responses. The reasons for the different outcomes of the Kane and Engle (Engle, 2002) and Larson and Perry studies could thus rest on the nature of the measure of working memory capacity. The tasks used by Kane and colleagues require that participants keep track of a list of words while performing a separate cognitive activity, whereas those of Larson and Perry require continuously updating the same three counters. The key difference between these two types of tasks may be that the goal (update set of three counters) is constant in the mental counters test, but varies (e.g., switch between evaluating arithmetical expressions and remembering words) in the working memory capacity tasks. This suggests that the ability to sustain attention to one task in the face of interference or distraction from another task is the key component in the relationship among intelligence, working memory capacity, and attention.

The question of how attention, memory, and intelligence are related is an intriguing one. Memory tasks (e.g., the backward digit span task discussed in more detail in Chapter 12) have long been included in intelligence test batteries. However, the key processes related to intelligence may be attentional rather than memorial in nature. As discussed in Chapter 7, the processes involved in memory tasks, such as retrieving items in memory or keeping subsets of information active, rely on attention.

ATTENTION, MEMORY, AND EMOTION ▲

Attention and memory can be affected by the emotional state of the observer. An illustration of this can be found in the conditioning of monkeys to fear certain stimuli. If a monkey that has never experienced any danger observes an adult showing a fear reaction to stimuli that are natural dangers to monkeys, such as a snake or a crocodile, the naïve monkey will show fear to toy snakes or crocodiles presented by an experimenter. However, if the fear-inducing stimulus is normally harmless, such as flowers or a toy rabbit, the naïve monkey does not learn fear (Mineka, 1992). Learning (and, presumably, memory) for fear-based stimuli seems to have an evolutionary basis (this might explain why relatively many people have a phobia for spiders and so few a phobia for flies). Whether or not seen from an evolutionary perspective, emotion and cognition are intertwined. Emotion can color our perceptions and bias our memories, and severe emotional disorders lead to distortions in information processing.

Mood-Congruent Memory

Think of the saddest thing that happened to you when you were a child. If you are successful in doing this, you will be more likely to remember sad or negative words or events mentioned in this section. Thinking about sad events tends to induce a negative mood, and mood can bias memory. Research on the effects of mood on attention and memory have shown that people tend to remember information that is congruent with their mood state better than information that is incongruent with the current state (see, e.g., Bower, 1981). One theory proposed to account for these effects supposes that memory consists of nodes connected together by associations of various strengths (Bower, 1981). These interconnected nodes represent concepts, emotions, and experiences, and the activation of one node spreads activation to other nodes connected to it. Thus, activation of an emotion will tend to activate things associated with that emotion. This, in turn, leads to more attention and better memory for activated items.

When negative or anxious emotions are so intense as to be pathological (as in depression and anxiety, respectively), information processing may be distorted. It has been proposed that anxious individuals have a "danger" schema that leads them to selectively attend to and process threat-related information, and that depressed individuals have a negative self-schema that leads to enhanced processing of negative information and maintenance of the negative state (Beck, 1967, 1976). The theories of both Bower (1981) and Beck suggest that mood or emotion can influence where attention is allocated and what is most likely to be remembered.

Memory and Depression

One of the characteristics of depression is frequent negative thoughts. In fact, the tendency to dwell and elaborate on negative thoughts seems to affect the memory of depressed individuals. When asked to remember lists of words in which some items are negative (the others may be neutral or positive), depressed individuals remember disproportionately many of the items related to negative occurrences, especially information that refers to the self or the depressed state. This bias for negative words is generally found only for explicit memory tests, and not for implicit tests. This dissociation suggests that it is elaboration of the negative items that leads to the selective remembering, and not a bias to pay more attention to the negative words when they are presented. It also appears that the memory bias of depression is tied to the particular state of the individual (i.e., whether or not the individual is in a depressive episode). People prone to depression do not show a bias for depression-related material when they are not currently depressed (Bradley & Mathews, 1988). The dependence of the retrieval bias on mood state has also been shown to vary in a cyclical way. Diurnal depressives—depressives whose state of depression tends to follow a 24-hour cycle—are more likely to retrieve a negative memory in response to a positive cue as the day wears on and their depression grows (Clark & Teasdale, 1982).

It has been argued that the tendency to dwell on depression-related information and, thus, to remember it better, may serve the function of evaluating failures or losses, thus providing the basis for reflection and eventual improvement of the behavior or circumstances that led to the depression (Mineka, 1992). However, this tendency to dwell on negative thoughts can form part of a vicious cycle in which negative events lead to negative thoughts, negative thoughts lead to a more depressed state, and the depressed state prevents a person from experiencing positive events. It is, of course, overly simplistic to think that positive thoughts alone will cure depression, but finding a way not to dwell on negative thoughts may help to break a downward spiral (J. D. Teasdale, 1988).

Examining the effects of mood induction on memory in depressives who are currently in remission may provide insight into the cognitive biases that make some people vulnerable to depression (Mineka & Nugent, 1995). For example, Gilboa and Gotlib (1997) compared the effects of mood induction (remembering sad autobiographical events) on attention and memory in individuals who either had or had not suffered from depression. Although they found no differences in attention to negative stimuli between the two groups (as measured by performance in an emotional Stroop task in which the color of emotional or neutral words must be named), they found that people who had suffered from depression in the past remembered disproportionately more of the negative words that had been presented in the Stroop task. Previously depressed participants also reported more persistent negative affect following the negative mood induction procedure than did never-depressed participants. The authors concluded that memory biases and affect-regulation style may play a causal role in susceptibility to depression.

Attention, Memory, and Anxiety

According to the theories of Bower (1981) and Beck (1967, 1976), mentioned earlier, suffering from emotional disorders such as depression or anxiety should lead to biases in selecting and processing information. As described, depressed individuals do show a bias toward remembering negative events; however, little evidence has been found that depressed individuals pay more attention to negative information. That is, attention is not more easily captured by negative than by neutral stimuli (see Mineka & Nugent, 1995, for a review). People with anxiety disorders show the opposite pattern of results: Their attention is easily captured by threat-related stimuli, but they are not any more likely to remember the threat-related material. The attentional bias of persons with anxiety disorders toward potential sources of threat has been shown with a variety of techniques. In one method, called dot-probe detection, two words are presented at a time, one above the other, for a brief period of time (see, e.g., MacLeod, Mathews, & Tata, 1986). Some of the words are neutral, and others are related to threat (e.g., fire, spider). The subject's task is to read the upper word aloud. Following the presentation of some of the words, a small dot is presented at the location of one of the words and the subject presses a key as quickly as possible as soon as they see this dot-probe. In general, RTs to the dot-probe are faster when the probe is presented at the location of the word that must be read aloud, presumably because that location is attended. However, anxious individuals show the fastest dot-probe RTs to probes presented at the location of threat-related words, regardless of their position. This result suggests that their attention is captured by the threat stimuli.

Even though anxious persons show an attentional bias to threat-related words, their memory for these words is not consistently better than for neutral or positive words. Although research results are rather mixed regarding whether memory biases are sometimes found in anxious individuals, it seems that such individuals tend to avoid rehearsal of negative information and therefore do not show the advantage for remembering it that might be expected, especially when one considers that the information tends to capture attention (Mineka & Nugent, 1995). The apparent tendency of anxiety to induce an early, selective attentional bias for threat followed by avoidance of more elaborate processing of the threat may reflect the nature of a "danger detection" system. It is obviously in our best interest to be able to quickly detect and react to threats in the environment. It must also be possible to quickly "reset" this system in order to be able to continue to monitor for danger (see, e.g., Beck, 1967, 1976). However, some have argued that the evolutionary value of such an acute danger detection system has been lost, and that anxiety disorders reflect the maladaptive nature of an attentional bias for threat (Williams, Mathews, & MacLeod, 1996). Just as dwelling on depressing thoughts may prolong or worsen depression, over-acute sensitivity to threat might lead to a heightened awareness of potential danger, which in turn strengthens anxiety.

▲ SUMMARY

As for any other cognitive ability, differences in attention between (and within) individuals can be observed. The literature on individual differences in attention is complex, and is made even more complicated by the facts that attention itself is multifaceted and that not all researchers use the same terms for describing the different aspects of attention. Whether one speaks of selective or focused attention, divided attention or timesharing, or executive control or task set, robust differences between individuals have been found. One of these differences is the ability to switch attention on cue from one source of information to another. This ability is correlated with general intelligence, and may be predictive of eventual success in a variety of complex tasks. Another difference is the ability to divide attention between two tasks. This ability can to some extent be trained, and leads to positive transfer on complex tasks. However, it is a well-established fact that the ability to divide attention decreases across the lifespan.

Our ability to pay attention depends on a number of factors, including time of day, subjective energy level, and mood. These factors can influence both general arousal level and strategic aspects of performance, especially those involving rehearsal of information. Rehearsal strategies differ within an individual, and the ability to actively maintain information in working memory also varies considerably between individuals. The relations between working memory capacity and executive attention, and between executive attention and intelligence, appear to be stable and could lead to a revision of our thinking about the nature of intelligence. Much work is still needed to determine the extent to which intelligence can be conceived of as a basic ability to pay attention in an efficient manner.

NOTES ▲

1. A discussion of theories of intelligence is beyond the scope of this book. Basically, general intelligence (*g*) is considered to consist of two types of intelligence: culturally derived knowledge, or general crystallized intelligence, and the ability to reason and to solve novel problems, or general fluid intelligence.

2. Because neural maturation proceeds along a caudal to frontal gradient such that the development of anterior systems of attention occurs later than that of posterior systems, late-selection processes, thought to depend on anterior systems, should develop more slowly in childhood that the posterior, early-selection systems (Huang-Pollock et al., 2002).

3. The results of the Gopher, Weil, and Bareket (1994) study have been criticized by Roessingh (2002), who argues that differential drop-out rates may have exaggerated the differences between the experimental and control groups.

4. Structural equation modeling is based on the statistical analysis of correlations between large numbers of tests. Alternative models are conceived and then tested to see whether they can produce the patterns of correlations observed between the tests. Models may contain latent variables, which are variables derived from different tests that purportedly measure the same construct. Causal relationships between latent variables can be determined by fitting the models to obtained data.

CHAPTER **11**

THE COGNITIVE NEUROSCIENCE OF ATTENTION

by Robert D. Melara

The scientific study of human attention has advanced greatly during the past decade owing, in part, to the emergence of the new field of cognitive neuroscience. The goal of cognitive neuroscience is to isolate the physiological and anatomical bases of human cognition in the nervous system. We can view cognitive neuroscience as the intersection of two well-established disciplines—neuroscience and cognitive psychology—each bringing its own concepts and tools to the task of understanding the processes of cognition. Much of this book has been devoted to detailing the results of behavioral research and its implications for theories of attention. Research in the cognitive neuroscience of attention asks how neural processes in the brain might account for many of these behavioral results, and how the brain's physiology might inform or constrain the theories of attention. In this chapter, we will review some of the major findings about attention to emerge from this field. These findings address several important and longstanding issues about how human attention operates.

▲ TOOLS OF THE COGNITIVE NEUROSCIENTIST

In Chapter 2 we introduced several of the techniques and measures that cognitive neuroscientists use to study the functional properties of the brain as participants engage in various cognitive tasks. These techniques include measuring event-related potentials (ERPs), positron emission tomography (PET) scanning, and functional magnetic resonance imaging (fMRI). Each of these techniques can be used in tandem with the usual behavioral measures of reaction time and accuracy. But each provides additional information that can be extremely beneficial in understanding specific properties of attention. The ERP waveform, for example, has excellent temporal resolution. It can track changes in cognitive processing in the brain at the level of milliseconds (see Figure 2.13 in Chapter 2, p. 52). ERP components thus are very helpful in identifying the temporal sequence of cognitive processing. Functional MRI has excellent spatial resolution. It can track the location of cognitive activity to within a few millimeters of brain tissue. Functional MRI images thus are extremely useful in identifying the areas of the brain responsible for specific cognitive processes and how these areas are interconnected during the performance of an attention task.

Measurement Strengths and Limitations

In several of the studies we will review in this chapter, the investigators recorded both the electrophysiological (ERP) and hemodynamic (fMRI) responses of participants engaged in cognitive tasks. The two types of data complement each other. Each of the current noninvasive procedures is characterized by its strength in capturing one aspect of neural processing—either its temporal or spatial properties—and its weakness in capturing the other aspect. To understand why, let us consider the ERP and fMRI techniques in greater detail.

ERP waveforms are a direct measure of the electrical activity produced by one or more local groups of aligned pyramidal neurons firing in synchrony. Each local neural group is a *neural generator* of a scalp-recorded ERP component. A recording electrode measures the sum of activity (post-synaptic potentials) from all active neural generators, attenuated by the tissue and bone that lie between the generators and the scalp. The changes across time in the neural activity to a stimulus can be measured with great precision, being constrained primarily by the sampling rate of the recording (e.g., a sampling rate of 1,000 Hz measures ERP waveforms at a resolution of 1 ms). Thus, the temporal resolution of ERPs is extremely high, an important methodological advantage when one considers that most cognitive processes last less than one second. However, the spatial resolution of ERPs—their accuracy in identifying the anatomical loci of neural generators—is severely limited in ordinary applications. Indeed, depending on how the pyramidal cells are aligned in the folds of brain tissue, an ERP component may show its strongest amplitude at a scalp location far removed from its actual source. For example, one ERP component called MMN (described in the section "Mismatch Negativity: The Automatic Detection of Change") arises in the temporal lobe but, due to the frontal orientation of the generator's electric field, is measured best from an electrode placed over an anterior site. Thus, whereas ERPs reflect millisecond-by-millisecond changes in bioelectric activity, electrode location is an ambiguous guide to the source of the underlying neural generators.

Functional MRI gauges changes in regional cerebral blood flow as participants perform cognitive or motor tasks. During task performance, MR scans are taken by sending radio-frequency signals through a head coil as the participant is centered in a strong magnetic field. Using a sophisticated computer program, functional brain images are constructed from variation in a specific type of MR signal known as the blood oxygen level–dependent (BOLD) contrast signal. Whenever neurons fire, the cells' mitochondria engage in aerobic (oxygen-requiring) metabolism. Blood carrying oxygen-laden hemoglobin soon flows to these active regions to meet the metabolic needs of the neurons. The BOLD signal measures how long certain hemoglobin atoms take to return to the orientation of the scanner's magnetic field. The BOLD signal varies inversely with the amount of oxygen-free (deoxygenated) hemoglobin contained in a region of tissue.

BOLD signals are indirect measures of local neural activity because they lag by several seconds behind the actual neural response. At first, aerobic consumption from neural firing causes a drop in local oxygen levels (i.e., a negative BOLD signal; Thompson, Peterson, & Freeman, 2003). It then usually takes an additional 1–4 seconds for blood flow to begin reaching the site of neural activation. The arrival of blood to a region causes a decrease in deoxygenated hemoglobin, which is measured in fMRI by a boost in the BOLD signal. The rise in the BOLD signal occurs too slowly to provide useful information about the time course of neural generators. Yet, fMRI does provide unparalleled precision in isolating the spatial coordinates of hemodynamic activity in most regions of brain (with the notable exceptions of the orbitofrontal cortex and the anterior temporal cortex; see Buckner & Logan, 2001). Using computational procedures common in traditional MRI applications, the source of oxygen changes can be mapped to within several millimeters of brain tissue.

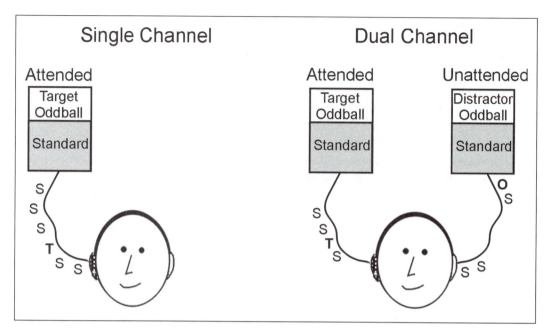

Figure 11.1   The single- and dual-channel oddball paradigms. In both cases, the participant responds to a target oddball presented in the attended channel (ear) among a stream of frequently occurring standards. In the dual-channel task, a separate stream of standards and distractor oddballs is presented asynchronously in the unattended channel.

We can see, then, that ERP and fMRI measurements are burdened by opposite limitations. When used together, however, their complementary strengths offer an unsurpassed view of the spatial and temporal properties of neural generators that underlie specific cognitive processes.

The Oddball Paradigm

Chapter 2 introduced a research paradigm that cognitive neuroscientists often have relied upon in studying human attention: the oddball paradigm. Figure 11.1 depicts two different forms of this paradigm: the single-channel oddball task and the dual-channel oddball task. A *channel* refers to a distinguishing feature of the stimuli used for presentation and, sometimes, for identification. In the depiction in Figure 11.1, the channels are the ears to which sounds are presented. An *oddball* refers to a distinctive or deviant stimulus presented in a channel among a set of standard stimuli. For example, in a single-channel task, a deviant (oddball) sound having a relatively high pitch might be periodically interspersed throughout a stream of standard sounds all having the same, low pitch. In a dual-channel task, different streams of standard and oddball stimuli are presented to the two channels.

The oddball paradigm affords the cognitive neuroscientist a great deal of flexibility in studying attention. For example, physiological measures can be taken separately to standard and oddball stimuli, whether or not a participant is asked to pay attention or respond to those stimuli. Thus, researchers can study the physiological effects of paying attention to stimuli. As we shall see, the single-channel oddball task has been used extensively to isolate preattentive or automatic processes of cognition.

MISMATCH NEGATIVITY: THE AUTOMATIC DETECTION OF CHANGE ▲

Certain cognitive processes can occur without effort and without focal attention. Neisser (1967) termed these processes *preattentive*. They also are called automatic because neither effort nor attention can prevent them from occurring (Posner & Snyder, 1975). When automatic processes are studied using behavioral techniques alone, only the consequences of such processes can be observed, not the processes themselves. In the Stroop color-word task (see Chapter 5), for example, the automatic process of knowing a word's meaning is inferred from the disruptive effects irrelevant words have on the speed and accuracy of color naming.

Detecting change in an otherwise uniform environment is thought to be another automatic process. Indeed, the ability to detect change preattentively would appear necessary for the very purpose of soliciting our attention, such as when the abrupt onset of a light quickly orients us to it (Jonides & Yantis, 1988). Cognitive neuroscientists have been able to study change detection directly by making separate ERP measurements to standards and oddballs in a single-channel task. During the course of the task, the repeated presentations of standards create a context of perceptual uniformity. The infrequent appearance of the oddball signals a perceptual change, a mismatch with the current context, which disrupts the uniformity. To examine how detection of this mismatch is expressed electrophysiologically, the average ERP waveform to the oddball stimulus can be compared with the average ERP waveform to the standard stimulus.

This was the approach taken by Sams, Paavilainen, Alho, and Näätänen (1985) in an investigation of auditory mismatch. Participants in their study were presented with sounds at a rate of one every second. Most (80%) of the sounds were standards, a 1,000-Hz pure tone. An oddball sound of either 1,004, 1,008, 1,016, or 1,032 Hz was presented unpredictably (though after at least three standards) and infrequently (20%). To ensure that the participants paid no attention to the sounds, they were asked to read a book during the task. Recordings were made at midline locations on the scalp (Fz and Cz), and voltage was measured relative to a

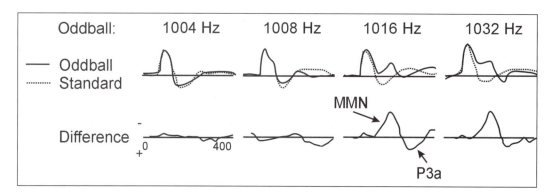

Figure 11.2   ERP results from Sams et al. (1985) measured from the Fz location. An MMN response is generated by oddball tones that deviate sufficiently from the standard tone (1,000 Hz), and the MMN response increases with the magnitude of the deviance. Larger deviants (1,016 Hz and 1,032 Hz) also produce a P3a orienting response. (Note that negativity in voltage is plotted upward.)

SOURCE: Data from Sams et al., 1985.

reference electrode placed on the nose. The results for the Fz location appear in Figure 11.2. Notice that the standard and oddball waveforms do not line up exactly. There is relatively more negativity in voltage to the oddball approximately 200 ms after the onset of the sound. This is the mismatch negativity or MMN. It reflects the brain's response to a mismatch in the perceptual context established by the standard. This mismatch response can occur in the absence of attention, for example, is, while the participant is reading a novel or watching a video (Kraus et al., 1995). It will even occur when the participant is asleep (Sabri, de Lugt, & Campbell, 2000), under anesthesia (Csépe, Karmos, & Molnár, 1989; Van Hooff et al., 1995), or in a coma (Kane, Curry, Butler, & Cummins, 1993)!

Notice in Figure 11.2 that the magnitude of MMN grows with the physical difference between the standard and the oddball stimulus. The MMN did not appear for a 1,004-Hz oddball, was small for a 1,008-Hz oddball, and was largest for the 1,032-Hz oddball. In a separate behavioral experiment, Sams et al. (1985) showed that their participants could just barely detect the difference between the standard and the 1,008-Hz oddball. Within a certain range, the MMN response corresponds closely to a participant's perceptual discrimination ability as measured by, say, the signal-detection statistic d'.

Involuntary Orienting

The MMN still will occur if the participant pays attention to the stimuli, but it will be augmented by another negativity called the N2b. The MMN also can act as an attention switch, diverting an observer to a previously unattended stimulus. Notice in Figure 11.2, for example, that the MMN is followed by an increased positivity in the electrophysiological response to the oddball, especially for the physically most deviant sounds (1,016 Hz and 1,032 Hz). Here the deviant oddball has attracted the observers' attention, producing an ERP component called P3a. Rare or unusual stimuli often will cause an observer to orient. The orientation is expressed in P3a, and it often is preceded by MMN. Thus, MMN may reflect the nonconscious detection of change or novelty, which then may trigger conscious realization, reflected in P3a (Schröger, 1996).

Neural Generators of Change Detection

Insight into the neural sources of MMN and P3a has come from an approach that combines ERPs and fMRI. Opitz et al. (2002), for example, presented complex tones to participants in an oddball paradigm as they watched a cartoon video. During a tonal sequence, three types of oddballs were intermixed with repeated presentations of a standard tone, the three oddballs reflecting small, medium, or large degrees of physical deviation from the standard. Participants were tested in two different measurement sessions. In one session, the tones were presented while ERP recordings were taken from electrodes placed on the scalp and nose, the usual technique for measuring MMN and P3a. In the other session, the tones were presented while the participants lay on their backs in an MR scanner and performed the task while functional scans were taken. The reconstructed images were *event related,* meaning that a separate functional scan was made of the brain's BOLD response to each of the four types of signals in the oddball paradigm: the standard and each of the three deviant oddballs. Event-related fMRI scans thus could be meaningfully compared with ERPs because each is a measure of brain activity to a specific stimulus type.

The neural activation to the tonal mismatch was measured by taking the difference between the standard and each oddball, using either the electrical potentials or the BOLD contrast signal. The ERP differences revealed an MMN response followed by a P3a response. The magnitude of each of these ERP components corresponded to the magnitude of the oddball's physical deviance from the standard, a finding similar to that reported by Sams et al. (1985; see Figure 11.2). The fMRI scans, which are depicted in Figure 11.3, revealed that each tonal mismatch activated regions of the superior temporal gyrus in both hemispheres. These brain regions correspond to the human auditory cortex. This result indicates that automatic change detection is primarily a sensory phenomenon.

The fMRI scans also revealed, however, that the medium and large oddballs activated the right prefrontal cortex. One interpretation of this finding is that the

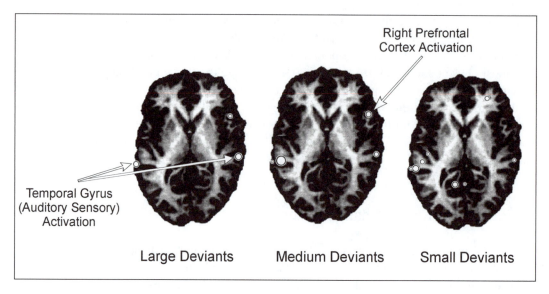

Figure 11.3   The neural activation to tonal mismatch. The white circles indicate areas of difference in activation to the standard and the oddball signal. All deviants activated the superior temporal gyrus in both hemispheres, areas that include the auditory cortex. Medium and large deviants additionally activated the right prefrontal cortex, perhaps corresponding to the P3a orienting response.

SOURCE: Based on data from Opitz et al., 2002.

larger oddballs drew attention to themselves by triggering neural generators in the frontal lobe, which gave rise to the P3a orienting response. As will be seen, much of the control of human attention occurs in the prefrontal cortex. The study by Optiz and colleagues demonstrates how the joint use of ERPs and fMRI can be an extremely powerful approach for the cognitive neuroscientist to specify both the temporal sequence and the spatial location of cognitive processes in the brain. In terms of auditory change detection, an automatic sensory response in the auditory cortex 100–200 ms after stimulus presentation often is followed by an attentional orienting response in the frontal lobe 100–200 ms later.

▲ SELECTIVE ATTENTION

The single-channel oddball task has been valuable in characterizing the course and loci of processing when disruptive stimuli in an otherwise homogenous context elicit our attention. Under many circumstances, however, attention is not passively elicited, but purposefully directed toward a stimulus of interest. For example, suppose we are trying to console a distraught friend at a noisy party. The party activities may be very distracting, making it necessary for us to concentrate fully on each word spoken by our serious friend, while at the same time trying to ignore all of the party's diversions. This is a task of selective attention (see Chapter 3). To investigate the brain processes active during tasks of selective attention, a dual (or multiple) channel oddball task is required.

The Dual-Channel Oddball Task

In a dual-channel task, a participant is asked to direct his or her attention to the stimuli presented in one channel (e.g., sounds in the left ear) while ignoring irrelevant stimuli presented in the other channel (sounds in the right ear). The oddball in the attended channel is the *target;* the stimuli in the unattended channel are *distractors* (see the right panel of Figure 11.1, p. 336). The investigator compares the neural processing of stimuli in the attended and unattended channels.

Behavioral measurements of the speed and accuracy to identify oddballs can be made in conjunction with physiological measurements. However, because it is impossible to make behavioral measurements of distractors (i.e., if a participant responded behaviorally to a distractor, then it would be a target), physiological measurements provide the cognitive neuroscientist with a means of studying the cognitive processing of unattended stimuli. Distractor processing can be studied more effectively in this way than by limiting measurements to the indirect behavioral effects of distractors on subsequent targets.

Channel Separation

Hillyard and his colleagues (e.g., Hansen & Hillyard, 1980, 1983; Hillyard, Hink, Schwent, & Picton, 1973; Schwent & Hillyard, 1975) have used the dual-channel oddball task to evaluate several competing theories of selective attention. Recall from Chapter 3 that Broadbent (1958) and Treisman (1960) conceived of selective attention as a funnel or filter to screen apart stimuli exhibiting certain targeted properties (e.g., a male's voice in a room filled with female voices). These theorists argued that such filtering must occur at a relatively early (sensory) stage of stimulus processing. By contrast, other theorists, such as Deutsch and Deutsch (1963) and Norman (1968), suggested that selection operates only later in stimulus processing, after perception, on elaborated stimulus representations established by long-term learning, such as the representations of a word's meaning. Still other theorists, such as Johnston and Heinz (1978), hypothesized that selection is flexible, and so is able to operate either early or late in stimulus processing, depending on the observer's task goals and capacity limitations.

To evaluate these theories, Hillyard et al. (1973) developed an ingenious approach. Participants heard a sequence of tones presented randomly to one ear or the other. The participants were asked to pay attention and detect targets in one ear and to ignore tones in the other ear. In one condition they listened to the tones in the left ear; in another condition they listened to tones in the right ear. Hillyard et al. compared the electrophysiological recordings to tones in, say, the left ear when participants were paying attention to them (the attended channel) with recordings to the same tones in the same ear when participants were ignoring them (the unattended channel). These recordings then were used to measure the onset of *channel separation;* that is, the point in time at which physiological processing in the attended channel diverged electrically from processing in the unattended channel. Channel separation provided Hillyard and his colleagues with a relatively direct means of determining whether selection occurs early or late in processing and has led to a host of discoveries about the course of human selective attention.

Filtering Unidimensional Stimuli

A study by Hansen and Hillyard (1980) provides one example of how the channel-separation paradigm is used to investigate the locus of selection. Participants in this study listened to a stream of tones that were either short (51 ms) or long (102 ms) in duration, and either low or high in pitch. The selection task defined the two channels by tonal pitch: Participants were asked to attend to one of the pitches, and to press a key whenever tones with this pitch were long in duration. On some blocks of trials, the participants attended to the low-pitched tones, ignoring the high-pitched ones, and on other blocks they attended to the high-pitched tones, ignoring the low-pitched ones. To manipulate channel separation, Hansen and Hillyard varied the physical difference between the low-pitched and high-pitched tones. The low-pitched tone was always 300 Hz. The high-pitched tone was 350 Hz (50-Hz difference) on some blocks, 400 Hz (100-Hz difference) on other blocks, and 700 Hz (400-Hz difference) on still other blocks. For each of the three degrees of physical difference—50 Hz, 100 Hz, and 400 Hz—Hansen and Hillyard plotted the average ERP waveforms to tones in the attended and unattended channels, separately for low-pitched and high-pitched tones.

These plots are shown in Figure 11.4. The plots on the far left show the average ERP waveforms to the low-pitched tones during blocks on which participants attended to low-pitched tones (dark line), and during blocks on which participants attended to high-pitched tones (dotted line). The plots in the middle show

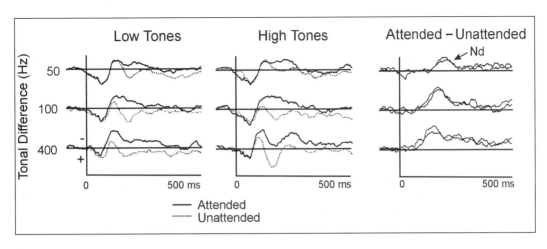

Figure 11.4   ERPs to high and low tones in the attended and unattended conditions of Hansen and Hillyard (1980). As shown in the rightmost panel, Nd peaks later and decays faster with a 50-Hz tonal difference than with a 400-Hz tonal difference. In each condition, channel separation begins by 200 ms after the onset of the tone. (Note that negativity in voltage is plotted upward.)

SOURCE: Data from Hansen & Hillyard, 1980.

the average ERP waveforms to the high-pitched tones during blocks on which participants attended to high-pitched tones (dark line), and during blocks on which participants attended to low-pitched tones (dotted line). The onset of channel separation can be seen in each plot as the point in time at which the attended channel's waveform and the unattended channel's waveform diverged from each other. Notice that the onset of channel separation corresponded inversely with the physical difference between the channels.

A convenient way to visualize channel separation is by subtracting the unattended waveform from the attended waveform. This creates a new waveform revealing the negative difference between the channels, abbreviated Nd by Hansen and Hillyard (1980). Plots of Nd are depicted in the far right panel of Figure 11.4. One can see that Nd peaks later and decays faster with a 50-Hz difference between channels than it does with a 400-Hz difference. But notice that even with the smallest physical difference, channel separation begins very early—by 200 ms after the onset of the tone. This finding led Hansen and Hillyard to conclude that the electrophysiological evidence is consistent with an early-selection model of attention.

Later research showed that channel separation begins as early as 25 ms after stimulus onset (McCallum et al., 1983; Woldorff & Hillyard, 1991), indicating that attending can exert its influence on the primary auditory cortex. Of course, it is conceivable that only simple sensory dimensions such as pitch can be selected so early in processing. Channels defined by more complex dimensions, such as word meaning or object category, might be separated only much later in processing. Nonetheless, the results of Hansen and Hillyard indicate that early channel separation is possible, suggesting that selection need not be delayed until the activation of more elaborate representations.

Hansen and Hillyard's (1980) results also demonstrate that attended and unattended channels become separated by a gradual process, one that can begin early but builds to a peak—the peak of Nd—before gradually diminishing over the course of a trial. It seems, then, that the filtering process does not involve the abrupt elimination of information in a rejected channel. This may explain why observers often will notice unattended signals (e.g., their name spoken in the rejected channel; Moray, 1959a): The access to long-term representations can begin before channel separation has peaked. Such incremental selection activity is in keeping with theories positing a slow suppression of unattended information, such as the filter attenuation theory proposed by Treisman (1960; see Chapter 3). At least one recent theory of attention has incorporated the idea of gradual inhibition into a computational model of selection processes (Melara & Algom, 2003).

Filtering Multidimensional Stimuli

Often in everyday life we are required to direct our attention to stimuli having a certain combination of qualities. We might be searching the library stacks for a book with both an odd size and a specific jacket cover. Or, we might be listening at the airport for a boarding announcement from a specific male flight attendant standing at a specific gate. In these cases, the targeted stimuli are multidimensional, defined by a conjunction of features (e.g., size and hue, pitch and location). Attention researchers have been interested in understanding how perceivers identify multidimensional stimuli for the purpose of filtering targets from distractors.

Garner (1974) distinguished conceptually between two types of multidimensional stimuli. Those composed of separable dimensions, such as size and hue, were thought to be selected by a separate analysis of the individual features of the stimulus (e.g., large and red), whereas those composed of integral dimensions, such as brightness and hue, were thought to be filtered as wholes, with individual dimensions analyzed only later in processing. Later research by Melara and his colleagues (Melara & Day, 1992; Melara & Marks, 1990a; Melara, Marks, & Potts, 1993), however, indicated that all multidimensional stimuli, whether integral or separable, are subjected to a similar analysis of the constituent psychological dimensions. On this view, selection of multidimensional targets proceeds by evaluating each stimulus dimension separately, with the speed of evaluation determined by the relative discriminability or salience of each dimension (see Melara & Algom, 2003).

Hansen and Hillyard (1983) were concerned with understanding how selection unfolds when targets are defined according to multiple dimensions varying in relative discriminability. They again used the onset of channel separation to measure differential processing of targets and distractors. However, now each target was designated according to two dimensions—pitch and location—with a specific value on each dimension defining each of two channels.

Within each block of trials, participants heard a stream of tones that varied randomly in pitch (low or high), location (left side or right side), and duration (short or long). Participants were asked to press a key when they detected a long duration oddball having a specific conjunction of pitch (P) and location (L; e.g., high pitch in the left ear). The four possible combinations of pitch and location were tested as targets in separate blocks. The target was given the notation P+L+. A distractor having only pitch in common with the target was P+L−. A distractor with only location in common was P−L+. A distractor with neither feature in common was P−L−. In separate conditions, Hansen and Hillyard (1983) varied the difficulty in discrimination of pitch and location. In the *pitch-easy, location-easy* condition, values along both dimensions were easily discriminated. In the *pitch-easy, location-hard* condition, the two sound locations were relatively difficult to distinguish, whereas in the *pitch-hard, location-easy* condition, the two auditory frequencies were relatively difficult to distinguish.

Figure 11.5 depicts the ERP waveforms to the target (P+L+) and the three distractors (P+L−,P−L+, and P−L−) in each of the three conditions. The onset of channel separation in each condition occurred early, beginning by 200 ms after stimulus onset. Importantly, the onset of filtering was determined by the relative discriminability of the stimulus dimensions. In the *pitch-easy, location-easy* condition, all three distractors were separated from the target by approximately 100 ms after stimulus onset. In the *pitch-easy, location-hard* condition, however, only the distractors different in pitch from the target (i.e., P−L+ and P−L−) were filtered that early; separation of the distractor having a pitch in common with the target (P+L−) was delayed by another 75 ms. Similarly, in the *pitch-hard, location-easy* condition, only the distractors different in location from the target (i.e., P+L− and P−L−) were filtered by 100 ms; the distractor having a location in common with the target (P−L+) took another 100 ms to separate.

These results demonstrate that selection of multidimensional stimuli occurs on a dimension-by-dimension basis, not holistically. All distractors that differ from a target along an easily discriminable dimension are quickly separated in processing, regardless of whether the distractor shares a value in common with the target on the less discriminable dimension. However, it is difficult to reject a distractor

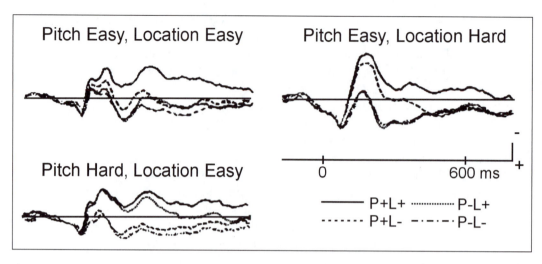

Figure 11.5   ERPs to the target (P+L+) and each of the three distractors (P+L−, P−L+, and P−L−) in the three conditions of Hansen and Hillyard (1983). In *pitch-easy, location-easy*, all three distractors were separated quickly from the target. In *pitch-easy, location-hard*, only the distractors different in pitch (i.e., P−L+ and P−L−) were filtered quickly. In *pitch-hard, location-easy*, only the distractors different in location (i.e., P+L− and P−L−) were filtered quickly. (Note that negativity in voltage is plotted upward.)

Source: Data from Hansen & Hillyard, 1983.

that mismatches a target along a less discriminable dimension, and that difficulty leads to a delay in channel separation.

In a more recent study, Woods and Alain (2001) used the Hansen and Hillyard (1983) paradigm to study the processing stages involved in the integration of multidimensional stimuli. A target tone was defined by a specific combination of pitch, location, and duration: P+L+D+. Distractors could differ from the target on a single dimension (e.g., P−L+D+), two dimensions (e.g., P−L−D+), or on all three dimensions (i.e., P−L−D−). The researchers found that three stages of channel separation could be distinguished in the ERP waveforms according to the number of dimensional values a distractor had in common with the target: (1) An early stage of sensory analysis (60–120 ms after onset) signaling a single common value; (2) an intermediate stage of conjunction analysis (120–220 ms) indicating a pairing of values; and (3) a late stage of "jackpot analysis" (200–720 ms) signaling a match on all three dimensions. These results indicate that attentional systems first analyze the dimensions of complex stimuli separately and in parallel, and only later identify interactions among certain combinations of sought-after dimensional values.

THE DUALITY OF SELECTION ▲

Many of the current computational models of selective attention tend to conceive of attentional processes only in terms of an increased activation or excitation of targeted experiences (see, e.g., J. D. Cohen, Dunbar, & McClelland, 1990; J. D. Cohen & Servan-Schreiber, 1992; Kimberg & Farah, 1993; but see Melara & Algom, 2003). Of course, enhanced target excitation seems an obvious outcome of selection processes, because often we find ourselves consciously directing our attention toward one specific feature of our environment (e.g., a friend's voice). Moreover, excitatory processes would appear necessary to activate and maintain specific targets, such as a telephone number, in our working memory (Goldman-Rakic, 1998) while we engage in other activities (e.g., searching for a pen and paper to write the number down). Not surprisingly, then, evidence of channel separation in the dual-channel oddball task usually has been interpreted as indicating an intentional boost in activation directed toward the target channel (Hillyard et al., 1973; Näätänen, 1982; Woods & Alain, 2001). For example, Näätänen (1982) refers to the cognitive forces causing channel separation as *processing negativity,* emphasizing that the difference in activity between attended and unattended channels resides in the increased negativity applied to targets.

It is important to realize, though, that the mechanisms underlying channel separation can, in principle, also be inhibitory. After all, in an oddball task the difference in voltage between target and distractor waveforms can just as well be due to increased positivity in the unattended channel as to increased negativity in the attended channel. Computational models of attention cannot easily distinguish between hypothetical systems that use solely excitatory processes and those that use a combination of excitatory and inhibitory processes. The two types of systems often will yield identical predicted outcomes (Melara & Algom, 2003). Even hemodynamic indices such as the BOLD response in fMRI may fail to differentiate excitatory from inhibitory activations because either process will elevate local metabolic activity (Raichle, 2001). Electrophysiological techniques therefore are necessary to establish whether channel separation entails processes specific to the unattended channel. Unfortunately, achieving the goal of assessing the relative amounts of electrophysiological negativity (to the attended channel) or electrophysiological positivity (to the unattended channel) has proven difficult, primarily because various attempts to establish a neutral baseline condition have been unsatisfactory (Alho, Woods, & Algazi, 1994; Michie, Solowij, Crawford, & Glue, 1993).

Inhibition Revealed by Attentional Training

Melara, Rao, and Tong (2002) recently took a new approach to the question of the duality of selection. They asked whether enhanced inhibitory processing could

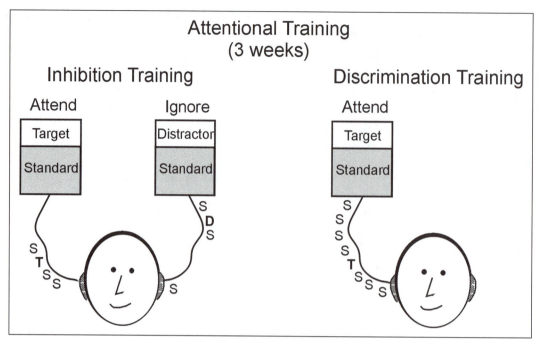

Figure 11.6   Schematic diagram of the attentional training given by Melara et al. (2002). Discrimination training involved practice of a single-channel oddball task (right panel). Inhibition training involved practice of a dual-channel oddball task (left panel) that was made progressively more difficult during the course of each training session by increasing the loudness of the distractor (D) relative to the target (T).

SOURCE: Adapted from Melara, Rao, & Tong, 2002.

be the source of an improvement in channel separation resulting from selection training. The design used by Melara et al. is depicted in Figure 11.6. The participants performed a single-channel oddball task and a dual-channel oddball task both before and after several weeks of training. In each case, the target oddball was a tone slightly higher in pitch than a standard tone. In the dual-channel tasks, the target oddball was presented to only one ear, and a distractor oddball was presented asynchronously to the other ear (the standard tone could be presented in either ear). The distractor oddball had a salient pitch compared with the target and the standard. Participants listened for the target in the attended ear, pressing a key whenever they detected one.

Two types of training were compared. Participants undergoing discrimination training practiced detecting targets without distraction. They repeated the single-channel oddball task for several hours a week for 3 weeks. Participants undergoing inhibition training practiced suppressing increasing levels of distraction in their

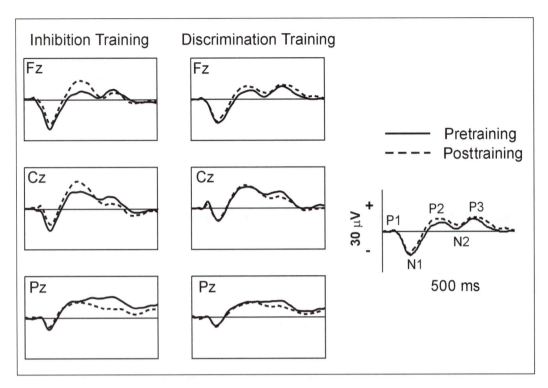

Figure 11.7   Pre- and posttraining ERPs to the distractor in the study of Melara et al. (2002). Note the enhanced positivity after training at Fz and Cz in the P1, N1, and P2 components for participants receiving inhibition training, a reflection of their improved inhibitory processing of distractors. Also note the diminution after training at Pz in the P3 component for participants receiving inhibitory training, an indication of decreased distractor salience from improved inhibitory processing. (Note that positivity in voltage is plotted upward.)

SOURCE: Adapted from Melara, Rao, & Tong, 2002.

unattended ear. In each of the three training sessions, these participants performed the dual-channel oddball task for four consecutive blocks of trials, with the attended ear at progressively more difficult signal-to-noise ratios relative to the unattended ear (i.e., +24 dB, +16 dB, +8 dB, and 0 dB).

After the training sessions, the group receiving the inhibitory training showed a marked behavioral improvement in their selection performance, relative both to their pretest performance and to the posttest performance of participants receiving discrimination training. Participants who underwent inhibitory training now were faster and more sensitive in detecting the targets in the face of distraction. Most important, the physiological effects of their training were confined to processes in the unattended channel. As shown in Figure 11.7, after inhibitory training these participants evinced elevated levels of ERP activity to the distractor oddball. The inhibitory ERP component peaked approximately 200 ms after distractor onset. Its magnitude was correlated positively with the participants' level of success in attending selectively to the target channel.

The results of Melara et al.'s (2002) study indicate that inhibitory training enhances channel separation by boosting the inhibitory processing to distractors. One conclusion from this study is that excitatory processing alone is insufficient to explain channel separation in selective attention tasks.

▲ THE SOURCES OF SELECTIVE CONTROL

Posner (1995; Posner & DiGirolamo, 2000) has advised that any neural theory of attention should distinguish between those brain regions responsible for implementing attentional control—the *sources* of attention—and those sensory, perceptual, memory, or motor regions whose activity is modulated by such control—the *sites* of attention. Which brain regions serve as the sources of excitatory and inhibitory control in selective attention? Knight and his colleagues (e.g., Knight, Grabowecky, & Scabini, 1995; Knight, Hillyard, Woods, & Neville, 1981; Knight, Scabini, & Woods, 1989; Knight, Staines, Swick, & Chao, 1999) have developed a powerful method for identifying the physiological loci of selection processes: Their approach combines the *neurophysiological* study of selective attention with the *neuropsychological* study of brain damage.

The Logic of Lesion Studies

The guiding principle in the field of neuropsychology is that the human brain is organized into specialized regions of function. Neuropsychologists study patients suffering from localized brain lesions (e.g., from a stroke or brain tumor) as a means of pinpointing the unique functions of individual brain areas. Anatomical images of the brain (e.g., from CAT or MRI scans) are used to classify patients by the type and location of their lesions. Neuropsychologists administer cognitive tests to the patients to probe for specific losses or deficits in functioning. The goal is to connect the type and location of lesion to the specific form of cognitive deficit. Of course, patients will vary in the exact location and extent of damage to a circumscribed area of the brain. However, by examining groups of patients with similarly located lesions, neuropsychologists often find similar losses in cognitive performance. One interpretation is that the

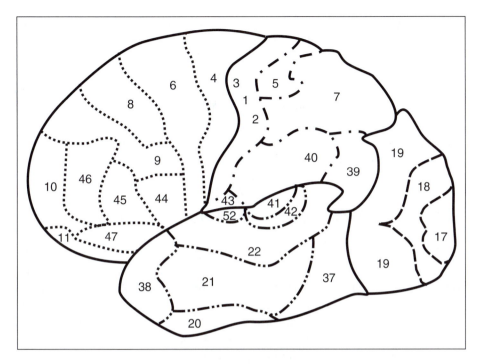

Figure 11.8   A subset of the 52 brain areas identified by Brodmann based on the organization and cell types found in the cerebral cortex. The human prefrontal cortex comprises the frontal eye fields (area 6), the orbitofrontal cortex (areas 11, 12 [hidden behind 11], and 47), and the dorsolateral prefrontal cortex (areas 9, 10, 44, 45, and 46).

SOURCE: Adapted from Brodmann, 1909.

damaged brain area normally is responsible for carrying out the now lost cognitive function.

Divisions of the Prefrontal Cortex

Knight and his colleagues evaluated channel separation in patients suffering from lesions to the prefrontal cortex. This is a region of the frontal lobe of special interest to attention researchers. The human prefrontal cortex has three major subdivisions, all of which receive their primary input from the dorsomedial area of the thalamus, a subcortical structure that serves as an early transfer point for sensory input. One subregion of the prefrontal cortex is the frontal eye fields. This division corresponds to posterior area 6 of Brodmann's (1909) labeling scheme (see Figure 11.8). A second division of the prefrontal cortex, the orbitofrontal subregion, includes the anterior areas 11, 12, and 47 of the frontal lobe. This region has been linked to the control of emotional responses. By far the largest subregion of the frontal lobe is the dorsolateral prefrontal cortex. It corresponds to Brodmann's areas 9, 10, 44, 45, and 46. The dorsolateral prefrontal cortex has reciprocal connections to visual, auditory, and somatosensory association areas in the parietal and temporal lobes. Damage to this subregion has been strongly implicated in problems in attention and memory, both in humans and in other primates (Goldman-Rakic, 1996; Goldman-Rakic, Selemon, & Schwartz, 1984; Jacobsen, 1935; Petrides, 1995).

Effects of Prefrontal Damage on Channel Separation

Knight et al. (1981) studied patients with right-sided or left-sided lesions in the dorsolateral prefrontal cortex. The patients performed a dual-channel oddball task in which short-duration standard tones were presented to both ears; the patients were asked to detect longer-duration target oddballs presented to a predesignated ear. They were quite poor at this task, detecting only 57% of targets, compared with an 85% hit rate for control participants. The patients also showed much weaker channel separation than the controls.

Channel separation in patients with right-hemisphere damage was smaller than in patients with left-hemisphere damage, implying that the control of selective attention is lateralized in the frontal lobe in favor of the larger right prefrontal cortex. Interestingly, the unattended stimuli presented contralaterally to the side of the lesion revealed enhanced sensory processing, as expressed in the sensory N100 component (the auditory ERP component occurring approximately 100 ms after stimulus onset), indicating that the lesions had sparked a *disinhibition* of the distracting stimuli. Unlike lesions in the temporal lobe (Knight, Hillyard, Woods, & Neville, 1980), the prefrontal lesions only modulated the amplitude of the auditory N100 component, rather than eliminating it, suggesting that the dorsolateral prefrontal cortex is concerned primarily with modulating perceptual responses, rather than with perceptual coding per se.

Prefrontal Control of Selection Duality

A study by Chao and Knight (1998) demonstrates that the dorsolateral prefrontal cortex exerts two separate kinds of attentional influence: excitatory control of targets and inhibitory control of distractors. Participants in their study were asked to compare two everyday sounds (e.g., a sneeze, a dog bark, dishwasher noise) separated by a delay, responding "yes" if the sounds matched and "no" if the sounds were different. The interval between the sounds was filled with silence or with distracting tones. Patients with damage to the dorsolateral prefrontal cortex experienced much more interference from the distracting tones than did a group of age-matched control participants, responding more slowly and less accurately relative to the silent interval.

Two important electrophysiological results were obtained in this study. First, relative to controls, the patients showed enhanced electrical activation of the distracting tones 20–40 ms after stimulus onset. Such early activation has a locus in the primary auditory cortex, indicating the disinhibition of sensory processing. Second, the patients displayed a reduced N1 component to the targets, particularly over posterior scalp locations and in the lesioned hemisphere. This finding suggests that an intact prefrontal cortex is responsible for boosting the activation of attended stimuli, particularly in sensory association areas in the same hemisphere.

Role of Prefrontal Cortex in Attention Disorders

The dorsolateral prefrontal cortex also has been implicated in the selective attention problems found in other groups of individuals. Chao and Knight (1997) showed, for example, that elderly subjects experience the same set of electrophysiological effects in the delayed matching task as prefrontal subjects. Similarly, children with attention-deficit hyperactivity disorder (ADHD) exhibit lower metabolic activity in this region (Zametkin et al., 1990), and may suffer from a mutation of certain dopamine receptor genes expressed there (Holmes et al., 2000; McCracken et al., 2000). Compared with children without ADHD, children with the disorder show dramatically reduced levels of channel separation in the dual-channel oddball task, especially at electrode locations over the frontal lobe, suggesting that the attention deficits in these children emerge from abnormal prefrontal development (Satterfield, Schell, Nicholas, & Backs, 1988; Satterfield et al., 1990).

The Anterior Cingulate Cortex

The prefrontal cortex is not the only area of the frontal lobe involved in attentional control. Research with the Stroop task has shown that the anterior region of the cingulate cortex is activated by distraction. In a study by Leung et al. (2000), for example, participants classified the colors of Stroop stimuli during fMRI scanning. The task involved infrequent presentations of distracting incongruent stimuli interspersed among frequent presentations of congruent stimuli. BOLD activation was tracked separately to the two types of stimuli in an event-related fMRI design. Differences in the BOLD signal represented increased hemodynamic activation to the incongruent stimuli. Distracting stimuli activated areas of the dorsolateral prefrontal cortex (Brodmann areas 44, 45, and 46), as well as the anterior cingulate cortex (Brodmann area 32), suggesting joint selection control between regions, at least in certain selective attention situations.

▲ THE SITES OF SELECTIVE CONTROL

In recent years, studies of selective attention have shifted from a predominance of auditory paradigms to a concentration on the attentional effects of processing visual stimuli. One reason for this shift is that the neurophysiology of the primate visual system (including humans) is known in much greater detail than the primate auditory system. Thus, scientists understand relatively more about the cognitive functions of those visual sites potentially under attentional control. For example, hemodynamic and electrophysiological recordings have revealed that selective control can reach each of several levels of the visual system. Indeed, attention has been shown to selectively influence the processing of (1) individual visual features, such as color and orientation; (2) the conjunctions of such features; and (3) integrated whole objects, such as faces and houses. Thus, at least in the visual modality, the sites of selective control are numerous, covering functionally distinct areas of the occipital, parietal, and temporal lobes.

The Spatial Mapping of Selective Attention

Brefczynski and DeYoe (1999) investigated attention-modulated activation in the primary and extra-primary (striate and extra-striate) visual cortices. Participants situated in an MR scanner were asked to maintain their gaze on a central location while viewing colored bar gratings oriented vertically or horizontally. The gratings were arranged as small segments of pie slices within a set of concentric circles. The participants were asked to identify by keypress the specific conjunctions of color and orientation (e.g., blue and vertical) in segments targeted by an auditory cue. They also were asked to ignore the distractor gratings appearing simultaneously at other, nontarget segments.

In the course of a block of trials, attention was directed to target segments of increasingly greater eccentricity from the central point of fixation. The investigators were interested in mapping the anatomical sources of the hemodynamic response as attention was shifted progressively away from the fixation point. This goal requires an event-related analysis of the physiological signal, which was achieved by correlating the BOLD response in time (cross-correlation) with a waveform representing the pattern of changing auditory cues in the sequence of trials.

Brefczynski and DeYoe (1999) found that attention was directed to regions of both higher and lower visual processing. As the cued segment appeared farther from the point of fixation, the BOLD response shifted in lockstep fashion to progressively more anterior regions of the primary visual cortex (area V1). This result suggested that spatially directed attention influences the earliest levels of visual processing. Most interesting, the effects of attention tracked precisely the careful retinotopic mapping of neural responses known to characterize this cortical region.

The strongest BOLD response found by these investigators, across a cortical terrain spanning most of the occipital and temporal lobes, was in the ventral portion of area V4. This region, part of the extra-striate cortex, is known to contain cells that respond selectively to wavelength (color) and orientation (Desimone & Schein, 1987). Here again, the authors discovered that the effects of attention on hemodynamic activity corresponded to the retinotopic mapping of neurons in this area. The result suggests that attention facilitates the actual conjoining of visual features into whole objects, in this case the features of color and orientation (see Treisman & Gelade, 1980).

Selection of Object-Based Representations

Much of the early research in cognitive neuroscience examined the influence of attention on simple physical properties of stimuli: color, pitch, location, orientation, duration, and so forth. Recent behavioral studies in cognitive psychology, however, imply that attention can operate on mental representations at the level of the perceptual object itself (see, e.g., Desimone & Duncan, 1995; Nakayama, He, & Shimojo, 1995; see also Chapter 3). An especially interesting implication of this finding is that areas responsible for early processing of stimulus features (e.g., motion) are functionally connected via attention to areas responsible for higher-level processing of specific objects (e.g., houses). This notion was tested recently in an intriguing fMRI study conducted by O'Craven, Downing, and Kanwisher (1999) that suggests that areas coding high-level perceptual representations can serve as a site of selective control.

Previous neuroimaging research by Kanwisher and her colleagues uncovered specialized areas for processing of specific object categories. Kanwisher, McDermott, and Chun (1997), for example, reported that an area within the right fusiform gyrus was selectively activated in humans by viewing human faces (but see Gauthier et al., 1999). This area is close to the region often damaged by lesion in patients with *prosopagnosia*, an inability to recognize familiar faces (De Renzi, 1997). Epstein and Kanwisher (1998) found that an area within the parahippocampal gyrus was selectively activated by the passive viewing of spatial layouts (e.g., an empty room). This

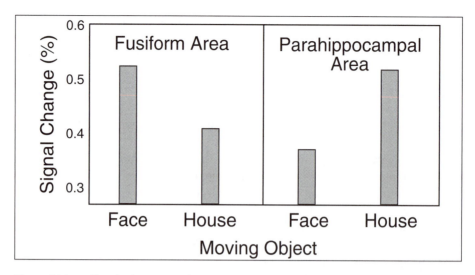

Figure 11.9   Signal change in the BOLD response when attending to direction of movement. The signal change was relatively greater in the fusiform (face selective) area when the face moved and relatively greater in the parahippocampal (house/layout selective) area when the house moved.

SOURCE: Adapted from O'Craven, Downing, & Kanwisher, 1999.

area also responds, albeit more weakly, to the passive viewing of houses (Epstein, Harris, Stanley, & Kanwisher, 1999). O'Craven, Downing, and Kanwisher (1999) exploited these different specializations by presenting participants with stimuli containing a partially transparent picture of a face superimposed on a picture of a house. Overlaying the objects ensured that both face and house occupied identical spatial locations, preempting a role for spatial selection in the results. On each trial, either the face or the house would move slightly in one direction. Participants were asked to attend to the direction of motion of the moving object.

The next paragraph follows. Relative to a condition involving passive viewing of the stimuli, attention to the moving object caused increased blood oxygenation in area V5, an extra-striate region selectively sensitive to motion. The important question, however, was whether focusing on motion also activated the object-selective extra-striate areas. To answer this question, an event-related analysis was required to sort the BOLD contrast signals by the type of moving stimulus: faces or houses. The hemodynamic response to a stimulus usually occurs about 4–6 seconds after the stimulus appears. Thus, the event-related analysis was used to track and group the BOLD signals measured 4–6 seconds after each face or house appeared.

The results are shown in Figure 11.9. As can be seen in the figure, even though the participants were attending only to the direction of motion, the BOLD signal was greater in the fusiform (face selective) area when the face moved than when the house moved (left panel). Similarly, the BOLD signal was greater in the parahippocampal (house/layout selective) area when the house moved than when the face moved (right panel). Of course, because of the sluggish temporal resolution of fMRI (see the section "Measurement Strengths and Limitations" earlier in the chapter), it is difficult to determine whether the results indicate (1) a functional connection between area V5 and object selective areas (i.e., attending to a feature triggers object-level processing) or (2) the orienting effect of motion on the object in motion (i.e., motion elicits attention to objects). Nevertheless, the results of O'Craven et al. (1999) demonstrate that attention can modulate (either directly or indirectly) areas that code complex, higher-order representations of stimuli.

Target Versus Distractor Activation in Lateral Intraparietal Cortex

Although fMRI has proven to be a powerful technique for identifying the representational units on which attention acts, it has not yet enabled researchers to differentiate between the excitatory and inhibitory processes that separate stimulus representations in the posterior cortex. To address this issue, cognitive neuroscientists have turned to single-cell recordings of primates as they engage in attention tasks. One possible site of visual attention is in the posterior parietal lobes. As we discuss later, both Posner and Petersen (1990) and Mesulam (2000) considered this region essential for shifting attention from one part of the visual field to another. A recent study by Bisley and Goldberg (2003) suggests, however, that attentional processing in the parietal lobes also may serve to distinguish relevant from irrelevant channels of activation.

Bisley and Goldberg (2003) used tiny implant electrodes to record the activity of 40 individual parietal neurons in the lateral intraparietal area (LIP; see the top panel of Figure 11.10). Their participants were two monkeys who performed a spatial cuing task (see Chapter 3). As shown at the bottom of Figure 11.10, on each trial a white dot appeared in one of the four quadrants of a computer screen, cuing the monkey to the likely location of an upcoming target. The target was an open ring, called a Landolt C, either oriented normally (C) or mirror reversed (Ɔ). The monkeys were trained to make go/no-go responses, moving their eyes toward the target in response to C (go), but staying fixated on the center of the screen in response to Ɔ (no-go). On certain trials, a distractor dot appeared after the cue dot, but just before the target C, in a quadrant opposite to the cue. The inter-stimulus interval (ISI) between the distractor and the target

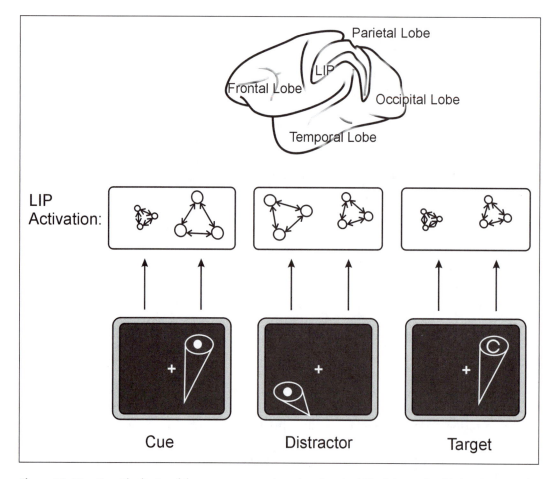

Figure 11.10 Top: The brain of the macaque monkey showing the LIP of the parietal lobe. Bottom: The magnitude of excitatory activity to LIP neurons (represented by the size of triangles in the upper panel) as a function of the locus of spatial attention in the Bisley and Goldberg (2003) cuing task. First, attention is oriented toward the location of the cue (left panels); next, attention is drawn to the location of the distractor in the opposite quadrant (middle panels); finally, attention is directed to the location of the target (right panels).

was 200, 700, or 1,200 ms, the distractor otherwise appearing in the same location as the impending target.

The monkey's behavioral performance was measured by the amount of contrast between the Landolt C and background needed for the monkey to achieve 75% response accuracy. Lower contrast thresholds indicate better behavioral

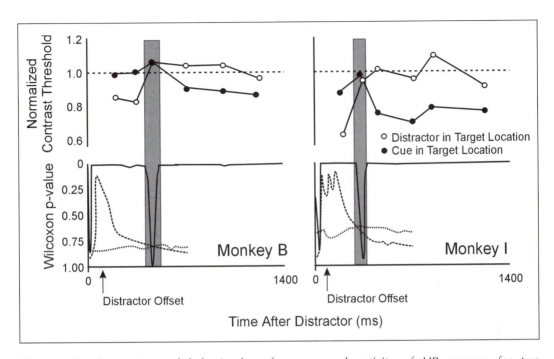

Figure 11.11 Comparison of behavioral performance and activity of LIP neurons for two monkeys (B and I) in Bisley and Goldberg's (2003) spatial cuing task. Top: Contrast thresholds of the monkeys as a function of ISI to trials in which the distractor appeared in the target's location (and the cue was in the opposite location; white circles) and trials in which the cue appeared in the target's location (and the distractor was opposite; black circles). Bottom: Responses of LIP neurons to the distractor (dashed line) in the target's location (cue opposite) and to the cue (dotted line) in the target's location (distractor opposite). The black line represents P values from a statistical test (Wilcoxon paired signed-rank test) comparing LIP activity to the distractor and the cue. The vertical gray column shows the period of time during which no statistical difference was found in the LIP activity to distractor and cue. Note that this period also was characterized by an absence of behavioral differences (see top panels).

SOURCE: Data from Bisley & Goldberg, 2003.

performance. The top of Figure 11.11 shows each monkey's behavioral performance as a function of the ISI between distractor and target in each of the two conditions. At the short ISI, each monkey's performance was better when the distractor appeared in the target's location (and the cue was in the opposite location; white circles) than when the cue appeared in the target's location (and the distractor was opposite; black circles). At the long ISIs, however, performance was relatively better when the cue correctly signaled the target's location.

The reason for this pattern of performance can be understood from the neural activity in LIP. The bottom of Figure 11.11 shows traces of activity in LIP cells sensitive to the location where a target would appear (but had not yet appeared) at that point in time in which a distractor was presented. The dashed line shows the activation caused by the distractor in the target's location (cue opposite); the dotted line shows the activation caused by a cue in the target's location (distractor opposite). Evidently, the distractor initially caused increased activation relative to the cue, an indication of orienting to the distractor, but later showed relatively weak activation. The monkeys' behavioral performance followed this neural pattern precisely, evincing an early performance advantage from the distractor when the distractor's activation was greater than the cue's, a late performance advantage from the cue when the cue's activation was greater than the distractor's, and no performance advantage when activations of distractor and cue were equal.

Bisley and Goldberg's (2003) results suggest that behavioral performance in visual attention tasks can be closely linked to activation patterns in the posterior parietal cortex. Neural activation here has a winner-take-all effect on performance, with relevant and irrelevant signals battling for priority in attention. Their results indicate that attentional control (and behavioral performance) is achieved by the relations between signal or channel activations, and not by the absolute level of activation in any one channel.

▲ ATTENTIONAL NETWORKS

In humans, damage to LIP, together with other posterior areas of the parietal cortex, often is associated with the syndrome known as *unilateral neglect*. In this disorder, the patient's attention is easily drawn and held by stimuli in the ipsilesional visual field (the visual space on the same side as the lesion). However, the patient tends to ignore (neglect) stimuli in the contralesional visual field. The most common form of the disorder is left-side neglect, produced by an extensive lesion in the parietal lobe of the right hemisphere. When severe, a patient may leave an abnormally large left margin while writing, fail to copy the left side of a scene when drawing, or leave the left side of a plate filled with undisturbed food when eating. In a cuing paradigm, such a patient will suffer a substantial delay in responding to targets on the left side of a visual display if cued incorrectly to the right side of the display (Posner, Walker, Friedrich, & Rafal, 1984). The famous Italian film director Federico Fellini showed in his drawings an awareness of the left-side neglect he suffered after a stroke: A cartoon of a man staring at his right limbs bore the caption

"Where is the left?" ("Dové la sinistra?"; Cantagallo & Della Sala, 1998). Interestingly, patients whose lesions are restricted to the right frontal lobe also may display the symptoms of unilateral neglect.

The phenomenon of unilateral neglect and other neuropsychological syndromes has led several cognitive neuroscientists to theorize networks of interacting neural systems to explain both disordered and normal attentional functioning (Büchel & Friston, 1997; Mesulam, 2000; Posner & Petersen, 1990; Shimamura, 2000). In this section, we will review several of the most prominent theories. They differ in their specific proposals, but they all share an organizing framework in using previous research to explicitly distinguish the sources and sites of attentional control.

Posner's Orienting Network

The abnormal delay that neglect patients suffer in responding to targets when incorrectly cued led Posner and his colleagues to propose a functional role for the parietal lobe in *disengaging* attention from its current locus (Posner et al., 1984). This network forms one component of a hypothesized tripartite system used by humans to orient their attention, voluntarily or involuntarily, to events of current importance in their environment. Data from patients with other neuropsychological disorders suggested to Posner (1988; Rafal & Posner, 1987) that the pulvinar nucleus is responsible for the specific act of *engaging* attention to significant environmental stimuli. A final component of the orienting system is required to *move* attention between a disengaged and a newly oriented stimulus. Results with patients suffering from midbrain lesions implicated the superior colliculus as the neural circuit of attentional movement. Posner and DiGirolamo (2000) have argued that the three constituents of the orienting system—namely, the posterior parietal lobe, the pulvinar nucleus, and the superior colliculus—act collectively as an attentional source operating on separate sites within the visual system, such as on the ventral pathway in object recognition tasks (e.g., visual search).

Mesulam's Attentional System

The network system proposed by Mesulam (2000) reserves a greater role than Posner's for the frontal lobe in the control of attentional processes. Mesulam emphasizes that almost all attentional tasks, regardless of sensory modality, involve metabolic activity in the prefrontal cortex, especially Brodmann areas 9, 44, and 46 (i.e., dorsolateral prefrontal cortex; see Figure 11.8, p. 351). He thus considers the prefrontal cortex to be the primary source of top-down modulation in both divided and selective attention tasks. Driving the attentional network from the bottom up is the ascending reticular activating system (ARAS), a diffuse set of neurons in the brainstem that includes the reticular formation and its connections to and from the frontal lobe. The prefrontal cortex and ARAS work cooperatively in the everyday tasks that require attention. When detecting a novel stimulus in the environment, for example, Mesulam (2000) asserts that first the prefrontal cortex is required to register the identity and significance of the stimulus. Descending projections to the reticular formation then trigger a boost in arousal tone, which serves to speed the flow of sensory information through the thalamus and on to sensory/perceptual regions of the posterior cortex.

Figure 11.12 provides a schematic overview of Mesulam's (2000) proposed system in the context of an auditory selective attention task. Top-down and bottom-up influences are focused on modality- and domain-specific regions of the posterior cortex, including (depending on the target of attention) the auditory cortices (Brodmann areas 41 and 42), the visual areas V4 (color, orientation), V5 (motion), fusiform gyrus (possibly face specific), and parahippocampus (possibly house specific). In spatial attention, Mesulam accords special status to area LIP for encoding covert shifts of attention from one part of the visual field to another. This idea fits with the observation that damage to area LIP is associated with severe cases of unilateral neglect. The modulation of LIP activity via its connections to the frontal lobe (including the frontal eye fields) may entail a battle between excitatory and inhibitory processes, as suggested by the research of Bisley and Goldberg (2003). Indeed, Mesulam claims that, across modalities, selective attention always works optimally when the frontal influences on domain-specific regions involve a duality of processes: increased activity to neurons coding attended stimuli and suppressed activity to neurons coding unattended stimuli.

Büchel and Friston's Path Network

The results of lesion, ERP, and fMRI studies have underscored the role of the prefrontal cortex in modulating activity in posterior sensory areas. One approach for examining the network connections between a prefrontal source and sensory/perceptual sites is to employ techniques of mathematical modeling on physiological data. Büchel and Friston (1997) have modeled the regional changes in cerebral blood flow, as measured by fMRI, using a statistical approach called path analysis. In a path analysis of functional activation, covariations in the BOLD contrast signal among different brain regions are incorporated into and evaluated by a formal model of how one region affects another.

Büchel and Friston (1997) were interested in how attention to moving visual stimuli modulates the extra-striate area V5. Single-cell recordings of the macaque monkey analogue of V5, the medial temporal area MT, indicate that this region

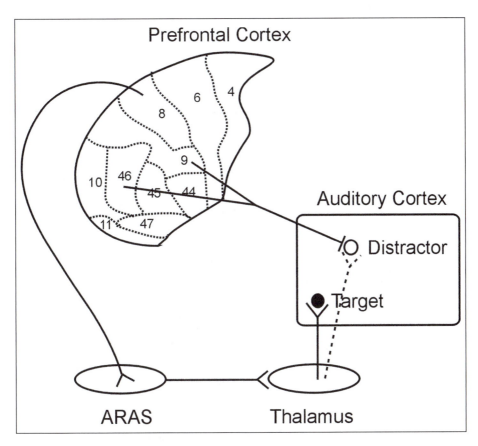

Figure 11.12   Mesulam's (2000) framework of attention control in the context of an auditory selective attention task. The prefrontal cortex registers the identity and significance of the stimulus (i.e., target, distractor). Top-down activation of ARAS enhances arousal tone, which speeds the bottom-up flow of sensory information through the thalamus and on to the auditory cortex. Prefrontal projections to the sensory cortex suppress activity to neurons coding distractor stimuli.

is strongly involved in the early processing of visual motion. Büchel and Friston collected fMRI scans of three human participants as they viewed an array of moving dots during fMRI scanning. In the attention condition, the participants were instructed to detect changes in the speed of the dots' motion. In the passive viewing (nonattention) condition, they were asked merely to watch the dots. Relative to passive viewing, the researchers found that attention caused an increased hemodynamic response in three areas: the right dorsolateral prefrontal cortex, area V5, and the striate cortex (area V1).

A path analysis of these three regions uncovered effective connections between V1 and V5 and between the prefrontal cortex and V5. In particular, the structural model revealed that attention modulated the degree of hemodynamic activation in area V5 via projections from the dorsolateral prefrontal cortex. One interpretation of this modeling result is that V5 is a sensory/perceptual site of attentional signals from the prefrontal cortex. The success of path analysis and other formal modeling techniques in accounting for such complex patterns of physiological data has established them as a valuable new tool for evaluating theorized attentional networks.

Dynamic Filtering: A General Purpose Attentional Network

How is attention orchestrated? One venerable hypothesis places the control of attention in an executive system operating from the frontal lobe. This notion appears in Baddeley's (1986) theory of working memory, responsible for controlling the flow of information into storage buffers (see Chapter 7). One potential difficulty for theories that posit executive systems is an inability to explain the intelligent behavior behind the executive control. To suggest that decisions about selection, for example, are in the hands of an intelligent executive is to beg the question of how selection occurs. In the extreme, the idea of an executive is equivalent to positing a little man in the head, a homunculus, who makes all decisions using a little man in his head, and so on to infinity. Obviously, such an explanation of selective control is no explanation at all.

Research on the neurophysiology and neuropsychology of attention, however, has shed light on possible mechanisms of executive control. Shimamura (1994, 2000) recently proposed an updated version of Broadbent's (1958) filter theory that fits with the new evidence from cognitive neuroscience. He calls it *dynamic filtering theory*. According to this view, a filtering mechanism in the prefrontal cortex handles the constant flood of information to the perceptual systems by accentuating selected signals and suppressing irrelevant signals. Different filters are applied to different selection situations. Filters that act on sensory qualities, such as pitch, motion, or spatial location, may be innate. Filters that act on more abstract representations, such as word categories or object categories (e.g., houses), are acquired through experience, and may be represented as patterns of activation in the prefrontal cortex.

Importantly, Shimamura (2000) considers all filters to operate according to the same basic principle. Relying on the reciprocal connections that exist between the prefrontal cortex and the posterior association cortices, he posits that executive control is maintained by the combination of excitation of target signals and inhibition of distractor signals. Such a simple, direct mechanism avoids the thorny philosophical problem of conceiving of a central executive as an intelligent being inside the head. Just as a thermostat controls room temperature through a nonintelligent sensitivity to current environmental conditions, so too an array of prefrontal filters can, in principle, monitor and control the constant flow of information through sensory systems.

At present, dynamic filtering theory is simply a framework for conceptualizing attention, not a detailed model of the processing course of attentional experience in all its varieties. Yet the theory may help us to consider how attentional processes relate to other aspects of executive control. For example, one reason why we attend to certain events or objects is to keep them active in our memory for further processing. Shimamura (2000) believes that one way to maintain information in memory is to set and leave a filter fixed for some period of time. He thinks that the ability to shift quickly from one task to another may amount to a proficiency in replacing one filter with another. Because different filters serve different cognitive functions and outcomes by activating posterior representations of differing complexity (e.g., features vs. objects), the wide variety of attentional disorders may arise from the numerous ways filtering can fail in the posterior cortex.

SUMMARY ▲

The evidence from cognitive neuroscience reviewed in this chapter indicates that selection operates by a combination of excitatory and inhibitory processes that can act very early in perception by segregating attended from unattended information. It is interesting that, in a sense, the evidence largely conforms to the seminal ideas of early sensory filtering proposed 45 years ago by Broadbent (1958). Of course, all of the results described here were collected after Broadbent advanced his theory. The brain research has served to qualify his views in several ways. For example, we now know that the filtering (1) is gradual, not abrupt; (2) occurs in both the attended channel and the unattended channel, but using different processes; (3) can begin at different times in processing, depending on factors such as stimulus discriminability; and (4) can operate both on simple sensory dimensions and on complex object representations. We also know that control of these filtering operations probably rests with the dorsolateral prefrontal cortex (and perhaps also the anterior cingulate cortex).

The purpose of this chapter has been to highlight several of the many gains made to date in our understanding of the physiology of attention, insights gleaned from implementing the versatile toolkit of the cognitive neuroscientist. The toolkit will continue to expand in the years to come, and will continue to provide modern researchers with a special glimpse into the intricate mechanisms of attention. In a real sense, then, the field of cognitive neuroscience has permitted us to peer into the black box inside our skull so as to better grasp its mysteries.

CHAPTER **12**

DISORDERS OF ATTENTION

with Edward de Haan and Roy Kessels

A man who recently suffered a stroke behaves strangely in the hospital. He appears to be fully awake and conscious but he takes no notice of anything that happens to his left. In contrast, he reacts in a normal fashion to events taking place to his right. The problem is not that he cannot see to the left, as he is free to move his eyes and head. Still, he ignores people who talk to him while standing on his left side, he does not eat the food on the left half of his plate, and he does not shave the left half of his own face. In the next bed lies a man who has just recovered consciousness after a severe head injury incurred during a car crash. Despite the fact that he is now fully awake, he is disoriented and unable to tell his name, where he is, or what the date is. A few months later, his condition has improved and he is oriented in "time, place, and person." However, he still finds it very difficult to concentrate on the task at hand and his mind wanders off easily; as a result he is unable to return to his previous employment.

Although at first sight patients such as these appear to exhibit behavior that most of us would associate with Hollywood films, such behaviors are, unfortunately, quite common. If you were to visit a neurology ward, the chance is great that you would encounter patients similar to the ones just described. A number of factors contribute to the increasing interest of psychologists in people with cognitive deficits following brain trauma. First, the number of people with a brain injury resulting from concussion is substantial and growing. The volume of road traffic continues to increase, and so does the number of accidents. In addition, life expectancy continues to increase, and with this increase comes a proportional increase in diseases associated with age, such as dementias and stroke. Improved medical care means that more victims of disease or accidents survive, only to suffer long-term cognitive deficits. Finally, a number of clinical phenomena that have traditionally been interpreted as psychiatric in origin, such as schizophrenia and autism, have now been associated with brain pathology. The combined effect of these separate factors is that there is a growing number of people with brain dysfunction, many of whom will become chronic patients (Keefe, 1995).

Attention deficits are among the most common effects of brain disease or injury, occurring in as many as 80% of patients (Lezak, 1995). Subjective complaints about attention problems are common, and both patients and their families often notice that the patient has more trouble concentrating than before the injury. Large-scale studies on the cognitive consequences of different types of brain damage have confirmed that a wide variety of attention deficits might be present following injury, and assessment of these deficits requires a varied battery of attention tests. Most of the tests used in clinical settings are based on tasks used to study attention in research settings, such as the Stroop task and vigilance tests. However, because patients might suffer from a variety of additional problems (such as impaired motor control), a number of specialized tests have been developed.

As the previous chapters have made clear, attention is not a unitary function. In clinical settings, very different attention deficits may emerge, depending on a number of factors such as the cause of brain dysfunction and the location of the damage. Most clinical researchers and practitioners divide attention function into four groups: alertness, vigilance (or sustained attention), selective attention, and divided attention. However, interest in executive function (and problems therein) is increasing. This chapter will focus on the attention deficits that follow the major categories of brain damage, including developmental disorders, stroke, head trauma, dementia, and schizophrenia.

▲ DEVELOPMENTAL ATTENTION DISORDERS

Developmental disorders are cognitive or behavioral problems that present themselves in childhood. Because of the variability in symptoms associated with these disorders, diagnosis is often based on excluding other possible causes for the problems. Developmental disorders may be relatively specific, affecting one cognitive function (such as the influence of dyslexia on reading), but often they are more generalized and affect a broad spectrum of cognitive functions (see, e.g., Bishop, 1992). For instance, *autism* affects a number of mental processes, including perception and attention, resulting in severe impairments in social interaction. Many developmental disorders have a familial or genetic component. This means that children of parents who suffer from a developmental disorder have a higher than normal chance of developing the same problem.

With an incidence in the western world of about 3 to 5% (Barkley, 1990), attention-deficit hyperactivity disorder (ADHD) is one of the most prevalent developmental disorders affecting attentional processing (see Chapter 2 for a discussion of ADHD in relation to arousal, and Chapter 11 for a neural processing account of ADHD). This is a broadly defined syndrome that, as the term indicates, is characterized by severe impairments in attention (e.g., difficulty sustaining attention and avoidance of tasks requiring sustained effort) and behavior (e.g., interrupts or intrudes on others and has difficulty waiting turn). Children (and adults) with ADHD have difficulty in attending to relevant cues in the environment and maintaining attention for prolonged periods of time. They are often fidgety and restless, and may be overtly aggressive. Their schoolwork is often disorganized, and they encounter problems in playing with other children.

Diagnosis of ADHD is somewhat subjective,[1] and may be complicated by the presence of other problems, such as learning disabilities or conduct disorder. Moreover, the expression of the condition depends on the situation. A common observation is that the hyperactive child who is often a burden to his environment may quietly play computer games for hours on end. When a child suffering from ADHD is tested with standard clinical tests for selective or sustained attention, he or she may perform normally, perhaps because the examiner is a stranger with authority and the user of reinforcers, such as the promise of sweets. As soon as the child has left the clinic, the hyperactive behavior will reappear and directly affect cognitive abilities. Thus, the essence of ADHD is that children who suffer from it are able to perform cognitive tasks, but not to their full potential. This means, in practical terms, that the diagnosis of ADHD is made on the basis of clinical interviews, as well as checklists and/or questionnaires, rather than solely on the basis of objective performance tests. In order to reach a diagnosis with some confidence, clinicians will want to see reports from at least two environments, in most cases the home and the school situation (Barkley, 1991).

Research on the cognitive basis of ADHD began in the 1970s, first using tests of vigilance in which responses had to be made to infrequent, visual targets (Sykes, Douglas, & Morgenstern, 1973). Although ADHD children performed worse on vigilance tests than children without the syndrome (showing both more misses and more false alarms), suggesting a problem with sustained attention, early research shed little light on the nature of the processes that were impaired in ADHD. More recent studies have shown that basic information processes such as stimulus encoding, comparison, and response selection are intact in ADHD children (see Logan, Schachar, & Tannock, 2000, for a review). The search for the basis of ADHD has thus moved on to exploring processes that control basic information processes—that is, executive control processes, and, in particular, the ability to inhibit responses.

Perhaps the most promising line of research in ADHD in the last 10 years has been that using the stop-signal paradigm (see Chapter 5). Children who suffer from ADHD have trouble stopping on stop-signal trials, even though they have no difficulty perceiving the stop signal. They tend to fail to withhold responses more frequently than children without ADHD, and when they do manage to stop, it takes them longer (Schachar & Logan, 1990). Moreover, medication that improves the symptoms of ADHD (the stimulant methylphenidate) also improves stopping-task performance (Tannock et al., 1989). The finding that the same treatment that reduces the symptoms of ADHD also improves stopping performance suggests that the ability to exercise inhibitory control may be the central deficit in ADHD (Logan, Schachar, & Tannock, 2000; see also Barkley, 1997; see also Box 2.1 in Chapter 2).

Three factors suggest that ADHD has a biological basis. First, there is evidence for a dysfunctional neurotransmitter system that results in lower catecholamine levels in the brain (see, e.g., Todd & Botteron, 2001). This is in line with the paradoxical clinical observation that stimulants, such as methylphenidate, actually help ADHD children to slow down and concentrate. Second, neuroimaging studies have shown reduced blood flow in the prefrontal cortices, and event-related potential (ERP) studies (reviewed in Swanson et al., 1998) show that ADHD sufferers show abnormalities in the components associated with enhancing relevant and blocking irrelevant stimuli. Third, there is a clear familial factor, with about 30% of the parents of children with ADHD suffering from this disorder themselves. Children with ADHD often grow up to become adults with ADHD. Adult ADHD has been largely ignored until recently, with the identification of ADHD as a precursor of clinical conditions ranging from alcoholism to sociopathology (Hallowell & Ratey, 1994).

Linking clinical symptoms of ADHD to cognitive processes and to neural networks of attention may lead to a better understanding of the biological basis of ADHD. Swanson and colleagues (Swanson et al., 1998) advocate this approach within Posner and Raichle's (1994) theory of attentional networks in the brain. This theory assumes that distinct neural networks control the functions of alerting (inhibiting irrelevant or ongoing neural activity and exerting mental effort to establish a state of vigilance and readiness to react), orienting (facilitating some neural resources while inhibiting others in order to prepare for an expected type of input), and executive control (coordinating the processes of detecting targets, starting and stopping mental operations, and ordering multiple responses to direct behavior towards goals). Different symptoms of ADHD and the cognitive processes involved in their expression have been linked to each of these attentional networks. For example, difficulty in sustaining attention, as measured by continuous performance tests and reflecting vigilance level, can be related to dysfunction in the right frontal network that subserves alerting. Such an integrated approach will be necessary to reconcile the many theories that have been proposed to account for ADHD.

ATTENTION DEFICITS DUE TO FOCAL LESIONS AND HEMORRHAGE ▲

About 150 per 100,000 people suffer a first-time *cerebrovascular disease* or *stroke* each year (G. G. Brown, Baird, Shatz, & Bornstein, 1996). Stroke is a major cause of death and disability in the western world, affecting primarily older people (9 out of 10 stroke patients are older than 65). There are two main types of cerebrovascular disease. An *ischemic infarct* involves the obstruction of an artery, and a *cerebral hemorrhage* is the result of a burst blood vessel. Infarcts are four times more frequent than hemorrhage. A large number of subtypes of infarct can be distinguished, but the most important ones are (1) embolic infarct in a major cerebral artery, (2) lacunar infarct in one of the smaller perforating arterioles, and (3) watershed infarct due to low perfusion pressure in an artery, which results in insufficient blood supply to the areas that are furthest away (Powers, 1990). The symptoms of an infarct are determined by the location, size, and type of infarct. Large embolic infarcts may occur in any of the cerebral arteries and often destroy a substantial area of gray matter (more than 2 cm^2), causing substantial motor, perceptual, and/or cognitive deficits. Watershed infarcts tend to affect the same cortical regions as embolic infarcts and may produce clinical signs such as motor weakness or language problems. Lacunar infarcts, which are found in the deep white matter of the brain, tend to cause only transient motor impairments. Until recently, it was thought that lacunar infarcts did not produce any long-lasting cognitive impairments, but it is now clear that there is some decrease in mental abilities, notably attentional functioning, probably as a result of metabolic changes (Van Zandvoort, Kappelle, Algra, & De Haan, 1998). In general, infarcts result in a general decline of mental functioning that is somewhat independent of the affected brain structure as well as specific location-dependent deficits.

Two main types of hemorrhage can be distinguished. The first is a subarachnoidal hemorrhage in the protective layers surrounding the brain. This nearly always produces severe and unusual headache due to pressure on the brain.

Given timely diagnosis and surgery to relieve the pressure, the patient might escape with little cognitive or physical impairment. A second type of hemorrhage is intracerebral, and is caused by a burst blood vessel, often as the result of an arterial venous malformation, such as an aneurysm, or a traumatic blow to the head. Arterial venous malformations may occur anywhere in the subcortical regions and the occipital, temporal, parietal, or frontal lobes and can result in a wide variety of attention deficits. In addition to the deficits that may follow posterior brain lesions, described later in this chapter, deficits following hemorrhage may include impairments in arousal and in selective, divided, and sustained attention. In addition, frontal lobe damage may lead to problems in executive function.

Because not all patients show the same symptoms following stroke or hemorrhage, cognitive deficits are usually studied by having large numbers of patients complete a battery of neuropsychological tests. Poor performance on tests of memory (approximately 20–30% of patients), attention (30–50%), and language (20–40%) is common (see, e.g., Hochstenbach et al., 1998). Moreover, patients report a reduced quality of life (as measured by an index that looks at the subjective repercussions of physical and mental impairments in daily life (De Haan et al., 1995).

The nature of any attention deficits in stroke patients depends on the location of the infarct. Infarcts in the *posterior cerebral artery* affect the occipital lobe and the posterior part of the temporal lobe, which may cause visual field defects and other visual deficits. The function of attention in detecting visual stimuli is partly dependent on intact processing of the occipital lobe, and patients with a posterior cerebral artery infarct may experience problems in this respect. Infarcts in the *middle cerebral artery* may produce lesions in a large cortical area involving extensive sections of the temporal, parietal, and frontal lobes. Middle cerebral artery infarcts are relatively common and are responsible for diverse and severe cognitive deficits affecting language, memory, and attention. Both posterior and middle cerebral artery infarcts are associated with neglect, extinction, and Balint's syndrome, all of which will be discussed in the following sections.

Neglect

The clinical phenomenon of hemispatial neglect, introduced in Chapter 11, is a relatively frequent clinical occurrence, and is one of the most intriguing disorders following brain damage. In its most florid form, the patient does not acknowledge any stimulation from the side contralateral to the damaged hemisphere, whether the stimulation is visual, auditory, or even tactile. The problem is not caused by primary sensory or motor deficits; the patients can, in principle, see the stimuli and perform the appropriate responses. However, *hemianopia* (i.e., blindness in one visual field) and *hemiplegia* (motor dysfunction in one half of the body) often

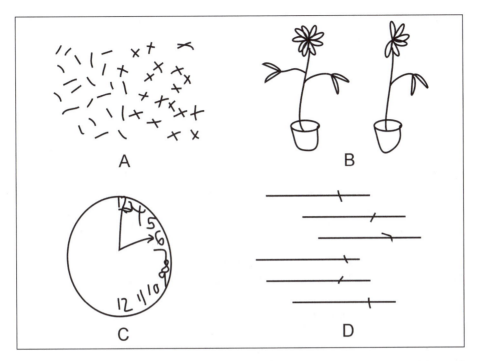

Figure 12.1   Examples of a test performance of a neglect patient on four widely used clinical tests: (A) the cancellation task, (B) the copying task, (C) clock drawing, and (D) line bisection.

co-occur with neglect, making it difficult to diagnose in some cases. Another factor that can complicate diagnosis further is that several single-case studies indicate the possibility that neglect is sometimes restricted to a single modality (e.g., visual or auditory) or a certain type of stimulus (e.g., pictures vs. text; Heilman, Watson, & Valenstein, 1985; Robertson & Marshall, 1993). Left and right hemisphere lesions may cause neglect for the right and left half of space, respectively, but right-hemisphere neglect tends to be more common, more severe, and more persistent (Robertson & Halligan, 1999).

The diagnosis of neglect is often made on the basis of simple paper and pencil tests. Figure 12.1 shows the most common types of tests used to diagnose neglect (see also Lezak, 1995). In cancellation tasks, in which all stimuli of a given sort are to be crossed out, right-hemisphere neglect patients fail to cross out elements toward the left side of the paper, and in copying and free drawing, right-hemisphere neglect is indicated by omission of details that are present on the left side of the original. Finally, in the line-bisection task, right-hemisphere neglect patients place the middle of a horizontal line significantly to the right, presumably because they do not perceive the left side of the line properly. It is important to realize that the patient performs these tasks while sitting at a table without any restriction of eye, head, or body movements. This stresses that the crux of the problem is not perceptual, but reflects a failure to attend to the left.

In some circumstances—for instance, when a specific training method is considered—in-depth assessment is recommended to chart the characteristics of the neglect symptoms. One fine-grained method to assess neglect is based on measurement of the extent of the perception distortions in the affected visual field (Robertson & Marshall, 1993). This method requires adjusting the length of a horizontal bar in one visual field to match the length of a bar in the other visual field. The degree of mismatch between the two bars is a quantitative measure of the severity of the visual neglect.

Neglect is apparent not only in the perceptual domain, but also in the motor behavior of the patient. For example, patients are slower to start and execute hand movements towards the unattended side (Heilman, Bowers, et al., 1985; Mattingley, Phillips, & Bradshaw, 1994). In most patients, perceptual and motor neglect co-occur, but distinct symptoms affecting only perception or motor behavior have been described. In addition, there are indications that perceptual neglect is more often associated with parietal lesions, whereas motor neglect is associated with damage to the frontal lobe (see, e.g., Na et al., 1998; Nakagawa et al., 1998). It should be stressed that the parietal and frontal areas involved in neglect are parts of the same attentional network (see, e.g., Paus, Jech, & Thompson, 1997).

Like normal selective attention, neglect can be space-based or object-based (see Chapter 3). Neglect patients with lesions in the right hemisphere asked to copy a drawing with several elements (e.g., a house, a tree, and the sun) will often fail to include objects located to the left in the original, but may also fail to draw the left side of objects that are actually to the right of other objects. Similarly, neglect in reading (a condition sometimes referred to as *neglect dyslexia*) is characterized by missed words at the beginning of each line and by misreadings of the initial letters of those words that are detected. These findings show that the left side of space, as well as the left side of objects—even when in the right hemifield—may be neglected (Driver, Baylis, Goodrich, & Rafal, 1994; Driver & Pouget, 2000).

Neglect can be described as a deficit in overt orienting in that patients fail to make head or eye movements in the contralesional direction. In addition, tests based on the peripheral cuing procedure (see Chapter 3), in which a noninformative spatial cue precedes target presentation, indicate that covert orienting may also be impaired. Relative to normal subjects, neglect patients show problems in the disengagement of attention from the ipsilesional to the contralesional side. That is, the difference between the cued and uncued conditions on the contralesional side of space is much larger than this difference on the ipsilesional side. To put it differently, when patients with a right hemisphere lesion are attending a stimulus, they have no problem diverting their attention to something else appearing towards the right. However, they appear to be stuck to the stimulus they are attending to when a new stimulus appears to the left (Morrow & Ratcliff, 1988; Posner, 1994).

By definition, neglect is not a sensory perception problem, although many neglect patients have visual field defects, as well. One widely cited source of evidence for the contention that neglect is not a perceptual deficit, but an inability to divert attention to the left, is a clinical experiment carried out by Bisiach and Luzzatti (1978) with a patient who suffered from severe hemispatial neglect. The patient had been living in Milan all his life and therefore was well acquainted with the main square. At one end of the square there is a cathedral and at the other end the City Hall. When the patient was asked to think of the square while looking at it from the perspective of the City Hall, he described the different buildings on the right side while ignoring the ones on the left. Subsequently, when the patient was asked to mentally cross the square and face it from the opposite side, he did not report most of the buildings mentioned earlier but adequately described the previously neglected side. Apparently, neglect not only affects what we can attend to in the outside world but also what we can imagine. Imagery and perception are related and may partly depend on the same processes. Thus, it could be argued that Bisiach and Luzzatti's finding does not provide conclusive evidence that neglect is not due to a perceptual problem. More direct evidence for the attentional nature of the problem comes from priming studies indicating subconscious processing of "neglected" stimuli. Priming studies indicate that the brain may actually process information that is neglected even though no conscious experience of that information emerges. For instance, when pictures are used as primes for words, presenting a picture of a loaf of bread in the neglected visual field speeds up the recognition of the word "BUTTER" in the attended part of the visual field (Berti & Rizzolatti, 1992; McGlinchey-Berroth et al., 1993). Thus, it seems that neglect patients can sometimes process neglected information at least to a semantic level. As in the case of the attentional blink (see Chapter 7), a persistent problem remains at the level of becoming consciously aware of the information. Lack of awareness in neglect patients extends to the very recognition of the problem that is so readily apparent to an outside observer: If one points out to a patient that he or she has neglect, the initial reaction is often one of incomprehension. In the same way that we are not aware of "missing" items presented behind us, the neglect patient is often not aware of any reduction in the attended visual field. This lack of insight into the problem can seriously hamper attempts to teach the patient compensatory strategies. Only after a patient realizes that he or she is ignoring part of the world can compensation kick in, allowing the symptoms of the problem to be alleviated.

Extinction

Most neglect patients recover relatively quickly, but some may exhibit other deficits even after the neglect disappears. One such deficit, first described at the end of the 19th century (Oppenheim, 1885), is *extinction*. Extinction, which may also occur in people who have never suffered from neglect, is a subtle deficit that affects the detection of stimuli presented in the visual field contralateral to the damaged hemisphere. As long as there is only one stimulus present anywhere in the visual field, recognition of that stimulus proceeds normally. However, when two stimuli are presented simultaneously, the patient will often fail to detect the stimulus in the field contralateral to the damage. Assessment of extinction in the clinic is straightforward. The patient is seated on a stool with his back toward the examiner and asked to look straight ahead. The examiner can then detect visual extinction by briefly moving her two index fingers simultaneously in the left and the right peripheral visual fields of the patient (this is called the "confrontation" method for investigating visual field defects). Tactile extinction can be assessed by simultaneously tapping the left and right shoulders of the patient, and, finally, auditory extinction can be indexed via bilateral presentation of sounds. According to Vallar et al. (1994), these bedside testing routines are probably the most sensitive way to detect the occurrence of a unilateral stroke. At the same time, subtle forms of extinction might be missed with these simple tasks. More sensitive methods using computer-controlled presentation of stimuli are required to detect these less pronounced forms of extinction.

Extinction is not the result of a sensory deficit, as demonstrated by the fact that a single stimulus will be detected normally (Driver & Vuilleumier, 2001). Rather, it appears to be an attention deficit. One finding consistent with the attentional nature of the deficit is that the symptoms of extinction can be dramatically reduced by instructing patients to ignore the ipsilesional stimulus. Thus, paying extra attention to the contralesional side improves the detection on that side while the ipsilesional stimuli are still detected accurately. Unfortunately, patients do not use this strategy spontaneously, and it is very difficult to teach them to use it. As is the case with neglect patients, they don't know what they're missing.

Balint's Syndrome

Balint's syndrome is a classic neurological syndrome characterized by difficulty in fixating the eyes, executing controlled movements, and processing visual scenes. This syndrome, first described by Balint (1909), is the result of bilateral damage to the superior posterior parietal lobes. Because it results from two separate infarcts at more or less the same place in each hemisphere, it occurs only rarely. The syndrome is so characteristic that it allows a clinician to deduce the location of brain lesions on the basis of the observed pathological behavior. Balint observed that bilateral damage to the posterior parietal lobes results in three distinct pathological behavior patterns: ocular apraxia, optic ataxia, and simultanagnosia.

Ocular apraxia is a problem in eye movements in which the patient finds it very difficult to fixate on a certain position in space. The eyes continue to wander, unable to settle down at any given point. Because a primary disorder in the execution of eye movements can be ruled out, the central problem appears to be visuo-motor integration.

Optic ataxia is a disorder in visually guided motor behavior. The patient is not able to point accurately to a specific position in space or to grasp an object. The reason to assume that this disorder is a problem in linking visual information and motor planning is that these patients actually perform normally when their eyes are closed. The traditional method of assessment is to ask the patient to point to the finger of the examiner with his eyes open and to his own nose with his eyes closed. Assessment is slightly more accurate when the patient is asked to indicate more distant targets, such as the nose of a doctor standing on the other side of the room. In any case, the deficit is so pronounced that it is easy to detect deviations from normal performance.

Simultanagnosia, the third sign of Balint's syndrome, refers to an inability to simultaneously perceive the different aspects of an object or a visual scene (Wolpert, 1924). As if glued to one detail, patients are unable to change their focus of interest from position to position and are unable to see the "whole picture." As a result, they suffer from severe visual recognition impairments. The usual test to diagnose simultanagnosia involves showing the patient line drawings of complex scenes and asking him or her to give an account of what is depicted. The typical simultanagnosic will describe a number of details, but in an unrelated manner. Severe simultanagnosia will render the patient completely object agnosic in that the different aspects of an object cannot be combined to support recognition.

Although the constellation of these three symptoms define Balint's syndrome and indicate bilateral damage to the parietal lobes, any of them may also occur in isolation (De Renzi, 1982). Of these three disorders, only simultanagnosia is in essence an attention disorder (Farah, 2000). Perception as such is intact, but the attention system does not seem to be able to direct perception so that an integrated representation of the outside world can be achieved. In Posner's terms (see Posner, Walker, Friedrich, & Rafal, 1984), the problem in hemispatial neglect is that the patient is unable to disengage his attention in order to move it to the contralesional side. In Balint's syndrome there are bilateral lesions, such that these patients suffer from a bi-directional disengagement deficit. Balint's syndrome, in this view, is a demonstration of the role of selective attention in perception: Without it, the perceptual system wanders aimlessly, unable to integrate separate visual elements.

▲ ATTENTION DEFICITS FOLLOWING HEAD INJURY

Head injuries due to accidents are, unfortunately, very common, with an incidence in the western world of about 100 cases per 100,000 people per year. Men are more often the victims of traumatic head injury than women, and the average age of the victim is about 23 years (NIH Consensus Development Panel, 1999). The young age of the victims means that most of these patients will survive, but many will suffer severe chronic cognitive deficits throughout the remainder of their lives.

Traumatic Brain Injury

An important distinction exists between closed and penetrating head injuries (Grafman & Salazar, 1987). Penetrating head injuries, such as gunshot wounds, are more likely to be survived when the subcortical brain structures are spared. This means that victims of cortical wounds have a much higher rate of survival. Because damage tends to be restricted to particular cortical regions, attentional and other cognitive deficits are common in these patients. The nature of any cognitive deficits will depend crucially on the site and the size of the damaged area. Thus, assessment of these deficits requires across the board evaluation of attentional functioning, comparable to the procedures used in patients with intracerebral hemorrhage.

Closed head injury is said to have occurred when a person suffers a blow to the head and the skull remains intact. Technically, classification requires that there was actual contact between the head and another object (for instance, the dashboard in a car accident). The damage incurred to the brain after a closed head injury is complex and includes both primary and secondary damage. Primary damage includes bruising and laceration of the brain. Because the brain is surrounded by protective layers to dampen the effect of head movements, the brain can, within limits, move around within the skull. When the deceleration of the head is such that the movement can no longer be absorbed, the brain hits the inside of the skull. The bruising of that part of the brain that has been in contact with the often rough inside surface of the skull is called the *coup* effect. The momentum of the brain leads to a subsequent movement in the opposite direction within the skull, culminating in a collision between brain tissue and the skull at the other end. This resulting bruising of the brain is called the *contrecoup* effect. The typical car accident victim who hits the dashboard with his forehead suffers from a coup effect in the frontal lobe and a contrecoup effect in the occipital lobe (see Figure 12.2).

In addition to the linear forces that cause the coup and contrecoup effects, a closed head injury often causes rotational movement of the brain within the skull. These rotational movements may cause laceration in brain tissue. There are some

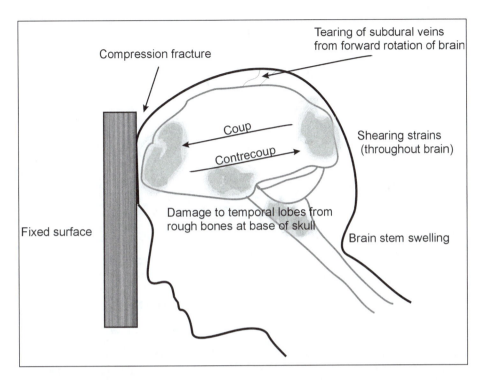

Figure 12.2   Schematic diagram of the so-called coup–contrecoup effect and resulting brain injury in the prefrontal cortex, occipital regions, and temporal lobe.

differences between these two types of primary damage. Bruised areas of the brain tend to be localized, cortical, and visible with modern imaging techniques such as MRI. Lacerations cause widespread, diffuse axonal damage in cortical and subcortical structures and are difficult to detect with brain imaging. The latter point is important because it implies that closed head injury may cause cognitive impairments that are not necessarily expected on the basis of neuroimaging evidence (Kesler, Adams, & Bigler, 2000). Closed head injury may result in secondary damage in the form of lacerated blood vessels, which can lead to intracerebral hemorrhage, or swelling of the brain. This damage can obstruct blood flow in the smaller blood vessels, which may lead to tissue loss, and in severe cases, the swelling may result in an increase in intracranial pressure. Because high intracranial pressure may result in coma and death, it is imperative to monitor patients with a closed head injury closely during the first 24 hours after the accident.

   In nearly all cases of closed head injury, but, per definition, not in whiplash, there is an episode in which the patient loses consciousness. This "coma" is measured in terms of depth and duration. The most common measure of the level of

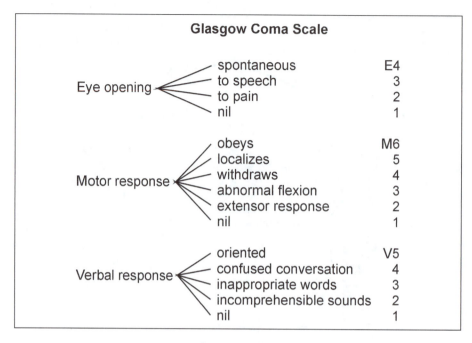

Figure 12.3 The Glasgow Coma Scale. The EMV (eye opening, motor response, and verbal response) score gives an indication of the patient's level of consciousness.

consciousness (or depth of coma) is the Glasgow Coma Scale (Teasdale & Jennett, 1974; see Figure 12.3), which measures the reactivity of a patient using three different responses: eye opening (E), motor (M), and verbal (V). Coma is defined as an E-M-V score of 1-5-2 or less. The second measure, the duration of coma, is scored in hours or days.

The severity of a closed head injury is reflected in the nature and severity of specific memory deficits. As a rule, a closed head injury patient suffers from severe amnesia upon awakening from coma. Encoding of new information is virtually impossible, the patient is often severely disoriented, and confabulation is not uncommon. The duration of this amnesia, known as post-traumatic amnesia (PTA), can be accurately determined because patients often experience a sensation of "waking up" only when they regain the ability to store new information. The depth and duration of coma and the duration of PTA are the most reliable indices of the severity of the closed head injury.

Although the damage incurred after a closed head injury is complex, the pattern of spared and impaired functioning is relatively consistent. First, both patients and their relatives often spontaneously report that the patient suffers attention-related problems. Memory problems and chronic tiredness are also prominent aftereffects of closed head injury. In one study of closed head injury, patients filled in a subjective complaints inventory 12 months after the accident (Van Zomeren & Van den Burg, 1985). The most important complaints concerned mental slowness, difficulties in concentration, and problems in carrying out two tasks simultaneously. Closed head injury patients may demonstrate problems at all levels of attentional functioning and often suffer from reduced levels of arousal and lack of energy. Several studies indicate deficits in divided attention manifested as complaints about difficulties in "doing two things at once." Finally, many clinical investigations have revealed disorders in executive functioning (Levine et al., 2000).

Whiplash

Whiplash may occur when the head is swung forward and backward, resulting in hyperflexion and hyperextension of the neck without direct contact of the head with another object. This type of injury occurs most commonly after rear-end collisions and may lead to a wide range of mild to moderate cognitive complaints, such as loss of concentration, heightened sensitivity to sound or light, forgetfulness, and the inability to perform two tasks at the same time. In most patients, the symptoms rapidly disappear and recovery is complete. However, in a minority of patients the complaints persist after several months or even years; this is referred to as *chronic whiplash syndrome* (Barnsley, Lord, & Bogduk, 1994). One of the hypotheses regarding the etiology of these complaints is that the sudden movement of the head may result in small lesions in the brain or the connecting subcortical white matter, thus affecting information processing. Neuroimaging findings, however, have failed to support this notion (see, e.g., Ronnen et al., 1996). The cognitive impairments can be objectively quantified using neuropsychological assessment. Typically, deficits in divided attention and concentration are found (e.g., as measured with the Paced Auditory Serial Addition Task [PASAT]; Kessels, Keyser, Verhagen, & Van Luijtelaar, 1998), as well as a heightened susceptibility to interference (assessed with the Stroop Color and Word Test). Although mild brain injury cannot be fully excluded, there is growing evidence that other factors, such as pain, fatigue, medication, and depression, also play an important role in the development and persistence of whiplash-associated complaints (Kessels, Aleman, Verhagen, & Van Luijtelaar, 2000).

Measuring Attention Deficits

Both stroke and head trauma (especially closed head injury) can result in a range of attention problems. These different attentional deficits may occur in any constellation, and the severity of the different complaints may vary. Deficits are often much more severe in the acute phase of the illness, becoming less prominent within 3 to 6 months. The more selective deficits following stroke, such as neglect and extinction, are uncommon after closed head injury. In contrast, long-term complaints of difficulty in concentration and susceptibility to distraction are common, which points to the need for a complete diagnostic battery for assessing the basis of the complaints in these patients (Stuss et al., 1999). Formal neuropsychological evaluation of chronic deficits routinely takes place 3 months after head injury. In most cases, these chronic deficits will not improve substantially during the patient's lifetime unless the patent is enrolled in a rehabilitation program.

Neurological patients in general, and closed head injury patients in particular, often complain about a lack of energy, which may be interpreted as an indication that arousal level is reduced relative to before the injury. Two types of arousal, or *cortical tone,* can be distinguished. First, *alertness* refers to a short-lived increase in preparedness to react to a specific stimulus. This can be tested behaviorally with a reaction time apparatus or physiologically using EEG recordings (Gronwall & Sampson, 1974). Second, the overall level of arousal, which fluctuates over days or weeks, can be measured with questionnaires, including questions such as "Do you feel that you have less energy at the end of the day?" Relatively low arousal levels, in turn, affect most cognitive functions. Patients often complain that the execution of a certain task is much more effortful and takes more time than it used to before the accident. It has been hypothesized that the overall level of arousal is related to the construct of *speed of information processing* (Kail & Salthouse, 1994; see Chapter 10). A sensitive task to evaluate speed of information processing is the Digit Symbol subtest of the Wechsler Adult Intelligence Scale (WAIS–III; Wechsler, 1997), in which the test-taker as quickly as possible assigns symbols to letters according to a key provided at the top of the test. Impairments are indicated by a significant increase in the time needed to fill in the correct symbols according to the key.

Poor concentration is a frequently reported problem in neurological patients, and can reflect trouble selectively attending to relevant stimuli while ignoring irrelevant ones. However, evidence for selective attention deficits is not always found. For example, Van Zomeren and Brouwer (1994) found that although chronic closed head injury patients were very slow at naming the colors of colored words in the Stroop task, they were also slow at naming the colors of colored blocks. Thus, rather than indicating a specific deficit in inhibiting an irrelevant dimension and selecting a relevant one, the relatively poor performance of these patients seemed largely to be due to a general reduction in mental processing speed.

Another recurrent complaint concerns difficulties in dual-task performance, which could be indicative of a deficit in divided attention. A well-known clinical test of divided attention is the Paced Auditory Serial Addition Task (PASAT; Gronwall,

1977). The PASAT involves the auditory (recorded on tape) presentation of a series of digits. As each digit is presented, the patient is required to add up the last two numbers and to report the sum. Therefore, the task entails a memory component (remember the last two digits) and an arithmetic component (addition). The test includes five conditions that differ in the speed of presentation of the digits. Closed head injury patients carry out this task in a very slow fashion, but this might largely be due to a general slowing down and not to problems in switching between the component tasks. In order to test this hypothesis, Veltman, Brouwer, Van Zomeren, and Van Wolffelaar (1996) either statistically or experimentally controlled for differences in the speed of information processing with respect to the individual tasks. When differences in speed of information processing were controlled for, patient groups did not show a greater divided-attention deficit than did normal controls. Thus, the problems patients report in performing more than one task at a time may be due to the relative difficulty of the component tasks.

Another aspect of attention often included in neurological test batteries is sustained attention. This is often measured using vigilance tasks such as a continuous performance test (CPT; see Borgaro et al., 2003, for a review) or the Bourdon dot-cancellation test (Van Zomeren & Brouwer, 1994; Vos, 1988). A popular version of the Bourdon test consists of 50 lines with 25 groups of three, four, or five dots each. The groups of four dots are defined as targets and the groups of three and five dots as distractors. Patients are required to mark all the targets, working as quickly and accurately as possible. Closed head injury patients are slow in detecting targets among nontargets, but their performance typically does not deteriorate with time on task, as would be expected if they suffered a specific impairment of sustained attention.

Finally, head injury patients often complain of everyday problems that could be construed as deficits in cognitive control. They complain about problems in planning behavior and about having lost their ability to react in a flexible manner, especially in new situations for which they have not developed well-rehearsed behavioral responses (Levine et al., 2000; Mateer, 1999). Cognitive control can be attributed to the supervisory attentional system (SAS; Shallice, 1988; see Chapter 9) or the central executive (Baddeley, 1998a; see Chapter 7). One commonly used test of executive function is the backward digit span. In this test of short-term memory capacity, lists of single digits are presented auditorily, and the task is to reproduce the sequence in the reverse order. The list length is gradually increased until an error is made in two consecutive lists of the same length. Backward digit span is commonly defined as one less than the number of digits on which the subject fails twice in a row. This test is thought to be sensitive to attention problems because it requires selecting and organizing the digits held in memory before they can be reported.

A widely used clinical test to assess executive function is the Wisconsin Card Sorting Test (Berg, 1948). In this task, patients have to sort a large number of cards that

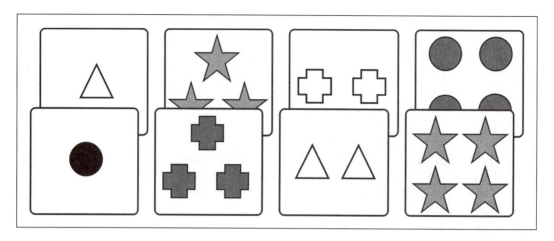

Figure 12.4   The Wisconsin Card Sorting Test. The cards are sorted by the test-taker according to either the color, number, or form of the elements using feedback from the experimenter (a "yes" or "no" as each card is placed) to discover the correct sorting rule.

differ in the shape, color, or number of elements printed on them (see Figure 12.4). The experimenter does not tell the patient what the sorting rule is, but does inform him or her whether each card is sorted correctly or not. Once a patient has discovered the correct sorting rule—for example, color (red on red, green on green, etc.)—the experimenter changes the rule without informing the patient (e.g., to shape). The typical error made by patients with executive disorders is "perseveration"; that is, the same sorting rule continues to be applied even though it no longer leads to correct responses. A more recently developed test along the same lines is the Brixton test (Burgess & Shallice, 1997). This test consists of a series of trials in which the patient is shown a card with two rows of six circles, one of which is filled and the rest of which are open. The task is to predict which of the 12 circles will be filled on the following card. This prediction is to be based on a rule that can be inferred from the preceding trials. The rule changes after every six trials. Both the detection of the fact that the previous rule no longer applies and the development of an alternative strategy require intact executive functioning, and are found to be difficult for patients with damage to frontal regions of the brain.

A final test used to test executive function is the Tower of Hanoi test (see Figure 12.5). The stimulus material consists of a board outfitted with three wooden pegs and a number of rings. The test begins with each of the rings in a certain configuration. Subsequently, a new configuration is shown to the patient, and the task is to change the positions of the rings in as few moves as possible and

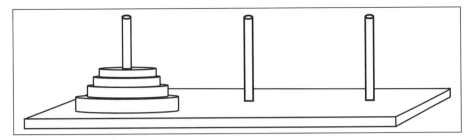

Figure 12.5   The Tower of Hanoi puzzle. The task is to move all of the discs to the right peg, moving only one disc at a time and never placing a larger disc on a smaller one. Alternatively, a patient may be shown a picture of a particular configuration of discs and asked to re-create it.

without violating the constraints that one can move only one ring at a time, and that a larger disk can never be placed on top of a smaller disk. The task requires planning ahead and mental simulation before actually moving the rings. A trial-and-error approach will almost inevitably lead to poor performance. Certain patients with frontal damage and patients who are severely depressed have difficulty carrying out this task.

DEMENTIA ▲

Generally speaking, the term *dementia* refers to an overall deterioration in mental functioning. According to the fourth edition of the *Diagnostic and Statistical Manual of Mental Disorders* (DSM–IV; American Psychiatric Association, 1994), dementia involves the development of multiple cognitive and behavior deficits, including memory impairment, and is frequently accompanied by deficits in visual perception, language, and attention. There are, broadly speaking, two types of dementia, one involving degeneration of cortical tissue and one that mainly affects subcortical regions. Within these categories, a number of different diseases have been identified. With increased life expectancy in the western world, the prevalence of dementia is rising rapidly. About 2 to 4% of the population is thought to suffer from Alzheimer's disease, the most prominent type of dementia.

Cortical Dementias

The main form of cortical dementia is Alzheimer's disease, which is thought to account for 50 to 60% of all cases of dementia (Gurland & Cross, 1986). The preliminary diagnosis of this disease is based on clinical features, such as mental status. Formal diagnosis can be made only on the basis of a postmortem examination. The disease expresses itself in the form of enlarged ventricles, cortical atrophy, and specific brain abnormalities such as senile plaques and tangles. As a result of the widespread, diffuse brain damage, Alzheimer's disease can result in a wide range of cognitive impairments, with memory problems and clumsiness at the forefront. Although the clinical picture may vary in individual patients, the consensus appears to be that the main attention problems in Alzheimer's disease center on a reduction in working memory or executive function. There is no evidence for a major problem in arousal, and these patients perform normally on vigilance tests (Parasuraman & Nestor, 1993). In addition, visuospatial attention impairments, such as neglect and extinction, are uncommon. Patients with dementia are somewhat slower than normal people on both simple and choice reaction time tasks, and show more variability in performance (Van Zomeren & Brouwer, 1994).

Problems of working memory and executive function are central to Alzheimer's disease. Alzheimer's disease patients show high degrees of perseveration on tests such as the Wisconsin card-sorting test and the fluency task. The fluency task is a test in which patients are asked to produce as many categorically or phonologically related items as possible within one minute (Lezak, 1995). The typical patient with a dysexecutive syndrome will often "get stuck" and as a result produce many repetitions. Deficits may also become apparent on selective attention tasks such as the Stroop test, in which Alzheimer's disease patients demonstrate difficulty in inhibiting the dominant response (reading) when naming colors on colored word cards.

A number of cortical degenerative syndromes selectively affect certain areas of the brain. These syndromes, which are much less prevalent than Alzheimer's disease, initially produce relatively specific clinical signs but often progress rapidly into a generalized dementia. For instance, in *Pick's disease,* the frontal lobes are affected first, resulting in higher-order cognitive deficits in planning and attention and dramatic changes in personality and behavior. Pick's disease is characterized by disrupted cognitive control, resulting in poor performance on tasks such as the Stroop, Brixton, and fluency tests. A rare syndrome, *posterior cortical atrophy,* commences with degeneration of the occipital, parietal, and temporal areas. The most prominent features of this syndrome include visual recognition deficits such as agnosia for objects and faces. These patients also often suffer from neglect or visual extinction.

Subcortical Dementias

The most prominent subcortical dementias result from Parkinson's and Huntington's disease. In addition, there is now an increasing group of patients who develop dementia in the context of acquired immune deficiency syndrome (AIDS). AIDS affects (via calcifications) the subcortical areas of the brain.

Parkinson's disease refers more to a class of syndromes than to one particular illness. The primary cause of the disease is degeneration of brain stem nuclei, notably the substantia nigra, but more widespread damage is common in the chronic phase of the disease. The damage to the substantia nigra leads to a depletion of the neurotransmitter dopamine. This means that in addition to subcortical dysfunction, one might expect deficits in other areas of the brain where dopamine is used, such as the frontal lobes. The most characteristic features of Parkinson's disease are motor abnormalities, such as tremor in the hands at rest, a "frozen" face, and difficulties in walking. At the onset of the disease, Parkinson's disease patients normally do not suffer from dementia, but with age the risk of developing cognitive impairments increases. At the age of 85 about 65% of Parkinson's patients suffer from dementia (Gibb & Luthert, 1994). The cognitive deficits include memory (especially motor learning) and selective attention dysfunction. Patients may experience a reduction in arousal that will affect their ability to concentrate for long periods of time, but the main problem appears to be a clear decrease in mental flexibility. Parkinson's disease patients demonstrate perseveration errors on tasks like the Wisconsin card-sorting and fluency tasks, and they find it difficult to shift attention between different aspects of a complex task (Gibb & Luthert, 1994).

Huntington's disease is a hereditary illness that can be diagnosed, before any clinical signs are apparent, on the basis of DNA analysis. The disease causes degeneration of the caudate nucleus, a subcortical structure in the striatum that is also connected to parietal and frontal cortical areas. The main clinical features are involuntary, repetitive movements (chorea) in the face, hands, and legs. Huntington's disease patients suffer, apart from a generalized reduction in mental speed (sometimes referred to as "bradyphrenia"), a number of distinct cognitive impairments. In the realm of memory functioning, they suffer from a selective deficit in the retrieval of information. This is apparent in a severe retrograde memory loss in addition to anterograde amnesia. They may encounter visual-perceptual problems and often show severe changes in personality and emotion. Huntington's disease patients also encounter problems in maintaining their concentration on tests of selective attention and suffer from executive function deficits (Lawrence et al., 1996).

Finally, patients suffering from a series of small infarcts, notably in subcortical areas, will present a dementia usually referred to as multi-infarct dementia. This is the second leading cause of cerebral degeneration, accounting for about 20% of all dementia cases. These patients often suffer from memory problems and may experience a variety of attention deficits depending on the specific areas that have been affected by the strokes. In sum, a whole range of impairments of attention may occur in the different types of dementia. In elderly people it is often difficult to establish whether poor performance on an attentional test is due to neurological damage or to old age, especially in the early stages of dementia. In such circumstances, it is advisable to test the patient a second time 6 months after the first test. The finding of substantial deterioration at the time of retesting strongly suggests that the attentional impairments are due to dementia.

▲ ATTENTION DEFICITS IN PSYCHIATRIC PATIENTS

Psychiatric conditions range from the more modest ailments such as phobias to complex conditions such as bipolar personality disorder. In many, if not all, of these conditions, disturbances of emotion and personality are accompanied by problems in cognitive functioning. Even when these cognitive effects are mild and diffuse, they can have significant repercussions for daily living and recovery. Here we focus on the two most common psychiatric illnesses: schizophrenia and depression.

Schizophrenia

Kraepelin, Barclay, and Robertson (1919) described a pattern of cognitive, emotional, and personality disorders for which they used the term *dementia prae-cox* (early dementia). The clinical signs of this so-called brain disease were auditory hallucinations, delusions, and disorientation in the acute phase, followed by cognitive retardation, flat affect, and social isolation in the chronic phase. Bleuler (1950), who stressed the psychological nature of the disease, introduced the term *schizophrenia* for this disorder. Both Kraepelin and Bleuler commented on the attention deficits in these patients. Today, schizophrenia is one of the most common psychiatric conditions, with the total number of people who at one time suffer from schizophrenia estimated at about 7 per 1,000. In approximately 30% of the cases, the patient recovers and the illness is confined to one psychotic episode.

The exact causes of schizophrenia are still unknown, but the most supported explanation is that a genetic factor, possibly strengthened by environmental factors in utero, disrupts the normal development of certain brain structures (notably the hippocampus, the amygdala, and some frontal lobe areas). The genetic component is apparent in monozygotic twin studies that have shown that the chance that such a twin will become schizophrenic, given that the other twin is schizophrenic, is 50%. The role of development is evident in the findings that events, such as viral infections, during pregnancy are associated with increased risk of developing the disease. The fact that, in the majority of cases, the disease will express itself during puberty in turn suggests a possible role of hormones. A final piece of evidence supporting the hypothesis that some brain areas develop abnormally is that modern neuroimaging studies have identified brain areas that are smaller or less developed in schizophrenics than is normal.

Although the early clinicians who were interested in schizophrenia were acutely aware of the cognitive deficits that accompany the disease, they tended to focus on problems within the realms of emotion and personality. Recent modern neuroimaging work demonstrating structural abnormalities in the brains of schizophrenic patients has, in part, redirected attention to cognitive impairments. It appears that schizophrenia affects most cognitive domains to some degree, but the areas that are impaired the most concern language, memory, attention, and executive functioning (Heinrichs & Zakzanis, 1998). With respect to memory, there is clear evidence for substantial memory deficits, notably affecting the ability to acquire new information. Schizophrenic patients perform poorly on tests for selective (e.g., the Stroop test) and sustained (e.g., the CPT) attention. It is, however, likely that these problems can be partially attributed to slowed mental speed (Van den Bosch, Rombouts, & Van Asma, 1996). Executive deficits have been demonstrated with a number of different tasks, such as the Wisconsin card-sorting task and the Brixton test. A relatively new task that tests for cognitive deficits is based on the work of Baddeley (1966), who observed that normal subjects find it difficult to respond in a random manner. You can easily demonstrate this to yourself by attempting to say the numbers from 1 to 10 in random order. You will probably find yourself actively seeking to avoid a strategy, such as saying first the odd and then the even numbers. In addition to the memory load imposed by the need to keep track of the numbers already said, demands are placed on cognitive control to generate seemingly random strings. The clinical random generation test involves two conditions. The first, *memory control,* condition is the standard digit span test to measure the capacity of short-term memory. Subsequently, the patient is given a range of numbers, say from 3 to 12, and is asked to produce the intervening digits in a random manner as if choosing lots from a hat. Patients find it especially difficult to say the numbers in a random manner and will usually adopt covert strategies to generate the numbers. Detection of such a strategy is easy because the number of possible strategies is limited. Schizophrenic patients, like those with frontal lobe lesions, are poor at formulating new strategies and performance will deteriorate quickly, with some digits repeated and others missed entirely. Even when the capacity of short-term memory is taken into account, their performance is impaired relative to normal controls.

Another attention defect associated with schizophrenia is illustrated with the phenomenon of *latent inhibition* (the inability to use a stimulus dimension in performing a task when that dimension had no relevance in a pretask). For instance, a pretask might consist of detecting the number "3" in a series of single digits in which the letter "e" occasionally occurs at random. When the letter "e" is subsequently correlated with the number "3" (e.g., "e" always occurs before "3" and thus acts as a warning that the 3 is about to appear), latent inhibition may occur such that people cannot make use of the correlation because the previously unimportant stimulus continues to be ignored. Several studies indicate that acute schizophrenics do not show latent inhibition (see, e.g., Rascle et al., 2001; Vaitl et al., 2002). Although there is some controversy regarding the robustness of the absence of this effect in schizophrenic patients, the paradigm has been used extensively by psychopharmacologists because it can be applied to animals as well as humans. Research, mainly on rats, suggests that the reduction of latent inhibition is due to depletion of the dopaminergic and serotonergic systems in the limbic system, notably the hippocampus (J. A. Gray et al., 1991). This latter observation fits with more recent observations using neuroimaging.

In sum, schizophrenia affects cognition and has a detrimental effect on attention. It reduces the speed of information processing; selective and sustained attention tasks are carried out more slowly than normal; and there are problems in higher-order executive functioning. Fortunately, new anti-psychotic drugs seem not only to have few side effects, but also to have a positive effect on cognitive impairments (Aleman & De Haan, 2000).

Depression

Depression, also discussed in Chapter 10, is a mood disorder that is characterized by negative feelings, loss of initiative, and a reduction in enjoyment in activities that would normally be considered pleasant. Depression affects cognition, resulting in, for instance, poor concentration and memory deficits, and disturbs the somatic system, often resulting in sleep deprivation and weight loss. According to the DSM–IV, the diagnosis "depression" requires that a subset of these symptoms be present for some time and affect normal living. Depression is one of the most frequently occurring psychiatric disorders. According to some estimates, as much as 10 to 30% of the population experiences at least one episode of depression. Endogenous depression is the result of a predisposition to depression and usually results in multiple depressive episodes. Depression can also be caused by an external event, such as the loss of a partner, although according to the clinical definition the episode should exceed 2 months in order to be classified as depression. It can also be caused by disease, such as disruption of the hormonal system, cancer, or stroke.

Several brain areas have been associated with depression, most notably the left temporal and the frontal lobes. The most common treatment is the use of medication. In some countries, the use of benzodiazepines (e.g., Valium) is still common. However, partly because benzodiazepines are very addictive, antidepressants such as serotonin uptake inhibitors are increasingly used instead. The disadvantage of these drugs is that it may take weeks before they show any effect. Medication-resistant depression is sometimes treated with electric convulsive (shock) therapy (ECT).

Obviously, this method, which basically triggers an epileptic fit, is rather crude, but it has proven to be effective. The fact that some patients request ECT treatment has led to a resurgence of the treatment after it had almost been abolished in the 1960s. A recent development is the use of transcranial magnetic stimulation (TMS) as a more humane form of ECT. In this technique (see Chapter 2), the application of a strong magnetic field over the scalp induces a localized current in the brain. There is some evidence that stimulation over the left dorsolateral frontal region relieves depression (Berman et al., 2000), although the effects have been, up until now, rather modest.

The cognitive declines observed in depression patients appear to be rather generalized. Studies comparing healthy people and depressed patients on a battery of neuropsychological tests often demonstrate subtle but significant reductions in performance in the majority of cognitive domains that have been evaluated. The most notable problems are found in language (e.g., word-finding difficulties), motor behavior (e.g., increased motor times on reaction time tasks), memory, and attention. Given the diffuse nature of the cognitive decline, it is perhaps not surprising that attention deficits are observed on tasks for selective and sustained attention. Attention span (digit span) and divided attention tend to be unimpaired, but there is some evidence suggesting that depressed patients have difficulty on problem-solving tasks, such as the Tower of Hanoi test.

Cognitive disturbances in depression are, to a degree, reversible, in contrast to those of some of the other patient groups that have been discussed in this chapter. That is, when a patient improves as a result of treatment, the performance on cognitive tasks also improves.

TREATMENT OF ATTENTION DEFICITS ▲

In recent decades, researchers have turned from merely documenting cognitive deficits to developing techniques to ameliorate their symptoms. In rehabilitation research, a distinction is made between impairments, disabilities, and handicaps (World Health Organization, 1980). *Impairments* are related to limitations in functions (comparable to organ defects in physical medicine); for example, a patient suffering from the long-term effects of closed head injury may have an impairment of attention. *Disabilities* refer to limitations in specific behaviors or skills such as reading the daily newspaper or participating in a conversation. Whereas impairments refer to cognitive functions, disabilities involve a particular context or task. A *handicap* reflects limitations the patient may experience as a result of a given disability. For example, a patient who cannot read the newspaper or engage in a conversation due to impaired attention may be handicapped in his or her social functioning. He or she might stop socializing or become partially dependent on the help of others. This distinction has proven to be useful in classifying treatment programs and in setting the goals of a specific treatment method. Generally, treatment programs are designed to improve performance of daily tasks and, as such, may focus on the development of compensatory strategies rather than the elimination of impairments.

Originally, the focus of research on the treatment of attentional dysfunction was at the level of impairments. It was thought that extensive training of cognitive tasks (e.g., tasks requiring attention) could help the patients to overcome their impairments. For example, patients suffering from mental slowing after closed head injury were trained over long periods of time on various reaction time tasks (see, e.g., Ponsford & Kinsella, 1988). Although such training procedures did tend to result in improvements in performance on the trained task, the treatment effects failed to generalize to other tasks, and therefore failed to have an impact on patients' everyday-life activities (i.e., their disability was not lessened). Although the efficacy of cognitive treatment procedures in which the brain is regarded as a "muscle" that must be trained is limited, such techniques are still prominent in various rehabilitation programs. Unfortunately, most evidence suggests that any observed improvement in impairment or disability in trained patients does not result directly from the treatment, but is due to spontaneous recovery or aspecific factors such as receiving attention from therapists or increases in motivation to actively cope with one's impairments (Robertson, 1999). Moreover, the high cost of the often lengthy programs (which may take weeks, months, or even years) limit the benefits of this approach.

Although results with aspecific cognitive training have been discouraging, somewhat more encouraging results have been found with training directed specifically at increasing alertness (e.g., using a warning stimulus to prepare a patient to respond to an imperative stimulus). For example, Sturm, Willmes, Orgass, and Hartje (1997) developed a test battery to train alertness (using an animated driving task with obstacle avoidance), vigilance (monitoring of a "radar" screen for changes), selective attention (choice reaction task embedded in a "safari" or "trap shooting" context), and divided attention (a flight simulator task in which three displays had to be monitored). Studies using this test battery showed that training was effective only when specifically matched to the individual's deficits. Such studies led Leclercq and Sturm (2002, p. 357) to conclude "(a) that it is very important to start an attention therapy with comprehensive diagnosis to work out the specific attention deficits the patient suffers from, and (b) that specific deficits have to be treated specifically."

Several promising treatments have been developed for neglect patients. For example, Robertson, North, and Geggie (2002) tested the efficacy of a "neglect alert device" to help neglect patients become more aware of the side of the neglect. This device consists of a hand-held button that must be pressed at regular intervals to keep it from emitting a beep. Carrying such a device for a period of time was shown to result in an improvement in the symptoms of neglect. Of course, it can only be used by patients who have near-normal motor function on the side of the neglect. An impairment-based treatment for neglect was developed by Pizzamiglio and colleagues (1998), who used optokinetic stimulation to train patients to more thoroughly scan the impaired visual field. In this procedure, the patient is seated in front of a large projection screen displaying visual stimuli with a background that moves slowly towards the direction of the impaired hemifield (in most cases the left visual field). Although early results were promising, the initial benefits did not generalize to real-life situations. Apparently, the positive effects of optokinetic stimulation in neglect are due to the development of compensatory strategies rather than a reduction of the actual impairment itself (Robertson & Heutink, 2002), and these compensatory strategies are observable only in a highly controlled laboratory setting.

Much research in neglect treatment is now focusing on the use of *prism adaptation*. This method requires subjects to wear glasses that contain prisms, causing an optical shift to the right of 10 degrees. Generally, subjects rapidly adapt to wearing these distorting glasses, and show an aftereffect of adaptation in which the world still seems to be shifted to the right. Neglect patients also show this effect, and, impressively, this adaptation effect results in a reduction of the symptoms of neglect that extends beyond the normal duration of adaptation (see Figure 12.6). Neglect patients have been shown to perform better on standard neuropsychological tests after adaptation (Rossetti et al., 1998), and show better performance on behavioral tasks such as removing sticky pieces of paper from their clothes or reaching toward common objects in a room (Frassinetti et al., 2002). Also, the effects have been found to alleviate a variety of symptoms of neglect, such as impaired imagery and motor performance, and inattention to personal features. However, not all aspects of neglect benefit from prism adaptation. For example, prism adaptation has been found not to have an effect on the reduced size matching (i.e., impaired estimation of the sizes of lines or objects) that is commonly found in neglect patients (Dijkerman, et al., in press). The mechanism of the improvement is not yet understood, but the beneficial effects of prism adaptation are most likely related to alterations in spatial or perceptual representations.

In the treatment of executive disorders, which are fairly common in patients with frontal-lobe injury, a disability-focused approach is often applied. Treatment procedures predominantly rely on techniques from behavioral therapy and are often less theory-driven than the previously addressed more "formal" attention treatments (Worthington, 2002). A main focus in rehabilitation of central executive function is on the restoration of self-regulatory control and the use of external cues to help patients learn to initiate, plan, and organize their behavior (Mateer, 1999), as well as to overcome problems in disinhibition and concept-shifting (i.e., the ability to change from one mental set to another in tasks such as the Wisconsin

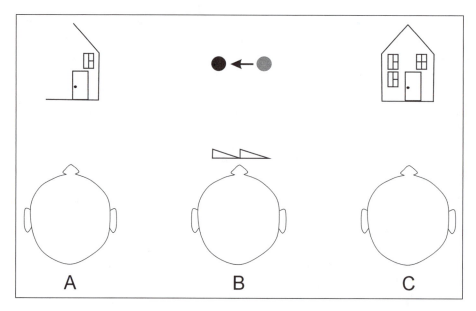

Figure 12.6   Schematic view of the effects of prism adaptation in neglect. Before adaptation, the patient shows inattention for stimuli in the left visual field (A). During adaptation, the patient wears glasses containing a prism that shifts the visual field 10° to the right (B); the location of the gray dot is visually transposed to the position indicated by the black dot. After removing the glasses, this adaptation results in a long-lasting reduction of the neglect-related symptoms (C).

card-sorting task). An example of a disability-oriented therapy for dysexecutive syndrome is *goal management training* (Robertson, 1996) to improve the self-regulation of goal-directed behavior. Basically, this therapy consists of teaching patients to use a top-down, structured protocol to keep them "on task." The protocol involves a series of five stages dealing with setting goals and determining if the proper steps have been taken to achieve these goals. Goal management training has been shown to improve performance on paper-and-pencil laboratory tasks, as well as in real-life situations, such as meal preparation (Levine et al., 2000).

In summary, it should be noted that recovery following treatment of attentional disorders may only be apparent. For example, a neglect patient may still have problems in attending to one side, but these may be masked by behavioral compensation. This becomes evident when some apparently recovered patients perform difficult tasks (such as pointing to the midpoint between two objects) or are simultaneously required to perform an attention-demanding task (Manley, 2002). In these cases, the attentional deficit can reappear. It has been suggested that difficulties in mobilizing attentional resources may contribute to the incidence of persistent problems (i.e., the lack of development of compensation) in those patients who never show recovery.

SUMMARY ▲

Whereas the rest of the book has concentrated on "normal" attention in typical healthy people, this chapter focused on disorders of attention. Attentional disorders may be developmental or may be the result of injury or illness. This chapter illustrates how the tasks, methods, and theories of the experimental study of attention have been applied to the study of disorders of attention. Several standard paradigms in experimental psychology, such as the Stroop task and reaction time tasks, have made their way into the toolkit of the clinical neuropsychologist, helping to delineate the precise nature of the different patterns of deficit. However, as this and earlier chapters emphasized, studying attentional disorders can also shed light on the nature of attention itself.

In recent years, many different training programs for the alleviation of attention deficits have been developed. In general, cognitive training programs aimed at improving impaired attentional functions have had limited effectiveness. More promising are impairment- and disability-oriented techniques such as the use of prism adaptation in neglect and goal management training for executive disorders. Although the basic processes of attention may seem quite simple, attention is a complex construct. There is much to be gained by studying patients in more detail to determine how the different processes of attention interact or are separately affected by disease or injury.

NOTE ▲

1. North American and European standards for diagnosis of ADHD differ. In both cases, diagnosis depends on the number of symptoms within the categories "inattention," and "hyperactivity/impulsivity."

REFERENCES

Abrams, R. A., & Dobkin, R. S. (1994). Inhibition of return: Effects of attentional cuing on eye movement latencies. *Journal of Experimental Psychology: Human Perception and Performance, 20*, 467–477.

Ackerman, P. L. (1988). Determinants of individual differences during skill acquisition: Cognitive abilities and information processing. *Journal of Experimental Psychology: General, 117*, 288–318.

Alderton, D. L., Wolfe, J. H., & Larson, G. E. (1997). The ECAT battery. *Military Psychology, 9*, 5–37.

Aleman, A., & De Haan, E. H. F. (2000). Antipsychotics and working memory in schizophrenia. *Science, 289*, 56–58.

Alho, K., Woods, D. L., & Algazi, A. (1994). Processing of auditory stimuli during auditory and visual attention as revealed by event-related potentials. *Psychophysiology, 31*, 469–479.

Allport, A. (1987). Selection for action: Some behavioral and neurophysiological considerations of attention and action. In H. Heuer & A. F. Sanders (Eds.), *Perspectives on perception and action* (pp. 395–419). Hillsdale, NJ: Erlbaum.

Allport, A., & Styles, E. A. (1990). Multiple executive functions, multiple resources? Experiments in shifting attentional control of tasks. Unpublished manuscript, Oxford University. (See E. A. Styles, *The psychology of attention.* Hove, UK: Psychology Press.)

Allport, A., Styles, E. A., & Hsieh, S. (1994). Shifting intentional set: Exploring the dynamic control of tasks. In C. Umiltà & M. Moscovitch (Eds.), *Conscious and nonconscious information processing: Attention and performance XV* (pp. 421–452). Cambridge, MA: MIT Press.

Allport, A., & Wylie, G. (2000). Task switching, stimulus-response bindings, and negative priming. In S. Monsell & J. Driver (Eds.), *Control of cognitive processes: Attention and performance XVIII* (pp. 35–70). Cambridge, MA: MIT Press.

Allport, D. A., Antonis, B., & Reynolds, P. (1972). On the division of attention: A disproof of the single channel hypothesis. *Quarterly Journal of Experimental Psychology, 24*, 225–235.

American Psychiatric Association. (1980). *Diagnostic and statistical manual of mental disorders* (3rd ed.). Washington, DC: Author.

American Psychiatric Association. (1994). *Diagnostic and statistical manual of mental disorders* (4th ed.). Washington, DC: Author.

Anderson, J. R. (1993). *Rules of the mind.* Hillsdale, NJ: Erlbaum.

Anderson, J. R., & Lebiere, C. (1998). *The atomic components of thought.* Mahwah, NJ: Erlbaum.

Anderson, K. J., & Revelle, W. (1982). Impulsivity, caffeine, and proofreading: A test of the Easterbrook hypothesis. *Journal of Experimental Psychology: Human Perception and Performance, 8,* 614–624.

Andre, A. D., & Wickens, C. D. (1990). Display-control compatibility in the cockpit: Guidelines for display layout analysis. *Technical Report: NASA Ames Research Center.* Moffett Field, CA.

Arbuthnott, K., & Frank, J. (2000). Executive control in set switching: Residual switch cost and task-set inhibition. *Canadian Journal of Experimental Psychology, 54,* 33–41.

Atienza, M., Cantero, J. L., & Gomez, C. M. (2000). Decay time of the auditory sensory memory trace during wakefulness and REM sleep. *Psychophysiology, 37,* 485–493.

Atkinson, R. C., & Shiffrin, R. M. (1968). Human memory: A proposed system and its control processes. In K. W. Spence (Ed.), *The psychology of learning and motivation: Advances in research and theory* (Vol. 2, pp. 89–195). New York: Academic Press.

Avolio, B., Kroeck, K., & Panek, P. (1985). Individual differences in information processing ability as a predictor of motor vehicle accidents. *Human Factors, 27,* 577–587.

Awh, E., Annlo-Vento, L., & Hillyard, S. A. (2000). The role of spatial selective attention in working memory for locations: Evidence from event-related potentials. *Journal of Cognitive Neuroscience, 12,* 840–847.

Awh, E., & Jonides, J. (1998). Spatial working memory and spatial selective attention. In R. Parasuraman (Ed.), *The attentive brain* (pp. 353–380). Cambridge, MA: MIT Press.

Awh, E., Jonides, J., & Reuter-Lorenz, P. A. (1998). Rehearsal in spatial working memory. *Journal of Experimental Psychology: Human Perception and Performance, 24,* 780–790.

Awh, E., Smith, E. E., & Jonides, J. (1995). Human rehearsal processes and the frontal lobes: PET evidence. In J. Grafman, K. Holyoak, & F. Boller (Eds.), *Structure and function of the prefrontal cortex* (pp. 97–119). New York: New York Academy of Sciences.

Baddeley, A. (1986). *Working memory.* New York: Oxford University Press.

Baddeley, A. (1998a). *Human memory: Theory and practice.* Boston: Allyn & Bacon.

Baddeley, A. (1998b). Recent developments in working memory. *Current Opinion in Neurobiology, 8,* 234–238.

Baddeley, A. D. (1966). The capacity of generating information by randomization. *Quarterly Journal of Experimental Psychology, 18,* 119–129.

Baddeley, A. D. (1996). Exploring the central executive. *Quarterly Journal of Experimental Psychology, 49A,* 5–28.

Baddeley, A. D., & Hitch, G. (1974). Working memory. In G. A. Bower (Ed.), *Recent advances in learning and motivation* (Vol. 8, pp. 46–89). New York: Academic Press.

Balakrishnan, J. D. (1998). Measures and interpretations of vigilance performance: Evidence against the detection criterion. *Human Factors, 40,* 601–623.

Balakrishnan, J. D. (1999). Decision processes in discrimination: Fundamental misrepresentations of signal detection theory. *Journal of Experimental Psychology: Human Perception and Performance, 25,* 1189–1206.

Balint, R. (1909). Seelenlähmung des "Schauens", optische Ataxie, räumliche Störung der Aufmerksamkeit. *Monatschrift für Psychiatrie und Neurologie, 25,* 51–81.

Ballard, J. C. (1996). Computerized assessment of sustained vigilance: A review of factors affecting vigilance performance. *Journal of Clinical and Experimental Neuropsychology, 18,* 843–863.

Banks, W. P., & Prinzmetal, W. (1976). Configurational effects in visual information processing. *Perception & Psychophysics, 19,* 361–367.

Banks, W. P., Roberts, D., & Ciranni, M. (1995). Negative priming in auditory attention. *Journal of Experimental Psychology: Human Perception and Performance, 21,* 1354–1361.

Barkley, R. A. (1990). *Attention deficit hyperactivity disorder: A handbook for diagnosis and treatment.* New York: Guilford Press.

Barkley, R. A. (1991). The ecological validity of laboratory and analogue assessment methods of ADHD symptoms. *Journal of Abnormal Child Psychology, 19,* 149–178.

Barkley, R. A. (1997). Attention-deficit/hyperactivity disorder. In E. J. Mash & L. G. Terdal (Eds.), *Assessment of childhood disorders* (3rd ed., pp. 71–129). New York: Guilford Press.

Barnsley, L., Lord, S., & Bogduk, N. (1994). Whiplash injury. *Pain, 58,* 283–307.

Bartz, W. H., Satz, P., & Fennell, E. (1967). Grouping strategies in dichotic listening: The effects of instructions, rate, and ear asymmetry. *Journal of Experimental Psychology, 74,* 132–136.

Baylis, G. C., & Driver, J. (1992). Visual parsing and response competition: The effect of grouping factors. *Perception & Psychophysics, 51,* 145–162.

Beatty, J. (1982). Phasic not tonic pupillary responses vary with auditory vigilance performance. *Psychophysiology, 19,* 167–172.

Beck, A. T. (1967). *Depression: Clinical, experimental, and theoretical aspects.* New York: Harper & Row.

Beck, A. T. (1976). *Cognitive therapy and the emotional disorders.* New York: International Universities Press.

Beilock, S. L., Carr, T. H., MacMahon, C., & Starkes, J. L. (2002). When paying attention becomes counterproductive: Impact of divided versus skill-focused attention on novice and experienced performance of sensorimotor skills. *Journal of Experimental Psychology: Applied, 8,* 6–16.

Bennett, K. B., & Flach, J. M. (1992). Graphical displays: Implications for divided attention, focused attention, and problem-solving. *Human Factors, 34,* 513–534.

Bennett, P. J., & Pratt, J. (2001). The spatial distribution of inhibition of return. *Psychological Science, 12,* 76–80.

Ben-Shakhar, G., & Sheffer, L. (2001). The relationship between the ability to divide attention and standard measures of general cognitive abilities. *Intelligence, 29,* 293–306.

Berg, E. A. (1948). A simple objective treatment for measuring flexibility in thinking. *Journal of General Psychology, 39,* 15–22.

Berlyne, D. E. (1974). Attention. In E. C. Carterette & M. P. Friedman (Eds.), *Handbook of perception (Vol. I: Historical and philosophical roots of perception*; pp. 123–147). New York: Academic Press.

Berman, R. M., Narasimhan, M., Sanacora, G., Miano, A. P., Hoffman, R. E., Hu, X. S., Charney, D. S., & Boutros, N. N. (2000). A randomized clinical trial of repetitive transcranial magnetic stimulation in the treatment of major depression. *Biological Psychiatry, 47,* 332–337.

Bertelson, P. (1967). The refractory period of choice reactions with regular and irregular interstimuli intervals. *Acta Psychologica, 27,* 45–56.

Bertelson, P., & Aschersleben, G. (1998). Automatic visual bias of perceived auditory location. *Psychonomic Bulletin & Review, 5,* 482–489.

Berti, A., & Rizzolatti, G. (1992). Visual processing without awareness: Evidence from unilateral neglect. *Journal of Cognitive Neuroscience, 4*, 345–351.

Besner, D., Stolz, J. A., & Boutilier, C. (1997). The Stroop effect and the myth of automaticity. *Psychonomic Bulletin & Review, 4*, 221–225.

Binet, A. (1890). La concurrence des états psychologiques. *Revue philosophique de la France et de l'étranger, 24*, 138–155.

Bishop, D. V. M. (1992). The underlying nature of specific language impairment. *Journal of Child Psychology and Psychiatry, 33*, 3–66.

Bisiach, E., & Luzzatti, C. (1978). Unilateral neglect of representational space. *Cortex, 14*, 129–133.

Bisley, J. W., & Goldberg, M. E. (2003). Neuronal activity in the lateral intraparietal area and spatial attention. *Science, 299*, 81–86.

Blattner, M., Sumikawa, D., & Greenberg, R. (1989). Earcons and icons: Their structure and common design principles. *Human-Computer Interaction, 4*, 11–44.

Bleuler, E. (1950). *Dementia praecox or the group of schizophrenias*. New York: International University Press.

Blumenthal, A. L. (1975). A reappraisal of Wilhelm Wundt. *American Psychologist, 30*, 1081–1088.

Blumenthal, A. L. (1980). Wilhelm Wundt and early American psychology. In R. W. Rieber (Ed.), *Wilhelm Wundt and the making of scientific psychology* (pp. 117–135). New York: Plenum.

Blumethal, A. L. (2001). A Wundt primer: The operating characteristics of consciousness. In R. W. Rieber & D. K. Robinson (Eds.), *Wilhlem Wundt in history: The making of scientific psychology* (pp. 121–144). New York: Kluwer/Plenum.

Bogaro, S., Pogge, D. L., DeLuca, V. A., Bilginer, L., Stokes, J., & Harvey, P. D. (2002). Convergence of different versions of the continuous performance text: Clinical and scientific implications. *Journal of Clinical and Experimental Neuropsychology, 25*, 283–292.

Bors, D. A., Stokes, T. L., Forrin, B., & Hodder, S. L. (1999). Inspection time and intelligence: Practice, strategies, and attention. *Intelligence, 27*, 111–129.

Botella, J. (1996). Decision competition and response competition: Two main factors in the flanker compatibility effect. In A. F. Kramer, M. G. H. Coles, & G. D. Logan (Eds.), *Converging operations in the study of visual selective attention* (pp. 503–518). Washington, DC: American Psychological Association.

Bower, G. H. (1981). Mood and memory. *American Psychologist, 36*, 129–148.

Bradley, B. P., & Mathews, A. (1988). Memory bias in recovered clinical depressives. *Cognition and Emotion, 2*, 235–245.

Braun, J. (1994). Visual search among items of different salience: Removal of visual attention mimics a lesion in extrastriate area V4. *Journal of Neuroscience, 14*, 554–567.

Brefczynski, J. A., & DeYoe, E. A. (1999). A physiological correlate of the 'spotlight' of visual attention. *Nature Neuroscience, 2*, 370–374.

Bregman, A. S. (1990). *Auditory scene analysis: The perceptual organization of sound*. Cambridge, MA: MIT Press.

Breitmeyer, B., Ehrenstein, A., Pritchard, K., Hiscock, M., & Crisan, J. (1999). The roles of location specificity and masking mechanisms in the attentional blink. *Perception & Psychophysics, 61*, 798–809.

Brewster, S. (2003). Nonspeech auditory output. In J. A. Jacko & A. Sears (Eds.), *The human-computer interaction handbook: Fundamentals, evolving technologies, and emerging applications* (pp. 220–239). Mahwah, NJ: Lawrence Erlbaum.

Brickner, M., & Gopher, D. (1981). *Improving time-sharing performance by enhancing voluntary control on processing resources.* Technical report AFOSR-77-3131C. Haifa, Israel: Technion—Israel Institute of Technology.

Brickner, M. S. (1989). Apparent limitations of head-up displays and thermal imaging systems. In R. S. Jensen (Ed.), *Proceedings of the Fifth International Symposium on Aviation Psychology* (pp. 703–707). Columbus, OH: Ohio State University.

Broadbent, D. E. (1954). The role of auditory localization in attention and memory span. *Journal of Experimental Psychology, 47,* 191–196.

Broadbent, D. E. (1956). Successive responses to simultaneous stimuli. *Quarterly Journal of Experimental Psychology, 8,* 142–152.

Broadbent, D. E. (1958). *Perception and communication.* London: Pergamon Press.

Broadbent, D. E. (1971). *Decision and stress.* Oxford, UK: Academic Press.

Broadbent, D. E. (1982). Failures of attention in selective listening. *Journal of Experimental Psychology, 44,* 428–433.

Broadbent, D. E., & Broadbent, M. H. (1987). From detection to identification: Response to multiple targets in rapid serial visual presentation. *Perception & Psychophysics, 42,* 105–113.

Broadbent, D. E., Cooper, P. F., FitzGerald, P., & Parkes, K. R. (1982). The Cognitive Failures Questionnaire (CFQ) and its correlates. *British Journal of Clinical Psychology, 21,* 1–16.

Brodmann, K. (1909). *Vergleichende Lokalisationlehre der Grosshirnrinde in ihren Prinzipien dargestellt auf Grund des Zellenbaues.* Leipzig: Barth.

Brouwer, W. H., Withaar, F. K., Tant, M. L. M., & Van Zomeren, A. H. (2002). Attention and driving in traumatic brain injury: A question of coping with time-pressure. *Journal of Head Trauma Rehabilitation, 17,* 1–15.

Brown, G. G., Baird, A. D., Shatz, M. W., & Bornstein, R. A. (1996). The effects of cerebral vascular disease on neuropsychological functioning. In I. Grant & K. M. Adams (Eds.), *Neuropsychological assessment of neuropsychiatric disorders* (2nd ed., pp. 342–378). New York: Oxford University Press.

Brown, I. D., Tickner, A. H., & Simmonds, D. C. (1969). Interference between concurrent tasks of driving and telephoning. *Journal of Applied Psychology, 53,* 419–424.

Büchel, C., & Friston, K. J. (1997). Modulation of connectivity in visual pathways by attention: Cortical interactions evaluated with structural equation modeling and fMRI. *Cerebral Cortex, 7,* 768–778.

Buchtel, H. A., & Butter, C. M. (1988). Spatial attentional shifts: Implications for the role of polysensory mechanisms. *Neuropsychologica, 26,* 499–509.

Buckner, R. L., & Logan, J. M. (2001). Functional neuroimaging methods: PET and fMRI. In R. Cabeza & A. Kingstone (Eds.), *Handbook of functional neuroimaging of cognition* (pp. 27–48). Cambridge, MA: MIT Press.

Bundesen, C. (1990). A theory of visual attention. *Psychological Review, 97,* 523–547.

Bundesen, C., Pedersen, L. F., & Larsen, A. (1984). Measuring efficiency of selection from briefly exposed visual displays: A model for partial report. *Journal of Experimental Psychology: Human Perception and Performance, 10,* 329–339.

Burgess, P. W. (2000). Real-world multitasking from a cognitive neuroscience perspective. In S. Monsell & J. Driver (Eds.), *Control of cognitive processes: Attention and performance XVIII* (pp. 465–472). Cambridge, MA: MIT Press.

Burgess, P. W., Alderman, N., Evans, J., Emslie, H., & Wilson, B. A. (1998). The ecological validity of tests of executive function. *Journal of the International Neuropsychological Society, 4*, 547–558.

Burgess, P. W., & Shallice, T. (1997). *The Hayling and Brixton Tests*. Suffolk, UK: Thames Test Valley.

Bushnell, M. C., Duncan, G. H., Dubner, R., Jones, R. L., & Maixner, W. (1985). Attentional influences on noxious and innocuous cutaneous heat detection in humans and monkeys. *Journal of Neuroscience, 5*, 1103–1110.

Butcher, P. R., Kalverboer, A. F., & Geuze, R. H. (1999). Inhibition of return in very young infants: A longitudinal study. *Infant Behavior & Development, 22*, 303–319.

Butler, B. E., & Currie, A. (1986). On the nature of perceptual limits in vision: A new look at lateral masking. *Psychological Research, 48*, 201–209.

Cabeza, R., Dolcos, F., Prince, S. E., Rice, H. J., Weissman, D. H., & Nyberg, L. (2003). Attention-related activity during episodic memory retrieval: A cross-function fMRI study. *Neuropsychologia, 41*, 390–399.

Cantagallo, A., & Della Sala, S. (1998). Preserved insight in an artist with extrapersonal spatial neglect. *Cortex, 34*, 163–189.

Card, S. K. (1982). User perceptual mechanisms in the search of computer command menus. *Proceedings of human factors in computer systems* (pp. 190–196). Gaitherburg, MD: SIGCHI.

Carlson, R. A. (1997). *Experienced cognition*. Mahwah, NJ: Erlbaum.

Carlson, R. A., & Sohn, M.-H. (2000). Cognitive control of multistep routines: Information processing and conscious intentions. In S. Monsell & J. Driver (Eds.), *Control of cognitive processes: Attention and performance XVIII* (pp. 443–464). Cambridge, MA: MIT Press.

Carlson, R. A., Sullivan, M. A., & Schneider, W. (1989). Practice and working memory effects in building procedural skill. *Journal of Experimental Psychology: Learning, Memory, and Cognition, 15*, 517–526.

Carpenter, W. B. (1852). On the influence of suggestion in modifying and directing muscular movement, independently of volition. *Proceedings of the Royal Institution of Great Britain, 1,* 147–153.

Carrier, L. M., & Pashler, H. (1995). Attentional limits in memory retrieval. *Journal of Experimental Psychology: Learning, Memory, and Cognition, 21*, 1339–1348.

Carter, R. C., & Cahill, M. C. (1979). Regression models of search time for color-coded information displays. *Human Factors, 21*, 293–302.

Casey, S. (1993). *"Set phasers on stun" and other true tales of design, technology, and human error*. Santa Barbara, CA: Aegean.

Castiello, U., & Umiltà, C. (1990). Size of the attentional focus and efficiency of processing. *Acta Psychologica, 73,* 195–209.

Cave, K. R., & Pashler, H. (1995). Visual selection mediated by location: Selecting successive visual objects. *Perception & Psychophysics, 57,* 421–432.

Cepeda, N. J., Cave, K. R., Bichot, N. P., & Kim, M.-S. (1998). Spatial selection via feature-driven inhibition of distractor locations. *Perception & Psychophysics, 60,* 727–746.

Chandler, P., & Sweller, J. (1996). Cognitive load while learning to use a computer program. *Applied Cognitive Psychology, 10,* 151–170.

Chao, L. L., & Knight, R. T. (1997). Prefrontal deficits in attention and inhibitory control with aging. *Cerebral Cortex, 7,* 63–69.

Chao, L. L., & Knight, R. T. (1998). Contribution of human prefrontal cortex to delay performance. *Journal of Cognitive Neuroscience, 10,* 167–177.

Chapanis, A., & Lindenbaum, L. E. (1959). A reaction time study of four control-display linkages. *Human Factors, 1,* 1–7.

Cheal, M., & Lyon, D. R. (1991). Central and peripheral precuing of forced-choice discrimination. *The Quarterly Journal of Experimental Psychology, 43A,* 859–880.

Chen, Y., & Blanchard-Fields, F. (2000). Unwanted thought: Age differences in the correction of social judgments. *Psychology and Aging, 15,* 475–482.

Cherry, E. C. (1953). Some experiments on the recognition of speech, with one and with two ears. *Journal of the Acoustical Society of America, 25,* 975–979.

Chervin, R. D., Archbold, K. H., Dillon, J. E., Panahi, P., Pituch, K. J., Dahl, R. E., & Guilleminault, C. (2002). Inattention, hyperactivity, and symptoms of sleep-disordered breathing. *Pediatrics, 109,* 449–456.

Chun, M. M., & Potter, M. C. (1995). A two-stage model for multiple target detection in rapid serial visual presentation. *Journal of Experimental Psychology: Human Perception and Performance, 21,* 109–127.

Clark, D. M., & Teasdale, J. D. (1982). Diurnal variation in clinical depression and accessibility of memories of positive and negative experiences. *Journal of Abnormal Psychology, 91,* 87–95.

Clark, V. P., & Hillyard, S. A. (1996). Spatial selective attention affects early extrastriate but not striate components of the visual evoked potential. *Journal of Cognitive Neuroscience, 8,* 387–402 .

Cohen, A., & Ivry, R. (1989). Illusory conjunctions inside and outside the focus of attention. *Journal of Experimental Psychology: Human Perception and Performance, 15,* 650–663.

Cohen, A., Ivry, R. I., & Keele, S. W. (1990). Attention and structure in sequence learning. *Journal of Experimental Psychology: Learning, Memory, and Cognition, 16,* 17–30.

Cohen, A., Ivry, R., Rafal, R., & Kohn, C. (1995). Response code activation by stimuli in the neglected visual field. *Neuropsychology, 9,* 165–173.

Cohen, J. D., Dunbar, K., & McClelland, J. L. (1990). On the control of automatic processes: A parallel distributed processing account of the Stroop effect. *Psychological Review, 97,* 332–361.

Cohen, J. D., & Servan-Schreiber, D. (1992). Context, cortex, and dopamine: A connectionist approach to behavior and biology in schizophrenia. *Psychological Review, 99,* 45–77.

Colle, H. A., & Reid, G. B. (1998). Context effects in subjective mental workload ratings. *Human Factors, 40,* 591–600.

Colavita, F. B. (1974). Human sensory dominance. *Perception & Psychophysics, 16,* 409–412.

Coltheart, M. (1983). Ecological necessity of iconic memory. *The Behavioral and Brain Sciences, 6,* 17–18.

Compton, B. J., & Logan, G. D. (1993). Evaluating a computational model of perceptual grouping by proximity. *Perception & Psychophysics, 53,* 403–421.

Connelly, S. L., & Hasher, L. (1993). Aging and the inhibition of spatial location. *Journal of Experimental Psychology: Human Perception and Performance, 19*, 1238–1250.

Connelly, S. L., Hasher, L., & Kimble, G. A. (1992, November) *The suppression of identity and spatial location*. Paper presented at the 33rd annual meeting of the Psychonomic Society, St. Louis, MO.

Conrad, R., & Hull, A. J. (1964). Information, acoustic confusion and memory span. *British Journal of Psychology, 55,* 429–432.

Conway, A. R. A., Cowan, N., & Bunting, M. F. (2001). The cocktail party phenomenon revisited: The importance of working memory capacity. *Psychonomic Bulletin & Review, 8,* 331–335.

Conway, A. R. A., Tuholski, S. W., Shisler, R. J., & Engle, R. W. (1999). The effect of memory load on negative priming: An individual differences investigation. *Memory & Cognition, 27*, 1042–1050.

Corbetta, M. (1998). Functional anatomy of visual attention in the human brain: Studies with positron emission tomography. In R. Parasuraman (Ed.), *The attentive brain* (pp. 95–122). Cambridge, MA: MIT Press.

Corteen, R. S., & Wood, B. (1972). Autonomic responses to shock-associated words in an unattended channel. *Journal of Experimental Psychology, 94,* 308–313.

Cowan, N. (1984). On short and long auditory stores. *Psychological Bulletin, 96,* 341–370.

Cowan, N. (1988). Evolving conceptions of memory storage, selective attention, and their mutual constraints within the human information-processing system. *Psychological Bulletin, 104,* 163–191.

Cowan, N. (1995). *Attention and memory: An integrated framework.* New York: Oxford University Press.

Craik, F. I. M. (1977). Age differences in human memory. In J. Birren & K. Schaie (Eds.), *Handbook of the psychology of aging* (pp. 384–420). New York: Van Nostrand Reinhold.

Crossley, M., & Hiscock, M. (1992). Age-related differences in concurrent task performance of normal adults: Evidence for a decline in processing resources. *Psychology and Aging, 7*, 499–506.

Csépe, V., Karmos, G., & Molnár, M. (1989). Subcortical evoked potential correlates of early information processing: Mismatch negativity in cats. In E. Basar & T. H. Bullock (Eds.), *Springer series in brain dynamics 2* (pp. 279–289). Berlin: Springer Verlag.

Dai, H. (1989). *Detection of unexpected sounds*. Unpublished doctoral dissertation. Northeastern University, Boston.

Dai, H., Scharf, B., & Buus, S. (1991). Effective attenuation of signals in noise under focused attention. *Journal of the Acoustical Society of America, 89,* 2837–2842.

Danziger, K. (2001). Wundt and the temptations of psychology. In R. W. Rieber & D. K. Robinson (Eds.), *Wilhlem Wundt in history: The making of scientific psychology* (pp. 69–94). New York: Kluwer/Plenum.

Darwin, C. J., Turvey, M. T., & Crowder, R. G. (1972). An auditory analogue of the Sperling partial report procedure: Evidence for brief auditory storage. *Cognitive Psychology, 3,* 255–267.

Davis, R. (1957). The human operator as a single channel information system. *Quarterly Journal of Experimental Psychology, 9*, 119–129.

Dawson, M. E., & Schell, A. M. (1982). Electrodermal responses to attended and nonattended significant stimuli during dichotic listening. *Journal of Experimental Psychology: Human Perception and Performance, 8*, 315–324.

Deatherage, B. H., & Evans, T. R. (1969). Binaural masking: Backward, forward and simultaneous effects. *Journal of the Acoustical Society of America, 46,* 362–371.

De Fockert, J. W., Rees, G., Frith, C. D., & Lavie, N. (2001). The role of working memory in visual selective attention. *Science, 291,* 1803–1806.

De Haan, R. J., Limburg, M., Van der Meulen, J. H. P., Jacobs, H. M., & Aaronson, N. K. (1995). Quality of life after stroke. *Stroke, 26,* 402–408.

De Jagger, J. J. (1970). *Reaction time and mental processes* (J. Brozek & M S. Sibinga, Translators). Nieuwkoop, Netherlands: B. De Graf. (Original work published 1865)

De Jong, R. (1993). Multiple bottlenecks in overlapping task performance. *Journal of Experimental Psychology: Human Perception and Performance, 19,* 965–980.

De Jong, R. (2000). An intention-activation account of residual switch costs. In S. Monsell & J. Driver (Eds.), *Control of cognitive processes: Attention and performance XVIII* (pp. 357–376). Cambridge, MA: MIT Press.

De Jong, R., Berendsen, E., & Cools, R. (1999). Goal neglect and inhibitory limitations: Dissociable causes of interference effects in conflict situations. *Acta Psychologica, 101,* 379–394.

De Jong, R., Coles, M. G. H., Logan, G. D., & Gratton, G. (1990). In search of the point of no return: The control of response processes. *Journal of Experimental Psychology: Human Perception and Performance, 16,* 164–182.

De Jong, R., Liang, C.-C., & Lauber, E. (1994). Conditional and unconditional automaticity: A dual-process model of effects of spatial stimulus-response correspondence. *Journal of Experimental Psychology: Human Perception and Performance, 20,* 731–750.

De Renzi, E. (1982). *Disorders of space exploration and cognition.* Chichester, UK: Wiley.

De Renzi, E. (1997). Prosopagnosia. In T. E. Feinberg & M. J. Farah (Eds.), *Behavioral neurology and neuropsychology* (pp. 245–255). New York: McGraw-Hill.

Desimone, R., & Duncan, J. (1995). Neural mechanisms of selective attention. *Annual Review of Neuroscience, 18,* 193–222.

Desimone, R., & Schein, S. J. (1987). Visual properties of neurons in area V4 of the macaque: Sensitivity to stimulus form. *Journal of Neurophysiology, 57,* 835–868.

D'Esposito, M., Zarahn, E., & Aguirre, G. K. (1999). Event-related functional MRI: Implications for cognitive psychology. *Psychological Bulletin, 125,* 155–164.

Deutsch, J. A., & Deutsch, D. (1963). Attention: Some theoretical considerations. *Psychological Review, 70,* 80–90.

Dijkerman, H. C., McIntosh, R. D., Milner, A. D., Rossetti, Y., Tilikete, C., & Roberts, R.C. (in press). Ocular scanning and perceptual size distortion in hemispatial neglect: Effects of prism adaptation and sequential stimulus presentation. *Experimental Brain Research.*

Di Lollo, V. (1977). Temporal characteristics of iconic memory. *Nature, 267,* 241–243.

Donchin, E., & Coles, M. G. H. (1988). Is the P300 component a manifestation of context updating? *Behavioral and Brain Sciences, 11,* 357–427.

Donchin, E., Ritter, W., & McCallum, W. C. (1978). Cognitive psychophysiology: The endogenous components of the ERP. In E. Callaway, P. Tueting, & S. H. Koslow (Eds.), *Brain event-related potentials in man* (pp. 349–441). New York: Academic Press.

Donders, F. C. (1868/1969). On the speed of mental processes. In W. G. Koster (Ed.), *Acta Psychologica, 30, Attention and performance II* (pp. 412–431). Amsterdam: North-Holland.

Donk, M. (1994). Human monitoring behavior in a multiple-instrument setting: Independent sampling, sequential sampling or arrangement-dependent sampling. *Acta Psychologica, 86,* 31–55.

Donk, M. (1999). Illusory conjunctions are an illusion: The effects of target-nontarget similarity on conjunction and feature errors. *Journal of Experimental Psychology: Human Perception and Performance, 25,* 1207–1233.

Dowling, W. S., Lung, K. M., & Herrbold, S. (1987). Aiming attention in pitch and time in the perception of interleaved melodies. *Perception & Psychophysics, 41,* 642–656.

Downing, P., Liu, J., & Kanwisher, N. (2001). Testing cognitive models of visual attention with fMRI and MEG. *Neuropsychologia, 39,* 1329–1342.

Driver, J. (1996). Enhancement of selective listening by illusory mislocation of speech sounds due to lip-reading. *Nature, 381,* 66–68.

Driver, J., Baylis, G. C., Goodrich, S. J., & Rafal, R. D. (1994). Axis-based neglect of visual shapes. *Neuropsychologia, 32,* 1353–1365.

Driver, J., & Pouget, A. (2000). Object-centered visual neglect, or relative egocentric neglect? *Journal of Cognitive Neuroscience, 12,* 542–545.

Driver, J., & Spence, C. J. (1994). Spatial synergies between auditory and visual attention. In C. Umiltà & M. Moscovitch (Eds.), *Attention and performance XV: Conscious and nonconscious information processing* (pp. 311–331). Cambridge, MA: MIT Press.

Driver, J., & Spence, C. J. (1998). Attention and the crossmodal construction of space. *Trends in Cognitive Sciences, 2,* 254–262.

Driver, J., & Tipper, S. P. (1989). On the nonselectivity of "selective" seeing: Contrasts between interference and priming in selective attention. *Journal of Experimental Psychology: Human Perception and Performance, 15,* 304–314.

Driver, J., & Vuilleumier, P. (2001). Unconscious processing in neglect and extinction. In B. De Gelder, E. H. F. De Haan, & C. A. Heywood (Eds.), *Out of mind: Varieties of unconscious processes* (pp. 107–139). London: Oxford University Press.

Duncan, J. (1980). The locus of interference in the perception of simultaneous stimuli. *Psychological Review, 87,* 272–300.

Duncan, J. (1984). Selective attention and the organization of visual information. *Journal of Experimental Psychology: General, 113,* 501–517.

Duncan, J. (2001). Frontal lobe function and the control of visual attention. In J. Braun, C. Koch & J. L. Davis (Eds.), *Visual attention and cortical circuits* (pp. 69–88). Cambridge, MA: MIT Press.

Duncan, J., Emslie, H., Williams, P., Johnson, R., & Freer, C. (1996). Intelligence and the frontal lobe: The organization of goal-directed behavior. *Cognitive Psychology, 30,* 257–303.

Duncan, J., & Humphreys, G. W. (1989). Visual search and stimulus similarity. *Psychological Review, 96,* 433–458.

Duncan, J., Martens, S., & Ward, R. (1996). Restricted attentional capacity within but not between sensory modalities. *Nature, 379,* 808–810.

Dutta, A., & Walker, B. N. (1995, November). *Persistence of the PRP effect: Evaluating the response-selection bottleneck.* Poster presented at the 36th Meeting of the Psychonomic Society, Los Angeles, CA.

Easterbrook, R. A. (1959). Effects of emotion on cue utilization and organization of behavior. *Psychological Review, 66,* 183–201.

Eccles, J. C. (1977). *The understanding of the brain* (2nd ed.). New York: McGraw-Hill.

Egan, J., Carterette, E., & Thwing, E. (1954). Some factors affecting multichannel listening. *Journal of the Acoustic Society of America, 26*, 774–782.

Eggemeier, F. T., & Wilson, G. F. (1991). Performance-based and subjective assessment of workload in multi-task environments. In D. L. Damos (Ed.), *Multiple-task performance* (pp. 217–278). London: Taylor & Francis.

Eggemeier, F. T., Wilson, G. F., Kramer, A. F., & Damos, D. L. (1991). Workload assessment in multi-task environments. In D. L. Damos (Ed.), *Multiple-task performance* (pp. 207–216). London: Taylor & Francis.

Ehrenstein, A., Schweickert, R., Choi, S., & Proctor, R. W. (1997). Scheduling processes in working memory: Instructions control the order of memory search and mental arithmetic. *Quarterly Journal of Experimental Psychology, 50A*, 766–802.

Ehrenstein, A., Walker, B. N., Czerwinski, M., & Feldman, E. M. (1997). Some fundamentals of training and transfer: Practice benefits are not automatic. In M. A. Quiñones & A. Ehrenstein (Eds.), *Training for a rapidly changing workplace: Applications of psychological research* (pp. 119–147). Washington, DC: American Psychological Association.

Eijkman, E., & Vendrik, A. J. H. (1965). Can a sensory system be specified by its internal noise? *Journal of the Acoustical Society of America, 37*, 1102–1109.

Eimer, M., Cockburn, D., Smedley, B., & Driver, J. (2001). Crossmodal links in endogenous spatial attention are mediated by common external locations: Evidence from event-related brain potentials. *Experimental Brain Research, 13*, 398–411.

Eimer, M., & Schröger, E. (1998). ERP effects of intermodal and crossmodal links in spatial attention. *Psychophysiology, 35*, 313–327.

Elander, J., West, R., & French, D. (1993). Behavioral correlates of individual differences in road-traffic crash risk: An examination of methods and findings. *Psychological Bulletin, 113*, 279–294.

Elio, R. (1986). Representation of similar well-learned cognitive procedures. *Cognitive Science, 10*, 41–73.

Endsley, M. R. (1995a). Measurement of situation awareness in dynamic systems. *Human Factors, 37*, 65–84.

Endsley, M. R. (1995b). Toward a theory of situation awareness in dynamic systems. *Human Factors, 37*, 32–64.

Endsley, M. R., & Kiris, E. O. (1995). The out-of-the-loop performance problem and level of control in automation. *Human Factors, 37*, 381–394.

Engle, R. W. (2002). Working memory capacity as executive attention. *Current Directions in Psychological Science, 11,* 19–23.

Engle, R. W., Kane, M. J., & Tuholski, S. W. (1999). Individual differences in working memory capacity and what they tell us about controlled attention, general fluid intelligence, and the functions of the prefrontal cortex. In A. Miyake & P. Shah (Eds.), *Models of working memory: Mechanisms of active maintenance and executive control* (pp. 102–134). New York: Cambridge University Press.

Engle, R. W., Tuholski, S., Laughlin, J., & Conway, A. R. (1999). Working memory, short-term memory and general fluid intelligence: A latent variable approach. *Journal of Experimental Psychology: General, 128*, 309–331.

Enns, J. T., & Girgus, J. S. (1985). Developmental changes in selective and integrative visual attention. *Journal of Experimental Child Psychology, 40*, 319–337.

Enns, J. T., & Rensink, R. A. (1990). Sensitivity to three-dimensional orientation in visual search. *Psychological Science, 1*, 323–326.

Entin, E. E., & Serfaty, D. (1999). Adaptive team coordination. *Human Factors, 41*, 312–325.

Epstein, R., Harris, A., Stanley, D., & Kanwisher, N. (1999). The parahippocampal place area: Recognition, navigation, or encoding? *Neuron, 23*, 115–125.

Epstein, R., & Kanwisher, N. (1998). A cortical representation of the local visual environment. *Nature, 392*, 598–601.

Erev, I., & Gopher, D. (1999). A cognitive game-theoretic analysis of attention strategies, ability, and incentives. In D. Gopher & A. Koriat (Eds.), *Attention and performance XVII: Cognitive regulation of performance: Interaction of theory and application* (pp. 343–371). Cambridge, MA: MIT Press.

Eriksen, B. A., & Eriksen, C. W. (1974). Effects of noise letters upon the identification of a target letter in a nonsearch task. *Perception & Psychophysics, 16*, 143–149.

Eriksen, C. W. (1995). The flankers task and response competition: A useful tool for investigating a variety of cognitive problems. In C. Bundesen & H. Shibuya (Eds.), *Visual selective attention, Visual Cognition, 2* (pp. 101–118). Hillsdale, NJ: Erlbaum.

Eriksen, C. W., & Hoffman, J. E. (1973). The extent of processing of noise elements during selective encoding from visual displays. *Perception & Psychophysics, 14,* 155–160.

Eriksen, C. W., & Murphy, T. D. (1987). Movement of attentional focus across the visual field: A critical look at the evidence. *Perception & Psychophysics, 42,* 299–305.

Eriksen, C. W., & St. James, J. D. (1986). Visual attention within and around the field of focal attention: A zoom lens model. *Perception & Psychophysics, 40,* 225–240.

Eriksen, C. W., & Webb, J. M. (1989). Shifting of attentional focus within and about a visual display. *Perception & Psychophysics, 45,* 175–183.

Eriksen, C. W., & Yeh, Y. (1985). Allocation of attention in the visual field. *Journal of Experimental Psychology: Human Perception and Performance, 11,* 583–597.

Exner, S. (1882). Zur Kenntniss von der Wechselwirkung der Erregungen im Centralnervensystem. *Archiv für die gesamte Physiologie des Menschen und der Tiere, 28*, 487–506.

Farah, M. J. (2000). *The cognitive neuroscience of vision. Fundamentals of cognitive neuroscience*. Malden, MA: Blackwell.

Fechner, G. T. (1860). *Elemente der Psychophysik*. Leipzig: Breitkopf and Härtel. (Translated by H. E. Adler, *Elements of psychophysics*. New York: Holt, Rinehart, & Winston, 1966.)

Fischer, E., Haines, R. F., & Price, T. A. (1980). Cognitive issues in head-up displays. NASA Technical Paper 1711. Moffett Field, CA: NASA Ames Research Center.

Fischer, G. (1991). The importance of models and making complex systems comprehensible. In M. J. Tauber & D. Ackermann (Eds.), *Mental models and human-computer interaction 2* (pp. 3–36). Amsterdam: North-Holland.

Fitts, P. M., & Seeger, C. M. (1953). S-R compatibility: Spatial characteristics of stimulus and response codes. *Journal of Experimental Psychology, 46,* 199–210.

Flach, J. M. (2001). A meaning processing approach to analysis and design. In M. J. Smith, G. Salvendy, D. Harris, & R. J. Koubek (Eds.), *Usability evaluation and interface design: Cognitive engineering, intelligent agents, and virtual reality* (Vol. 1, pp. 1405–1409). Mahwah, NJ: Erlbaum.

Folkard, S. (1975). Diurnal variation in logical reasoning. *British Journal of Psychology, 66,* 1–8.

Folkard, S., & Monk, T. H. (1979). Time of day and processing strategy in free recall. *Quarterly Journal of Experimental Psychology, 31,* 461–475.

Folkard, S., & Monk, T. H. (1980). Circadian rhythms in human memory. *British Journal of Psychology, 71,* 295–307.

Fox, E. (1995). Negative priming from ignored distractors in visual selection: A review. *Psychonomic Bulletin & Review, 2,* 145–173.

Foyle, D. C., Dowell, S. R., & Hooey, B. L. (2001). Cognitive tunneling in head-up display (HUD) superimposed symbology: Effects of information location. In R. S. Jensen (Ed.), *Proceedings of the Eleventh Symposium on Aviation Psychology* (pp. 143:1–143:6). Columbus, OH: Ohio State University.

Foyle, D. C., McCann, R. S., Sanford, B. D., & Schwirzke, M. F. J. (1993). *Proceedings of the Human Factors and Ergonomics Society 37th Annual Meeting* (pp. 1340–1344). Santa Monica, CA: Human Factors and Ergonomics Society.

Foyle, D. C., Sanford, B. D., & McCann, R. S. (1991). Attentional issues in superimposed flight symbology. In R. S. Jensen (Ed.), *Proceedings of the Sixth Symposium on Aviation Psychology* (pp. 577–582). Columbus, OH: Ohio State University.

Francis, G. (2000). Designing multifunction displays: An optimization approach. *International Journal of Cognitive Ergonomics, 4,* 107–124.

Frankmann, J. P., & Adams, J. A. (1962). Theories of vigilance. *Psychological Bulletin, 59,* 257–272.

Frassinetti, F., Angeli, V., Meneghello, F., Avanzi, S., & Ladavas, E. (2002). Long-lasting amelioration of visuospatial neglect by prism adaptation. *Brain, 125,* 608–623.

Freud, S. (1922). *Introductory lectures on psychoanalysis*. London: George Allen and Unwin.

Galton, F. (1883). *Inquiries into human faculty and its development*. London: Macmillan.

Garner, W. R. (1974). *The processing of information and structure*. Hillsdale, NJ: Erlbaum.

Gauthier, I., Tarr, M. J., Anderson, A. W., Skudlarski, P., & Gore, J. C. (1999). Activation of the middle fusiform "face area" increases with expertise in recognizing novel objects. *Nature Neuroscience, 2,* 568–573.

Gaver, W. (1997). Auditory interfaces. In M. Helander, T. Landauer, & P. Prabhu (Eds.), *Handbook of human-computer interaction* (2nd ed., pp. 1003–1042). Amsterdam: Elsevier.

Geffen, G., & Sexton, M. A. (1978). The development of auditory strategies of attention. *Developmental Psychology, 14,* 11–17.

Geiselman, R. E., & Bagheri, B. (1985). Repetition effects in directed forgetting: Evidence for retrieval inhibition. *Memory & Cognition, 13,* 57–62.

Gernsbacher, M. A. (1993). Less skilled readers have less efficient suppression mechanisms. *Psychological Science, 4,* 294–298.

Gernsbacher, M. A., & Robertson, R. R. W. (1995). Reading skill and suppression revisited. *Psychological Science, 6,* 165–169.

Gibb, W. R. G., & Luthert, P. J. (1994). Dementia in Parkinson's disease and Lewy body disease. In A. Burns & R. Levy (Eds.), *Dementia* (pp. 719–737). London: Chapman & Hall Medical.

Gibson, J. J. (1941). A critical review of the concept of set in contemporary experimental psychology. *Psychological Bulletin, 38,* 781–817.

Gilboa, E., & Gotlib, I. H. (1997). Cognitive biases and affect persistence in previously dysphoric and never-dysphoric individuals. *Cognition and Emotion, 11,* 517–538.

Gilliom, J. D., & Sorkin, R. D. (1974). Sequential vs simultaneous two-channel signal detection: More evidence for a high-level interrupt theory. *Journal of the Acoustical Society of America, 56*, 157–164.

Glucksberg, S., & Cowan, G. N., Jr. (1970). Memory for nonattended auditory material. *Cognitive Psychology, 1,* 149–156.

Goldman-Rakic, P. S. (1996). Regional and cellular fractionation of working memory. *Proceedings of the National Academy of Sciences, 93,* 13473–13480.

Goldman-Rakic, P. S. (1998). The prefrontal landscape: Implications of functional architecture for understanding human mentation and the central executive. In A. C. Roberts, T. W. Robbins, and L. Weiskrantz (Eds.), *The prefrontal cortex: Executive and cognitive function* (pp. 87–102). Oxford: Oxford University Press.

Goldman-Rakic, P. S., Selemon, L. D., & Schwartz, M. L. (1984). Dual pathways connecting the dorsolateral prefrontal cortex with the hippocampal formation and parahippocampal cortex in the Rhesus monkey. *Neuroscience, 12,* 719–743.

Goldsmith, M. (1998). What's in a location? Comparing object-based and space-based models of feature integration in visual search. *Journal of Experimental Psychology: General, 127,* 189–219.

Gopher, D. (1982). A selective attention test as a predictor of success in flight training. *Human Factors, 24,* 173–183.

Gopher, D. (1993). The skill of attention control: Acquisition and execution of attention strategies. In D. E. Meyer & S. Kornblum (Eds.), *Attention and performance XIV* (pp. 299–322). Cambridge, MA: MIT Press.

Gopher, D. (1994). Analysis and measurement of mental load. In G. d'Ydewalle, P. Edlen, & P. Bertelson (Eds.), *International perspectives on psychological science, Vol. 2: The state of the art* (pp. 265–291). Hove, UK: Erlbaum.

Gopher, D., & Barzilai, O. (1993). The effect of knowledge levels on operators response to malfunctions and technical problems in the system. *Proceedings of the IEEE: Systems, Man and Cybernetics, 1,* 185–190.

Gopher, D., & Braune, R. (1984). On the psychophysics of workload: Why bother with subjective measures? *Human Factors, 26,* 519–532.

Gopher, D., Brickner, M., & Navon, D. (1982). Different difficulty manipulations interact differently with task emphasis: Evidence for multiple resources. *Journal of Experimental Psychology: Human Perception and Performance, 8,* 146–157.

Gopher, D., & Donchin, E. (1986). Workload—An examination of the concept. In K. R. Boff, L. Kaufman, & J. P. Thomas (Eds.), *Handbook of perception and human performance* (Vol. 2, pp. 41-1–41-49). New York: Wiley.

Gopher, D., & Kahneman, D. (1971). Individual differences in attention and the prediction of flight criteria. *Perceptual and Motor Skills, 33,* 1335–1342.

Gopher, D., Weil, M., & Bareket, T. (1994). Transfer of skill from a computer game trainer to flight. *Human Factors, 36,* 387–405.

Gopher, D., Weil, M., & Siegel, D. (1989). Practice under changing priorities: An approach to training of complex skills. *Acta Psychologica, 71,* 147–177.

Gottsdanker, R., & Stelmach, G. E. (1971). The persistence of psychological refractoriness. *Journal of Motor Behavior, 3,* 301–312.

Grafman, J., & Salazar, A. M. (1987). Methodological considerations relevant to the comparison of recovery from penetrating and closed head injuries. In H. S. Levin, J. Grafman, & H. M. Eisberg (Eds.), *Neurobehavioral recovery from closed head injury* (pp. 43–54). New York: Oxford University Press.

Gratton, G., Coles, M. G., Sirevaag, E. J., & Eriksen, C. W. (1988). Pre- and poststimulus activation of response channels: A psychophysiological analysis. *Journal of Experimental Psychology: Human Perception and Performance, 14,* 331–344.

Gray, J. A., Feldon, J., Rawlins, J. N. P., Hemsley, D. R., & Smith, A. D. (1991). The neuropsychology of schizophrenia. *Behavioral and Brain Sciences, 14,* 20–84.

Gray, J. A., & Wedderburn, A. A. I. (1960). Grouping strategies with simultaneous stimuli. *Quarterly Journal of Experimental Psychology, 12,* 180–184.

Gray, R., & Tan, H. Z. (2002). Dynamic and predictive links between touch and vision. *Experimental Brain Research, 145,* 50–55.

Green, D. M. (1961). Detection of auditory sinusoids of uncertain frequencies. *Journal of the Acoustical Society of America, 33,* 897–903.

Green, D. M., & Swets, J. A. (1966). *Signal detection theory and psychophysics.* New York: Wiley.

Greenberg, G. Z., & Larkin, W. D. (1968). Frequency-response characteristic of auditory observers detecting signals of a single frequency in noise: The probe-signal method. *Journal of the Acoustical Society of America, 44,* 1513–1523.

Greenwald, A. G. (1970). Sensory feedback mechanisms in performance control: With special reference to the ideo-motor mechanism. *Psychological Review, 77,* 73–99.

Greenwald, A. G. (1972). On doing two things at once: Time sharing as a function of ideomotor compatibility. *Journal of Experimental Psychology, 94,* 52–57.

Greenwald, A. G. (in press). On doing two things at once: III. Confirmation of perfect time-sharing when simultaneous tasks are ideomotor compatible. *Journal of Experimental Psychology: Human Perception and Performance.*

Greenwald, A. G., & Shulman, H. G. (1973). On doing two things at once: II. Elimination of the psychological refractory period effect. *Journal of Experimental Psychology, 101,* 70–76.

Gronwall, D., & Sampson, H. (1974). *The psychological effects of concussion.* Auckland, New Zealand: Auckland University Press.

Gronwall, D. M. (1977). Paced auditory serial-addition task: A measure of recovery from concussion. *Perceptual and Motor Skills, 44,* 367–373.

Gugerty, L. J. (1997). Situation awareness during driving: Explicit and implicit knowledge in dynamic spatial memory. *Journal of Experimental Psychology: Applied, 3,* 42–66.

Gurland, B. J., & Cross, P. S. (1986). Public health perspectives on clinical memory testing of Alzheimer's disease and related disorders. In L. W. Poon (Ed.), *Handbook for clinical memory assessment of older adults* (pp. 11–20). Washington, DC: American Psychological Association.

Haier, R. J., Siegel, B. V., Jr., Nuechterlein, K. H., Hazlett, E., Wu, J. C., Paek, J., et al. (1988). Cortical glucose metabolic rate correlates of abstract reasoning and attention studied with positron emission tomography. *Intelligence, 12,* 199–217.

Hallowell, E. M., & Ratey, J. J. (1994). *Driven to distraction.* New York: Pantheon Books.

Hamilton, W. (1859). *Lectures on metaphysics and logic (Vol. 1: Metaphysics).* Edinburgh & London: Blackwood.

Handy, T. C., & Mangun, G. R. (2000). Attention and spatial selection: Electrophysiological evidence for modulation by perceptual load. *Perception & Psychophysics, 62,* 175–186.

Hankey, J. M., & Dingus, T. A. (1990). A validation of SWAT as a measure of workload induced by changes in operator capacity. In *Proceedings of the Human Factors Society 34th Annual Meeting* (pp. 112–115). Santa Monica, CA: Human Factors Society.

Hansen, J. C., & Hillyard, S. A. (1980). Endogenous brain potentials associated with selective auditory attention. *Electroencephalography and Clinical Neurophysiology, 49,* 277–290.

Hansen, J. C., & Hillyard, S. A. (1983). Selective attention to multidimensional auditory stimuli. *Journal of Experimental Psychology: Human Perception and Performance, 9,* 1–19.

Hansen, J. P. (1995). Representation of system invariants by optical invariants in configural displays for process control. In P. Hancock, J. Flach, J. Caird, & K. Vicente (Eds.), *Logical applications of the ecological approach to human-machine systems* (pp. 208–233). Hillsdale, NJ: Erlbaum.

Hart, S. G., & Staveland, L. (1988). Development of NASA task load index (TLX): Results of empirical and theoretical research. In P. A. Hancock, & N. Meshkati (Eds.), *Human mental workload* (139–183). Amsterdam: Elsevier.

Hasher, L., Zacks, R., & May, C. P. (1999). Inhibitory control, circadian arousal, and age. In D. Gopher & A. Koriat (Eds.), *Attention and performance XVII: Cognitive regulation of performance: Interaction of theory and application* (pp. 653–675). Cambridge, MA: MIT Press.

Haxby, J. V., Courtney, S. M., & Clark, V. P. (1998). Functional magnetic resonance imaging and the study of attention. In R. Parasuraman (Ed.), *The attentive brain* (pp. 123–142). Cambridge, MA: MIT Press.

Heaton, R. K., Grant, I., & Mathews, C. G. (1991). *Comprehensive norms for expanded Halstead-Reitan battery.* Odessa, FL: Psychological Assessment Resources.

Hebb, D. O. (1949). *The organization of behavior.* New York: Wiley-Interscience.

Hedge, A., & Marsh, N. W. (1975). The effect of irrelevant spatial correspondence on two-choice response-time. *Acta Psychologica, 39,* 427–439.

Heil, M., Osman, A., Wiegelmann, J., Rolke, B., & Hennighausen, E. (2000). N200 in the Eriksen-task: Inhibitory executive process? *Journal of Psychophysiology, 14,* 218–225.

Heil, M., Wahl, K., & Herbst, M. (1999). Mental rotation, memory scanning, and the central bottleneck. *Psychological Research, 62,* 48–61.

Heilman, K. M., Bowers, D., Cosslet, H. B., Whelan, H., & Watson, R. T. (1985). Directional hypokinesia: Prolonged reaction times for leftward movements in patients with right hemisphere lesions and neglect. *Neurology, 35,* 855–859.

Heilman, K. M., Watson, R. T., and Valenstein, E. (1985). Neglect and related disorders. In K. M. Heilman & E. Valenstein (Eds.), *Clinical neuropsychology* (2nd ed., pp. 243–293). New York: Oxford University Press.

Heinrichs, R. W., & Zakzanis, K. K. (1998). Neurocognitive deficit in schizophrenia: A quantitative review of the evidence. *Neuropsychology, 12,* 426–445.

Heinze, H. J., Luck, S. J., Mangun, G. R., & Hillyard, S. A. (1990). Visual event-related potentials index focused attention within bilateral arrays. I. Evidence for early selection. *Electroencephalography and Clinical Neurophysiology, 75,* 511–527.

Heinze, H. J., Mangun, G. R., Burchert, W., & Hinrichs, H. (1994). Combined spatial and temporal imaging of brain activity during visual selective attention in humans. *Nature, 372,* 543–546.

Heister, G., Schroeder-Heister, P., & Ehrenstein, W. H. (1990). Spatial coding and spatio-anatomical mapping: Evidence for a hierarchical model of spatial stimulus-response compatibility. In R. W. Proctor & T. G. Reeve (Eds.), *Stimulus-response compatibility: An integrated perspective* (pp. 117–143). Amsterdam: North-Holland.

Heller, M. A. (1992). Haptic dominance in form perception: Vision versus proprioception. *Perception, 21,* 655–660.

Hellier, E. J., Edworthy, J., & Dennis, I. (1993). Improving auditory warning design: Quantifying and predicting the effects of different warning parameters on perceived urgency. *Human Factors, 35,* 693–706.

Hempel, T., & Altınsoy, E. (in press). Multimodal user interfaces: Designing media for the auditory and tactile channels. In R. W. Proctor & K. -P. L. Vu (Eds.), *Handbook of human factors in web design.* Mahwah, NJ: Erlbaum.

Hendy, K. C., Hamilton, K. M., & Landry, L. N. (1993). Measuring subjective workload: When is one scale better than many? *Human Factors, 35,* 579–601.

Herbart, J. F. (1824–1825). *Psychologie als Wissenschaft neu gegründet auf Erfahrung, Metaphysik und Mathematik.* Königsberg: Unzer.

Hick, W. E. (1952). On the rate of gain of information. *Quarterly Journal of Experimental Psychology, 4,* 11–26.

Hillyard, S. A., Hink, R. F., Schwent, V. L., & Picton, T. W. (1973). Electrical signs of selective attention in the human brain. *Science, 182,* 177–180.

Hillyard, S. A., & Kutas, M. (1983). Electrophysiology of cognitive processing. *Annual Review of Psychology, 34,* 33–61.

Hirst, W., Spelke, E. S., Reaves, C. C., Caharack, G., & Neisser, U. (1980). Dividing attention without alternation or automaticity. *Journal of Experimental Psychology: General, 109,* 98–117.

Hochstenbach, J., Mulder, T., Van Limbeek, J., Donders, R., & Schoonderwaldt, H. (1998). Cognitive decline following stroke: A comprehensive study of the cognitive decline following stroke. *Journal of Clinical and Experimental Neuropsychology, 20,* 503–517.

Hockey, G. R. J. (1993). Cognitive energetical control mechanisms in the management of work demands and psychological health. In A. D. Baddeley & L. Weiskrantz (Eds.), *Attention: Selection, awareness, and control: A tribute to Donald Broadbent* (pp. 328–345). New York: Oxford University Press.

Hoffman, J. E., Nelson, B., & Houck, M. R. (1983). The role of attentional resources in automatic detection. *Cognitive Psychology, 15,* 379–410.

Holland, J. D., Hutchins, E. L., & Weitzman, L. (1984). STEAMER: An interactive inspectable simulation-based training system. *AI Magazine, 5*(2), 15–27.

Holmes, J., Payton, A., Barrett, J. H., Hever, T., Fitzpatrick, H., Trumper, A. L., et al. (2000). A family-based and case-control association study of the dopamine D4 receptor gene and dopamine transporter gene in attention deficit hyperactivity disorder. *Molecular Psychiatry, 5,* 523–530.

Hommel, B. (1993a). The relationship between stimulus processing and response selection in the Simon task: Evidence for a temporal overlap. *Psychological Research/Psychologische Forschung, 55*, 280–290.

Hommel, B. (1993b). The role of attention for the Simon effect. *Psychological Research/Psychologische Forschung, 55*, 208–222.

Hommel, B. (1998). Automatic stimulus-response translation in dual-task performance. *Journal of Experimental Psychology: Human Perception and Performance, 24*, 1368–1384.

Hommel, B., Müsseler, J., Aschersleben, G., & Prinz, W. (2001). The theory of event coding (TEC): A framework for perception and action planning. *Behavioral and Brain Sciences, 24*, 849–937.

Hopfinger, J. B., & Mangun, G. R. (1998). Reflexive attention modulates processing of visual stimuli in human extrastriate cortex. *Psychological Science, 9*, 441–447.

Houghton, G., & Tipper, S. P. (1994). A model of inhibitory mechanisms in selective attention. In D. Dagenbach & T. H. Carr (Eds.), *Inhibitory processes in attention, memory, and language* (pp. 53–112). San Diego: Academic Press.

Huang-Pollock, C. L., Carr, T. H., & Nigg, J. T. (2002). Development of selective attention: Perceptual load influences early versus late attentional selection in children and adults. *Developmental Psychology, 38*, 363–375.

Humphreys, G. W., Ford, E. M. E., & Francis, D. (2000). The organization of sequential actions. In S. Monsell & J. Driver (Eds.), *Control of cognitive processes: Attention and performance XVIII* (pp. 427–442). Cambridge, MA: MIT Press.

Humphreys, G. W., & Müller, H. (1993). Search via recursive rejection (SERR): A connectionist model of visual search. *Cognitive Psychology, 25*, 43–110.

Humphreys, M. S., & Revelle, W. (1984). Personality, motivation, and performance: A theory of the relationship between individual differences and information processing. *Psychological Review, 91*, 153–184.

Hyman, R. (1953). Stimulus information as a determinant of reaction time. *Journal of Experimental Psychology, 45*, 188–196.

Inuzuka, Y., Osumi, Y., & Shinkai, H. (1991). Visibility of head up display (HUD) for automobiles. In *Proceedings of the Human Factors Society 35th Annual Meeting* (pp. 1574–1578). Santa Monica, CA: Human Factors Society.

Irwin-Chase, H., & Burns, B. (2000). Developmental changes in children's abilities to share and allocate attention in a dual task. *Journal of Experimental Child Psychology, 77*, 61–85.

Isreal, J. B., Wickens, C. D., Chesney, G. L., & Donchin, E. (1980). The event-related brain potential as an index of display-monitoring workload. *Human Factors, 22*, 211–224.

Ivry, R. B., Franz, E. A., Kingston, A., & Johnston, J. C. (1998). The psychological refractory period effect following callosotomy: Uncoupling of lateralized response codes. *Journal of Experimental Psychology: Human Perception and Performance, 24*, 463–480.

Ivry, R. B., & Hazeltine, E. (2000). Task switching in a callosotomy patient and in normal participants: Evidence for response-related sources of interference. In S. Monsell & J. Driver (Eds.), *Control of cognitive processes: Attention and performance XVIII* (pp. 401–423). Cambridge, MA: MIT Press.

Iwata, H. (2003). Haptic interfaces. In J. A. Jacko & A. Sears (Eds.), *The human-computer interaction handbook: Fundamentals, evolving technologies, and emerging applications* (pp. 206–219). Mahwah, NJ: Erlbaum.

Jacobsen, C. F. (1935). Functions of frontal association areas in primates. *Archives of Neurology and Psychiatry*, 33, 458–569.

James, W. (1890). *The principles of psychology* (Vol. 1). New York: Holt. (Reprinted in 1950 by Dover Press, New York)

Jameson, A. (2003). Adaptive interfaces and agents. In J. A. Jacko & A. Sears (Eds.), *The human-computer interaction handbook: Fundamentals, evolving technologies, and emerging applications* (pp. 305–330). Mahwah, NJ: Lawrence Erlbaum.

Jastrow, J. (1890). *The time-relations of mental phenomena*. New York: N. D. C. Hodges.

Jensen, A. R. (1998). *The g factor: The science of mental ability*. Westport, CT: Praeger.

Jentsch, F., Barnett, J., Bowers, C. A., & Salas, E. (1999). Who is flying this plane anyway? What mishaps tell us about crew member role assignment and air crew situation awareness. *Human Factors, 41*, 1–14.

Jersild, A. T. (1927). Mental set and shift. *Archives of Psychology*, Whole No. 89, pp. 5–82.

Jevons, W. S. (1871). The power of numerical discrimination. *Nature, 3*, 281–282.

Jiménez, L., & Méndez, C. (1999). Which attention is needed for implicit sequence learning? *Journal of Experimental Psychology: Learning, Memory, and Cognition, 25*, 236–259.

Johnson, A. (2003). Procedural memory and skill acquisition. In A. F. Healy & R. W. Proctor (Eds.), *Experimental psychology* (pp. 499–523). Volume 4 in I. B. Weiner (Editor-in-Chief), *Handbook of psychology*. New York: Wiley.

Johnson, H. M. (1994). Processes of successful intentional forgetting. *Psychological Bulletin, 116*, 274–292.

Johnson, M. H. (1998). Developing an attentive brain. In R. Parasuraman (Ed.), *The attentive brain* (pp. 427–443). Cambridge, MA: MIT press.

Johnson, R. (1993). On the neural generators of the P300 component of the event related potential. *Psychophysiology, 30*, 90–97.

Johnston, W. A., & Heinz, S. P. (1978). Flexibility and capacity demands of attention. *Journal of Experimental Psychology: General, 107*, 420–435.

Jolicœur, P. (1999). Restricted attentional capacity between sensory modalities. *Psychonomic Bulletin & Review, 6*, 87–92.

Jolicœur, P., & Dell'Acqua, R. (1999). Attentional and structural constraints on visual encoding. *Psychological Research, 62*, 154–164.

Jones, D. G., & Endsley, M. R. (1996). Sources of situation awareness errors in aviation. *Aviation, Space, and Environmental Medicine, 67*, 507–512.

Jonides, J. (1981). Voluntary versus automatic control over the mind's eye movement. In J. B. Long & A. D. Baddeley (Eds.). *Attention and performance IX* (pp. 187–203). Hillsdale, NJ: Erlbaum.

Jonides, J., & Mack, R. (1984). On the cost and benefit of cost and benefit. *Psychological Bulletin, 96*, 29–44.

Jonides, J., & Yantis, S. (1988). Uniqueness of abrupt visual onset in capturing attention. *Perception & Psychophysics, 43*, 346–354.

Jordan, T. C. (1972). Characteristics of visual and proprioceptive response times in the learning of a motor skill. *Quarterly Journal of Experimental Psychology, 24*, 536–543.

Joseph, J. S., Chun, M. M., & Nakayama, K. (1996). Attentional requirements in a "preattentive" feature search task. *Nature, 379*, 805–807.

Judd, C. H. (1917). *Psychology: General introduction*. Boston: Ginn.

Juola, J. F., Koshino, H., & Warner, C. B. (1995). Tradeoffs between attentional effects of spatial cues and abrupt onsets. *Perception & Psychophysics, 57,* 333–342.

Kahneman, D. (1973). *Attention and effort*. Englewood Cliffs, NJ: Prentice Hall.

Kahneman, D., Ben-Ishai, R., & Lotan, M. (1973). Relation of a test of attention to road accidents. *Journal of Applied Psychology, 58,* 113–115.

Kahneman, D., Treisman, A., & Burkell, J. (1983). The cost of visual filtering. *Journal of Experimental Psychology: Human Perception and Performance, 9,* 510–522.

Kail, R., & Salthouse, T. A. (1994). Processing speed as a mental capacity. *Acta Psychologica, 86,* 199–225.

Kalyuga, S., Chandler, P., & Sweller, J. (1999). Managing split-attention and redundancy in multimedia instruction. *Applied Cognitive Psychology, 13,* 351–371.

Kane, M. J., Bleckley, M. K., Conway, A. R. A., & Engle, R. W. (2001). A controlled-attention view of working memory capacity. *Journal of Experimental Psychology: General, 130,* 169–183.

Kane, M. N., Curry, S. H., Butler, S. R., & Cummins, B. H. (1993). Electrophysiological indicator of awakening from coma. *The Lancet, 341,* 688.

Kanwisher, N., McDermott, J., & Chun, M. M. (1997). The fusiform face area: A module in human extrastriate cortex specialized for face perception. *Journal of Neuroscience, 17,* 4302–4311.

Karlin, L., & Kestenbaum, R. (1968). Effects of number of alternatives on the psychological refractory period. *Quarterly Journal of Experimental Psychology, 20,* 167–178.

Kato, H., Ito, H., Shima, J., Imaizumi, M., & Shibata, H. (1992). Development of hologram head-up display (SAE Tech Paper 920600). In *Electronics display technology and information systems* (SP-904, pp. 21–27). Warrendale, PA: Society of Automotive Engineers.

Keefe, R. S. E. (1995). The contribution of neuropsychology to psychiatry. *American Journal of Psychiatry, 152,* 6–15.

Keele, S. W. (1967). *Attention and human performance*. Pacific Palisades, CA: Goodyear Press.

Kesler, S. R., Adams, H. F., & Bigler, E. D. (2000). SPECT, MR and quantitative MR imaging: Correlates with neuropsychological and psychological outcome in traumatic brain injury. *Brain Injury, 14,* 851–857.

Kessels, R. P. C., Aleman, A., Verhagen, W. I. M., & Van Luijtelaar, E. L. J. M. (2000). Cognitive functioning after whiplash injury: A meta analysis. *Journal of the International Neuropsychological Society, 6,* 271–278.

Kessels, R. P. C., Keyser, A., Verhagen, W. I. M., & Van Luijtelaar, E. L. J. M. (1998). The whiplash syndrome: A psychophysiological and neuropsychological study towards attention. *Acta Neurologica Scandinavica, 97,* 188–193.

Kieras, D. E., Meyer, D. E., Ballas, J. A., & Lauber, E. J. (2000). Modern computational perspectives on executive mental processes and cognitive control: Where to from here? In S. Monsell & J. Driver (Eds.), *Control of cognitive processes: Attention and performance XVIII* (pp. 679–712). Cambridge, MA: MIT Press.

Kimberg, D. Y., & Farah, M. J. (1993). A unified account of cognitive impairments following frontal lobe damage: The role of working memory in complex, organized behavior. *Journal of Experimental Psychology: General, 122,* 411–428.

Kimberg, D. Y., & Farah, M. J. (2000). Is there an inhibitory module in the prefrontal cortex? Working memory and the mechanisms underlying cognitive control. In S. Monsell & J. Driver (Eds.), *Control of cognitive processes: Attention and performance XVIII* (pp. 739–751). Cambridge, MA: MIT Press.

Kingstone, A., & Pratt, J. (1999). Inhibition of return is composed of attentional and oculomotor processes. *Perception & Psychophysics, 61*, 1046–1054.

Klein, R., & Shore, D. I. (2000). Relations among modes of visual orienting. In S. Monsell & J. Driver (Eds.), *Control of cognitive processes: Attention and performance XVIII* (pp. 195–208). Cambridge, MA: MIT Press.

Klein, R. M., & Taylor, T. L. (1994). Categories of cognitive inhibition with reference to attention. In D. Dagenbach & T. H. Carr (Eds.), *Inhibitory processes in attention, memory, and language* (pp. 113–150). San Diego, CA: Academic Press.

Kleitman, N., & Jackson, D. P. (1950). Body temperature and performance under different routines. *American Journal of Applied Psychology, 3*, 309–328.

Knight, R. T., Grabowecky, M. F., & Scabini, D. (1995). Role of human prefrontal cortex in attention control. In H. H. Jasper, S. Riggio, & P. S. Goldman-Rakic (Eds.), *Epilepsy and the functional anatomy of the frontal lobe* (pp. 21–36). New York: Raven.

Knight, R. T., Hillyard, S. A., Woods, D. L., & Neville, H. J. (1980). The effects of frontal and temporal-parietal lesions on the auditory evoked potentials in man. *Electroencephalography and Clinical Neurophysiology, 50,* 112–124.

Knight, R. T., Hillyard, S. A., Woods, D. L., & Neville, H. J. (1981). The effects of frontal cortex lesions on event-related potentials during auditory selective attention. *Electroencephalography and Clinical Neurophysiology, 52,* 571–582.

Knight, R. T., Scabini, D., & Woods, D. L. (1989). Prefrontal cortex gating of auditory transmission in humans. *Brain Research, 504*, 338–342.

Knight, R. T., Staines, W. R., Swick, D., & Chao, L. L. (1999). Prefrontal cortex regulates inhibition and excitation in distributed neural networks. *Acta Psychologica, 101*, 159–178.

Korteling, J. (1991). Effects of skill integration and perceptual competition on age-related difference in dual-task performance. *Human Factors, 33*, 35–44.

Korteling, J. (1993). Effects of age and task similarity on dual-task performance. *Human Factors, 35*, 99–114.

Koshino, H., Warner, C. B., & Juola, J. F. (1992). Relative effectiveness of central, peripheral, and abrupt-onset cues in visual attention. *The Quarterly Journal of Experimental Psychology, 45A,* 609–631.

Kraepelin, E., Barclay, R. M., & Robertson, G. M. (Eds.). (1919). *Dementia praecox and paraphrenia*. Edinburgh: E & S Livingstone.

Kramer, A. F., Hahn, S., & Gopher, D. (1999). Task coordination and aging: Explorations of executive control processes in the task switching paradigm. *Acta Psychologica, 101*, 339–378.

Kramer, A. F., Humphrey, D. G., Larish, J. F., Logan, G. D., & Strayer, D. L. (1994). Aging and inhibition: Beyond a unitary view of inhibitory processing in attention. *Psychology and Aging, 9*, 491–512.

Kramer, A. F., & Jacobson, A. (1991). Perceptual organization and focused attention: The role of objects and proximity in visual processing. *Perception & Psychophysics, 50*, 267–284.

Kramer, A. F., Larish, J. F., & Strayer, D. L. (1995). Training for attentional control in dual task settings: A comparison of young and old adults. *Journal of Experimental Psychology: Applied, 1*, 50–76.

Kramer, A. F., Larish, J. F., Weber, T. A., & Bardell, L. (1999). Training for executive control: Task coordination strategies and aging. In D. Gopher & A. Koriat (Eds.), *Cognitive regulation of performance: Interaction of theory and application: Attention and performance XVII* (pp. 617–652). Cambridge, MA: MIT Press.

Kramer, A. F., Trejo, L. J., & Humphrey, D. G. (1995). Assessment of mental workload with task-irrelevant auditory probes. *Biological Psychology, 40,* 83–100.

Kraus, N., McGee, T., Carrell, T., King, C., Tremblay, K., & Nicol, T. (1995). Central auditory system plasticity associated with speech discrimination training. *Journal of Cognitive Neuroscience, 7,* 25–32.

Külpe, O. (1904). Versuche über Abstraktion. *Bericht über den Kongress für experimentele Psychologie, 1,* 56–68.

LaBerge, D. (1983). Spatial extent of attention to letters and words. *Journal of Experimental Psychology: Human Perception and Performance, 9,* 371–379.

LaBerge, D., & Brown, V. (1989). Theory of attentional operations in shape identification. *Psychological Review, 96,* 101–124.

LaBerge, D., Carlson, R. L., Williams, J. K., & Bunney, B. G. (1997). Shifting attention in visual space: Tests of moving-spotlight models versus an activity-distribution model. *Journal of Experimental Psychology: Human Perception and Performance, 23,* 1380–1392.

Lahey, B. B. (1995). *Psychology: An introduction* (5th ed.). Madison, WI: Brown & Benchmark.

Lane, D. M. (1982). The development of selective attention. *Merrill Palmer Quarterly, 28,* 317–337.

Lange, L. (1888). Neue Experimente über den Vorgang der einfachen Reaction auf Sinneseindrücke. *Philosophische Studien (Wundt), 4,* 479–510.

Lange, N. (1888). Beiträge zur Theorie der sinnlichen Aufmerksamkeit und der actieven Apperception. *Philosophische Studien (Wundt), 4,* 390–422.

Larish, I., & Wickens, C. D. (1991). *Divided attention with superior and separated imagery: Implications for head-up displays.* (Tech Rep. ARL 91-4/NASA-HUD-91-1). Savoy, IL: University of Illinois Institute of Aviation, Aviation Research Lab.

Larson, G. E., & Perry, Z. A. (1999). Visual capture and human error. *Applied Cognitive Psychology, 13,* 227–236.

Lasswell, J. W., & Wickens, C. D. (1995). *The effects of display location and dimensionality on taxi-way navigation.* (Tech. Rep. ARL (91-5/NASA-HUD-95-2) Savoy, IL: University of Illinois Institute of Aviation, Aviation Research Lab.

Lavie, N. (1995). Perceptual load as a necessary condition for selective attention. *Journal of Experimental Psychology: Human Perception and Performance, 21,* 451–468.

Lavie, N., & Fox, E. (2000). The role of perceptual load in negative priming. *Journal of Experimental Psychology: Human Perception and Performance, 26,* 1038–1052.

Lavie, N., & Tsal, Y. (1994). Perceptual load as a major determinant of the locus of selection in visual attention. *Perception & Psychophysics, 56,* 183–197.

Lavie, P., Gopher, D., & Wollman, M. (1987). Thirty-six hour correspondence between performance and sleepiness cycles. *Psychophysiology, 24,* 430–438.

Lawrence, A. D., Sahakian, B. J., Hodges, J. R., Rosser, A. E., Lange, K. W., & Robbins, T. W. (1996). Executive and mnemonic functions in early Huntington's disease. *Brain, 119*, 1633–1645.

Leclercq, M., & Sturm, W. (2002). Rehabilitation of attention disorders: A literature review. In M. Leclercq & P. Zimmerman (Eds.), *Applied neuropsychology of attention* (pp. 341–364). London: Psychology Press.

Lee, E., & MacGregor, J. (1985). Minimizing user search time in menu retrieval systems. *Human Factors, 27*, 157–162.

Leibniz, G. W. (1765). Nouveaux essays sur l'entendement humain. In R. E. Raspe (Ed.), *Oeuvres philosophiques de feu M. Leibnitz*. Amsterdam & Leipzig: Schreuder.

Leibniz, G. W. (1948/1985). *Textes inédits*. G. Grua (Ed.). New York: Garland.

Leonards, U., Sunaert, S., Van Hecke, P., & Orban, G. A. (2000). Attention mechanisms in visual search—An fMRI study. *Journal of Cognitive Neuroscience, 12*, 61–75.

Leung, H.-C., Skudlarski, P., Gatenby, J. C., Peterson, B. S., & Gore, J. C. (2000). An event-related functional MRI study of the Stroop color word interference task. *Cerebral Cortex, 10*, 552–560.

Levine, B., Robertson, I. H., Clare, L., Carter, G., Hong, J., Wilson, B. A., et al. (2000). Rehabilitation of executive functioning: An experimental-clinical validation of goal management training. *Journal of the International Neuropsychological Society, 6*, 299–312.

Levy, F. (1980). The development of sustained attention (vigilance) and inhibition in children: Some normative data. *Journal of Child Psychology and Psychiatry, 21*, 77–84.

Lezak, M. D. (1995). *Neuropsychological assessment* (3rd ed.). New York: Oxford University Press.

Lien, M.-C., & Proctor, R. W. (2000). Multiple spatial correspondence effects on dual-task performance. *Journal of Experimental Psychology: Human Perception and Performance, 26*, 1260–1280.

Lien, M.-C., & Proctor, R. W. (2002). Stimulus-response compatibility and psychological refractory period effects: Implications for response selection. *Psychonomic Bulletin & Review, 9*, 212–238.

Lien, M.-C., Proctor, R. W., & Allen, P. A. (2002). Ideomotor compatibility in the psychological refractory period effect: 29 years of oversimplification. *Journal of Experimental Psychology: Human Perception & Performance, 28*, 396–409.

Lien, M.-C., Proctor, R. W., & Ruthruff, E. (in press). Still no evidence for perfect timesharing with two ideomotor compatible tasks: An observation on Greenwald (2003). *Journal of Experimental Psychology: Human Perception and Performance*.

Logan, G. D. (1981). Attention, automaticity, and the ability to stop a speeded choice response. In J. Long & A. D. Baddeley (Eds.), *Attention and performance IX* (pp. 205–222). Hillsdale, NJ: Lawrence Erlbaum.

Logan, G. D. (1988). Toward an instance theory of automatization. *Psychological Review, 95*, 492–527.

Logan, G. D. (1990). Repetition priming and automaticity: Common underlying mechanisms? *Cognitive Psychology, 22*, 1–35.

Logan, G. D. (1994). On the ability to inhibit thought and action: A user's guide to the stop signal paradigm. In D. Dagenbach & T. H. Carr (Eds.), *Inhibitory processes in attention, memory, and language* (pp. 189–239). San Diego: Academic Press.

Logan, G. D. (1995). Linguistic and conceptual control of visual spatial attention. *Cognitive Psychology, 28*, 103–174.

Logan, G. D. (1996). The CODE theory of visual attention: An integration of space-based and object-based attention. *Psychological Review, 103,* 603–649.

Logan, G. D. (2002). An instance theory of attention and memory. *Psychological Review, 109,* 376–400.

Logan, G. D., & Compton, B. J. (1998). Attention and automaticity. In R. D. Wright (Ed.), *Visual attention. Vancouver studies in cognitive science* (Vol. 8, pp. 108–131). New York: Oxford University Press.

Logan, G. D., & Cowan, W. B. (1984). On the ability to inhibit thought and action: A theory of an act of control. *Psychological Review, 91,* 295–327.

Logan, G. D., & Delheimer, J. A. (2001). Parallel memory retrieval in dual-task situations: II. Episodic memory. *Journal of Experimental Psychology: Learning, Memory, and Cognition, 27,* 668–685.

Logan, G. D., & Etherton, J. L. (1994). What is learned during automatization? The role of attention in constructing an instance. *Journal of Experimental Psychology: Learning, Memory, and Cognition, 20,* 1022–1050.

Logan, G. D., & Irwin, D. E. (2000). Don't look! Don't touch! Inhibitory control of eye and hand movements. *Psychonomic Bulletin & Review, 7,* 107–112.

Logan, G. D., Schachar, R. J., & Tannock, R. (2000). Impulsivity and inhibitory control. *Psychological Science, 8,* 60–64.

Logan, G. D., & Schulkind, M. D. (2000). Parallel memory retrieval in dual-task situations: I. Semantic memory. *Journal of Experimental Psychology: Human Perception and Performance, 26,* 1072–1090.

Logan, G. D., Taylor, S. E., & Etherton, J. L. (1999). Attention and automaticity: Toward a theoretical integration. *Psychological Research, 62,* 165–181.

Logan, G. D., & Zbrodoff, N. J. (1979). When it helps to be misled: Facilitative effects of increasing the frequency of conflicting stimuli in a Stroop-like task. *Memory & Cognition, 7,* 166–174.

Logie, R., Baddeley, A., Mané, A., Donchin, E., & Sheptak, R. (1988). Working memory in the acquisition of complex cognitive skills. In A. M. Colley & J. R. Beech (Eds.), *Cognition and action in skilled behaviour* (pp. 361–377). Amsterdam: North-Holland.

Lorist, M. M., & Tops, M. (in press). Caffeine and effects on cognition, with special attention to adenosine-dopamine interactions. *Brain and Cognition.*

Loschky, L. C., & McConkie, G. W. (2002). Investigating spatial vision and dynamic attentional selection using a gaze-contingent multiresolutional display. *Journal of Experimental Psychology: Applied, 8,* 99–117.

Lotze, H. (1852). *Medicinische Psychologie oder Physiologie der Seele.* Leipzig: Weidmann.

Lotze, H. (1885). *Outlines of psychology* (C. L. Herrick, Trans.). Minneapolis: S. M. Williams.

Lovie, A. D. (1983). Attention and behaviourism. *British Journal of Psychology, 74,* 301–310.

Lowe, G. (1968). Auditory detection and recognition in a two-alternative, directional uncertainty situation. *Perception & Psychophysics, 4,* 278–280.

Lu, C.-H., & Proctor, R. W. (1995). The influence of irrelevant location information on performance: A review of the Simon and spatial Stroop effects. *Psychonomic Bulletin & Review, 2,* 174–207.

Lu, Z.-L., & Dosher, B. A. (1998). External noise distinguishes attention mechanisms. *Vision Research, 38,* 1183–1198.

Luck, S. J., Fan, S., & Hillyard, S. A. (1993). Attention-related modulation of sensory-evoked brain activity in a visual search task. *Journal of Cognitive Neuroscience, 5,* 188–195.

Luck, S. J., & Girelli, M. (1998). Electrophysiological approaches to the study of selective attention in the human brain. In R. Parasuraman (Ed.), *The attentive brain* (pp. 71–94). Cambridge, MA: MIT Press.

Lukas, J. H. (1981). The role of efferent inhibition in human auditory attention: An examination of the auditory brainstem potential. *International Journal of Neuroscience, 12,* 137–145.

Lundberg, U., & Frankenhaeuser, M. (1978). Psychophysiological reactions to noise as modified by personal control over noise intensity. *Biological Psychology, 6,* 51–59.

Luria, A. R. (1980). *Higher cortical functions in man*. Oxford, UK: Basic Books.

MacDonald, P. A., Joordens, S., Seergobin, K. N. (1999). Negative priming effects that are bigger than a breadbox: Attention to distractors does not eliminate negative priming, it enhances it. *Memory & Cognition, 27,* 197–207.

Mackworth, J. F. (1969). *Vigilance and habituation*. Middlesex, England: Penguin.

Mackworth, N. (1950). *Researches on the measurement of human performance*. Medical Research Council Special Report Series No. 268. London: H. M. S. O.

Mackworth, N. H. (1948). The breakdown of vigilance during prolonged visual search. *Quarterly Journal of Experimental Psychology, 1,* 6–21.

Mackworth, N. H. (1961). Researches on the measurement of human performance. In H. W. Sinaiko (Ed.), *Selected papers on human factors in the design and use of control systems* (pp. 174–331). (Reprinted from Medical Research Council Special Report Series 268, London: H. M. Stationary Office, 1950.)

Mackworth, N. H. (1965). Visual noise causes tunnel vision. *Psychonomic Science, 3,* 67–68.

MacLeod, C., Mathews, A., & Tata, P. (1986). Attentional biases in emotional disorders. *Journal of Abnormal Psychology, 95,* 15–20.

MacLeod, C. M. (1992). The Stroop task: The "gold standard" of attentional measures. *Journal of Experimental Psychology: General, 121,* 12–14.

Maki, W. S., Frigen, K., & Paulson, K. (1997). Associative priming by targets and distractors during rapid serial visual presentation: Does word meaning survive the attentional blink? *Journal of Experimental Psychology: Human Perception and Performance, 23,* 1014–1034.

Malebranche, N. (1674/1980). *De la recherché de la vérité*/The search after truth. Columbus, OH: Ohio State University Press.

Mané, A., Adams, J. A., & Donchin, E. (1989). Adaptive and part-whole training in the acquisition of a complex perceptual-motor skill. *Acta Psychologica, 71,* 179–196.

Mané, A., & Donchin, E. (1989). The space fortress game. *Acta Psychologica, 71,* 17–22.

Mangun, G. R., Hansen, J. C., & Hillyard, S. (1987). The spatial orienting of attention: Sensory facilitation or response bias? In R. Johnson, Jr., J. W. Rohrbaugh, & R. Parasuraman (Eds.), *Current trends in event-related potential research* (pp. 118–124). Amsterdam: Elsevier.

Mangun, G. R., & Hillyard, S. A. (1991). Modulations of sensory-evoked brain potentials indicate changes in perceptual processing during visual-spatial priming. *Journal of Experimental Psychology: Human Perception and Performance, 17,* 1057–1074.

Manley, T. (2002). Cognitive rehabilitation for unilateral neglect: Review. *Neuropsychological Rehabilitation, 12*, 289–310.

Martens, S., Wolters, G., & Van Raamsdonk, M. (2002). Blinks of the mind: Memory effects of attentional processes. *Journal of Experimental Psychology: Human Perception and Performance, 28*, 1275–1287.

Mateer, C. A. (1999). The rehabilitation of executive disorders. In D. S. Stuss, G. Winocur, & I. H. Robertson (Eds.), *Cognitive neurorehabilitation* (pp. 314–332). Cambridge, UK: Cambridge University Press.

Matthews, G., & Davies, D. R. (2001). Individual differences in energetic arousal and sustained attention: A dual-task study. *Personality and Individual Differences, 31,* 575–589.

Matthews, G., Davies, D. R., & Lees, J. (1990). Arousal, extraversion and resource availability. *Journal of Personality and Social Psychology, 59*, 150–168.

Matthews, G., Jones, D. M., & Chamberlain, A. G. (1990). Refining the measurement of mood: The UWIST Mood Adjective Checklist. *British Journal of Psychology, 81*, 629–639.

Matthews, G., & Westerman, S. J. (1994). Energy and tension as predictors of controlled visual and memory search. *Personality and Individual Differences, 17*, 617–626.

Mattingley, J. B., Phillips, J. G., & Bradshaw, J. L. (1994). Impairments of movement execution in unilateral neglect: A kinematic analysis of directional bradykinesia. *Neuropsychologia, 32*, 1111–1134.

May, C. P., Zacks, R. T., Hasher, L., & Multhaup, K. S. (1999). Inhibition in the processing of garden-path sentences. *Psychology and Aging, 14*, 304–313.

Maylor, E. A., & Rabbitt, P. M. A. (1987). Effect of alcohol on rate of forgetting. *Psychopharmacology, 91*, 230–235.

McCallum, W. C., Curry, S. H., Cooper, R., Pocock, P. V., & Papakostopoulos, D. (1983). Brain event-related potentials as indicators of early selective processes in auditory target localization. *Psychophysiology, 20*, 1–17.

McCann, R. S., Foyle, D. C., & Johnston, J. C. (1993). Attentional limitations with head-up displays. *Proceedings of the 7th International Symposium on Aviation Psychology* (pp. 71–75). Columbus, OH: Ohio State University.

McCann, R. S., & Johnston, J. C. (1992). Locus of the single-channel bottleneck in dual-task interference. *Journal of Experimental Psychology: Human Perception and Performance, 18*, 471–484.

McClelland, J. L. (1979). On the time relations of mental processes: An examination of systems of processes in cascade. *Psychological Review, 86*, 287–330.

McCloskey, M., & Watkins, M. J. (1978). The seeing-more-than-is-there phenomenon: Implications for the locus of iconic storage. *Journal of Experimental Psychology: Human Perception and Performance, 4,* 553–564.

McConkie, G. W., & Rayner, K. (1976). Identifying the span of the effective stimulus in reading: Literature review and theories of reading. In H. Singer & B. Ruddell (Eds.), *Theoretical models and processes of reading* (pp. 137–162). Newark, NJ: International Reading Association.

McCracken, J. T., Smalley, S. L., McGough, J. J., Crawford, L., Del'Homme, M., Cantor, R. H., et al. (2000). Evidence for linkage of a tandem duplication polymorphism upstream of the dopamine D4 receptor gene (DRD4) with attention deficit hyperactivity disorder (ADHD). *Molecular Psychiatry, 5*, 531–536.

McDonald, J. E., Stone, J. D., & Liebelt, L. S. (1983). Searching for items in menus: The effects of organization and type of target. *Proceedings of the Human Factors Society 27th Annual Meeting* (pp. 289–338). Santa Monica, CA: Human Factors and Ergonomics Society.

McDonald, J. J., Teder-Saelejaervi, W. A., & Hillyard, S. A. (2000). Involuntary orienting to sound improves visual perception. *Nature, 407*, 906–908.

McDowd, J. (1986). The effects of age and extended practice on divided attention performance. *Journal of Gerontology, 41*, 764–769.

McGlinchey-Berroth, R., Milberg, W. P., Verfaellie, M., Alexander, M., & D'Esposito, M. (1993). Semantic processing in the neglected visual field: Evidence from a lexical decision task. *Cognitive Neuropsychology, 10*, 79–108.

McGurk, H., & MacDonald, J. (1976). Hearing lips and seeing voices. *Nature, 264,* 746–748.

McLeod, P. (1978). Does probe RT measure central processing demand? *Quarterly Journal of Experimental Psychology, 30*, 83–89.

McRae, R. (1976). *Leibniz: Perception, apperception, & thought*. Toronto: University of Toronto Press.

Meiran, N. (2000). Reconfiguration of stimulus task sets and response task sets during task switching. In S. Monsell & J. Driver (Eds.), *Control of cognitive processes: Attention and performance XVIII* (pp. 377–399). Cambridge, MA: MIT Press.

Melara, R. D., & Algom, D. (2003). Driven by information: A tectonic theory of Stroop effects. *Psychological Review, 110,* 422–471.

Melara, R. D., & Day, D. J. A. (1992). Primacy of dimensions in vibrotactile perception: An evaluation of early holistic models. *Perception & Psychophysics, 52*, 1–17.

Melara, R. D., & Marks, L. E. (1990a). Perceptual primacy of dimensions: Support for a model of dimensional interaction. *Journal of Experimental Psychology: Human Perception and Performance, 16*, 398–414.

Melara, R. D., & Marks, L. E. (1990b). Processes underlying dimensional interactions: Correspondences between linguistic and nonlinguistic dimensions. *Memory & Cognition, 18*, 477–495.

Melara, R. D., Marks, L. E., & Potts, B. C. (1993). Early-holistic processing or dimensional similarity? *Journal of Experimental Psychology: Human Perception and Performance, 19*, 1114–1120.

Melara, R. D., Rao, A., & Tong, Y. (2002). The duality of selection: Excitatory and inhibitory processes in auditory selective attention. *Journal of Experimental Psychology: Human Perception and Performance, 28*, 279–306.

Merkel, J. (1885). Die zeitliche Verhaltnisse der Willenstatigkeit [The temporal relations of activities of the will]. *Philosophische Studien, 2*, 73–127.

Mesulam, M.-M. (2000). Attentional networks, confusional states, and neglect syndromes. In M.-M. Mesulam (Ed.), *Principles of behavioral and cognitive neurology* (pp. 174–256). New York: Oxford University Press.

Meyer, D. E., & Kieras, D. E. (1997a). A computational theory of executive cognitive processes and multiple-task performance: Part 1. Basic mechanisms. *Psychological Review, 104*, 3–65.

Meyer, D. E., & Kieras, D. E. (1997b). A computational theory of executive cognitive processes and multiple-task performance: Part 2. Accounts of psychological refractory-period phenomena. *Psychological Review, 104*, 749–791.

Meyer, V., Gross, C. G., & Teuber, H. (1963). Effect of knowledge of site of stimulation on the threshold for pressure sensitivity. *Perceptual and Motor Skills, 16*, 637–640.

Michie, P. T., Solowij, N., Crawford, J. M., & Glue, L. C. (1993). The effects of between-source discriminability on attended and unattended auditory ERPs. *Psychophysiology, 30*, 205–220.

Mihal, W. L., & Barrett, G. V. (1976). Individual differences in perceptual information processing and their relation to automobile accident involvement. *Journal of Applied Psychology, 61*, 229–233.

Miller, G. A. (1956). The magical number seven plus or minus two: Some limits on our capacity for processing information. *Psychological Review, 63*, 81–97.

Miller, J. (1987). Priming is not necessary for selective-attention failures: Semantic effects of unattended, unprimed letters. *Perception & Psychophysics, 41*, 419–434.

Miller, J. (1991). Channel interaction and the redundant-targets effect in bimodal divided attention. *Journal of Experimental Psychology: Human Perception and Performance, 17*, 160–169.

Miller, J., & Hackley, S. A. (1992). Electrophysiological evidence for temporal overlap among contingent mental processes. *Journal of Experimental Psychology: General, 121*, 195–209.

Milliken, B., Tipper, S. P., & Weaver, B. (1994). Negative priming in a spatial localization task: Feature mismatching and distractor inhibition. *Journal of Experimental Psychology: Human Perception and Performance, 20*, 624–646.

Mineka, S. (1992). Evolutionary memories, emotional processing and the emotional disorders. In D. Medin (Ed.), *The psychology of learning and motivation* (Vol. 28, pp. 161–206). New York: Academic Press.

Mineka, S., & Nugent, K. (1995). Mood-congruent memory biases in anxiety and depression. In D. L. Schacter (Ed.), *Memory distortion: How minds, brains, and societies reconstruct the past* (pp. 173–193). Cambridge, MA: Harvard University Press.

Miron, D., Duncan, G., & Bushnell, M. C. (1989). Effects of attention on the intensity and unpleasantness of thermal pain. *Pain, 39*, 345–352.

Mondor, T. A., Breau, L. M., & Milliken, B. (1998). Inhibitory processes in auditory selective attention: Evidence of location based and frequency based inhibition of return. *Perception & Psychophysics, 60*, 296–302.

Monsell, S. & Driver, J. (2000). Banishing the control homunculus. In S. Monsell & J. Driver (Eds.), *Control of cognitive processes: Attention and performance XVIII* (pp. 3–32). Cambridge, MA: MIT Press.

Moore, C. M. (1994). Negative priming depends on probe-trial conflict: Where has all the inhibition gone? *Perception & Psychophysics, 56*, 133–147. See also "Negative priming depends on probe-trial conflict: Where has all the inhibition gone?": Erratum. *Perception & Psychophysics, 56*, 721.

Moore, C. M., Yantis, S., & Vaughan, B. (1998). Object-based visual selection: Evidence from perceptual completion. *Psychological Science, 9*, 104–110.

Moore, J. J., & Massaro, D. W. (1973). Attention and processing capacity in auditory recognition. *Journal of Experimental Psychology, 99*, 49–54.

Moray, N. (1959a). Attention in dichotic listening: Affective cues and the influence of instructions. *Quarterly Journal of Experimental Psychology, 11*, 56–60.

Moray, N. (1959b). *Attention: Selective processes in vision and hearing*. London: Hutchinson Educational.

Moray, N. (1969). *Listening and attention*. Baltimore: Penguin.

Moray, N. (1975). A data base for theories of selective listening. In P. M. A. Rabbitt & S. Dornic (Eds.), *Attention and performance V* (pp. 119–135). Hillsdale, NJ: Erlbaum.

Moray, N. (1986). Monitoring behavior and supervisory control. In K. R. Boff, L. Kaufman, & J. P. Thomas (Eds.), *Handbook of perception and human performance* (Vol. 2: *Cognitive processes and performance*, pp. 40-1–40-51). New York: Wiley.

Moray, N., Bates, A., & Barnett, T. (1965). Experiments on the four-eared man. *Journal of the Acoustical Society of America, 38,* 196–201.

Morrow, L. A., & Ratcliff, G. (1988). The disengagement of covert attention and the neglect syndrome. *Psychobiology, 16,* 261–269.

Moruzzi, G., & Magoun, H. W. (1949). Brain stem reticular formation and activation of the EEG. *Electroencephalography and Clinical Neurophysiology, 1,* 455–473.

Moss, C. F., & Carr, C. E. (2003). Comparative psychology of audition. In M. Gallagher & R. J. Nelson (Eds.), *Biological psychology*. Vol. 4 in I. B. Weiner (Editor-in-Chief) *Handbook of psychology* (pp. 71–107). New York: Wiley.

Mowrer, O. H., Rayman, N. N., & Bliss, E. L. (1940). Preparatory set (expectancy)—An experimental demonstration of its 'central' locus. *Journal of Experimental Psychology, 26,* 357–372.

Mudd, S. A., & McCormick, J. (1960). The use of auditory cues in a visual search task. *Journal of Applied Psychology, 44,* 184–188.

Mulhern, G. (1997). Cognitive processes, mental abilities and general intelligence. In C. Cooper & V. Varma (Eds.), *Processes in individual differences* (pp. 149–163). London: Routledge.

Müller, H. J., & Rabbitt, P. M. A. (1989). Reflexive and voluntary orienting of visual attention: Time course of activation and resistance to interruption. *Journal of Experimental Psychology: Human Perception and Performance, 15,* 315–330.

Murray, D. J., & Ross, H. E. (1982). Vives (1538) on memory and recall. *Canadian Psychology, 23,* 22–31.

Na, D. L., Adair, J. C., Williamson, D. J. G., Schwartz, R. L., Haws, B., & Heilman, K. M. (1998). Dissociation of sensory-attentional from motor-intentional neglect. *Journal of Neurology, Neurosurgery and Psychiatry, 64,* 331–338.

Näätänen, R. (1982). Processing negativity: An evoked-potential reflection of selective attention. *Psychological Bulletin, 92,* 605–640.

Näätänen, R. (1992). *Attention and brain function*. Hillsdale, NJ: Erlbaum.

Naito, E., & Matsumura, M. (1996). Movement-related potentials associated with motor inhibition under different preparatory states during performance of two visual stop signal paradigms in humans. *Neuropsychologia, 34,* 565–573.

Najjar, L. (2001). E-commerce user interface design for the Web. In M. J. Smith, G. Salvendy, D. Harris, & R. J. Koubek (Eds.), *Usability evaluation and interface design: Cognitive engineering, intelligent agents, and virtual reality* (Vol. 1, pp. 843–847). Mahwah, NJ: Erlbaum.

Nakagawa, Y., Tanabe, H., Kazui, H., Kato, A., Yoshimine, Y., Yamada, K., & Hayakawa, T. (1998). Motor neglect following damage to the supplementary motor area. *Neurocase, 4,* 55–63.

Nakayama, K., & Silverman, G. H. (1986). Serial and parallel processing of visual feature conjunctions. *Nature, 320,* 264–265.

Nakayama, K., He, Z., & Shimojo, S. (1995). Visual surface representation: A critical link between lower-level and higher-level vision. In S. M. Kosslyn & D. N. Osherson (Eds.), *An invitation to cognitive science: Visual cognition* (Vol. 2, pp. 1–70). Cambridge, MA: MIT Press.

Nash, E. B., Edwards, G. W., Thompson, J. A., & Barfield, W. (2000). A review of presence and performance in virtual environments. *International Journal of Human-Computer Interaction, 12,* 1–41.

Naveh-Benjamin, M., & Jonides, J. (1984). Maintenance rehearsal: A two-component analysis. *Journal of Experimental Psychology: Learning, Memory, and Cognition, 10,* 369–385.

Navon, D. (1984). Resources—A theoretical soup stone? *Psychological Review, 91,* 216–234.

Navon, D., & Gopher, D. (1979). On the economy of the human-processing system. *Psychological Review, 86,* 214–255.

Navon, D., & Miller, J. (2002). Queuing or sharing? A critical evaluation of the single-bottleneck notion. *Cognitive Psychology, 44,* 193–251.

Neely, J. H. (1977). Semantic priming and retrieval from lexical memory: Roles of inhibitionless spreading activation and limited-capacity attention. *Journal of Experimental Psychology: General, 106,* 226–254.

Neill, W. T., & Valdes, L. A. (1992). Persistence of negative priming: Steady state or decay? *Journal of Experimental Psychology: Learning, Memory, and Cognition, 18,* 565–576.

Neill, W. T., Valdes, L. A., Terry, K. M., & Gorfein, D. S. (1992). Persistence of negative priming: II. Evidence for episodic trace retrieval. *Journal of Experimental Psychology: Learning, Memory, and Cognition, 18,* 993–1000.

Neisser, U. (1967). *Cognitive psychology.* New York: Appleton-Century-Crofts.

Neisser, U. (1976). *Cognition and reality.* San Francisco: Freeman.

Neisser, U., & Becklen, R. (1975). Selective looking: Attending to visually specified events. *Cognitive Psychology, 7,* 480–494.

Neumann, O. (1984). Automatic processing: A review of recent findings and a plea for an old theory. In W. Prinz & A. F. Sanders (Eds.), *Cognition and motor processes* (pp. 255–293). Berlin: Springer.

Neumann, O. (1987). Beyond capacity: A functional view of attention. In H. Heuer & A. F. Sanders (Eds.), *Perspectives on perception and action* (pp. 361–394). Hillsdale, NJ: Erlbaum.

Newell, K. M., Carlton, M. J., Fisher, A. T., & Rutter, B. G. (1989). Whole-part training strategies for learning the response dynamics of microprocessor-driven simulators. *Acta Psychologica, 71,* 197–216.

Newman, R. L. (1995). *Head-up displays: Designing the way ahead.* Aldershot, UK: Avebury Aviation.

Nicolas, S., Gyselinck, V., Murray, D. J., & Bandomir, C. A. (2002). French descriptions of Wundt's laboratory in Leipzig in 1886. *Psychological Research, 66,* 208–214.

Nicoletti, R., & Umiltà, C. (1985). Responding with hand and foot: The right/left prevalence in spatial compatibility is still present. *Perception & Psychophysics, 38,* 211–216.

Nicoletti, R., & Umiltà, C. (1989). Splitting visual space with attention. *Journal of Experimental Psychology: Human Perception and Performance, 15,* 164–169.

Nieminen, T., & Summala, N. (1994). Novice and experienced drivers' looking behaviour and primary task control while doing a secondary task. *Proceedings of the Human Factors and Ergonomics Society 38th Annual Meeting* (pp. 852–856). Santa Monica, CA: The Human Factors and Ergonomics Society.

Nieuwenhuis, S., Ridderinkhof, K. R., de Jong, R., Kok, A., & van der Molen, M. W. (2000). Inhibitory inefficiency and failures of intention activation: Age related decline in the control of saccadic eye movements. *Psychology and Aging, 15*, 635–647.

NIH Consensus Development Panel on Rehabilitation of Persons With Traumatic Brain Injury. (1999). Rehabilitation of persons with traumatic brain injury. *Journal of the American Medical Association, 282*, 974–983.

Nikolic, M. I., & Sarter, N. (2001). Peripheral visual feedback: A powerful means of supporting effective attention allocation in event-driven, data-rich environments. *Human Factors, 43*, 30–38.

Ninio, A., & Kahneman, D. (1974). Reaction time in focused and in divided attention. *Journal of Experimental Psychology, 103*, 394–399.

Nissen, M. J., & Bullemer, P. (1987). Attentional requirements of learning: Evidence from performance measures. *Cognitive Psychology, 19*, 1–32.

Norman, D. A. (1968). Towards a theory of memory and attention. *Psychological Review, 75*, 522–536.

Norman, D. A. (1969). Memory while shadowing. *Quarterly Journal of Experimental Psychology, 21*, 85–93.

Norman, D. A. (1981). Categorization of action slips. *Psychological Review, 88*, 1–15.

Norman, D. A. (1988). *The psychology of everyday things.* New York: Basic Books.

Norman, D. A., & Shallice, T. (1986). Attention to action: Willed and automatic control of behavior. In R. J. Davidson, G. E. Schwartz, & D. Shapiro (Eds.), *Consciousness and self-regulation* (Vol. 4, pp. 1–18). New York: Plenum Press.

Noy, Y. I. (1997). Human factors in modern traffic systems. *Ergonomics, 40*, 1016–1024.

O'Craven, K. M., Downing, P. E., & Kanwisher, N. (1999). fMRI evidence for objects as the units of attentional selection. *Nature, 401*, 584–587.

Ollman, R. T. (1966). Fast guesses in choice-reaction time. *Psychonomic Science, 6*, 155–156.

Opitz, B., Rinne, T., Mecklinger, A., von Cramon, D. Y., & Schröger, E. (2002). Differential contribution of frontal and temporal cortices to auditory change detection: fMRI and ERP results. *NeuroImage, 15*, 167–174.

Oppenheim, H. (1885). Ueber eine durch eine klinische bisher nicht verwerthete Untersuchungsmethode ermittelte Form der Sensibilitätstörung bei einseitigen Erkrankungen des Grosshirns. *Neurologisches Centralblatt, 4*, 529–533.

Osman, A., Kornblum, S., & Meyer, D. E. (1990). Does motor programming necessitate response execution? *Journal of Experimental Psychology: Human Perception and Performance, 16*, 183–198.

Osman, A., Lou, L., Muller-Gethmann, H., Rinkenauer, G., Mattes, S., & Ulrich, R. (2000). Mechanisms of speed-accuracy tradeoff: Evidence from covert motor processes. *Biological Psychology, 51*, 173–199.

Osman, A., & Moore, C. M. (1993). The locus of dual task interference: Psychological refractory effects on movement related brain potentials. *Journal of Experimental Psychology: Human Perception and Performance, 19*, 1292–1312.

Paap, K. R., & Cooke, N. J. (1997). Design of menus. In M. Helander, T. K. Landauer, & P. Prabhu (Eds.), *Handbook of human-computer interaction* (2nd ed., pp. 533–572). Amsterdam: North-Holland.

Pachella, R. G. (1974). The interpretation of reaction time in information processing research. In B. Kantowitz (Ed.), *Human information processing: Tutorials in performance and cognition* (pp. 41–82). Hillsdale, NJ: Erlbaum.

Palmer, S. E. (2003). Visual perception of objects. In A. F. Healy & R. W. Proctor (Eds.), *Experimental psychology*. Vol. 4 in I. B. Weiner (Editor-in-Chief), *Handbook of psychology* (pp. 179–212). New York: Wiley.

Palomares, M., Pelli, D. G., & Majaj, N. J. (in press). Crowding is unlike ordinary masking: Distinguishing feature detection and integration. *Journal of Vision.*

Paquet, L., & Craig, G. L. (1997). Evidence for selective target processing with a low perceptual load flankers task. *Memory & Cognition, 25*, 182–189.

Parasuraman, R. (1984). The psychobiology of sustained attention. In J. S. Warm (Ed.), *Sustained attention and human performance* (pp. 61–101). London: Wiley.

Parasuraman, R., & Davies, D. R. (1977). A taxonomic analysis of vigilance performance. In R. R. Mackie (Ed.), *Vigilance theory, operational performance, and physiological correlates* (pp. 559–574). New York: Plenum.

Parasuraman, R., & Nestor, P. G. (1993). Preserved cognitive operations in early Alzheimer's disease. In J. Cerella, J. M. Rybash, et al. (Eds.), *Adult information processing: Limits on loss* (pp. 77–111). San Diego, CA: Academic Press.

Parasuraman, R., Warm, J. S., & See, J. E. (1998). Brain systems of vigilance. In R. Parasuraman (Ed.), *The attentive brain* (pp. 221–256). Cambridge, MA: MIT Press.

Parducci, A. (1965). Category judgment: A range-frequency model. *Psychological Review, 72*, 407–418.

Paschal, F. C. (1941). The trend in theories of attention. *Psychological Review, 48*, 383–403.

Pashler, H. (1998). *The psychology of attention*. Cambridge, MA: MIT Press.

Pashler, H. (2000). Task switching and multitask performance. In S. Monsell & J. Driver (Eds.), *Control of cognitive processes: Attention and performance XVIII* (pp. 275–423). Cambridge, MA: MIT Press.

Pashler, H., & Johnston, J. C. (1989). Chronometric evidence for central postponement in temporally overlapping tasks. *Quarterly Journal of Experimental Psychology, 41A*, 19–45.

Pashler, H., Luck, S. J., Hillyard, S. A., Mangun, G. R., O'Brien, S., & Gazzaniga, M. S. (1994). Sequential operation of the disconnected cerebral hemispheres in "split-brain" patients. *NeuroReport, 5*, 2381–2384.

Pashler, H. A. (1984a). Evidence against late selection: Stimulus quality effects in previewed displays. *Journal of Experimental Psychology: Human Perception and Performance, 10*, 429–448.

Pashler, H. A. (1984b). Processing stages in overlapping tasks: Evidence for a central bottleneck. *Journal of Experimental Psychology: Human Perception and Performance, 10*, 358–377.

Patterson, R. D. (1974). Auditory filter shape. *Journal of the Acoustical Society of America, 55*, 802–809.

Paus, T., Jech, R., & Thompson, C. J. (1997). Transcranial magnetic stimulation during positron emission tomography: A new method for studying connectivity of the human cerebral cortex. *Journal of Neuroscience, 17*, 3178–3184.

Pavani, F., Spence, C., & Driver, J. (2000). Visual capture of touch: Out-of-the-body experiences with rubber gloves. *Psychological Science, 11*, 353–359.

Pavlov, I. P. (1960). *Conditioned reflexes.* New York: Dover.

Perlman, G. (1984). Making the right choices with menus. *Proceedings of INTERACT '84* (pp. 291–295). London: IFIP.

Perrot, D., Cisneros, J., McKinley, R. L., & D'Angelo, W. R. (1996). Aurally aided visual search under virtual and free-field listening conditions. *Human Factors, 38,* 702–715.

Petrides, M. (1995). Impairments on nonspatial self-ordered and externally ordered working memory tasks after lesions of the mid-dorsal lateral part of the lateral frontal cortex of monkey. *Journal of Neuroscience, 15*, 359–375.

Pew, R. (1995). The state of situational awareness measurement: Circa 1995. In D. J. Garland & M. R. Endsley (Eds.), *Proceedings of an international conference on experimental analysis and measurement of situation awareness* (pp. 7–15). Daytona Beach, FL: Embry-Riddle Aeronautical University Press.

Pillsbury, W. B. (1908). *Attention.* (Reprinted in 1973 by Arno Press, New York)

Pivik, R. T., Broughton, R. J., Coppola, R., Davidson, R. J., Fox, N., & Nuwer, M. R. (1993). Guildelines for the recording and quantitative analysis of electroencephalographic activity in research contexts. *Psychophysiology, 30*, 547–558.

Pizzamiglio, L., Perani, D., Cappa, S. F., Vallar, G., Paolucci, S., Grassi, F., et al. (1998). Recovery of neglect after right hemispheric damage: H2(15).O positron emission tomographic activation study. *Archives of Neurology, 55*, 561–568.

Pohlmann, L. D., & Sorkin, R. D. (1976). Simultaneous three-channel signal detection: Performance and criterion as a function of order of report. *Perception & Psychophysics, 20*, 179–186.

Ponds, R. W. H. M., Brouwer, W. B., & van Wolffelaar, P. C. (1988). Age differences in divided attention in a divided-attention task. *Journal of Gerontology, 43*, 151–156.

Ponsford, J. L., & Kinsella, G. (1988). Evaluation of a remedial programme for attentional deficits following closed-head injury. *Journal of Clinical and Experimental Neuropsychology, 10*, 693–708.

Posner, M. I. (1978). *Chronometric explorations of mind.* Hillsdale, NJ: Erlbaum.

Posner, M. I. (1980). Orienting of attention. *Quarterly Journal of Experimental Psychology, 32*, 3–25.

Posner, M. I. (1982). Cumulative development of attentional theory. *American Psychologist, 37*, 168–179.

Posner, M. I. (1988). Localization of cognitive operations in the human brain. *Science, 240*, 1627–1631.

Posner, M. I. (1994). Neglect and spatial attention. *Neuropsychological Rehabilitation, 4*, 183–187.

Posner, M. I. (1995). Attention in cognitive neuroscience: An overview. In M. S. Gazzaniga (Ed.), *The cognitive neurosciences* (pp. 615–624). Cambridge, MA: MIT Press.

Posner, M. I, & Boies, S. J. (1971). Components of attention. *Psychological Review, 78*, 391–408.

Posner, M. I., & Cohen, Y. P. C. (1984). Components of visual orienting. In H. Bouma & D. Bouwhuis (Eds.), *Attention and performance X* (pp. 531–566). London: Erlbaum.

Posner, M. I., & DiGirolamo, G. J. (2000). Cognitive neuroscience: Origins and promise. *Psychological Bulletin, 126*, 873–889.

Posner, M. I., & Keele, S. W. (1969). Attention demands of movement. In *Proceedings of the 16th International Congress of Applied Psychology* (pp. 418–422). Amsterdam: Swets & Zeitlinger.

Posner, M. I., & Mitchell, R. F. (1967). Chronometric analysis of classification. *Psychological Review, 74,* 392–409.

Posner, M. I., & Petersen, S. E. (1990). The attention system of the human brain. *Annual Review of Neuroscience, 13,* 25–42.

Posner, M. I., & Raichle, M. E. (1994). *Images of mind.* New York: Scientific American.

Posner, M. I., & Snyder, C. R. R. (1975). Attention and cognitive control. In R. L. Solso (Ed.), *Information processing and cognition: The Loyola symposium* (pp. 55–85). Hillsdale, NJ: Erlbaum.

Posner, M. I., Snyder, C. R. R., & Davidson, B. J. (1980). Attention and the detection of signals. *Journal of Experimental Psychology: General, 109,* 160–174.

Posner, M. I., Walker, J. A., Friedrich, F. J., & Rafal, R. D. (1984). Effects of parietal lobe injury on covert orienting of visual attention? *Journal of Neuroscience, 4,* 1863–1874.

Posner, M. I., Walker, J. A., Friedrich, F. A., & Rafal, R. D. (1987). How do the parietal lobes direct covert attention? *Neuropsychologia, 25,* 135–145.

Potter, M. C. (1976). Short-term conceptual memory for pictures. *Journal of Experimental Psychology: Human Learning and Memory, 2,* 509–522.

Potter, M. C. (1993). Very short-term conceptual memory. *Memory & Cognition, 21,* 156–161.

Potter, M. C. (1999). Understanding sentences and scenes: The role of conceptual short-term memory. In K. Coltheart (Ed.), *Fleeting memories: Cognition of brief visual stimuli* (pp. 13–46). London: MIT Press.

Powers, W. J. (1990). Stroke. In A. L. Pearlman & R. C. Collins (Eds.), *Neurobiology of disease* (pp. 339–355). New York: Oxford University Press.

Prechtl, H., & Beintema, D. (1964). The neurological examination of the full-term newborn infant. *Little Club clinics in developmental medicine, 12.* London: Heineman.

Pringle, H. L., Irwin, D. E., Kramer, A., & Atchley, P. (2001). The role of attentional breadth in perceptual change detection. *Psychonomic Bulletin & Review, 8,* 89–95.

Prinzmetal, W. (1981). Principles of feature integration in visual perception. *Perception & Psychophysics, 30,* 330–340.

Prinzmetal, W., & Banks, W. P. (1977). Good continuation affects visual detection. *Perception & Psychophysics, 21,* 389–395.

Prinzmetal, W., Ivry, R. B., Beck, D., & Shimuzu, N. (2002). A measurement theory of illusory conjuctions. *Journal of Experimental Psychology: Human Perception and Performance, 28,* 251–269.

Proctor, R. W. (1981). A unified theory for matching-task phenomena. *Psychological Review, 88,* 291–326.

Proctor, R. W. & Dutta, A. (1995). *Principles of skill acquisition and human performance.* Newbury Park, CA: Sage.

Proctor, R. W., & Reeve, T. G. (Eds.). (1990). *Stimulus-response compatibility: An integrated perspective.* Amsterdam: North-Holland.

Puel, J. L., Bonfils, P., & Pujol, R. (1988). Selective attention modifies the active micromechanical properties of the cochlea. *Brain Research, 447,* 380–383.

Puleo, J. S., & Pastore, R. E. (1978). Critical-band effects in two-channel auditory signal detection. *Journal of Experimental Psychology: Human Perception and Performance, 4,* 153–163.

Rabbitt, P., Banerji, N., & Szymanski, A. (1989). Space Fortress an IQ test? *Acta Psychologica, 71*, 179–211.

Rabbitt, P. M. (1990). Age, IQ and awareness, and recall of errors. *Ergonomics, 33*, 1291–1305.

Rafal, R., Calabresi, P., Brennan, C., & Sciolto, T. (1989). Saccade preparation inhibits reorienting to recently attended locations. *Journal of Experimental Psychology: Human Perception and Performance, 15*, 673–685.

Rafal, R., & Henik, A. (1994). The neurology of inhibition: Integrating controlled and automatic processes. In D. Dagenbach & T. H. Carr (Eds.), *Inhibitory processes in attention, memory, and language* (pp. 1–51). San Diego: Academic Press.

Rafal, R. D., & Posner, M. I. (1987). Deficits in human visual spatial attention following thalamic lesions. *Proceedings of the National Academy of Sciences, 84*, 7349–7353.

Raichle, M. E. (2001). Functional neuroimaging: A historical and physiological perspective. In R. Cabeza & A. Kingstone (Eds.), *Handbook of functional neuroimaging of cognition* (pp. 3–26). Cambridge, MA: MIT Press.

Rascle, C., Mazas, O., Vaiva, G., Tournant, M., Raybois, O., Goudemand, M., & Thomas, P. (2001). Clinical features of latent inhibition in schizophrenia. *Schizophrenia Research, 51*, 149–161.

Rasmussen, G. (1946). The olivary peduncle and other fibrous projections of the superior olivary complex. *Journal of Comparative Neurology, 84*, 141–219.

Rasmussen, J. (1983). Skills, rules, and knowledge; signals, signs, and symbols, and other distinctions in human performance models. *IEEE Transactions on Systems, Man, and Cybernetics, SMC-13*, 257–266.

Rasmussen, J. (1985). The role of hierarchical knowledge representation in decisionmaking and system management. *IEEE Transactions on Systems, Man, and Cybernetics, SMC-15*, 234–243.

Raymond, J. E., Shapiro, K. L., & Arnell, K. M. (1992). Temporary suppression of visual processing in an RSVP task: An attentional blink? *Journal of Experimental Psychology: Human Perception and Performance, 18*, 849–860.

Read, L. E., & Proctor, R. W. (in press). Spatial stimulus–response compatibility and negative priming. *Psychonomic Bulletin & Review.*

Reason, J. (1979). Actions not as planned: The price of automatization. In G. Underwood & R. Stevens (Eds.), *Aspects of consciousness,* Vol. 1 (pp. 67–89). London: Academic Press.

Reason, J. (1993). Self-report questionnaires in cognitive psychology: Have they delivered the goods? In A. Baddeley & L. Weiskrantz (Eds.), *Attention: Selection, awareness, and control* (pp. 406–423). Oxford: Oxford University Press.

Reid, G. B., Shingledecker, C. A., & Eggemeier, F. T. (1981). Application of conjoint measurement to workload scale development. *Proceedings of the Human Factors Society 25th Annual Meeting* (pp. 522–526). Santa Monica, CA: Human Factors Society.

Reingold, E. M., Loschky, L. C., McConkie, G. W., & Stampe, D. M. (2003). Gaze-contingent multi-resolutional displays: An integrative review. *Human Factors, 45*, 307–328.

Reisberg, D., Scheiber, R., & Potemken, L. (1981). Eye position and the control of auditory attention. *Journal of Experimental Psychology: Human Perception and Performance, 7*, 318–323.

Remington, R., & Pierce, L. (1984). Moving attention: Evidence for time invariant shifts of visual selective attention. *Perception & Psychophysics, 35*, 393–399.

Rensink, R. A., O'Regan, J. K., & Clark, J. J. (1997). To see or not to see: The need for attention to perceive changes in scenes. *Psychological Science, 8,* 368–373.

Ribot, T. (1890). *The psychology of attention*. Chicago: Open Court Press.

Ridderinkhof, K. R., Band, G. P. H., & Logan, G. D. (1999). A study of adaptive behavior: Effects of age and irrelevant information on the ability to inhibit one's actions. *Acta Psychologica, 101*, 315–337.

Rieber, R. W. (Ed.). (1980). *Wilhelm Wundt and the making of a scientific psychology*. New York: Plenum.

Rieber, R. W., & Robinson, D. K. (Eds.). (2001). *Wilhelm Wundt in history: The making of scientific psychology*. New York: Kluwer/Plenum.

Rieger, M., & Gauggel, S. (1999). Inhibitory after-effects in the stop signal paradigm. *British Journal of Psychology, 90*, 509–518.

Riggio, L., & Kirsner, K. (1997). The relationship between central cues and peripheral cues in covert visual orientation. *Perception & Psychophysics, 59,* 885–899.

Roberts, S., & Sternberg, S. (1993). The meaning of additive reaction-time effects: Tests of three alternatives. In D. E. Meyer & S. Kornblum (Eds.), *Synergies in experimental psychology, artificial intelligence, and cognitive neuroscience: Attention and performance XIV* (pp. 611–653). Cambridge, MA: MIT Press.

Robertson, I. H. (1996). *Goal management training: A clinical manual.* Cambridge, UK: PsyConsult.

Robertson, I. H. (1999). The rehabilitation of attention. In D. S. Stuss, G. Winocur, & I. H. Robertson (Eds.), *Cognitive neurorehabilitation* (pp. 302–313). Cambridge, UK: Cambridge University Press.

Robertson, I. H., & Halligan, P. W. (1999). *Spatial neglect: A clinical handbook for diagnosis and treatment*. Hove, UK: Psychology Press.

Robertson, I., & Heutink, J. (2002). Rehabilitation of unilateral neglect. In W. Brouwer, E. van Zomeren, I. Berg, A. Bouma, & E. de Haan (Eds.), *Cognitive rehabilitation: A clinical neuropsychological approach* (pp. 207–221). Amsterdam: Boom.

Robertson, I. H., & Marshall, J. C. (1993). *Unilateral neglect: Clinical and experimental studies*. Hove, UK: Erlbaum.

Robertson, I. H., North, N., & Geggie, C., (2002). Spatio-motor cueing in unilateral neglect: Three single-case studies of its therapeutic effectiveness. *Journal of Neurology, Neurosurgery, and Psychiatry, 55*, 799–805.

Robinson, D. K. (2001). Reaction-time experiments in Wundt's institute and beyond. In R. W. Rieber & D. K. Robinson (Eds.), *Wilhelm Wundt in history: The making of scientific psychology* (pp. 161–204). New York: Kluwer/Plenum.

Roessingh, J. J. M. (2002). *The acquisition of complex skills.* Unpublished doctoral dissertation. Utrecht, Netherlands: Helmholtz Institute.

Rogers, R. D., & Monsell, S. (1995). Costs of a predictable switch between simple cognitive tasks. *Journal of Experimental Psychology: General, 124*, 207–231.

Ronnen, H. R., De Korte, P. J., Brink, P. R. G., Van der Bijl, H. J., Tonino, A. J., & Franke, C. L. (1996). Acute whiplash injury: Is there a role for MR imaging?—A prospective study of 100 patients. *Radiology, 201*, 93–96.

Rosenbaum, D. A. (1991). *Human motor control*. San Diego, CA: Academic Press.

Rossetti, Y., & Revonsuo, A. (Eds.). (2000). *Beyond dissociation: Interaction between dissociated implicit and explicit processing*. Amsterdam: John Benjamins.

Rossetti, Y., Rode, G., Pisella, L., Farne, A., Li, L., Boisson, D., & Perenin, M.T. (1988). Prism adaptation to a rightward optical deviation rehabilitates left hemispatial neglect. *Nature, 395*, 166–169.

Roswarski, T. E., & Proctor, R. W. (2003). Intrahemispherical activation, visuomotor transmission, and the Simon effect: Comment on Wascher et al. (2001). *Journal of Experimental Psychology: Human Perception and Performance, 29*, 152–158.

Rudmann, D. S., & Strybel, T. Z. (1999). Auditory spatial facilitation of visual search performance: Effect of cue precision and distractor density. *Human Factors, 41,* 146–160.

Ruthruff, E., Johnston, J. C., & Van Selst, M. (2001). Why practice reduces dual-task interference. *Journal of Experimental Psychology: Human Perception and Performance, 27*, 3–21.

Ruthruff, E., Johnston, J. C., Van Selst, M., Whitsell, S., & Remington, R. (2003). Vanishing dual-task interference after practice: Has the bottleneck been eliminated or is it merely latent? *Journal of Experimental Psychology: Human Perception and Performance, 29*, 280–289.

Ruthruff, E., Miller, J., & Lachman, T. (1995). Does mental rotation require central mechanisms? *Journal of Experimental Psychology: Human Perception and Performance, 21*, 552–570.

Sabri, M., de Lugt, D. R., & Campbell, K. B. (2000). The mismatch negativity to frequency deviants during the transition from wakefulness to sleep. *Canadian Journal of Experimental Psychology, 54*, 230–242.

Salamé, P., & Baddeley, A. (1987). Noise, unattended speech and short-term memory. *Ergonomics, 30,* 1185–1193.

Salas, E., & Cannon-Bowers, J. A. (1997). Methods, tools, and strategies for team training. In M. A. Quiñones & A. Ehrenstein (Eds.), *Training for a rapidly changing workplace: Applications of psychological research* (pp. 249–279). Washington, DC: American Psychological Association.

Salthouse, T. A., & Meinz, E. J. (1995). Aging, inhibition, working memory, and speed. *Journals of Gerontology: Series B: Psychological Sciences and Social Sciences, 50B*, P297–P306.

Salthouse, T. A., & Miles, J. D. (2002). Aging and time-sharing aspects of executive control. *Memory & Cognition, 30*, 572–582.

Sams, M., Paavilainen, P., Alho, K., & Näätänen, R. (1985). Auditory frequency discrimination and event-related potentials. *Electroencephalography and Clinical Neurophysiology, 62*, 437–448.

Sanders, A. F. (1983). Towards a model of stress and human performance. *Acta Psychologica, 53*, 61–97.

Sanders, A. F. (1990). Issues and trends in the debate on discrete vs. continuous processing of information. *Acta Psychologica, 74*, 123–167.

Sanders, A. F. (1997). A summary of resource theories from a behavioral perspective. *Biological Psychology, 45*, 5–18.

Sanders, A. F. (1998). *Elements of human performance*. Mahwah, NJ: Erlbaum.

Sarter, N. B. (2000). The need for mulitsensory interfaces in support of effective attention allocation and highly dynamic event-driven domains: The case of cockpit automation. *International Journal of Aviation Psychology, 10*, 231–245.

Sarter, N. B., & Woods, D. D. (1995). "How in the world did we ever get into that mode?" Mode error and awareness in supervisory control. *Human Factors, 37*, 5–19.

Satterfield, J. H., Schell, A. M., Nicholas, T., & Backs, R. W. (1988). Topographic study of auditory event-related potentials in normal boys and boys with attention deficit disorder with hyperactivity. *Psychophysiology, 25,* 591–606.

Satterfield, J. H., Schell, A. M., & Nicholas, T. W., Satterfield, B. T., & Freese, T. E. (1990). Ontogeny of selective attention effects on event-related potentials in attention-deficit hyperactivity disorder and normal boys. *Biological Psychiatry, 28*, 879–903.

Schachar, R, J., & Logan, G. D. (1990). Impulsivity and inhibitory control in normal development and childhood psychopathology. *Developmental Psychology, 26*, 710–720.

Scharf, B. (1988). The role of listening in the measurement of hearing. In S. D. G. Stephens (Ed.), *Advances in audiology* (pp. 13–26). Basel, Switzerland: Karger.

Scharf, B. (1998). Auditory attention: the psychoacoustical approach. In H. Pashler (Ed.), *Attention* (pp. 75–117). Hove, UK: Psychology Press.

Scharf, B., & Buus, S. (1986). Audition I: Stimulus, physiology, thresholds. In K. Boff, L. Kaufman, & J. Thomas (Eds.), *Handbook of perception and performance* (Vol. I, pp. 14-1–14-71). New York: Wiley.

Scharf, B., Quigley, S., Aoki, C, Peachey, N., & Reeves, A. (1987). Focused auditory attention and frequency selectivity. *Perception & Psychophysics, 42*, 215–223.

Schmidt, M., Postma, A., & De Haan, E. (2000). Interactions between exogenous auditory and visual spatial attention. *Quarterly Journal of Experimental Psychology, 53A,* 105–130.

Schneider, W., & Detweiler, M. (1987). A connectionist/control architecture for working memory. In G. H. Bower (Ed.), *The psychology of learning and motivation* (Vol. 21, pp. 53–119). San Diego, CA: Academic Press.

Schneider, W., & Detweiler, M. (1988). The role of practice in dual-task performance: Toward workload modeling in a connectionist/control architecture. *Human Factors, 30*, 539–566.

Schneider, W., & Fisk, A. D. (1982). Concurrent automatic and controlled visual search: Can processing occur without resource cost? *Journal of Experimental Psychology: Learning, Memory, and Cognition, 8*, 261–278.

Schneider, W., & Shiffrin, R. M. (1977). Controlled and automatic human information processing: I. Detection, search, and attention. *Psychological Review, 84*, 1–66.

Schröger, E. (1996). A neural mechanism for involuntary attention shifts to changes in auditory stimulation. *Journal of Cognitive Neuroscience, 8*, 527–539.

Schweickert, R. (1983). Latent network theory: Scheduling of processes in sentence verification and the Stroop effect. *Journal of Experimental Psychology: Learning, Memory, and Cognition, 9*, 353–383.

Schweickert, R., & Boruff, B. (1986). Short-term memory capacity: Magic number or magic spell? *Journal of Experimental Psychology: Learning, Memory, and Cognition, 12*, 419–425.

Schweickert, R., & Wang, Z. (1993). Effects on response time of factors selectively influencing processes in acyclic task networks with OR gates. *British Journal of Mathematical and Statistical Psychology, 46,* 1–30.

Schwent, V. L., & Hillyard, S. A. (1975). Evoked potential correlates of selective attention with multichannel auditory inputs. *Electroencephalography and Clinical Neurophysiology, 38,* 131–138.

Seagull, J., & Gopher, D. (1997). Training head movement in visual scanning: An embedded approach to the development of piloting skills with helmet-mounted displays. *Journal of Experimental Psychology: Applied, 3,* 163–189.

See, J. E., Howe, S. R., Warm, J. S., & Dember, W. N. (1995). Meta-analysis of the sensitivity decrement in vigilance. *Psychological Bulletin, 117,* 230–249.

Selcon, S. J., & Taylor, R. M. (1990). Evaluation of the situational awareness rating technique (SART) as a tool for aircrew systems design. In *Situational awareness in aerospace operations* (AGARD-CP-478, pp. 5-1–5-8). Neuilly-sur-Seine, France: NATO-AGARD.

Senders, J. W. (1983). *Visual scanning processes.* Tilburg, Netherlands: University of Tilburg Press.

Shallice, T. (1988). *From neuropsychology to mental structure.* New York: Cambridge University Press.

Shallice, T., & Burgess, P. W. (1991). Deficits in strategy application following frontal lobe damage in man. *Brain, 114,* 727–741.

Shannon, C. E., & Weaver, W. (1949). *The mathematical theory of communication.* Urbana, IL: University of Illinois Press.

Shebilske, W., Goettl, B., & Regian, J. W. (1999). Executive control of automatic processes as complex skills develop in laboratory and applied settings. In D. Gopher & A. Koriat (Eds.), *Cognitive regulation of performance: Interaction of theory and application: Attention and performance XVII* (pp. 401–432). Cambridge, MA: MIT Press.

Shiffrin, R. M., Diller, D., & Cohen, A. (1996). Processing visual information in an unattended location. In A. F. Kramer & M. G. H. Coles (Eds.), *Converging operations in the study of visual selective attention* (pp. 225–245). Washington, DC: American Psychological Association.

Shiffrin, R. M., & Grantham, D. W. (1974). Can attention be allocated to sensory modalities? *Perception & Psychophysics, 15,* 460–474.

Shiffrin, R. M., & Schneider, W. (1977). Controlled and automatic human information processing: II. Perceptual learning, automatic attending, and a general theory. *Psychological Review, 84,* 127–190.

Shimamura, A. P. (1994). Memory and frontal lobe function. In M. S. Gazzaniga (Ed.), *The cognitive neurosciences* (pp. 803–813). Cambridge, MA: MIT Press.

Shimamura, A. P. (2000). The role of the prefrontal cortex in dynamic filtering. *Psychobiology, 28,* 207–218.

Shiu, L.-P., & Kornblum, S. (1996). Negative priming and stimulus-response compatibility. *Psychonomic Bulletin & Review, 3,* 510–514.

Simon, J. R. (1990). The effects of an irrelevant directional cue on human information processing. In R. W. Proctor & T. G. Reeve (Eds.), *Stimulus-response compatibility: An integrated perspective* (pp. 31–86). Amsterdam: North-Holland.

Simon, J. R., & Small, A. M., Jr., (1969). Processing auditory information: Interference from an irrelevant cue. *Journal of Applied Psychology, 53,* 433–435.

Simons, D. J. (2000). Current approaches to change blindness. *Visual Cognition, 7,* 1–15.

Simons, D. J., & Levin, D. T. (1998). Failure to detect changes to people in a real-world interaction. *Psychonomic Bulletin & Review, 5,* 644–649.

Singh, I. L., Molloy, R., & Parasuraman, R. (1993). Individual differences in monitoring failures of automation. *Journal of General Psychology, 120*, 357–373.

Sklar, A. E., & Sarter, N. B. (1999). Good vibrations: Tactile feedback in support of attention allocation and human-automation coordination in event-driven domains. *Human Factors, 41*, 543–552.

Smith, M. C. (1967). Theories of the psychological refractory period. *Psychological Bulletin, 67*, 202–213.

Snyder, J. J., & Kingstone, A. (2000). Inhibition of return and visual search: How many separate loci are inhibited? *Perception & Psychophysics, 62*, 452–458.

Sohn, M. H., & Carlson, R. A. (2000). Effects of repetition and foreknowledge in task set reconfiguration. *Journal of Experimental Psychology: Learning, Memory, and Cognition, 26*, 1445–1460.

Sokolov, E. N. (1963). *Perception and the conditioned reflex*. New York: Macmillan.

Somberg, B. L., & Picardi, M. C. (1983). Locus of information familiarity effect in search of computer menus. *Proceedings of the Human Factors Society 27th Annual Meeting* (pp. 826–830). Santa Monica, CA: Human Factors Society.

Sommer, W., Leuthold, H., & Schubert, T. (2001). Multiple bottlenecks in information processing? An electrophysiological examination. *Psychonomic Bulletin & Review, 8*, 81–88.

Sorkin, R. D. (1987). Design of auditory and tactile displays. In G. Salvendy (Ed.), *Handbook of human factors* (pp. 549–576). New York: Wiley.

Sorkin, R. D., Pohlmann, L. D., & Gilliom, J. D. (1973). Simultaneous two-channel signal detection. III. 630- and 1400-Hz signals. *Journal of the Acoustic Society of America, 53*, 1045–1050.

Spearman, C. (1927). *The abilities of man*. New York: Macmillan.

Spelke, E., Hirst, W., & Neisser, U. (1976). Skills of divided attention. *Cognition, 4*, 215–230.

Spence, C., Nichols, M. E. R., Gillespie, N., & Driver, J. (1998). Cross-modal links in exogenous covert spatial orienting between touch, audition, and vision. *Perception & Psychophysics, 60*, 544–557.

Spence, C. J., & Driver, J. (1994). Covert spatial orienting in audition: Exogenous and endogenous mechanisms. *Journal of Experimental Psychology: Human Perception and Performance, 20*, 555–574.

Spence, C. J., & Driver, J. (1996). Audiovisual links in endogenous covert spatial attention. *Journal of Experimental Psychology: Human Perception and Performance, 22*, 1005–1030.

Spence, C. J., & Driver, J. (1997a). Audiovisual links in exogenous covert spatial orienting. *Perception & Psychophysics, 59*, 1–22.

Spence, C. J., & Driver, J. (1997b). On measuring selective attention to an expected sensory modality. *Perception & Psychophysics, 59*, 389–403.

Spence, C. J., & Driver, J. (2000). Attracting attention to the illusory location of a sound: Reflexive crossmodal orienting and ventriloquism. *NeuroReport, 11*, 2057–2061.

Sperandio, J. C. (1971). Variation of operator's strategies and regulating effects on workload. *Ergonomics, 14*, 571–577.

Sperling, G. (1960). The information available in brief visual presentations. *Psychological Monographs: General and Applied, 74*, 1–29.

Spieler, D. H., Balota, D. A., & Faust, M. E. (1996). Stroop performance in healthy younger and older adults and in individuals with dementia of the Alzheimer's type. *Journal of Experimental Psychology: Human Perception and Performance, 22*, 461–479.

Spitz, G. (1988). Flexibility in resource allocation and the performance of time-sharing tasks. *Proceedings of the Human Factors Society 32nd Annual Meeting* (pp. 1466–1470). Santa Monica, CA: Human Factors Society.

Squire, L. R. & Cohen, N. J. (1984). Human memory and amnesia. In G. Lynch, J. L. McGaugh, & N. M. Weinberger (Eds.), *Neurobiology of learning and memory* (pp. 3–64). New York: Guilford.

Stankov, L. (1983). Attention and intelligence. *Journal of Educational Psychology, 75*, 471–490.

Stankov, L., & Horn, J. L. (1980). Human abilities revealed through auditory tests. *Journal of Educational Psychology, 72*, 19–42.

Stanney, K., & Salvendy, G. (1998). Aftereffects and sense of presence in virtual environments: Formulation of a research and development agenda. *International Journal of Human-Computer Interaction, 10*, 135–187.

Stein, B. E., London, N., Wilkinson, L. K., & Price, D. D. (1996). Enhancement of perceived visual intensity by auditory stimuli: A psychophysical analysis. *Journal of Cognitive Neuroscience, 8*, 497–506.

Stein, B. E., & Meredith, M. A. (1993). The merging of the senses. Cambridge, MA: MIT Press.

Sternberg, S. (1966). High-speed scanning in human memory. *Science, 153*, 652–654.

Sternberg, S. (1969). The discovery of processing stages: Extensions of Donders' method. In W. G. Koster (Ed.), *Attention and performance II, Acta Psychologica, 30*, 276–315.

Sternberg, S. (1998). Discovering mental processing stages: The method of additive factors. In D. Scarborough & S. Sternberg (Eds.), *Methods, models, and conceptual issues: An invitation to cognitive science, Vol. 4. An invitation to cognitive science* (pp. 703–863). Cambridge, MA: MIT Press.

Stevens, S. S. (1975). *Psychophysics: Introduction to its perceptual, neural, and social prospects.* New York: Wiley.

Stewart, L., Ellison, A., Walsh, V., & Cowey, A. (2001). The role of transcranial magnetic stimulation (TMS) in studies of vision, attention and cognition. *Acta Psychologica, 107*, 275–291.

Strayer, D., Wickens, C., & Braune, R. (1987). Adult age differences in speed and capacity of information processing: 2. An electrophysiological approach. *Psychology and Aging, 2*, 99–110.

Strayer, D. L., & Kramer, A. F. (1990). Attentional requirements of automatic and controlled processing. *Journal of Experimental Psychology: Learning, Memory, and Cognition, 16*, 67–82.

Stroop, J. R. (1992). Studies of interference in serial verbal reactions. (Reprinted from *Journal of Experimental Psychology, 18*, 643–662, 1935.) *Journal of Experimental Psychology: General, 121*, 15–23.

Strybel, T. Z., Boucher, J. M., Fujawa, G. E., & Volp, C. S. (1995). Auditory spatial cueing in visual search tasks: Effects of amplitude, contrast and duration. *Proceedings of the Human Factors and Ergonomics Society 39th Annual Meeting* (pp. 109–113). Santa Monica, CA: Human Factors and Ergonomics Society.

Sturm, W., Willmes, K., Orgass, B., & Hartje, W. (1997). Do specific attention deficits need specific training? *Neuropsychological Rehabilitation, 7*, 81–103.

Stuss, D. T., Binns, M. A., Carruth, F. G., Levine, B., Brandys, C. E., Moulton, R. J., et al. (1999). The acute period of recovery from traumatic brain injury: Posttraumatic amnesia or posttraumatic confusional state? *Journal of Neurosurgery, 90*, 635–643.

Swanson, J., Posner, M. I., Cantwell, D., Wigal, S., Crinella, F., Filipek, P., et al. (1998). Attention-deficit/hyperactivity disorder: Symptom domains, cognitive processes, and neural networks. In R. Parasuraman (Ed.), *The attentive brain* (pp. 445–460). Cambridge, MA: MIT Press.

Sweller, J. (1994). Cognitive load theory, learning difficulty and instructional design. *Learning and Instruction, 4*, 295–312.

Swets, J. A. (1998). Separating discrimination and decision in detection, recognition, and matters of life and death. In D. Scarborough & S. Sternberg (Eds.), *Methods, models, and conceptual issues: (An invitation to cognitive science, Vol. 4,* pp. 635–702). Cambridge, MA: The MIT Press.

Sykes, D. H., Douglas, V. I., & Morgenstern, G. (1973). Sustained attention in hyperactive children. *Journal of Child Psychology and Psychiatry and Allied Disciplines, 14*, 213–220.

Takeda, Y., & Yagi, A. (2000). Inhibitory tagging in visual search can be found if search stimuli remain visible. *Perception & Psychophysics, 62*, 927–934.

Tan, H. Z., & Pentland, A. (2001). Tactual displays for sensory substitution and wearable computers. In W. Barfield & T. Caudell (Eds.), *Fundamentals of wearable computers and augmented reality* (pp. 579–598). Mahwah, NJ: Erlbaum.

Tanner, W., & Norman, R. (1954). The human use of information: II. Signal detection for the case of an unknown signal parameter. *Transactions of the Institute of Radio Engineering, Professional Group on Information Theory, 4*, 222–227.

Tannock, R., Schachar, R. J., Carr, R. P., Chajczyk, D., & Logan, G. D. (1989). Effects of methylphenidate on inhibitory control in hyperactive children. *Journal of Abnormal Child Psychology, 17*, 473–491.

Tatler, B. W. (2001). Characterising the visual buffer: Real-world evidence for overwriting early in each fixation, *Perception, 30*, 993–1006.

Teasdale, G., & Jennett, B. (1974). Assessment of coma and impaired consciousness: A practical scale. *Lancet, 2*(7872), 81–84.

Teasdale, J. D. (1988). Cognitive vulnerability to persistent depression. *Cognition and Emotion, 2*, 247–274.

Teder-Sälejärvi, W. A., McDonald, J. J., Di Russo, F., & Hillyard, S. A. (2002). An analysis of audio-visual crossmodal integration by means of event-related potential (ERP) recordings. *Cognitive Brain Research, 14*, 106–114.

Telford, C. W. (1931). Refractory phase of voluntary and associative responses. *Journal of Experimental Psychology, 14*, 1–35.

Theeuwes, J. (1989). Effects of location and form cuing on the allocation of attention in the visual field. *Acta Psychologica, 72*, 177–192.

Theeuwes, J. (1991). Exogenous and endogenous control of attention: The effect of visual onsets and offsets. *Perception & Psychophysics, 49*, 83–90.

Theeuwes, J. (1995). Abrupt luminance change pops out; abrupt color change does not. *Perception & Psychophysics, 57*, 637–644.

Thompson, J. K., Peterson, M. R., & Freeman, R. D. (2003). Single-neuron activity and tissue oxygenation in the cerebral cortex. *Science, 299*, 1070–1072.

Tipper, S. P. (2001). Does negative priming reflect inhibitory mechanisms? A review of conflicting views. *Quarterly Journal of Experimental Psychology, 54A,* 321–343.

Tipper, S. P., & Baylis, G. C. (1987). Individual differences in selective attention: The relation of priming and interference to cognitive failure. *Personality and Individual Differences, 8,* 667–675.

Tipper, S. P., Brehaut, J. C., & Driver, J. (1990). Selection of moving and static objects for the control of spatially directed action. *Journal of Experimental Psychology: Human Perception and Performance,16,* 492–504.

Tipper, S. P., & Cranston, M. (1985). Selective attention and priming: Inhibitory and facilitatory effects of ignored primes. *Quarterly Journal of Experimental Psychology, 37A,* 591–611.

Tipper, S. P., Driver, J., & Weaver, B. (1991). Object-centered inhibition of return of visual attention. *Quarterly Journal of Experimental Psychology: Human Experimental Psychology, 43A,* 289–298.

Tipper, S. P., Lortie, C., & Baylis, G. C. (1992). Selective reaching: Evidence for action-centered attention. *Journal of Experimental Psychology: Human Perception and Performance, 18,* 891–905.

Tipper, S. P., MacQueen, & Brehaut, J. C. (1988). Negative priming between response modalities: Evidence for the central locus of inhibition in selective attention. *Perception & Pyschophysics, 43,* 45–52.

Tipper, S. P., & Weaver, B. (1998). The medium of attention: Location-based, object-centred, or scene-based? In R. D. Wright (Ed.), *Visual attention* (pp. 77–107). New York: Oxford University Press.

Tipper, S. P., Weaver, B., Jerreat, L. M., & Burak, A. L. (1994). Object-based and environment-based inhibition of return of visual attention. *Journal of Experimental Psychology: Human Perception and Performance, 20,* 478–499.

Titchener, E. B. (1908). *Psychology of feeling and attention.* New York: MacMillan. (Reprinted in 1973 by Arno Press, New York).

Todd, R. D., & Botteron, K. N. (2001). Is attention-deficit/hyperactivity disorder an energy deficiency syndrome? *Biological Psychiatry, 50,* 151–158.

Toet, A., Kooi, F. L., Bijl, P., & Valeton, J. M. (1998). Visual conspicuity determines human target acquisition performance, *Optical Engineering, 37,* 1969–1975.

Tombu, M., & Jolicoeur, P. (2002). All-or-none bottleneck versus capacity sharing accounts of the psychological refractory period phenomenon. *Psychological Research, 66,* 274–286.

Tombu, M., & Jolicoeur, P. (2003). A central capacity sharing model of dual-task performance. *Journal of Experimental Psychology: Human Perception and Performance, 29,* 3–18.

Townsend, J. T. (1972). Some results concerning the identifiability of parallel and serial processes. *British Journal of Mathematical & Statistical Psychology, 25,* 168–199.

Townsend, J. T., & Ashby, G. (1983). *Stochastic modeling of elementary psychological processes.* New York: Cambridge University Press.

Treat, J., Tumbas, N., McDonald, S., Shinar, D., Hume, R., Mayer, R., et al. (1979). *Tri-level study of the causes of traffic accidents: Executive summary* (National Technical Information Services Tech. Rep. No. DOT HS-805 099). Bloomington: University of Indiana.

Treisman, A. (1960). Contextual cues in selective listening. *Quarterly Journal of Experimental Psychology, 12*, 242–248.

Treisman, A. (1964a). The effect of irrelevant material on the efficiency of selective listening. *American Journal of Psychology, 77*, 533–546.

Treisman, A. (1964b). Monitoring and storage of irrelevant messages in selective attention. *Journal of Verbal Learning and Verbal Behavior, 3*, 533–546.

Treisman, A. (1964c). Verbal cues, language, and meaning in attention. *American Journal of Psychology, 77*, 206–214.

Treisman, A. (1991). Search, similarity, and integration of features between and within dimensions. *Journal of Experimental Psychology: Human Perception and Performance, 17*, 652–676.

Treisman, A. (1998). The perception of features and objects. In R. D. Wright (Ed.), *Visual attention* (pp. 26–54) New York: Oxford University Press.

Treisman, A., & Davies, A. (1973). Dividing attention to ear and eye. In S. Kornblum (Ed.), *Attention and performance IV* (pp. 101–117). New York: Academic Press.

Treisman, A., & Gelade, G. (1980). A feature-integration theory of attention. *Cognitive Psychology, 12*, 97–136.

Treisman, A., & Riley, J. G. A. (1969). Is selective attention selective perception or selective response? A further test. *Journal of Experimental Psychology, 79*, 27–34.

Treisman, A., & Sato, S. (1990). Conjunction search revisited. *Journal of Experimental Psychology: Human Perception and Performance, 16*, 459–478.

Treisman, A., & Schmidt, H. (1982). Illusory conjunctions in the perception of objects. *Cognitive Psychology, 14*, 107–141.

Treisman, A. M. (1969). Strategies and models of selective attention. *Psychological Review, 76*, 282–299.

Treisman, A. M. (1986). Properties, parts, and objects. In K. R. Boff & L. Kaufman (Eds.), *Handbook of perception and human performance, Vol. 2: Cognitive processes and performance* (pp. 1–70). New York: Wiley.

Tsal, Y. (1983). Movement of attention across the visual field. *Journal of Experimental Psychology: Human Perception and Performance, 9*, 523–530.

Tsal, Y., & Lamy, D. (2000). Attending to an object's color entails attending to its location: Support for location-special views of visual attention. *Perception & Psychophysics, 62*, 960–968.

Tsang, P. S., & Vidulich, M. A. (1994). The roles of immediacy and redundancy in relative subjective workload assessment. *Human Factors, 36*, 503–513.

Tufano, D. R. (1997). Automative HUDS: The overlooked safety issues. *Human Factors, 39*, 303–311

Tuholski, S. W., Engle, R. W., & Baylis, G. C. (2001). Individual differences in working memory capacity and enumeration. *Memory & Cognition, 29*, 484–492.

Tulving, E. (1985). How many memory systems are there? *American Psychologist, 40*, 385–398.

Turvey, M. T. (1973). On peripheral and central processes in vision: Inferences from an information-processing analysis of masking with patterned stimuli. *Psychological Review, 80*, 1–52.

Tzelgov, J., Henik, A., & Berger, J. (1992). Controlling Stroop effects by manipulating expectations for color words. *Memory & Cognition, 20*, 727–735.

Ulrich, R., Mattes, S., & Miller, J. (1999). Donders's assumption of pure insertion: An evaluation on the basis of response dynamics. *Acta Psychologica, 102*, 43–75.

Umiltà, C., & Nicoletti, R. (1985). Attention and coding effects in S-R compatibility due to irrelevant spatial cues. In M. I. Posner & O. S. M. Marin (Eds.), *Attention and Performance XI* (pp. 456–471). Hillsdale, NJ: Erlbaum.

Underwood, G. (1974). Moray vs. the rest: The effects of extended shadowing practice. *Quarterly Journal of Experimental Psychology, 26*, 368–372.

Uttal, W. R. (2001). *The new phrenology: The limits of localizing cognitive processes in the brain*. Cambridge, MA: MIT Press.

Vaitl, D., Lipp, O., Bauer, U., Schulerk, G., Stark, R., Zimmermann, M., & Kirsch, P. (2002). Latent inhibition and schizophrenia: Pavlovian conditioning of autonomic responses. *Schizophrenia Research, 55*, 147–58

Vallar, G., Rusconi, M. L., Bignamini, L., Geminiani, G., & Perani, D. (1994). Anatomical correlates of visual and tactile extinction in humans: A clinical CT scan study. *Journal of Neurology, Neurosurgery, and Psychiatry, 57*, 464–470.

Van den Bosch, R. J., Rombouts, R. P., & Van Asma, M. J. O. (1996). What determines continuous performance test performance? *Schizophrenia Research, 22*, 643–651.

Van der Heijden, A. H. C. (1992). *Selective attention in vision.* London, New York: Routledge.

Van der Heijden, A. H. C. (1993). The role of position in object selection in vision. *Psychological Research, 56*, 44–58.

Van der Lubbe, R. H. J., Jaskowski, P., Wauschkuhn, B., & Verleger, R. (2001). Influence of time pressure in a simple response task, a choice-by-location task, and the Simon task. *Journal of Psychophysiology, 15*, 241–255.

Van der Lubbe, R. H. J., Keuss, P. J. G., & Stoffels, E.-J. (1996). Threefold effect of peripheral precues: Alertness, orienting, and response tendencies. *Acta Psychologica, 94*, 319–337.

Van der Lubbe, R. H. J., & Woestenburg, J. C. (1997). Modulation of early ERP components with peripheral precues: A trend analysis. *Biological Psychology, 45*, 143–158.

Van der Veer, G. C., & Puerta Melguizo, M. d. C. (2003). Mental models. In. J. Jacko & A. Sears (Eds.), *The human-computer interaction handbook: Fundamentals, evolving technologies, and emerging applications* (pp. 52–80). Mahwah, NJ: Erlbaum.

Van Duren, L. L., & Sanders, A. F. (1988). On the robustness of the additive factors stage structure in blocked and mixed choice reaction designs. *Acta Psychologica, 69*, 83–94.

Van Hooff, J. C., De Beer, N. A. M., Brunia, C. H. M., Cluitmans, P. J. M., Korsten, H. H. M., Tavilla, G., & Grouls, R. (1995). Information processing during cardiac surgery: An event related potential study. *Electroencephalography and Clinical Neurophysiology, 96*, 433–452.

Van Oeffelen, M. P., & Vos, P. G. (1982). Configurational effects on the enumeration of dots: Counting by groups. *Memory & Cognition, 10*, 396–404.

Van Selst, M. A., Ruthruff, E., & Johnston, J. C. (1999). Can practice eliminate the Psychological Refractory Period effect? *Journal of Experimental Psychology: Human Perception and Performance, 25*, 1268–1283.

Van Zandt, T., & Ratcliff, R. (1995). Statistical mimicking of reaction time data: Single-process models, parameter variability, and mixtures. *Psychonomic Bulletin & Review, 2*, 20–54.

Van Zandt, T., & Townsend, J. T. (1993). Self-terminating versus exhaustive processes in rapid visual and memory search: An evaluative review. *Perception & Psychophysics, 53*, 563–580.

Van Zandvoort, M., Kappelle, L. J., Algra, A. & De Haan, E. H. F. (1998). A decreased capacity for mental effort after a single supertentorial lacunar infarct may affect performance in everyday life. *Journal of Neurology, Neurosurgery and Psychiatry, 65*, 697–702.

Van Zomeren, A. H., & Brouwer, W. H. (1994). *Clinical neuropsychology of attention*. New York: Oxford University Press.

Van Zomeren, A. H., & Van den Burg, W. (1985). Residual complaints of patients two years after severe head injury. *Journal of Neurology, Neurosurgery, & Psychiatry, 48*, 21–28.

Vandenberghe, R., Duncan, J., Arnell, K. M., Bishop, S. J., Herrod, N. J., Owen, A. M., et al. (2000). Maintaining and shifting attention within right or left hemifield. *Cerebral Cortex, 10*, 706–713.

Vandenberghe, R., Duncan, J., Dupont, P., Ward, R., Poline, J.-B., Bormans, G., et al. (1997). Attention to one or two features in left or right visual field: A positron emission tomography study. *Journal of Neuroscience, 17*, 3739–3750.

Veltman, J. A., & Guillard, A. W. K. (1993). Pilot workload evaluated with subjective and physiological measures. In K. Brookhuis, C. Weikert, J. Moraal, & D. de Waard (Eds.), *Aging and human factors* (pp. 107–128). Groningen, NL: University of Groningen Traffic Control Centre.

Veltman, J. C., Brouwer, W. H., Van Zomeren, A. H., & Van Wolffelaar, P. C. (1996). Central executive aspects of attention in subacute severe and very severe closed head injury patients: Planning, inhibition, flexibility, and divided attention. *Neuropsychology, 10*, 357–367.

Verleger, R. (1997). On the utility of P3 latency as an index of mental chronometry. *Psychophysiology, 34*, 131–156.

Vicente, K. J. (1999). *Cognitive work analysis: Toward safe, productive, and healthy computer-based work*. Mahwah, NJ: Erlbaum.

Vicente, K. J. (2002). Ecological interface design: Progress and challenges. *Human Factors, 44*, 62–78.

Vicente, K. J., & Rasmussen, J. (1992). Ecological interface design: Theoretical foundations. *IEEE Transactions on Systems, Man, and Cybernetics, 22*, 589–606.

Vicente, K. J., Thornton, D. C., & Moray, N. (1987). Spectral analysis of sinus arrhythmia: A measure of mental effort. *Human Factors, 29*, 171–182.

Vidulich, M. A. (2000). Testing the sensitivity of situation awareness metrics in interface evaluations. In M. R. Endsley & D. J. Garland (Eds.), *Situation awareness analysis and measurement* (pp. 227–246). Hillsdale, NJ: Erlbaum.

Virzi, R. A., & Egeth, H. E. (1985). Toward a translational model of Stroop interference. *Memory & Cognition, 13*, 304–319.

Visser, T. W. A., Bischof, W. F., & Di Lollo, V. (1999). Attentional switching in spatial and nonspatial domains: Evidence from the attentional blink. *Psychological Bulletin, 125*, 458–469.

Vives, J. L. (1538/1948). On the soul and on life. In J. L. Vives, *Obras completas* (translated into Spanish by L. Riber). Madrid: M. Aguilar.

Vogel, E. K., & Luck, S. J. (2000). The visual N1 component as an index of a discrimination process. *Psychophysiology, 37*, 190–203.

Vogel, E. K., Luck, S. J., & Shapiro, K. L. (1998). Electrophysiological evidence for a postperceptual locus of suppression during the attentional blink. *Journal of Experimental Psychology: Human Perception and Performance, 24*, 1656–1674.

Volpe, C., E., Cannon-Bowers, J. A., Salas, E., & Spector, P. E. (1996). The impact of cross-training on team functioning: An empirical investigation. *Human Factors, 38,* 87–100.

von Helmholtz H. (1894a). Über den Ursprung der richtigen Deutung unserer Sinneseindrücke (The origin of the correct interpretation of our sensory impressions). Translated in R. M. Warren & R. P. Warren (1968). *Helmholtz on perception, its physiology, and development* (pp. 249–260). New York: Wiley.

von Helmholtz, H. (1894b). *Handbuch der physiologischen Optik.* Hamburg/Leipzig: L. Vos.

Von Wright, J. M. (1968). Selection in visual immediate memory. *Quarterly Journal of Experimental Psychology, 20,* 62–68.

Vos, P. G. (1988). *Bourdon-Vos Test.* Lisse, Netherlands: Swets & Zeitlinger.

Vu, K.-P. L., & Proctor, R. W. (2001). Determinants of right-left and top-bottom prevalence for two-dimensional spatial compatibility. *Journal of Experimental Psychology: Human Perception and Performance, 27,* 813–828.

Vu, K.-P. L., & Proctor, R. W. (2002). The prevalence effect in two-dimensional stimulus-response compatibility is a function of the relative salience of the dimensions. *Perception & Psychophysics, 6,* 815–828.

Walker, B. N., & Ehrenstein, A. (2000). Pitch and pitch change interact in auditory displays. *Journal of Experimental Psychology: Applied, 6,* 15–30.

Ward, L. M. (1994). Supramodal and modality-specific mechanisms for stimulus-driven shifts of auditory and visual attention. *Canadian Journal of Experimental Psychology, 48,* 242–259.

Ward, L. M., McDonald, J. J., & Golestani, N. (1998). Crossmodal control of attention shifts. In R. D. Wright (Ed.), *Visual attention* (pp. 232–268). New York: Oxford University Press.

Ward, L. M., McDonald, J. J., & Lin, D. (2000). On asymmetries in crossmodal spatial attention orienting. *Perception & Psychophysics, 62,* 1258–1264.

Warm, J. S., Dember, W. N., & Hancock, P. A. (1996). Vigilance and workload in automated systems. In R. Parasuraman & M. Mouloua (Eds.), *Attention and human performance: Theories and applications* (pp. 183–200). Mahwah, NJ: Erlbaum.

Wascher, E., Schatz, U., Kuder, T., & Verleger, R. (2001). Validity and boundary conditions of automatic response activation in the Simon task. *Journal of Experimental Psychology: Human Perception and Performance, 27,* 731–751.

Wassermann, E. M., & Lisanby, S. H. (2001). Therapeutic application of repetitive transcranial magnetic stimulation: A review. *Clinical Neurophysiology, 112,* 1367–1377.

Watson, D. G., & Humphreys, G. W. (1997). Visual marking: Prioritizing selection for new objects by top down attentional inhibition of old objects. *Psychological Review, 104,* 90–122.

Watson, D. G., & Humphreys, G. W. (1998). Visual marking of moving objects: A role for top-down feature based inhibition in selection. *Journal of Experimental Psychology: Human Perception and Performance, 24,* 946–962.

Watson, D. G., & Humphreys, G. W. (2000). Visual marking: Evidence for inhibition using a probe-dot detection paradigm. *Perception & Psychophysics, 62,* 471–481.

Watson, F. (1915). The father of modern psychology. *Psychological Review, 22,* 333–353.

Weber, E. H. (1978). *The sense of touch.* Contains *De Tactu* (1834), translated by H. E. Ross, and *Der Tastsinn und das Gemeingefühl* (1846), translated by D. J. Murray. New York: Academic Press.

Weber, T. A., Kramer, A. F., & Miller, G. A. (1997). Selective processing of superimposed objects: An electrophysiological analysis of object-based attentional selection. *Biological Psychology, 45,* 159–182.

Wechsler, D. (1997). *Wechsler Adult Intelligence Scale–Third Edition: Administration and scoring manual.* San Antonio, TX: Psychological Corporation.

Weintraub, D. J., & Ensing, M. (1992). *Human factors issues in head-up display: The book of HUD.* SOAR CSERIAC 92-2. Wright Patterson AFB, OH: CSERIAC.

Weintraub, D. J., Haines, R. F., & Randle, R. J. (1984). The utility of head-up displays: Eye-focus versus decision time. *Proceedings of the 28th Annual Meeting of the Human Factors Society* (pp. 529–533). Santa Monica, CA: Human Factors Society.

Weintraub, D. J., Haines, R. F., & Randle, R. J. (1985). Head-up display (HUD) utility, II: Runway to HUD transitions monitoring eye focus and decision times. *Proceedings of the 29th Annual Meeting of the Human Factors Society* (pp. 615–619). Santa Monica, CA: Human Factors Society.

Welch, J. C. (1898). On the measurement of mental activity through muscular activity and the determination of a constant of attention. *American Journal of Physiology, 1,* 253–306.

Welford, A. T. (1952). The "psychological refractory period" and the timing of high-speed performance: A review and a theory. *British Journal of Psychology, 43,* 2–19.

Welford, A. T. (1980). On the nature of higher-order skills. *Journal of Occupational Psychology, 53,* 107–110.

Weltman, G., Smith, J. E., & Egstrom, G. H. (1971). Perceptual narrowing during simulated pressure-chamber exposure. *Human Factors, 13,* 99–107.

Wertheim, A. H. (2002). *Eccentric perceptibility and contrast reduction as components of visual conspicuity.* (Tech. Rep. TM-02-C054). TNO-Human Factors, Soesterberg, Netherlands.

West, R., & Baylis, G. C. (1998). Effects of increased response dominance and contextual disintegration on the Stroop interference effect in older adults. *Psychology and Aging, 13,* 206–217.

West, R. L. (1996). An application of prefrontal cortex function theory to cognitive aging. *Psychological Bulletin, 120,* 272–292.

Wickelgren, W. A. (1977). Speed-accuracy tradeoff and information processing dynamics. *Acta Psychologica, 41,* 67–85.

Wickens, C. D. (1980). The structure of attentional resources. In R. Nickerson (Ed.), *Attention and performance VIII* (pp. 239–257). Hillsdale, NJ: Erlbaum.

Wickens, C. D. (1984). Processing resources in attention. In R. Parasuraman & D. R. Davies (Eds.), *Varieties of attention* (pp. 63–102). New York: Academic Press.

Wickens, C. D. (1991). Processing resources and attention. In D. L. Damos (Ed.), *Multiple-task performance* (pp. 3–34). London: Taylor & Francis.

Wickens, C. D. (1999). Cognitive factors in aviation. In F. T. Durso (Ed.), *Handbook of applied cognition* (pp. 247–282). Chichester, UK: Wiley.

Wickens, C. D., & Andre, A. D. (1990). Proximity compatibility and information display: Effects of color, space, and objectness on information integration. *Human Factors, 32,* 61–77.

Wickens, C. D., & Carswell, C. M. (1995). The proximity compatibility principle: Its psychological foundation and relevance to display design. *Human Factors, 37,* 473–494.

Wickens, C. D., Gordon, S. E., & Liu, Y. (1998). *An introduction to human factors engineering.* New York: Longman.

Wickens, C., D., Helleberg, J., & Xu, X. (2002). Pilot maneuver choice and workload in free flight. *Human Factors, 44,* 171–188.

Wickens, C. D., & Hollands, J. G. (2000). *Engineering psychology and human performance* (3rd ed.). Upper Saddle River, NJ: Prentice Hall.

Wickens, C. D., Hyman, F., Dellinger, J., Taylor, H., & Meador, M. (1986). The Sternberg memory search task as an index of pilot workload. *Ergonomics, 29,* 1371–1383.

Wickens, C. D., & Long, J. (1995). Object vs. space-based models of visual attention: Implication for the design of head-up displays. *Journal of Experimental Psychology: Applied, 1,* 179–194.

Wickens, C. D., Martin-Emerson, R., & Larish, J. (1993). Attentional tunneling and the head-up display. *Proceedings of the 7th International Symposium on Aviation Psychology.* Columbus, OH: Ohio State University.

Wijers, A. A., Lange, J. J., Mulder, G. & Mulder, L. J. M. (1997). An ERP study of visual spatial attention and letter target detection for isoluminant and nonisoluminant stimuli. *Psychophysiology, 34,* 553–565.

Wikman, A.-S., Nieminen, T., & Summala, N. (1998). Driving experience and time-sharing during in-car tasks on roads of different width. *Ergonomics, 41,* 358–372.

Wilkinson, R. T. (1962). Muscle tension during mental work under sleep deprivation. *Journal of Experimental Psychology, 64,* 565–571.

Wilkinson, R. T. (1963). Interaction of noise with knowledge of results and sleep deprivation. *Journal of Experimental Psychology, 66,* 332–337.

Williams, J. M. G., Mathews, A., & MacLeod, C. (1996). The emotional Stroop task and psychopathology. *Psychological Bulletin, 120,* 3–24.

Wilson, J. R. (1997). Virtual environments and ergonomics: Needs and opportunities. *Ergonomics, 40,* 1057–1077.

Woldorff, M. G., & Hillyard, S. A. (1991). Modulation of early auditory processing during selective listening to rapidly presented tones. *Electroencephalography and Clinical Neurophysiology, 79,* 170–191.

Woldorff, M. G., Hillyard, S. A., Gallen, C. C., Hampson, S. R., & Bloom, F. E. (1998). Magneto-encephalographic recordings demonstrate attentional modulation of mismatch related neural activity in human auditory cortex. *Psychophysiology, 35,* 283–292.

Wolfe, J. M. (1994). Guided Search 2.0: A revised model of visual search. *Psychonomic Bulletin & Review, 1,* 202–238.

Wolfe, J. M. (1998). What can 1 million trials tell us about visual search? *Psychological Science, 9,* 33–39.

Wolfe, J. M., Cave, K. R., & Franzel, S. L. (1989). Guided search: An alternative to the modified feature integration model for visual search. *Journal of Experimental Psychology: Human Perception and Performance, 15,* 419–433.

Wolfe, J. M., & Pokorny, C. W. (1990). Inhibitory tagging in visual search: A failure to replicate. *Perception & Psychophysics, 48,* 357–362.

Wolpert, J. (1924). Die Simultanagnosie: Störung der Gesamtauffassung. *Zeitschrift für die Gesamte Neurologie und Psychiatrie, 93,* 397–425.

Wolters, N. C. W. & Schiano, D. J. (1989). On listening where we look: The fragility of a phenomenon. *Perception & Psychophysics, 45,* 184–186.

Woods, D. D. (1991). The cognitive engineering of cognitive representations. In G. R. S. Weir & J. L. Alty (Eds.), *Human-computer interaction and complex systems* (pp. 169–188). London: Academic Press.

Woods, D. L., & Alain, C. (2001). Conjoining three auditory features: An event-related brain potential study. *Journal of Cognitive Neuroscience, 13,* 492–509.

Woods, D. L., Alain, C., Diaz, R., Rhodes, D., & Ogawa, K. H. (2001). Location and frequency cues in auditory selective attention. *Journal of Experimental Psychology: Human Perception and Performance, 27,* 65–74.

Woodworth, R. S. (1899). The accuracy of voluntary movement. *Psychological Review, 3* (Monograph Supplement), 1–119.

Woodworth, R. S. (1938). *Experimental psychology.* New York: Holt.

World Health Organization. (1980). *International classification of impairments, disabilities, and Handicaps (ICIDH): A manual of classification relating to the consequences of disease.* Geneva: Switzerland: Author.

Worthington, A. (2002). *Rehabilitation of executive deficits: The effect on disability.* Paper presented at the Conference on Effectiveness of Rehabilitation of Cognitive Deficits, Cardiff, UK.

Wright, R. D., & Richard, C. M. (1996). Inhibition of return at multiple locations in visual space. *Canadian Journal of Experimental Psychology, 50,* 324–327.

Wright, R. D., & Richard, C. M. (1998). Inhibition-of-return is not reflexive. In R. D. Wright (Ed.), *Visual attention. Vancouver studies in cognitive science* (Vol. 8, pp. 330–347). New York: Oxford University Press.

Wundt, W. (1880). *Grundzüge der physiologischen Psychologie* (Vol. II, 2nd ed.). Leipzig: Engelmann.

Wundt, W. (1883). Über psychologische Methoden. *Philosophische Studien, 10,* 1–38.

Wundt, W. (1900). *Die Sprache.* Leipzig: Engelmann.

Wundt, W. (1907a). *Lectures on human and animal psychology.* New York: Macmillan. (Trans. from the 2nd German edition by J. B. Creighton & E. B. Titchener.)

Wundt, W. M. (1907b). *Outlines of psychology* (3rd rev. English ed., C. H. Judd, trans.). Leipzig: Engelmann.

Wundt, W. (1912). *An introduction to psychology.* London: Allen & Unwin.

Yantis, S. (1988). On analog movements of visual attention. *Perception & Psychophysics, 43,* 203–206.

Yantis, S. (2000). Goal-directed and stimulus-driven determinants of attentional control. In S. Monsell & J. Driver (Eds.), *Control of cognitive processes: Attention and performance XVIII* (pp. 73–103). Cambridge, MA: MIT Press.

Yantis, S. (2003). To see is to attend. *Science, 299,* 54–56.

Yantis, S., & Hilstrom, A. P. (1994). Stimulus-driven attentional capture: Evidence from visual search. *Journal of Experimental Psychology: Human Perception and Performance, 20,* 95–107.

Yantis, S., & Johnson, D. N. (1990). Mechanisms of attentional priority. *Journal of Experimental Psychology: Human Perception and Performance, 16,* 812–825.

Yantis, S., & Jonides, J. (1984). Abrupt visual onsets and selective attention: Evidence from visual search. *Journal of Experimental Psychology: Human Perception and Performance, 10*, 601–621.

Yeh, Y. Y., & Wickens, C. D. (1988). Dissociation of performance and subjective measures of workload. *Human Factors, 30*, 111–120.

Yellott, J. I. (1971). Correction for fast guessing and the speed-accuracy tradeoff in choice reaction time. *Journal of Mathematical Psychology, 8*, 159–199.

Yellott, J. I., Jr. (1967). Correction for guessing in choice reaction time. *Psychonomic Science, 8*, 321–322.

Yerkes, R. M., & Dodson, J. D. (1908). The relation of strength of stimulus to rapidity of habit formation. *Journal of Comparative Neurology and Psychology, 18*, 459–482.

Zametkin, A. J., Nordahl, T. E., Gross, M., King, A. C., Semple, W. E., Rumsey, J., et al. (1990). Cerebral glucose metabolism in adults with hyperactivity of childhood onset. *New England Journal of Medicine, 323*, 1361–1366.

Zwahlen, H. T., Adams, C. C., Jr., & DeBald, D. P. (1988). Safety aspects of CRT touch panel controls in automobiles. In A. G. Gale, M. H. Freeman, C. M. Haselgrave, P. Smith, & S. P. Taylor (Eds.), *Vision in vehicles II* (pp. 335–344). Amsterdam: North-Holland.

AUTHOR INDEX

SUBJECT INDEX

ABOUT THE AUTHORS

Addie Johnson is Professor of Human Performance and Ergonomics at the University of Groningen, The Netherlands. She received a Ph.D. in cognitive psychology from Purdue University in 1993. She conducts research in attention, memory, and skill acquisition, with applications in the field of ergonomics. In addition, Dr. Johnson is active in several professional societies and has served on a number of editorial boards. She is currently Secretary of the Dutch Ergonomics Society.

Robert W. Proctor is Professor of Psychology at Purdue University in West Lafayette, Indiana. He received a Ph.D. in psychology from the University of Texas at Arlington in 1975. He conducts research on basic and applied aspects of human performance, with an emphasis on stimulus–response compatibility effects and the relation between perception and action. Dr. Proctor is a member of several journal editorial boards, coauthor of four books, and coeditor of two edited volumes. He is a fellow of the American Psychological Association and the American Psychological Society, and an honorary fellow of the Human Factors and Ergonomics society.

Attention: *Theory and Practice* is Johnson and Proctor's second book together. The first, *Skill Acquisition and Human Performance*, was published by Sage in 1995. They can be reached at the following addresses:

Addie Johnson
Dept. of Experimental and Work
    Psychology
University of Groningen
Grote Kruisstraat 2/1
9712 TS Groningen
The Netherlands
A.Johnson@ppsw.rug.nl

Robert W. Proctor
Department of Psychological Sciences
Purdue University
703 Third Street
West Lafayette, IN 47907-2081
proctor@psych.purdue.edu

ABOUT THE CONTRIBUTING AUTHORS

Edward H. F. de Haan is Professor at the University of Utrecht.
Department of Psychonomics
Heidelberglaan 2
3584 CS Utrecht, The Netherlands

Roy P. C. Kessels is Assistant Professor at the University of Utrecht.
Department of Psychonomics
Heidelberglaan 2
3584 CS Utrecht, The Netherlands

Robert D. Melara is Associate Professor at Purdue University.
Department of Psychological Sciences
Purdue University
703 Third Street
West Lafayette, IN 47907-2081

Mark R. Nieuwenstein is a graduate student at the University of Utrecht.
Department of Psychonomics
Heidelberglaan 2
3584 CS Utrecht, The Netherlands

Kim-Phuong L. Vu is a postdoctoral researcher at Purdue University.
Department of Psychological Sciences
Purdue University
703 Third Street
West Lafayette, IN 47907-2081